ROCKY MOUNTAIN NATIONAL PARK

The Complete Hiking Guide

Text and Photography by **Lisa Foster**

*R*enaissance MOUNTAINEERING
RENAISSANCEMOUNTAINEERING.COM

INTERNATIONAL STANDARD BOOK NUMBER:
978-0-615-52684-3

For more information about this fine book from Renaissance Mountaineering's Book Division, please contact your local bookstore, call us at 970-235-1264, or visit us on the web at *renaissancemountaineering.com*.

EDITORS: Jenna Samelson Browning, Martha Ripley Gray, and Elizabeth Train

BOOK AND OVERVIEW MAP DESIGNER (PP. 14–15)
Rebecca Finkel, F + P Graphic Design

PRODUCTION MANAGER: Craig Keyzer

OTHER CONTRIBUTORS: Hike maps created by Steve Volker using Global Mapper GIS software. (GIS trail and boundary data were obtained from the NPS and overlaid onto digitized USGS 7.5-minute quadrangles of RMNP.) Regional maps designed and reproduced from TOPO! TrailSmart software by Alex Kostadinov.

STATISTICS: Steve Volker, Alex Kostadinov, and Lisa Foster

PUBLISHED BY:
Renaissance Mountaineering, LLC
Book Division
PO Box 1212
Estes Park, CO 80517 USA

Printed in China by Hing Yip Printing Co., Ltd.

Maps created with TOPO! software © 2005 National Geographic maps. TOPO! users can download information from the National Geographic MapXchange for use with TOPO! and GPS receivers. To learn more, visit www.nationalgeographic/topo.

LIBRARY OF CONGRESS CATALOGING-IN-PUBLICATION DATA:
Foster, Lisa
  Rocky Mountain National Park : the complete hiking guide / by Lisa Foster.
    p. cm.
  Includes index.
  ISBN-13: 978-0-615-52684-3
  1. Hiking—Colorado—Rocky Mountain Park—Guidebooks.
  2. Rocky Mountain National Park (Colo.)—Guidebooks. I. Title.
  GV199.42.C6R6524 2005
  917.88'690433—dc22
                                          2005000545

PLEASE NOTE: Risk is always a factor in backcountry and high-mountain travel. Many of the activities described in this book can be dangerous, especially when weather is adverse or unpredictable, and when unforeseen events or conditions create a hazardous situation. The author has done her best to provide the reader with accurate information about backcountry travel, as well as to point out some of its potential hazards. It is the responsibility of the users of this guide to learn the necessary skills for safe backcountry travel, and to exercise caution in potentially hazardous areas, especially on glaciers and avalanche-prone terrain. The author and publisher disclaim any liability for injury or other damage caused by backcountry traveling or performing any other activity described in this book.

The author and publisher of this book have made every effort to ensure the accuracy and currency of its information. Nevertheless, books can require revisions. Please feel free to let us know if you find information in this book that needs to be updated, and we will be glad to correct it for the next printing. Your comments and suggestions are always welcome.

FRONT COVER:
Hiking in the North Inlet
photograph by John Fielder

TITLE PAGE:
Ypsilon and Fairchild Mountains from Mount Tileston

BACK COVER:
Hallett Peak at sunrise
photograph by John Fielder

Opposite: Steve Volker photographing from the summit of Elk Tooth, Wild Basin

Dedication

This book is dedicated to Ronny Jordan Campbell,
with whom I first explored and learned to love these mountains.

Thank you for your friendship,
for saving my life on the east face of 'Little No Name,'
and for teaching me the beauty of mountaineering.

Brian Verhulst approaching Lava Cliffs

Acknowledgments

This book took a considerable amount of effort to produce. I want to thank the following people for their friendship and their individual contributions to this book. Most of them helped in ways they didn't even realize.

My special thanks goes sincerely to: God, for creating this amazing landscape and for keeping me out of harm's way while exploring it. Alex Kostadinov, who helped me climb these mountains and worked diligently and selflessly on the maps, destinations chart, and editing of my manuscript; without him, this book would not have been completed on time. My parents, Steve and Cathy Foster, and my sisters, Laura Foster, Carolyn Olson, and Stephanie Foster, for their undying support and encouragement in all my endeavors. Steve Volker for his hard work on the maps and destinations chart, and for his excellent hiking companionship; our friendship was forged on the landscape of Rocky Mountain National Park (RMNP) and shall endure. Ron Thomas of RMNP for his help with private-property issues and maps. Larry Gamble of RMNP for his friendship and help with trail and trailhead relocation information. Mark Daniel of RMNP for his help with matters on the west side of the Park. Jim Detterline of RMNP for taking me ice climbing for the first time (back in the day) and for his willingness to share his expertise on this beautiful Park. Larry Frederick of RMNP for help with trailhead issues. Dave Larsen of RMNP for helping with trail details. My friend Brian Biggs for help

Spruce Lake

with road mileages and photograph selection. Brad Brandewie for his answering-machine pep talks, inspirational attitude about climbing, and friendship. Michelle Chase for digging deep and going on grueling death marches in the pouring rain, for her editorial help, and, of course, her friendship. Bob Chase, my friend and climbing mentor, for exploring much of the vertical terrain in RMNP with me. Melissa Gargano for her unselfish, enduring friendship; her support was much needed and appreciated. Steve Lawlor for being my friend and hero, and for getting me up there. Pete Daniels for making my life more comedic, for hanging it out there with me on the vertical blue, and for his friendship. My friends Dale and Laurel Hatcher for their support and patience. Elizabeth Mills and Eryn Victoria Mills for their friendship and inspiration. Enda Mills Kiley for perpetuating the significance of her father's work. Lester Moore for his excellent photographs. Cindy Hirschfeld for logistical help with getting this book started. John Fielder, Linda Doyle, Jenna Browning, Craig Keyzer, Martha Gray, Elizabeth Train, Rebecca Finkel, and everyone else at Westcliffe Publishers for bringing this book to fruition. Special thanks to Fran Marshall and Daniel Ortiz of National Geographic for their professionalism and courtesy in granting the user license for National Geographic maps.

And to my climbing and hiking partners: Joshua "Zagnut" Agan, Macey Bray, Jim Cleary, Maureen Cleary, Ken Dunn, Kellie Falbo, Tony Falbo, John Haugh, Karla Mosier, Judy Lovdokken Thomas, Clint Lamb, Jonathan Ramsey, Lindsey Landers, Pat and Mike Arneson, Marisa Howe, Bob Hostetler, Lionel Olson, Brian and Melissa Verhulst, Kari Lennartson, Keith Brown, Rick Bachand, Sandy White, Lorraine Carter, Buff Carter, Andrew Mason, Leigh Mason, Shane Cole, Guillaume Dargaud, Jennifer Dargaud, Mike Ellison, Linda Wold, Elizabeth Francois, Tom McQuade, Andy Neff, Joanne Skidmore, Bronson MacDonald, Todd Burke, Celia Shacklett, Martin Karl Strausbaugh, Clinton "Ship" Sander, Ron Williams, Kathleen Theriault, David Bailey, Renee Van Horn, Chelsea Van Horn, Peter Van Horn, Chris Bechard, Molly Kemper, Geoffrey Smith, Jami Hamilton, Stephanie Sutton, Mike Poland, Bob VonNormann, John Norris, Tom Kuepers, Jan Kuepers, Ed Phillips, Andrea Charlebois, Jorin Botte, and Drew Gunn.

Contents

Foreword.   9

Preface. 11

RMNP Regional Map. 14

Introduction. 17

How to Use This Guide 22

▓ REGION 1 East Side Central   28

▓ REGION 2 Mummy Range 118

▓ REGION 3 Wild Basin 174

▓ REGION 4 Longs Peak Group 221

▓ REGION 5 Eastern Perimeter. 247

▓ REGION 6 West Side Central 270

▓ REGION 7 Southwest Corner 309

▓ REGION 8 Never Summer Mountains. 323

APPENDIX A: Glossary. 362

APPENDIX B: Destinations Chart 364

Index. 387

About the Author/Photographer 400

Above: Bob and Michelle Chase cross over the Big Thompson River
Opposite: 'Sprague Tarn' and Rainbow Lake from the Continental Divide

Foreword

The alpine paradise of Rocky Mountain National Park draws 3.5 million visitors annually to enjoy its features, which include a plethora of waterfalls and swiftwater passages, 147 lakes of various colors and depths, and 100 peaks towering above the 11,000-foot treeline —with 14,259-foot Longs Peak as the spectacular centerpiece. Most travel Trail Ridge Road, the nation's highest contiguous road, which traverses the width of the Park. However, many infrequently traveled areas remain, where one might expect to find few, if any, fellow human travelers. To truly experience these areas, you must get out of the car and wander on foot. The Park officially advertises "more than 360 miles of trails." Some are short and heavily civilized, while others offer access to the most remote and pristine areas of the Park.

As a former Park ranger, my backcountry patrol beat covered popular routes such as the East Longs Peak Trail, as well as little-known cross-country zones such as Forest Canyon, where the greenback cutthroat trout was rediscovered in the 1960s after it had been considered extinct since the 1930s, and where mischievous black bears roamed. Interestingly, the Park received the majority of its so-called "Bigfoot" sightings in this area! I was assigned to cover Forest Canyon for an entire workweek at times. The peace and tranquility of this area inspired me to throw the typewriter into my backpack, as it was the only place in the Park where I could sequester myself and catch up on overdue reports.

I have now been enjoying the backcountry of RMNP for 26 years, yet there are still numerous untrodden corners and little-used trails to discover as new treasures. Lisa Foster is the consummate scholar and guide to these places. Aside from being an accomplished mountaineer and technical climber, she has served as a National Park Biological Science Technician in Resource Management, a journalist, filmmaker, hiking guide, and more, which has given her a unique perspective on the geography, natural history, and human legacy of RMNP.

Lisa shares this perspective in her guidebook, which explains the well-known trails and sights of the Park, as well as detailing almost unknown paths and challenging off-trail scrambles. For example, her description of the well-worn Keyhole Route, the sole nontechnical route to the summit of Longs Peak, is the best description I've seen and is the next best thing to hiring a guide. The uncluttered maps and clear photographs amply support the descriptions without taking away the adventure.

In May 2005, Lisa and I hiked along the obscure trail to 'Hidden Falls' to catch a final water ice climb for the season. Her enthusiasm for the Park was unbounded, and we shared information about the little points of interest along the way. After the climb, we continued to an old outlaw cabin for a grand view of the expansive valley of the North St. Vrain Creek below. We gazed over the sun-draped features all around us and enjoyed a quiet moment in an uninhabited corner of America's fourth-busiest park. I have had the pleasure of sharing adventures among the Park's features and personally being guided by Lisa Foster. Now, with her guidebook in your hand, you will have that chance, too.

—DR. JIM DETTERLINE
Retired Longs Peak Ranger, RMNP

Opposite: Lake of the Clouds from Mount Cirrus

Preface

Welcome to the most comprehensive hiking guide ever written about Rocky Mountain National Park. Whether you want to introduce your two-year-old to the beauty of nature on a smooth, level path, or you want to hike 20 miles off-trail to submerge yourself in the wilderness and embrace true adventure in epic proportions, this book is for you.

I wrote this book because I love RMNP. To me, it is the most special section of preserved land on earth. My goal is that this book will aid visitors in exploring this extraordinary landscape, and inevitably, that they will learn to love it as much as I do.

This guide is unique because, unlike any other, it provides information about every named destination in RMNP, as well as many with unofficial names. It also contains selected destinations near the border of RMNP in Roosevelt National Forest, Comanche Peak Wilderness, Never Summer Wilderness, Indian Peaks Wilderness, Colorado State Forest, and Arapaho National Forest.

Without a doubt, this is the most extensively field-checked hiking book available for RMNP. I have not included a hike that I did not personally accomplish. The fact that I hiked each and every route myself lends consistency to the descriptions and ensures an unparalleled level of accuracy.

The idea for this guidebook had been lingering in my thoughts for more than a decade, but it wasn't until 2004 that I made a commitment to myself to bring the project into reality. That summer, I set out to finish hiking to every named destination in RMNP. It was an intimidating task, and it took a lot out of me, as well as the various souls who unwarily agreed to accompany me on some of the longer, more strenuous hikes. In the wake of my relief at completing my goal, I wrote the following letter to friends, which sums up my liberation from that phase of writing the book:

"Well, I can hardly believe it, but I did it. The list of 100 hikes that seemed so daunting at the beginning of the season has officially been completed. This summer was plagued with rain, hail, lightning danger, illness, and more rain. But somehow, by the grace of God, I got it done.

At the beginning of the summer, it rained straight for two months. We switched the schedule around to accommodate this by hiking to all the places on the list in the trees. By 10 a.m. every day the clouds were already rolling in. No place to hide up on the tundra, so we stuck to the trees. Since the weather pattern of building clouds, hail, and rain did not relent, we started leaving at 2, 3, and 4 a.m. to get up the peaks and down into the trees before the tempest hit. In August we were blessed with 10 straight days of fair weather and it was truly glorious. Lots of peaks were climbed. By late August I contracted my little sister Stephanie's pneumonia and viral bronchitis, which hit me really hard, but I couldn't stop. September traditionally brings shorter days, but the thunderstorms usually disappear. Unfortunately for me, in this wet, wet year, September acted like June. All summer long I have been tagging summits and running from the storms. September was no exception. Completing all the destinations on the west side of the Park before Trail Ridge Road closed was particularly stressful. The road was shut down in late June for a hailstorm and on Labor Day Weekend for a snowstorm. A couple of weeks ago I completed my last hike over there and now can rest comfortably as it snows, rains, hails, or whatever it will because I don't care.

Opposite: A scenic winter view from McGregor Mountain

The last two weekends were a crazy hiking frenzy to complete the list before the snow came. On the second to last weekend Steve Lawlor and I went down to Watanga Lakes and hiked all of those peaks on the southern border of the Park that are difficult to access. I can't believe Steve could tolerate the violent coughing fits that accompany this illness I have. It must be as horrible to listen to as it is to endure. The higher elevations particularly affected my lungs. But we got all the peaks we went for. This week Josh Agan and I climbed Elk Tooth and then traversed that gnarly ridge over to Ogalalla, all under questionable skies, but luckily it didn't rain. We descended Cony Pass (steep!) and hiked out in the dark. The next day Alex Kostadinov and I left at 4 a.m. and hightailed it up to the Continental Divide, then cruised over to that elusive pinnacle, The Cleaver. As intimidated as I have always been about this sharp, precipitous, seldom-climbed feature, it turned out to be an easy Class 3 scramble to the top. Then we booked it over to the saddle between Mount Alice and the highpoint of the "false Pilot Mountain." We descended a loose scree gully and traversed out over grassy ledges to the lower, more jagged true summit of Pilot Mountain. An exposed Class 4 scramble took us to the top, the last named summit I had to climb in RMNP. The sky was so dark we just signed the summit register, which has been there since 1974, and scooted down as fast as we could. It started to rain just as we were downclimbing some Class 4 slabs, but we made it down to the tundra and rushed into the trees before it really unleashed. It poured rain the whole 7-mile hike out, but the rangers at the Thunder Lake Cabin welcomed us in and offered us tea.

As I trod my last steps across the footbridge to the Wild Basin Trailhead, I felt a gulping sense of relief. The weather was horrendous, but for the first time all summer, I didn't care. Let it snow, let it rain, let it freeze into ice. I did it. The grueling

Bench Lake

death marches are over. The days of back-to-back 20-mile hikes are gone. Now I can rest, sit at my computer, and write my book.

But now I miss it. It's kind of sad to think that I have been to every named destination in RMNP. This summer was a joyous journey into the unknown. Now it is known. I saw about 30 moose, most of them in the wildest places, and I was alone. My moments spent with the moose, them checking me out, me holding my ground, regarding each other, were some of the most special and intriguing minutes I have ever had. When Steve Volker and I were in Spruce Canyon, walking along a suspended log, and suddenly we saw the little black-as-night bear cub scurry up the tree, with me asking "Where do you think his mother is?" and Steve looking about 10 feet away from us and saying calmly, "Right there," and to see her, all beautiful and cinnamon-colored, bounding downhill, away from us, with her cub safely hanging on a limb, was remarkable.

I am transitioning between a summer of unbelievable wilderness experience to sitting at a desk, staring at a computer screen, and I hope I can do

Longs Peak framed by The Gable

it. To write this book—to put down into words the thrill of the peaks, the serenity of the forest, and the excitement of the unknown around the next bend, across the river, down the talus slope, or around that next gendarme—will be a challenge and an experience. I hope I'm girl enough for the task. Wish me luck."

So began the process of writing this book, which proved to be harder and much more grueling than any 20-mile death march! But in the end, with this book that you hold in your hands, it was all worth it.

RMNP belongs to all of us. It is our public land, our heritage, and our legacy. It has been preserved for our enjoyment. It is an unspoiled natural playground conserved because we *need* wilderness. It allows us to escape the grind of daily life and leave our worries behind. It is not riddled with development, not characterized by right angles, and not limited to tame adventure. It is a wild place, and for good or bad, adventure will be met in this arena. We must continue to preserve it for future generations so that they, too, might come here and get immersed in adventure, whether it be spending an unplanned, cold night on a rocky ledge and surviving, taking that breathtaking dip into an alpine lake, or sliding almost out of control down a steep snowfield. You may revel in the sunset atop a distant peak, hear the sweet songbirds croon at a mystic lake, or wake up refreshed after a night on the banks of a rushing river.

Whatever your experience, I hope this book will help you to get there. You will no doubt come back a richer person, more at peace, and ready to face the other elements of your life. Good luck, be safe, and most of all, *have fun*. See you out there!

— LISA FOSTER
Estes Park, Colorado

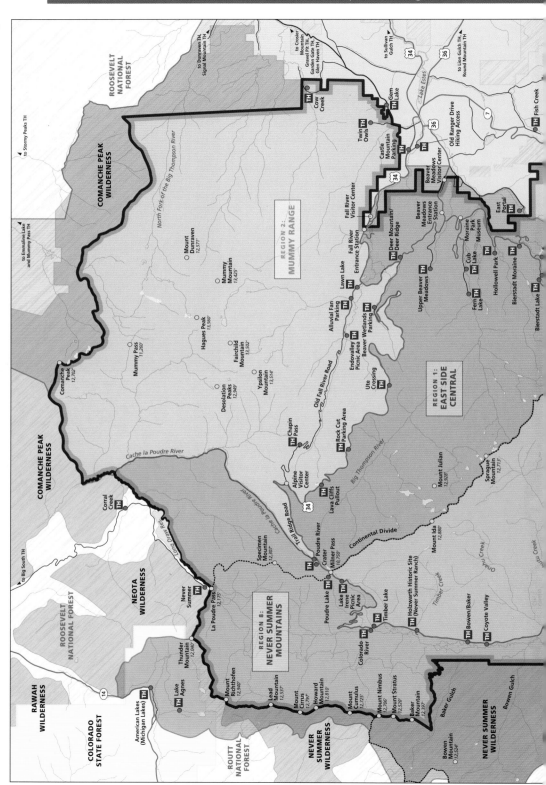

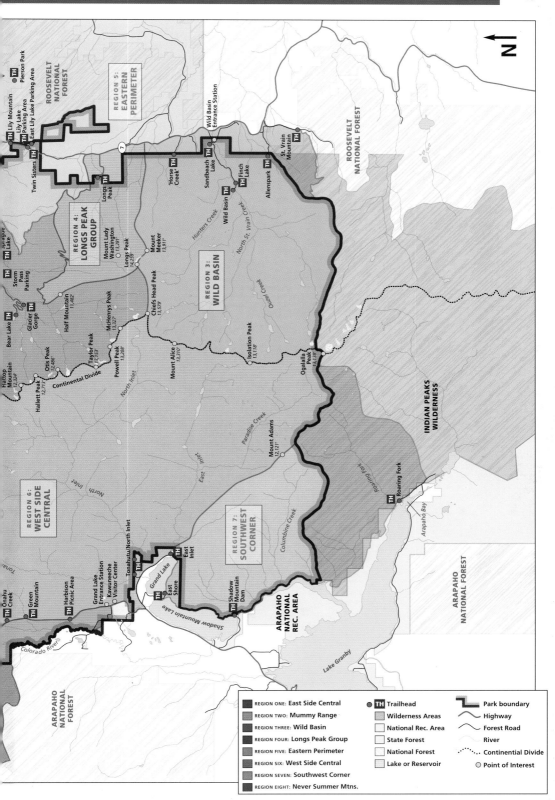

ROOSEVELT NATIONAL FOREST

Pierson Park
Lily Mountain
Lily Lake Parking Area
East Lily Lake Parking Area
REGION 5: EASTERN PERIMETER
Twin Sisters
Wild Basin Entrance Station
St. Vrain Mountain
REGION 4: LONGS PEAK GROUP
'Horse Creek'
Sandbeach Lake
Finch Lake
Allenspark
Longs Peak
Hunters Creek
North St. Vrain Creek
Wild Basin
Mount Lady Washington 13,281'
Mount Meeker 13,911'
Longs Peak 14,259'
Ouzel Creek
REGION 3: WILD BASIN
Chiefs Head Peak 13,579'
ROOSEVELT NATIONAL FOREST
McHenrys Peak 13,327'
Half Mountain 11,482'
Isolation Peak 13,118'
Ogalalla Peak 13,138'
Powell Peak 13,208'
Taylor Peak 13,153'
Mount Alice 13,310'
Continental Divide
Hallett Peak 12,713'
Otis Peak 12,486'
Flattop Mountain 12,324'
Bear Lake
Glacier Gorge
Storm Pass Parking
Sprague Lake
North Inlet
Paradise Creek
Mount Adams 12,121'
INDIAN PEAKS WILDERNESS
Roaring Fork
Roaring Fork
East Inlet
Columbine Creek
REGION 7: SOUTHWEST CORNER
Arapaho Bay
REGION 6: WEST SIDE CENTRAL
North Inlet
Tonahutu/North Inlet
East Inlet
East Shore
Shadow Mountain Dam
Shadow Mountain Lake
Grand Lake
Grand Lake Entrance Station
Kawuneeche Visitor Center
Harbison Picnic Area
Green Mountain
Onahu Creek
Onahu Creek
Colorado River
Tonahutu Creek
Lake Granby
ARAPAHO NATIONAL REC. AREA
ARAPAHO NATIONAL FOREST
ARAPAHO NATIONAL FOREST

REGION ONE: **East Side Central**
REGION TWO: **Mummy Range**
REGION THREE: **Wild Basin**
REGION FOUR: **Longs Peak Group**
REGION FIVE: **Eastern Perimeter**
REGION SIX: **West Side Central**
REGION SEVEN: **Southwest Corner**
REGION EIGHT: **Never Summer Mtns.**

TH Trailhead
Wilderness Areas
National Rec. Area
State Forest
National Forest
Lake or Reservoir

Park boundary
Highway
Forest Road
River
Continential Divide
Point of Interest

Longs Peak from The Spearhead

Introduction

Rocky Mountain National Park (RMNP) is a veritable treasure trove of scenic splendor that attracts more than three million people each year. Most visitors experience RMNP during the summer season, usually from June through September. But RMNP offers wonderful adventures year-round; those wishing to escape the crowds might consider a trip during the shoulder seasons or the winter.

Hiking is one of the main activities for visitors to RMNP. It is also the best way to experience the astonishing majesty of this spectacular landscape. Hiking gets people out there: on the trails, atop the peaks, to the lakes. By hiking you get to feel the brush of the wind, the warmth of the sun on your skin, the beauty of the changing weather. There is no way to step off the treadmill and call it a day. You must experience everything the hike has to offer.

In close proximity to large centers of population, RMNP is remarkably accessible by paved roads that wind into the very heart of the mountains. This convenient road network offers the visitor the ability to enter RMNP's wilderness easily and economically, with relatively little time expended. Strategically located trailheads provide tactical starting points for hikes that penetrate deep into the forests and high up on the peaks, all of which are possible to complete in one day. Indescribable grandeur awaits virtually steps from your car. Most of the mountains have at least one nontechnical route to the summit, making RMNP a hiker's paradise.

This guidebook presents a total of 686 route descriptions for 440 destinations. In these pages you'll find details such as how to reach the trailhead; hiking descriptions; whether the hike follows a road, a trail, or is off-trail; if it is suitable for families or those with disabilities; relevant history; and other pertinent information to access any of the destinations in RMNP.

The hikes within this guide range from very easy (your great-grandmother could do these) to extremely strenuous (for experts only), with everything in between. There is something for everyone in this book. Each reader will be able to find a hike to suit his or her desires, abilities, and time frame.

RMNP offers almost 400 miles of hiking trails. They range from paved paths to long, rocky, strenuous trails that climb relentlessly to their destinations. RMNP has an exceptional trail crew and most of the trails are well built and easy to follow. The majority of the hikes in this guide utilize the extensive trail system. However, many hikes start on a trail but end up off-trail, requiring the hiker to bushwhack through forests or travel cross-country above treeline.

All route descriptions in this guidebook assume summer conditions, and many require a high level of fitness on the hiker's part.

ON THE TRAIL

Hiking in RMNP is exciting and fun, but it takes place in an alpine environment, which involves inherent risks that need to be considered in order to ensure a safe and pleasant experience for you and the members of your party. The written hiking descriptions are intended to supplement the hiker's knowledge, and the information provided is not a substitute for your own good judgment and skill. Ultimately, only you are responsible for your safety.

Route conditions change from year to year, potentially making them dangerous. Varying weather conditions can alter the nature of any route in this guide, making it unsafe. However, potential hazards can be easily avoided when the proper precautions are taken.

ASSESSMENT OF ABILITY   Fair assessment of your ability and that of the weakest member of your group will help you to maximize your time in RMNP, and to effectively use this guidebook for choosing the best hike for your party. Consider whether any disabilities or medical conditions might prevent a person from performing ordinary tasks at high elevations. Consider how much time your group has on a particular day. Consider the children and elderly in your group. Consider the group's collective outdoor experience.

DEHYDRATION, DRINKING WATER, and **GIARDIA**   Colorado's low humidity and dry atmosphere can lead to dehydration. Be sure to carry enough drinking water to prevent dehydration as you exert energy while hiking.

Do not drink untreated water from the lakes or streams in RMNP. Invisible to the human eye, the microscopic organism *Giardia lamblia* can cause serious illness. It is present in all water systems in RMNP. Boil water or use a filter to purify water taken from RMNP water sources, or simply carry enough purified water.

ALTITUDE SICKNESS   At high elevations, there is less oxygen in the air. Reduced oxygen intake can cause an illness commonly known as altitude sickness. The effects of altitude affect everyone differently. Take time to let your body acclimatize to RMNP's high elevation. Start by selecting shorter hikes with less elevation gain and work your way up to the more difficult hikes. Pay attention to symptoms of altitude sickness, which include shortness of breath, nausea, dizziness, weakness, and loss of appetite, and take precautions to prevent them.

HYPOTHERMIA   The lowering of the body's core temperature to dangerous levels is called hypothermia. Exposure to wetness, wind, and cold temperatures can all contribute to this condition. You can prevent hypothermia by staying warm and dry. Carry raingear and extra layers of clothing, including a hat and gloves, to help combat hypothermia in wet and cold conditions.

EXPOSURE TO HIGH-ALTITUDE SUN   Sunscreen, sunglasses, and a hat are important ways to fight the fatigue and illness that can plague a hiker as a result of sunburn. Remember that ultraviolet rays are stronger at higher elevations and the sun can be intense and severe.

SUMMER WEATHER   Although characterized by clear, sunny mornings, stormy afternoons, and cool nights, RMNP's weather is unpredictable. Observe current weather conditions before hiking and consider the long-range weather forecast. The weather in RMNP can change rapidly. Even if you begin hiking on a clear, cloudless day, adverse weather can move in quickly, so prepare for any type of weather conditions. Summer snowstorms are not uncommon at high altitude. Summer daytime temperatures average in the mid-70s (Fahrenheit), but be prepared for temperatures ranging between 30° and 90° F.

LIGHTNING   Lightning poses a real threat to hikers in RMNP. Lightning kills more people each year in the United States than any other weather-related hazard. Thunderstorms build in RMNP's high country almost every afternoon during the summer months. Start hiking early in the day to ensure that you can return below treeline before afternoon thundershowers and lightning move in. Lightning typically strikes the highest object in an area. Don't be the highest object around and don't stand next to the highest object for protection. Seek the safety of your car, the forest, or the lowest point in the terrain on which you are hiking.

PETS   Dogs and other pets are not allowed on the trails or in the backcountry of RMNP. Leashed pets are allowed on some roads in RMNP during certain times of the year. For detailed information, please contact RMNP (see the end of this Introduction).

A summer thundershower

WILDLIFE   The animals that live in RMNP are wild and free. It is a treat to view them in their natural habitat, but be aware that they can pose a threat to visitors. To avoid negative conflict between animals and humans, do not approach or feed wildlife. Respect the animal's territory and take care not to disturb its movement. Don't interfere when an animal is feeding, and don't disturb the interaction between animals. Some people find it exciting to feed wildlife. It's a bad idea, though, and here's why:

- Animals bite and carry disease.
- Feeding animals draws them to close contact with people, which causes them to gradually lose their fear of humans. This is potentially problematic for both animals and humans.
- Dependence on human-provided food can cause starvation and make the animal more susceptible to predation.
- Altering the animal's natural methods might disrupt ecosystems and have far-ranging effects in ways that we can't initially see.

Mammals that live in RMNP include black bears, mountain lions, elk, deer, moose, bighorn sheep, squirrels, and chipmunks. Common sightings of elk and deer attract hordes of wildlife enthusiasts. It is extremely rare, however, to see a bear or mountain lion. For information about what to do in case of an encounter with large mammals, inquire at one of RMNP's visitor centers.

FALLING TREES   Falling trees are always a hazard when traveling in forested areas. In recent years, RMNP has been experiencing an outbreak of several species of bark beetles that has exacerbated the potential for falling trees. Bark beetles are native insects that have shaped the forests of North America for thousands of years. The current outbreak is largely due to the fact that average winter temperatures in RMNP have been higher than normal in the last decade, which has prevented beetle eggs and larvae from being eliminated naturally. Couple that with recent prolonged periods of low precipitation, and the outcome is a forest with trees that are weakened structurally, and more prone to collapse in periods of high winds. To protect yourself from being injured while hiking in the forest, the National Park Service urges visitors to follow these guidelines to avoid the risks associated with falling trees:

Notchtop Mountain looms over Odessa Lake

- Be aware of your surroundings. Avoid dense patches of dead trees. They can fall without warning.
- Be particularly watchful when it is windy or following a snowstorm when tree branches are heavy with snow. Stay out of the forest when there are strong winds that could blow trees down. If you are already in the forest when the wind increases, hike to a clearing out of reach of any potentially falling trees.
- Avoid parking or camping in areas where trees could fall. Place tents and park vehicles in areas where they will not be hit if trees fall.
- Do not rely on cell phones for safety. There is no coverage in many areas of the Park.
- Remember, safety is your responsibility!

INSECTS Mosquitoes, flies, and ticks are all found in RMNP. You can deter these pests with insect repellent containing DEET.

WHAT TO BRING The essentials recommended for any day hike, include, but are not limited to:

- Water
- Extra clothes for layering
- Sunscreen and lip balm
- Sunglasses
- Raingear
- Food

- Map and compass
- Flashlight and extra batteries
- First-aid kit
- Pocketknife
- Waterproof matches or a lighter

Coyote near Moraine Park

PARK INFORMATION

All overnight stays in RMNP require a permit, but no permit is needed for day hiking or climbing. A fee is charged to enter RMNP. The National Park Service has strict regulations governing all activity within RMNP. These necessary guidelines protect this pristine landscape from the millions of visitors it receives annually. Park rules change regularly. To receive updated, detailed information, contact RMNP at (970) 586-1206, visit the website at www.nps.gov/romo, or write to Rocky Mountain National Park, Information Office, 1000 US 36, Estes Park, CO 80517. Visitor and hiker shuttle busses are available during the summer season from Estes Park and throughout the National Park.

LEAVE NO TRACE

To protect the natural conditions of RMNP's backcountry, the National Park Service recommends adhering to Leave No Trace outdoor ethics. Leave No Trace is a national nonprofit organization that is dedicated to educating people about responsible use of the outdoors. It recommends simple techniques for minimum-impact travel in Colorado's fragile, high-alpine environments. *The member-driven Leave No Trace Center for Outdoor Ethics teaches people how to enjoy the outdoors responsibly. This copyrighted information has been reprinted with permission: www.LNT.org*

- Plan Ahead and Prepare
- Travel and Camp on Durable Surfaces
- Dispose of Waste Properly
- Leave What You Find

- Minimize Campfire Impacts
- Respect Wildlife
- Be Considerate of Other Visitors

How to Use This Guide

ORGANIZATION

This book consists of eight chapters, each covering a distinct geographical area of RMNP. The color-coded chapters are organized in sections. After a brief introduction to the region of the Park, a table of contents provides at-a-glance reference to the main "subregions," and to a selection of my favorite hiking destinations within those subregions. Symbols next to the highlighted destinations indicate whether the hikes are particularly suitable for families 🖼, for the disabled, including those in wheelchairs 🖼, or whether special equipment is recommended 🖼 (meaning the hike is more challenging, possibly technical). Regional maps introduce each of the eight chapters and detailed hike maps appear where applicable throughout the text (see Maps, p. 27).

The Hiking Destinations section describes all the named geographical features in RMNP; unofficial place-names appear in single quotes. For hikers who wish to picnic at a scenic lake or waterfall, or climb a summit, the destinations are categorized into two subsections: The names of lakes, waterfalls, wetlands, and other water features appear in blue, whereas peaks, glaciers, passes, meadows, and other landforms appear in brown. The feature's elevation is listed next to its name, and references to the map or maps on which it appears are listed below it. Where possible, the destinations are grouped in a geographical fashion; for instance, lakes dotting a drainage are presented together. Historical information is sprinkled throughout the text.

These symbols appear with each destination to indicate what you can expect from the hike:

- **T** the destination is accessed by a trail
- **OT** the destination is accessed by off-trail means
- **R** the destination is on a road
- 🖼 hikes suitable for families
- 🖼 destinations that provide access to the disabled
- 🖼 recommended use of equipment such as a helmet, ice axe, crampons, and/or rope

Hiking descriptions begin with a brief introduction, followed by detailed information about how to execute the hike. The descriptions note distances between points (see Mileages, p. 26), trail difficulty and conditions, intersecting trails, and natural features; additional information may be found in the Destinations Chart (see Appendix B, p. 364). Note that even though I have personally visited every destination in this book, things change, and landslides, avalanches, flash floods, fires, and dying and falling trees can alter the face of the landscape, affecting the routes described and the difficulty of established trails. If the destination has more than one route or access point, they are listed subsequently. For routes that climb to a summit, a difficulty rating by grade and class is included (see Ratings, opposite). For each destination, the easiest possible route is always described; additional routes listed may be more difficult.

The Trailheads and Trails sections toward the end of each region provide information about the starting points for hikes and how to reach them, and profile the trails within the region. The section called Other Points of Interest describes any of the region's other unique features.

APPENDICES

In the back of the book is a highly detailed Destinations Chart (p. 366). For each hiking destination, this chart lists the destination and its page number in the book; the one-way distance of the hike (except when noted, e.g., for loop trails); the trailhead or access point; the route used for access; the starting elevation; the ending elevation; the absolute change in elevation gain or loss; difficulty ratings of Grade and Class; and snow or ice ratings, if applicable (see Ratings, below). Many destinations have multiple routes, so information for each route is included on a separate line. Destinations with unofficial names appear in single quotes. Note that the Trail/Route column, which provides pertinent information for each hike, highlights additional details to aid the reader in determining the exact line of ascent for which the statistics were calculated.

This chart is an extremely useful tool for planning a hike. Information necessary to determine which hike best suits your needs is at your fingertips. This comprehensive, one-of-a-kind table lists hundreds of routes that have never before had easy reference information published about them.

Also in the back of the book, a glossary (p. 362) aids in understanding climbing terms that might not be commonly known.

RATINGS

A rating system is a tool that helps a hiker or climber choose a route within his or her abilities that also presents a desirable level of challenge. The inherently subjective nature of this system makes consistency between hiking/climbing guidebooks and other sources, such as National Park Service information, difficult to achieve. In general terms, routes are usually rated by community consensus. Typically guidebook authors have not climbed every route described and must rely on the opinions of others. However, for this guidebook, I have climbed every route I describe; therefore, my ratings are more consistent unto themselves.

This guidebook employs a rating system for all routes that ascend a peak. In general, I don't rate hikes to lakes, waterfalls, meadows, parks, or other features that aren't summits. The ratings of the climbs in this guidebook assume good weather, dry conditions, and adequate equipment.

This book uses the nationally accepted Yosemite Decimal System (YDS) to rate a route's difficulty. Each rating has two main parts, Grade and Class. The term "grade" is a commitment rating; it is used to rate a route's

The Chasm Lake Spur Trail

SNOW/ICE DESIGNATIONS

Snow steepness reflects the angle of snow on a particular route. I have used these ratings in the chart as rough guidelines to describe the general difficulty of snow travel along a given route.

• **Easy Snow (ES):** angle of snow up to 30 degrees

• **Moderate Snow (MS):** angle of snow between 30 and 45 degrees

• **Steep Snow (SS):** angle of snow greater than 45 degrees

Alpine ice designations are assigned to routes that ascend ice slopes. All routes in this category are technical and are defined as follows:

• **AI1:** easy, low-angle ice

• **AI2:** a sustained ice slope with an angle of at least 55 to 60 degrees

• **AI3:** a sustained ice slope with an angle of ice between 70 and 80 degrees

overall difficulty, generally described by the length of time it takes to complete and how much elevation gain is involved. The term "class" is used to describe the route's most difficult section. Grade and Class are useful ways to determine if a route is suitable for the experience of an individual or group. Additionally, a detailed analysis of the overall route description as explained in the chapters is another helpful method for assessing the qualities of each route.

On certain routes, a note about snow steepness is included. I have used the following ratings as rough guidelines to describe the general difficulty of snow travel. "Easy snow" describes a route for which the angle of the snow is up to 30 degrees. "Moderate snow" describes a route for which the angle of the snow is between 30 and 45 degrees. "Steep snow" describes a route for which the angle of the snow is greater than 45 degrees. "Alpine ice" describes routes that ascend ice slopes; all routes in this category are technical. Please note that all snow routes in this guide require some technical knowledge and training. When using an ice axe or crampons, you need to know what you are doing. Seek professional guidance if you are a novice.

Rocks near Sprague Pass

Les Moore scrambles up Class 4 terrain, Arrowhead Arête, McHenrys Peak

A GENERAL OVERVIEW OF THE YDS

The YDS rates only the most difficult move on a route. This means that a Class 4 route might only have one move of Class 4 climbing to be rated as such. However, be prepared for the more common scenario that a climb has multiple moves, or sections of moves, at the difficulty for which it was rated.

CLASS

This scale rates routes with a number from 1 to 5.15, with 1 being the easiest classification. Classes 1 through 4 are written with a single digit only. Class 5 is broken down into fractions, from 5.0 to 5.15. In Class 5, the word "class" is usually dropped and the routes are described with the number only.

Classes 1 and 2 are used to describe hiking routes only. Classes 3, 4, and 5 are in the climbing category, where movement becomes more complicated than walking. An ascent in this range involves simple (Class 3) to extremely difficult (Class 5) climbing techniques. When a "+" sign is listed after the class, such as Class 2+, this means that the route is either a sustained Class 2 (with multiple moves at that difficulty), or the route falls somewhere between the two classifications (more difficult than Class 2, but not as difficult as Class 3). The most difficult route discussed in this guide is 5.6; this is out of the realm of hiking, necessitating the skill and experience of seasoned technical climbers.

Class 1: This rating includes hiking along a maintained trail or hiking cross-country over terrain that is no more difficult than walking along a trail.

Class 2: This rating describes off-trail hiking, including bushwhacking, hiking up talus slopes, or negotiating marshy terrain. The use of hands for movement is not necessary in this class.

Class 3: This class leaves the range of walking and enters the realm of climbing, utilizing the most basic technical climbing methods. The most common technique used to ascend a Class 3 route is called "scrambling," which requires the use of hands for upward movement.

Class 4: This class describes intermediate technical climbing, although many experienced climbers opt to forgo the use of a rope when a climb is rated Class 4. Good climbing skills, the use of hands for upward movement, and thoughtful hand and foot placements are all required. A fall on Class 4 terrain could be serious or even fatal.

Class 5: This is serious technical climbing. A rope and natural or artificial protection are recommended on all routes within this category. Plenty of previous experience and well-honed climbing skills are required to ascend routes in this class safely.

Grade I: A route in this category can be of any technical difficulty, but it should only require a few hours to complete. Grade I describes a short day climb.

Grade II: A route in this category can be of any technical difficulty, but it is a day climb, requiring a half-day or more to complete.

Grade III: A route in this category can be of any technical difficulty, but it requires a full day to complete. Routes of this grade are long day climbs.

Grade IV: This category generally applies to a route that is at least as hard as 5.7 and is a very long day climb, expected to take the entire day. There are no Grade IV routes in this guide.

Exposure can be present in any class of hiking or climbing. This is a subjective fear and it affects people differently. Exposure, and the fear of it, can make a route within a certain class feel exponentially more difficult.

GRADE

This scale rates routes for their overall difficulty, in terms of length and commitment. They are described as Grade I to Grade IV, with Grade I being the easiest. The highest grade on a route in this guide is Grade III.

MILEAGES

Measuring mileage is an inexact science. With any method, there is a margin of error.

TRAILS

Trail mileages were meticulously calculated using measurements from United States Geological Survey (USGS) topographical maps. These mileages might—and probably do in most cases—conflict with information in other guidebooks or information supplied by the National Park Service, such as on signs encountered along the trail in the back-country. The mileages listed here were calculated uniformly, with painstaking attention to detail. However, the maps from which they were derived are not always accurate; sometimes trails are marked slightly incorrectly on the maps, such as the Lion Lake Trail in Wild Basin. In these cases, Global Positioning System (GPS) and Geographic Information Systems (GIS) information was used to supplement map information in an attempt to gain the most accurate mileages available for RMNP.

Mount Alice

ROADS

Let's face it, consistency between vehicle odometers is just not there. The road mileages in this book were taken in different vehicles at different times. I personally drove each leg of road in this guide and took down the mileage. These distances are as accurate as possible, but your vehicle could register a slightly different number. The mileage numbers are simply general references, but should be reliable within a few tenths of a mile in most cases.

MAPS

Each of the eight chapters covers a distinct geographical area of RMNP, color-coded and shown on the overview map on p. 14. A regional map of the area covered is included at the beginning of every chapter, and grid coordinates provided in the text pinpoint the location of each destination. These maps are general, listing roads, trailheads, visitor centers, major features, and major trails. The contour interval on the regional maps is 80 feet. The following symbols appear on the regional maps:

Eric Salerno on the west summit of Mount Meeker

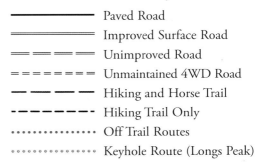

▲ 🅿 Campground, Picnic Area	────────── Paved Road
🚹 🚻 Ranger Station, Restrooms	══════════ Improved Surface Road
🚤 🏠 Boat Ramp, Livery	═ ═ ═ ═ ═ Unimproved Road
♿ 🏞 Handicap Access, Interpretive Trail	= = = = = = = = Unmaintained 4WD Road
ⓒⓓ •─• Continental Divide Trail, Gate	━ ━ ━ ━ Hiking and Horse Trail
🅗 🖼 Trailhead, Scenic Overlook	-·-·-·-·-· Hiking Trail Only
❓ Information (Visitor Center)	················ Off Trail Routes
	∘∘∘∘∘∘∘∘∘∘∘∘∘∘ Keyhole Route (Longs Peak)

Additionally, throughout the chapters are maps of select areas that require more detail than that depicted on the regional maps. These maps highlight routes to high-profile, sought-after destinations and provide a more comprehensive picture of the Park's terrain and destinations. These detailed hike maps have 40-foot contour intervals and have certain routes, as described in the text, drawn in as red dotted lines to aid navigation to a particular summit or destination. The routes are not established trails, but are off-trail routes depicting an invisible line of ascent, describing the best way to access the destination. Established trails appear on these maps as black dashed lines.

The maps in this book are meant to introduce a route and shouldn't serve as your sole guide in the field. For this purpose, I recommend the USGS 7.5-minute topographical quadrangles that cover specific areas of RMNP.

Sky Pond

East Side Central

This chapter describes some of the most popular and highly acclaimed destinations in RMNP. East Side Central includes the area east of Milner Pass, north of Wild Basin, and south of Trail Ridge Road. The region showcases the steep, beautiful, glacially carved eastern faces of the mountains that lie along the Continental Divide, as well as pristine lake valleys and forested canyons. The destinations in this region draw millions of people to Estes Park each year. Well-maintained roads and strategically located trailheads aid visitors in accessing this natural wonderland. Bear Lake, Glacier Gorge, and Loch Vale are stunningly scenic areas that offer everything from easy walks to strenuous technical challenges. There is truly something for everyone in this exciting region of RMNP

Andrews Tarn from Andrews Glacier

Hayden Spire

SUBREGIONS with Highlighted Hiking Destinations

GLACIER BASIN 33
  Sprague Lake 33

BIERSTADT MORAINE 34
    Bierstadt Lake 34

HOLLOWELL PARK 35

MORAINE PARK 36
    The Pool 37
    Cub Lake 38

BEAVER MEADOWS 40

DEER RIDGE 40
    Deer Mountain 40

HIDDEN VALLEY 41

TRAIL RIDGE 42
  Toll Memorial 43
    Ute Trail 44

GLACIER GORGE 46
    Alberta Falls 46
    Mills Lake 49
    Black Lake 49
    McHenrys Peak 56
    Chiefs Head Peak 59

LOCH VALE... 62
  🚶 The Loch 62
    Timberline Falls................................. 63
    Glass Lake...................................... 64
    Sky Pond....................................... 64
    Andrews Tarn.................................. 65
  ⛰ Andrews Glacier 66
    Taylor Peak..................................... 67
  ⛰ Powell Peak.................................... 68

CHAOS CANYON 69
  🚶 Lake Haiyaha 71
    Otis Peak....................................... 71

TYNDALL GORGE 72
 ♿🚶 Bear Lake 72
  🚶 Nymph Lake 73
  🚶 Dream Lake 73
  🚶 Emerald Lake................................. 74
    Flattop Mountain 75
    Hallett Peak 76

ODESSA GORGE................................. 78
  🚶 Fern Falls..................................... 78
    Fern Lake 79
    Odessa Lake 80
    Lake Helene 81
  ⛰ Notchtop Mountain 84

TOURMALINE GORGE 86
  ⛰ Little Matterhorn 87
    Gabletop Mountain 88

SPRUCE CANYON 89
    Spruce Lake 89
    Sprague Mountain 93
    Stones Peak.................................... 94

FOREST CANYON 94

HAYDEN GORGE 97
  ⛰ Cracktop 100
    Mount Julian 102
    Terra Tomah Mountain 102

GORGE LAKES................................. 103
    Rock Lake..................................... 104
    Arrowhead Lake 105
    Highest Lake 106
    Mount Ida 106
    Chief Cheley Peak............................. 107

TRAILHEADS 108

TRAILS 110

OTHER POINTS OF INTEREST 114

*John Haugh
in Loch Vale*

*Gabletop Mountain
from Spruce Lake*

*Michelle Chase and
Todd Burke descending
to Forest Canyon from
Trail Ridge Road*

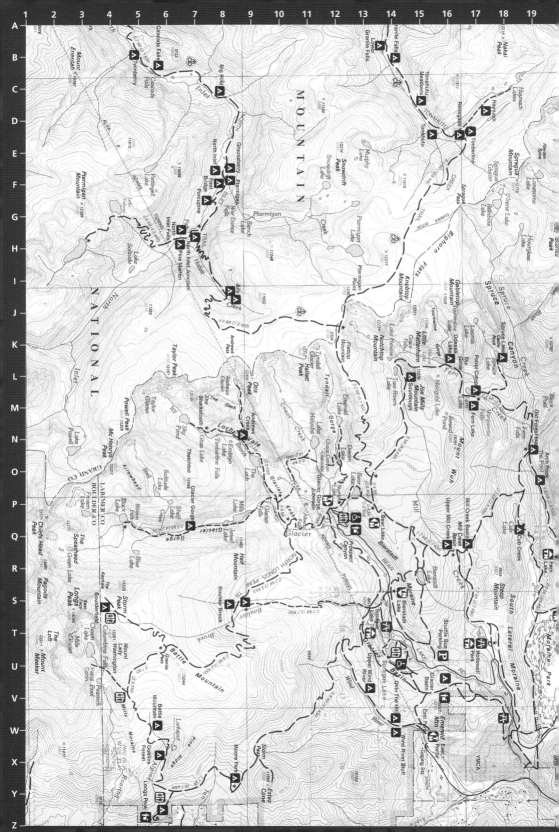

Distance in miles

N

© 2003 National Geographic

Map created with TOPO!®

GLACIER BASIN   *Regional map p. 30 (T, 14)*

LAKES

Sprague Lake   8,700 feet

T 🚶 ♿   *Regional map p. 30 (U, 14)*

This extremely popular, shallow lake provides inspiring views of the Continental Divide and is a great location for children to explore and view pond life. A level, 0.5-mile wheelchair-accessible path made of hard-packed dirt and lined with logs circles the lake. The path offers benches for resting and observation decks that protrude over the water, providing great views of the lake and mountain scenery. A large parking lot serves the destination, which is located 0.3 mile south of Bear Lake Road. The enchanting stroll around the lake is enjoyable for hikers of all abilities, including families, seniors, and disabled persons. Ducks frequent the lake and chipmunks and golden-mantled ground squirrels play in the nearby forest. Birds such as Clark's nutcrackers, gray jays, and Steller's jays are common sights. Dragonflies, beetles, and midges add to the thriving insect life in the pond. Frogs can be heard on quiet evenings. Beaver and muskrat rove nearby.

Abner Sprague, an early guide and Estes Park historian, and his wife, Alberta, ran a resort in Glacier Basin from 1910 to 1940. The tourist trade served them well and the Sprague Lodge was a popular place. They dammed Boulder Brook to establish two ponds in order to provide good fishing opportunities for their many guests. Along with fishing, guests enjoyed picnicking and hiking, as well as the peaceful atmosphere of a mountain resort. Only one of the fishponds remains today, carrying the name Sprague Lake in honor of the couple.

Sprague Lake Nature Trail Access

The Sprague Lake Nature Trail begins at the east end of the parking lot. The best views of the Continental Divide are found on the east side of the lake, the point farthest from the parking lot on the loop trail. Cross a footbridge and head southeast along the lakeshore. The trail meanders along the shoreline through trees to a marshy area. A well-kept boardwalk elevates the trail through the marsh. Resting benches on the boardwalk provide good views of Hallett Peak and Bierstadt Moraine to the west.

A painter at Sprague Lake

The trail continues to a junction with the path to wheelchair-accessible backcountry campsites. Continue along the east side of the lake to the junction with a spur trail to Glacier Basin Campground, which lies 1 mile to the northeast. Here, a wooden bridge crosses the outlet of the lake. Sweeping views of the Continental Divide can be seen to the west. An incredible panorama of high mountain peaks unfolds from Storm Peak, Half Mountain, Thatchtop, Taylor Peak, Otis Peak, Hallett Peak, and Flattop Mountain, extending all the way to Notchtop Mountain. Continue along the path and pass a pond on the north side of the trail. Soon a spur loop trail to a fishing pier and observation deck cuts away from the main path. A little farther is the turnoff for another trail that leads to Glacier Basin Campground. The loop continues and leads back to the parking lot. Sunrise and sunset are favorable times to visit Sprague Lake and experience the wonder of a mountain lake with grand views.

Opposite: Alberta Falls (see p. 46)

BIERSTADT MORAINE   *Regional map p. 30 (R, 14)*

Bierstadt Moraine is one of the most dramatic lateral moraines in RMNP. It has a steep south side that rises above Bear Lake Road and a gentle north side bordered by Mill Creek Basin and Hollowell Park. Bierstadt Lake lies on the plateau on top of the moraine, formed behind a dam built by glacial action.

LAKES

Bierstadt Lake   9,416 feet
T *Regional map p. 30 (R, 15)*

Nestled in a depression atop a large moraine and surrounded by conifers, picturesque Bierstadt Lake offers spectacular views that stretch from Notchtop Mountain to Longs Peak. The best view of Longs Peak is from the north side of the lake. A small sandy beach lining the eastern shore is a great spot to relax

Half Mountain, Thatchtop, Cathedral Spires, and Otis Peak from Bierstadt Moraine

and have lunch. The shallow outer edges of the lake are filled with sedges that grow in and out of the water. Four main trail systems serve Bierstadt Lake. All the routes that lead to the lake are moderate in difficulty and afford a pleasant hiking experience.

Bierstadt Lake Trailhead Access   From the Bierstadt Lake Trailhead (p. 108), follow the Bierstadt Lake Trail (p. 111) as it leads through dense lodgepole pine forest, then zig-zags quite steeply up Bierstadt Moraine. Large, sparse aspen groves and outstanding views of the Continental Divide highlight this strenuous climb. Crest the top of the moraine where the trail levels out and continues through lodgepole pines to a trail junction. Follow the signs to Bierstadt Lake. A lovely 0.6-mile wooded trail circles the lake.

Bierstadt Lake was named in honor of Albert Bierstadt, the famous 19th-century painter who came to Estes Park in 1876 with the Earl of Dunraven. Bierstadt's art glorified the Rocky Mountains. He rose to fame through his highly romanticized images of the West, which he portrayed on large-scale canvases. The earl commissioned Bierstadt to paint a landscape of Estes Park and Longs Peak, for which he allegedly paid an incredible sum of $15,000. The earl transported the painting to Europe to decorate the Dunraven Castle. The earl's business manager, Theodore Whyte, escorted Bierstadt around the Estes Park area and showed him many of the natural wonders. Abner Sprague gave credit to Whyte for naming the lake because Bierstadt showed a particular interest in it.

Bierstadt Moraine Trailhead Access   This trail climbs the eastern end of Bierstadt Moraine. This route is less crowded and more parking opportunities make it advantageous when Bear Lake and Bierstadt Lake parking areas are full. From the trailhead at the west end of RMNP's Park and Ride Lot (p. 108), follow the forested trail west 0.3 mile to a trail junction. The left-hand fork leads 1.3 miles southwest to the Bierstadt Lake Trailhead. The right-hand fork climbs west 0.9 mile to Bierstadt Moraine and the trail that circles Bierstadt Lake. Follow signs to the lake.

Bear Lake Access   This route is 0.7 mile longer than the trail from Bierstadt Lake Trailhead but it is less strenuous. Bear Lake is 34 feet higher than Bierstadt Lake so this route ambles gently downhill. From the Bear Lake Trailhead (p. 108), follow the Flattop Mountain Trail (pp. 75, 112) for 0.4 mile to the junction with the trail to Bierstadt Lake. Follow the trail toward Bierstadt Lake as it climbs for a short distance and then descends along easy, forested terrain for 0.75 mile to the junction with the trail to Mill Creek Basin. Turn east (right) and follow the trail toward Bierstadt Lake for 0.6 mile to the junction with the Bierstadt Lake Trail. Follow signs to Bierstadt Lake.

Hollowell Park Access This route ascends the north side of Bierstadt Moraine and is one of the most scenic ways to reach Bierstadt Lake. Vibrant willows along Mill Creek combine with brilliant aspen trees to make this a colorful autumn hike. The Mill Creek Basin Trail in Hollowell Park also showcases the dense carpet of sagebrush on the east side of Steep Mountain and a dramatic view of Longs Peak rising to the south above the heavily forested moraine.

From the Hollowell Park Trailhead (p. 109), hike along the wide, flat trail that leads to Mill Creek Basin (p. 113). The trail leads through a lovely open meadow, then enters the trees and skirts the south side of Steep Mountain, following Mill Creek. Turn southwest (left) at a trail junction and follow the trail that leads toward Upper Mill Creek and Bierstadt Lake. Cross Mill Creek and climb up the north side of Bierstadt Moraine. Follow the signs toward Bierstadt Lake at the next trail junction and climb through the forest, hiking away from Mill Creek. Another junction prompts the hiker to head east toward Bierstadt Lake. Arrive at the lake and follow a small path that leads directly to the water's edge.

HOLLOWELL PARK
Regional map p. 30 (T, 18)

This marshy, open meadowland along Mill Creek lies at 8,400 feet at the eastern foot of Steep Mountain and on the south side of South Lateral Moraine. It provides access to Steep Mountain, South Lateral Moraine, and the Mill Creek Basin Trail system.

A spelling error in the interpretation of original homestead land records resulted in the frequently encountered misspelling, "Hallowell Park." However, descendents of George C. Hollowell, for whom the park is named, have requested that the error be corrected in all references. George Hollowell was a Loveland rancher who grazed cattle in Hollowell Park during the late 1800s and early 1900s. Through the years Hollowell Park was the site of a variety of logging operations, sawmills, ranches, and camps.

PEAKS AND OTHER DESTINATIONS

Mill Creek Basin 9,000 feet
T *Regional map p. 30 (Q, 17)*

Mill Creek Basin is a scenic, open meadow along pretty Mill Creek, northwest of Bierstadt Lake. It is situated on a ridge high above and southeast of Cub Lake, and it is home to two NPS backcountry campsites.

Hollowell Park Access From the Hollowell Park Trailhead (p. 109), hike along the wide, flat trail that leads to Mill Creek Basin. The trail heads through a lovely open meadow, then enters the trees and skirts the south side of Steep Mountain, following

Snow-dusted trees in Hollowell Park

Mill Creek. Bear west (right) at the trail junction and hike to lovely Mill Creek Basin, 1.9 miles from the trailhead.

Access from The Pool Locate the major trail junction immediately west of The Pool (follow the route description, p. 37). Turn southeast (left) and follow the trail 2.5 miles to Mill Creek Basin. This trail climbs very steeply through the forest with intermittent but superb views of Cub Lake and Moraine Park. It then crests a plateau for a short distance and drops steeply downhill to the pretty aspen- and pine-lined meadow of Mill Creek Basin.

Bear Lake Access   From the Bear Lake Trailhead (p. 108), follow the Flattop Mountain Trail (pp. 75, 112) for 0.4 mile to the junction with the trail to Bierstadt Lake. Hike along the trail toward Bierstadt Lake as it climbs for a short distance and then descends along easy, forested terrain for 0.75 mile to the junction with the trail to Mill Creek Basin. Continue north for 1 mile to pretty Mill Creek Basin.

South Lateral Moraine 8,720 feet
OT *Regional map p. 30 (T, 18)*

Glacial erratics and rounded boulders ornament this beautiful, forested moraine, which is one of the most dramatic lateral moraines in RMNP. A glacial advance that also formed Moraine Park pushed it up into a 1.8-mile-long ridge that separates Moraine Park from Hollowell Park.

South Slope GRADE I CLASS 2   From the Hollowell Park Trailhead (p. 109), strike off-trail to the northwest and climb steeply up the moraine for 320 vertical feet to a highpoint. Take the time to explore the ridgetop of the moraine.

Steep Mountain 9,538 feet
T **OT** *Regional map p. 30 (S, 18)*

This small mountain lies between Cub Creek and Mill Creek, at the western end of the South Lateral Moraine in Hollowell Park. A short, steep bushwhack provides access to the top.

East Slope GRADE I CLASS 2   From the Hollowell Park Trailhead (p. 109), hike 0.4 mile along the wide, flat trail that leads through a lovely open meadow. At the point where the trail turns south to contour around Steep Mountain, break away from the trail and hike up Steep Mountain's eastern flank. This open, rocky slope is covered with low-lying plants and sagebrush. A pretty aspen grove flourishes in a small gully that runs west up the hillside.

Continue hiking up the steep grade and enter the trees. Keep heading west and upslope to a group of rock outcroppings on the southeastern rib of the peak. From this vantage, intimate views of Hallett Peak and the Continental Divide stand out to the southwest. A slightly more distant view of Longs Peak rises to the south. Contour around the rocky section to a beautiful plateau. Continue west to the summit. Huge panoramic views abound from this small mountaintop. They include Moraine Park, the Mummy Range, massive Stones Peak, the Continental Divide, and Longs Peak.

MORAINE PARK   *Regional map p. 31 (T, 20)*

Moraine Park (8,040 feet) is a low-elevation meadow located along Bear Lake Road. The braided streams of the Big Thompson River and Cub Creek meander through the wide-open valley. South Lateral Moraine rises on the south edge of Moraine Park. Elk, deer, and coyotes frequent Moraine Park, making it a great place to view wildlife. Road-side pullouts offer access to this beautiful meadow and picnic tables dot the perimeter.

Moraine Park is a perfect example of a glacially carved valley that was formed when a glacier dragged up rock debris below the ice, excavating the large basin. The 'Grassy Knoll' is an 8,099-foot hill in the middle of Moraine Park and is a perfect example of a roche moutonnée, a mass of hard rock that resisted erosion but was abraded, smoothed, and shaped by the glacier. The name "roche moutonnée," French for "sheep-shaped rock" or "fleecy rock," was applied because the mounds resemble the rounded backs of sheep. The 'Grassy Knoll' is a small island of forest surrounded by the large meadow. Moraine Park has seen the hand of man, and was the former site of ranches, resorts, and even a golf course. It is now restored to a natural meadow, perfect for exploration.

LAKES AND FALLS

Windy Gulch Cascades   8,600 feet

T **OT**   *Regional map p. 31 (Q, 20)*

This small, steep waterfall in Windy Gulch tumbles out of a cleft in the steep cliffs north of the Fern Lake Trail, then spills through a boulder field. The creek then crosses the trail and joins the Big Thompson River. Tucked behind a rock wall, the cascades are difficult to see from the trail.

From the Fern Lake Trailhead (p. 108), follow the Fern Lake Trail (see Fern-Odessa Trail, pp. 79, 111) 0.4 mile to the point where the Windy Gulch creek crosses the trail. There are several seasonal rivulets that cross the trail, so look sharply for the correct stream. Leave the trail and bushwhack upslope to the north, fighting through bramble and over a boulder field, which can be wet and treacherous in times of high water. Hike 0.1 mile to the base of the cascade. The view is spectacular from the rocks near the top of the falls, but some adventurous scrambling is required to get there. Scramble north up a weakness in the cliffs to the east of the falls to reach the top of the cascade (Class 3).

The Pool   8,300 feet

T   **[icon]**   *Regional map p. 30 (O, 19)*

The Pool is a churning body of water cupped into a granite bowl carved out by the incessant swirling of the Big Thompson River. The Pool is a pleasant family destination that involves an easy stroll along the level and beautiful Fern Lake Trail, which only gains 150 feet of elevation from the trailhead to The Pool.

From the Fern Lake Trailhead (p. 108), follow the Fern Lake Trail (see Fern-Odessa Trail, pp. 79, 111) as it travels along the banks of the scenic Big Thompson River. Good views of Gabletop and Sprague Mountains appear through the trees. Continue west along the Fern Lake Trail and enjoy the serenity of the tranquil forest. About a mile from the trailhead, the path weaves through a group of massive boulders called Arch Rocks. The trail then becomes slightly steeper in sections and leads to The Pool, 1.75 miles from the trailhead. This frothy body of churning water lies just downstream from the point where Spruce and Fern Creeks join the Big Thompson River. Nature's forces are still at work, carving The Pool deeper into the bedrock. Search the rocks above The Pool for a comfortable place to sit and take in the beauty of the area.

> The Pool was originally called "Funston Pool," but the U.S. Board on Geographic Names shortened the appellation in 1932. Frederick Funston spent the summer of 1889 in the area, and he and a friend pulled off the stunt of reportedly catching a record 312 trout from the little pool in one day. When Funston fell into The Pool, his friends christened it after him. Funston later went on to achieve fame for his work as a general during the Spanish-American War.

'Jaws Falls' (Technical)   9,000 feet

T   **[icon]**   *Regional map p. 30 (O, 19)*

This feature is located on the cliffs north of the Fern Lake Trail. It is not a true waterfall. In summer, seeping water gently washes over steep slabs and creates a glistening dark sheen on the rock walls. In winter, the seep creates a thick, wide icefall that hangs over a recessed cave. The

Alex Kostadinov climbing 'Jaws Falls'

icicles that hang over the cave look like fangs, giving the formation its name. The south-facing icefall does not always form, and when it does, it is of interest only to technical ice climbers. Hikers can enjoy the view of the striking formation from a forested viewpoint on the Fern Lake Trail, located 1.1 miles from the trailhead between Windy Gulch Cascades and Arch Rocks.

Cub Creek Beaver Ponds   8,120 feet

T **[图]** *Regional map p. 30 (S, 19)*

This series of beaver ponds lies west of Moraine Park along Cub Creek. It's a fun family destination. From the Cub Lake Trailhead (p. 108), follow the Cub Lake Trail (below and p. 111) south over level terrain as it skirts the western edge of Moraine Park. The trail climbs a small hill and curves sharply, then descends and heads west along Cub Creek to the group of beaver ponds on the south side of the trail, 0.9 mile from the trailhead.

Cub Lake   8,620 feet

T **[图]** *Regional map p. 30 (Q, 19)*

Cub Lake is a great destination for families. The short, pleasant hike leads through a shady forest. Noted for the striking yellow pond lilies that bloom in July and August, this area offers abundant wildflowers, river scenery, and excellent bird-watching opportunities. Because the lake is rich in organic sediments, many aquatic plants flourish here; the lily pads that make this lake famous are no exception, as they colorfully cover most of the water's surface.

From the Cub Lake Trailhead (p. 108), follow the Cub Lake Trail (p. 111) south to a substantial log footbridge that crosses Big Thompson River. Good views of Stones Peak, Sprague Mountain, and Gabletop Mountain can be seen from the bridge. The trail continues south over level terrain and skirts the western edge of Moraine Park. Various wildflowers thrive in the marshy areas during summer. The trail climbs a small hill and curves sharply, heading west along Cub Creek. Beaver ponds along the stream offer a refuge and a source of drinking water for wildlife. Steep Mountain, true to its name,

lies to the south. The trail becomes slightly steeper and then climbs through aspen trees before entering a dense forest. Wind through the scenic pine forest to a short uphill section that tops out at the lake. Cub Lake is festooned with yellow pond lilies. Views of Stones Peak and Sprague Mountain make an impressive backdrop and provide good photo opportunities. The trail continues west beyond Cub Lake for 0.4 mile to the Mill Creek Basin Trail and 1.1 miles to the Fern Lake Trail.

Carolyn and Stephanie Foster enjoy a summer evening at Cub Lake

Arch Rocks 8,220 feet

T **⚐** *Regional map p. 30 (O, 19)*

The peaceful hike to Arch Rocks is an easy walk along the banks of Big Thompson River, highlighted by impressive rocky precipices, good views, and a beautiful pine forest. Tilted at odd angles, these huge, orange-red granite boulders reach almost 40 feet in height. The monoliths are distorted into interesting crescent shapes that almost seem to fit together like a puzzle. It is interesting to ponder how the rocks broke apart and settled into their current position. The megaliths probably fell from the imposing cliffs on the north side of the trail after the last ice age ended. The mammoth stones tower over the Fern Lake Trail as it weaves between them, and the area provides a good, easy-to-get-to destination for families.

From the Fern Lake Trailhead (p. 108), the Fern Lake Trail (see Fern-Odessa Trail, pp. 79, 111) follows the Big Thompson River and is relatively flat and easy all the way to Arch Rocks. Along the way, look west through the trees for good views of Gabletop and Sprague Mountains. To the north of the trail rise the tall, rocky crags. A little over a mile from the trailhead, the path weaves through Arch Rocks' group of massive boulders. Fascinating examples of gravity at work, the towering boulders seem alien in the environment of the quiet, shady forest.

Eagle Cliff Mountain 8,906 feet

OT *Regional map p. 31 (W, 20)*

Easily recognizable by the distinctive rock dome that ornaments the northeastern side of the summit, Eagle Cliff Mountain stands formidably at the eastern end of Moraine Park. It is a notable Estes Park landmark tucked just inside the eastern border of RMNP. Situated directly north of the YMCA of the Rockies, this small summit is climbed by hundreds of YMCA guests each year. Game paths and unofficial trails crisscross this diminutive peak, but no official trails lead to the top. The rocky dome that makes up the summit of Eagle Cliff Mountain may have been a favorite roosting place for eagles when they were more abundant in the area.

> The Ute and Arapaho Indians were known for trapping eagles in the mountains near Estes Park. Their method was to conceal the hunter in a brush-covered pit atop a mountain summit. They placed raw meat on the brush roof of the pit, and captured eagles as they descended to take the bait. Historical reports indicate that some individuals caught up to 100 eagles with this technique. Some accounts claim that the summit of Longs Peak was used for this purpose, though John Wesley Powell expedition members found no evidence of this use of the mountain when they climbed it in 1868.

Northwest Slope GRADE I CLASS 2   From the Moraine Park Museum, located 1.3 miles south on Bear Lake Road, leave the parking lot and climb steeply through cactus, sage, and scrubbrush on the abrupt northwest slope. This slope can be a breeding ground for ticks in the months of April and May. Ticks thrive in the low-lying vegetation that covers the hillside, so wear light-colored clothing and perform a tick-check after hiking. Choose the path of least resistance and hike uphill, avoiding the numerous rock outcrops that dot the hillside. Weave between the cliffs to find the easiest way to the summit. Hike in a switchback pattern to help prevent erosion and make the ascent easier. Climb over 750 vertical feet to the rocky slabs and boulders that make up the summit. Gain the highest point and enjoy the panoramic view.

BEAVER MEADOWS *Regional map p. 31 (U, 22)*

Beaver Meadows (8,440 feet) is an open meadowland located east of Beaver Mountain between Moraine Park and Deer Ridge. It is a pretty place to take short walks. A dirt road, open during the summer to public vehicle access, stretches west through the meadow and ends at a turnaround loop at the Upper Beaver Meadows Trailhead. When the dirt road is closed, a small pullout on the east side of Trail Ridge Road provides parking to access this area. A maze of low-elevation trails leaves from different points in Beaver Meadows. Get out and explore these trails, well marked by signs.

PEAKS

Beaver Mountain 10,491 feet
T **OT** *Regional map p. 31 (P, 22)*

This small, forested peak is a heavily wooded rampart of Trail Ridge and rises above the western end of Beaver Meadows, dividing the Beaver Brook and Windy Gulch drainages. The hike to the summit is short, but more than 2,000 feet of elevation gain and the absence of a continuous trail leading to the craggy summit make it a challenging day hike. It provides impressive views of Moraine Park, Upper Beaver Meadows, and Windy Gulch.

East Slope GRADE I CLASS 2   A loop trail circles from Upper Beaver Meadows road along the eastern flank of Beaver Mountain. Though the trail does not go to the top of the peak, it affords convenient access to the eastern slope and a prominent ridge that leads to the summit. From the Upper Beaver Meadows Trailhead (p. 110), hike south on the Ute Trail (p. 44) as it skirts the western margin of Upper Beaver Meadows. The trail enters a beautiful forest of ponderosa and Douglas fir, making its way to a trail junction near Windy Gulch. The Ute Trail continues to climb to Trail Ridge Road, 3,000 feet higher and 6.3 miles from the trailhead. The trail that loops around Beaver Mountain forks to the north, traversing the eastern slope of the peak. Follow the loop trail as it contours along the east side of the mountain to a small clearing marked by a horse hitch rack.

From this point, break away from the trail and bushwhack west up the wooded slope of Beaver Mountain. Gain 350 vertical feet and crest a rock outcrop that offers good views into Windy Gulch and Moraine Park. From here the obvious ridgeline ascends to the top of Beaver Mountain. Negotiate the rocky spine of the ridge as it dips and rises, and hike west toward the summit. Nearly 0.5 mile before the mountain crest, reenter the forest and climb through a uniform stand of young lodgepole pines, similar in size and mystifyingly beautiful. More rocky outcrops appear near the summit. Climb to the highpoint for worthwhile and far-reaching views of the Mummy Range to the north and the Continental Divide to the southwest.

DEER RIDGE *Regional map p. 31 (Y, 24)*

PEAKS

Deer Mountain 10,013 feet
T *Regional map p. 31 (V, 25)*

Deer Mountain is the highest point along the broad slope known as Deer Ridge, which extends west from Estes Park into RMNP. Although the mountain is flanked on all sides by steep forest, the summit is a broad tableland of trees interspersed with granite domes—the highest of which is located on the mountain's south side. Though not an exceptionally high summit, Deer Mountain is strategically positioned to offer extraordinary views of the high peaks of RMNP. It is bordered on the north by Fall River and on the south by Beaver Brook. The mountain is heavily treed, but various viewpoints on the trail offer scenic vistas of the surrounding meadows and high peaks.

Deer Mountain/Deer Ridge Trailhead Access

GRADE II CLASS 1   Two trails lead to the summit and a trail system nearly circumnavigates the base of this low-elevation mountain. From the Deer Mountain/ Deer Ridge Trailhead (p. 109), hike northeast along the trail through a magnificent grove of ponderosa

Eastern Deer Ridge is dotted with many rocky high points, the tallest of which is pretty 'Mount Washburne' (8,763 feet), located east of Deer Mountain on private land. This small, unofficially named subsummit is a popular destination for area residents, but it cannot be accessed without permission. It is most prominent when viewed from the Beaver Meadows Visitor Center.

pine for 0.1 mile to a trail junction. The North Deer Mountain Trail leads north to loop around the north side of Deer Mountain and also leads to spur trails that access

The snowy summit of Deer Mountain

Horseshoe Park and Aspenglen Campground. Follow the signs east toward Deer Mountain. The trail soon emerges onto an arid grassy slope with superb views of Beaver Meadows and the high mountain scenery stretching from Longs Peak to Notchtop Mountain. The trail switchbacks amid a stand of aspen, then heads northwest through increasingly dense Douglas fir and lodgepole pine forest. Several sections of the trail offer open views looking northwest toward Horseshoe Park and the magnificent Mummy Range.

The trail continues to switchback up the slope, eventually leveling off before beginning a gradual descent eastward across the forested summit mesa. The trail loses roughly 100 feet of elevation in 0.8 mile before reaching a major junction in the Deer Ridge Trail system. The Deer Mountain Trail continues east and descends toward Deer Ridge, Estes Park, Oldman Mountain, and the connection with North Deer Mountain Trail. The Deer Mountain summit spur trail turns southwest and climbs 0.25 mile to Deer Mountain summit. Turn southwest (right) and follow the summit spur trail as it climbs very steeply up the hillside through the forest. Continue to the summit for grand views of Estes Park to the east. Picturesque gnarled limber pines frame fine vistas over Beaver Meadows and Moraine Park. A little exploring of the wooded summit area reveals several scenic highpoints.

HIDDEN VALLEY   *Regional map p. 31 (N, 26)*

The Hidden Valley Picnic and Snow Play Area (9,240 feet) is located on Trail Ridge Road (US 34), 6.7 miles west of RMNP Beaver Meadows Visitor Center. Before 1900, Abner Sprague ran a sawmill in the valley. Dan Griffith took over the sawmill business in 1907, and in 1915 a fire that started in a sawdust pile blazed and burned much of Hidden Valley. In 1941, locals installed a primitive tow lift, establishing Hidden Valley Ski Area. Construction of a lodge and lifts was completed in 1955. Though controversial, the ski area operated until March 1992. In 2003 and 2004, the NPS dismantled the ski lodge and built a covered picnic shelter, a warming hut, and restroom facilities for the Hidden Valley Picnic and Snow Play Area. Short hikes and nature strolls through the deforested ski runs provide moderate day hiking.

OTHER DESTINATIONS

Hidden Valley Beaver Wetlands   9,160 feet

T **▧** **▧** *Regional map p. 31 (Q, 28)*

This area (formerly called Hidden Valley Beaver Ponds) allows visitors to experience a lush, riparian ecosystem that was once the home of several beaver colonies. Beaver dams once blocked the stream flow of Hidden Valley Creek, creating ponds. Beaver abandoned the dams and moved elsewhere, and with time, the dams decayed and the ponds drained, leaving fertile soil that allowed sedges and grasses to grow. In the future, this marshy area with mountain views will become a lush meadow, unless the beavers return to restart the cycle.

From the Beaver Wetlands parking pullout (p. 108) on Trail Ridge Road, an asphalt path leads downhill to the Beaver Wetlands Boardwalk. The very short boardwalk ends in an observation deck with benches.

TRAIL RIDGE   *Regional map p. 31 (J, 27)*

LAKES

Poudre Lake   10,758 feet

R *Regional map p. 31 (west of A, 34; off of map)*

This large lake is a long finger of water on the east side of the Continental Divide at Milner Pass and is the headwaters of the Cache la Poudre River. Trail Ridge Road skirts the northwest shore of the lake and Milner Pass parking lot is located on the south side. There is no trail around the lake but hikers can explore the marshy shore or hike on the Ute Trail for a short distance to access the southeastern end of the lake.

Iceberg Lake   11,860 feet

OT *Regional map p. 31 (D, 33)*

Millions of people view this lake from the Lava Cliffs parking area, but few visitors take the time to hike down to it, probably because there is no trail. From the Lava Cliffs Pullout on Trail Ridge Road (p. 109), hike north over tundra and descend through a grouping of rock mounds over loose, jagged lava rocks for 0.2 mile to the lake. A smaller lake lies just west of Iceberg Lake, and together they provide good foreground material for photo opportunities of the Mummy Range. The striking 300-foot-high walls of Lava Cliffs rise to the west. During the summer, RMNP restricts access to the snowfields above Iceberg Lake and east of Lava Cliffs for visitor safety. Approach Iceberg Lake via the outlet to avoid the closed area.

Iceberg Lake

PEAKS AND OTHER DESTINATIONS

Forest Canyon Pass   11,320 feet

T *Regional map p. 31 (west of A, 33; off of map)*

Forest Canyon Pass lies at the head of Forest Canyon and is the headwaters to the Big Thompson River. It stands between the Cache la Poudre River and Big Thompson River drainages. It can be reached from the Alpine Visitor Center (AVC) or Milner Pass.

From the western end of the parking lot for the AVC (Region 2, p. 166), which is 21.6 miles west of the Beaver Meadows Visitor Center on Trail Ridge Road, cross to the west side of Trail Ridge Road and access the trail to Milner Pass. Descend southwest along the trail for 2.3 miles to Forest Canyon Pass.

From the Poudre Lake Trailhead (p. 109), hike 0.9 mile southeast along the trail to the junction with the Mount Ida Trail. Turn northeast and climb through the forest along the Ute Trail for 1.5 miles to Forest Canyon Pass.

Lava Cliffs   12,000 feet

OT *Regional map p. 31 (D, 33)*

This beautiful 300-foot wall causes countless visitors to stop at the scenic overlook on Trail Ridge Road and take notice. Reddish-brown and vertical, the cliffs were formed by volcanic action. The hike to the base of the wall is pleasant and short.

Hike north from the Lava Cliffs Pullout (p. 109) over tundra, then weave through some unique-looking mounds made of stacked lava rocks. Pick a route over the loose, jagged shale to the base of the wall. Iceberg Lake and its unnamed neighbor lie below to the east. The rock on the cliffs is loose and crumbling, but still attracts technical rock climbers. The first technical ascent of Lava Cliffs took place in 1962. When steep snowfields exist above Iceberg Lake, they are closed by RMNP for visitor safety. Approach Lava Cliffs and Iceberg Lake via the lake's outlet when the closure is in effect.

Toll Memorial   12,304 feet

T 🚶 🧗 *Regional map p. 31 (F, 30)*

Tundra World Nature Trail Access   The Tundra World Nature Trail is a high-altitude hike through the amazing world of alpine tundra. Perfect for families, the paved asphalt path climbs for 0.5 mile and 194 vertical feet to reach the Toll Memorial.

From the Rock Cut Parking Area (p. 109), locate the trail on the north side of Trail Ridge Road. Hike northeast up the trail as it climbs strenuously past placards that describe the area's natural history. The trail levels off and leads to a junction. Turn southeast (right) and hike to the base of several scenic mushroom-shaped rocks. These unique formations were created when the granite stems eroded more quickly than the schist caps. The bulging towers are made of multicolored rock, with white bases and darker caps covered with yellow lichen.

Backtrack to the main trail and continue northeast to the Toll Memorial, located at the end of the path. Climb up a rocky cleft past a memorial plaque commemorating Roger Wolcott Toll, RMNP superintendent from 1921 to 1928. He was a civil engineer, naturalist, and mountaineer who manifested his love of the high country by helping Trail Ridge Road to become a reality. Scramble to the top of the rock outcrop for a panoramic view and to utilize the large, round metal plate that serves as a mountain finder. This "Trail Ridge Mountain Index" lies at 12,304 feet and is used to sight landmarks up to 60 miles away. The rock outcrop is a small, lofty summit with unequalled views of the expansive tundra world of RMNP.

The "Trail Ridge Mountain Index" at the Toll Memorial

Sundance Mountain   12,466 feet
OT *Regional map p. 31 (I, 29)*

This large mountain lies between Fall River and the Big Thompson River. It has substantial north and south slopes that rise above the waterways. Trail Ridge Road traverses across the middle of the southern slope, providing quick access to the open summit. The peak offers stupendous views of both Fall River and Big Thompson drainages and the high-altitude peaks that flank them. About three million people a year drive over Trail Ridge Road and pass below the summit of this regal peak, but only a few get out of their vehicles and make the short jaunt to the top.

Southeast Slope GRADE I CLASS 2   From the parking pullout at Ute Crossing (p. 110) the east (12,375 feet) and west (12,466 feet) summits of Sundance Mountain stand out to the northwest. Cross Trail Ridge Road to the north and gain the southeast slope of Sundance Mountain. Hike north (and gently!) over the fragile alpine tundra for 1 mile to the eastern summit, then traverse west for 0.8 mile to the highest (western) summit. To dramatically shorten this hike, park along Trail Ridge Road 1.4 miles west of Ute Crossing and simply hike north for 0.3 mile to the summit.

Ute Trail
T *Regional map p. 31 (M, 24)*

Ute Trail is a lengthy 16.8-mile passageway from Upper Beaver Meadows to Farview Curve. The trail climbs steeply from Upper Beaver Meadows through Windy Gulch to Timberline Pass. This is most likely the steep section where Arapaho children walked (see sidebar below). It continues to climb along Tombstone Ridge to Ute Crossing on Trail Ridge Road. This is a popular section of the trail. The trail is less distinct from this point to Gore Range Overlook, but still exists. It crosses Trail Ridge Road at Ute Crossing and picks up on the north side of the road. It travels northeast between Point 12,036' and Sundance Mountain. The trail crosses and recrosses the road to skirt south of the Toll Memorial, then climbs northwest to Iceberg Pass. It cuts across the switchbacks at Tundra Curves, then climbs north to Point 12,355', located north of Iceberg Lake. It contours northwest to Gore Range Overlook, then descends southwest through Forest Canyon Pass to Milner Pass, where it crosses the Continental Divide. Between Milner Pass and Lake Irene, the Ute Trail becomes hard to distinguish, then picks up again to skirt Lake Irene on the southeast side. It then continues southwest to Farview Curve, where the trail ends.

Most people enjoy hiking the Ute Trail in sections. The two most popular segments are from Upper Beaver Meadows to Ute Crossing, and from the Alpine Visitor Center (AVC) to Milner Pass. The trail from AVC (which is an abandoned vehicle road that was closed when Trail Ridge Road replaced it in 1932) connects with the Ute Trail as it travels southwest from

In 1914, an innovative expedition to identify key geographical features by their original Arapaho names was organized. Members of the Colorado Mountain Club solicited three Arapaho men from a reservation in Wyoming to take a two-week pack trip around the Estes Park—Grand Lake region with several locals. Two of the Native Americans had lived in the region during their youth, but did not speak English. The third man was part Arapaho, and came as an interpreter. Oliver Toll diligently recorded the stories they told and, in particular, the regional place names they remembered from their childhood. Although his important book, *Arapaho Names and Trails,* was not published until 1962, dozens of Indian names were placed on area features as a direct result of this trip.

Today, RMNP showcases one of the greatest concentrations of Indian place names in the United States. The Arapahos called Trail Ridge, or Tombstone Ridge, "Child's Trail," which is shortened from "Where the Children Walked," referring to their impression that the route was so steep in places that children had to dismount from the horses and walk. The trail followed the approximate course of today's Ute Trail.

Gore Range Overlook toward Forest Canyon Pass. This slight variation is a popular way to access the lower section of the Ute Trail.

Historically, a section of the Ute Trail traveled southwest from the Gore Range Overlook on Trail Ridge Road (located 20.6 miles west of the Beaver Meadows Visitor Center (BMVC) in Estes Park) for 1.5 miles through open country to Forest Canyon Pass. However, the historical Ute Trail from the Gore Range Overlook is now closed. Gore Range Overlook is classified as a Tundra Protection Area, and the NPS requires that hikers access the western section of the Ute Trail from the Alpine Visitor Center (AVC). This popular hike leaves from Fall River Pass at the AVC, located 21.6 miles west of BMVC.

Ute Trail (Upper Beaver Meadows to Ute Crossing)   This hike is usually managed with a car shuttle between the two starting points to avoid the redundant return hike. The hike is either a one-way uphill adventure from Upper Beaver Meadows, or a steep, downhill journey from Ute Crossing, or both. It is described here as an uphill hike; simply reverse the directions to start from Ute Crossing on Trail Ridge Road.

From the Upper Beaver Meadows Trailhead (p. 110), hike south on the Ute Trail as it skirts along the western margin of Upper Beaver Meadows. The trail enters a beautiful forest of ponderosa and Douglas fir, leading to a trail junction near Windy Gulch. From here, the Ute Trail turns southwest and climbs steeply along the southwestern flank of Beaver Mountain, gaining elevation rapidly to Timberline Pass at 11,484 feet. The trail leaves the trees and gains Tombstone Ridge. This open, windswept region of tundra is historically interesting because it still has remains of rock game-drive walls that were used by prehistoric people to kill elk, bison, or bighorn sheep for food and clothing. From Timberline Pass, hike 1.9 miles northwest across open tundra with grand views of Forest Canyon and Longs Peak to Ute Crossing on Trail Ridge Road.

Ute Trail (Fall River Pass at AVC to Milner Pass)   This hike is usually managed with a car shuttle between the two starting points to avoid the redundant return hike. The hike is either a one-way uphill adventure from Milner Pass, or a steep, downhill journey from AVC. It is described here as a downhill hike; simply reverse the directions to start from Milner Pass at Poudre Lake. Fall River Pass at the AVC is located 21.6 miles west of BMVC. From the western end of the AVC parking lot (Region 2, p. 166), cross to the west side of Trail Ridge Road and access the trail to Milner Pass. This smooth, wide path above treeline is very scenic, offering wonderful views of Specimen Mountain. Pass three small ponds, which provide nice reflections of the surrounding land and sky. The trail passes through krummholz, willows, and low , stunted trees

to Forest Canyon Pass (11,320 feet), 2.3 miles from the AVC. Look southeast into the head of Forest Canyon and the origin of the Big Thompson River. From Forest Canyon Pass, the trail descends more rapidly through a lovely forest where elk are frequently seen. Descend 1.5 miles southwest to the junction with the Mount Ida Trail, then turn northwest and follow the trail 0.9 mile to Poudre Lake at Milner Pass.

Forest Canyon Pass

Timberline Pass 11,484 feet
T *Regional map p. 31 (M, 24)*

Located at the head of Windy Gulch, Timberline Pass lies at the southeastern edge of Tombstone Ridge. From Ute Crossing (p. 110), hike southeast along the Ute Trail (p. 44) for 1.9 miles to Timberline Pass. From the Upper Beaver Meadows Trailhead (p. 110), hike uphill on the Ute Trail (p. 45) as it climbs 4.2 miles to Timberline Pass.

Tombstone Ridge 11,691 feet to 11,722 feet
T **OT** *Regional map p. 31 (M, 25)*

Tombstone Ridge is the large, windswept tundra ridge between Timberline Pass and Trail Ridge Road. It has several distinct highpoints, the three highest of which are Point 11,691', Point 11,630', and Point 11,722'. An early traveler originally named it because he thought the rocky outcrops that crown the ridge resembled tombstones. The area is historically significant because it is the site of rock game-drive walls that prehistoric people used to kill elk, bison, or bighorn sheep for food and clothing. There are dozens of game-drive sites on and near the Continental Divide in Colorado.

From Ute Crossing (p. 110), climb southeast along the Ute Trail (p. 44) for 0.5 mile to Point 11,691'. Descend 0.4 mile to the south and cross Ute Trail to climb to Point 11,630', then rejoin Ute Trail and travel 1 mile southeast to climb Point 11,722'.

GLACIER GORGE *Regional map p. 30 (Q, 7)*

Loch Vale and Glacier Gorge have historically been referred to as 'The Wild Gardens.' The grinding movement of glaciers scoured out the 3.5-mile-long valley of Glacier Gorge. Glacier Creek originates from snowfields and lakes at the southern headwall of the gorge and flows northeast to join the Big Thompson River. The gorge has two distinct sections: upper Glacier Gorge, which is a stark, treeless basin formed by the steep walls of Storm Peak, Longs Peak, Pagoda Mountain, Chiefs Head Peak, McHenrys Peak, and Arrowhead; and lower Glacier Gorge, which lies in the trees and is formed by the impressive east face of Thatchtop and the long ridge between Storm Peak and Half Mountain. Nine majestic high-alpine tarns dot the landscape of Glacier Gorge, carved deeply into the bedrock during the last ice age. The majestic setting draws thousands of people to visit nearby Mills, Jewel, Black, and Frozen Lakes each year.

LAKES AND FALLS

Alberta Falls 9,400 feet
T 🚶 *Regional map p. 30 (Q, 11); hike map p. 48.*

This lovely, 25-foot-high cascade in Glacier Creek is the most popular waterfall in RMNP. A moderate, well-maintained trail serves this scenic spot, a great place for picnicking. Half Mountain rises to the south and provides an impressive backdrop to the rushing water. Aspen trees in the foreground have framed thousands of photos taken at this waterfall. This is a good hike for children and anyone desiring a short, rewarding hike in RMNP.

From the Glacier Gorge Trailhead (p. 109), follow the trail as it climbs southwest 0.25 mile to Glacier Gorge Junction (p. 114). Turn south (left) and follow Loch Vale Trail as it meanders through groves of pretty aspen trees and crosses two bridges. Continue as the

> Early Estes Park guide and historian Abner Sprague named this beautiful waterfall for his wife, Alberta. A mapmaker, he named many of the natural features in RMNP and noted them on his maps in the early 1900s. Abner and Alberta ran a resort in Glacier Basin from 1910 to 1940.

trail climbs slightly to a dramatic overlook of Glacier Creek. Large, colorful rock walls form a small canyon through which the creek flows. Continue hiking up some switchbacks to Alberta Falls. The water noisily rushes over large slabs of granite and huge boulders into a pool, then cascades through a few more drops to funnel north down Glacier Creek. Alberta Falls is a popular place to relax in the cooling spray kicked off by the cascade.

Glacier Falls 9,880 feet

T **OT** 🥾 *Regional map p. 30 (P, 9); hike map p. 48*

Glacier Falls spills through a rocky canyon in Glacier Creek north of Mills Lake. It is located less than 20 yards west of the Glacier Gorge Trail, but few people leave the trail to check it out. The stream tumbles 30 feet through an inviting and beautiful canyon carved from granite walls. This is one of the most impressive spots along Glacier Creek. Downed trees, interesting boulders, and exposed bedrock highlight the waterfall.

From the Glacier Gorge Trailhead (p. 109), follow the trail as it climbs southwest 0.25 mile to Glacier Gorge Junction (p. 114). Turn south (left) and follow the Loch Vale Trail for 1.75 miles to the prominent junction between Loch Vale Trail and Glacier Gorge Trail. Turn south (left) and follow the Glacier Gorge Trail toward Mills Lake. Hike for 0.3 mile to a footbridge that crosses Glacier Creek. Leave the trail and bushwhack south along the west bank of Glacier Creek for 20 yards to the base of the tiny cascade.

Ribbon Falls 10,580 feet

T *Regional map p. 30 (P, 5); hike map p. 55*

Ribbon Falls is a picturesque cascade in Glacier Creek, set magnificently against the dramatic backdrop of McHenrys Peak's sheer northeastern face. It was originally dubbed "Silver Slide" because the shallow water rushes over smooth slabs and sweeps into a grassy marshland, looking slightly iridescent in the sunlight as it cascades over the sloping granite. A lush, blossoming meadow precedes the falls, alive with the colors of bistort, chiming bells, yarrow, aspen daisies, arnica, and ragwort.

From Mills Lake (follow route description, p. 49), hike south along the Glacier Gorge Trail (p. 112) as it skirts the east shore and continues to parallel Glacier Creek. Boardwalks provide dry crossings of marshy areas. The trail climbs steeply, weaving through the forest and over intermittent rocky slabs. At a point 2 miles beyond Mills Lake, the trail leaves the forest and enters an open meadow where Ribbon Falls shimmers amid the blossoming wildflowers.

Ribbon Falls

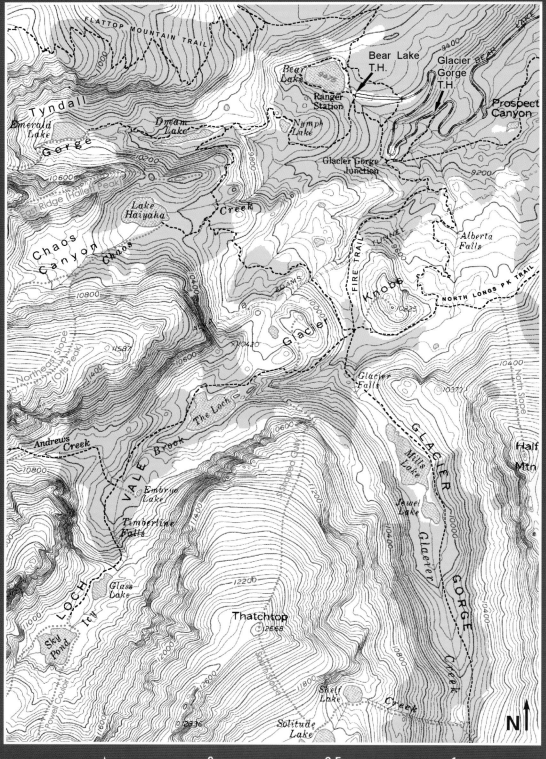

FLATTOP MOUNTAIN TRAIL

Tyndall
Gorge

Emerald
Lake

Dream
Lake

Bear
Lake

Ranger
Station

Bear Lake
T.H.

Glacier
Gorge
T.H.

Prospect
Canyon

Nymph
Lake

Glacier Gorge
Junction

East Ridge (Hallett Peak)

Lake
Haiyaha

Creek

Chaos
Canyon

Chaos

Alberta
Falls

TUNNEL

FIRE TRAIL

Knobs

NORTH LONGS PK TRAIL

Northeast Slope
(Otis Peak)

ADAMS

Glacier

Glacier
Falls

GLACIER

Mills
Lake

Half
Mtn

The Loch

Andrews Creek

VALE

Brook

Embryo
Lake

Timberline
Falls

Jewel
Lake

GORGE

Glass
Lake

LOCH

Icy

Shapely Gully

South Slope

Thatchtop

Creek

Sky
Pond

Powell Couloir

Shelf
Lake

Solitude
Lake

N

Magnetic North
11.5 degrees

N

0   0.5   1

Distance in miles

Mills Lake 9,940 feet

T 🚶 *Regional map p. 30 (P, 9); hike map p. 48.*

Considered by many to be the prettiest lake in RMNP, Mills Lake lies on the northern end of Glacier Gorge, a strikingly beautiful U-shaped valley carved by repeated glaciation. Longs Peak, Pagoda Mountain, and Chiefs Head Peak provide an impressive backdrop to this lovely high mountain lake, while Thatchtop and Half Mountain flank it on the west and east.

From the Glacier Gorge Trailhead (p. 109), follow the trail as it climbs southwest 0.25 mile to Glacier Gorge Junction (p. 114). Turn south (left) and follow the Loch Vale Trail for 1.75 miles to the prominent junction between Loch Vale Trail and Glacier Gorge Trail. Turn south (left) and follow the Glacier Gorge Trail toward Mills Lake. Descend slightly to a bridge and cross Icy Brook. The trail climbs a steep hillside of bedrock and leads to another footbridge that crosses Glacier Creek. Continue south along the trail to a shelf of exposed bedrock. Follow cairns (rock piles that mark the trail) along the rocky trail to the northeast shore of Mills Lake. Amazing views of the Glacier Gorge headwall rise dramatically to the south. The serene mountain lake provides several scenic picnic spots. The trail continues beyond Mills Lake for 2.7 miles to Black Lake.

Named for Enos Mills, who is commonly considered the "Father of Rocky Mountain National Park," the lake is one of several features christened for this pioneer. Mills fought for years to establish a national park in the area. A well-known guide and naturalist, he used public speaking as a tool to promote his ideas. He owned and operated the Longs Peak Inn in the early 1900s and guided countless people to the summit of Longs Peak. Enos Mills' dream became a reality on September 4, 1915, when he attended the dedication ceremony for the newly established Rocky Mountain National Park.

Mills Lake

Jewel Lake 9,940 feet

T 🚶 *Regional map p. 30 (P, 8); hike map p. 48*

Jewel Lake lies a few hundred yards south of Mills Lake, inconspicuously located in a swampy meadow full of bog grasses and surrounded by a thick forest. It receives little attention because of its close proximity to the more famous Mills Lake, but it is a pleasant destination in its own right. Unlike Mills Lake, with its rocky shoreline and big views, Jewel Lake remains more secluded. A narrow channel of water separates Mills and Jewel Lakes.

From Mills Lake (follow route description above), follow the Glacier Gorge Trail (p. 112) south as it skirts the east shore and leads 0.4 mile to Jewel Lake. Leave the trail and hike west over marshy ground to explore the shoreline of this little lake.

Black Lake 10,620 feet

T *Regional map p. 30 (P, 4); hike map p. 55*

Black Lake is a deep tarn near treeline in upper Glacier Gorge. Dark granite cliffs rise ominously above the water, giving the lake its dark complexion. McHenrys Peak rises majestically above the rock cliffs that ring the lake, and Arrowhead stands as a sentinel to the northwest.

From Mills Lake (follow route description, p. 49), hike south along the Glacier Gorge Trail (p. 112) as it skirts the east shore and continues to parallel Glacier Creek. Boardwalks provide dry crossings of marshy areas. The trail weaves through forest and over intermittent rocky slabs, then climbs steeply up a stone staircase constructed by the hardworking RMNP trail crew. Continue for 2 miles to Ribbon Falls, which cascades down granite slabs. Climb south along the trail as it rises above the falls and negotiates a small rock cliff. Top out at the outlet to Black Lake and hop across strategically placed boulders to the northern shore of the lake.

Black Lake and McHenrys Peak

Blue Lake   11,140 feet

T **OT**   *Regional map p. 30 (R, 5); hike map p. 55*

Blue Lake sits obscurely atop a large shelf below the steep northwestern slope of Storm Peak. This secluded and rarely visited lake remains neglected only because of its proximity to better-known lakes serviced by a good trail. The hike follows the Glacier Gorge Trail to Black Lake and beyond before becoming a short off-trail jaunt over tundra and boulders to reach the breathtaking setting of this high alpine lake.

From Mills Lake (follow route description, p. 49), hike south on the Glacier Gorge Trail (p. 112) for 2.2 miles to Black Lake. Scramble over the rocks at the outlet of Black Lake and follow the trail as it climbs up the drainage to the east. This stream flows from Green Lake at the head of Glacier Gorge. Near the crest of a rise, the trail turns south toward the upper reaches of the valley. Strike away from the trail and travel northeast over tundra to the rock bench that harbors Blue Lake, 0.6 mile from Black. The lake, nestled high above the main drainage of Glacier Gorge, offers a spectacular view of the steep, glacially carved valley below. This vantage offers a dramatic vista of Arrowhead and McHenrys Peak, made even more remarkable by the angle of view and the vertical relief to the valley floor.

Jim Cleary looks out over Blue Lake

Frozen Lake   11,580 feet

T **OT**   *Regional map p. 30 (P, 3); hike map p. 55*

Nestled at the base of a permanent snowfield, Frozen Lake is deeply set into a granite shelf, sheathed in ice well into the summer. The sheer north face of Chiefs Head Peak and the rocky northwest flank of The Spearhead block the sun from the lake for much of the day, making it typically free of ice only during the month of August. Frozen Lake is tied with Solitude Lake as the largest of Glacier Gorge's high-altitude tarns.

From Mills Lake (follow route description, p. 49), follow the Glacier Gorge Trail (p. 112) south for 2.2 miles to Black Lake. The huge glacial shelf that towers above Black Lake is home to Blue, Frozen, Green, and 'Italy' Lakes. Scramble over the rocks at the outlet of Black Lake and follow the trail as it climbs east up the drainage. This stream flows from Green Lake at the head of Glacier Gorge. The trail crosses the creek and turns south, breaching a short granite cliff to access the broad glacial shelf of upper Glacier Gorge.

The well-defined trail ends here, and some route finding is necessary to bushwhack through the dense shrubbery that grows over the large rock slabs of the upper gorge. Several routes marked by cairns penetrate toward different destinations in the upper basin. Hike southwest and cross-country toward The Spearhead, an impressive triangle-shaped spur at the end of the ridge extending north from Chiefs Head Peak. The Spearhead stands between Green and Frozen Lakes. Scramble over the shelf and skirt The Spearhead on the north. Climb up long, low-angled slabs to reach a rock bench, then hike southwest to scenic Frozen Lake.

Green Lake 11,540 feet
T **OT** *Regional map p. 30 (Q, 2); hike map p. 55*

This emerald-colored alpine tarn represents the upper headwaters of Glacier Creek. It is cupped in a granite bowl formed by The Spearhead, Chiefs Head Peak, Pagoda Mountain, and Longs Peak. From Mills Lake (follow route description, p. 49), follow the Glacier Gorge Trail (p. 112) south for 2.2 miles to Black Lake. On the lake's east side, a creek flows from Green Lake at the head of Glacier Gorge. Follow the trail east up the drainage until it crosses the creek and turns south, breaching a short granite cliff to top out on the broad glacial shelf of upper Glacier Gorge. The trail ends at the crest of the plateau, and some route finding is necessary to bushwhack through the dense shrubbery that grows over the large rock slabs of the upper gorge. Hike south, negotiating krummholz, marshy areas, large granite slabs and boulders for 0.8 mile to Green Lake.

'Italy Lake' 11,620 feet
T **OT** *Regional map p. 30 (Q, 2); hike map p. 55*

This unofficially named lake lies south of Green Lake in upper Glacier Gorge. Paul Nesbit, a former Longs Peak climbing guide, named this lake in his 1946 pamphlet, "Longs Peak: Its Story and a Climbing Guide." From Green Lake (follow route description above), hike south among large boulders for 0.1 mile to tiny 'Italy Lake.'

Shelf Lake (11,220 feet) and Solitude Lake (11,420 feet)
T **OT** *Regional map p. 30 (P, 6); hike maps pp. 48, 55*

Shelf and Solitude Lakes lie in a hanging glacial valley, hidden on a rock shelf high above the popular Glacier Gorge Trail. Each year, thousands of people pass just a half-mile below this gorge without realizing the wonder and beauty that is cupped in the small basin between Thatchtop and Arrowhead. Thatchtop, the large, bulky mountain that divides Loch Vale and Glacier Gorge, forms the north wall of the basin. Arrowhead is the prominent rock ridge that extends a half-mile northeast of impressive McHenrys Peak and forms the south side of the basin. Shelf Creek cascades magnificently over a granite shelf, pooling into scoured-out depressions to form bean-shaped Solitude Lake and round, colorful Shelf Lake.

Frozen cascade between Shelf and Solitude Lakes

From Mills Lake (follow route description, p. 49), hike south along the Glacier Gorge Trail (p. 112) as it skirts the east shore and continues to parallel Glacier Creek. Continue south for 1.5 miles to a meadow at 10,240 feet. The meadow is immediately north of the point where Shelf Creek empties into Glacier Creek. Leave the trail and bushwhack along the north end of the meadow to the creek. A huge flat rock provides an uncomplicated crossing of Glacier Creek. A climber's trail starts on the west side of Glacier Creek. Cairns intermittently mark the trail, and although it's faint in places, the path is relatively easy to follow in the absence of snow. (Note: Park policy prohibits the use of cairns unless they are historic, and Park staff are charged to remove unauthorized cairns when they find them. Therefore, cairns may not exist along this, or any other route from year to year.) The intermittent climber's path climbs steadily through stunted trees and up boulder fields along the north side of Shelf Creek for 0.5 mile to a rocky ledge system below the lakes. Cross the creek and top out at Shelf Lake, perched on a distinct granite bench.

> Arapaho legend tells the story of a group of bison that climbed up the southeast slope of Thatchtop (most likely the Shelf Creek drainage, as this is the least steep aspect of the large mountain), and got caught there by deep snow. The people were able to snowshoe up the drainage and kill many of the animals. An Arapaho man interviewed in 1914 said that because of this occurrence, they called Thatchtop the "Buffalo Climb."

The cascades between the two lakes are powerful and beautiful. From Shelf Lake, ascend southwest over rock slabs along the side of cascading Shelf Creek to lovely Solitude Lake, augmented by the stark, cathedral-like walls of Arrowhead. The north face of McHenrys Peak and the east face of Powell Peak form the granite headwall from which Shelf Creek flows. The summit of Thatchtop rises 0.6 mile to the north.

PEAKS AND OTHER DESTINATIONS

Half Mountain   11,482 feet
T **OT**   *Regional map p. 30 (R, 9); hike map p. 48*

Half Mountain represents the northern terminus of the majestic ridgeline that extends north from Longs Peak. Originally dome-shaped, Half Mountain was split in half by the glacier that carved the magnificent lake valley of Glacier Gorge. Though much smaller, Half Mountain bears many similarities to the famous Half Dome in Yosemite National Park. Half Mountain's steep and convoluted west face offers a multitude of technical climbing routes. The north and east faces relent, providing wonderful off-trail hiking opportunities to the top of this strategically located peak. Half Mountain reveals an intimate look at Glacier Gorge and the high peaks that form its boundaries. Wide-ranging views stretch from Longs Peak to Thatchtop. Unique, sculpted limber pines ornament the slopes of Half Mountain.

A limber pine on Half Mountain

North Slope GRADE I CLASS 2   From the Glacier Gorge Trailhead (p. 109), follow the trail as it climbs southwest for 0.25 mile to Glacier Gorge Junction (p. 114). Turn south (left) and follow the Loch Vale Trail as it meanders through groves of pretty aspen trees and crosses two bridges, then climbs to Alberta Falls. Continue south beyond Alberta Falls as the Loch Vale Trail contours around East Glacier Knob and leads for 0.8 mile to the junction with the North Longs Peak Trail.

Follow the North Longs Peak Trail as it heads east and crosses a footbridge that spans

Glacier Creek. Suspended above the riverbed, the bridge offers a unique view of the creek spilling over a short step in the granite. The creek is carved into colorful rock walls that stand 20 feet high. The trail continues, skirting the northern flank of Half Mountain. It's tempting to start climbing the hillside shortly after the bridge, but the northwest slope of Half Mountain is riddled with large boulders and steep cliffs that make it difficult to ascend. Continue along the North Longs Peak Trail for about 0.5 mile before leaving the trail to climb the northern aspect of Half Mountain. The farther east you travel on the North Longs Peak Trail, the gentler Half Mountain's broad slope becomes; but, at the same time, the forest gets thicker, which can be a hindrance on the lower section of the mountainside.

Strike off-trail and hike south through the forest, negotiating the boulder fields and steep, rugged terrain. Gnarled limber pines and stunted shrubs augment the stark scene of broken rock. Climb upward for about 0.7 mile to Half Mountain's summit ridge. The sheer west face drops away steeply, revealing the grandeur of Glacier Gorge. Scramble up blocks along the summit ridge to the top.

Thatchtop   12,668 feet

T **OT** *Regional map p. 30 (O, 7); hike maps pp. 48, 55*

Thatchtop

Thatchtop is the bulkhead that separates the Glacier Gorge and Loch Vale drainages. This important, prominent peak sports technical ice climbs on its north and east sides and holds a commanding position in a popular area of RMNP. Two Class 2 hiking routes climb to the top of this beautiful mountain.

S-Shaped Gully GRADE II CLASS 2   This hike is straightforward but long. It ascends what is commonly known as the 'S-Shaped Gully,' a winding, steep ravine that snakes up Thatchtop's north side. From the Glacier Gorge Trailhead (p. 109), follow the trail as it climbs southwest 0.25 mile to Glacier Gorge Junction (p. 114). Turn south (left) and follow the Loch Vale Trail for 1.75 miles to the prominent junction between the Loch Vale Trail and the Glacier Gorge Trail. Continue southwest along the Loch Vale Trail for 0.3 mile to the first switchback.

Leave the trail 20 yards northeast (downhill) of the first switchback and descend southeast to Icy Brook. Cross the creek and climb the hillside to the base of the rock cliffs on Thatchtop's northwest side. During winter, these steep rocks provide a number of 60- to 100-foot ice-climbing routes. Skirt the cliffs on the northeast (left) and access a wide gully that climbs south up the hillside. Continue up the slope as it narrows and becomes steeper. Shortly, the gully opens up into a wide, boulder-strewn basin. Contour upslope to the southwest (right) and climb up the precipitous gulch as it narrows again and leads into an obvious couloir filled with loose rocks. This is the S-shaped gully that penetrates the lower cliffs and provides access to the gentle upper slopes of Thatchtop. Scramble 800 vertical feet up the steep ravine. The gully tops out amid thick krummholz and leads to Thatchtop's uncomplicated summit slopes.

From here, hike south up the windswept tundra and talus slopes for 0.8 mile to the summit. The jagged northeast ridge of Powell Peak extends impressively to the south, and grand views of the Continental Divide stretch to the west and south. Shelf and Solitude Lakes pool in a granite basin directly southeast of the summit. This summit is one of few that allows unobstructed vistas of both Glacier Gorge and Loch Vale.

South Slope GRADE II CLASS 2   From Solitude Lake (follow route description, p. 51), climb north up a steep, loose boulder slope for 0.6 mile to the summit of Thatchtop.

Arrowhead   12,640+ feet

T **OT** *Regional map p. 30 (O, 4); hike map p. 55*

This beautiful rock rampart forms the western cliff of upper Glacier Gorge. It is a spur ridge that runs for 0.5 mile northeast from mighty McHenrys Peak. The highpoint on the ridge is the summit of Arrowhead at 12,640+ feet, not to be confused with a lower summit (Point 12,387') that lies farther east along the ridge and is more visible from Glacier Gorge. There is no easy route to the summit of this interesting bulwark of rock. The main difficulty is in the route finding. The Class 3+ route is complicated to find and somewhat difficult to follow. When the easiest route is found, this is a fun scramble to a worthy destination.

Northwest Face GRADE II CLASS 3+
From Solitude Lake (follow route description, p. 51), skirt the lake on the north side and hike south-west over tundra and rock slabs for 0.5 mile to a tiny pool in Shelf Creek. The valley continues southwest to the headwall formed by the precipitous east face of Powell Peak and the dramatic north face of McHenrys Peak. Several prominent gullies on the south side of the upper valley seem like enticing alleyways to gain access to the ridge, but they are all technical. The most promising-looking gully is a deep chimney below the Arrowhead-

Lisa Foster ascending Arrowhead's Northwest Face Route.
Photo by Les Moore

McHenrys saddle, but this route is technical as well. The easiest route is a ledge system to the northeast (left) of this gully. The ledge system is difficult to find because it doesn't look like the path of least resistance from below. From the small pond, the north face of Arrowhead appears intimidating, but a weakness provides passage. Persistence in route finding will eventually reveal the Class 3+ ledge system.

Head southeast from the pond and ascend blocky ledges up Arrowhead's north-west face that ultimately lead to easier ground. Commit to an ascending southwestern traverse (climber's right) along a series of rock ledges. This route is Class 3 overall, with several semi-exposed Class 3+ moves. The ledges give way to a Class 2 boulder slope that leads to the ridge between Arrowhead and McHenrys Peak. The ridge drops away dramatically on the south side. Sweeping views down the south face of Arrowhead are breathtaking. The views of Glacier Gorge and Longs Peak are simply incredible from this vantage. Protruding rocks jut south from the ridge to allow views into the mighty abyss. Turn northeast and climb up the blocky, jagged ridge (Class 2) to the distinct summit of Arrowhead.

Stone Man Pass 12,500 feet

T **OT** **⬩** *Regional map p. 30 (O, 4); hike map p. 55*

Easily visible from the glacial shelf above Black Lake, the human-shaped rock figure of Stone Man stands out on the ridge connecting Chiefs Head and McHenrys Peaks. Stone Man Pass is the 12,500-foot saddle at the north end of this ridge. Take care not to mistake it with the lowest point on the ridge, which lies south of Stone Man above steep cliff walls. Stone Man Pass is north of Stone Man, directly below the steep southeast ridge of McHenrys Peak, and has a steep scree gully leading up to it. In early summer this gully is filled with snow, which can be avalanche-prone in May and June. When the snow stabilizes, usually by mid-July, crampons and an ice axe are recommended for the ascent. A steep, rounded bulge forms near the top in some years. When the snow melts out, it is a long scramble up the dirt and rubble that fills the gully. Short cliffs can be easily avoided to keep the difficulty at Class 2.

⬩ **Northeast Slope** GRADE II CLASS 2   From Black Lake (follow route description, p. 49), scramble across the rocks at the outlet and follow the trail as it climbs up the drainage to the east. Cross the stream and hike southwest as the well-defined trail dissipates. From here, route find and bushwhack west through the dense shrubbery that intermingles with the large rock slabs of the upper gorge, heading toward Stone Man Pass. If Stone Man Pass is free of snow, it's a nontechnical scramble up steep, loose rock to the summit of the pass.

McHenrys Peak 13,327 feet

T **OT** **⬩** *Regional map p. 30 (N, 3); hike map p. 55*

This impressive mountain lies along the Continental Divide and towers above Black Lake and the western section of upper Glacier Gorge. Its broken southwest face rises above Lake Powell, the headwaters to North Inlet. The north face remains hidden in the southern reaches of the Shelf and Solitude Lake basin. McHenrys Notch is the deep, U-shaped barrier set between the north and west faces of McHenrys Peak. The views from atop McHenrys are astounding. Glacier Gorge unveils a long string of alpine lakes, while Ptarmigan Mountain and Andrews Peak stand out to the west.

South Slope via Stone Man Pass GRADE II CLASS 3   This is the shortest, easiest route to the summit of McHenrys Peak. It requires good route finding to locate the easiest passage up the south face. From Stone Man Pass (follow route description above), hike northwest onto McHenrys' south side. Several chutes bordered by rock ribs rise skyward to the north. Traverse across the boulder-strewn slope and climb into the second gully northwest of Stone Man Pass. This channel can be avalanche-prone when filled with snow. An intermittent cairn trail weaves up the ravine and along the dirt and rock ledges (Class 3) that lead to the top. There are few nontechnical routes up the south face of this peak. Most other options include strenuous Class 4 and/or minor Class 5 climbing. Finding the correct gully is the key to making this hike nontechnical. Carefully study the landscape and choose the correct gully. The gully tops out on McHenrys Peak's southeast ridge. Scramble northwest to the summit (Class 2).

⬩ **Arrowhead Arête** GRADE II CLASS 4+   This beautiful route ascends the serrated ridge that connects McHenrys Peak and Arrowhead. The ridge has a sheer drop-off to Glacier Gorge on the southeast, and a broken, sloping northwest face. Some sections of the ridge are extremely steep, and a rope is highly recommended. If the ridge is wet or icy, it becomes much more difficult.

From the Arrowhead-McHenrys saddle (see Arrowhead's Northwest Face route description, p. 54), climb southwest along the ridge that rises majestically toward McHenrys Peak. This ridge is easy at first, but soon becomes steep and challenging. Stay below the ridgeline on the northwest (right) side of the ridge. Negotiate a route up broken slabs to a steep section of precipitous rock separated by steep gullies (Class 4+). Carefully traverse up the slabs and across the gullies to the ridge crest immediately northwest of the summit. Here the ridge relents and Class 2 scrambling leads southeast to the top.

McHenrys Notch (Technical) 12,820 feet

T **OT** ◪ Regional map p. 30 (N, 4); hike map p. 55

McHenrys Notch is one of the most difficult features to access in RMNP. It is a deep, impressive gash in the Continental Divide, located between McHenrys and Powell Peaks. To stand in the notch is a special experience—one in which the hiker is many miles from a trail, isolated from any human's view, tucked within a majestic setting of stark rock, hard snow, and plentiful views of a remote sparkling lake and abundant high peaks.

McHenrys Notch Loop GRADE II CLASS 5.3 The loop required to traverse the notch is long and arduous. It requires an ascent of McHenrys Peak, which, matched against other RMNP peaks over 13,000 feet by their easiest routes, is one of the most difficult to climb. Dropping into the notch requires stringent route finding, and even then it enters into the realm of Class 5 climbing, prompting most hikers to use a rope. After all of that, an ascent of Powell Peak must be made and a long hike over tundra and talus must be undertaken to reach Andrews Glacier, which might require crampons and an ice axe for a safe descent, depending on conditions. After carefully negotiating all this terrain, the hiker then faces a 4.7-mile hike to the trailhead. As with most investments of time and effort, this hike is a rewarding endeavor reserved for the most hearty and ambitious hikers. Seclusion and majestic mountain glory await anyone willing to undertake the journey to this magical destination.

From the summit of McHenrys Peak (follow route description, opposite), descend northwest toward McHenrys Notch. Easy at first, the downclimbing becomes more difficult when the route passes a prominent highpoint on the ridge. As you look into the notch, it is difficult to see the length of the technical section until you start downclimbing it. The slabs offer moderate 5.3 climbing, making rock-climbing shoes or a rope appealing. Descend for 400 vertical feet of technical rock scrambling and reach easier ground just above the flat section of the notch.

Once you're in the notch, Lake Powell glistens below to the south, and the imposing cliffs of Powell Peak tower to the northwest. Descend slightly west and gain the south slope of Powell Peak. Negotiate a way over rock ribs to an obvious gully that shoots up toward the summit slopes of Powell. Climb this nontechnical gully to the Continental Divide and walk 100 yards to the summit of Powell Peak.

From Powell Peak, skirt below the Continental Divide along relatively easy ground to contour around Taylor Peak. Curve and descend along the rock and tundra slope for 2.5 miles to Andrews Pass, located between Otis and Taylor Peaks. Take care not to mistake the numerous other snow gullies along the Continental Divide for Andrews Glacier.

Andrews Glacier is the most moderate snow descent from the Continental Divide. In summer, it is possible to walk up or down Andrews Glacier on soft snow without crampons. By late summer the snow melts and the dark, dirty glacial ice becomes exposed. Crampons are then necessary to find purchase on the moderately steep ice.

Descend to Andrews Tarn at the base of the glacier. From here, follow the trail along Andrews Creek to the confluence with Icy Brook. Join the Loch Vale Trail and hike to the Glacier Gorge Trailhead.

Descent from Powell Peak GRADE II CLASS 2   This is the easiest route into McHenrys Notch. From Powell Peak (follow route description, p. 68), hike southeast 100 yards to the top of a gully on the southeast face. The gully is steep but nontechnical. Scramble down loose rocks and dirt to some rock ribs on the west side of McHenrys Notch, then scramble east across the ribs to the Notch.

McHenrys Notch Couloir GRADE II CLASS 2 STEEP SNOW   This classic couloir climbs the northwest face of McHenrys Peak and ends at McHenrys Notch. From Solitude Lake (follow route description, p. 51), skirt the lake on the north side and hike southwest through krummholz, over tundra, rock slabs, and seasonal snowfields up the Shelf Creek valley for 1 mile to the headwall. The couloir is hidden behind a rock fin until you are directly under it. Assess the conditions carefully, as the couloir is prone to avalanche. In typical years, it is in the best condition in mid-June, after the snow stabilizes and the cornice disappears. Crampons, a helmet, and an ice axe are recommended for this route. The couloir averages 45 degrees, but reaches 55 degrees at a bulge near the top. Climb up steep snow for 900 vertical feet to the bulge. Crest the bulge and top out on the flat base area of the notch. Lake Powell and Mount Alice lie to the south. The huge rock walls that form the notch rise grandly above the level platform.

The Spearhead   12,575 feet

T OT *Regional map p. 30 (Q, 3); hike map p. 55*

The Spearhead is a triangular-shaped rock spur that extends north from Chiefs Head Peak and ends in an abrupt, highly recognizable 975-foot face. The formation has

a distinctive, pointed summit and a half-mile-long serrated ridge that connects it to Chiefs Head. It stands prominently in upper Glacier Gorge and rises majestically above two striking alpine tarns. There are many technical routes to the summit of this imposing feature, but a couple of Class 3 routes climb to within 15 feet of the summit and allow hikers to enjoy the thrill of climbing this amazing piece of granite and enjoy the wide view of Glacier Gorge. However, several highly exposed Class 4 moves are needed to reach the true summit. Most hikers are content to take in the view from the rocks below the summit scramble.

Northwest Slope GRADE II CLASS 4   If the path of least resistance is followed, this route is Class 2 to the ridge below the summit. If not, the route is Class 3. Several Class 4 moves are required to reach the true summit. From Mills Lake (follow route description, p. 49), hike south on the Glacier Gorge Trail (p. 112) for 2.2 miles to Black Lake. On the lake's east side is a drainage that flows from Green Lake at the head of Glacier Gorge. Hike east up the gully until the trail crosses the creek and turns south, breaching a short granite cliff to top out on the broad glacial shelf of upper Glacier Gorge.

Green Lake, The Spearhead, and McHenrys Peak from the summit of Pagoda Mountain

The trail ends at the crest of the plateau, and some route finding is necessary to bushwhack through the dense shrubbery that grows over the large rock slabs of the upper gorge. Several routes marked by cairns lead to different destinations in the upper basin. Hike southwest and cross-country toward The Spearhead.

Continue southwest to a ramp between The Spearhead and Frozen Lake. Choose the path of least resistance and climb south on the ramp around the cliffs on The Spearhead's northwest face. Locate a narrow scree gully that leads southeast to the broad talus slope on The Spearhead's west side. The gully has a short Class 2 cliff section in it. Climb up talus for 600 vertical feet to gain the south ridge of The Spearhead. This is the serrated ridge that extends north from Chiefs Head Peak. Stay below (west) of the ridge crest and scramble north toward the summit. Cross to the east side of the ridge by passing through a hole in the ridge to access the last few moves to the top. The actual summit of The Spearhead is a small, pointed rock tower that requires a few moves of highly exposed Class 4 scrambling. Do not underestimate this final section. The top is so exposed and the view so spectacular that it's worth spending some time here soaking up the dramatic scenery.

East Gully GRADE II CLASS 4   Ascending the East Gully Route and descending the Northwest Slope Route makes a nice "tour de Spearhead" for adventurous hikers. From Green Lake (follow route description, p. 51), scramble southwest over large boulders to the base of The Spearhead. A wide, east-facing gully located 0.25 mile south of The Spearhead's summit provides a Class 3+ scramble up to the south ridge. Once at the ridge, hop over to the west side and follow the Northwest Slope Route (p. 58) to the summit.

Chiefs Head Peak   13,579 feet
T **OT** *Regional map p. 30 (Q, 1); hike maps p. 55 and Region 3, p. 192*
Crowning Glacier Gorge with its broad north face, this mighty peak is the third highest in RMNP. It stands between Glacier Gorge and Wild Basin about 250 yards east of the Continental Divide. Its broken south face towers majestically over the Lion Lakes basin. It can be reached from Wild Basin or Glacier Gorge.

Southeast Slope GRADE II CLASS 2   From the Sandbeach Lake Trailhead (see Region 3, p. 215), follow the Sandbeach Lake Trail (p. 181) 4.2 miles to Sandbeach Lake. Hike around the north side of the lake and bushwhack northwest up the densely wooded slope of Mount Orton. Top out on the bulge of Mount Orton's east side and follow the gentle rock-and-tundra slope northwest to the stony summit. Descend northwest for 0.6 mile to the expansive North Ridge. Follow the spine of the broad tundra-and-talus ridge as it climbs for 1 mile to the base of Chiefs Head Peak's southeastern slope. Here the route gets steeper and climbs chunky talus for 0.6 mile to the summit of Chiefs Head Peak.

West Ridge GRADE II CLASS 2   From the Wild Basin Trailhead (see Region 3, p. 215), follow the Thunder Lake Trail (p. 191) 4.5 miles to the Lion Lake Trail. Follow the Lion Lake Trail 1.75 miles to Lion Lake No. 1, where the trail ends. Hike along the east shore of the lake and continue over rock slabs and marshy areas past Trio Falls to Lion Lake No. 2, then continue through krummholz and over rock steps to Snowbank Lake.

From here, hike northwest toward the obvious, broad ramp that leads to the sizeable saddle between Chiefs Head Peak and Mount Alice. In July, wildflowers ornament this extremely scenic ramp. A faint path leads up the ramp to the saddle, 1.1 miles from Snowbank Lake. Turn east on the saddle and clamber up talus to a point where the slope narrows and leads along the west ridge to the summit of Chiefs Head Peak, 1.2 miles from the saddle.

East Ridge GRADE II CLASS 2   From the top of the Chiefs Head–Pagoda Couloir (follow route description below), turn west and scramble up large granite blocks (Class 2) for 0.6 mile to the summit.

Northwest Ridge GRADE II CLASS 3   From Stone Man Pass (follow route description, p. 56), descend slightly on the west side of the pass, then turn south and locate a talus-and-tundra ramp that skirts the vertical, flat-faced cliffs along the ridge crest. The ramp leads to a cluster of rock faces. Hike to the base of these short towers and negotiate a route up gully systems to gain the easy talus slope on the west face of Chiefs Head. The climbing through this maze of cliffs should not exceed Class 3. After passing through the cliff section, turn southeast and walk up talus for 0.7 mile to the summit.

Chiefs Head–Pagoda Couloir   12,860 feet

T OT ⛰   *Regional map p. 30 (R, 1); hike maps p. 55; Region 3, p. 192; and Region 4, p. 228*

This is the north-facing snow gully between Pagoda Mountain and Chiefs Head Peak. It provides access to the technical west ridge of Pagoda Mountain and the Class 2 east ridge of Chiefs Head Peak. It is also worthy of a climb just for the sake of it, without climbing anything else. It holds snow into August, and when the snow melts it becomes an undesirable route up rubble and loose scree.

⛰ **Green Lake Access** GRADE II CLASS 2 STEEP SNOW   From Green Lake (follow route description, p. 51), hike south over large boulders to the base of the couloir. A helmet, ice axe, and crampons are recommended, and if the snow in the couloir is hard or icy, a rope might be necessary. Ascend the steep 45- to 60-degree snow in the gully for 900 vertical feet to the rocks that make up the saddle between the two peaks.

Pagoda Mountain   13,497 feet

T OT   *Regional map p. 30 (R, 1); hike maps p. 55; Region 3, p. 192; and Region 4, p. 228*

This awesome, pyramid-shaped peak at the southern end of Glacier Gorge is the seventh highest peak in RMNP. It has sheer north and southwest faces and a wicked west ridge that are all technical. However, the east side of the peak and the northeast ridge provide nontechnical access to Pagoda Mountain. Pagoda can be approached from Glacier Gorge or Wild Basin. Both routes reach the summit via the northeast ridge.

Glacier Gorge and Tower 1 and 2 of Keyboard of the Winds from Pagoda Mountain

Glacier Gorge Access (Pagoda–Keyboard Col to Northeast Ridge) GRADE II CLASS 3   From Black Lake (follow route description, p. 49), skirt the lake on the northeast shore and hike east up the drainage, following the trail to a point where it crosses the creek and turns south. Climb a short granite cliff to the broad glacial shelf of upper Glacier Gorge. The trail ends here.

Bushwhack south through dense bushes and over large rock slabs toward Pagoda Mountain. Angle southeast over boulders and talus toward the base of a large gully between Pagoda Mountain and Keyboard of the Winds, which leads to the Pagoda–Keyboard Col. Pick a route up the talus-filled gully and skirt some steep, short cliffs at the bottom. These cliffs are easily avoided. Climb 900 vertical feet up the gully to some moderate Class 3 climbing moves near the top. Scramble to the notchlike saddle (the col) between Pagoda Mountain and Keyboard of the Winds. Turn southwest and climb along the southeast side of the blocky ridge (Class 2) for 300 yards to the summit.

Wild Basin Access (Southeast Gully to Northeast Ridge) GRADE II CLASS 2   From the Sandbeach Lake Trailhead (see Region 3, p. 215), follow the Sandbeach Lake Trail (p. 181) for 3.25 miles to a bridge that crosses Hunters Creek. Leave the trail and locate a faint path that travels northwest along the east side of the creek. The trail climbs through the trees and is somewhat hard to follow. When the path disappears, keep bushwhacking northwest to break out of the trees and negotiate marshy terrain to a shallow, unnamed lake at 11,200 feet. Hiking to this lake requires arduous bushwhacking through thick willows and over deep, soggy terrain.

From the shallow lake, hike north through willows, krummholz, large boulder fields, and marsh into the mighty high alpine basin at the base of Pagoda Mountain, Longs Peak, and Mount Meeker. The sheer, striated walls of Pagoda Mountain's southern rib are astoundingly beautiful. Skirt these walls and hike northwest to the base of a broad gully that climbs 900 vertical feet (Class 2) to the notchlike saddle (the Pagoda–Keyboard Col) between Pagoda Mountain and Keyboard of the Winds. Turn southwest and climb along the southeast side of the blocky ridge (Class 2) for 300 yards to the summit.

Keyboard of the Winds   13,200+ feet

T **OT** *Regional map p. 30 (S, 2); hike map Region 4, p. 228*

Keyboard of the Winds is the long, serrated ridge between Longs Peak and Pagoda Mountain. It is composed of seven main towers that rise above 13,000 feet. Five of the towers are technical, but the two at the southwest end of the ridge, closest to Pagoda Mountain, offer enjoyable Class 2 scrambling up their southeast faces. The feature was so named because wind howls through the gaps between the towers and creates noisy songlike sounds as it funnels around lofty Longs Peak.

Keyboard of the Winds

Tower 1 and Tower 2 GRADE II CLASS 3
Towers 1 and 2 are the two towers at the southwest end of Keyboard of the Winds. From Black Lake (follow route description, p. 49), skirt the lake on the northeast shore and follow a trail east up the drainage until it crosses the creek and turns south, then climbs a short granite cliff to gain the broad glacial shelf of upper Glacier Gorge. The trail ends at the crest of the plateau. Bushwhack south through dense bushes and over large rock slabs toward Pagoda Mountain. Angle southeast over boulders and talus toward the base of a large gully between Pagoda Mountain and Keyboard of the Winds, which leads to the Pagoda–Keyboard Col. Pick a route up the talus-filled gully and skirt some steep, short cliffs at the bottom. These cliffs are easily avoided. Climb 900 vertical feet up the gully to some moderate Class 3 climbing moves near the top. Scramble to the notchlike saddle (the col) between Pagoda Mountain and Keyboard of the Winds.

Hike northeast to the sloping boulder field on the southeast side of Tower 1. Climb northwest over large boulders (Class 2) to the top. A substantial drop-off on the southwest makes this exciting. Scramble out to the summit of Tower 1 to enjoy extreme exposure and a dizzying view into the abyss of Glacier Gorge. To reach Tower 2, continue northeast from the base of Tower 1 to the base of Tower 2. Climb northwest over large boulders (Class 2) to the summit. Towers 3–7 present varying technical challenges.

LOCH VALE   *Regional map p. 30 (N, 9)*

The two-mile-long gorge of Loch Vale, literally meaning "lake valley," runs southwest from The Loch to the eastern headwall of Taylor Peak. Upper Loch Vale is a gorgeous alpine canyon ringed by sheer granite towers, steep snowfields, and precipitous rock faces. It is home to two pristine alpine tarns and a dramatic waterfall. Lower Loch Vale is a wooded valley dwarfed beneath the broken south face of Otis Peak's northeast ridge, and the beautiful, craggy slopes of Thatchtop's north face.

Of the numerous glacially carved valleys in RMNP, Loch Vale ranks as one of the most scenic and spectacular. Icy Brook flows through the valley, originating at mighty Taylor Glacier. The Cathedral Spires are tall, beautiful rocks that soar beyond The Loch, dominating the scene to the southwest.

LAKES AND FALLS

The Loch   10,180 feet

⬛ 🚶 *Regional map p. 30 (O, 9); hike map p. 48*

The Loch is the lowest of three spectacular lakes in scenic Loch Vale. Its moderate approach and spectacular mountain scenery make it one of the most popular destinations in RMNP.

From the Glacier Gorge Trailhead (p. 109), follow the trail as it climbs southwest 0.25 mile to Glacier Gorge Junction (p. 114). Turn south (left) and follow the Loch Vale

The Loch

Trail as it meanders through groves of pretty aspen trees and crosses two bridges. Proceed to Alberta Falls, 0.8 mile from the trailhead. Continue southwest as the trail swings around the south side of Glacier Knobs and leads to a major trail junction between the Loch Vale and Glacier Gorge Trails. Bear southwest (right) at this intersection and follow the Loch Vale Trail as it climbs above Icy Brook to a major switchback in the trail. This small overlook provides a breathtaking view of the narrow gully carved by Icy Brook.

> Abner Sprague named The Loch and Loch Vale after a Kansas City banker with the surname "Locke." Sprague altered the spelling of the name to represent the Scottish word for lake. Sprague, an early Estes Park historian, prolifically named hundreds of natural features during the early 1900s.

The trail climbs through a few more switchbacks to a scenic open area immediately northeast of the lake. Climb steps up the trail and crest the rise that leads to a level shelf cradling the lake. The huge rock walls that tower above The Loch augment the irregular shoreline. This is a majestic and splendid setting.

Embryo Lake   10,380 feet

T **OT**   *Regional map p. 30 (N, 8); hike maps pp. 48, 70*

This tiny, shallow pond lies southwest of The Loch at the foot of Thatchtop's northwest face. From The Loch (follow route description, opposite), continue along the Loch Vale Trail as it skirts the lake on the north and leads for 0.6 mile to the junction with Andrews Creek Trail. Leave the trail and bushwhack east 30 yards to an open meadow. Find a way to cross Icy Brook and hike east up over a forested knoll for 150 yards to the marshy shore of Embryo Lake.

Timberline Falls   10,480 feet

T   *Regional map p. 30 (N, 8); hike maps pp. 48, 70*

Timberline Falls is an impressive feature located in one of the most beautiful and pristine valleys in RMNP. The cascade dances and tumbles over a set of dark, broken cliffs for 270 feet, sending spray in all directions, creating a misty wonderland blessed by wet moss and colorful wildflowers. The hike to the lush meadowland at the base of the falls is a wonderful journey that includes a hike past The Loch, a pretty mountain lake set amid high rocky crags and serene pine forest.

From The Loch (follow route description, opposite), continue along the Loch Vale Trail (p. 112) as it skirts the lake on the north side and leads through forest, with intermittent openings in the canopy offering good vistas of the imposing cliffs of Cathedral Wall. At a point 0.6 mile from The Loch, the trail crosses Andrews Creek on a set of rough-hewn logs and branches off, with a spur path heading west over bedrock toward Andrews Glacier. Follow the main trail as it continues south toward Sky Pond, crossing some plank boards that elevate the hiker over bog grasses and wet areas. Continue through the forest to the open area below the falls. The trail weaves through stunted trees near the meadow edge and then climbs through a modest boulder field.

The falls are magnificent, a delicate cascade of water spilling down a broken granite wall. Several forks in the flow

The scramble down the west side of Timberline Falls

create a braided effect as water rushes over the polished stone. The water splashes into a basin at the bottom, pooling there briefly before splitting off into separate rivulets that penetrate the lush meadow below the falls. In early summer, sculpted snowdrifts prevail on the broken cliffs and the falls wash over them, slowly disintegrating them until they disappear in mid-July. Impressive views to the northeast reveal The Loch, 270 vertical feet below and more than 1 mile away. The granite precipices of Thatchtop dominate the view to the south. Water spills out of Glass Lake to feed the waterfall.

Glass Lake   10,820 feet
T *Regional map p. 30 (N, 7); hike maps pp. 48, 70*

This awesome alpine lake lies on a rocky shelf in upper Loch Vale. Fancifully called 'Lake of Glass' by most locals, it requires a sporting 280-vertical-foot ascent of the cliffs on the west side of Timberline Falls. From Timberline Falls (follow route description, p. 63), climb up the indistinct trail that ascends the steep, broken cliff immediately west of the cascade. The route becomes extremely difficult and hazardous when these rocks are icy or snowy. For most of the summer the rocks are wet from the spray off the falls, which makes them slick. Use extreme caution when ascending the cliffs. Scramble up the initial section of the wall, which is most difficult in times of high water when runoff from the falls forces hikers farther west onto more challenging rock. The climbing should not exceed Class 3. Negotiate the rough, unmaintained route up broken benches of loose rock to a small cleft that leads to easier ground. Scramble up the last section of low rock steps to the glorious alpine shelf that is home to Glass Lake.

Sky Pond   10,900 feet
T *Regional map p. 30 (M, 6); hike maps pp. 48, 70*

Set near the headwall of Loch Vale and fed by runoff from Taylor Glacier, Sky Pond is the premier alpine tarn in Loch Vale. Stark rock faces and slender granite towers adorn the impressive glacial cirque that surrounds the lake. Snow clings year-round to the sheer cliffs, and the isolated setting is simply magical. The hike to Sky Pond is an adventurous journey into one of the most beautiful basins in the world.

Unnamed pool near Sky Pond

From Glass Lake (follow route description above), follow an unmaintained, roughly cairned trail that climbs up rock slabs on the northwest side of the lake. The route descends from these slabs to skirt the western lakeshore and push through thick, low-lying bushes to a small cliff face. The trail climbs the face (Class 2) and gains a rock ledge above the southwest side of Glass Lake. Hike across the ledge to a narrow tree gully that passes a large boulder and leads to an open boulder field. Continue to follow cairns across the boulder field and hike along the trail as it continues south along undulating topography of tundra and boulders. A noisy cascade highlights the scene. The trail surmounts another small boulder field and tops out on a rocky bench slightly above Sky Pond. The grand mountain scenery of Taylor and Powell Peaks combines with the majesty of the Cathedral Spires to make this a truly special place.

Andrews Tarn   11,380 feet

T   *Regional map p. 30 (L, 8); hike map p. 70*

This chilly, deep alpine lake lies at the base of Andrews Glacier. For most of the year, ice that breaks away from the glacier floats in the frigid waters. From the junction of Loch Vale Trail (p. 112) and Andrews Creek Trail (p. 110), follow the Andrews Creek Trail west as it climbs rock slabs and carved steps in the steep hillside. Continue through the primeval forest until the trail pops out above treeline into a gorge bordered on the north by the impressive walls of Otis Peak. The trail weaves through an active avalanche path lined with battered trees and debris. The trail follows Andrews Creek into the scenic rock basin and climbs the steep boulder headwall east of Andrews Tarn. Climb to the rocky bowl that holds the lake, situated magnificently at the base of Andrews Glacier.

PEAKS AND OTHER DESTINATIONS

East Glacier Knob (10,225 feet) and **West Glacier Knob** (10,280+ feet)

T **OT**   *Regional map p. 30 (P, 10); hike map p. 48*

Glacier Knobs are a series of granite domes just north of the confluence of Icy Brook and Glacier Creek, near the major trail junction between Loch Vale and Glacier Gorge Trails. Many visitors pass by these lovely rock bulges without giving much thought to climbing them; such an ascent requires a bit of scrambling but offers magnificent views into Loch Vale and Glacier Gorge drainages, showcasing the impressive high peaks that form their boundaries. The Knobs are fun to climb and offer an unusual, solitary excursion in what is otherwise a well-traveled area. Steep walls and cliffs guard the summits of these landmarks, and it takes persistence to find the nontechnical routes up them. However, each knob is graced with at least one nontechnical route suitable for hikers of moderate ability.

> Sculpted by the glaciers that formed the neighboring valleys, the Glacier Knobs are formed of biotite schist, conspicuously banded rock marked by alternating layers of contrasting composition. Geologists theorize that after the last ice age, the Pleistocene Era, the earth warmed, causing heavy ice to move downstream, carving U-shaped valleys and creating obvious natural formations. The Glacier Knobs lie at the end of two valleys, left behind by the force of moving rivers of ice.

East Glacier Knob—West Slope GRADE I CLASS 2   From the Glacier Gorge Trailhead (p. 109), follow the trail 0.8 mile to Alberta Falls. From here the trail climbs switchbacks and swings west around the south side of East Glacier Knob. Hike to a point 50 yards east of the major trail junction between Loch Vale and Glacier Gorge Trails. Leave the trail and bushwhack north along the base of the cliff band on the west side of East Glacier Knob. Descend through the forest past a series of short cliffs and low-angled slabs rising up to steeper granite walls. Look sharply for a nontechnical cleft in these walls that leads to the summit slope of East Glacier Knob. The gully is choked with trees and nasty bushes in the lower reaches. Climb over large boulders and up the gully. If the correct gully is found, the climbing does not exceed Class 2. Top out on the broad dome that leads to the summit. Hike southeast over low-angled slabs to the highest point. Brilliant vistas of Glacier Gorge and sweeping views of Estes Park unfold. West Glacier Knob and the rock ramparts of Otis Peak's east face stand out to the west.

West Glacier Knob—South Slope GRADE I CLASS 2   To reach West Glacier Knob and the pretty little "sub-knob" on its southwest side, return to the Loch Vale Trail and locate the major junction with the Loch Vale and Glacier Gorge Trails. Follow the Loch Vale Trail west 0.2 mile to the site of a miniature, lush grotto on the north side of the trail. Leave the trail and bushwhack north to the rocky summit of the "sub-knob."

This requires delicate rock scrambling near the top. This tiny vantage offers an intimate and unusual bird's-eye view of The Loch, one of the most popular lakes in RMNP. Descend the north side of the "sub-knob" and hike east to the top of West Glacier Knob. The route is straightforward and does not require any scrambling.

The Gash 11,540 feet
T **OT** *Regional map p. 30 (M, 8); hike map p. 70*

The Gash is a wide ravine north of The Sharkstooth. A permanent snowfield feeds a creek that flows north through The Gash to join Andrews Creek. The Gash is used as an access gully to technical climbing routes on The Sharkstooth.

From the junction of Loch Vale Trail (p. 112) and Andrews Creek Trail (p. 110), follow the Andrews Creek Trail west 0.7 mile to the bottom of The Gash, which is obvious to the south. Leave the trail and hike south over large boulders, skirting some short, steep cliffs on the west. Follow the drainage as the ravine narrows and becomes steeper. A faint trail leads to the base of The Sharkstooth.

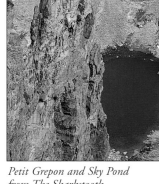

The Sharkstooth (Technical) 12,630 feet
◩ *Regional map p. 30 (M, 7); hike map p. 70*

This appropriately named spire lies at the head of The Gash among the majestic Cathedral Spires that rise magnificently above Sky Pond. All of the routes up The Sharkstooth are technical, and this jagged pinnacle is recognized as a goal for those wishing to climb all the named summits in RMNP. Of them, The Sharkstooth is the most challenging. The easiest route to the top of the formation is East Gully, a 5.4 rock route that ascends a broad gully on the east side of The Sharkstooth. This is the standard descent for parties climbing other routes on The Sharkstooth. Loose rock in the gully can make this ascent hazardous. Refer to a climbing guidebook for details.

Petit Grepon and Sky Pond from The Sharkstooth

Andrews Glacier 11,680 feet
T **OT** **◩** *Regional map p. 30 (L, 8); hike map p. 70*

This beautiful glacier is one of the largest in RMNP, and it is the easiest to climb. It also serves as the headwaters to Andrews Creek. Andrews Glacier averages a modest 20 degrees (though in lean snow years the glacier can exceed 35 degrees), and in good snow conditions this is an easy climb or line of descent to or from the Continental Divide. However, each year hikers attempt the glacier unprepared for less-than-perfect conditions and find themselves in trouble on unyielding, steep ice. Crampons and an ice axe for self-arresting are recommended for this route. In good snow conditions, these tools are unnecessary for a safe experience on the glacier. But when conditions turn hard-packed or icy, negotiating the glacier becomes much more challenging, and these tools are necessary for safety. A fall on Andrews Glacier is very serious, leading to a wild slide into rocks or Andrews Tarn. It is also important to remember that Andrews Glacier is *not* a snowfield, but a living glacier. Between July and October, crevasses and/or bergschrunds open up on the upper reaches of the glacier, and these features are of even greater concern in lean snow years. Anyone traveling on Andrews Glacier must be prepared to avoid such features and be experienced in recognizing and mitigating the hazards presented by open crevasses. These skills are especially important when descending the glacier in late summer.

Glacier Gorge Access GRADE II CLASS 2 MODERATE SNOW From the Glacier Gorge Trailhead (p. 109), follow the Loch Vale Trail for 2.8 miles to The Loch. Continue west along the trail for 0.6 mile to the point where the trail crosses Andrews Creek on a series of footbridges. Immediately after the stream crossing is the junction with the Andrews Creek Trail. Turn north (right) and hike 1 mile to Andrews Tarn. Skirt the lake on the south side to reach the base of Andrews Glacier, where the trail ends. The conditions on Andrews Glacier change every season. It is typically steeper in the middle, with a gentler slope on the south side. Climb up snow or ice for about 0.4 mile and 580 vertical feet to the bulge below Andrews Pass.

Flattop Mountain Access GRADE II CLASS 2 MODERATE SNOW Andrews Glacier can also be reached from the Flattop Mountain Trail. From the Bear Lake Trailhead (p. 108), follow the Flattop Mountain Trail (pp. 75, 112) for 4.4 miles to the summit of Flattop Mountain. From the summit, hike south across talus and tundra, skirting Tyndall Glacier and Hallett Peak on the west. Continue south beyond Chaos Canyon, and don't mistake 'Chaotic Glacier,' a steep snowfield at the headwall of Chaos Canyon, for Andrews Glacier. 'Chaotic Glacier' is much steeper and unreasonable to descend without a rope. Hike beyond Otis Peak to Andrews Pass, 1.6 miles from Flattop Mountain. From Andrews Pass, descend northeast on tundra to the bulge at the top of Andrews Glacier.

Andrews Pass 11,980 feet

T **OT** *Regional map p. 30 (K, 8); hike map p. 70*

Andrews Pass, a gorgeous tundra-laden saddle between Otis and Taylor Peaks, is located along the Continental Divide at the head of Andrews Glacier. Andrews Pass can be reached via Andrews Glacier (follow route description, opposite), Flattop Mountain (follow route description, p. 75), or from the North Inlet Trailhead (see Region 6, p. 303). From the Bear Lake Trailhead (p. 108), follow the Flattop Mountain Trail (p. 112) for 4.4 miles to the summit of Flattop Mountain. From the summit, hike south across talus and tundra for 1.6 miles to Andrews Pass. From North Inlet, follow the North Inlet Trail (see Region 6, p. 306) 11 miles to the broad tundra slopes west of Andrews Pass at 11,720 feet. Leave the trail and climb east over talus and tundra for 0.4 mile to Andrews Pass.

View from the summit of Taylor Peak

Taylor Peak 13,153 feet

T **OT** *Regional map p. 30 (L, 6); hike maps pp. 55, 70*

This major summit has gentle north, west, and south slopes, but its sheer east face casts a shadow on the upper reaches of Loch Vale. The summit knob slightly overhangs the imposing 1,000-foot east face, which stands above a glacially carved cirque that spans 180 degrees and is one of the most impressive in RMNP.

Northwest Slope GRADE II CLASS 2 This route can be reached via Flattop Mountain or Andrews Glacier. Follow one of the routes to Andrews Pass (above). From Andrews Pass, climb southeast up the huge, expansive talus slopes for a little over a mile to the summit of Taylor Peak.

Taylor Glacier (Technical) 11,800 feet

◿ *Regional map p. 30 (M, 5); hike maps pp. 55, 70*

Taylor Glacier is the narrow snow/ice finger that rises southwest from the base of Taylor Peak's east face for 1,400 vertical feet to the Continental Divide. It serves as the headwaters of Icy Brook and is very scenic when viewed from any destination in Loch Vale. The base of the glacier is wide and low-angle, but the top is narrow and reaches 60 degrees. Conditions on the glacier vary from soft snow to hard, dirty glacial ice. The glacier tops out in a narrow gully that is full of loose rock and leads to the Continental Divide. Sometimes a sizeable snow cornice blocks this gully. In any conditions, this route is technical. It is rated Alpine Ice 3, which requires technical equipment and a rope. In soft snow conditions, hardcore skiers actually descend this steep headwall.

Powell Peak   13,208 feet
T **OT** **⟋**   *Regional map p. 30 (M, 5); hike map p. 55*

Powell Peak is located along the Continental Divide, northwest of McHenrys Peak. The great hulk of Thatchtop hides Powell's indistinct summit from view from most vantages. Powell Peak has a striking north face that soars above beautiful Sky Pond, a vertical east face at the headwall of the Shelf and Solitude Lake gorge, and gentle west and south slopes.

West Slope   GRADE II CLASS 2   This is the easiest route up Powell Peak. This route can be reached via Flattop Mountain or Andrews Glacier. Follow one of the routes to Andrews Pass (p. 67). From Andrews Pass, climb southeast up the huge, expansive talus slopes on the west side of Taylor Peak. Stay low and skirt Taylor on the west. Continue southeast over talus and tundra to Powell Peak, 2.5 miles from Andrews Pass.

⟋ Powell Couloir   GRADE II CLASS 2 STEEP SNOW   Powell's north face has several long snow couloirs that lead to the upper talus slope below the summit. The easiest of these is the eastern-most gully, which doesn't normally produce a cornice. This route varies greatly in condition. It ranges from a serious ice climb to a strenuous snow climb. In soft snow conditions a rope and crampons might not be necessary, but avalanche conditions can exist. The headwall of the couloir approaches 70 degrees. In the easiest conditions, this is a demanding and difficult climb up a steep snow slope. An ice axe, crampons, and helmet are recommended, both for the ascent of the couloir, and for the descent of Andrews Glacier.

From Sky Pond (follow route description, p. 64), the Powell couloirs are visible to the south. Climb above Sky Pond to the south toward the couloirs. Enter the eastern couloir and climb up snow for 1,000 vertical feet to the upper section of the gully. Here the snow gets considerably steeper for a few body lengths before it tops out on the rocky slope. Hike on the talus for 100 yards to Powell Peak's splendid summit. To descend, use the West Slope Route for Powell Peak (follow route description above), then descend Andrews Glacier (p. 66).

⟋ Thatchtop–Powell Ridge   GRADE II CLASS 5.2   This route traverses the extremely exposed, serrated ridge between Thatchtop and Powell Peak. Climbing this ridge is a real adventure. The ridge can be used to access either peak. In either direction, it's a fun, sporty route with plenty of exposure. The jagged ridge is narrow and knife-edged in several places, and a rope is recommended for one crucial, exposed, steep section.

Thatchtop–Powell Ridge

From the summit of Thatchtop (follow route description, p. 53), hike southwest to the beginning of the ridge, which is easy at first, traversing across blocky terrain. The ridge quickly gets narrower and steeper, with a vertical drop on the southeast side and exposed, broken slabs on the northwest side. Follow the path of least resistance, staying on the northwest side of the ridge and using small ledges to climb upward. As the ridge approaches Point 12,836', it gets very steep and highly exposed for one committing, 200-foot section (Class 5.2). Many parties opt to use a rope here. The ridge continues southwest, getting slightly easier but remaining hugely exposed. Follow the ridge until the difficulty eases, then enjoy nice scrambling to the Continental Divide. Turn south for 200 yards to reach the summit of Powell Peak.

CHAOS CANYON   *Regional map p. 30 (N, 10)*

This quiet, secluded, and boulder-filled gorge is formed by the convoluted south side of Hallett Peak and the sloping, precipitous north side of Otis Peak, which sports scenic and steep north-facing ramparts. 'Chaotic Glacier,' an unofficially named, extremely steep patch of snow and ice, ornaments the headwall of the rocky gorge. Until the mid-1990s, this magnificent canyon received little attention except from occasional hikers and mountaineers. At that time, technical rock climbers discovered the secret of Chaos Canyon's remarkable car- and house-sized blocks of granite; these "boulderers" weaved their way through the boulder-choked valley in search of good climbing routes. Today, climbers from all over the globe flock to Chaos Canyon to test their mettle on the multitude of granite boulders that offer some of the world's finest bouldering. Set against a backdrop of high mountain peaks and steep snowfields, the location is one of grandeur and beauty.

LAKES AND FALLS

Chaos Canyon Cascades   9,840 feet

T **OT**   *Regional map p. 30 (N, 11)*

Set in an open ravine lush with dense green vegetation, this long, gentle waterfall in Chaos Creek cascades almost 500 feet over short, low-angle steps hidden from view of the trail east of Lake Haiyaha. From the Bear Lake Trailhead (p. 108), hike on the Emerald Lake Trail (p. 111) for 1 mile to the junction with the trail to Lake Haiyaha. Follow the Lake Haiyaha Trail 0.8 mile to the footbridge that spans Chaos Creek. Cross the creek and another small tributary, then leave the trail and bushwhack east, following a faint game trail down the slope. The route becomes very steep and slick with dense vegetation. Hike 0.1 mile from the Lake Haiyaha Trail to arrive at the cascades, lined with mountain bluebells, cow parsnip, parrot's beak, and asters. The stream fans out at the base of some recognizable rock outcrops southwest of Nymph Lake.

Michelle Chase at Chaos Canyon Cascades

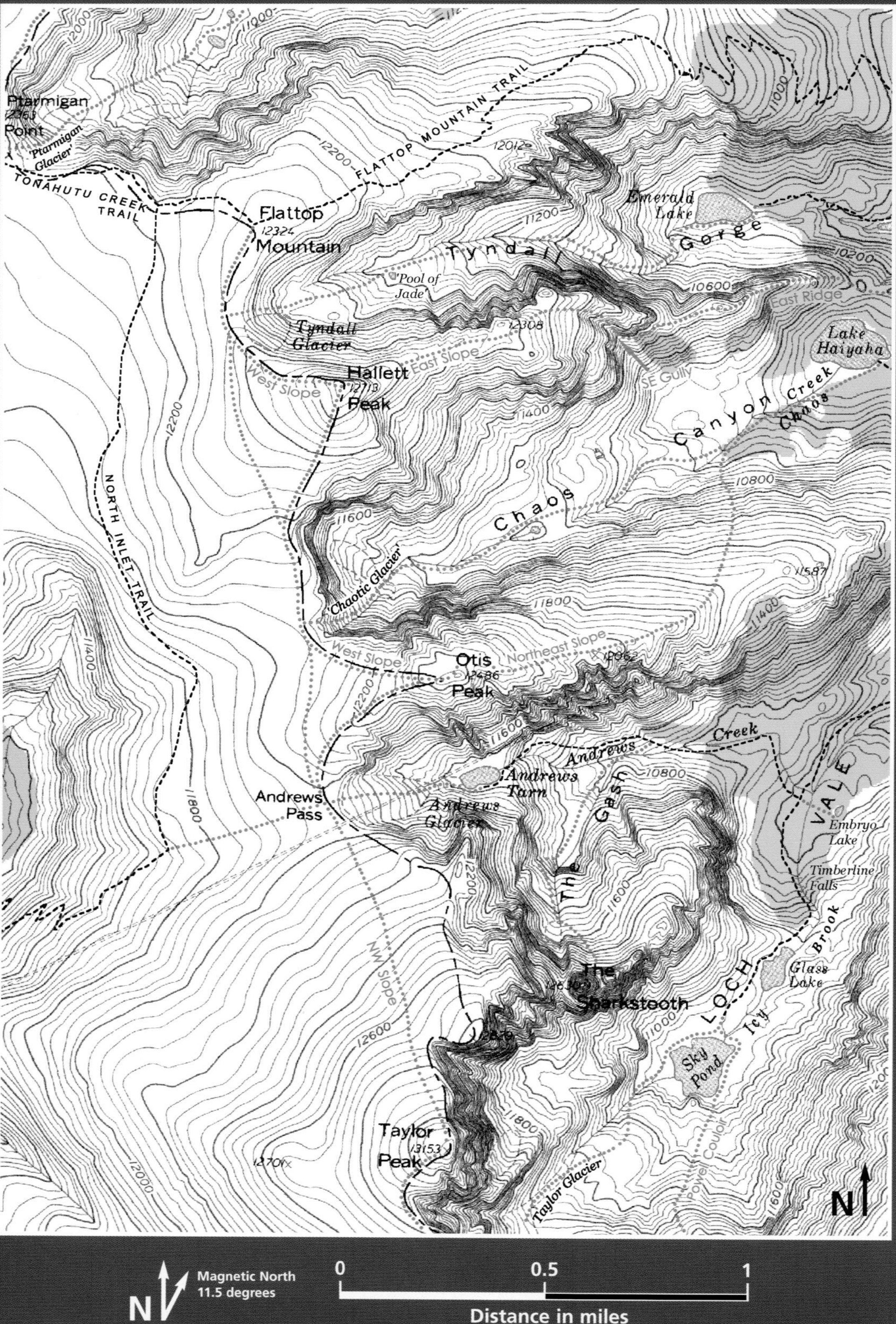

Ptarmigan
Point
2363
'Ptarmigan
Glacier'

TONAHUTU CREEK
TRAIL

FLATTOP MOUNTAIN TRAIL

12012

Flattop
Mountain
12324

Emerald
Lake

T y n d a l l

G o r g e

'Pool of
Jade'

East Ridge

10200

10600

Tyndall
Glacier

12308

Lake
Haiyaha

West Slope

East Slope

SE Gully

Hallett
Peak
12713

11400

Canyon Creek

Chaos

NORTH INLET TRAIL

11600

C h a o s

10800

'Chaotic Glacier'

11597

11800

12200

West Slope

Northeast Slope

1400

Otis
Peak
12486

11600

11963

Creek

Andrews

10800

Andrews
Tarm

V A L E

12200

Andrews
Pass

Andrews
Glacier

The

Gash

Embryo
Lake

11800

Timberline
Falls

11600

NW Slope

Icy

Brook

L O C H

Glass
Lake

The
Sharkstooth

12630

11000

Sky
Pond

12600

Powell Circuit

Taylor
Peak
13153

12701

11800

Taylor Glacier

1600

11400

12200

12000

11800

11400

N

Magnetic North
11.5 degrees

N

0   0.5   1

Distance in miles

Lake Haiyaha 10,220 feet

T **[hiker]** *Regional map p. 30 (N, 11); hike maps pp. 48, 70*

Nestled in the rocky confines of lower Chaos Canyon, Lake Haiyaha lies in an unspoiled subalpine setting amid the distinctive geometry of the jumbled rocks that brought the canyon fame. Enormous boulders left behind by the glacier that carved the ravine distinguish Lake Haiyaha and set it apart in appearance from any other lake in Rocky Mountain National Park.

Bear Lake Access   From the Bear Lake Trailhead (p. 108), walk the Emerald Lake Trail (p. 111) for 1 mile to the junction with the Lake Haiyaha Trail. Turn southwest (left) and follow the Lake Haiyaha Trail as it climbs along the steep hillside through thick subalpine forest and traverses the eastern flank of a ridge extending from Hallett Peak. Impressive views of Nymph and Bear Lakes come into view. The unimproved trail from Glacier Gorge joins the path 0.25 mile from the lake. Turn northwest and hike to Lake Haiyaha, set amongst gnarled limber pines and picturesque tilted boulders.

Glacier Gorge Access   This route, slightly longer than the route from Bear Lake, follows an unimproved trail. This is the preferred winter route because the route from Bear Lake presents an avalanche hazard. From the Glacier Gorge Trailhead (p. 109), follow the Loch Vale Trail (p. 112) past Alberta Falls to the junction with Loch Vale and Glacier Gorge Trails, 2 miles from the trailhead. Turn north and follow the sign to the unimproved trail to Lake Haiyaha. The trail rambles along the north side of West Glacier Knob and climbs through the forest, rising and descending with the hilly topography. Continue in a winding, northwesterly direction to a trail junction 0.2 mile southeast of Lake Haiyaha. Turn northwest (left) and hike to Lake Haiyaha. Bypass the shallow pools amid large rocks southeast of the lake and scramble over boulders to the best vantage of the pristine alpine tarn, amplified by this rugged, unspoiled wilderness.

PEAKS AND OTHER DESTINATIONS

Otis Peak 12,486 feet

T **OT** *Regional map p. 30 (L, 9); hike maps pp. 48, 70*

This massive peak lies slightly east of the Continental Divide, 1.1 miles southeast of Hallett Peak and 0.6 mile northeast of Andrews Pass. It has gentle west slopes and a long northeast ridge that is bordered by steep north and south faces.

West Slope GRADE II CLASS 2   The West Slope Route can be reached from either Flattop Mountain or Andrews Pass. From Flattop Mountain (follow route description, p. 75), leave the trail and hike south across the broad talus and tundra slopes west of Hallett Peak's summit dome. Skirt Tyndall Glacier, Hallett Peak, and 'Chaotic Glacier', and hike for 1.4 miles to reach the west slope of Otis Peak. From Andrews Pass (follow route description, p. 67), climb north 0.25 mile over talus, skirting the headwall of Andrews Glacier to the west slope of Otis Peak. From the west slope of Otis Peak, turn east and climb up the boulder slope for 0.25 mile to the summit of Otis Peak.

Northeast Slope GRADE II CLASS 2   This route approaches Otis Peak from Chaos Canyon. From Lake Haiyaha (follow route description above), leave the trail and skirt the lake on the southeast side. Hike southwest into Chaos Canyon, weaving through the maze of car-sized boulders, hugging the north slope of Otis Peak's massive northeast ridge. Several viable gullies ascend the north side of the ridge and top out between the two major false summits (Point 11,587' and Point 12,062') east of Otis Peak. Choose a gully and climb 800 vertical feet in 0.4 mile to the ridge. The gullies are filled with loose rubble but are nontechnical. Turn southwest and skirt Point 12,062' on the north. Continue southwest up talus for 0.4 mile to the summit.

'Chaotic Glacier' (Technical) 11,810 feet

T **OT** ▨ *Regional map p. 30 (L, 10); hike map p. 70*

Lake Haiyaha Access GRADE II CLASS 2 STEEP SNOW This unofficially named permanent snowfield lies at the southwest end of Chaos Canyon, on the east side of the Continental Divide. The steepest section of the snowfield averages between 50 and 60 degrees and ranges from firm snow to solid ice, depending on the season. The snowfield is rated Alpine Ice 2, Steep Snow. A rope is recommended for an ascent, as are crampons, an ice axe, and a helmet.

From Lake Haiyaha (follow route description, p. 71), hike west through the chaotic boulder fields and past a small, unnamed pond for 1.5 miles to the base of the snowfield. Choose a route and climb 0.3 mile up the snowfield to the Continental Divide at 12,060 feet. Descend via Andrews Glacier (p. 66) or the Flattop Mountain Trail (p. 75).

TYNDALL GORGE *Regional map p. 30 (M, 12)*

The craggy south side of Flattop Mountain, the steep headwall of Tyndall Glacier, and the impressive, renowned north face of Hallett Peak form the beautiful rocky valley of Tyndall Gorge. It is home to Tyndall Glacier, 'Pool of Jade,' Emerald Lake, and Dream Lake. Numerous mountaineering and technical rock- and ice-climbing challenges abound on the steep faces and gullies in the gorge.

LAKES

Bear Lake 9,475 feet

T ⛹ ♿ *Regional map p. 30 (P, 12); hike map p. 48*

Bear Lake is without a doubt the most popular lake in RMNP. A paved road dead-ends into a huge parking lot 100 yards east of the spectacular, high-altitude lake. A wide trail of firm, packed dirt circles the lake, complete with self-guided nature trail signs. Obtain a pamphlet for the self-guided tour at the Beaver Meadows Visitor Center on US 36. Hallett Peak's sheer, highly recognizable north face looms above Bear Lake in a dramatic display of natural wonder.

Bear Lake

Bear Lake Nature Trail   From the parking lot at the Bear Lake Trailhead (p. 108), hike west 100 yards on the Bear Lake Nature Trail to reach the shore of the lake. The striking north face of Hallett Peak provides an impressive backdrop to the round lake. Follow the loop trail 0.65 mile around the lake, taking in the changing panorama of peaks at every turn. From the north shore, enjoy a breathtaking view of Glacier Gorge and Longs Peak, the highest mountain in RMNP. Discover wildlife, flowers, and dramatic mountain scenery on this lovely walk. Great for families, the loop trail provides benches for resting and taking in the view.

Nymph Lake 9,700 feet

T [hiker icon] *Regional map p. 30 (O, 12); hike map p. 48*

Nymph Lake is a small, scenic pond located 0.6 mile southwest of Bear Lake. The forested shores of the lake provide views over the treetops of Hallett Peak, Flattop Mountain, Longs Peak, and the large, bulky mountain simply referred to as Thatchtop. Pond lilies ornament the lake, and birds and small mammals frequent the area. A gentle, asphalt-paved trail leads to the lake, a wonderful destination for hikers of all abilities. The colorful pond lilies that abundantly adorn Nymph Lake in the summer gave the tiny pool of water its name. It was originally called Lily Pad Lake, but somewhere along the line this was changed to Nymph, which is short for *Nymphaea polysepala,* the original scientific name for the flowering plant.

From the parking lot at the Bear Lake Trailhead (p. 108), cross a footbridge and turn south (left), bypassing the spur trail that leads downhill for 0.5 mile to Glacier Gorge Junction. Locate the Emerald Lake Trail and follow the path as it climbs steadily through a pleasant, dense forest. Sporadic views of Longs Peak can be seen through the trees. The trail levels out near the top of a rise before arriving at pretty Nymph Lake.

Dream Lake 9,900 feet

T [hiker icon] *Regional map p. 30 (N, 12); hike map p. 48*

This narrow, long lake stretches for 0.2 mile from east to west and lies in the shadow of majestic Hallett Peak. It is a wonderful, scenic family destination and a great place for a summer picnic. The mythical, dreamlike setting with magnificent mountain scenery no doubt inspired the name.

From the Bear Lake Trailhead (p. 108), follow signs and hike along the asphalt-paved trail for 0.6 mile to Nymph Lake. From Nymph Lake the trail climbs more steeply and passes through a beautiful grove of aspen. A vantage overlooking Nymph Lake offers impressive panoramas to the east and south, stretching from the rocky outcrops on Rams Horn Mountain to Longs Peak. The trail switchbacks and traverses a south-facing slope and then continues to a bridge that spans Tyndall Creek. Shortly thereafter a junction directs the way to Lake Haiyaha, which splits off to the southwest, and the fork that leads west to Dream and Emerald Lakes.

Dream Lake

Michelle Chase at Emerald Lake

Turn west (right) and cross a footbridge to reach Dream Lake.

Magnificent in every way, Dream Lake's shoreline is dotted with picturesque gnarled limber pines. Stark and prominent, the dramatic rock face of Hallett Peak fills the scene with grandeur. The craggy south side of Flattop Mountain displays its impressive rock fins and Tyndall Glacier glistens between the two peaks.

Emerald Lake 10,100 feet

T [🚶] Regional map p. 30 (M, 12); hike maps pp. 48, 70

Truly a gem among RMNP's alpine tarns, Emerald Lake is nestled in a rocky amphitheater at the eastern edge of beautiful Tyndall Gorge. It offers spectacular views of the dramatic north face of Hallett Peak, and an intimate perspective of Flattop Mountain's not-so-flat south side, which is riddled with steep, snow-filled gullies separated by magnificent rock spires. Cupped into a deep basin at the foot of an impressive talus field, Emerald Lake offers a sense of alpine majesty that allures hikers to visit the scene and drink in the unique mountain splendor. A long, cascading waterfall flows over rocks on the west side of the lake.

From Dream Lake (follow the route description, p. 73), continue as the trail skirts the shoreline of long Dream Lake and hike west for 0.7 mile to Emerald Lake. Trees adorn the lake's east side, and a stark talus field forms the western shoreline. Though this lake is an extremely popular destination, it still imparts a sense of isolation because of the austere alpine setting. Tyndall Gorge stretches out to the west and rises to the Continental Divide.

'Pool of Jade' 11,580 feet

T [OT] Regional map p. 30 (not shown on map); hike map p. 70

This tiny, jade-colored tarn lies on a rocky bench in majestic Tyndall Gorge between Emerald Lake and Tyndall Glacier. From Emerald Lake (follow route description above), leave the trail and climb up steep talus on the south side of the lake, then turn west and

hike below the three main buttresses of Hallett Peak's dramatic north face. Weave between large boulders and boulder-hop over Class 2 terrain and across some intermittent snowfields that persist for most of the summer. Tyndall Creek flows through the gorge and is delimited by dense patches of krummholz. Lush grottos and pretty stream features such as coves and clear stream channels make this area very scenic.

In the upper reaches of Tyndall Gorge, smooth horizontal slabs on the north side of the creek are easier to negotiate than the large

'Pool of Jade'

boulders of the south side. Cross the creek to gain the rock slabs and work westward past the third buttress of Hallett Peak. 'Pool of Jade' is on the next bench to the west. It is set in a stark valley of large granite boulders and ridges with great views of Hallett Peak's north face and Tyndall Glacier.

PEAKS AND OTHER DESTINATIONS

Flattop Mountain 12,324 feet

T *Regional map p. 30 (K, 12); hike map p. 70*

The Flattop Mountain Trail

This mountain is one of the most popular to hike in RMNP. It is also one of the few summits with a well-maintained trail all the way to the top. The trail is very popular in summer because it is one of the easiest ways to reach the Continental Divide. It is the gateway to two spectacular, lengthy hikes that cross the divide, essentially providing wilderness foot travel between Estes Park and Grand Lake. The large, flat summit area that inspired Flattop Mountain's name is the largest in RMNP and provides access to numerous other high destinations, as well as a nontechnical passage to the west side of RMNP. Flattop Mountain has gentle east and west sides, complete with trails that lead up them to reach the summit from both Grand Lake and Bear Lake. These two trails are often connected as a through-hike across the Continental Divide between these two points. Flattop has steep north and south faces that provide multiple technical climbing routes.

Flattop Mountain Trail Access GRADE I CLASS 1   From the Bear Lake Trailhead (p. 108), follow the Flattop Mountain Trail (p. 112) for 0.4 mile to the junction with the trail to Bierstadt Lake. Turn west (left) and climb along the Flattop Mountain Trail as it rises above Bear Lake, offering spectacular views of Glacier Gorge and Longs Peak. Continue west on the Flattop Mountain Trail for 0.5 mile to the junction with the Fern-Odessa Trail. Turn south (left) at the fork, following the Flattop Mountain Trail as it climbs through the forest at a moderate grade to Dream Lake Overlook. Located in the crook of a switchback along the trail, this overlook gives a bird's-eye view of Dream Lake, hundreds of feet below.

The trail continues and climbs through stunted trees near timberline. The terrain changes to open, rocky tundra. Arrive at the Emerald Lake overlook and experience the impressive view of the lake, 1,250 vertical feet below the trail that skirts the rim. The steep drop lends a sense of vertigo to the scene and illustrates the immensity of Tyndall Gorge.

The Flattop Mountain Trail continues to zigzag westward through rocky tundra, providing incredible views of the surrounding mountains and valleys. Climb to a horse hitch rack on a prominent flat area that offers an impressive vantage of Tyndall Glacier. Continue to climb to the large expanse of Flattop Mountain's summit. It is difficult to distinguish the true summit amid the flat field of uneven boulders. The true summit lies near the rim of Tyndall Gorge, simply a boulder that rises higher than the rest. On the west side of Flattop Mountain's summit is a major trail junction between the Flattop Mountain Trail, North Inlet Trail, and Tonahutu Creek Trail.

North Inlet Trail Access GRADE II CLASS 1   From the North Inlet Trailhead near Grand Lake (see Region 6, p. 303), follow the North Inlet Trail (see Region 6, p. 306)

7.7 miles to the junction of the Lake Nanita Trail. Continue northeast on the North Inlet Trail as it climbs steep switchbacks along the banks of Hallett Creek. Climb out of the forest and ascend open, sharp switchbacks up the naked hillside, then follow the trail as it sweeps northward to cross the open tundra slopes west of the Continental Divide to the junction with Flattop Mountain Trail, 5.6 miles from the Lake Nanita Trail junction.

Continental Divide Crossing (Flattop Mountain–North Inlet/Tonahutu Creek)

T *Regional map p. 30 (P, 12 to A, 5)*

This one-day hike climbs Flattop Mountain, crosses the Continental Divide, then descends along either the North Inlet Trail to the North Inlet Trailhead or the Tonahutu Creek Trail to the Green Mountain Trailhead. It is a fun hike that essentially provides wilderness foot travel between Estes Park and Grand Lake. A vehicle shuttle is necessary for this hike. It involves approximately 2,875 vertical feet of elevation gain and 3,825 vertical feet of elevation loss over 17.7 miles.

From the Bear Lake Trailhead (p. 108), follow the Flattop Mountain Trail (p. 112) 4.4 miles to the summit of Flattop Mountain on the Continental Divide. Go west 0.3 mile on the trail to the major trail junction between Flattop Mountain Trail, North Inlet Trail, and Tonahutu Creek Trail. From here, follow either the Tonahutu Creek Trail or the longer North Inlet Trail. For the Tonahutu Creek Trail, hike 9.75 miles west to the Green Mountain Trail and follow the Green Mountain Trail 1.8 miles west to the Green Mountain Trailhead. For the North Inlet Trail, head south, then west, for 13.3 miles to the North Inlet Trailhead.

Hallett Peak　12,713 feet

T **OT** *Regional map p. 30 (L, 11); hike map p. 70*

The conspicuously banded north face of Hallett Peak is composed of 1.7-billion-year-old schist and was formed from the metamorphosis of ancient layers of clay and sand deposited before the Rocky Mountains were even formed. Glaciers from comparatively recent times carved away much of the rock, leaving behind the glistening waters and majestic cliffs of Tyndall Gorge. The impressive north face of Hallett Peak dominates the view from Dream, Emerald, and Bear Lakes, and is one of the best and most photographed scenes in all of RMNP. The non-technical summit dome is on the Continental Divide and caps the more technical north, south, and east faces of the peak, which sport numerous technical rock- and ice-climbing routes. Hallet Peak's summit, a rounded mass of talus, is easily reached by a rewarding hiking route.

Hallett Peak

West Slope GRADE II CLASS 2 This is the easiest route to the top of Hallett Peak. From the Bear Lake Trailhead (p. 108), follow the Flattop Mountain Trail (p. 112) 4.4 miles to the summit of Flattop Mountain. From here, Hallett Peak's rocky summit dome lies to the southeast, 390 feet higher. Leave the trail and hike south across the flat boulder field, skirting the headwall of Tyndall Glacier and Tyndall Gorge. Continue southeast and climb up granite boulders that constitute the moderately steep summit of Hallett Peak. A tall summit cairn marks the top. Surrounded on all sides by spectacular, seemingly endless mountain scenery, this summit deserves the acclaim it receives from all who climb it. The views stretch from Grand Lake and the Never Summer Mountains in the west to an incredible panorama including Wild Basin to the south, the Eastern Plains, and the Mummy Range to the north.

East Ridge, Southeast Gully, and East Slope GRADE II CLASS 2 This fun route traverses Hallett Peak's east ridge to a technical section, which it avoids by skirting to the southeast side and ascending a long, nontechnical gully to reach the broad east slope of Hallett Peak. From the Bear Lake Trailhead (p. 108), follow the Emerald Lake Trail (p. 111) for 1 mile to the junction with the Lake Haiyaha Trail. Turn southwest (left) and follow the Lake Haiyaha Trail as it climbs along the steep hillside through thick subalpine forest and traverses the eastern flank of a ridge extending from Hallett Peak.

Leave the trail and bushwhack to the top of the ridge. Follow the rocky, undulating ridge west for 0.9 mile. Several sections of exposed Class 2 climbing make this an exciting traverse. The ridge comes to a lowpoint immediately east of a large, technical cliff band that prevents easy access along the crest of the east ridge. Descend slightly and skirt the steep, bulging cliff that juts out to the southeast. Hike southwest around the bulge to a large, nontechnical, rubble-filled gully that shoots up the southeast face of Hallett Peak's east ridge. Enter the gully and climb 600 vertical feet to the broad talus slope east of the summit. Turn west and enjoy Class 2 hiking for 0.7 mile to the summit of Hallett Peak.

Tyndall Glacier 12,200 feet
T **OT** 🗻 *Regional map p. 30 (L, 11); hike map p. 70*
Because it is visible from the Bear Lake parking lot, Tyndall Glacier is probably the most famous and most photographed glacier in RMNP. It lies at the head of Tyndall Gorge between Hallett Peak and Flattop Mountain, and is a miniature remnant of the mighty glacier that carved out Tyndall Gorge. The glacier's size varies from year to year, but it is generally 0.4 mile long and 0.3 mile wide. Ascending or descending Tyndall Glacier is serious business and requires crampons and an ice axe (and the experience and ability to use them) for most of the year. A helmet is recommended. Tyndall Glacier provides a wonderful mountaineering ascent up a beautiful body of living ice. Steepness ranges from 35 to 45 degrees, with the steepest section on the south side below the slope of Hallett Peak.

🗻 **Tyndall Glacier** GRADE II CLASS 2 STEEP SNOW From 'Pool of Jade' (follow route description, p. 74), continue over the expansive boulder fields to the base of Tyndall Glacier. There are numerous ways to ascend the glacier. It's even possible to avoid the snow and ice altogether and scramble up loose gully systems on the north side of the glacier. Choose a route compatible with the experience of the group and climb steep snow and ice to the crevasses at the top of the glacier. The crevasses are easy to cross. From the boulder-strewn headwall above the glacier, hike north for 0.3 mile to access the Flattop Mountain Trail.

Tyndall Glacier Overlook GRADE I CLASS 2 This route accesses Tyndall Glacier from above. From Flattop Mountain (follow route description, p. 75), turn south and hike 0.2 mile over boulders and tundra to the headwall of Tyndall Gorge, which provides a nice overview of the glacier.

ODESSA GORGE *Regional map p. 30 (L, 16)*

LAKES AND FALLS

Fern Falls 8,800 feet
T [icon] *Regional map p. 30 (N, 19)*

Fern Falls cascades through a forested gorge, spilling over large boulders and fallen trees, creating a lush, mossy grotto along the popular Fern Lake Trail. The falls are so raucous that it is difficult to communicate near them without shouting. A fine mist gently floats away from the rushing water, providing a refreshing spray on hot days.

Pteridium ferns proliferate along the Big Thompson River and Fern Creek. The trailside scenery is carpeted with these plants, making the area names quite appropriate.

From the Fern Lake Trailhead (p. 108), follow the Fern Lake Trail (see Fern-Odessa Trail, p. 111) 1.75 miles to The Pool. Immediately west of The Pool is the intersection with the trail toward Cub Lake and Mill Creek Basin. Continue west along the Fern Lake Trail as it climbs more steeply along the side of a ravine. Cross Fern Creek and continue hiking to Fern Falls, 0.9 mile beyond The Pool. The falls lie along a switchback in the trail, which continues toward Fern and Odessa Lakes.

Marguerite Falls 9,420 feet
T **OT** *Regional map p. 30 (M, 18); hike map p. 85*

Marguerite Falls is one of those obscure destinations within a stone's throw from a highly traveled backcountry area. Most visitors to the wildly popular Fern Lake region bypass this subtle drop in Fern Creek without even realizing the waterfall is mere steps away through the thick coniferous forest of spruce and fir. Fern Creek descends from Odessa Lake and passes through Fern Lake before tumbling through dense forest on its way to join the Big Thompson River near The Pool. The creek flows over several sets of steps, and discerning exactly which cascading bit of water is Marguerite Falls represents the fun of off-trail exploration in a wild area, with no signs directing or cajoling the hiker to a popular destination. Modest in scope, this tiny cascade surges through the woods, jumping boulders and downed trees, the water murmuring and babbling as it drops over ledges amid a charming wooded scene.

Dr. William Workman practiced medicine in Denver near the turn of the 20th century. An avid fisherman, he spent several months each year in Estes Park. He built the Fern Lodge (also called Fern Lake Lodge) in 1910–1911 and made the Fern Lake area famous, inviting hundreds of visitors to explore RMNP's natural beauty from the comfort of the lodge. He was instrumental in naming many of the Fern Creek drainage features. Some of his capricious designations were later changed through the prudence of the Colorado Geographic Board and other agencies. Workman whimsically named lakes, falls, mountains, and other landmarks for his daughters, his wives, friends, and his general fancy. He named Grace Falls and Odessa Lake for his daughters, Fern Falls for his third wife, Marguerite Falls for a friend's wife, and Lake Helene for the daughter of a Denver lawyer who summered in Estes Park.

From the Fern Lake Trailhead (p. 108), follow the Fern Lake Trail (see Fern-Odessa Trail, p. 111) for 3.8 miles to Fern Lake. Hike to the outlet on the lake's northeastern shore for commanding views of

Notchtop Mountain and Little Matterhorn. Cross the long wooden footbridge and turn north to bushwhack along Fern Creek. Travel cross-country through the thick forest for 0.1 mile to Marguerite Falls. Negotiating a route through the dense woods to the falls is a short journey, but it requires fighting through underbrush, avoiding sharp tree limbs, walking over slick pine duff, and climbing over downed logs.

Grace Falls 10,260 feet

T **OT** *Regional map p. 30 (K, 14); hike map p. 85*

Nestled in beautiful Odessa Gorge below Notchtop Mountain, this tall, narrow waterfall tumbles gracefully over dark rock slabs. The Fern Creek headwaters flow from the permanent snowfields that cling to the precipitous slope east of the Continental Divide at Ptarmigan Point. The creek meanders through the ravine, pooling into two unnamed tarns before streaming over bedrock and tumbling through a broken granite step that forms Grace Falls. In winter, heavy snows and cold temperatures combine to transform the waterfall into an expanding ice formation. The ice sculpture grows in scope as the season progresses, covering the width of the broad granite crag and revealing bare rock behind picturesque ice curtains. Grace Falls is a lovely destination in winter or summer. Winter brings more difficulties in traveling through possible avalanche terrain and over unsteady slopes, but the wintry look of the falls is worth the effort in stable conditions. Ice climbers flock to the flow to scale the large, sustained pillar in the middle of the formation and to try their skills on the thinner ice sheets draped on steep rock.

From the Bear Lake Trailhead (p. 108), follow the Flattop Mountain Trail (pp. 75, 112) 0.9 mile to the junction with the Fern-Odessa Trail. Follow the Fern-Odessa Trail as it climbs steadily through the forest along the northern flank of Flattop Mountain. Cross Mill Creek and hike along the southern slope of Joe Mills Mountain. The trail descends, then makes a sweeping turn to the north to skirt the west side of Joe Mills Mountain. Just as the trail begins to loop north toward Odessa and Fern Lakes, leave the trail and drop down in a westerly direction over steep, rocky terrain for 0.2 mile (there might be remnants of an old trail in this area). The best view is from the marshy meadow at the base of Grace Falls, located in the middle of the gorge, north of Notchtop Mountain.

Fern Lake 9,540 feet

T *Regional map p. 30 (L, 17); hike map p. 85*

Fern Lake is one of the most popular lakes in RMNP. Served by a well-maintained trail, the lake provides commanding views of both Notchtop Mountain and Little Matterhorn. The area, rich in history, was home to the famous Fern Lodge (also called Fern Lake Lodge).

Built in 1910–1911 by Dr. William Workman, Fern Lodge served as a haven for scores of visitors over the years. In February 1916, members of the Estes Park Outdoor Club invited the leaders of the Colorado Mountain Club (CMC) to the lake. After that, the lodge, then run by Clifford Higby, opened for about two weeks each winter to function as a base for skiing, snowshoeing, and sledding. Encouraged by the NPS, the CMC developed ski trails and toboggan slides and continued its well-advertised winter outings there until 1934.

In a fanciful 1917 newspaper campaign by the *Denver Post*, Agnes Lowe, a 20-year-old summer resident of Estes Park, dressed in a leopard skin and disappeared into the wilds of RMNP. The newspaper touted her as a "modern Eve," and her story and photographs were widely circulated to the public. During her frolic, she was escorted to Fern Lodge by a ranger to rest from the rigors of the wilderness and the media. She returned to civilization after a week, and the publicity stunt that brought her fame across the country drew attention and controversy to the newly designated national park.

Fern Lodge closed permanently in 1959, and in 1964 the secondary buildings were removed. In later years, vandalism plagued the lodge, causing the NPS to finally burn it to the ground in 1976. The Fern Lake Patrol Cabin, which now stands near the lake, is used for official NPS business. The cabin was placed on the National Register of Historic Places in 1989.

From the Fern Lake Trailhead (p. 108), follow the Fern Lake Trail (see Fern-Odessa Trail, p. 111) for 2.6 miles to Fern Falls. Continue along the Fern Lake Trail as it rises at a sustained grade through the thick forest for 1.2 miles to the junction with the spur trail to Spruce Lake. Pass the junction and climb a short, steep hill to top out above Fern Lake. The Fern Lake Patrol Cabin lies to the south. Descend along the trail to a footbridge at the north end of the lake for grand views of the surrounding mountains.

Odessa Lake   10,020 feet
T *Regional map p. 30 (K, 15); hike map p. 85*

This distinctive subalpine lake is set like a crown jewel in lovely Odessa Gorge, below the dramatic scenery of the rugged rock walls and snowfields of upper Fern Creek drainage. The lake lies in the deep, glacially carved rift that extends north from 'Ptarmigan Glacier' to Forest Canyon. The famous shape of Little Matterhorn highlights the scene. Flattop Mountain's conspicuous rock walls and snow gullies cling to the Continental Divide and add grandeur to this remarkable setting. Odessa Lake is accessed from either the Fern Lake Trailhead or Bear Lake Trailhead. The Bear Lake route is shorter and has less total

NPS rangers cross Fern Creek near Odessa Lake

elevation gain, and it involves a substantial descent into Odessa Gorge; the Fern Lake route is a continuous uphill journey that allows the hiker to enjoy nearly the entire length of the beautiful Fern Creek drainage.

Fern Lake Access   From the Fern Lake Trailhead (p. 108), follow the Fern Lake Trail (see Fern-Odessa Trail, p. 111) 3.8 miles to Fern Lake. Hike to the outlet on the lake's northeastern shore for commanding views of Notchtop Mountain and Little Matterhorn. Continue south along the trail as it skirts Fern Lake on the east side and climbs through a scattered boulder field, then reenters the forest and climbs for 1 mile to the turnoff to Odessa Lake. Follow the Odessa Lake spur trail south and cross Fern Creek on a footbridge. Continue upstream through a shady gorge to Odessa Lake. Notchtop Mountain governs the scene with granite grandeur and its namesake notch.

Bear Lake Access   From the Bear Lake Trailhead (p. 108), follow the Flattop Mountain Trail (pp. 75, 112) 0.9 mile to the junction with the Fern-Odessa Trail. Follow the Fern-Odessa Trail as it climbs steadily through the forest along the northern flank of Flattop Mountain. Cross Mill Creek and hike along the southern slope of Joe Mills Mountain. The trail descends, then makes a sweeping turn to the north to skirt the west side of Joe Mills Mountain. Follow the trail as it loops north and descends to the turnoff to Odessa Lake. Follow the Odessa Lake spur trail south and cross Fern Creek on a footbridge. Continue upstream through a shady gorge to Odessa Lake.

Round Pond 10,340 feet
T **OT** *Regional map p. 30 (M, 16); hike map p. 85*

This tiny pond lies on a flat bench north of Mill Creek between the forested slopes of Joe Mills Mountain and Mount Wuh. From the Bear Lake Trailhead (p. 108), follow the Flattop Mountain Trail (pp. 75, 112) 0.9 mile to the junction with the Fern-Odessa Trail. Continue straight ahead, following the Fern-Odessa Trail as it climbs steadily through the forest along the northern flank of Flattop Mountain. Continue along the trail until Joe Mills Mountain comes into view to the northwest. Just before the path crosses Mill Creek, leave the trail and descend north into the Mill Creek drainage. Bushwhack through a rocky meadow into the thick forest and contour north around the northeast slope of Joe Mills Mountain for 0.6 mile to Round Pond.

Marigold Lake 10,220 feet
T **OT** *Regional map p. 30 (L, 16); hike map p. 85*

This tiny pool of water lies on a small, forested bench on the steep hillside north of Joe Mills Mountain. From the Bear Lake Trailhead (p. 108), follow the Flattop Mountain Trail (pp. 75, 112) 0.9 mile to the junction with the Fern-Odessa Trail. Continue along the Fern-Odessa Trail as it climbs steadily through the forest along the northern flank of Flattop Mountain, then swings north around the west side of Joe Mills Mountain and begins to descend. Hike north to 10,200 feet, then leave the trail and bushwhack northeast up the steep hillside for 0.2 mile to pretty Marigold Lake. The shallow lake is dotted with granite boulders sticking up out of the water, and the forest comes right to the waterline.

Lake Helene 10,580 feet
T **OT** *Regional map p. 30 (K, 14); hike map p. 85*

Lake Helene is a tiny mere below a rocky amphitheater formed by Notchtop and Flattop Mountains. It offers a commanding view of Notchtop and reflects the grandeur of the scenery in its shallow waters.

Bear Lake Access From the Bear Lake Trailhead (p. 108), follow the Flattop Mountain Trail (pp. 75, 112) 0.9 mile to the junction with the Fern-Odessa Trail. Continue following the Fern-Odessa Trail as it climbs steadily through the forest along the northern flank of Flattop Mountain. Cross Mill Creek and hike along the southern slope of Joe Mills Mountain. The trail descends toward Lake Helene. The lake lies just off-trail to the southwest, immediately before the main trail swings north around the western slope of Joe Mills Mountain. A short fisherman's path breaks away from the main trail and leads 0.1 mile to the northwest shore of pretty Lake Helene. The gentle slopes of Flattop Mountain dominate the area to the south, and a unique perspective of Joe Mills Mountain can be seen from the lake's south side. Notchtop Mountain rules the scene with its granite majesty and magnificent characteristic notch.

Fern Lake Access From the Fern Lake Trailhead (p. 108), follow the Fern-Odessa Trail (p. 111) 5.6 miles to a point directly north of Lake Helene. This is the point where the trail swings east around the southern slope of Joe Mills Mountain. A short fisherman's path breaks away from the main trail and leads 0.1 mile to the northwest shore of Lake Helene.

Two Rivers Lake 10,620 feet
T **OT** *Regional map p. 30 (L, 14); hike map p. 85*

This pretty lake represents the headwaters of Mill Creek and is located south of the Fern-Odessa Trail. It is set in a small river basin northeast of Lake Helene. From the

Bear Lake Trailhead (p. 108), follow the Flattop Mountain Trail (p. 112) 0.9 mile to the junction with the Fern-Odessa Trail. Follow the Fern-Odessa Trail as it climbs steadily through the forest along the northern flank of Flattop Mountain. Cross Mill Creek and hike along the southern slope of Joe Mills Mountain. Pass the NPS Sourdough backcountry campsite and travel downhill along the trail for 200 yards to a point where it is possible to drop off the trail and bushwhack south a short distance to Two Rivers Lake. Walk through a boulder field and marshy terrain to reach the east end of the lake. Marigold Pond and an unnamed pool lie to the northeast. From the west end of the lake, it is a short stroll through forest and marsh to reach pretty Lake Helene. An unmaintained path on the northwest side of Lake Helene leads back to the Fern-Odessa Trail.

Marigold Pond   10,580 feet
T **OT** *Regional map p. 30 (not shown on map); hike map p. 85*

Two tiny ponds lie northeast of Two Rivers Lake along Mill Creek. The larger, northeasternmost pool is Marigold Pond. From Two Rivers Lake (follow route description, p. 81), follow the drainage northeast through marsh and boulder fields 0.1 mile to Marigold Pond.

PEAKS AND OTHER DESTINATIONS

Mount Wuh   10,761 feet
T **OT** *Regional map p. 30 (N, 16)*

Mount Wuh is the rocky-topped highpoint on an inconspicuous wooded ridge west of Mill Creek Basin and east of Fern Lake. The Fern-Odessa and Mill Creek Basin Trails circumvent Mount Wuh's graceful slopes. This is a special destination, secluded and isolated even though it's less than a mile from a popular and often crowded trail system.

South Slope GRADE I CLASS 2   From the Bear Lake Trailhead (p. 108), follow the Flattop Mountain Trail (p. 112) 0.9 mile to the junction with the Fern-Odessa Trail. Continue straight ahead, following the Fern-Odessa Trail as it climbs steadily through the forest along the northern flank of Flattop Mountain. Mount Wuh is the long, forested ridge north of the trail. The summit, obscured from view, is at the western edge of the ridge crest. Continue on the trail until Joe Mills Mountain comes into view to the northwest.

Just before the path crosses Mill Creek, leave the trail and descend north into the Mill Creek drainage. Bushwhack through a rocky meadow into the thick forest that surrounds Mount Wuh. Hike north up the slope to access the ridge. Follow the rolling crest to the highpoint. A large rock cairn marks the true summit. Strategically situated between Mill Creek Basin and the Fern Creek drainage, the summit offers intimate and stupendous views of Moraine Park, Forest Canyon, Stones Peak, Gabletop Mountain, Little Matterhorn, Notchtop Mountain, and Flattop Mountain.

Joe Mills Mountain   11,078 feet
T **OT** *Regional map p. 30 (M, 15); hike map p. 85*

This small peak offers an intimate view of the high peaks surrounding Odessa Gorge, and requires a tough, trailless 0.25-mile scramble over boulders to get to the top.

South Slope GRADE I CLASS 2   From the Bear Lake Trailhead (p. 108), follow the Flattop Mountain Trail (pp. 75, 112) 0.9 mile to the junction with the Fern-Odessa Trail. Follow the Fern-Odessa Trail as it climbs steadily through the forest along the northern flank of Flattop Mountain. Cross Mill Creek and hike along the southern slope of Joe Mills Mountain. At the junction with the trail to the NPS Sourdough backcountry campsite, follow the spur trail north to the campsite. Be considerate of any campers and avoid their camp. A trail of sorts goes beyond the campsite and climbs north through the forest toward Joe Mills Mountain. The trail dissipates among a boulder field. Continue climbing north over rocky terrain through patches of gnarled trees to the summit of Joe Mills Mountain for a great panoramic view of the area.

Ptarmigan Point   12,363 feet

T **OT** *Regional map p. 30 (J, 13); hike map p. 70*

Ptarmigan Point is the rounded rock knob at the southeastern end of Bighorn Flats, 0.9 mile west of Flattop Mountain. It lies on the Continental Divide above Ptarmigan Glacier, which sits at the southwestern headwall of Odessa Gorge. It is not a pronounced summit, rising only 200 vertical feet above Ptarmigan Pass. It can be reached via the Tonahutu Creek Trail, which skirts southwest of Ptarmigan Point.

Tonahutu Creek Trail Access GRADE I CLASS 1   From the summit of Flattop Mountain (follow route description, p. 75), hike 0.3 mile west to the trail junction between Flattop Mountain Trail, Tonahutu Creek Trail, and North Inlet Trail. Follow the Tonahutu Creek Trail west as it descends over tundra and talus for 0.5 mile to Ptarmigan Pass. Leave the trail and climb 0.2 mile northwest to the summit.

Ptarmigan Pass   12,180 feet

T **OT** *Regional map p. 30 (I, 12)*

This lowpoint on the Continental Divide lies on the broad tundra slope west of Flattop Mountain. The pass lies between Ptarmigan Creek drainage and Odessa Gorge. The Tonahutu Creek Trail traverses east to west across the pass. From the summit of Flattop Mountain (follow route description, p. 75), hike west 0.3 mile to the trail junction between Flattop Mountain Trail, Tonahutu Creek Trail, and North Inlet Trail. Follow the Tonahutu Creek Trail west as it descends over tundra and talus for 0.5 mile to Ptarmigan Pass. It is also possible to access Ptarmigan Pass from Lake Helene, then by climbing 'Ptarmigan Glacier' (see hike description below).

'Ptarmigan Glacier'   11,900 feet

T **OT** **⬦** *Regional map p. 30 (I, 12); hike map p. 70*

This unofficially named, permanent snowfield is a remnant of the large glacier that carved Odessa Gorge. It faces northeast and is located north of Ptarmigan Pass at the headwall of Odessa Gorge. The snowfield's east side is moderate, while the west side is quite steep. A large bergschrund opens near the top in late summer. Crampons, an ice axe, and a helmet are recommended for this route.

Odessa Gorge Access GRADE I CLASS 2 MODERATE SNOW   From the Bear Lake Trailhead (p. 108), follow the Flattop Mountain Trail (pp. 75, 112) for 0.9 mile to the junction with the Fern-Odessa Trail. Follow the Fern-Odessa Trail northwest for 2.2 miles to the turnoff for the fisherman's path to Lake Helene. Turn south on the fisherman's path and hike 0.1 mile to Lake Helene. Cross the outlet stream and locate a faint climber's

> Joe Mills Mountain was named for an innovative Estes Park man who takes a back seat historically to his more famous brother. Enoch Josiah "Joe" Mills was born 10 years after Enos Mills, who is commonly considered to be the father of RMNP. The brothers were instrumental in the fight to preserve the area and were inexhaustible lecturers on the nature circuit. Joe followed in his brother's footsteps and moved to Estes Park to work at the Longs Peak Inn for their uncle, Elkanah Lamb. When he arrived in Loveland by train in 1896, the 16-year-old decided to travel to Estes Park by bicycle instead of by the four-horse stage. He immediately fell in love with the area and came back for summer seasons between his schooling and his career as an athlete and a coach. In 1909 he married Ethel Steere and they homesteaded on the western slope of Twin Sisters Mountain.

trail that leaves the west side of the lake and leads southwest into upper Odessa Gorge. Scramble through dense shrubs and over rock slabs for 0.5 mile to two pretty, unnamed lakes at 10,950 feet. Here the faint trail disappears altogether. Hike southwest over large boulders, up and over a large rock moraine to reach the base of 'Ptarmigan Glacier.'

The wide snowfield presents a variety of ascent options. For some parties, a rope might be necessary under certain conditions. Climb 600 vertical feet up the snowfield to Ptarmigan Pass and the Continental Divide. Either descend the snowfield or hike east on the Tonahutu Creek Trail to the summit of Flattop Mountain, then descend the Flattop Mountain Trail to the Bear Lake Trailhead.

Notchtop Mountain 12,160+ feet

T **OT** ⬦ *Regional map p. 30 (K, 14); hike map p. 85*

This beautiful peak is beset on three sides by steep, soaring cliffs nearly 1,200 feet high. The jagged mountain juts out into Odessa Gorge 0.2 mile east of the Continental Divide, to which it is connected by a serrated northwest ridge. The stunning, 100-foot-deep namesake notch stands near the eastern end of this

ridge. The notch separates the true summit on the west side of the gap from 'Notch Spire' (12,129 feet), a slightly lower pinnacle on the east side of the notch. The summits of Notchtop Mountain and 'Notch Spire' are nearly the same height—within 35 feet of each other. The USGS topographical maps only list the elevation of 'Notch Spire,' leading to the common misconception that 'Notch Spire' is the true summit.

Neither the summit of Notchtop Mountain nor the summit of 'Notch Spire' is easy to reach. The routes listed here are rated Class 4, but that is true only if the path of least resistance is found. A rope and a helmet are recommended. Good route-finding skills are a must to ascend this mountain by the easiest routes. It is extremely easy to wander into exposed, Class 5 terrain at any point along the Northwest Ridge Route. If the rock is wet or snowy, this route becomes dangerous and technical. The least difficult routes meet at the 12,120-foot saddle on the Northwest Ridge below the Continental Divide, then follow the Northwest Ridge Route to gain either

Notchtop Mountain   summit.

Southeast Gully to Northwest Ridge GRADE I CLASS 4 From Lake Helene (follow route description, p. 81), cross the outlet stream and locate a faint climber's trail that leaves from the west side of the lake and leads southwest into upper Odessa Gorge. Scramble through dense shrubs and over rock slabs for 0.5 mile to two scenic, unnamed lakes at 10,950 feet. Turn west and scramble over rocky terrain, skirting below the sheer south face of Notchtop Mountain and gaining a southeast-facing gully. Climb up the steep, grassy scree gully, which presents several sections of Class 4 scrambling over short rock obstacles. The hardest of these is a 15-foot section that approaches Class 5 climbing. Continue to the top of the gully, which ends at the 12,120-foot saddle below the Continental Divide. To reach the summit, refer to the following route description (Northwest Ridge Route).

Continental Divide to Northwest Ridge Route GRADE I CLASS 4 From Ptarmigan Pass (follow route description, p. 83), hike north, then northeast over tundra and talus

N

11,800

×1227

Tonahutu Creek Trail

To Sprague Pass

CONTINENTAL

Bighorn Flats

12,000

DIVIDE

To Spruce Pass

To Hallett Pk.

Spruce Creek

SPRUCE CANYON

10,800

11,000

10,600

10,880

12,200

SW Slope

SW Slope

11,000

9,800

Knobtop Mountain
11,331

Gabletop Mtn

Castle Rock

To Flattop Mtn.

Notchtop Mountain
12,129

11,000

Tourmaline Lake

Tourmaline Gorge

Little Matterhorn
11,586

Grace Falls

10,800

Loomis Lake

Primrose Pond

10,200

Gorge Lakes

Odessa Lake

The Gable

10,600

Fern

Spruce Lake

12,000

11,900

Lake Helene

10,600

12,000

Two Rivers Lake

Joe Mills Mountain
×11,078

Marigold Lake

Patrol Cabin

Fern Lake

9,000

Fern-Odessa Trail

Marigold Pond

Creek

Marguerite Falls

11,200

Round Pond

10,000

N

Magnetic North
11.5 degrees

0   0.5   1

Distance in miles

for 0.7 mile to 12,280 feet along the Continental Divide, immediately northwest of Notchtop Mountain's northwest ridge. Hike slightly north to locate a steep, rocky slope that leads down to the 12,120-foot saddle at the top of the Southeast Gully.

From here, traverse southeast along the south side of the ridge on highly exposed Class 4 terrain. Follow the path of least resistance and angle upward to the summit of Notchtop Mountain. From the summit, it's an easy scramble east down to the famous notch, but it's a tricky, exposed scramble to reach the summit of 'Notch Spire.'

To climb 'Notch Spire,' descend slightly on the south side of the notch and locate broken terrain that provides the only nontechnical option. Climb southeast up an exposed ramp system, then turn north and scoot toward the summit over highly exposed slabs. The exposure in this area can make the climbing seem more challenging.

Knobtop Mountain   12,331 feet

T **OT**   *Regional map p. 30 (J, 15); hike map p. 85*

This pile of granite boulders lies along the Continental Divide overlooking Odessa Gorge and is reached by an uncomplicated hiking route. It offers an impressive overview of jagged Notchtop Mountain, as well as expansive vistas of Bighorn Flats and the wide tundra plateau near Flattop Mountain. A wonderful perspective of Longs Peak stands out to the southeast.

Southwest Slope GRADE I CLASS 2   This is the easiest route to Knobtop Mountain. From Ptarmigan Pass (follow route description, p. 83), hike north over tundra and talus for 1 mile to the summit.

TOURMALINE GORGE   *Regional map p. 30 (J, 15)*

Tourmaline Gorge is a striking cirque framed by the impressive walls of Little Matterhorn and Gabletop Mountain. Tourmaline Creek, which originates at a permanent, unnamed snowfield nestled high in the gorge, flows east to Odessa Lake. This rugged, trailless creek valley is home to Tourmaline Lake.

Macey Bray snowshoes past Tourmaline Lake in late May

LAKES

Tourmaline Lake 10,580 feet
T **OT** *Regional map p. 30 (J, 15); hike map p. 85*

Tucked into an amphitheater of large boulders and stunted trees, Tourmaline Lake glistens below the summits of Knobtop and Gabletop Mountains. The rugged glacial valley is a wonderful place to view the Colorado state flower during the summer. Columbines flourish in the basin's boulder fields and are particularly impressive in July.

From lovely Odessa Lake (follow route description, p. 80), skirt west along the northwestern shore, following a faint path to the point where Tourmaline Creek empties into Odessa Lake. Leave the path and turn west, climbing through thick forest along a faded, intermittent footpath. The footpath is hard to follow and leads west into the lush valley, climbing through marsh and over boulder fields. Near the lake the forest opens up and reveals the majesty of Tourmaline Gorge, with the rock ramparts of Gabletop Mountain rising impressively behind this pretty alpine tarn. Joe Mills Mountain can be seen across the valley to the southeast. Follow the creek to beautiful Tourmaline Lake, 0.5 mile from Odessa Lake.

PEAKS

Little Matterhorn 11,586 feet
T **OT** *Regional map p. 30 (K, 15); hike map p. 85*

Little Matterhorn is the northeastern end of a spur ridge that extends from Knobtop Mountain. The jagged ridge forms the south side of Tourmaline Gorge and lies 0.3 mile southwest of Odessa Lake in Odessa Gorge. The peak has steep and broken north, east, and south faces. It is a fun, challenging peak to climb.

The Southwest Ridge that serves as the primary access extends northeast from the Continental Divide. It can be reached from the Continental Divide or from scree gullies that ascend the north or south sides of the ridge.

Continental Divide Access to Southwest Ridge GRADE I CLASS 3 From Knobtop Mountain (follow route description, opposite), descend north over tundra and talus for 0.2 mile to the start of the Southwest Ridge. Descend northeast (Class 3) to an obvious notch in the ridge. Large scree gullies climb the north and south sides to also reach this notch. This is the shared point for the three access routes that reach the Southwest Ridge (see South Side Access below for complete route description).

North Side Access to Southwest Ridge GRADE I CLASS 3 From Tourmaline Lake (follow route description above), bushwhack 0.3 mile southwest through Tourmaline Gorge, bypassing the sharp cliffs on Little Matterhorn's Southwest Ridge and locating a large, steep, northeast-facing scree gully that ascends the north side of the ridge and leads to the notch. The gully is immediately east of the large face of Point 12,080'. This steep, loose gully can hold a lot of snow into early summer. A few rock obstacles must also be bypassed (Class 3). Take care when ascending this gully. If steep snow persists, an ice axe and crampons might be necessary (see below for complete route description).

South Side Access to Southwest Ridge GRADE I CLASS 3 This route is slightly easier than the north side access. From the base of Grace Falls (follow route description, p. 79), bushwhack and scramble west 0.5 mile, bypassing the sharp cliffs on Little Matterhorn's Southwest Ridge and locating a large, southeast-facing scree gully that ascends the south side of the ridge and leads to the notch. From this shared point, the objective is to traverse northeast along the ridge to the summit of Little Matterhorn. The ridge crest is blocky and extremely exposed. Careful route finding is required to keep the climbing difficulty at Class 3. Climb up, down, and around the obstacles along the ridge, traversing rock ledges and bypassing large granite blocks. The high exposure is dizzying. The summit is a small knob atop the main tower near the northeast end of the ridge.

Gabletop Mountain   11,939 feet

T **OT** *Regional map p. 30 (J, 16); hike map p. 85*

This blocky-topped mountain is located between Spruce Canyon and Tourmaline Gorge. It has two scenic northeastern arms that form the Loomis Lake gorge and terminate at Castle Rock and The Gable. It is a fun mountain to climb, and can be reached from either the Continental Divide or Tourmaline Gorge.

Southwest Slope GRADE I CLASS 2   This long hike approaches Gabletop Mountain from the Continental Divide. From Knobtop Mountain (follow route description, p. 86), descend north over tundra and talus, contouring around the headwall of Tourmaline Gorge, for 0.8 mile to the summit of Gabletop Mountain.

Southeast Slope GRADE I CLASS 2   This route is more difficult than the Southwest Slope Route, but it is also more varied. From Tourmaline Lake (follow route description, p. 87), skirt the lake on the north side and hike west over large boulders, skirting

short cliffs when necessary. Locate a broad talus slope that leads northwest to Gabletop Mountain's upper limits. The slope is rocky and several short cliffs need to be circumvented or climbed. Continue up and enter a gully system that gradually narrows and leads to a break in the summit blocks of Gabletop Mountain. Climb the narrow passageway over grass and rocks to a notch between the summit blocks. Scramble up stacked granite boulders to the summit. The rock on this mountain is very aesthetic.

Mike Poland and Ronny Campbell on Gabletop Mountain

The Gable   11,040+ feet

T **OT** *Regional map p. 30 (L, 16); hike map p. 85*

The Gable is the highest pyramid of rocks among a set of stately ramparts that form the eastern end of a long ridge extending northeast from Gabletop Mountain. It is a marvelous destination that sees few ascents. Superb views of the Fern and Spruce Creek drainages are the reward for bushwhacking through thick krummholz and up steep slopes to stand at the apex of this beautiful stack of rocks.

North Slope GRADE I CLASS 2   From Spruce Lake (follow route description, opposite), skirt the lake on the north side by following a faint trail that leads into the gully southwest of the lake. From Spruce Lake's inlet, find a rough path that follows the stream southwest to a small pool, unofficially called 'Primrose Pond.' Loomis Lake, a large alpine tarn cupped at the base of Gabletop Mountain's dramatic east face, lies 0.2 mile farther upstream. Bushwhack to the south side of 'Primrose Pond' and look for a weakness in the rock walls above. Climb through the forest to the base of the cliffs, then pick a route over the broken wall. If the path of least resistance is chosen, the hillside should present no technical difficulties, so avoid the steeper sections and choose ledges and gullies that penetrate the cliff system.

Climb above the crag and fight through the dense krummholz that plagues the upper slopes. The low-lying shrubbery is quite thick and difficult to negotiate, but it is essentially unavoidable. Small pockets of barren rocky patches are enticing but short-lived before the krummholz becomes overwhelming once again. Continue the struggle to a boulder field that leads to the striking rock towers near The Gable.

The Gable sports a small, exposed summit. Between The Gable and the nearest outcrop to the west is a marvelous cleft ornamented with yellow lichen that offers a sneak peek at Longs Peak and Odessa Lake shimmering below. Explore all the outcrops to take advantage of the unique views.

SPRUCE CANYON *Regional map p. 30 (J, 18)*

Spruce Canyon, an incredibly rugged gorge located northeast of the Continental Divide, is formed by the massive southeast slopes of Stones Peak and the northeastern ridge of Gabletop Mountain. Spruce Creek originates at Sprague Pass and flows northeast through the valley for 3.6 miles to join Big Thompson River near The Pool. This trailless paradise presents arduous bushwhacking along Spruce Creek for intrepid hikers. Rock slabs, thick forest, downed trees, rugged boulder fields, wet bogs, and dense vegetation combine to make this a tough place to walk. A narrow section of the canyon creates some steep, tricky terrain close to the creek. Spruce Canyon provides access to a large glacial shelf on the southwest side of Stones Peak that is home to several high alpine tarns.

LAKES

Spruce Lake 9,660 feet

T *Regional map p. 30 (K, 18); hike map p. 85*

Located in a modest triangle of paradise between Fern and Spruce Creeks, Spruce Lake lies northeast of the Continental Divide and 0.6 mile northwest of Fern Lake. Though it has a heavily treed shoreline, the lake's east side offers great views of the nearby mountains. The stark granite face of Gabletop Mountain rises to the southwest. Castle Rock, a prominent rock spire that crowns a nearby ridge, stands out to the west. This popular destination is a favorite spot for anglers in the summer.

From the Fern Lake Trailhead (p. 108), follow the Fern Lake Trail (see Fern-Odessa Trail, p. 111) as it gently parallels the Big Thompson River. Cross a small stream that flows out of Windy Gulch and look to the north to catch a glimpse of Windy Gulch Cascades. After 1 mile, weave through the tall, jumbled blocks of Arch Rocks and continue along to a small basin of water aptly named

Castle Rock as seen from Spruce Lake

The Pool, located 1.75 miles from the trailhead. Beyond The Pool, the trail climbs steadily for 0.9 mile to Fern Falls. Another uphill stretch of trail leads to the junction with the unimproved trail to Spruce Lake. Fern Lake lies directly south of this junction, a few hundred yards farther and up over a small rise.

The unimproved trail to Spruce Lake winds through the thick forest in a northwesterly direction for 1 mile, and although the path is not as well defined as Fern Lake Trail, it is relatively easy to follow. At one point the trail leads through a boulder field, and cairns show the way along the indistinct section. Closer to Spruce Lake, the trail travels through several marshy areas, and plank-board walkways elevate the hiker above the bog. Spruce Lake is lovely, with spruce and fir trees covering the ridges and mountain slopes, remaining a beautiful green color year-round.

Loomis Lake (10,220 feet) and 'Primrose Pond' (10,140 feet)
T **OT** *Regional map p. 30 (J, 17); hike map p. 85*

Loomis Lake is the origin of the southernmost tributary to Spruce Creek, which in turn flows into the Big Thompson River. It is one of two lakes located high in the basin southwest of Spruce Lake. The smaller of the two, unofficially referred to as 'Primrose Pond,' is a quaint pool amid a rich forest with a rocky shoreline. Higher, deep in the cirque, lies Loomis Lake, a striking alpine tarn flanked on three sides by rocky cliffs. Intimate views of the beautiful east face of Gabletop Mountain, The Gable, and Castle Rock can be seen from this stark, watery vantage.

From Spruce Lake (follow route description, p. 89), hike to the southwest shore and follow the drainage along a faint trail that climbs into the Loomis Lake basin, marked sparsely by rock cairns. The trail is somewhat hard to follow. Bushwhack up the drainage, staying on the north (right-hand) side of the creek for 0.6 mile to 'Primrose Pond.' Interesting rocks dot the landscape. Continue hiking up the faint path to Loomis Lake, 0.8 mile from Spruce Lake and 0.2 mile from 'Primrose Pond.' Loomis Lake is a third of the size of Spruce Lake, but is twice as deep. Glacially polished rocks on the northeastern shore provide a good picnic site.

Irene Lake 11,860 feet
T **OT** *Regional map p. 30 (G, 18); hike map p. 96*

This lovely, triangle-shaped tarn lies about 50 yards northeast of 'Sprague Tarn' and is about 20 vertical feet higher. From 'Sprague Tarn' (follow route description, p. 92), hike northeast over a small rise to reach the lake. Short rock cliffs rise out of the water and show the previous high water marks. A grassy landing on the southwest shore provides a nice spot for lunch.

Rainbow Lake 11,740 feet
T **OT** *Regional map p. 30 (G, 17); hike map p. 96*

This multicolored tarn lies 100 yards below and to the southeast of 'Sprague Tarn.' The obvious depth levels of its shallow shoreline show distinct gradients of color. The water reflects different colors according to depth, giving it a rainbow look. The east face of Point 12,348' rises magnificently above the lake. A mostly mossy slope to the west is home to a modest waterfall flowing from 'Sprague Tarn' into Rainbow Lake.

Continental Divide Access GRADE II CLASS 3 This fun route from the Continental Divide descends a rib separating 'Sprague Tarn' and Rainbow Lake. From Sprague Pass (follow route description, p. 93), climb northwest up the sustained tundra-and-talus slope for 0.5 mile to Point 12,348'. Leave the divide and scramble down a prominent rock rib (Class 3) that extends north and stands between 'Sprague Tarn'

Looking down on Rainbow Lake and 'Sprague Tarn' from the Continental Divide

and Rainbow Lake. Descend 0.25 mile to the base of 'Sprague Tarn.' Turn east and scramble 0.1 mile over a rocky moraine to Rainbow Lake.

Spruce Canyon Access   GRADE II CLASS 2

This route can be accessed from Spruce Lake or Sprague Pass. From the northeast end of Spruce Lake (follow the route description on p. 89), leave the trail and bushwhack northwest to 9,800 feet. Contour northwest to the north side of Castle Rock. Descend into Spruce Canyon, negotiating rock slabs and thick forest to Spruce Creek. Turn southwest and bushwhack 1.5 miles to the point where the drainage from Rainbow Lake joins Spruce Creek. Turn northwest and bushwhack up the steep slope for 0.5 mile to Rainbow Lake.

From Sprague Pass (follow route description, p. 93), hike slightly north on the Continental Divide to 11,800 feet, then contour north across steep terrain on the east side of the divide until it is reasonable to descend northeast to the Rainbow Lake shelf. Climb northwest to Rainbow Lake.

Hourglass Lake   11,220 feet

[T] [OT] *Regional map p. 30 (G, 19); hike map p. 96*

Hourglass Lake is 0.2 mile long and bulges at the west end. It has a narrow neck between its east and west sides, which causes it to resemble the shape of an hourglass. It lies below the stately rock towers that decorate the southern shoulder of Stones Peak. Krummholz, grass, and stunted trees ornament the shoreline.

Spruce Canyon Access   GRADE II CLASS 2

This route can be accessed from either Spruce Lake or Sprague Pass. From the northeast end of Spruce Lake (follow route description, p. 89), leave the trail and bushwhack northwest to 9,800 feet. Contour northwest to the north side of Castle Rock. Descend into Spruce Canyon, negotiating rock slabs and thick forest to Spruce Creek. Turn southwest and bushwhack 1.4 miles to a meadow at 10,520 feet. Turn northwest and bushwhack up the steep slope for 0.5 mile to Hourglass Lake. This is easier than following the creek that flows from Hourglass Lake, a route beleaguered by difficult rock sections.

Sprague Pass Access   From Sprague Pass (follow route description, p. 93), hike slightly north on the Continental Divide to 11,800 feet, then

Hourglass Lake

contour north across steep terrain on the east side of the divide until it is reasonable to descend northeast to the Rainbow Lake shelf. From Rainbow Lake, descend 0.5 mile northeast over steep, grassy terrain to Hourglass Lake. The route is a bit complicated and takes some route finding to circumvent a series of short, steep cliffs.

Sprague Glacier (12,100 feet) and 'Sprague Tarn' (11,860 feet)

T **OT** *Regional map p. 30 (F, 18); hike map p. 96*

Sprague Glacier lies on the east side of the Continental Divide, 0.5 mile southeast of Sprague Mountain. A beautiful, icy lake lies at the base of the glacier, unofficially named 'Sprague Tarn.' Rising upward for 500 vertical feet, the glacier makes a picturesque backdrop to the four alpine lakes below it.

Continental Divide Access GRADE II CLASS 3 This fun route from the Continental Divide descends along a rib separating 'Sprague Tarn' and Rainbow Lake. From Sprague Pass (follow route description, opposite), climb northwest up the sustained tundra-and-talus slope for 0.5 mile to Point 12,348', which provides amazing views of Spruce Canyon, 'Sprague Tarn,' and Rainbow, Irene, and Hourglass Lakes. Leave the divide and scramble down the prominent rock rib (Class 3) that extends north and stands between 'Sprague Tarn' and Rainbow Lake. Descend 0.25 mile to the base of 'Sprague Tarn.'

Rainbow Lake Access GRADE II CLASS 2 This route can be accessed from either Spruce Lake or Sprague Pass. From Rainbow Lake (follow route description, p. 90), hike west up a rocky moraine, to the north of a modest waterfall, for 0.1 mile to 'Sprague Tarn.'

PEAKS AND OTHER DESTINATIONS

Castle Rock 10,640+ feet

T **OT** *Regional map p. 30 (K, 18); hike map p. 85*

The beautiful spire of Castle Rock rises west of Spruce Lake. Standing at the end of a ridge that extends northeast from Gabletop Mountain, Castle Rock forms the north-west side of the superb alpine cirque that is home to attractive Loomis Lake. Castle Rock is an exciting feature to climb. Its picturesque, craggy ridgeline offers a sporty scramble out to its highest point. It showcases outstanding views into rugged Spruce Canyon and the terrain that surrounds popular Spruce Lake. From a point near the summit of Castle Rock, the rocks near The Gable perfectly outline Longs Peak in a wonderful display of natural framing.

Castle Rock

South Gully to West Ridge GRADE I CLASS 2

At Spruce Lake (follow route description, p. 89), Castle Rock highlights the scene, majestically towering over the mountain lake. Skirt Spruce Lake on the north side by following a faint trail that leads into the gully above the lake. From Spruce Lake's inlet, find a rough path that follows the stream southwest to 'Primrose Pond' (p. 90). Bushwhack around the north side of 'Primrose Pond' and gain a wide, tree-choked gully riddled with boulder fields and downed trees. The gully has no trail and is quite steep. It tops out to the west of a prominent rock face and narrows to a small V-slot with plenty of loose rock and dirt. Scramble up the slot to the ridgeline and hike east along the forested crest to a series of rock outcrops. Skirt the first prominence on the north side for spectacular views into Spruce Canyon. Deep, vertical ravines drop from the crest into the forested depths of the gorge. Continue east and note the views of Longs Peak, framed nicely by The Gable, the stately rock rampart that forms the east end of Gabletop Mountain's southeast ridge.

The final scramble involves stepping across a very narrow fissure between rock outcrops and then walking along a slender rock bridge to the wide summit. The scramble is not difficult, but it does offer some exposure. Another rock outcrop lies farther east of the summit, but it is much lower and involves technical climbing to reach.

Sprague Pass   11,708 feet
T **OT**   *Regional map p. 30 (G, 17); hike map p. 96*
Sprague Pass lies at the head of Spruce Canyon, 1 mile southeast of Sprague Mountain at the northwest edge of Bighorn Flats. It can be approached from the Tonahutu Creek Trail or Spruce Canyon.

Tonahutu Creek Trail Access   From Ptarmigan Pass (follow route description, p. 83), descend along the Tonahutu Creek Trail for 1.2 miles to 11,920 feet on Bighorn Flats. Leave the trail here and hike northwest over intermittent grass and boulder fields, skirting patches of dense krummholz for 1 mile to Sprague Pass.

Spruce Canyon Access   From the northeast end of Spruce Lake (follow route description, p. 89), leave the trail and bushwhack northwest to 9,800 feet. Then contour northwest to the north side of Castle Rock. Descend into Spruce Canyon, negotiating rock slabs and thick forest to Spruce Creek. Turn southwest and bushwhack 1.8 miles to the base of Sprague Pass. Spruce Canyon presents very difficult bushwhacking along Spruce Creek. Thick forest, downed trees, rugged boulder fields, wet bogs, and dense vegetation combine to make this an arduous journey. A narrow section of the canyon forces the hiker to negotiate some tricky terrain close to the creek. Break out of treeline and scramble up rocky topography to the base of the pass. A steep snowfield persists below the pass in early summer. Skirt the snow and hike up the loose, dirty, rocky headwall to top out on the tundra.

Sprague Mountain   12,713 feet
T **OT**   *Regional map p. 30 (F, 18); hike map p. 96*
This beautiful mountain is 1 mile northwest of Sprague Pass, and from most vantages is dwarfed by its higher, larger neighbor, Stones Peak. The summit overlooks the lovely lake basin below Sprague Glacier. It can be accessed from the Green Mountain Trailhead on the west side of the Continental Divide, or the Bear Lake Trailhead on the east side of the divide.

Southeast Ridge GRADE II CLASS 2   From Sprague Pass (follow route description above), climb northwest up the sustained tundra-and-talus slope for 0.5 mile to Point 12,348', which provides amazing views of Spruce Canyon, 'Sprague Tarn,' and Rainbow, Irene, and Hourglass Lakes. Continue northwest for 0.5 mile to the summit of Sprague Mountain.

South Slope GRADE II CLASS 2   From the Green Mountain Trailhead (see Region 6, p. 303), follow the Green Mountain Trail (see Region 6, p. 304) 1.8 miles to the Tonahutu Creek Trail. Follow the Tonahutu Creek Trail for 5.3 miles to treeline. Leave the trail and scramble north up a steep slope to gain the rounded boulder field that leads 1 mile to the summit of Sprague Mountain.

Stones Peak 12,922 feet
T **OT** *Regional map p. 31 (H, 20); hike map p. 96*

This huge mountain towers over Hayden Gorge, Forest Canyon, and Spruce Canyon. It has massive west, northeast, and south slopes, and its eastern aspect is cut by the deep cleft of the Hidden River drainage. The broad summit area has two separate highpoints and a lower, distinct tip at the end of its eastern arm unofficially called 'Stony Point' (12,298 feet). Because the valleys that surround it don't have trails, the easiest route to Stones Peak is via Sprague Mountain, but that route is very long.

Southwest Ridge GRADE II CLASS 2   From Sprague Mountain (follow route description, p. 93), traverse and descend east 0.2 mile to Point 12,680'. Turn northeast and descend 0.4 mile to a saddle southwest of Point 12,358', a rocky mound that can either be climbed or skirted to reach the southwest ridge of Stones Peak. Climb the steep, rounded southwest ridge for 0.6 mile to the summit of Stones Peak.

Spruce Canyon Access GRADE II CLASS 2   From the northeast end of Spruce Lake (follow route description, p. 89), leave the trail and bushwhack northwest to 9,800 feet. Contour northwest to the north side of Castle Rock. Descend into Spruce Canyon, negotiating rock slabs and thick forest to Spruce Creek. Cross the creek and bushwhack northwest up the densely forested slope to the southeast ridge of 'Stony Point,' located on the north side of the steep Hidden River drainage. Hidden River originates high on the slopes of Stones Peak and flows southeast through a steep-walled gorge, then tumbles abruptly through the forest of Spruce Canyon to join Spruce Creek on the valley floor. Climb above treeline and hike northwest along the ridge for 1.2 miles to Point 12,736'. Turn southwest and hike 0.7 mile to the summit of Stones Peak, skirting the headwall of the Hidden River basin.

Hourglass Lake Access (South Slope) GRADE II CLASS 2   From the west end of Hourglass Lake (follow route description, p. 91), climb northwest up steep talus for 0.4 mile to the saddle between Point 12,358' and the southwest ridge of Stones Peak. Climb the steep, rounded southwest ridge for 0.4 mile to the summit of Stones Peak.

Eureka Ditch 11,870 feet
T **OT** *Regional map p. 30 (F, 16)*

This 0.75-mile-long canal across Bighorn Flats, the large summit upland that stretches from Sprague Pass to Ptarmigan Point, was dug in 1902 to collect water and redirect it into Spruce Canyon. In 1996, a creative agreement regained the water rights for RMNP, and an effort was made to fill in the ditch. This task was difficult to achieve because of the rocky nature of the plateau, and the scar still remains, filled with boulders in an attempt to stop the flow of water. From Ptarmigan Pass (follow route description, p. 83), follow the Tonahutu Creek Trail (see Region 6, p. 307) 1.5 miles across Bighorn Flats, then leave the trail and hike north 0.1 mile to locate the start of Eureka Ditch.

FOREST CANYON *Regional map p. 31 (H, 26)*

Forest Canyon is a deep valley carved by the Big Thompson River, which originates at Forest Canyon Pass. It is undoubtedly one of the most pristine drainages in all of Colorado. The canyon stretches southeast from the pass for 9.3 miles to The Pool, west of Moraine Park. Visitors traveling along Trail Ridge Road can gaze across the 1.7-mile-wide gulf of forest at the high peaks along and near the Continental Divide. There are no trails into Forest Canyon; it represents the most rugged terrain in RMNP. Destinations within Forest Canyon are hard to reach. Descending to the river from Trail Ridge Road involves 2,100 vertical feet of descent through heavily forested terrain. At the southeast end of the canyon, 150-foot cliffs guard the entrance. At the northwest end, marshy, boggy terrain makes access difficult. Once you are in the canyon, the true nature of this unspoiled forest wilderness reveals itself. It requires bush-whacking through dense under-brush, scrambling over downed timber, and negotiating a route through thick, unrelenting forest.

Carolyn and Lionel Olson in Forest Canyon

LAKES

Black Pool 9,060 feet
T **OT** *Regional map p. 31 (M, 20)*

Black Pool, a tiny dark pond hidden on an elevated bench, is tucked into the narrow end of the "V" created by the confluence of the Big Thompson River and Spruce Creek. Precipitous cliffs guard access to this pretty pond from The Pool, a famous land-mark along the Fern Lake Trail. Located less than 0.5 mile from one of the most popular trails in RMNP, this gorgeous watery gem is probably visited by only one or two people each year. Though short, the steep, off-trail descent down into Spruce Canyon combines with a bridgeless crossing of swift Spruce Creek and a difficult ascent to the forested bench for a challenging exercise in bushwhacking. Named for its dark complexion, Black Pool is surrounded by lush green grasses and is ornamented with yellow pond lilies.

From the Fern Lake Trail-head (p. 108), take the Fern Lake Trail (see Fern-Odessa Trail, p. 111) 1.75 miles to The Pool. This frothy body of churning water lies just downstream of where Spruce and Fern Creeks join the Big Thompson River. At the trail junction west of The Pool, take the right-hand fork and continue hiking west along the Fern Lake Trail to the first switchback. Leave the trail and bushwhack through a thick forest that is choked with fallen trees as well as deep underbrush.

Alex Kostadinov views Forest Canyon from rocks by Black Pool

Head north and downhill toward Spruce Creek. Cross the creek on a convenient fallen log (this is a dangerous practice so take extreme care) and negotiate a route north up the steep hillside. Look south for an unusual view of Fern Falls cascading through the densely forested hillside. Climb toward some rock outcrops, staying to the east of Point 9,249'. Gain the obvious bench to the west of a grouping of beautiful rock mounds that provides a good overlook of the forest. Hike northwest along the bench to Black Pool and enjoy the serenity of a spot that is seldom visited. The extremely rugged and remote Forest Canyon unfolds to the northwest.

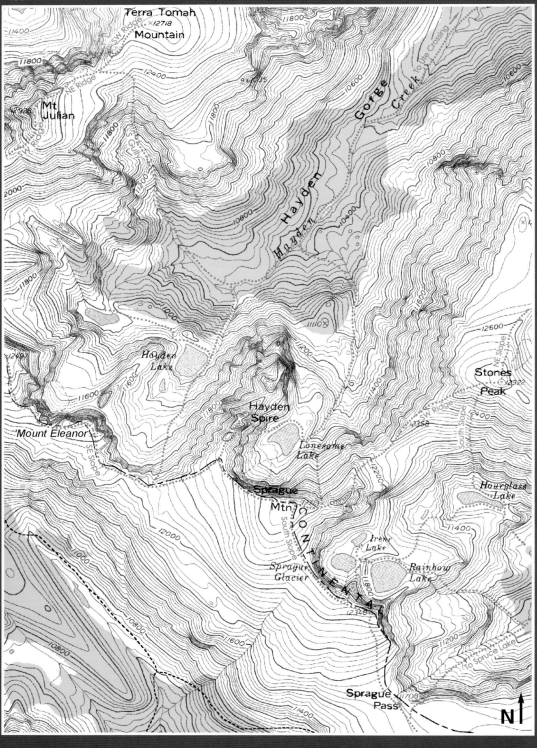

Terra Tomah
Mountain
×12718

Mt
Julian
12928

Hayden
Gorge
Creek

To Ute Crossing

SW Ridge

NE Ridge

SW Ridge

11400

11800

12000

11800

11800

12400

10600

10800

10600

11800

10800

10800

10400

10400

11200

Hayden
Lake

Hayden
Spire

Stones
Peak
12922

12600

NE Slope

SW Ridge

12358

12400

South Slope

'Mount Eleanor'

12493

11600

11800

11803

11200

11400

Lonesome
Lake

Hourglass
Lake

Sprague
Mtn

CONTINENTAL

South Slope

Sprague
Glacier

Irene
Lake

Rainbow
Lake

11800

11400

11200

To Spruce Lake

12000

11600

11000

10800

10800

11600

11400

12348

Sprague
Pass
11708

N

Magnetic North
11.5 degrees

N

0   0.5   1

Distance in miles

Forest Lake   10,298 feet
OT *Regional map p. 31 (F, 26)*

This awesome, forested lake lies in the middle of rugged Forest Canyon, on the southwest side of the Big Thompson River near the northeastern flank of mighty Terra Tomah Mountain. Far from any trail, it is difficult to reach.

From the Forest Canyon Overlook parking pullout (p. 116), located 2.9 miles west of Rainbow Curve on Trail Ridge Road, hike west across the tundra and descend into the sparse tree stands of the upper canyon. Locate a thickly forested creek drainage and skirt the rim of the ravine to prevent getting sucked into the tree-choked gully. Bushwhack southwest for 1,950 vertical feet to the Big Thompson River. Scout the riverbank for a good crossing, possibly on a fallen log. This is a dangerous practice so take care. Across the river, climb steeply southwest through the much thicker forest to a bench that holds Forest Lake. Contour southwest to the marshy shoreline of the lake.

OTHER DESTINATIONS

Raspberry Park   9,000 feet
T **OT** *Regional map p. 31 (K, 22)*

Thriving with wild raspberry shrubs, this densely forested region is located in Forest Canyon at the confluence of Lost Brook and the Big Thompson River. Lost Brook originates high on the slopes of Stones Peak and flows northeast over very steep terrain to Raspberry Park. From Black Pool (follow route description, p. 95), hike northwest along a forested bench, descending gradually into Forest Canyon. The initial section of the forest is pleasantly sparse and is easy to negotiate. Closer to the river, however, the true nature of Forest Canyon is revealed. Fight through thick underbrush, over downed timber, and through unyielding forest. Continue upriver to Raspberry Park, 1.5 miles from Black Pool.

HAYDEN GORGE
Regional map p. 31 (F, 22)

Hayden Gorge is a special place. It is a remote, pristine, forested valley formed on the southeast by the steep northwest slopes of Stones Peak, and on the northwest by the ridge that connects Cracktop, Mount Julian, and Terra Tomah Mountain. Hayden Creek flows from lakes at the southwestern headwall of the gorge for 2.9 glorious miles to join the Big Thompson River in rugged Forest Canyon. Though easily seen across the abyss of Forest Canyon from Trail Ridge Road, this unspoiled and trailless wilderness is preserved through difficulty of access and is reserved for only the most hearty nature lovers.

Hayden Gorge

Trail Ridge Road Access From the Ute Crossing parking pullout (p. 110), located 2 miles west of Rainbow Curve on Trail Ridge Road, leave the road and bushwhack southwest, descending over open tundra to enter the stunted trees below the road. Continue to descend over steep terrain on the west side of an unnamed creek drainage. Negotiate steep, difficult, densely forested terrain for 1.25 miles to Big Thompson River. Look for the safest crossing of the river, either by wading (the river is deep and swift in early summer) or on a fallen log that acts as a natural bridge. Both of these practices are dangerous, so take care. Cross the river and hike northwest to Hayden Creek. Follow Hayden Creek southwest into Hayden Gorge.

Continental Divide Access Access to Hayden Gorge is from either the west side of the Continental Divide via the Green Mountain Trailhead, or the east side of the divide via Sprague Pass. From the Green Mountain Trailhead (see Region 6, p. 303), follow the Green Mountain Trail (see Region 6, p. 304) 1.8 miles to the Tonahutu Creek Trail. Follow the Tonahutu Creek Trail northeast for 5.3 miles to treeline. Leave the trail and scramble north up a steep slope to gain the rounded boulder field that leads 1.2 miles to the Continental Divide at 12,360 feet. For the East Side Access from Sprague Pass (follow route description, p. 93), climb northwest up the sustained tundra-and-talus slope for 1.2 miles, skirting Sprague Mountain on the southwest. From the Continental Divide at 12,360 feet, locate a loose, dirty scree gully that descends very steeply to the north. Slide down this gully on loose rubble to a huge field of large boulders southwest of Hayden Lake.

LAKES

Hayden Lake   11,140 feet
T OT   Regional map p. 31 (E, 20); hike maps pp. 96, 101
Hayden Lake is a large tarn on a glacial bench northwest of Hayden Spire.

Continental Divide Access This route can be accessed from the east (see Bear Lake Trailhead to Flattop Mountain, p. 75) or the west (Poudre Lake Trailhead at Milner Pass to Mount Ida, p. 106). Take either route and traverse along the Continental Divide to 12,360 feet, located 1.2 miles northwest of Sprague Pass. Locate a loose, dirty scree gully that descends very steeply to the north. Slide down this gully on loose rubble to a huge field of large boulders southwest of Hayden Lake.

Weave through the maze of boulders and descend past an unnamed pond to the south shore of beautiful Hayden Lake. A lovely, oval-shaped, unnamed lake on the other side of a rock ridge northwest of Hayden Lake is well worth visiting. To reach it, circle around to the northwest side of Hayden Lake, then contour west along the northeast end of the ridge for 0.3 mile. Descend to the east shore of the unnamed lake. This shallow lake is stunning. A braided stream flows below the surface, creating aesthetic patterns in the sandy bottom. The broken face of 'Mount Eleanor' rises to the south.

Hayden Gorge Access Use the Trail Ridge Road Access for Hayden Gorge (follow route description above) to reach lower Hayden Gorge. From the confluence of Hayden Creek and the Big Thompson River, bushwhack southwest for 2.9 miles along the magnificent wonderland of Hayden Creek to Hayden Lake. The bushwhacking in this gorge is arduous and the climb to the lake travels through thick forest and up large boulder fields.

Lonesome Lake 11,700 feet
T **OT** *Regional map p. 30 (F, 19); hike map p. 96*

This high alpine tarn is cupped below precipitous walls and a permanent snowfield in a
rugged gorge east of Hayden Spire and north
of Sprague Mountain.

Lower Hayden Gorge Access Use the Trail
Ridge Road Access for Hayden Gorge (follow
route description, opposite) to access lower
Hayden Gorge. From the confluence of
Hayden Creek and the Big Thompson River,
bushwhack southwest for 2.6 miles along the
magnificent wonderland of Hayden Creek to
the point where the stream from Lonesome

Lonesome Lake

Lake joins Hayden Creek. Bushwhack south up the stream for 1.2 miles to Lonesome
Lake, climbing up steep boulder fields and through rugged terrain to the stark rock
bowl that holds the lake.

Sprague Mountain Access From Sprague Mountain (follow the route description on
p. 93), traverse and descend east for 0.1 mile to a small lowpoint on the ridge that
is immediately southwest of Point 12,680'. Turn north and then scramble down a steep
boulder slope for 0.5 mile to Lonesome Lake.

PEAKS

Hayden Spire 12,480+ feet
T **OT** **△** *Regional map p. 30 (E, 19); hike map p. 96*

This elegant summit is the high pinnacle on a ridge that extends northeast from the
Continental Divide and juts out into Hayden Gorge. It is the highest tower amid a
group of spires along the jagged, serrated ridge. Hayden Spire is flanked on the northwest by Hayden Lake drainage and on the southeast by Lonesome Lake drainage. The
summit spire is not easy to reach. The steep southwest face of the summit block thwarts
easy passage along a Class 3 ridge that leads northeast from the divide. Reaching the
summit involves technical, Class 5 climbing, and a rope and helmet are recommended.

△ Continental Divide Access (Technical) GRADE II CLASS 5.6   Access to Hayden Spire is
possible from either the west side of the Continental Divide from the Green Mountain
Trailhead, or the east side of the divide via Sprague Pass. From the Green Mountain
Trailhead (see Region 6, p. 303), follow the Green Mountain Trail (see Region 6,
p. 304) 1.8 miles to the Tonahutu Creek Trail. Follow the Tonahutu Creek Trail
northeast for 5.3 miles to treeline. Leave the trail and scramble north up a steep slope
to gain the rounded boulder field that leads 1.2 miles to the Continental Divide at
12,360 feet. For the eastern access from Sprague Pass (follow route description, p. 93),
climb northwest up the sustained tundra-and-talus slope for 1.2 miles, skirting Sprague
Mountain on the southwest.

From the Continental Divide at 12,360 feet, descend slightly and then traverse
northeast on exposed ledges along the southeast face of Hayden Spire. Serious exposure
above Lonesome Lake makes this traverse exciting. Follow the path of least resistance
to a gully that leads up to the northeast ridge of Hayden Spire. The gully offers easy
climbing until it reaches a chockstone that must be bypassed. Climb past the chockstone (5.6) and continue upward to gain the northeast ridge. Climb southwest up
broken terrain (5.4) to the beautiful summit block of Hayden Spire.

◩ **Hayden Gorge Access (Technical)** GRADE II CLASS 5.4   From Lonesome Lake (follow the route description, p. 99), scramble northwest up an obvious, steep, scree-filled gully to a notch below and northeast of Hayden Spire. Turn southwest and climb up slabs and over broken terrain (5.4) to easier terrain north of the summit. Scramble up blocks to the top of Hayden Spire.

'Mount Eleanor' 12,360+ feet
T **OT** *Regional map p. 31 (C, 21); hike maps pp. 96, 101*
This unofficially named summit lies on the Continental Divide, 1.7 miles southeast of Chief Cheley Peak and 1.3 miles northwest of Sprague Mountain. It overlooks Hayden Gorge and has a permanent snowfield on its steep northwest face. This is a fun peak to tag when following the Milner Pass to Bear Lake Traverse (p. 107).

Northwest Ridge GRADE II CLASS 2   From Chief Cheley Peak (follow route description, p. 107), descend southeast over talus and tundra for 1.7 miles to the summit of 'Mount Eleanor.'

Southeast Ridge GRADE II CLASS 2   From Sprague Pass (follow the route description on p. 93), hike northwest up the tundra and talus slope, skirting Sprague Mountain on the southwest. Continue over gentle terrain to the summit of 'Mount Eleanor.'

Cracktop 12,766 feet
T **OT** ◩ *Regional map p. 31 (C, 22); hike map p. 101*
This beautiful peak lies just east of the Continental Divide, 0.6 mile east of Chief Cheley Peak. It has a cracked top, split by the impressive, 900-vertical-foot couloir that makes a curving gash down the northeast face of the peak. The couloir is highly visible from Trail Ridge Road.

Southwest Ridge GRADE II CLASS 2+   From Chief Cheley Peak (follow route description, p. 107), scramble southeast across the summit ridge and then descend and skirt the headwall above Highest Lake. Hike east to a small saddle northeast of the Continental Divide. Climb northeast up blocky talus with some exposure (Class 2+) to the summit of Cracktop.

◩ **Cracktop Couloir (Technical)** GRADE III CLASS 5.0–5.6 STEEP SNOW   This is an amazing snow climb up the gully that splits the summit of Cracktop. It is in best condition in early summer when snow fills the couloir in its entirety. In mid- to late summer, the upper section of the couloir melts out, exposing a short but steep section of broken rock that is wet with running water and requires technical rock climbing skills to ascend. Depending on how much rock is exposed, the climbing ranges from 5.0 to 5.6 and is easier when dry (rare) and sporting when drenched. When completely snow-filled, the couloir begins with moderate snow climbing to the sharp turn in the gully at 12,000 feet. The route gets dramatically steeper (50–60 degrees) and climbs 700 additional vertical feet to the saddle below the summit. Crampons, an ice axe, a helmet, and rope are recommended for this climb.

There are two approaches to the base of the couloir. Follow either Forest Canyon Pass Access (p. 104) or Mount Ida Access (p. 103) to the Gorge Lakes. From Azure Lake, contour southeast for 0.5 mile to the base of the couloir at 11,800 feet. Climb southwest up the couloir for 0.2 mile and 200 vertical feet to the sharp curve at 12,000 feet. Continue upward, negotiating rock and snow as the conditions dictate. The final push at the top becomes quite steep to the notch below the summit.

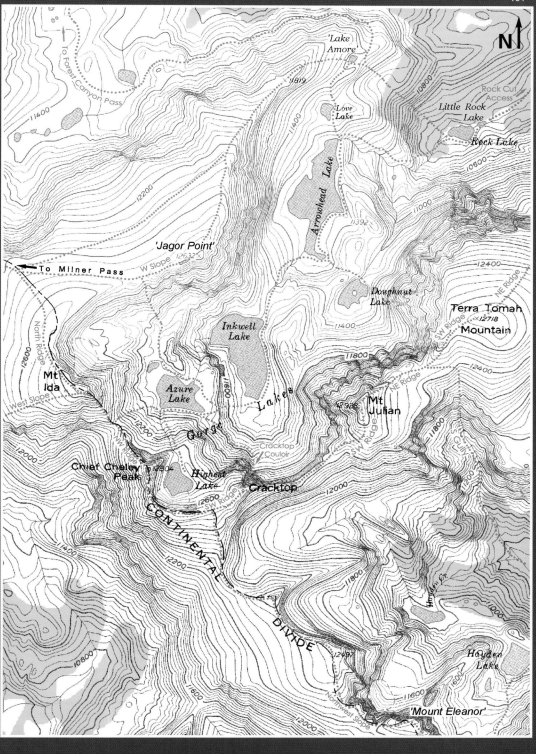

N

'Lake Amore'

Rock Cut Access

Little Rock Lake

Rock Lake

11819

Love Lake

To Forest Canyon Pass

11400

10800

10600

Arrowhead Lake

12200

11400

11392

11000

'Jagor Point'

W Slope 12632

To Milner Pass

Doughnut Lake

12400

NE Ridge

Terra Tomah Mountain 12718

North Ridge

12600

Inkwell Lake

11400

11800

SW Ridge

Mt Ida

Azure Lake

11600

Lakes

Gorge

13088

Mt Julian

NE Ridge

SW Ridge

West Slope

12200

12400

12000

Cracktop Couloir

11800

Couloir

Chief Cheley Peak 12804

Highest Lake

Cracktop

12000

12000

12000

CONTINENTAL

SW Ridge

12600

12200

11800

11400

Hayden Cr.

11000

10800

DIVIDE

11600

11600

12400

Northwest Slope

12493

Hayden Lake

'Mount Eleanor'

12000

Magnetic North 11.5 degrees

N

0   0.5   1

Distance in miles

Mount Julian 12,928 feet

T **OT** *Regional map p. 31 (D, 23); hike maps pp. 96, 101*

This majestic mountain lies along the beautiful, broken ridge that runs perpendicularly to the Continental Divide and connects Cracktop, Mount Julian, and Terra Tomah Mountain, forming the southeastern wall of the Gorge Lakes valley and the northwestern wall of Hayden Gorge. Mount Julian has a steep, broken northwest face that rises impressively above Inkwell Lake and jagged southwest (Class 3) and northeast (Class 2) ridges that connect it to its neighboring peaks.

Southwest Ridge GRADE II CLASS 3 This is the ridge connecting Mount Julian and Cracktop, which runs northeast from the Continental Divide. From the summit of Cracktop (follow route description, p. 100), descend northeast over blocky, broken terrain with huge exposure and sharp drops on either side. Choose the path of least resistance on either side of the ridge (Class 3) and descend to the saddle southwest of Mount Julian. Climb northeast up talus to the summit of Mount Julian (Class 2).

Northeast Ridge GRADE II CLASS 3 This is the 0.7-mile-long Class 2 ridge between Mount Julian and Terra Tomah Mountain. From Terra Tomah Mountain (follow route description below), descend along the wide tundra ridge to the saddle southwest of Terra Tomah, then climb southwest to the summit of Mount Julian.

South Gully to Northeast Ridge GRADE II CLASS 3 This route ascends Mount Julian or Terra Tomah Mountain from Hayden Gorge. A tributary to Hayden Creek originates on the southeast slopes of Mount Julian. From the junction of Hayden Creek and the Mount Julian tributary in the southwestern end of Hayden Gorge (see p. 98 for Trail Ridge Road Access), follow the tributary north through thick forest to 11,000 feet. Climb north up the steep, loose talus gully for 1,000 vertical feet to the talus slope southeast of the Julian–Terra Tomah saddle. The rock in this gully is extremely loose, making it hazardous for a large party because of the high potential of rockfall. Several short rock steps require Class 3 scrambling. Exit the gully and hike northwest to the Julian–Terra Tomah saddle. From here, either summit is a short jaunt up Class 2 tundra and talus.

Terra Tomah Mountain 12,718 feet

T **OT** *Regional map p. 31 (E, 24); hike maps pp. 96, 101*

This massive mountain is at the northeast end of a long spur that juts out 1.6 miles from the Continental Divide, also encompassing Cracktop and Mount Julian. Terra Tomah has vast, steep slopes but a broad, gentle summit plateau adorned with tundra that varies in color with the changing seasons. It is highly visible from Trail Ridge Road, but it is difficult to reach because no trails come close to this mighty peak. A unique glacial cirque deeply inset on its northeast side is very scenic.

Southwest Ridge GRADE II CLASS 3 This route is Class 3 only because the easiest accesses to it are Class 3. The ridge itself is Class 2. Follow a route to Mount Julian (above). From Mount Julian, descend over talus to the saddle between Julian and Terra Tomah. Then continue northeast up the gentle ridge to the summit.

Rock outcropping on Terra Tomah Mountain

Northeast Ridge GRADE II CLASS 3   This route approaches the peak from Forest Canyon. From Forest Lake (follow route description, p. 97), bushwhack southwest up the very steep grade of dirt, grass, and rocks to a series of boulder fields that makes up the north side of the mountain. Clamber up talus and boulders to gain the northeast ridge. Scramble west up to Point 11,643'. Above, the northeast ridge gets steep and is riddled with blocky humps of granite. Climb southwest through this section (Class 3), avoiding and skirting any serious technical difficulties. The ridge gives way to a moderate tundra slope that leads 0.5 mile southwest to the summit.

GORGE LAKES   *Regional map p. 31 (C, 24)*

Eight magnificent lakes and three unnamed tarns lie in a splendid alpine valley formed by the Cracktop–Mount Julian–Terra Tomah Mountain ridgeline and a rolling tundra ridge that extends northeast from Mount Ida. Highly visible from Trail Ridge Road, the lakes sit on irregular rock shelves. All of them are above treeline except Rock and Little Rock Lakes. Forest Lake is not part of the Gorge Lakes, but it lies within Forest Canyon northeast of the Gorge Lakes valley. No established trails lead into the gorge. The rugged and challenging access to the lakes starts from Mount Ida, Forest Canyon Pass, or from Trail Ridge Road at Rock Cut.

Mount Ida Access (from Saddle Southwest of 'Jagor Point')   From Milner Pass, follow the Mount Ida Trail (pp. 106, 113) for 4.2 miles to 12,400 feet, 0.7 mile northwest of Mount Ida's summit. From here, contour east along the gentle tundra ridge of 'Jagor Point' (p. 106) for 0.6 mile to a broad saddle between 'Jagor Point' and the Continental Divide. This saddle is above Inkwell Lake. Descend southeast over very steep, loose talus and boulders to a large bench between Azure and Inkwell Lakes. From here, climb south over boulder-strewn terrain to Azure and Highest Lakes. Extremely green in color, Highest Lake has a permanent snowfield rising above its southern shore. Descend north over rock steps to Inkwell Lake, then northeast to intriguing Doughnut Lake, named for its shape—the rock island in the middle representing the doughnut hole.

Descend steep, broken rock walls with scenic waterfalls cascading down them and through thick, stunted shrubs to Arrowhead Lake, encircled with dense krummholz. This is the largest of the Gorge Lakes and resembles the shape of an arrowhead. Its shimmering waters are the most obvious from Trail Ridge Road. This lake is long and has an irregular shoreline. It offers amazing views of Cracktop, Mount Julian, and Terra Tomah Mountain. Climb north to reach Love Lake or descend northeast into the forest to reach Rock and Little Rock Lakes. A campsite at Little Rock Lake is popular with anglers.

Mount Ida–Chief Cheley Peak Saddle Access   From the Mount Ida–Chief Cheley saddle at 12,350 feet (follow Northwest Ridge Route on Chief Cheley Peak, p. 107), descend northeast over steep talus or snow (which persists into July), for 0.3 mile and 450 vertical feet to the shore of Azure Lake. From Azure Lake, climb south up a rock bench to Highest Lake or descend north to the rest of the lakes.

Rock Cut Access   From the Rock Cut Parking Area (p. 109), descend abruptly into Forest Canyon over talus and tundra. This is a very steep route. Descend into thick forest and continue bushwhacking through rough terrain to the Big Thompson River. The challenge here is to find a way to cross the rushing creek. Fallen logs can act as natural bridges and are a good way to avoid getting wet, but crossing them can be a dangerous practice, so take care. The river is swift and the current is strong, so wading is also dangerous. Choose the option that best suits the abilities of your party.

Get to the south side of the river and hike southwest toward the obvious Gorge Lakes valley. The forest is thick and the ascent is laborious. A scenic meadow at the confluence of the stream from Forest Lake and the creek that flows from the Gorge Lakes is about the midway point. Continue southwest to Little Rock Lake. A fisherman's path leads to Rock Lake from here. Climb above treeline in the valley to reach Arrowhead Lake and continue to climb up rock benches to reach the other lakes.

Forest Canyon Pass Access   This route is less desirable than the Mount Ida Access because it crosses the marshy pond valley one drainage northwest of Gorge Lakes and can be extremely challenging, unless a drought dries the landscape. From Forest Canyon Pass (follow route description, p. 42), leave the trail and hike cross-country to the southeast. One option is to skirt Point 11,961' on the southwest and contour southeast above two drainages to reach the broad ridge northwest of Gorge Lakes. The other option is to skirt northeast of Point 11,961' and cross both drainages, fighting through wet marshland to the northeast end of the broad ridge, then skirting it to enter Gorge Lakes valley from the northeast. Either option involves careful route finding to follow the path of least resistance.

LAKES

Little Rock Lake   10,300 feet
OT *Regional map p. 31 (E, 26); hike map p. 101*

This tiny pond lies immediately east of Rock Lake in lower Gorge Lakes valley. From the Rock Cut Parking Area (p. 109), access Gorge Lakes through Forest Canyon, via the route description for Rock Cut Access (p. 103).

Rock Lake   10,300 feet
OT *Regional map p. 31 (D, 26); hike map p. 101*

This lake is popular with hardcore anglers who aren't afraid to bushwhack to enjoy a pristine, off-the-beaten-path fishing spot. It is located in the forest at the northeast end of the Gorge Lakes valley. A NPS backcountry campsite services this area. Follow one of the Gorge Lakes access routes on p. 103 to Arrowhead Lake. From here, descend east over challenging terrain for 0.6 mile to pretty Rock Lake. Or, from 'Lake Amore' (follow route description below), bushwhack southeast and descend 0.6 mile to

Rock Lake. Another alternative is to start at the Rock Cut Parking Area (p. 109) and hike to Gorge Lakes through Forest Canyon, following Rock Cut Access to Gorge Lakes (p. 103). From Little Rock Lake, follow the rough path for 0.1 mile southwest to Rock Lake.

'Lake Amore'   11,380 feet
OT *Regional map p. 31 (C, 26); hike map p. 101*

Surrounded by lush grass, this shallow, unnamed lake lies on a small bench 160 feet higher and north of Love Lake. From Point 11,819' along the north ridge of 'Jagor Point' (follow route description, p. 106), which forms the northwestern wall of the Gorge Lakes valley, descend 400 vertical feet northeast over tundra to the lake. From Love Lake (follow route description, opposite), climb 0.25 mile north up the gentle tundra bench to the little pond.

Steve Volker at 'Lake Amore'

Love Lake 11,260 feet
OT *Regional map p. 31 (C, 26); hike map p. 101*

This beautiful lake lies on a lush tundra bench 120 vertical feet north of Arrowhead Lake and provides wonderful views of the Gorge Lakes valley. It is located on the east side of the northeast ridge that runs perpendicularly to the Continental Divide and forms the northwest side of the Gorge Lakes valley. From Point 11,819' along the north ridge of 'Jagor Point' (follow route description, p. 106), hike 540 vertical feet down to the lake.

Mike Arneson and Pat Heier hiking near Love and Arrowhead Lakes

Arrowhead Lake 11,120 feet
OT *Regional map p. 31 (C, 25); hike map p. 101*

This is the largest of the Gorge Lakes and is the one most easily seen from Trail Ridge Road. Roughly shaped like an arrowhead, it's 0.6 mile long, 0.25 mile wide, and provides wonderful views of Mount Julian and Cracktop. From Rock Lake (follow Forest Canyon Pass or Rock Cut Access to the Gorge Lakes, pp. 103–104), scramble west up rocky terrain to the north shore of Arrowhead Lake, which is plagued by dense krummholz and shrubs. From Love Lake (follow route description above), descend south over grass and talus to the low-lying trees that surround Arrowhead Lake.

Doughnut Lake 11,260 feet
OT *Regional map p. 31 (D, 24); hike map p. 101*

This charming lake lies on a rock bench above the main gorge, nestled against the steep western flank of Terra Tomah Mountain. It has a rock island in the middle, serving as the "doughnut hole" of this round lake. Follow one of the Gorge Lakes access routes (p. 103) to Arrowhead Lake. From the south end of Arrowhead Lake, scramble southeast up steep rock for 0.1 mile and 240 vertical feet to Doughnut Lake.

Inkwell Lake 11,460 feet
OT *Regional map p. 31 (C, 23); hike map p. 101*

This is the second largest lake in the gorge. It lies on a large rock bench midway between Arrowhead Lake and Highest Lake. Follow Mount Ida Access (p. 103) to Gorge Lakes to reach Inkwell Lake. Hike southwest over a steep, broken rock shelf for 0.2 mile to Azure Lake, or descend northeast over a series of rock steps laced with waterfalls and greenery for 0.4 mile to Arrowhead Lake.

Azure Lake 11,900 feet
OT *Regional map p. 31 (B, 23); hike map p. 101*

This is the second highest lake in the gorge, and it lies directly below the steep east slopes of Mount Ida. From the small saddle (follow Northwest Ridge route on Chief Cheley Peak, p. 107) between Mount Ida and Chief Cheley Peak, scramble down talus and scree for 0.3 mile and 450 vertical feet to the lake. From here, it's possible to climb south 500 vertical feet to Highest Lake or descend northeast 450 vertical feet to Inkwell Lake.

Highest Lake 12,420 feet

OT *Regional map p. 31 (B, 22); hike map p. 101*

As its name implies, this lake is the highest in the gorge. It remains a deep jade color year-round. A permanent snowfield rises south of the lake, and snow and ice persist on the surface of the tarn for much of the summer. A fun Class 3 rock rib rises from the northwest shore and climbs southwest to the summit of Chief Cheley Peak. This is a good escape route from the gorge to the Continental Divide. From Azure Lake (follow one of the Gorge Lakes access routes, p. 103), climb south up a rock bench for 0.1 mile to Highest Lake.

PEAKS AND OTHERS DESTINATIONS

Mount Ida 12,880+ feet

T **OT** *Regional map p. 31 (A, 23); hike map p. 101*

This modest peak lies 4.9 miles from Milner Pass along the Continental Divide and overlooks the striking alpine basin of Gorge Lakes. Most of the hike to the summit is above treeline on stunning alpine tundra.

North Ridge GRADE I CLASS 2   From the Poudre Lake Trailhead at Milner Pass (p. 109), the trail leaves the southern end of Poudre Lake and ascends steeply up a hillside as it switchbacks through thick subalpine forest for 0.9 mile to a trail junction. Bear south (right) at the junction and follow the Mount Ida Trail to treeline. The trail then begins a long, gentle ascent on the southwest side of the ridge crest, traveling over expansive tundra slopes interspersed with rock outcroppings. The path becomes intermittent and somewhat difficult to follow, skirting highpoints on the Continental Divide. Continue climbing over rock and tundra to Mount Ida, which is strategically located to offer intimate views of Chief Cheley Peak, Cracktop, Mount Julian, and Terra Tomah Mountain. The panorama encompasses Lake Granby far to the southwest, and the peaks of the Mummy Range to the northeast. The Never Summer Mountains rise prominently to the west. The sharp, rocky precipices and shining bodies of water that form the Gorge Lakes drainage stand out directly below Mount Ida's rocky northwest side.

West Slope GRADE II CLASS 2   This route accesses Mount Ida from the Timber Lake drainage. Though longer and more strenuous, it has the advantage of offering a more secluded experience than the popular trail from Milner Pass. From the Timber Lake Trailhead (see Region 6, p. 304), located 6.6 miles west of Milner Pass on Trail Ridge Road, follow the Timber Lake Trail (see Region 6, p. 299) 5 miles to Timber Lake. Leave the trail and circle around to the south side of the lake. Climb southeast up the broad tundra slopes and gain a large saddle that separates the Julian Lake and Timber Lake valleys. The view of Julian Lake is magnificent, and Longs Peak stands out prominently to the southeast. From here, climb east up the gentle tundra slope for 0.75 mile to Mount Ida's summit.

'Jagor Point' 12,632 feet

T **OT** *Regional map p. 31 (B, 24); hike map p. 101*

This important, unofficially named summit lies northeast of Mount Ida and 0.9 mile east of the Continental Divide. The north ridge of 'Jagor Point' forms the northwestern wall of the Gorge Lakes valley.

West Slope GRADE I CLASS 2   From the Poudre Lake Trailhead at Milner Pass (p. 109), the trail leaves the southern end of Poudre Lake and ascends steeply up a hillside as it switchbacks through thick subalpine forest for 0.9 mile to a trail junction. Bear south (right) at the junction and follow Mount Ida Trail to treeline. The trail then begins a long, gentle ascent on the southwest side of the ridge crest, traveling over expansive tundra slopes interspersed with rock outcroppings. The path becomes intermittent and somewhat difficult to follow, skirting highpoints on the Continental Divide. At a point 4.2 miles from the trailhead and 0.7 mile northwest of Mount Ida, turn northeast and follow the west ridge of 'Jagor Point' for 0.9 mile to the summit.

Chief Cheley Peak   12,804 feet

T **OT** *Regional map p. 31 (A, 22); hike map p. 101*

This mountain is a rounded talus hump that soars above Highest and Julian Lakes. Located along the Continental Divide 0.5 mile southeast of Mount Ida, it provides an arresting overview of the Gorge Lakes.

Northwest Ridge GRADE II CLASS 2   From the summit of Mount Ida (follow route description, opposite), scramble southeast down a blocky ridge. This steep, broken slope made of large granite blocks requires a little route finding to locate the easiest descent. Continue 0.2 mile to the deep saddle between Mount Ida and Chief Cheley Peak. From here, climb 0.25 mile up the steep talus slope to the northwest ridge and follow it to the summit.

Continental Divide Traverse (Milner Pass to Bear Lake)

T **OT** *Regional map pp. 30–31 (A, 23 to P, 13)*

This fun, one-day traverse of the Continental Divide starts from Milner Pass and traverses 12.6 miles southeast to the summit of Flattop Mountain; it then finishes with a descent of the Flattop Mountain Trail for 4.4 miles to the Bear Lake Trailhead. The route can easily be reversed to go from Bear Lake to Milner Pass. Either choice requires a vehicle shuttle between Milner Pass and Bear Lake. The hike involves a lot of up and down, with 4,500 vertical feet of elevation gain and 5,800 vertical feet of elevation loss. Mount Ida, Chief Cheley Peak, and Flattop Mountain are mandatory summits, but the traverse can be modified to include up to 12 peaks (Cracktop, Mount Julian, Terra Tomah Mountain, 'Mount Eleanor,' Point 12,497', Hayden Spire, Sprague Mountain, Knobtop Mountain, and Ptarmigan Point), depending on the desires and fitness of the party.

Elk at rest on the Continental Divide

Continental Divide Traverse GRADE II CLASS 2 From the Poudre Lake Trailhead at Milner Pass (p. 109), follow the North Ridge Route to Mount Ida (opposite) and the Northwest Ridge Route up Chief Cheley Peak (above). Then descend southeast from Chief Cheley Peak and either turn northeast to take in the summits of Cracktop, Mount Julian, and Terra Tomah (follow the route descriptions on pages 100 and 102, and then backtrack to the Continental Divide), or contour southeast to Point 12,497' and 'Mount Eleanor.'

Continue over tundra and talus to the west slope of Sprague Mountain. Climb to the summit of Sprague, then descend 1.1 miles southeast to Sprague Pass. From here, either hike south to access the Tonahutu Creek Trail and follow it southeast as it climbs across Bighorn Flats to

Flattop Mountain, or hike cross-country and southeast up the gently sloping Bighorn Flats for 1.6 miles to Knobtop Mountain. From Knobtop Mountain, hike south for 0.8 mile and climb to the highest rock outcrop at Ptarmigan Point, then descend to the Tonahutu Creek Trail and climb east 0.7 mile to the summit of Flattop Mountain. Descend east on the the Flattop Mountain Trail for 4.4 miles to Bear Lake.

TRAILHEADS

Bear Lake Trailhead
This trailhead is at 9,450 feet and provides access to the Emerald Lake Trail (which includes Nymph and Dream Lakes), Lake Haiyaha Trail, Fern-Odessa Trail, Flattop Mountain Trail, and a trail to Bierstadt Lake. From the RMNP Beaver Meadows Visitor Center on US 36, drive west 1.1 miles to the Beaver Meadows Entrance Station. Pass the kiosk and continue 0.2 mile to Bear Lake Road. Turn south (left) and drive 9.2 miles to the huge Bear Lake parking lot. Bear Lake lies 100 yards west of the parking lot.

Beaver Wetlands Parking
This small parking pullout is on the north side of Trail Ridge Road, at 9,140 feet, and provides access to the Hidden Valley Beaver Wetlands boardwalk. From the RMNP Beaver Meadows Visitor Center on US 36, follow US 36 west 6.1 miles to Beaver Wetlands Parking.

Hidden Valley Beaver Wetlands boardwalk

Bierstadt Lake Trailhead
This trailhead lies at 8,860 feet and provides access to the Bierstadt Lake Trail. From the RMNP Beaver Meadows Visitor Center on US 36, follow US 36 west for 1.1 miles to the Beaver Meadows Entrance Station. Pass the kiosk and drive 0.2 mile to Bear Lake Road. Turn south (left) and drive 6.7 miles to the Bierstadt Lake Trailhead, located on the north side of the road.

Park and Ride Lot (Bierstadt Moraine Trailhead)
This large parking lot on Bear Lake Road lies at 8,820 feet and provides shuttle bus service to selected destinations within RMNP. The Bierstadt Moraine Trailhead lies at the west end of the lot. From the RMNP Beaver Meadows Visitor Center on US 36, follow US 36 west for 1.1 miles to the Beaver Meadows Entrance Station. Pass the kiosk and drive 0.2 mile to Bear Lake Road. Turn south (left) and drive 5 miles to the Park and Ride Lot, located on the west side of the road.

Cub Lake and Fern Lake Trailheads
These two trailheads are located in Moraine Park within 0.9 mile of each other. The Cub Lake Trailhead lies at 8,080 feet and provides access to the Cub Lake Trail. The Fern Lake Trailhead lies at 8,150 feet and provides access to Fern Lake Trail, which is called the Fern-Odessa Trail at its southern end. From the RMNP Beaver Meadows Visitor Center on US 36, drive west for 1.1 miles to the Beaver Meadows Entrance Station. Pass the kiosk and drive 0.2 mile to Bear Lake Road. Turn south (left) and drive 1.3 miles to

Moraine Park Road. Turn west (right) and drive 0.6 mile to the junction with Moraine Park Campground Road (straight ahead) and the road to Fern and Cub Lake Trailheads (on the left). Turn south (left) and drive 1.3 miles to the Cub Lake Trailhead. Continue west along the road for 0.9 mile to the Fern Lake Trailhead. During winter, the last stretch of the road to the Fern Lake Trailhead is closed and an alternate parking area is located 0.7 mile to the east. If the road is closed, park in the lot near the restrooms and hike west along the level road to the Fern Lake Trailhead.

Deer Mountain/Deer Ridge Trailhead
This trailhead lies at 8,920 feet and provides access to the Deer Ridge Trail system, which includes the North Deer Mountain Trail and the Deer Mountain Trail. From the RMNP Beaver Meadows Visitor Center on US 36, follow US 36 west for 4.2 miles to Deer Ridge Junction and the trailhead. From the Fall River Entrance Station on US 34, drive west, then south, on US 34 for 4 miles to Deer Ridge Junction and the trailhead.

Glacier Gorge Trailhead
This trailhead lies at 9,180 feet and provides access to the Loch Vale Trail, Glacier Gorge Trail, North Longs Peak Trail, and Glacier Creek Trail. From the RMNP Beaver Meadows Visitor Center on US 36, drive west 1.1 miles to the Beaver Meadows Entrance Station. Pass the kiosk and continue for 0.2 mile to Bear Lake Road. Turn south (left) and drive 8.3 miles to the Glacier Gorge Trailhead.

Hollowell Park Trailhead
This trailhead lies at 8,180 feet and provides access to the Mill Creek Basin Trail system and Steep Mountain. From the RMNP Beaver Meadows Visitor Center on US 36, follow US 36 west for 1.1 miles to the Beaver Meadows Entrance Station. Pass the kiosk and drive 0.2 mile to Bear Lake Road. Turn south (left) and drive 3.6 miles to the Hollowell Park turnoff. Turn west (right) and drive 0.2 mile to the parking turn-around at the trailhead.

Lava Cliffs Pullout on Trail Ridge Road
This parking pullout is located on the north side of Trail Ridge Road at 12,080 feet and provides access to Lava Cliffs and Iceberg Lake. From the RMNP Beaver Meadows Visitor Center near Estes Park, drive 4.2 miles west on US 36 until it turns into Trail Ridge Road (US 34) at Deer Ridge Junction. Continue west on Trail Ridge Road through the heart of RMNP for 15.3 miles to the Lava Cliffs Pullout.

Poudre Lake Trailhead at Milner Pass
This trailhead lies on the Continental Divide at 10,758 feet and provides access to the Ute Trail and the Mount Ida Trail. From the RMNP Beaver Meadows Visitor Center near Estes Park, drive 4.2 miles west on US 36 until it turns into Trail Ridge Road (US 34) at Deer Ridge Junction. Continue west on Trail Ridge Road through the heart of RMNP for 21.8 miles to the trailhead at Milner Pass. From Grand Lake, drive north on US 34 for 17.9 miles to the trailhead.

Rock Cut Parking Area
This parking area lies at 12,110 feet and provides access to the Tundra World Nature Trail to the Toll Memorial and Forest Canyon. From the RMNP Beaver Meadows Visitor Center near Estes Park, drive 4.2 miles west on US 36 until it turns into Trail Ridge Road (US 34) at Deer Ridge Junction. Continue west on Trail Ridge Road through the heart of RMNP for 13.2 miles to Rock Cut.

TRAILHEADS/TRAILS

Sprague Lake Trailhead
This trailhead lies at 8,700 feet and provides access to the Sprague Lake Nature Trail, Wind River Trail, Glacier Basin, Glacier Creek Trail, Boulder Brook Trail, and Storm Pass Trail. From the RMNP Beaver Meadows Visitor Center on US 36, follow US 36 west for 1.1 miles to the Beaver Meadows Entrance Station. Pass the kiosk and drive 0.2 mile to Bear Lake Road. Turn south (left) and drive 5.7 miles to the Sprague Lake turnoff. Turn south (left) and drive 0.3 mile to the large Sprague Lake parking lot.

Storm Pass Trail Parking
This parking pullout lies at 8,820 feet and provides access to the northern end of the Storm Pass Trail. From the RMNP Beaver Meadows Visitor Center on US 36, follow US 36 west for 1.1 miles to the Beaver Meadows Entrance Station. Pass the kiosk and drive 0.2 mile to Bear Lake Road. Turn south (left) and drive 6.5 miles to the parking pullout on the south side of the road.

Upper Beaver Meadows Trailhead
This trailhead lies at 8,440 feet and provides access to the Ute Trail, Windy Gulch, Beaver Mountain, Upper Beaver Meadows, Moraine Park, and Deer Ridge Trail system. From the RMNP Beaver Meadows Visitor Center on US 36 near Estes Park, drive west on US 36 for 1.8 miles to the Upper Beaver Meadows turnoff. Turn west (left) and then drive 1.5 miles to the Upper Beaver Meadows Trailhead. This 1.5-mile dirt road is open during the summer to public vehicle access, but is closed by a locked gate during the winter. When the road is closed, park at a small pullout on the east side of Trail Ridge Road and walk along the dirt road to the trailhead.

Ute Crossing
This trailhead is at 11,440 feet and provides access to both the Ute Trail and Sundance Mountain. From the RMNP Beaver Meadows Visitor Center near Estes Park, drive 4.2 miles west on US 36 until it turns into Trail Ridge Road (US 34) at Deer Ridge Junction. Continue west on Trail Ridge Road for 10.2 miles to Ute Crossing, located on the south side of the road, 2 miles west of Rainbow Curve.

TRAILS

Andrews Creek Trail
This trail splits off from the Loch Vale Trail in the heart of Loch Vale, 0.6 mile southwest of The Loch. It climbs steeply north up rock slabs and follows Andrews Creek, then swings west and climbs steep terrain for 1 mile to Andrews Tarn.

Bear Lake Nature Trail
See Bear Lake, p. 72.

Beaver Meadows Trail System
This confusing system of trails meanders in and around Beaver Meadows. From the Upper Beaver Meadows Trailhead, a series of short loop trails services the north end of Beaver Meadows. The Ute Trail leads southwest, then northwest, from the trailhead for 6.3 miles to Ute Crossing on Trail Ridge Road. Several trails along Upper Beaver Meadows road serve different destinations. At a point 0.75 mile west of US 36 along Upper Beaver Meadows road, a spur trail leads north for 1.1 miles to Deer Ridge Junction. At a point 1.4 miles west along this road, a trail leads north 1.3 miles to Deer Ridge Junction; another trail splits off from this trail and loops west, then south, to traverse the eastern

flank of Beaver Mountain, connecting with the Ute Trail in Windy Gulch. Yet another unmarked trail leaves the NPS Housing and Utility area near the Beaver Meadows Visitor Center and leads west to cross Bear Lake Road 0.3 mile south of US 36; it then continues west and splits off, with one track leading to Moraine Park and another that leads to the Upper Beaver Meadows Trailhead.

Bierstadt Lake Trail
This trail leaves the Bierstadt Lake Trailhead and climbs up the south side of Bierstadt Moraine for 1.3 miles to Bierstadt Lake.

Boulder Brook Trail
A spur trail leads southwest from Sprague Lake for 0.7 mile to reach the start of the Boulder Brook Trail. It can also be reached from the Storm Pass Trail Parking on Bear Lake Road. The Storm Pass Trail leads south for 0.4 mile to the Boulder Brook Trail, which continues south and parallels Boulder Brook, climbing 2.4 miles to the junction with the North Longs Peak Trail.

Ronny Campbell and Pat Lawhan explore rocks near the Boulder Brook Trail

Cub Lake Trail
The trail leaves Cub Lake Trailhead and travels south, then west, for 2.4 miles to Cub Lake.

Deer Ridge Trail System
Deer Mountain and Deer Ridge are both serviced by an extensive trail system. The North Deer Mountain Trail leaves Deer Ridge Junction and skirts along the north slope of Deer Mountain, looping back on itself along Deer Ridge, then climbing up the east side of the mountain to the trail junction with the Deer Mountain Trail and the summit spur trail. The Deer Mountain Trail leaves Deer Ridge Junction and climbs the west side of the mountain for 2.9 miles to arrive at the same trail junction. The summit spur trail climbs steeply southwest for 0.25 mile to the top. Another trail extension leads from the North Deer Mountain Trail on the south side of Deer Ridge for 1.8 miles to US 36, 0.8 mile west of the Beaver Meadows Entrance Station. Two other spur trails leave from a trail intersection that is 0.1 mile north of Deer Ridge Junction and lead to Little Horseshoe Park, Lawn Lake Trailhead, and Aspenglen Campground.

Emerald Lake Trail
This is perhaps the most popular trail in RMNP. The path leads from Bear Lake to three magnificent lakes, each of them pristine and picturesque. Nymph, Dream, and Emerald Lakes are the most visited backcountry pools in RMNP. From Bear Lake, the trail leads 0.6 mile to Nymph Lake, continues 0.5 mile to centrally located Dream Lake, then extends west 0.7 mile to Emerald Lake at the eastern end of Tyndall Gorge.

Fern-Odessa Trail
This trail makes an 8.4-mile semicircle from the Fern Lake Trailhead in the north to the Bear Lake Trailhead in the south. It is simply called the Fern Lake Trail on the northern end. The trails to Bierstadt Lake and Mill Creek Basin can be utilized to connect the Fern-Odessa Trail back to itself in a full circle.

TRAILS

'Fire Trail'

This unimproved 'Fire Trail' was developed for national park search-and-rescue and fire crews and serves as a shortcut to the Loch Vale and Glacier Gorge Trails, bypassing Alberta Falls. It follows a small tributary of Glacier Creek and shaves 0.6 mile one-way off the distance. It rejoins the Loch Vale Trail immediately east of the major trail junction with the Loch Vale, Glacier Gorge, and Lake Haiyaha Trails.

From the Glacier Gorge Trailhead, follow the trail as it climbs southwest 0.25 mile to Glacier Gorge Junction (p. 114). Turn south (left) and follow the Loch Vale Trail as it meanders through groves of pretty aspen trees and crosses two bridges. At the second bridge, leave the trail and turn southwest to locate the rocky path that leads upward through the forest. The 'Fire Trail' climbs steeply up the wide ravine between East Glacier Knob and West Glacier Knob for 1 mile. It hugs the flank of the eastern 'Knob' and rises rapidly through the forest. Follow this trail past a rock bench that offers a scenic overlook of the drainage below, and reenter the forest. Continue south to intersect the Loch Vale Trail.

Flattop Mountain Trail

This trail leaves Bear Lake and climbs west for 4.4 miles to the summit of Flattop Mountain on the Continental Divide. It is one of the most popular and highly used trails in RMNP, and is one of few that access a summit.

Glacier Creek Trail

This trail begins near Glacier Gorge Junction (0.25 mile southwest of the Glacier Gorge Trailhead) and descends northeast past some beautiful unnamed waterfalls into Prospect Canyon. It continues northeast to a junction with the Boulder Brook Trail (2.2 miles from Glacier Gorge Junction) and then skirts south of Sprague Lake and leads 0.25 mile to the Storm Pass Trail. It then travels northeast for 1.6 miles to Glacier Basin Campground.

Glacier Gorge Trail

This trail starts at the major junction of the Loch Vale and Glacier Gorge Trails, 2 miles from the Glacier Gorge Trailhead. It descends south to cross Icy Brook, then climbs south into Glacier Gorge for 0.7 mile to Mills Lake. From there the trail continues 2.2 miles south to Black Lake, where it ends.

Lake Haiyaha Trail

This trail leaves the Dream Lake Trail slightly east of Dream Lake and climbs south around the east ridge of Hallett Peak for 1 mile to access the 0.2-mile spur trail that leads northwest to Lake Haiyaha. The Lake Haiyaha Trail then continues southeast as an unimproved trail for 1.1 miles to join the Loch Vale Trail near the major junction of the Loch Vale and Glacier Gorge Trails.

Loch Vale Trail

From the Glacier Gorge Trailhead, this trail climbs southwest for 0.25 mile (NPS rounds this mileage up to 0.3 mile) to Glacier Gorge Junction, then turns south for 0.5 mile to Alberta Falls. It then skirts the Glacier Knobs and leads 1.2 miles to the major junction of the Loch Vale and Glacier Gorge Trails. From there it climbs southwest

Pat Lawhan overlooks Glacier Creek at the junction of the Loch Vale and North Longs Peak Trails

Cub Lake from the Mill Creek Basin Trail

into Loch Vale, passing The Loch after 0.9 mile and continuing another mile to the base of Timberline Falls. From here the trail becomes less distinct and much more difficult but continues past Glass Lake and ends at Sky Pond, 0.5 mile from Timberline Falls.

Mill Creek Basin Trail

From the Hollowell Park Trailhead, the Mill Creek Basin Trail travels west into Hollowell Park and skirts the east side of Steep Mountain. The trail then travels through the flat valley of Mill Creek and climbs up onto the north side of Bierstadt Moraine to a trail junction. From here, both trails lead west to Mill Creek Basin, 1.7 miles from the trailhead.

Mount Ida Trail

This trail climbs southeast from Milner Pass to the north ridge of Mount Ida. The trail deteriorates and becomes faint and somewhat difficult to follow on the high-altitude tundra slopes west of the Continental Divide, but provides access to the summit of beautiful Mount Ida, 4.9 miles from Milner Pass.

Sprague Lake Nature Trail

See Sprague Lake, p. 33.

Tundra World Nature Trail

See Toll Memorial, p. 43.

Ute Trail

See Ute Trail, p. 44.

'Winter Loch Vale Trail'

The Loch Vale Trail travels along the south side of Glacier Knobs to reach the major trail junction between the Loch Vale and Glacier Gorge Trails. In the winter, when freezing temperatures and deep snows fill in creek drainages, it is much easier to follow the 'Winter Loch Vale Trail,' which climbs southwest up a drainage between East and West Glacier Knobs, cutting 0.6 mile one-way from the distance. This alternate route is very popular in winter, and often a hard-packed snowshoe trail leads up the drainage.

TRAILS/OTHER POINTS OF INTEREST

This variation is slightly different from the 'Fire Trail,' which is a well-worn trail that begins in the same place but climbs up the hillside to the east. The 'Winter Loch Vale Trail' follows the drainage for most of the way to top out at the major junction between the Loch Vale and Glacier Gorge Trails.

From the Glacier Gorge Trailhead, follow the trail as it climbs southwest 0.25 mile to Glacier Gorge Junction (below). Turn south (left) and follow the Loch Vale Trail as it meanders through groves of pretty aspen trees and crosses two bridges. At the second bridge, turn southwest and follow the small tributary to Glacier Creek 1 mile up the drainage. The route reconnects with the Loch Vale Trail 50 feet east of the junction between the Loch Vale and Glacier Gorge Trails.

OTHER POINTS OF INTEREST

Glacier Basin

Home to the popular NPS Glacier Basin Campground, this wide open, glacially carved basin lies at 8,688 feet, 5 miles southwest along Bear Lake Road. Estes Park historian and lodge operator Abner Sprague originally called it "Bartholf Park" for his friend Frank Bartholf in 1877. The U.S. Board on Geographic Names changed it to "Glacier Basin" in 1961, but geologists still use the name Bartholf for the ancient glacier that is responsible for carving the deep valley of spectacular Glacier Gorge. The modern Andrews, Tyndall, and Taylor Glaciers sit high in cirques originally excavated by this ancient glacier. Trails from Glacier Basin lead to Moraine Park, Sprague Lake, East Portal, and Glacier Gorge Junction.

Glacier Gorge Junction

At 9,240 feet, this was the site of the former Glacier Gorge Trailhead until it was moved 0.25 mile (NPS rounds this up to 0.3 mile) northeast in 2004. It is now important because it is the site of a major trail junction. Here, a spur trail to Bear Lake leads north 0.5 mile, and the Loch Vale Trail (which in turn connects to the Glacier Gorge Trail) leads south. At a point 100 feet northeast of Glacier Gorge Junction is the intersection between the Glacier Creek Trail and the trail to the Glacier Gorge Trailhead.

Hondius Park

Named for early homesteader Pieter Hondius, this small meadow (8,300 feet) is located west of the RMNP Fall River Entrance Station, tucked into a U-shaped nook of land between the road to Aspenglen Campground and the sweeping curve in US 34.

Prospect Canyon

Glacier Creek carved this deep river canyon (9,015 feet), which is visible from a scenic overlook on Bear Lake Road. From the RMNP Beaver Meadows Visitor Center on US 36, drive west 1.1 miles to the Beaver Meadows Entrance Station. Pass the kiosk and continue 0.2 mile to Bear Lake Road. Turn south (left) and drive 7.7 miles to the parking pullout, located on the south side of the road. Prospect Canyon can also be accessed via the Glacier Creek Trail. From the Glacier Gorge Trailhead, follow the Glacier Creek Trail northeast for 1.9 miles to Prospect Canyon.

Tuxedo Park

This small valley (7,920 feet) is located off Bear Lake Road south of Moraine Park and north of the YMCA of the Rockies. It is the site of an RMNP residential housing area but also offers a small public picnic area near the road.

TRAIL RIDGE ROAD

Trail Ridge Road holds the distinction of being the highest continuous paved highway in the United States. It traverses RMNP for nearly 50 miles from east to west, crossing the Continental Divide at picturesque Milner Pass. It is above treeline for much of the way, and the highest point is a lofty 12,183 feet. Opened to vehicle travel in 1932, this marvel of early engineering provides access to countless hiking destinations. It is the premier summer driving route in RMNP. From about mid-October to Memorial Day weekend, it closes each year between Many Parks Curve on the east side of the Continental Divide and the Timber Lake Trailhead on the west. Numerous key overlooks and waypoints are of interest to RMNP visitors:

Deer Ridge Junction
At 8,940 feet, this is the eastern end of Trail Ridge Road, and is the junction of US 34 and US 36, 4.2 miles west of the RMNP Beaver Meadows Visitor Center.

Hidden Valley
At 9,240 feet, this is the site of a former lift-operated ski area. The location now provides hiking in summer and sledding, snowshoeing, and backcountry skiing in winter. The turnoff to Hidden Valley is 6.7 miles west of the RMNP Beaver Meadows Visitor Center.

Many Parks Curve
From the large parking pullout (9,620 feet) located 8.3 miles west of the RMNP Beaver Meadows Visitor Center, cross Trail Ridge Road at the marked crosswalk to access the paved, rock-walled path that provides an overview of several mountain parks, including Horseshoe Park, Beaver Meadows, and Moraine Park.

The Mummy Range from Hidden Valley

TRAIL RIDGE ROAD POINTS OF INTEREST

Rainbow Curve

This large parking pullout (10,829 feet) is located 12.4 miles west of the RMNP Beaver Meadows Visitor Center and provides restrooms and a grand overview of the high peaks of the majestic Mummy Range.

Forest Canyon Overlook

This parking lot (11,716 feet) is located 15.3 miles west of the RMNP Beaver Meadows Visitor Center on the south side of Trail Ridge Road. This area is one of four Tundra Protection Areas located along Trail Ridge Road. A short asphalt-paved path leads across the fragile tundra to an observation deck. Forest Canyon, Hayden Gorge, Gorge Lakes, and the high peaks along the Continental Divide are breathtaking from this vantage. For the protection of the alpine tundra in this area, and by order of the superintendent, visitors may not walk off trails or away from the parking lot for 100 yards in any direction. Hikers interested in bushwhacking into Forest Canyon in order to reach any number of backcountry destinations from the proximity of Forest Canyon Overlook must do so from a point outside the Tundra Protection Area perimeters.

Rock Cut

Rock Cut (12,110 feet) is the only location along Trail Ridge Road where much blasting was required to create a passageway. It is located 17.4 miles west of the RMNP Beaver Meadows Visitor Center, and is one of four Tundra Protection Areas located along Trail Ridge Road. It offers great views of the Never Summer Mountains and Forest Canyon. This is the trailhead for the Tundra World Nature Trail and the Toll Memorial.

Iceberg Pass to Tundra Curves

Trail Ridge Road climbs 300 feet through the beautiful, expansive, twisting Tundra Curves (11,830 feet), which provide sweeping, panoramic views of the surrounding valleys and peaks. Iceberg Pass (11,827 feet) has two small parking areas on either side of Trail Ridge Road.

Lava Cliffs Pullout

This wide parking pullout (12,080 feet) is located 19.5 miles west of the RMNP Beaver Meadows Visitor Center, and overlooks the rust-colored 300-foot cliffs that were carved out of the hillside by glacial action. Iceberg Lake and a smaller, unnamed tarn lie east below the cliffs.

Highest Point on Trail Ridge Road

At 12,183 feet in elevation, this spot is located 1.5 miles south of the Alpine Visitor Center. There is no parking or stopping in this location.

Gore Range Overlook

This overlook is on the south side of Trail Ridge Road, 1 mile west of Lava Cliffs. It provides a view of the majestic Gore Range, about 60 miles away to the southwest. It also overlooks Forest Canyon Pass and the Never Summer Mountains to the west. The Gore Range Overlook is one of four Tundra Protection Areas located along Trail Ridge Road. For the protection of the alpine tundra in this area, and by order of the superintendent, visitors may not walk off trails or away from the parking lot for 100 yards in any direction.

Fall River Pass/Alpine Visitor Center (AVC)

This site (11,796 feet) is located 21.6 miles west of the RMNP Beaver Meadows

The "Great Divide" separates drainage to the Atlantic from drainage to the Pacific. It traverses America from Alaska almost to Cape Horn

Milner Pass

Visitor Center, and is home to the AVC and Trail Ridge Store. Fall River Pass stands between the Fall River and Cache la Poudre River drainages. It is one of four Tundra Protection Areas located along Trail Ridge Road.

Medicine Bow Curve
This sharp curve (11,640 feet) is located on the descent of Trail Ridge Road into Kawuneeche Valley, 22.1 miles west of the RMNP Beaver Meadows Visitor Center. The overlook provides enticing views of Cache la Poudre River valley, the Never Summer Mountains, and the Medicine Bow Mountains to the northwest, which extend into Wyoming.

Milner Pass/Poudre Lake
Milner Pass (10,758 feet) is the point where Trail Ridge Road crosses the Continental Divide. It's 26 miles west of the RMNP Beaver Meadows Visitor Center and 17.9 miles north of Grand Lake. Poudre Lake lies along the road on the east side of the Continental Divide. The Poudre Lake Trailhead provides access to the Mount Ida and Ute Trails.

Farview Curve
This overlook (10,120 feet) is located 15.7 miles north of Grand Lake on US 34. The parking pullout provides wonderful views of Kawuneeche Valley, the Colorado River, and the Never Summer Mountains, including the Grand Ditch (see Region 8).

Holzwarth Historic Site/Never Summer Ranch
This site (8,884 feet) is located 9.4 miles north of Grand Lake on US 34, in the flat Kawuneeche Valley at the foot of the Never Summer Mountains. A scenic 0.5-mile walk from the trailhead to the Never Summer Ranch offers a history lesson about pioneers at the turn of the 20th century.

Mummy Range

Crystal Lake and
Fairchild Mountain

The Mummy Range dominates the northern section of RMNP and covers a huge area north of the Continental Divide. It is the largest geographical section of RMNP, ranging for 11 miles from Comanche Peak and Mirror Lake in the north to Sundance Mountain in the south, and 14 miles from Cache la Poudre River in the west to McGraw Ranch in the east. It has a large number of high summits, with seven named peaks rising to elevations greater than 13,000 feet.

The Mummy Range offers everything from low-lying foothills to pristine alpine tarns to lofty summits, including the highest point in Larimer County. From the northern end of Estes Park, the outline of the peaks resemble an Egyptian mummy lying on his back, nose tipped to the sky (formed by the summit of Mummy Mountain), with his chest extending northwest to Hagues Peak. This range offers something for everyone, from fun family destinations to some of the most remote backcountry destinations in RMNP. The peaks in this range have gentle, sloping west sides and precipitous eastern faces, illustrating the power of the ancient glaciers that formed the deep, lake-filled valleys.

Flower field in the
Mummy Range

SUBREGIONS with Highlighted Hiking Destinations

FALL RIVER PASS 123
  🚶 'Fall River Pass Mountain'........................ 123

OLD FALL RIVER ROAD 123
  🚶 Chasm Falls 124
    Chapin Pass 124
    Mount Chapin 124
    Mount Chiquita 125
    Ypsilon Mountain.............................. 125

HORSESHOE PARK 128
♿🚶 Alluvial Fan 129
  🚶 Fan Lake 129

ROARING RIVER 130
    Lawn Lake 131
    Crystal Lake.................................... 133
    Chipmunk Lake 133
    Ypsilon Lake 133
    Spectacle Lakes 134
    Bighorn Mountain 135
    Mount Tileston 135
    The Saddle 136
  ◺ Fairchild Mountain 136
    Hagues Peak.................................... 137
    Mummy Mountain 137

Mummy Pass Trail

CASTLE MOUNTAIN AREA 138

LUMPY RIDGE...................................... 139
  Gem Lake.. 140
  The Twin Owls 142
  'Balanced Rock'................................. 144

COW CREEK...................................... 145
  Bridal Veil Falls 145
  'Rabbit Ears'.................................... 147

NORTH BOUNDARY 147
  West Creek Falls 147

NORTH FORK OF THE BIG THOMPSON RIVER 149
  Lost Lake 150
  Deserted Village 152
  Mount Dickinson................................ 153
  Mount Dunraven 153
  Rowe Peak 155
  Stormy Peaks Pass............................... 156
  Stormy Peaks 156
  Sugarloaf Mountain 157
  Ramsey Peak 157

BULWARK RIDGE.................................. 159
  South Signal Mountain and Signal Mountain 159

COMANCHE PEAK AREA 159
  Cirque Lake and Emmaline Lake (CPWA)......... 159
  Mirror Lake 160
  Mummy Pass 161
  Fall Mountain 161
  Comanche Peak 162

DESOLATION PEAKS AREA 163
  Flatiron Mountain 165
  Desolation Peaks 165

TRAILHEADS 166

TRAILS 170

OTHER POINTS OF INTEREST 173

Spire on Mount Chapin

Lawn Lake

Upper Bridal Veil Falls

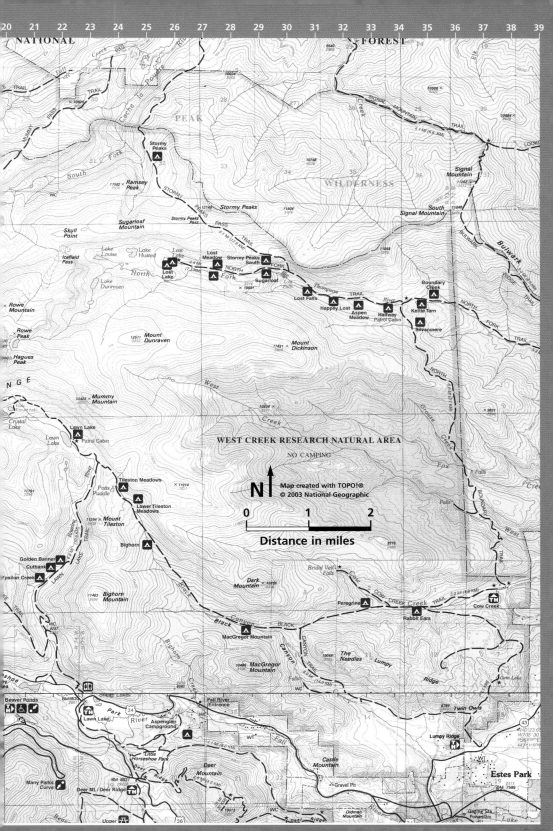

FALL RIVER PASS   *Regional map p. 120 (Q, 6)*

PEAKS AND OTHER DESTINATIONS

'Fall River Pass Mountain'   12,005 feet
T **🚶** *Regional map p. 120 (R, 7)*

From the Alpine Visitor Center (AVC, p. 166), a popular 0.3-mile path (the Alpine Ridge Trail) climbs steeply for 220 vertical feet to this unofficially named rocky outcrop that offers scenic views. Hundreds of people hike this trail on a summer day. The highpoint overlooks the Fall River to the south, the Mummy Range to the northeast, and the Medicine Bow Mountains to the north. AVC lies below at the pass.

The trail is extremely steep and starts at an altitude of 11,796 feet. Visitors coming from sea level and those with lung and heart conditions are not advised to attempt this short hike. The extreme altitude causes many people to experience health issues when trying to push themselves to climb this modest hill. Because of this phenomenon, locals have dubbed this point "Heart Attack Hill," though the NPS prefers the nickname "Huffer's Hill."

Marmot Point   11,909 feet
OT **🚶** *Regional map p. 120 (Q, 9)*

Marmot Point is a pretty, rounded tundra hump east of the Alpine Visitor Center (AVC) that provides good views of Chapin Creek and Fall River drainages. From the AVC (p. 166), hike east down Old Fall River Road for 0.7 mile to the first switchback from the top. From here, leave the dirt road and hike on tundra for 0.4 mile to the bald summit of Marmot Point, which provides great views of the Continental Divide. For those driving up Old Fall River Road, drive 8.3 miles from the Endovalley Picnic Area (p. 168) to a pullout on the northeast side of the road. Park and hike 0.4 mile to Marmot Point.

OLD FALL RIVER ROAD   *Regional map p. 120 (S, 13)*

This one-way 9-mile dirt road ascends from Endovalley to the Alpine Visitor Center and provides access to the Chapin Pass Trailhead. The road is closed seasonally from about mid-October to July 4th weekend.

FALLS

Thousand Falls   9,160 feet
OT *Regional map p. 120 (U, 18)*

Sundance Creek originates in Hanging Valley (formed by a small glacier that lacked the size and fortitude to gouge a larger valley, thus leaving the valley "hanging") on the northeast slopes of Sundance Mountain and flows 2.5 miles northeast to join Fall River near the Endovalley Picnic Area. Thousand Falls dances for 0.25 mile through the lower reaches of Sundance Creek, cascading 440 vertical feet over broken steps in 5- to 10-foot drop intervals. It is difficult to view the waterfall in its entirety because it is located amid an extremely thick forest.

From the Endovalley Picnic Area (p. 168), follow a fisherman's path west along the north side of Fall River to a bridge over Chiquita Creek. Pass a grassy pond and hike west on the fisherman's path, paralleling Fall River for 0.2 mile to a point where Sundance Creek joins Fall River on the south. Cross the river on fallen logs, and follow the remnants of an old trail that climbs along the east side of Sundance Creek for 0.1 mile to the lower section of the falls. Bushwhack southwest along the creek to take in the boisterous beauty of this long, forested cascade.

Opposite: Sunrise in the Roaring River Drainage

Chasm Falls 9,060 feet
T **[icon]** *Regional map p. 120 (U, 17)*

Chasm Falls is one of the prettiest waterfalls in RMNP. It is also the most highly visited, since it is easily accessed from Old Fall River Road and visitors can drive within a stone's throw of the site. The small cascade spills 25 feet through a narrow chute of multi-colored granite blocks before plunging spectacularly into a small pool.

From the Endovalley Picnic Area (p. 168), hike or drive west up Old Fall River Road for 1.4 miles to a large parking pullout above Chasm Falls. Here, a well-marked asphalt path leads downhill for 0.1 mile to the viewpoints that overlook the falls. The trail descends sharply, so use caution. Take care when attempting to hike down the polished rocks to the base of the falls. The falls rush through a narrow defile that was created when the stream eroded through granite potholes formed by grinding rocks swirling in the current after the Fall River Glacier retreated. From the falls, a trail follows Fall River downstream for 150 yards to the lower "trailhead" to Chasm Falls, located 0.9 mile west of the Endovalley Picnic Area on Old Fall River Road.

PEAKS AND OTHER DESTINATIONS

Willow Park 10,660 feet
R *Regional map p. 120 (S, 10)*

Willow Park is a pretty meadowland along Old Fall River Road, 6 miles west of the Endovalley Picnic Area. A gated side road leads west from the main road to the Willow Park Patrol Cabin. This historic structure was built in 1924 to accommodate work crews who shoveled out the road each spring. Teams of men would actually hand shovel a corridor through the 15- to 20-foot snow banks in order to accommodate vehicle traffic in June. The building is on the National Register of Historic Places and is utilized by NPS staff. Several social trails lead from the field near the cabin to explore Fall River, which flows through the meadow.

Chapin Pass 11,140 feet
T *Regional map p. 120 (R, 10)*

Chapin Pass is the forested lowpoint between Marmot Point and Point 11,407'. It is located north of Fall River at the headwaters of Chapin Creek, a tributary to the Cache la Poudre River. From the Chapin Pass Trailhead (p. 166), the Chapin Creek Trail (p. 171) climbs steeply for 0.2 mile to Chapin Pass. An obvious spur trail leaves Chapin Pass and travels east through the forest to top out above treeline and provide access to the high peaks of the Mummy Range. The Chapin Pass Trail descends north to Chapin Creek.

Mount Chapin 12,454 feet
T **OT** *Regional map p. 120 (R, 14); hike map p. 126*

This beautiful peak lies at the southern end of a long string of high peaks running southwest from Rowe Mountain. It is the lowest along this mountain chain and has gentle west and north slopes and a forested east ridge. Its craggy south side is riddled with rock fins and pinnacles that are easily seen from Fall River Road.

Rock spire on the south side of Mount Chapin

North Slope GRADE I CLASS 2 This is the easiest and shortest route up Mount Chapin. From the Chapin Pass Trailhead (p. 166), follow the Chapin Creek Trail (p. 171) as it climbs steeply for 0.2 mile to Chapin Pass. From here, do not drop downhill (north) into the Chapin Creek drainage. Instead, turn east (right) and follow a spur trail through dense forest for 0.75 mile to treeline. A faint trail continues east, contouring along the northwest side of Mount Chapin for 1.1 miles to the pass between Mounts Chapin and Chiquita. From this saddle, hike south for 0.3 mile over tundra and talus to the summit of Mount Chapin. Mount Chapin has a steep and impressive south side and the summit provides great views of Estes Park to the east.

East Ridge GRADE II CLASS 2 This is an interesting way to reach the summit of Mount Chapin, involving an arduous bushwhack to gain the mountain's forested east ridge, then a fun hike up the rock-strewn east face. It is considerably more difficult than the North Slope Route. From the Endovalley Picnic Area (p. 168), hike west on unpaved Old Fall River Road for 0.4 mile to a small bridge over Chiquita Creek. Leave the road and bushwhack northwest through difficult terrain to gain the forested east ridge of Mount Chapin. Several short cliff bands must be skirted on the east. Climb northwest along the rolling ridge, cresting Points 10,049' and 10,975' as the ridge broadens dramatically. Rise above treeline to climb the boulder-strewn east ridge that ascends steeply to the summit.

Mount Chiquita 13,069 feet

T OT *Regional map p. 120 (Q, 16); hike map p. 126*

Mount Chiquita is the lowest "thirteener" in RMNP and is considered the easiest one to climb in the Park. It soars above the Chiquita Creek drainage, and like its neighboring peaks, Mount Chiquita has a precipitous east face and a gentle, sloping west side.

Southwest Slope GRADE I CLASS 2 This is the easiest and shortest route up Mount Chiquita. From the Chapin Pass Trailhead (p. 166), follow the Chapin Creek Trail (p. 171) as it climbs steeply for 0.2 mile to Chapin Pass. From here, do not drop downhill (north) into the Chapin Creek drainage. Instead, turn east (right) and follow a spur trail through dense forest for 0.75 mile to treeline. A faint trail continues east and contours along the northwest side of Mount Chapin for 1.1 miles to the pass between Mounts Chapin and Chiquita. From here, hike northeast for 0.9 mile over tundra and talus to the summit.

East Ridge GRADE II CLASS 2 This route is longer and more difficult than the Southwest Slope Route, but it is the easiest way to climb Mount Chiquita from the east. From the Lawn Lake Trailhead (p. 168), follow the Lawn Lake Trail (p. 171) to the junction with the Ypsilon Lake Trail, 1.5 miles from the trailhead. Follow the Ypsilon Lake Trail northwest for 2.6 miles to a highpoint on the trail, just before the descent to pint-sized Chipmunk Lake. Mount Chiquita's east ridge is visible to the west. At this point, leave the trail and bushwhack west through the forest, then climb up talus for 0.7 mile to Point 12,005' on Chiquita's east ridge. Continue west from this point for 0.8 mile, then angle northwest and continue to gain elevation. The ridge is gentle and easy to follow at first, becoming increasingly steeper near the top. Continue 0.4 mile to the summit.

Ypsilon Mountain 13,514 feet

T OT *Regional map p. 120 (O, 17); hike map p. 126*

Ypsilon Mountain is the fifth highest peak in RMNP and second only to Hagues Peak in terms of height within the Mummy Range. It has gentle western slopes, as well as an extremely steep east face that was sheared away by glacial activity and is highlighted by vertical gullies that form the shape of a Y, thus giving the mountain its name.

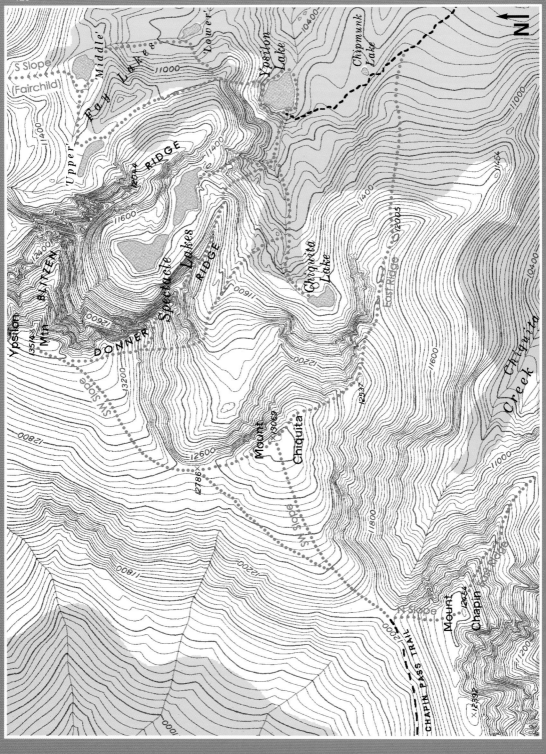

S Slope
(Fairchild)

Fay Lakes

Upper

Middle

Lower

Ypsilon Lake

Chipmunk Lake

11000

11400

RIDGE

11400

11600

11000

Ypsilon Mtn.

BINZEN

13514

12600

DONNER

Spectacle Lakes

RIDGE

13200

SW slope

12800

12786

12600

12200

11800

Chiquita Lake

Chiquita Creek

East Ridge

13005

11454

11400

11000

11600

11800

10400

Mount Chiquita

13069

12537

SW slope

12200

SW slope

12000

Mount Chapin

12454

Chapin Icefall Ridge

12200

11000

11200

11000

×12392

CHAPIN PASS TRAIL

N

N
Magnetic North
11.5 degrees

0   0.5   1

Distance in miles

Mrs. Frederick Chapin christened it "Ypsilon," the Greek word for "Y." The east face rises 2,100 vertical feet above Spectacle Lakes, forming a concave southeast-facing cirque that fans out more than 180 degrees.

Ypsilon Mountain

Southwest Slope GRADE I CLASS 2   This is the easiest and shortest route up Ypsilon Mountain. From the Chapin Pass Trailhead (p. 166), follow the Chapin Creek Trail (p. 171) as it climbs steeply for 0.2 mile to Chapin Pass. From here, do not drop downhill (north) into the Chapin Creek drainage. Instead, turn east (right) and follow a spur trail through dense forest for 0.75 mile to treeline. A faint trail continues east, contouring along the northwest side of Mount Chapin and ending at the pass between Mounts Chapin and Chiquita. Skirt low on another faint trail, and contour northeast below Mounts Chapin and Chiquita. Climb over boulders and tundra to the saddle between Mount Chiquita and Ypsilon Mountain. From here, hike up the broad southwest face of the peak to the summit, 4 miles from Chapin Pass. From the summit, hike southeast to the edge of the precipitous east face for an exciting look at Spectacle Lakes.

Donner Ridge GRADE II CLASS 3   This is the southeast ridge of Ypsilon Mountain. There are several ways to execute a hike using this ridge. One is to negotiate the entire length of the ridge, which has a lot of Class 3 scrambling around steep sections. The other is to climb the south face of the ridge and gain the ridge crest near 13,000 feet. This option presents Class 3 climbing on the south face but avoids all the difficulties along the crest of Donner Ridge. Both options begin on the west side of Ypsilon Lake, where a pretty waterfall tumbles over downed trees and jumbled rocks.

At Ypsilon Lake (follow route description, p. 133), cross a log footbridge and scramble up a faint trail that follows the cascading stream for 0.2 mile until the creek splits. From here, choose one of the options. To ascend the entire length of Donner Ridge, bushwhack northwest from the stream junction for 0.4 mile to crest Donner Ridge at 11,800 feet. Scramble northwest along the ridge (Class 3), avoiding any complexities by staying below the ridge crest on the southwest side. The difficulty of the ridge eases near 13,000 feet, and the rest is an easy hike to the summit. To avoid ascending the entire length of Donner Ridge, bushwhack west into the broad basin below Chiquita Lake. Hike through the forest and bypass Chiquita Lake on the north. Scramble northwest up rocky slopes to 12,000 feet, then turn north and climb the very steep south face of Donner Ridge. Ascend 1,000 vertical feet to the ridge top (Class 3). From here, the difficulties ease up and the summit is 0.5 mile to the north.

CCY Route (Mount Chapin, Mount Chiquita, and Ypsilon Mountain)
T **OT** *Regional map p. 120 (Q, 16); hike map p. 126*
This is a popular combination single-day hike up three high peaks of the Mummy Range, two of them soaring to elevations over 13,000 feet. The hike is committing because it is above treeline for most of the trek. Be prepared for high-altitude mountain weather. Leave early to avoid afternoon thundershowers, as the lightning hazard is particularly high on these exposed alpine summits. All three mountains have gentle, sloping west sides and steep, precipitous east faces, with Ypsilon Mountain being the highest and most dramatic.

CCY Route GRADE II CLASS 2   From the Chapin Pass Trailhead (p. 166), follow the Chapin Creek Trail (p. 171) as it climbs steeply for 0.2 mile to Chapin Pass. From here, do not drop downhill (north) into the Chapin Creek drainage. Instead, turn east (right) and follow a spur trail through dense forest for 0.75 mile to treeline. A faint trail continues east, contouring along the northwest side of Mount Chapin to the pass between Mounts Chapin and Chiquita. Another faint trail contours northeast below Chapin and Chiquita toward the saddle between Chiquita and Ypsilon Mountain. Follow the higher trail to the pass between Chapin and Chiquita. From this saddle, hike south for 0.3 mile to the summit of Mount Chapin.

Mount Chiquita lies to the northeast. Descend 400 vertical feet to the saddle between Chapin and Chiquita, then climb 1,000 vertical feet to Mount Chiquita's summit, 1.2 miles from Mount Chapin. A rock windbreak provides a wonderful spot to sit and relax while looking eastward at the dramatic views of Ypsilon Lake and Bighorn Mountain. There is no established trail between the peaks.

Ypsilon Mountain, the most impressive of them all, lies 1.25 miles northeast of Mount Chiquita. Descend 300 vertical feet to the saddle between Chiquita and Ypsilon, and hike northeast 700 vertical feet up the steep slope to the summit. Ypsilon Mountain's steep eastern cirque cradles Spectacle Lakes in a beautiful high-altitude basin. Great views of Desolation Peaks lie to the northwest. The rest of the rugged Mummy Range, including the spectacular Lawn Lake valley, spreads out to the northeast.

Mummy Kill

T **OT** *Regional map pp. 120–121 (R, 14 to M, 24)*

This is an ambitious one-day traverse of the Mummy Range's main-attraction summits. It takes in either six or eight peaks, depending on which variation is chosen. The shorter variation traverses 16 miles with 5,600 vertical feet of elevation gain. A car shuttle is required for this hike, with one vehicle left at the Lawn Lake Trailhead (p. 168) and another at the starting point at the Chapin Pass Trailhead (p. 166).

Mummy Kill Route GRADE II CLASS 3   From the Chapin Pass Trailhead, follow the CCY Route (above), to the summit of Ypsilon Mountain. From here, descend, traverse, and then climb northeast along an exposed, somewhat tricky Class 3 ridge to the summit of Fairchild Mountain. This traverse is the most difficult section of this long hike. From here, descend north to The Saddle, then climb the southwest ridge of Hagues Peak (for more details, see individual peak descriptions, pp. 136, 137, and 154–155).

From Hagues Peak, the longer variation presents itself. For extra credit, descend north to the east edge of Rowe Glacier Lake, climb north to Rowe Peak, then descend northwest to Rowe Mountain. This adds 2.1 miles and 700 vertical feet to the hike. Retrace the route back to Hagues Peak to continue.

From Hagues Peak, traverse southeast and descend to the saddle between Hagues and Mummy Mountain. Continue southeast to the summit of Mummy Mountain. Descend the Southeast Slope Route (follow route description, p. 138) to reach the Lawn Lake Trail, and hike out to the Lawn Lake Trailhead. Finish by retrieving the vehicle left at the Chapin Pass Trailhead and driving to Estes Park via Trail Ridge Road.

HORSESHOE PARK *Regional map p. 121 (V, 22)*

This flat 3.1-mile-long valley at 8,520 feet is one of the most beautiful open areas within RMNP. It stretches from the Endovalley Picnic Area on the west to the Fall River Entrance Station on the east. Fall River meanders through the long meadow, and Sheep Lakes, which lie at the northern end of the valley, draw thousands of visitors each season to view herds of majestic bighorn sheep. Horseshoe Park is the jumping-off point for hikes from the Lawn Lake Trailhead and also showcases Fan Lake and the Alluvial Fan. Old Fall River Road begins at the west end of the valley.

LAKES AND FALLS

Alluvial Fan 8,557 feet
T 🚶 ♿ *Regional map p. 121 (U, 20)*

An alluvial fan is a gradually sloping mass of rocks, sand, and debris that was deposited by moving water. When rushing water enters a valley and slows down, the debris spreads out like a fan. RMNP has a shining example of an alluvial fan, created by the 1982 Lawn Lake flood. Huge boulders that were carried down with the surge of water are strewn throughout the fan and provide interesting scenery in the flood-damaged area. New growth is taking hold amid the debris.

A gentle paved trail leads 0.5 mile from the East Alluvial Fan Parking Area to the West Alluvial Fan Parking Area. The trail winds through the debris fan and crosses a bridge over the cascading Roaring River. It climbs to a highpoint of 8,640 feet, then descends to the other parking lot.

Kids love to explore the stream and climb on the boulders lining this path. It's a marvelous place for children to experience the stunning power of nature's ability to alter the landscape. The deluge graphically tore away a huge section of hillside visible from Fall River Road. A fanned-out section of damaged landscape is riddled with huge boulders and dead trees, the Roaring River running its new course through the wreckage and into Horseshoe Park.

From the Alluvial Fan Parking (p. 166), hike along the Alluvial Fan Trail to witness the magnificence of nature's powerful landscaping tools. Take caution when climbing on the boulders and near the river. Watch children closely in this environment.

Horseshoe Falls 8,900 feet
T 🚶 *Regional map p. 121 (U, 22)*

Before the 1982 Lawn Lake flood, Horseshoe Falls was a pretty cascade that descended 320 feet over a quarter mile through the forest north of Horseshoe Park. The flood drastically redesigned the landscape, ripping away the forested riverbank and exposing raw earth, metamorphosing the falls into a broad cascade that flows down a series of rocky steps. The water dances over the huge boulders deposited by the raging torrent and spills out into an open, scenic alluvial fan. From the East Alluvial Fan Parking Area (p. 166), hike along the Alluvial Fan Trail 0.3 mile to enjoy the view of Horseshoe Falls.

Fan Lake (Historic) 8,560 feet
OT 🚶 *Regional map p. 121 (V, 21)*

Fan Lake no longer exists. This historic shallow lake used to lie in the flat valley of Horseshoe Park, created when debris from the Lawn Lake flood partially dammed the flow of Fall River. Restoration efforts by the NPS helped restore the natural hydrology of the area, and essentially eliminated this body of water. It was located about 0.1 mile south of the West Alluvial Fan Parking Area (p. 166).

Sheep Lakes 8,508 feet
R *Regional map p. 121 (V, 24)*

The bighorn sheep is the symbol of RMNP and the official mammal of Colorado. A large herd frequents the south slopes of Bighorn Mountain, often crossing US 34 to graze at Sheep Lakes, a group of shallow ponds in Horseshoe Park 1.75 miles west of the

Fall River Entrance Station. In the mid-1800s, the population of bighorn sheep in the area numbered in the thousands, but market hunters and disease from domestic sheep contributed to widespread population decline. By the 1960s, only about 140 sheep remained within RMNP. Efforts in 1977 and 1980 to transplant sheep in various areas of RMNP helped increase their numbers to nearly 500 today.

The sheep frequent the meadows surrounding Sheep Lakes, ingesting minerals found in lakeshore soils that restore nutrients depleted by a poor winter diet and the stress of lambing. Portions of the meadows that surround Sheep Lakes are closed year round. To reduce stress on the animals, the NPS provides "Bighorn Crossing Zones" in Horseshoe Park, allowing more animals to cross the highway safely. Both males and females have impressive horns. Mature rams have sets of curled horns, while ewes have straight spikes. Sheep horns continue to grow throughout an animal's lifespan and are not shed each year like deer and elk antlers.

ROARING RIVER   *Regional map p. 121 (Q, 22)*

LAKES

Potts Puddle   10,900 feet
T OT   *Regional map p. 121 (O, 24)*

Potts Puddle lies in a magical setting of tall pines and rough granite boulders at the head of Black Canyon. If it had been christened "Potts Lake," it undoubtedly would receive thousands of visitors each year. Its more famous neighbor Lawn Lake, only a mile away, is popular with hikers in both summer and winter. The puddle's insipid name and uncelebrated location just west of the Black Canyon Trail keep it secluded and relatively unvisited.

The name Potts Puddle grew out of a comedic stunt ranger Jack Moomaw played on a fellow NPS employee in the 1950s. Moomaw stocked the pond with 2,000 rainbow trout fry, withholding this crucial bit of information from avid angler Merlin Potts. Potts was studying bighorn sheep in the Mummy Range and chanced upon Mount Tileston's largest pond. His catch was so good that he ecstatically reported to Moomaw that he had found an abundant fishing hole. Moomaw, amused at Potts' excitement, didn't tell him the truth about the lake. In an effort to diminish the draw of other fisherman to his new secret stash, Potts dubbed it a "puddle." But word leaked out, and before long numerous anglers were searching for Potts Puddle. Before the end of that summer the pond had been fished barren, but the name Potts Puddle found its way onto the 1961 map.

The northern slopes of Mount Tileston drain into Tileston Meadows, a section of lush, grassy bog tucked neatly between the West Creek Research Natural Area and an inconspicuous ridge of small mountains on the east side of Roaring River. Mount Tileston's rocky slopes are home to several distinct ponds that are hidden among large boulder fields scattered within the sparse forest. Potts Puddle is the largest of these ponds and is actually a good-sized lake. It is situated a short distance off trail from several NPS backcountry campsites.

From the Lawn Lake Trailhead (p. 168), follow the Lawn Lake Trail (pp. 131, 171) for 5.6 miles to the junction with the Black Canyon Trail. Turn southeast (right) and follow the Black Canyon Trail for 0.7 mile to the Tileston Meadows campsites. Potts Puddle is located directly west of this site, up over a low, rocky ridge on the northeastern shoulder of Mount Tileston. Leave the trail and hike 0.1 mile to a rocky crest above the eastern shore of the lake. Descend to the shore for an imposing view of Mummy Mountain. Continue west from Potts Puddle to explore Mount Tileston's broad northern slopes, home to several other interesting, unnamed puddles and a few dry pond beds.

Lawn Lake   10,987 feet

T *Regional map p. 121 (N, 22); hike map p. 132*

Nestled below a semicircle of 13,000-foot peaks, Lawn Lake is the most popular backcountry destination in the Mummy Range, offering wonderful river scenery, astounding views, and a history lesson about the 1982 flood that dramatically changed the area and the valley below it. The Lawn Lake Trail follows the Roaring River, which was noticeably scarred by the deluge that felled trees, lifted heavy boulders, and graphically tore away the peaceful valley through which the river once flowed.

Lawn Lake Trail Access From the Lawn Lake Trailhead (p. 168), follow the Lawn Lake Trail (p. 171) as it climbs steeply along a ridge to an overlook of Roaring River. The floodwater had gained such momentum by this point that the hillside was ripped away, illustrating the immensity and power of the flood. Follow the ravaged streambed to the junction with the Ypsilon Lake Trail, 1.5 miles from the trailhead. Continue north on the Lawn Lake Trail along the west side of Bighorn Mountain. Excellent views of Longs Peak and Trail Ridge Road lie to the south. The trail gets steeper as it ascends several sets of switchbacks, leading to a sandy plateau that reveals the

In the early 1900s, Pingree Park pioneer Hugh Ramsey built an earthen dam at the outlet to Lawn Lake, 4.4 miles (as the crow flies) north of today's Alluvial Fan. The dam greatly enlarged the mountain lake and stored water used to irrigate the thirsty Eastern Plains. When RMNP was established in 1915, dams that predated the Park were allowed to remain on numerous mountain lakes within its borders.

Over time, water began to seep through the dirt and rock barrier around the outlet pipe at Lawn Lake, weakening the integrity of the dam. It collapsed on July 15, 1982, and water gushed out of the lake and down the once peaceful Roaring River drainage. The deluge carried boulders, trees, and earth down the river, ripping a deep scar into the land and redesigning Horseshoe Falls and Horseshoe Park. Three people died in the colossal flood that carried masses of debris down the Roaring and Fall Rivers. The torrent surged through downtown Estes Park, causing the greatest property loss in the town's history.

Lawn Lake

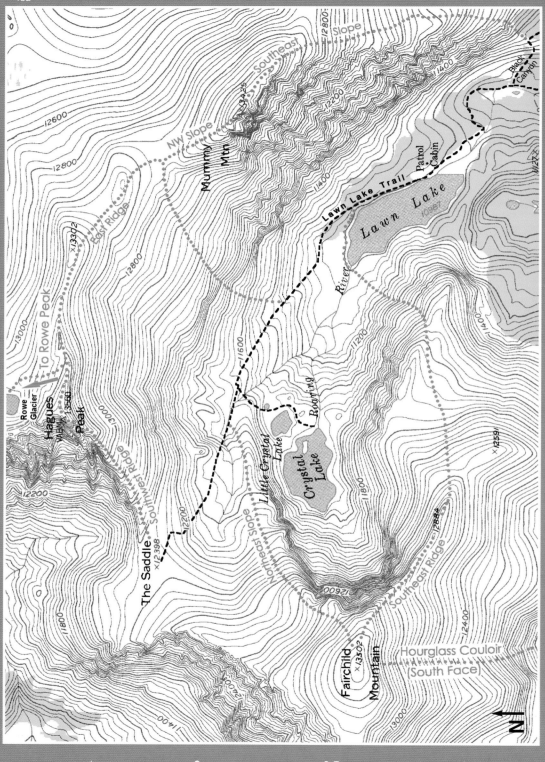

Mummy Mtn
×13425
Southeast Slope
NW Slope
East Ridge
×13302
To Rowe Peak
Rowe Glacier
Hagues Peak
×13560
WAHN
The Saddle
×12398
Southwest Ridge
Northeast Slope
Little Crystal Lake
Crystal Lake
Roaring River
Lawn Lake Trail
Lawn Lake
10987
Patrol Cabin
Black Canyon
Fairchild Mountain
×13502
Southeast Ridge
×12884
Hourglass Couloir (South Face)
×12591

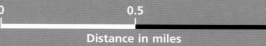

Magnetic North
11.5 degrees

N

0   0.5   1

Distance in miles

steep southwestern face of Mummy Mountain. Continue to the junction with the Black Canyon Trail, and then proceed 0.7 mile northwest to Lawn Lake. Immediately prior to reaching the lake, the ruined dam site comes into view. Lawn Lake is a lovely spot in which to view the grand peaks of the Mummy Range. It is surrounded on the west by Fairchild Mountain, on the north by Hagues Peak, and on the northeast by Mummy Mountain.

Black Canyon Trail Access   From the Lumpy Ridge Trailhead (p. 168), follow the Black Canyon Trail (p. 170) northwest for 8.9 miles to the junction with the Lawn Lake Trail. Follow the Lawn Lake Trail northwest 0.7 mile to Lawn Lake.

Little Crystal Lake   11,500 feet
T   *Regional map p. 121 (M, 20); hike map p. 132*

Little Crystal Lake lies northeast of Crystal Lake and is about a quarter of the size. The Crystal Lakes Trail skirts the eastern shore of this small pond en route to Crystal Lake.

Crystal Lake   11,500 feet
T   *Regional map p. 121 (M, 20); hike map p. 132*

Crystal Lake is a large alpine tarn set in a stark granite basin at the foot of Fairchild Mountain's dramatic east face. It is the headwaters of the Roaring River, surrounded by large boulders that are strewn about haphazardly. Long-lasting echoes resound off the sheer walls of the imposing northeast-facing cirque that cradles the lake.

From Lawn Lake (follow route description, p. 131), follow the trail toward The Saddle as it skirts along the northeast shore and continues beyond treeline into an open valley. One mile beyond Lawn Lake, the trail to Crystal Lakes splits off to the southwest, angling toward Fairchild Mountain's sheer face. Take this trail and hike to Little Crystal Lake, encircled by large boulders. Continue southwest to top out on a rock bench above the dark, deep waters of Crystal Lake.

Chipmunk Lake   10,660 feet
T **OT**   *Regional map p. 120 (Q, 18); hike map p. 126*

This tiny pond is surrounded by marsh and boulders on a flat bench along the Ypsilon Lake Trail, 0.5 mile southeast of Ypsilon Lake. A striking reflection of 13,502-foot Fairchild Mountain adds interest to this shallow mere. From its junction with the Lawn Lake Trail (pp. 131, 171), follow the Ypsilon Lake Trail (below) northwest for 2.7 miles to Chipmunk Lake.

Ypsilon Lake   10,540 feet
T   *Regional map p. 120 (P, 18); hike map p. 126*

Ypsilon Lake is nestled in a wooded corridor abutting a steep ridge that extends southeast from Ypsilon Mountain. Cascading tributaries babble down lush hillsides and spill into the lake. The shoreline is heavily forested, limiting the views of nearby mountains. Rock slabs protrude into the lake, and picturesque downed trees grace the shoreline.

From the Lawn Lake Trailhead (p. 168), follow the Lawn Lake Trail (p. 171) as it climbs steadily up a south-facing ridge. The trail levels off as it parallels the Roaring River, rising to the rim of a canyon that reveals the striking scar from the 1982 Lawn Lake flood. Follow the trail along the ravaged streambed to the junction with the Ypsilon Lake Trail, 1.5 miles from the trailhead. Turn south (left) and cross Roaring River on a log bridge. This is a good spot to view Ypsilon Mountain and the Y-shaped couloir that inspired its name.

The trail begins to climb away from the river through the dense lodgepole pine forest and levels off near a rocky outcrop with a spectacular view of Horseshoe Park.

Leave the trail to seek the best view at the overlook. The trail continues northwest to ascend a thickly forested hillside for nearly 2.6 miles to a sandy bench interspersed with boulders and trees. The trail meanders downward to Chipmunk Lake, then ascends a small rise. It then turns northeast and descends nearly 160 vertical feet to Ypsilon Lake, settled nicely on a heavily wooded bench.

Chiquita Lake 11,340 feet

T **OT** *Regional map p. 120 (Q, 16); hike map p. 126*

Cupped at the base of Mount Chiquita's broken east face, Chiquita Lake lies above the trees in a glacially scoured cirque. Interesting rock ramparts on the lake's western shore and a pagoda of dark granite streaked with light veins of rock add color to the stark amphitheater of stone and frigid water. From Ypsilon Lake (follow route description, p. 133), cross a log footbridge and hike along the west shore to the base of a pretty waterfall. Scramble up a faint trail that follows the cascading stream, then bushwhack west up the creek for 0.2 mile until the creek splits. Continue west along the southern (left) branch, ascending through a sparse forest and up a rocky shelf that embraces Chiquita Lake. Pass stands of stunted trees, lush alpine tundra, and pretty rivulets that cascade over glistening rock slabs. The route climbs steeply up to the shelf and tops out slightly above the remote glacial tarn on a rocky tundra bench.

Spectacle Lakes 11,340 feet

T **OT** *Regional map p. 120 (P, 17); hike map p. 126*

The Spectacle Lake basin is one of the most beautiful and inspiring places in RMNP. The two alpine tarns lie at the foot of the sheer, intimidating southeast face of Ypsilon Mountain, highlighted by a set of vertical snow gullies that form a Y-shaped imprint on the mountain's facade. The pair of lakes has a distinct eyeglass shape. This is a difficult hike that requires some route finding and, depending on the exact route followed, presents steep climbing along waterfalls and exposed scrambling up steep slabs.

From Ypsilon Lake (follow route description, p. 133), cross a log footbridge and hike along the west shore to the base of a pretty waterfall. Scramble up a faint trail on the north side of the cascading stream, then bushwhack northwest into a large alpine basin at the foot of a short waterfall that cascades down some granite slabs. Ascending this wet granite is the crux of the hike, and can be intimidating. Use caution and clamber up the rocks on the west side of the stream, ascending to a rocky shelf. From the top of the waterfall, scramble northwest along the outlet stream to 'Lower Spectacle Lake.' Skirt the lake on the west to continue along the broken rock bench to 'Upper Spectacle Lake.'

Fay Lakes

T **OT** *Regional map p. 120 (O, 18); hike map p. 126*

This pretty chain of three lakes: 'Lower Fay Lake' (10,740 feet); 'Middle Fay Lake' (11,020 feet); and 'Upper Fay Lake' (11,220 feet), lies in a remote, scenic valley between Ypsilon and Fairchild Mountains. The lakes are the headwaters of a major tributary to the Roaring River. From Ypsilon Lake (follow route description, p. 133), hike along the southern shore and cross the outlet stream. Bushwhack northeast through dense forest for 0.6 mile to the lowest and smallest of the

Ypsilon Mountain from Blitzen Ridge

Fay Lakes. This is easier said than done, as the thickly forested terrain does not provide any landmarks to lead the way.

From the lowest lake, follow the stream and climb cross-country to the north for 0.5 mile to round-shaped 'Middle Fay Lake.' Continue west for 0.3 mile to balloon-shaped 'Upper Fay Lake,' nestled at the base of Ypsilon Mountain's steep and jagged Blitzen Ridge.

PEAKS AND OTHER DESTINATIONS

Bighorn Mountain 11,463 feet
T **OT** *Regional map p. 121 (S, 23)*

At nearly 11,500 feet, the summit of Bighorn Mountain is situated just above treeline. The mountain rises like a fortress out of the forest, flanked on all sides by steep slopes of Engelmann spruce and subalpine fir. The large, rolling summit of Bighorn Mountain is a unique place to view bighorn sheep, as they frequently traverse the tundra on the summit plateau. A granite ridge stretches across the treeless summit of Bighorn Mountain, and it is difficult to discern which rocky vertex is actually the highest point. The true summit lies on the northern side of the crest, near the saddle dividing Bighorn and Tileston Mountains.

Mount Tileston lies just north of Bighorn Mountain and is 200 feet lower. Separating the two mountains is a 10,700-foot pass, which is the origin of an unnamed tributary to Black Canyon Creek. Astounding vistas can be seen from the summit of Bighorn Mountain, including the high peaks of the Mummy Range, intimate views of neighboring McGregor and Dark Mountains, and the striking formation of The Needles on Lumpy Ridge.

Northwest Slope GRADE II CLASS 2 From the Lawn Lake Trailhead (p. 168), follow the Lawn Lake Trail (p. 171) for 2.5 miles to the junction with the trail to Cutbank backcountry campsite. Hiking this far north avoids the steeper west slope of the mountain. At this junction, leave the trail and bushwhack southeast, directly up the dense forest of the mountain's northwest side. Emerge from the trees to a rocky, windswept slope that rises toward the summit. Hike in the direction of the obvious rock outcroppings on the northern end of the summit plateau. Watch for bighorn sheep grazing on the tundra near the top. A panoramic view of the Mummy Range to the north and west, as well as distant views of Longs Peak and Trail Ridge Road, are rewarding after the arduous ascent.

Mount Tileston 11,254 feet
T **OT** *Regional map p. 121 (P, 24)*

Hidden among the majesty of the Mummy Range, this wonderful peak is accessible from the popular Lawn Lake Trail. Though not exceptionally high, the summit is exposed and remarkable, offering privileged views of Mummy Mountain's jagged southwest face and a 360-degree panorama of RMNP.

Northwest Slope GRADE II CLASS 2 This route bypasses the steep, heavily treed western slope and ascends the gentler, sparsely forested northwest slope. From Lawn Lake Trailhead (p. 168), follow Lawn Lake Trail (p. 171) for 5.2 miles to an obvious open sandy plateau,

Keith Brown on the summit of Mount Tileston

enlarged by the power of the 1982 Lawn Lake flood as it swept through this area. This location is 0.4 mile south of the Black Canyon Trail junction. Leave the trail and bushwhack east up the slope of sparsely spaced trees to the crest of the ridge. From here, turn south and hike onto an open area decorated with gnarled limber pines. The summit is obvious to the south. Continue hiking on the smooth tundra to a rocky section that leads to the top. Hike up boulders to the summit.

Joanne Skidmore hiking from Lawn Lake to The Saddle

The Saddle 12,398 feet

T *Regional map p. 120 (L, 19); hike map p. 132*

This is the broad pass that lies between Fairchild Mountain and Hagues Peak, 2.3 miles northwest of Lawn Lake. A tributary to Hague Creek flows from the northern slope of The Saddle, and a tributary of the Roaring River flows from the southern slope. It is a great vantage from which to view the high peaks of the Mummy Range or to access the remote Hague Creek drainage. From Lawn Lake (follow the route description, p. 131), continue northwest along the trail as it skirts the lake to the northeast. Hike up into the gorgeous alpine valley below The Saddle. Pass the junction with the Crystal Lakes Trail and weave through rocky mounds to the base of The Saddle. Climb relatively steep terrain to the end of the trail as it peters out on open tundra slopes.

Fairchild Mountain 13,502 feet

T **OT** **[icon]** *Regional map p. 120 (M, 19); hike map p. 132*

Of the hundreds of named features in RMNP, few of them were designated by political persuasion. Fairchild Mountain is one exception, named for Lucius Fairchild, a three-time Wisconsin governor who never even visited the area. A couple of Fairchild's supporters came to Estes Park to climb and named the mountain for their hero. Somehow the name stuck. Fairchild Mountain is a rounded heap of granite with a sheer east face that forms a striking cirque cradling two alpine tarns. Though not technically difficult, this is a tough climb—nearly a mile of elevation gain and almost 18 miles round trip. The allure of this beautiful climb is augmented by superb views.

Marisa Howe and Michelle Chase on the final stretch to the summit of Fairchild Mountain

Northeast Slope GRADE II CLASS 2
From Lawn Lake (follow route description, p. 131), follow the trail that leads northwest to The Saddle, past the trail junction to Crystal Lakes, for 1.6 miles to 12,000 feet. The trail continues to The Saddle, but it is not necessary to go that far. Leave the trail and climb southwest up talus for 1 mile to the summit. The broad north slope of Fairchild has several rolling bulges on the way to the top.

Southeast Ridge GRADE II CLASS 2 This is a great spring descent route when the northeast-facing gully that rises to the southwest above Lawn Lake is filled with stable snow. This gully can be avalanche prone during winter. From Lawn Lake (follow route description, p. 131), circle around to the west side of the lake and hike southwest to the base of a prominent gully that climbs 1,500 vertical feet to Fairchild's southeast ridge between Point 12,884' and Point 12,591'. From here, turn northwest and ascend the nontechnical ridge for 0.7 mile to the summit.

◹ **Hourglass Couloir, South Face** GRADE II CLASS 2 MODERATE SNOW This beautiful hourglass-shaped gully climbs 2,500 vertical feet from Fay Lakes to the summit of Fairchild Mountain in 1 mile. This is a fun spring route but is not recommended after the snow melts out of the gully. It is an adventurous ski descent in stable spring conditions. Crampons and an ice axe are recommended for the ascent. From 'Middle Fay Lake' (follow route description, p. 134), hike north to the base of the couloir. Ascend the moderate snow slope to the point where it narrows dramatically (the neck of the hourglass) and the snow runoff forms a cascading stream. Climb up the stream and enter the broad upper snowfield. Continue to a small bulge below the summit slopes of the mountain. Crest the bulge and hike north over talus to the summit.

Hagues Peak   13,560 feet
T **OT** *Regional map p. 121 (K, 20); hike map p. 132*
This magnificent peak stands at the headwaters of three major drainages: Hague Creek, Roaring River, and the North Fork of the Big Thompson River. It's the highest peak in the Mummy Range and Larimer County, and the fourth highest in RMNP. It has a steep, convoluted west face rising above Hague Creek, but its other slopes are moderate.

Southwest Ridge GRADE II CLASS 2 From Lawn Lake (follow route description, p. 131), follow the trail along the lake's north shore and continue northwest for 2 miles to The Saddle. Turn northeast onto the broad southwest ridge of Hagues Peak. Climb over rough talus, staying on the southeast side of the ridge as it narrows near the summit. Some large granite blocks on the south side of the summit present a fun route-finding challenge. Clamber through the blocks to the top, 0.75 mile from The Saddle.

East Ridge GRADE II CLASS 2 From Lawn Lake (follow route description, p. 131), continue northwest along the trail for 1 mile as it skirts the northeast shore of the lake and climbs toward Crystal Lakes and The Saddle. Leave the trail near the Crystal Lake Trail turnoff at 11,400 feet. Turn northeast and hike cross-country over steep tundra and talus for 0.8 mile to a broad 12,920-foot saddle in the prominent ridge between Hagues Peak and Mummy Mountain. This saddle makes it possible to climb both peaks together. Mummy Mountain lies 500 yards southeast up a steep, rocky, Class 2 ridge. Turn northwest from the saddle and hike along the blocky ridge to Point 13,302', then continue west for 0.7 mile to Hagues Peak.

Mummy Mountain   13,425 feet
T **OT** *Regional map p. 121 (L, 23); hike map p. 132*
This beautiful thirteener has a remarkable, rugged southwest face that rises dramatically above the northeastern shore of Lawn Lake. The remaining slopes are gentle and expansive. This is a fun peak to climb in winter. The summit is spectacular, with panoramic views of the Mummy Range and the northeastern section of RMNP. Lawn Lake glistens below, and Fairchild Mountain's sheer east face rises grandly to the west.

Southeast Slope GRADE II CLASS 2   From the Lawn Lake Trailhead (p. 168), follow the Lawn Lake Trail (p. 171) 5.6 miles to the junction with the Black Canyon Trail. This trail intersection is 0.7 mile southeast of Lawn Lake. From here the striking southwest face of Mummy Mountain rises impressively skyward. From the junction, follow the Black Canyon Trail (p. 170) southeast 0.25 mile to the top of a tiny ridge at the foot of the southwest face. Leave the trail and climb steeply northeast over large boulders for 0.3 mile to a ridge crest where Mummy Mountain's broad, gentle southeast slope meets the rugged southwest face. Turn northwest and climb the gentle tundra slope over several false summits for 1.1 miles to Mummy Mountain's summit. This flowing slope is sometimes called the "hair" of the Mummy. High winds frequently sweep over this exposed slope, leaving bare tundra even in the winter months.

Northwest Slope GRADE II CLASS 2   From Lawn Lake (follow route description, p. 131), continue northwest along the trail for 1 mile as it skirts the northeast shore of the lake and climbs toward Crystal Lakes and The Saddle. Leave the trail near the Crystal Lake Trail turnoff at 11,400 feet. Turn northeast and hike cross-country over steep tundra and talus for 0.8 mile to a broad 12,920-foot saddle in the prominent ridge between Hagues Peak and Mummy Mountain. This saddle makes it possible to climb both peaks together. Several abrupt cliffs on Mummy Mountain's southwest side can be skirted on the west. From the saddle, turn southeast and climb a steep, rocky ridge for 500 yards to the summit of Mummy Mountain.

CASTLE MOUNTAIN AREA   *Regional map p. 121 (X, 31)*

PEAKS AND OTHER DESTINATIONS

Castle Mountain 8,834 feet
OT   *Regional map p. 121 (X, 31)*

This beautiful, turreted peak is located northwest of Estes Park and showcases a long ridge of tall rock towers, picturesque granite bulges, and bulky outcrops. Castle Mountain lies between the Black Canyon Creek and Fall River drainages, providing a wonderful vantage of the northern section of RMNP, including outstanding views of Lumpy Ridge. It also presents a unique, unobstructed view of the town of Estes Park. This is a fun mountain to climb, and it's interesting to explore the remarkable rock formations that dot the forested slopes and summit ridge of this low-elevation gem.

Southeast Slope GRADE I CLASS 2   There is no trail up this mountain, but the route crosses a couple of old, doubletrack dirt roads that are being reclaimed by nature as it follows an intermittent path marked by rock cairns. From Castle Mountain Parking (p. 166), hike north up the slope and into the forest. The route weaves northwest between rock outcrops as it ascends the moderately steep slope. Hike past rock blobs, knobs, stacks, and odd-shaped formations in a northerly direction. Contour upslope toward the steep granite walls that guard the summit. The west side of the summit block is quite steep, but the east side offers an easy scramble up some boulders and through bushes to a sandy plateau immediately below the top. Scramble up the summit rocks for a panoramic view. Castle Mountain is completely within RMNP, yet it offers an amazing overview of Estes Park. On the descent, it's fun to hike east below the ridge crest, exploring the rock outcrops that ornament the mountain's spine. Take care to stay within public land; private parcels are well marked.

Window Rock (8,530 feet)
and **Castle Rock** (8,669 feet)
on **Castle Mountain**

`OT` *Regional map p. 121 (X, 31)*

Three stacked, fluted rock spires form the southeast shoulder of Castle Mountain. This formation resembles the architecture of the Sydney Opera House and is home to the famous Castle Mountain "window." Climbing up to the window presents a good photo opportunity and the chance to peek through the hole in the rock toward Lumpy Ridge.

The highest of these fins is Castle Rock, just to the west of Window Rock. Technical rock climbers have explored these formations for years and have placed bolts on some of the rock faces. From Castle Mountain Parking (p. 166), hike northeast through the forest for 0.5 mile to the base of the rocks at 8,360 feet.

Window Rock

LUMPY RIDGE

Regional map p. 121 (U, 34)

Lumpy Ridge is the most prominent natural landmark in Estes Park. It flanks the town on its north side and forms a dramatic, rocky backdrop for the famous Stanley Hotel. This 3-mile-long strip of distinctive granite domes is a world-renowned Mecca for technical rock climbers. The natural formations of weathered granite oddities, towering blocks, and shapely domes ornament the ridge as it stretches from east to west.

Lumpy Ridge is encircled by a well-maintained trail system that provides a fine overview of the Black Canyon Creek and Cow Creek drainages. The loop around the Ridge offers a visit to popular Gem Lake, close-up views of the impressive rock formations that give Lumpy Ridge its name, and a look at secluded Cow Creek valley, which showcases one of the most beautiful aspen groves on the east side of RMNP. The Needles (10,068 feet) are the highest points on the ridge, while the most famous shape is the pronounced Twin Owls formation. Seen from Estes Park, these two granite towers resemble a pair of birds perched on a diagonal slab, which is called the "Roosting Ramp."

Elk grazing below Lumpy Ridge

The Arapaho Indians called Lumpy Ridge "Thatáá-ai-átah," which literally means "little lumps." No one who views the exposed granite knobs can dispute the appropriateness of the name. This distinct topography was formed by exfoliation caused by freezing and thawing. The historic MacGregor Ranch, a working cattle ranch at the southeast end of the Black Canyon, lies directly south of Lumpy Ridge.

LAKES AND FALLS

'MacGregor Falls' 8,380 feet
T 🚶 *Regional map p. 121 (U, 31)*

Also called 'Black Canyon Falls,' this cascade in Black Canyon Creek streams over a small granite cliff in a box canyon near historic MacGregor Ranch. The hike to the falls is not strenuous and leads through the meadow between Castle Mountain and Lumpy Ridge.

From the Lumpy Ridge Trailhead (p. 168), follow the Lumpy Ridge Trail (p. 172) as it climbs and then descends to the open meadows above MacGregor Ranch. Continue along the Black Canyon Trail (p. 170) as it meanders west along the base of Lumpy Ridge. About 1.7 miles from the trailhead, strike off-trail to the south, crossing through the meadow to a doubletrack dirt road that runs parallel to the trail. Follow the road west until it ends at the site of the previous Estes Park Public Water Supply, where there are a few buildings and a sign marking the trail that continues to 'MacGregor Falls.'

The narrow path is pleasant and gentle, paralleling Black Canyon Creek, and the peaceful forest and babbling stream add to the serene nature of this hike. A small cascade immediately prior to the falls is sometimes mistaken for 'MacGregor Falls,' but continue northwest to the tight canyon that conceals the pretty waterfall as it rushes over a granite slab. Cross the creek for the best view of the falls and enjoy the solitude and serenity of this destination.

Gem Lake 8,820 feet
T 🚶 *Regional map p. 121 (U, 37)*

Situated amid Lumpy Ridge's granite outcrops, this lake is about 5 feet deep. The weathering of exposed bedrock created this small pond, and it is one of the few lakes in RMNP not formed by glacial activity. The lake's low elevation and the southern exposure of the Gem Lake Trail make this a good year-round destination, though the trail can be hot and dusty during summer. Thousands visit this popular destination annually.

From the Lumpy Ridge Trailhead (p. 168), the Gem Lake Trail (p. 171) climbs into an open canyon and negotiates short switchbacks, weaving among forest and rocks. After 0.5 mile, the Gem Lake Trail reaches the junction with the trail that leads west toward The Twin Owls.

From this point, turn east (right) and follow the trail as it climbs at a moderate rate to a sandy area where several social paths break away from the Gem Lake Trail to explore a scenic grouping of huge boulders that overlooks Estes Park. These vistas are worth a quick diversion. Continue to follow the Gem Lake Trail northeast as it climbs over bedrock and up switchbacks to a rocky plateau that offers a sweeping view of Estes Park, Longs Peak, and the Continental Divide. From here, the trail swings north and traverses along the ridge to a sandy plateau, then descends into a rocky canyon. Short switchbacks lead to a rock bench and 'Paul Bunyan's Boot,' a rock formation that resembles a large boot propped on its heel with a hole in the sole.

Continue through the shady ravine as the trail crosses an intermittent stream, then climbs more steeply up multiple switchbacks and skirts along huge granite slabs. At the last switchback before the lake, stop to enjoy the grand overlook of the Estes Park valley. Follow the short, final stretch of rocky trail for 30 yards to the lake. Gem Lake is flanked on the northeast by weathered granite walls, creating an amphitheater-type setting. From a small, sandy beach on the western shore, a view of Twin Sisters Peaks is revealed.

Bronson MacDonald and Melissa Strong hike along the shore of Gem Lake

PEAKS AND OTHER DESTINATIONS

Lumpy Ridge Loop

T *Regional map p. 121 (T, 30 to T, 38)*

A system of trails completely encircles Lumpy Ridge, creating a loop hike that provides a nice overview of the area. From the Lumpy Ridge Trailhead (p. 168), follow the Lumpy Ridge Trail (p. 172) 0.7 mile northwest as it climbs and then descends to the open meadows above MacGregor Ranch. Continue along the Black Canyon Trail (p. 170) as it leads west and skirts the montane meadows of lower Black Canyon Creek. The trail skirts the MacGregor Ranch property and offers open views of Longs Peak to the south. Cattle graze in the sweeping landscape. Lumpy Ridge's rock cliffs rise north of the trail in a striking geologic display.

Travel west past trail junctions for the Lumpy Ridge rock formations, 'The Book' and 'The Pear,' and continue over level terrain until the trail enters the forest and then climbs steeply to a forested pass between Dark Mountain and Lumpy Ridge. A junction near the top of this saddle indicates that the Black Canyon Trail continues west-northwest toward Lawn Lake. This junction

Alexander MacGregor came to Estes Park in 1872 and fell in love with Clara Heeney, an art student who was traveling in the area. Clara's mother purchased land in Black Canyon, and after the couple's marriage in 1873, they moved to the Estes Valley and started Black Canyon Cattle Ranch. Over the years, the ranch was utilized for cattle, farming, and lodging for summer visitors.

In 1876 Clara became the first postmaster of Estes Park. The couple had three sons: George, Donald, and Halbert. George was with his father near Poudre Lake in 1896 when Alexander was struck and killed by lightning. Clara died in 1901, and Donald assumed care of the ranch. His daughter, Muriel, was the last MacGregor family trustee of the property. She never was married and was viewed by townsfolk to be a reserved spinster. Alone, she struggled to oversee the details and keep the ranch operating for 20 years, cash-poor but unwilling to sell. After Muriel's death in 1970, the MacGregor Trust was established. Negotiations between the National Park Service and the Trust resulted in an agreement for restoration and preservation and fulfilled Muriel's wish of maintaining a working cattle ranch with proceeds used for charities and educational purposes.

is 4.0 miles from the trailhead. Turn east (right) and follow the trail as it descends to Cow Creek, passing through thick forest and crossing an intermittent stream amid a small aspen grove. The trail then climbs to a plateau on the north side of Lumpy Ridge that reveals a lovely mountain meadow with the crags of Sheep Mountain to the northeast and an extensive aspen grove to the south.

Cross Cow Creek and hike through the quiet valley to the junction between Cow Creek Trail and the unnamed trail that leads southeast to Gem Lake. From the junction, turn south (right) and cross Cow Creek again, then follow the trail east toward Gem Lake. Climb steadily through the forest and pass the turnoff for the trail to 'Balanced Rock.' Stay on the main trail as it swings southwest to a saddle that allows passage through the crest of the ridge to arrive at Gem Lake. Gem Lake was formed by the weathering of exposed bedrock. From here, it's a simple 1.7-mile downhill trek to reach the Lumpy Ridge Trailhead.

The Twin Owls (Technical) 8,789 feet

T **OT** *Regional map p. 121 (V, 36)*

The Twin Owls are unmistakable rock formations at the eastern end of Lumpy Ridge. The two lofty rock towers are separated by a deep chimney on the south face and are perched on a long, diagonal ledge system called the "Roosting Ramp." The dual humps actually look like owls, especially from Estes Park.

There is no hiking route to the top of the formation, but there is an easy climbing route that sneaks up a chimney on the north side with a 30-foot section of mild Class 5 climbing. The Bowels of the Owls is a dark, damp, vertical cave located on the north side of the formation. Because the moves on this route are in a chimney where narrow rock walls on three sides provide a sense of security to climbers, most climbers do not feel the need for a rope to ascend or descend the cleft. If the route is wet or snowy, exposure above the Bowels becomes an issue and the route becomes dangerous. Use caution when taking inexperienced climbers up this route. Also beware that this route is used as a descent route for most of the technical rock climbs on The Twin Owls, which could present the problem of traffic congestion in the chimney. Because of its high use by climbers, the rock within the chimney is slick and polished.

The Twin Owls

⬙ **Bowels of the Owls** GRADE I CLASS 5.0   From the Lumpy Ridge Trailhead (p. 168), follow the Gem Lake Trail (p. 171) for 0.5 mile to the junction with the trail that leads toward The Twin Owls. Turn west (left) and follow that trail to the marked junction with the climbers' access trail to the Bowels of the Owls. Leave the main trail and hike up the steep access trail to the north side of The Twin Owls. Locate the largest, deepest, and easiest chimney on this face. The entrance to the Bowels of the Owls is a Class 3 scramble up a short step and into a slot that leads below some overhead chockstones to the base of the technical section of the chimney. There are several chimneys and clefts on the north side of the formation, so be careful to choose the correct one. If access to the chimney is more difficult than Class 3, you are in the wrong chimney, and much harder technical climbing will follow.

Once in the depth of the Bowels at the base of the chimney, squeeze up the back end of the chimney (Class 5.0) to a small ledge that traverses back out into the daylight on a sloping shelf. Because of a drop-off on the north side, this shelf is dangerous when wet, so use caution when navigating here. Scramble up a grooved channel to the cleft between the two summit blocks of The Twin Owls, then scramble to the top of the formation for an outstanding view.

The Needles   10,068 feet
T **OT** *Regional map p. 121 (U, 32)*

The Needles are a group of rock bulges and spires on the western edge of Lumpy Ridge. Sundance Buttress is the largest of the formations, surrounded by smaller rock knobs and granite fins that shape the ridge crest. Slightly east of Sundance Buttress, a slender pinnacle unofficially referred to as 'The Needle' represents the highest point on Lumpy Ridge. A good trail leads to the base of these rocks, and then a strenuous bushwhack gives way to the sporty scramble that is required to climb out to the tip of the highest needle formation.

South Gully to North Ridge GRADE I CLASS 2+   From the Lumpy Ridge Trailhead (p. 168), follow the Lumpy Ridge Trail (p. 172) 0.7 mile northwest as it climbs and then descends to the open meadows above MacGregor Ranch. From here, follow the Black Canyon Trail west for 1.9 miles to the junction with the climbers' trail to Sundance Buttress. Turn north (right) and follow the rough track to the base of the rock wall. Skirt the formation on the east (right) and gain the tree-choked gully between Sundance Buttress and 'The Needle.' Follow an extremely rough, unmaintained footpath up the ravine. This "trail" climbs through thick under-brush, over downed trees, and up small cliff sections. The gully tops out on the rolling summit plateau of Lumpy Ridge, riddled with rock knobs and domes. Hike to the east side of 'The Needle' and climb a steep, short step on the formation's east side to gain a narrow ridge that leads out to the highest point. A small rock cairn marks the highpoint. An exposed route out to the lower, southernmost point reveals a view of the sheer faces of Lumpy Ridge. Huge views of Estes Park and Lake Estes, Mount Meeker and Longs Peak, and the Continental Divide spread out in an impressive panorama.

Northwest Slope GRADE I CLASS 2+   This is a longer route, but it avoids the steep south face of The Needles. From the Lumpy Ridge Trailhead (p. 168), follow the Lumpy Ridge Trail (p. 172) 0.7 mile northwest as it climbs and then descends to the open meadows above MacGregor Ranch. From here, follow the Black Canyon Trail west for 3.3 miles to the junction with the trail from Cow Creek. Leave the trail and bushwhack southeast through thick forest and past numerous rock outcrops for 0.8 mile to the east side of 'The Needle.' Climb a steep, short step on the formation's east side to gain a narrow ridge that leads out to the highest point.

'Paul Bunyan's Boot'

'Paul Bunyan's Boot'   8,560+ feet

T **[hiker]** *Regional map p. 121 (U, 37)*

This unique rock formation lies 1.3 miles along the Gem Lake Trail from the Lumpy Ridge Trailhead. The 15-foot-high granite tower resembles a large boot propped on its heel with a hole in the sole. Refer to the route description for Gem Lake (p. 140) for hiking details.

'Balanced Rock'   8,863 feet

T *Regional map p. 121 (U, 36)*

'Balanced Rock' is among the most interesting of Lumpy Ridge's unique granite sculptures. Poised atop a slender plug of rock that sits on a gigantic boulder, this round, statuesque stone stretches toward the sky in a dramatic demonstration of nature's subtle balancing act. The hike to this chiseled formation highlights Lumpy Ridge's loveliest attributes: a visit to charming Gem Lake, ample scenery, fascinating rock sculptures, and the true serenity and quiescence of RMNP's low-altitude forest. The quiet solitude that typifies the north side of Lumpy Ridge (in contrast to the busy, highly visited south side) adds to the beauty and likability of this hike.

Lumpy Ridge Trailhead Access   From the Lumpy Ridge Trailhead (p. 168), follow the Gem Lake Trail (p. 171) for 1.7 miles to Gem Lake. The trail skirts along a small, sandy beach on the lake's western shore and continues through a gap in the rock walls, then it meanders along the ridge, weaving through the tranquil forest in an easterly direction before cutting back to the north and coming upon a level, sandy bench. Here the spur trail to 'Balanced Rock' diverges from the main trail, 1.6 miles from Gem Lake. At the sign, follow the spur trail to 'Balanced Rock' as it winds into the heart of Lumpy

Ridge. The trail, which is somewhat hard to follow, descends into a gorgeous wooded gulch that harbors the imposing bulk of 'Balanced Rock,' 1.1 miles from the trail junction.

Cow Creek Trailhead Access   From the Cow Creek Trailhead at McGraw Ranch (p. 167), follow the Cow Creek Trail (p. 171) 1.3 miles to a trail junction. Turn south (left) and follow the trail toward Gem Lake as it climbs steadily for 1.6 miles to a forested plateau and the junction with the spur trail to 'Balanced Rock.' Follow this spur trail for 1.1 miles to 'Balanced Rock.'

McGregor Mountain   10,486 feet

OT *Regional map p. 121 (U, 29)*

This sizable, low-elevation peak lies between the Black Canyon Creek and Fall River drainages, south of Dark Mountain. The off-trail hike to the summit offers a 360-degree panorama showcasing the spectacular Mummy Range, the majestic peaks of the Continental Divide, the Longs Peak area, Estes Park, and the technical rock climber's paradise of Lumpy Ridge. McGregor Mountain can be easily seen from several vantages in downtown Estes Park, and the signature

Summit area, McGregor Mountain

600-foot, low-angle rock dome that highlights the southwest side (McGregor Slab) makes it popular with climbers as well as hikers. Though normally spelled without the "a" in "Mac," the mountain is named for the colorful MacGregor family and lies northwest of historic MacGregor Ranch.

Southwest Slope GRADE I CLASS 2   From the Fall River Visitor Center on US 34 (Fall River Road), 5 miles west of Estes Park, cross the highway and hike north through a commercially operated campground. The owners of this resort are friendly and tolerant of climbers and hikers accessing McGregor Mountain through their land, but it's a good idea to stop by the office to ask for permission before continuing.

Hike through the campground and ascend a broad gully to the east of McGregor Slab. There is a faint trail up the gully, which is thick with downed trees and normally used as a descent route for rock climbers returning from McGregor Slab. Top out of the gully and continue bushwhacking northeast up the steep slope to the summit, which is adorned with lovely slabs of granite and gnarled, weathered trees.

COW CREEK *Regional map p. 121 (S, 34)*

FALLS

Bridal Veil Falls 8,880 feet
T ⚐ *Regional map p. 121 (R, 32)*

Located in a rocky valley on the east side of Dark Mountain, Bridal Veil Falls is a brilliant plume of whitewater cascading over a short but steep granite wall, swooshing down to a clear pool to create the illusion of a bride's flowing shroud. A common name

for a waterfall, Bridal Veil was an obvious choice for the distinctive flow of water that plummets more than 20 vertical feet from a broken granite crag, spraying up off the rocks at the base in a dazzling display of mist and roaring water. The hike parallels Cow Creek along a flat, easy trail and leads through open meadows before climbing into the rocky gorge that is home to the alluring waterfall. Spring is the best time of year to visit the falls, as heavy snowmelt creates a gushing torrent that is unequalled in other seasons.

From the Cow Creek Trailhead at McGraw Ranch (p. 167), hike west along the Cow Creek Trail (p. 171), which begins as a level double-track road, past the old barn and several other ranch buildings. The setting is aesthetic, with rustic buildings dwarfed by large granite crags in the midst of a healthy pine forest. Just beyond the structures is the junction with the North Boundary Trail. Continue along the Cow Creek Trail, with open meadows to the south and aspen and conifer forest covering the hillside to the north.

The trail narrows to singletrack as it passes the junction with the trail to 'Balanced Rock'

Joanne Skidmore and Bob Chase at upper Bridal Veil Falls

and Gem Lake, then it continues beyond the turnoff to the Rabbit Ears campsite. Continue west along the Cow Creek Trail to a trail junction nearly 2 miles from the trailhead. Leave the main trail and follow the path that splits off northwest toward Bridal Veil Falls. The trail gets steeper, enters the woods, and crosses the creek, leading to a hitch rack for horses, beyond which the animals are prohibited.

Old McGraw Ranch is steeped in history. Pioneered and homesteaded in the 1870s, it was called Indian Head Ranch until John McGraw bought the land in 1909. Used as a cattle ranch and later as a guest ranch, the property changed hands on a regular basis until the NPS purchased the 220-acre property in 1988.

In 1993, the NPS announced a plan to destroy the buildings and restore the land to its natural state. Immediate public outcry prompted the NPS to reassess the situation and seek public and private funds to restore the buildings and preserve their historical significance. Several proposals were considered, and finally an agreement was reached to establish the site as a research and learning center to be used by universities and other educational groups. The Continental Divide Research Learning Center was formally established in 2000.

The trail then climbs along some steep rock slabs and into a narrow gorge formed by broken granite walls. The falls rush over a short cliff, spraying water over the boulders that form the creek bed. Hike above the falls to picnic on the granite slabs and admire the rollicking upper section of the falls. The creek tumbles over several short steps and pools into picturesque basins before plummeting over the steep wall that forms the main section of the falls.

PEAKS AND OTHER DESTINATIONS

Sheep Mountain 9,794 feet
T **OT** Regional map p. 121 (R, 34)

Sheep Mountain is a broad summit plateau southeast of Point 9,776', north of Cow Creek. It has a sheer south face that is sometimes visited by technical rock climbers seeking adventure in secluded areas of RMNP. It has gentle north and west slopes that are perfect for hiking. Sheep Mountain overlooks Cow Creek and the north side of Lumpy Ridge, and though the forested summit offers limited views, the hike to the top is beautiful and rewarding.

Southeast Slope GRADE I CLASS 2   From the Cow Creek Trailhead (p. 167), follow the Cow Creek Trail (p. 171) beyond the ranch buildings to the junction with the North Boundary Trail. Though it is rare to see bighorn sheep here, elk and deer are abundant in this fertile valley. Continue west along the Cow Creek Trail for 1 mile until the sheer rock face of Sheep Mountain comes into view. Look to the east (right) of the face, and find the obvious tree-choked gully that ascends diagonally up the southeastern aspect of the mountain. Leave the trail and bushwhack north to reach the base of the gully. Force a route through the dense underbrush, downed trees, and standing forest traps in the ravine. Stay on the east side of the rift to minimize the difficulty of the bushwhacking.

Climb for nearly 900 vertical feet to gain the ridge that leads north to a distinctive set of rocky outcrops that offer good views of the distant Continental Divide and the satellite peaks of Estes Park. Continue north to reach the indistinct, rounded knoll that represents the summit. It is difficult to discern the highpoint, imperceptible amid the forest and rocks. Enjoy the views from the rock outcrops on the south side of the summit mound. This is a special summit, imparting a sense of seclusion, a reward for the thorny bushwhacking, and all-natural views, as nothing man-made is within sight. Though the distance from the trailhead is relatively short, this low-elevation summit offers a true sense of wilderness.

East Slope GRADE I CLASS 2   From the Cow Creek Trailhead (p. 167), hike west through McGraw Ranch to the junction with the North Boundary Trail (p. 172). Follow the North Boundary Trail as it climbs north at a steep grade for 0.7 mile to the top of a ridge extending east from Sheep Mountain. Leave the trail and bushwhack west for 1.4 miles to the summit of Sheep Mountain.

'Rabbit Ears'   8,290 feet
T | Regional map p. 121 (S, 35)

'Rabbit Ears' are a set of granite blocks that can be seen from the Rabbit Ears back-country campsite. The distinct rock formation is one large granite boulder with two pointed towers (the ears) balanced on top of it. From the Cow Creek Trailhead (p. 167), follow the Cow Creek Trail (p. 171) west for 1.4 miles to the junction with the Rabbit Ears campsite. Turn south and follow the campsite trail as it crosses the creek and climbs a short hill to the backcountry site. 'Rabbit Ears' can be seen to the south.

Dark Mountain   10,859 feet
T OT Regional map p. 121 (R, 29)

Tranquil and undisturbed, Dark Mountain is a small, forested summit sandwiched between the Cow Creek and Black Canyon Creek drainages. At only 10,859 feet, Dark Mountain seems like an easy jaunt up a "hill" by Rocky Mountain standards, but it is more demanding than it looks, and few people climb it. This modest peak has the honor of being RMNP's 100th highest summit. The route leading to the summit passes through two major life zones, with regions of open, montane vegetation and subalpine forest. Labeled Dark Mountain because it is completely wooded on all slopes, it casts a shadow over the Black Canyon, making that name even more appropriate.

Southeast Slope GRADE I CLASS 2   From the Cow Creek Trailhead (p. 167), follow the Cow Creek Trail (p. 171) for 3.5 miles to the junction with the Black Canyon Trail. From here, break away from the trail and bushwhack north to crest a small, forested ridge. Follow this ridge northwest for the final mile to the summit. This route gains roughly 1,700 vertical feet through heavily wooded forest. The summit is a secluded area of trees and rocks with a perfect view of the entire northeast corner of RMNP.

NORTH BOUNDARY

FALLS

West Creek Falls   8,140 feet
T Regional map p. 121 (P, 35)

This pretty cascade is one of RMNP's smallest named waterfalls. West Creek rushes swiftly through a dark granite channel, exploding over a rock slab and eddying out into a deep, clear pool before continuing southeast to join the North Fork of the Big Thompson River. This short hike begins at historic McGraw Ranch and climbs a steep ridge, then descends into the beautiful West Creek valley. The absolute change in elevation between the trailhead and the destination is 320 feet. However, because the trail climbs and then descends an extremely steep ridge before reaching the falls, the total gain for this hike is 890 feet.

The falls are located within the West Creek Research Natural Area—one of three such zones in RMNP. These research sites were established by the International Biological Program and included in a worldwide system of natural areas for scientific and educational purposes. In these areas, natural processes are allowed to predominate

Steve Volker enjoys the tranquility at West Creek Falls

and act as a baseline for man-caused changes measured elsewhere. Foot traffic is allowed but not encouraged, with only day-use activities authorized (no camping allowed).

From the Cow Creek Trailhead (p. 167), hike west through McGraw Ranch to the junction with the North Boundary Trail (p. 172). Follow the North Boundary Trail as it climbs north at a steep grade for 0.7 mile to the top of a ridge extending east from Sheep Mountain. A nice vantage of the West and Fox Creek drainages can be seen from here. The trail is rocky and very steep as it descends abruptly into the ravine, finally mellowing out in the somewhat level terrain of the West Creek drainage. Once on the valley floor, cross West Creek on a log footbridge and hike west along the trail as it parallels the brook for a short distance to another trail junction. At this intersection, the trail to West Creek Falls splits off from the North Boundary Trail and leads west, climbing along the creek through an alluring canyon for 0.5 mile to the waterfall. The scene at the falls is idyllic, as the stream first churns over a short cliff and spills into a circular pool of crystal clear water before flowing like a ribbon down polished granite slabs. There is a rough trail that ascends over rocks and tree roots on the north side of the falls. Climb up the hillside to stand on the dark slab at the top of the falls for a unique vantage of the area.

Fox Creek Falls   8,420 feet
T **OT**   *Regional map p. 121 (O, 37)*

Fox Creek Falls is a modest cascade that lies just outside the eastern boundary of RMNP in Roosevelt National Forest. It can be reached by way of an old, unmaintained trail that starts from private land west of Glen Haven, but permission must be gained to use this route. A pleasant legal alternative is to hike north from historic McGraw Ranch along the North Boundary Trail, then bushwhack east a short distance to the falls. Fox Creek originates on the south side of Mount Dickinson in the West Creek Research Natural Area of RMNP. It is joined by Grouse Creek and meanders east to

Glen Haven, where it contributes to the North Fork of the Big Thompson River. Fox Creek Falls is one of several short cascades that ornament the stream, located in a tight boxy canyon well surrounded by thick forest.

From the Cow Creek Trailhead at McGraw Ranch (p. 167), hike west along the level doubletrack road, past the ranch buildings, to the junction with the North Boundary Trail (p. 172). Turn north (right) and follow the North Boundary Trail as it climbs at a steep grade to the top of a ridge extending east from Sheep Mountain. The rocky, steep trail descends abruptly into the ravine, finally mellowing out in the somewhat level terrain of the West Creek drainage.

Cross West Creek and bypass the trail to West Creek Falls. Continue hiking north and climb another steep ridge that separates the West and Fox Creek drainages. Descend along the North Boundary Trail to Fox Creek and cross it on a footbridge. Leave the trail and turn east (right), bushwhacking along Fox Creek and picking a route through the dense, downed timber and narrowing canyon. A tiny cascade gushes around a large boulder before sweeping swiftly down the creek bed. Fox Creek Falls is farther east of this point. Bushwhack along the stream to a granite headwall that is about 25 feet high.

Diminutive Fox Creek Falls splash over two rock tiers to a moderately deep pool. A small tub collects the water near the top of the cascade before it fans out and tumbles over the rock slab. Hike down along the north side of the stream to view the waterfall in its entirety, which is difficult to do through the thick timber. Though Fox Creek Falls does not offer much in the way of scenic vistas, it is a pleasant spot in a box canyon surrounded by serene pine forest.

> The Earl of Dunraven was a wealthy Irish nobleman who came to Estes Park in 1872 for the superb hunting opportunities found there. He attempted to purchase the entire Estes Park valley as his own private hunting preserve. However, illegal land acquisitions that violated the homesteading laws eventually led to his demise and the loss of his land holdings in 1907. The Earl's resident manager, Theodore Whyte, hunted red fox with his imported Irish hounds in the North Fork area. Fox had been trapped in the region for years, chiefly for their valuable pelts, tragically diminishing the population. After the NPS banned hunting and trapping, the fox population has made a decent comeback, and it's possible to see them within the National Forest and RMNP.

NORTH FORK OF THE BIG THOMPSON RIVER

Regional map p. 121 (H, 27)

LAKES AND FALLS

'Kettle Tarn' 9,220 feet

T **OT** *Regional map p. 121 (J, 35)*

> Kettle Tarn is closed to public use and access from May 15 through August 31 every year. For the protection of the Boreal Toad, this closure extends 100 yards around the pond and the campsite. Please respect all wildlife closures issued by the NPS, as they are important in preserving our precious natural resources.

After a glacier leaves an area, the glacial drift left behind is comprised of rock and earth, and occasionally, an isolated mass of buried ice. When these ice lumps finally melt, the glacial till above it sinks into the depression and leaves a kettle-shaped hole. Usually these holes fill with water and become lakes. 'Kettle Tarn' is a perfect example of this geological phenomenon. It is a small, stagnant pond inundated by reed grasses and surrounded by thick forest, east of the ranger station on the North Fork of the Big Thompson River. With no inlet or outlet, it is fed by rainwater and snowmelt. It is a prolific breeding ground for the endangered species *Bufo boreas boreas,* or boreal toad.

From the Dunraven Trailhead (p. 167), follow the North Fork Trail (p. 172) west for 5.2 miles to the junction with the North Boundary Trail. Bushwhack east 0.1 mile to the small lake.

Lost Falls   9,840 feet

T **OT** *Regional map p. 121 (I, 30)*

Lost Falls

Lost Falls cascades 160 vertical feet over rock steps through a densely forested canyon along the North Fork of the Big Thompson River, south of Stormy Peaks and north of Mount Dickinson. The main section of the waterfall consists of a 40-foot drop that spills into a boulder-strewn section of river where the water sweeps around a protruding stone in a gorgeous natural display. The cool mist that is created by the water rushing over large boulders augments the scene. This is a special place that imparts a secluded feeling even though it is only a few hundred yards away from a major trail.

From the Dunraven Trailhead (p. 167), follow the North Fork Trail (p. 172) for 7.5 miles to the junction with the Stormy Peaks Pass Trail. Leave the trail and bushwhack 0.1 mile south and downhill to the river. Turn northwest and bushwhack upstream for 100 yards to the base of the main section of the cascade.

Lost Lake   10,714 feet

T *Regional map p. 121 (H, 26); hike map p. 151*

Lost Lake is a beautiful body of water set at the edge of treeline in a rugged gorge between Sugarloaf Mountain and Mount Dunraven. It is the lowest in a long string of lakes that feed the North Fork of the Big Thompson River, and since it lies at the end of a lengthy, maintained trail, it is the jumping-off point for numerous cross-country and mountaineering adventures. It is easy to feel pleasantly lost in this remote section of RMNP.

Like many alpine tarns, Lost Lake was dammed in 1911. Fortunately, the NPS fought to acquire the water rights in the 1970s and finally dismantled the dam in 1985. From the Dunraven Trailhead (p. 167), follow the North Fork Trail as it descends abruptly from the crest of a hill into the drainage of the North Fork. At the base of the ridge is a trail junction with a spur trail that heads downstream to Glen Haven. The North Fork Trail leads upstream along the North Fork through the peaceful forest. Soon the trail passes onto private land where a branch of the famous Cheley Camp is operated. The trail skirts a horse stable and riding arena. Continue along the trail as it winds upstream, crossing several bridges that span the creek. Three miles from the trailhead, the trail leads into an open meadow that is home to Deserted Village, the ruins of an old hunting resort. Continue west along the trail to the border between Comanche Peak Wilderness Area and RMNP.

Enter RMNP and hike to the junction with North Boundary Trail. A NPS patrol cabin is located a short distance south of this junction. Follow the North Fork Trail west through open meadows near several backcountry campsites, and continue 2.2 miles to the junction with Stormy Peaks Pass Trail. From this junction the North Fork Trail climbs west for 2.3 miles to Lost Lake.

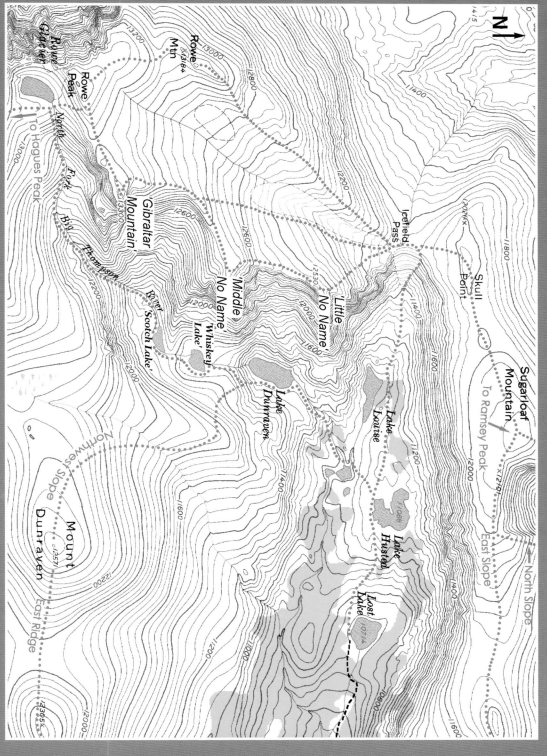

N

Magnetic North
11.5 degrees

N

0   0.5   1

Distance in miles

Lake Husted 11,088 feet

T **OT** *Regional map p. 121 (H, 25); hike map p. 151*

This beautiful, horseshoe-shaped lake lies west of Lost Lake on a tundra-covered bench. From Lost Lake (follow route description, p. 150), follow the trail as it skirts the south side of the lake and deteriorates near the water's western edge. Bushwhack northwest for 0.6 mile through stunted trees to the tundra at Lake Husted. A peninsula of grass-covered earthen mounds juts eastward into the water, and the shore is lined with grassy talus slopes.

Lake Louise 11,020 feet

T **OT** *Regional map p. 121 (H, 24); hike map p. 151*

This long lake lies east of Icefield Pass on a beautiful grassy bench. Stunted trees grace the north shore, and several smaller ponds lie 0.2 mile east of this pretty lake. From Lost Lake (follow route description, p. 150), follow the trail as it skirts the south side of the lake and deteriorates near the water's western edge. Climb west up tundra benches for 1.2 miles to Lake Louise, skirting south of Lake Husted and north of several unnamed ponds.

Lake Dunraven 11,260 feet

T **OT** *Regional map p. 121 (I, 23); hike map p. 151*

Lake Dunraven sits at the base of the abrupt east face connecting 'Little No Name' and 'Middle No Name,' the two unofficially named summits at the east edge of the Rowe Mountain massif. The lake is situated northwest of its namesake peak and is the starting point for a route up Mount Dunraven. From Lost Lake (follow route description, p. 150), follow the trail as it skirts the south side of the lake and disappears near the water's western edge. Climb west for 0.6 mile to Lake Husted, then angle southwest across the tundra bench for 0.3 mile to a grouping of unnamed ponds. From the southernmost pond, cross the creek and hike southwest, fighting through thick krummholz and aiming for the boulder-strewn headwall below Lake Dunraven. Climb up boulders for 0.4 mile to Lake Dunraven.

'Scotch Lake' (11,620 feet) and 'Whiskey Lake' (11,540 feet)

T **OT** *Regional map p. 121 (J, 23); hike map p. 151*

These unofficially named lakes lie above Lake Dunraven to the south. They are in the rocky canyon between the Rowe Mountain massif and Mount Dunraven. The North Fork of the Big Thompson River cascades noisily down this gully, spilling into 'Scotch' and 'Whiskey Lakes' before flowing over rocky steps into Lake Dunraven. From Lake Dunraven (follow route description above), scramble south 0.2 mile to 'Whiskey Lake' then continue south 0.1 mile to 'Scotch Lake.'

PEAKS AND OTHER DESTINATIONS

Deserted Village 8,180 feet

T **[🚶]** *Regional map p. 121 (off of map; east of J, 39)*

Located in Comanche Peak Wilderness Area, this charming spot along the North Fork of the Big Thompson River was once a hunting village, then it was a sawmill, and later, a destination resort. Now abandoned, this historical site showcases a dilapidated cabin near an open meadow—a pleasant setting for a summer picnic.

Jim Cleary and Phoebe Naughton at Deserted Village

From the Dunraven Trailhead (p. 167), take the North Fork Trail (p. 172) as it descends abruptly from the crest of a hill into the drainage of the North Fork of the Big Thompson River. At the base of the ridge is a junction with a spur trail that goes downstream to Glen Haven. The North Fork Trail leads upstream along the North Fork through the peaceful forest. Soon the trail passes onto private land where a branch of the famous Cheley Camp is operated. Follow the trail as it winds upstream, crossing several bridges that span the creek. The trail leads into an open meadow 3 miles from the trailhead, showcasing the ruins of Deserted Village near the river.

The ghost "village" was originally called Dunraven Park. In 1874 the Earl of Dunraven built a hunting supply cabin here. Near the turn of the twentieth century, the Simonds brothers ran a sawmill on the property. Fred Sprague bought the land in 1909 and established a resort there that is rumored to have been closed down by an outbreak of dysentery. The property changed hands again in 1914 when Norman Fuller bought it, but he only stayed one summer before abandoning the site. Since then these old buildings have been at the mercy of the elements.

Mount Dickinson   11,831 feet
T **OT** *Regional map p. 121 (K, 30)*

Mount Dickinson lies at the eastern end of a long ridge that runs east from Mount Dunraven. This wide ridge separates West Creek from the North Fork of the Big Thompson River.

Northeast Slope GRADE II CLASS 2   This route provides access to Mount Dickinson from the North Fork Trail (p. 172). From the Dunraven Trailhead (p. 167), follow the North Fork Trail west 6.2 miles to the Happily Lost backcountry campsite. Cross the river and bushwhack southwest through dense forest for 0.5 mile to gain a forested ridge that runs northeast from Mount Dickinson. Bushwhack southwest up the ridge for 0.3 mile to treeline, then head southwest up rocky slopes for 0.4 mile to the summit.

West Ridge GRADE II CLASS 2   This route first requires an ascent of Mount Dunraven (follow route description below). From the summit of Mount Dunraven, descend east for 0.5 mile to the saddle between Mount Dickinson and Point 12,305' (which is unofficially named 'Crown Rocks'). Climb east for 0.25 mile to 'Crown Rocks,' then descend along the pleasant, rolling ridge for 1.1 miles to the saddle west of Mount Dickinson. Scramble east and uphill for 0.4 mile to the summit.

Mount Dunraven   12,571 feet
T **OT** *Regional map p. 121 (K, 25); hike map p. 151*

This prominent, rounded mountain lies north of Mummy Mountain and south of Lost Lake. It is remote and secluded, located at the west end of a huge ridge that separates West Creek from the North Fork of the Big Thompson River.

Northwest Slope GRADE II CLASS 2   From Lake Dunraven (follow route description, opposite), hike to the east side of the lake, then turn southeast and climb the boulder field for 1.3 miles to the summit of Mount Dunraven. About a half-mile into the ascent, the route crosses a southern tributary to the North Fork of the Big Thompson River.

East Ridge GRADE II CLASS 2   This route utilizes the long, beautiful ridge between Mounts Dickinson and Dunraven. It is an enjoyable ridge-walk along a rocky crest, including the bonus of climbing 'Crown Rocks,' an unofficially named peak that is crowned by unique granite formations. From Mount Dickinson (follow the route description above), hike west down talus for 0.4 mile to a saddle. From here, climb west over undulating topography for 1.1 miles to 'Crown Rocks' at 12,305 feet. Descend 0.25 mile to the saddle between Mount Dunraven and 'Crown Rocks.' Climb west up a boulder slope for 0.5 mile to the summit.

Icefield Pass　11,840 feet

T **OT** 🏔 *Regional map p. 121 (H, 22); hike map p. 151*

This is the lush, green saddle between the Rowe Mountain massif and the Sugarloaf Mountain group. It lies between the South Fork of the Cache la Poudre River and the North Fork of the Big Thompson River drainages. It has a gentle, sloping west side and

Alex Kostadinov at Icefield Pass

a steep east side graced with a large permanent snowfield. The summit of the pass is an incredible place. Water flows from the permanent snowfield on Rowe Mountain to drain off Icefield Pass and feed the South Fork of the Cache la Poudre River. Grand views of Mummy Pass, Flint Pass, Hague Creek, the Rowe Mountain massif, and the pristine lakes of the North Fork of the Big Thompson River are breathtaking.

Stormy Peaks Pass Access GRADE II CLASS 2 From Stormy Peaks Pass (follow route description, p. 156), leave the trail and hike cross-country to the west. Travel over open tundra and talus slopes, skirting Point 11,820' on the north. Hike through this wildflower-and-grass paradise for 1.6 miles to Sugarloaf Mountain. Continue southwest across the tundra for 0.8 mile to Skull Point. From here, descend along grassy tundra for 0.25 mile to stunning Icefield Pass.

🏔 **Lake Louise Access** GRADE II CLASS 2 From Lake Louise (follow route description, p. 152), scramble northwest over boulder fields for 0.4 mile to the base of Icefield Pass. If snow conditions are favorable, the easiest ascent to the pass is on the south side of the permanent snowfield. The route climbs west up loose dirt and rock gullies for 520 vertical feet to the grassy saddle. Another option climbs up the loose, rocky gullies on the north side of the permanent snowfield. This slope is riddled with crumbling fins and rock ribs, which can be tricky to negotiate. In high snow years, the permanent snowfield may remain large enough to cover the entire east side of the pass, making it necessary to use the snow and ice to ascend to the pass. In this case, the ascent becomes much more difficult, possibly even technical, and an ice axe and crampons may be necessary.

Rowe Mountain　13,184 feet

T **OT** *Regional map p. 121 (J, 20); hike map p. 151*

This huge mountain has a modest summit but sports massive, sloping north and east sides that rise above Hague Creek and Mummy Pass Creek. The immensity of these grand slopes is best viewed from Flint Pass. Rowe Mountain also has a great east side that showcases three unnamed summits that have impressive east faces of their own. The three summits are 'Little No Name' (12,530 feet), which lies southwest of Lake Louise and southeast of Icefield Pass; 'Middle No Name' (12,760 feet), with a dramatic, broken face that rises east of Lake Dunraven; and 'Gibraltar Mountain' (13,300 feet), which is actually higher than the summit of Rowe Mountain. There are two permanent snowfields that grace the northeast slope of this mammoth peak, one of which is more than 0.7 mile long. The two most reasonable ways to reach this area are from Icefield Pass and Hagues Peak.

Icefield Pass Access GRADE II CLASS 2   From Icefield Pass (follow the route description on p. 154), hike southwest up green, grassy slopes on the east side of the long, permanent snowfield for almost 1 mile. The grass gives way to expansive boulder slopes. Contour southwest for 0.4 mile to the rocks below the summit. Clamber west up the rocks to the highpoint. This rocky outcrop may seem anticlimactic because it is noticeably lower than Rowe Peak and 'Gibraltar Mountain' to the southeast, but it provides wonderful views of the extreme northwestern section of RMNP.

Hagues Peak Access GRADE II CLASS 2   From the blocky summit of Hagues Peak (follow route description, p. 137), Rowe Glacier, 'Rowe Glacier Lake,' and the castlelike arête that connects Hagues Peak and Rowe Peak stand out magnificently to the north. Descend north over blocky boulders for 440 vertical feet and 0.4 mile to the east side of 'Rowe Glacier Lake.' Skirt the lake on the east side and climb northwest over snow or rocks (depending on the season) for 320 vertical feet and 0.25 mile to the summit of Rowe Peak. From here, descend northwest over rocky slopes for 0.5 mile to the rocks below Rowe Mountain's summit. Clamber west up the rocks to the highpoint.

Rowe Peak   13,400+ feet
T **OT** *Regional map p. 121 (J, 20); hike map p. 151*
This rocky crest lies north of Rowe Glacier at the head of the North Fork of the Big Thompson River. At more than 13,400 feet, it is the highest point on the enormous Rowe Mountain massif, which dominates the region north of Hagues Peak and east of Mount Dunraven. It stands out more impressively than Rowe Mountain's modest summit, and offers a fun hike to a scenic highpoint.

Icefield Pass Access GRADE II CLASS 2   From Icefield Pass (follow route description, opposite), hike southwest up green, grassy slopes on the east side of the long permanent snowfield. The grass gives way to expansive boulder slopes. Continue climbing southwest to crest the summit dome below Rowe Peak. Continue southwest to the highest point, which provides an exciting view of the Rowe Glacier cirque. Rowe Peak is 1.8 miles from Icefield Pass.

Hagues Peak Access GRADE II CLASS 2   From the blocky summit of Hagues Peak (follow route description, p. 137), Rowe Glacier, 'Rowe Glacier Lake,' and the castlelike arête that connects Hagues Peak and Rowe Peak stand out magnificently to the north. Descend north over blocky boulders for 440 vertical feet and 0.4 mile to the east side of 'Rowe Glacier Lake.' Skirt the lake on the east side and climb northwest over snow or rocks (depending on the season) for 320 vertical feet and 0.25 mile to the summit of Rowe Peak.

'Little No Name' (12,530 feet), 'Middle No Name' (12,760 feet), and 'Gibraltar Mountain' (13,300 feet)
T **OT** *Regional map p. 121 (H, 23; I, 22; J, 21); hike map p. 151*
These three unofficially named summits lie on the east side of the Rowe Mountain massif. They each have a very steep east side and look quite impressive from eastern vantages along the North Fork Trail. 'Little No Name' lies southwest of Lake Louise and southeast of Icefield Pass, 'Middle No Name' has a dramatic, broken face that rises east of Lake Dunraven, and 'Gibraltar Mountain' lies northeast of Rowe Peak and is the highest of the three unnamed summits.

Icefield Pass Access GRADE II CLASS 2   These summits are easily climbed from the northwest. From Icefield Pass (follow route description, p. 154), hike southeast up grassy boulder slopes for 0.4 mile to the summit of 'Little No Name.' From here, skirt along the edge of the dramatic eastern cliffs, hiking southwest for 0.4 mile to the summit of 'Middle No Name.' Continue to climb southwest, then turn south for 0.75 mile to impressive 'Gibraltar Mountain.'

Rowe Glacier (13,200 feet) and 'Rowe Glacier Lake' (13,100 feet)

T **OT** *Regional map p. 121 (J, 20); hike map p. 151*

This magnificent glacier is the northernmost glacier in RMNP and sits below the jagged, castlelike arête between Hagues Peak and Rowe Peak. It has numerous crevasses, and in late summer the top layer of snow melts to reveal the dirty glacial ice. Hagues Peak and Rowe Peak both offer outstanding overviews of the cirque headwall. A deep pond, unofficially named 'Rowe Glacier Lake,' sits at the base of the glacier. Chunks of ice break away from the glacier and float in the chilly water all summer.

Rowe Glacier and 'Rowe Glacier Lake'

Icefield Pass Access GRADE II CLASS 2

From Icefield Pass (follow route description, p. 154), hike southwest up expansive boulder slopes for 1.8 miles to Rowe Peak. Descend southeast over rock slopes for 320 vertical feet and 0.25 mile to the eastern side of 'Rowe Glacier Lake.' Rowe Glacier is superb from this vantage.

Hagues Peak Access GRADE II CLASS 2

From the blocky summit of Hagues Peak (follow route description, p. 137), descend north over blocky boulders for 440 vertical feet and 0.4 mile to the east side of 'Rowe Glacier Lake.'

Lake Dunraven Access GRADE II CLASS 2   From Lake Dunraven (follow route description, p. 152), bushwhack southwest up the North Fork drainage for 2 miles to 'Rowe Glacier Lake.'

Stormy Peaks Pass 11,660 feet

T *Regional map p. 121 (G, 27)*

This pass is a lowpoint between Stormy Peaks and the Sugarloaf Mountain massif, which separates the South Fork of the Cache la Poudre River from the North Fork of the Big Thompson River.

North Fork Access   From the Dunraven Trailhead (p. 167), follow the North Fork Trail (p. 172) 7.5 miles to the junction with Stormy Peaks Pass Trail (p. 173). Follow the Stormy Peaks Pass Trail northwest for 1.7 miles to Stormy Peaks Pass.

Pingree Park Access   From the Stormy Peaks Trailhead (p. 169), follow the Stormy Peaks Pass Trail (p. 173) southwest for 5.2 miles to Stormy Peaks Pass.

Stormy Peaks 12,148 feet

T **OT** *Regional map p. 121 (G, 28)*

This group of rocky outcrops lies northeast of Stormy Peaks Pass along the northern boundary of RMNP and overlooks Comanche Peak Wilderness Area and Pennock Creek to the north. The summit ridge runs west from Point 12,148' for 0.5 mile to Point 11,968' and is made up of large granite blocks. The highest point is on the west end of the ridge.

South Slope GRADE II CLASS 2   From Stormy Peaks Pass (follow route description, opposite), leave the trail and hike northeast over tundra to the base of the rocky ridge. Scramble north up large boulders for 400 vertical feet and 0.3 mile to the summit.

Sugarloaf Mountain   12,120 feet
T **OT** *Regional map p. 121 (G, 25); hike map p. 151*

Sugarloaf is a huge, rounded tundra mountain with massive west slopes, a steep south face, and a rugged glacial cirque on the north side. Two other named summits, Skull Point and Ramsey Peak, are located on its colossal slopes.

East Slope GRADE II CLASS 2   This is the easiest route to the summit of Sugarloaf. From Stormy Peaks Pass (follow route description, opposite), leave the trail and hike cross-country to the west over open tundra and talus slopes, skirting Point 11,820' on the north. Hike through the wildflower-and-grass paradise to a small bench below the slightly steeper east face of Sugarloaf. Climb up talus and tundra to the summit, 1.6 miles from Stormy Peaks Pass.

North Slope to East Slope GRADE II CLASS 2   This is a more direct route from the Stormy Peaks Trailhead than the East Slope Route, but it involves more off-trail hiking. From the Stormy Peaks Trailhead (p. 169), follow the Stormy Peaks Pass Trail (p. 173) for 4 miles to treeline. Leave the trail and hike cross-country to the south, then west, skirting the glacial cirque on the northeast side of Sugarloaf Mountain, for 1.3 miles to the summit.

Ramsey Peak   11,582 feet
T **OT** *Regional map p. 121 (F, 25)*

This cluster of rock outcrops is a sub-peak on Sugarloaf Mountain's massive north slopes. It overlooks Pingree Park to the north and separates two tributaries of the South Fork of the Cache la Poudre River.

South Slope GRADE II CLASS 2   From the summit of Sugarloaf Mountain (follow route description above), Ramsey Peak is hidden over a knoll to the north. Hike north over the tundra slope and descend along the west edge of an incredibly scenic glacial cirque. Scramble down the undulating rock slope for 0.5 mile to a saddle on the south side of Ramsey Peak. Climb 0.2 mile north up the rocky outcrops to the summit.

Northeast Slope GRADE II CLASS 2   From the Stormy Peaks Trailhead (p. 169), follow the Stormy Peaks Pass Trail (p. 173) southwest for 3.6 miles to 10,520 feet. Leave the trail and descend southwest through the forest for 0.2 mile to a tributary of the South Fork of the Cache la Poudre River. Cross the creek and climb southwest through the trees for 0.1 mile to crest the rocky northeastern slope of Ramsey Peak. Climb southwest up talus for 0.4 mile to the rocky summit.

Skull Point   12,040+ feet
T **OT** *Regional map p. 121 (G, 22); hike map p. 151*

Skull Point is a sub-summit on Sugarloaf Mountain's west slope, represented by a large stack of granite blocks that rises above the tundra. The top is comprised of a broken boulder divided into two parts by a tapered crack.

East Slope GRADE II CLASS 2   This is the easiest route to the summit of Skull Point. From Stormy Peaks Pass (follow route description, opposite), leave the trail and hike cross-country to the west over open tundra and talus slopes, skirting Point 11,820' on the north. Hike through the wildflower-and-grass paradise for 1.6 miles to Sugarloaf Mountain. Continue southwest across the tundra for 0.8 mile to Skull Point.

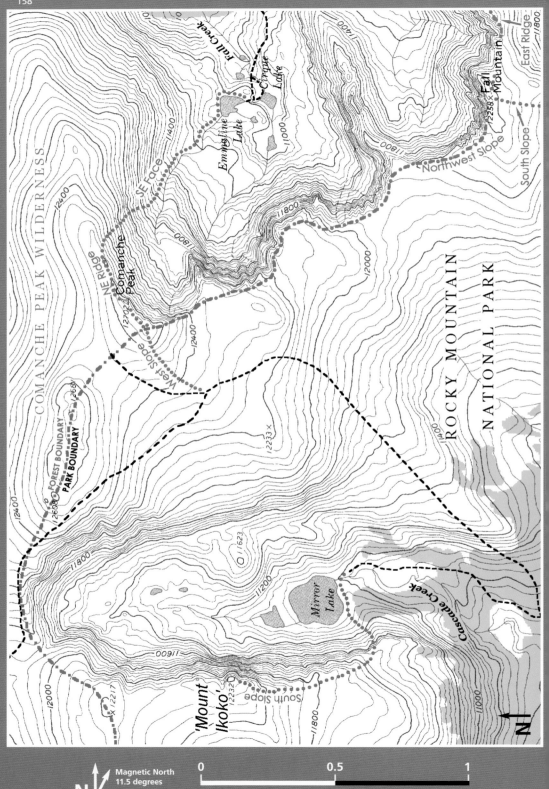

COMANCHE PEAK WILDERNESS

Fall Creek

Cirque Lake

Emmaline Lake

SE Face

NE Ridge

Comanche Peak

12702

West slope

ROCKY MOUNTAIN

NATIONAL PARK

Northwest Slope

Fall Mountain

×12258

East Ridge

South Slope

FOREST BOUNDARY

PARK BOUNDARY

×2608

×2663

×12233

×1623

Mirror Lake

11200

Cascade Creek

'Mount Ikoko'

×12232

South Slope

×12217

N

Magnetic North
11.5 degrees

0   0.5   1

Distance in miles

BULWARK RIDGE *Regional map p. 121 (H, 38)*

PEAKS

South Signal Mountain (11,248 feet) and Signal Mountain (11,262 feet)

T **OT** *Regional map p. 121 (F, 36)*

South Signal Mountain lies at the extreme northeastern corner of RMNP. The slightly higher Signal Mountain is located 0.6 mile northeast in neighboring Comanche Peak Wilderness Area, and together these sister peaks dominate the unspoiled terrain north of the North Fork of the Big Thompson River. The two summits peek out over the thickly forested landscape and offer a sweeping, unobstructed panorama of RMNP's northeastern section, with big views of the Mummy Range and an extensive perspective of eastern Comanche Peak Wilderness Area.

Southeast Slope to South Signal Mountain; Southwest Slope or Bulwark Ridge Trail to Signal Mountain GRADE II CLASS 2 From the Dunraven Trailhead (p. 167), pass the gate and hike northwest along the dirt road toward Cheley Camp for 0.2 mile to the Signal Mountain Trailhead (p. 169). From here, follow the Bulwark Ridge Trail (p. 170) for 5.1 miles to 11,000 feet. Leave the trail and hike cross-country over talus and tundra for 0.3 mile to the summit of South Signal Mountain. To reach Signal Mountain, hike northeast for 0.6 mile across the tundra to the rocky summit, or return to the Bulwark Ridge Trail at 11,000 feet and follow it 0.75 mile to the summit. A rare view of Rowe Glacier, Stormy Peaks, Twin Sisters, and Pingree Park unfolds from these spectacular peaks.

COMANCHE PEAK AREA *Regional map p. 120 (C, 18)*

LAKES

Cirque Lake (10,940 feet) and Emmaline Lake (11,020 feet)

T *Regional map p. 120 (C, 18); hike map p. 158*

These two beautiful alpine tarns lie majestically in a rugged mountain cirque, located just outside the northern boundary of RMNP in Comanche Peak Wilderness Area (CPWA). Huge, permanent snowfields and jagged rock towers create an astounding amphitheater surrounding these pretty lakes. Comanche Peak, the northernmost peak in RMNP, towers over the basin. The only drawback to visiting this stunning area from Estes Park is the lengthy drive to the trailhead. But possible sightings of moose, gorgeous scenery, and a refreshing view of the peaks that form the northern border of RMNP make this destination worthwhile.

From the Emmaline Lake/Mummy Pass Trailhead (p. 167), hike southwest along the doubletrack road for 0.5 mile to a gate, beyond which motorized vehicles are not allowed. Evidence of the 1994 'Hourglass Fire' abounds, with charred scars on living and dead trees and young aspen growing amid the old forest. A variety of colorful wildflowers also flourish in the regrowth area. Pass a trail junction with a spur path to Sky Ranch and continue toward Cirque Meadows. Cross a series of plank bridges

A stand of trees burned by the 1994 'Hourglass Fire'

spanning Fall Creek and come to the junction with the trail toward Mummy Pass. Continue southwest to Cirque Meadows, located 3.5 miles from the trailhead. This spectacular wetland provides impressive views of the majestic Mummy Range. Several campsites dot the perimeter of the meadow and an old logging road leads southwest. No horses or bikes are allowed beyond this point.

Hike northwest across the former dirt parking lot and cross a footbridge over Fall Creek, following a narrow trail into the forest. The route circles the north side of the meadow and enters Comanche Peak Wilderness Area. From here, it becomes much steeper and more demanding than the relatively easy stroll to Cirque Meadows. The trail climbs strenuously along Fall Creek, which showcases numerous scenic cascades. Continue upward through boulder fields surrounded by short rock ramparts and along the trail, which is marked intermittently by rock cairns.

Climb to a prominent shelf above boxy Cirque Lake and continue climbing up the granite bench for a few hundred yards to Emmaline Lake. Emmaline Lake is truly spectacular, surrounded by short cliff sections, riddled with small coves and fingers of water that extend from the main body. Magnificent scenery of jagged rock walls, steep snowfields, and impressive talus fields dominate the view. The summits of Comanche Peak and Fall Mountain hide behind the bulk of lower ridges and shoulders that extend toward the lake basin.

Mirror Lake 11,020 feet
T *Regional map p. 120 (D, 14); hike map p. 158*

Mirror Lake and the three pools that lie above it are some of the most sublime alpine lakes in RMNP. They lie in a spectacular gorge ringed by cliffs and adorned with rock spires and scenic tundra. This location is remote and pristine, and even though Mirror Lake is serviced by a good trail, relatively few people venture to the basin. In winter, the lake is almost impossible to access. Summer brings a gorgeous display of wildflowers and rugged alpine beauty to the hearty hiker who visits this area. The Corral Creek Trailhead near Long Draw Reservoir and the Mummy Pass Trailhead near Pingree Park both offer access to the Mummy Pass Trail, which leads to the Mirror Lake Trail. The Mirror Lake Trail (also called the Comanche Peak Trail) is a long pack trail that comes into RMNP from the north, which can be accessed from several starting points outside RMNP that add many miles to the trek.

Corral Creek Access From the Corral Creek Trailhead (p. 167), hike along the Corral Creek Trail (p. 171) for 1 mile to the junction between the Big South Trail and the Poudre River Trail. Follow the Poudre River Trail across the river on a substantial footbridge and enter RMNP. Hike along the level trail as it parallels the Cache la Poudre River for 0.8 mile to the junction with Mummy Pass Trail. Cross the river and head east through a scenic forest for 2.4 miles to the junction with Mirror Lake Trail. Travel north on the Mirror Lake Trail for 0.6 mile to the junction with the spur trail to Mirror Lake, and follow the spur north for 1 mile to scenic Mirror Lake.

A beautiful, good-sized alpine tarn lies 70 vertical feet above Mirror Lake to the north and affords the best photo opportunities in the basin. Hike north from Mirror Lake over rugged boulder fields and across the glacial moraines to reach the tarn. Two smaller pools, the true origin of Cascade Creek, lie above to the north, at the base of the impressive headwall of Mirror Lake gorge.

Pingree Park Access From the Emmaline Lake/Mummy Pass Trailhead (p. 167) in Pingree Park, follow the Mummy Pass Trail (p. 172) for 6.8 miles to Mummy Pass. Continue west along the Mummy Pass Trail for 1.8 miles to the junction with Mirror Lake Trail. Take the Mirror Lake Trail and travel north for 0.6 mile to the junction with the spur trail to Mirror Lake. Follow the spur trail north 1 mile to scenic Mirror Lake.

PEAKS AND OTHER DESTINATIONS

Mummy Pass   11,260 feet
T *Regional map p. 120 (G, 18)*

Mummy Pass lies on a high, treeless plateau that allows easy passage between Mummy Pass Creek, which drains into Hague Creek, and the South Fork of the Cache la Poudre River. The Mummy Pass Trail travels right over the pass between the two drainages. It is a scenic spot with good views of the Never Summer Range, especially jagged Nokhu Crags and impressive Mount Richthofen. The Mummy Pass Trail starts near the Corral Creek Trailhead by Long Draw Reservoir and ends at the Mummy Pass Trailhead near Pingree Park, or vice versa. The trail is lengthy and varied, offering wonderful hiking through the remote northern section of RMNP.

Corral Creek Access   From the Corral Creek Trailhead (p. 167), hike along the Corral Creek Trail (also known as the Corral Park Trail, p. 171), for 1 mile to the junction between the Big South Trail and the Poudre River Trail. Follow the Poudre River Trail across the river on a substantial footbridge and enter RMNP, continuing for 0.8 mile to the junction with Mummy Pass Trail. This trail crosses the river again and leads east through a scenic forest for 2.4 miles to the junction with Mirror Lake Trail. The Mummy Pass Trail continues northeast for 1.8 miles to the Mummy Pass.

Pingree Park Access   From the Emmaline Lake/Mummy Pass Trailhead (p. 167) in Pingree Park, follow the Mummy Pass Trail (p. 172) for 6.8 miles to Mummy Pass.

Fall Mountain   12,258 feet
T **OT** *Regional map p. 120 (E, 19); hike map p. 158*

Fall Mountain has gentle south slopes and a steep, rugged north face. The summit has an interesting cleavage plane with stacked, vertical, lichen-covered blocks of granite that break off in large flakes. It is a lovely mountain with a beautiful summit area.

Northwest Slope GRADE II CLASS 2   This route is used when climbing Comanche Peak and Fall Mountain together. From Comanche Peak (follow route description, p. 162), descend southeast on smooth, inviting tundra slopes for 1.7 miles to Fall Mountain. The entire ridge between the two peaks is heavily glaciated on the east side. Contour around the large rock formations at the headwalls of the cirques that punctuate this ridge.

East Ridge GRADE II CLASS 2   This is the shortest route from Pingree Park. From Emmaline Lake/ Mummy Pass Trailhead (p. 167), follow the Mummy Pass Trail (p. 172) for 5 miles to 11,400 feet. Leave the trail and hike cross-country along Fall Mountain's east ridge for 1.1 miles to the summit.

South Slope GRADE II CLASS 2   From the Corral Creek Trailhead, hike to Mummy Pass (follow route description above), then leave the trail and hike north for 1 mile up the broad tundra slope to the summit of Fall Mountain.

Cliffs near the summit of Fall Mountain

Comanche Peak   12,702 feet
T **OT** *Regional map p. 120 (C, 16); hike map p. 158*

This mighty peak lies on the border between Comanche Peak Wilderness Area and RMNP. It is the northernmost peak in RMNP and has gentle north and west slopes. It is connected to Fall Mountain by a rugged ridge that has a jagged east face.

West Slope GRADE II CLASS 2   From the Corral Creek Trailhead (p. 167), hike along the Corral Creek Trail (p. 171) for 1 mile to the junction between the Big South Trail and the Poudre River Trail. Follow the Poudre River Trail across the river on a substantial footbridge and enter RMNP. Continue for 0.8 mile to the junction with Mummy Pass Trail. This trail crosses the river again and leads east through a scenic forest for 2.4 miles to the junction with the Mirror Lake Trail. Turn north and follow the Mirror Lake Trail for 0.6 mile to the junction with the spur trail to Mirror Lake. Do not take the spur trail toward Mirror Lake, but continue northeast on the Mirror Lake Trail (also called the Comanche Peak Trail) for 2.1 miles to 12,400 feet. Leave the trail and hike over tundra for 0.4 mile to the summit area, comprised of two highpoints. The northeastern summit is higher.

Southeast Face to Northeast Ridge GRADE II CLASS 2   From Emmaline Lake (follow route description, p. 159), skirt the lake on the east and locate a faint path that snakes up the southeast face of Comanche Peak's northeast ridge. Continue northwest up the steep slope for 0.8 mile to the northeast ridge of Comanche. Turn southwest and hike 0.3 mile to the summit.

'Mount Ikoko'   12,232 feet
T **OT** *Regional map p. 120 (D, 13); hike map p. 158*

'Mount Ikoko' is the unofficial name of Point 12,232', located just northwest of Mirror Lake. 'Mount Ikoko' has an aesthetic, convoluted east face and is easily accessible from Mirror Lake. From the summit of 'Mount Ikoko,' a moderate hike along the tundra accesses Comanche Peak and Fall Mountain.

'Mount Ikoko'

South Slope GRADE II CLASS 2   From Mirror Lake (see route description, p. 160), cross the outlet and circle around to the west shore of the lake (no trail). Choose the path of least resistance and ascend a northeast-facing gully for 0.5 mile to a tundra slope that leads along the rolling plateau that rings the rugged Mirror Lake cirque. The tundra is alive with wildflowers in early summer, and wonderful rock outcrops adorn the alpine topography. This is a beautiful hike.

Once on the gentle tundra slopes at the western edge of the precipitous east face, hike north to the summit of 'Mount Ikoko.' Grand views of the Mummy Range, Neota Wilderness Area, and Comanche Peak Wilderness Area highlight the scene, made more impressive by an intimate look into the rugged alpine gap that is home to Mirror Lake and three lesser ponds.

To reach Comanche Peak and Fall Mountain, hike north from 'Mount Ikoko' over rolling tundra as it descends to the northern headwall of the Mirror Lake gorge. Continue hiking and climb southeast for 1.9 miles to Comanche Peak, which provides a commanding view of the area. From Comanche Peak, hike southeast to Fall Mountain, keeping west of the rugged ridge that connects the two. The dramatic glacial power that formed the Emmaline and Cirque Lakes basin is obvious below the sheer headwall to the east. From Fall Mountain, hike northwest and descend to the Mirror Lake Trail.

DESOLATION PEAKS AREA   Regional map p. 120 (M, 14)

LAKES

Hazeline Lake   11,100 feet
T **OT**   Regional map p. 120 (J, 13); hike map p. 164

Hazeline Lake is the largest and lowest in elevation of five bodies of water that lie at the base of the steep eastern flank of Flatiron Mountain. Set in an extremely remote and secluded location, this lake is difficult to reach. The majority of the hike is off-trail, and a lot of difficult bushwhacking combines with a tricky crossing of rugged Hague Creek to make this an arduous venture.

From the prominent junction of the Poudre River Trail and the Mummy Pass Trail, 1.8 miles east of the Corral Creek Trailhead (p. 167), cross the river and follow the Mummy Pass Trail as it travels along the north side of Hague Creek. At the junction with the trail to the NPS campsites Desolation and Flatiron, leave the main trail and follow the faint campsite path southeast alongside the creek to Flatiron Campsite. The trail fades rapidly east of this point. Continue east to the spot where the creek that flows out of Hazeline Lake joins Hague Creek. Look carefully for the correct drainage, as this is not the only stream in the vicinity.

Cross Hague Creek any way possible (this is a tricky crossing, as the forest does not reach the edge of the creek and there are no fallen logs to cross) and hike through the krummholz and marsh toward the forest. Follow the Hazeline Lake drainage through dense forest and climb steeply up the hillside. Negotiate the steep slope choked with fallen timber to the base of the bench that holds Hazeline Lake. This is a difficult bushwhack through challenging terrain. Top out on the bench to stand on the grassy shoreline of Hazeline Lake. Precipitous cliffs on the ridge north of Flatiron Mountain dominate the scene to the west. Stunted trees ornament the rock mounds on the south side of the lake. Hike south up the drainage to climb above treeline and into the stark, rocky gorge that is home to the four other ponds. This is an extremely scenic spot and is worth exploration.

PEAKS AND OTHER DESTINATIONS

Flint Pass   11,630 feet
T **OT**   Regional map p. 120 (H, 18)

This gorgeous, remote destination is a flat, narrow passageway between the expansive northwest slope of Rowe Mountain and some interesting rocky points on moraines to the northwest. It is small compared to neighboring Mummy Pass, but is a worthy goal. RMNP superintendent Roger W. Toll named the pass in 1927. Toll was an influential administrator from 1921 to 1929 who actively promoted tourism to the area. Toll found flint chips on the pass and speculated they were remnants of Native American arrowheads.

Corral Creek Access   From the prominent trail junction between the Mummy Pass Trail and the Mirror Lake Trail, 4.2 miles east of the Corral Creek Trailhead, hike east along the Mummy Pass Trail (p. 172) as it climbs through the forest. When the trail rises out of the trees and into the marshy, willow-filled expanse of Mummy Pass Creek,

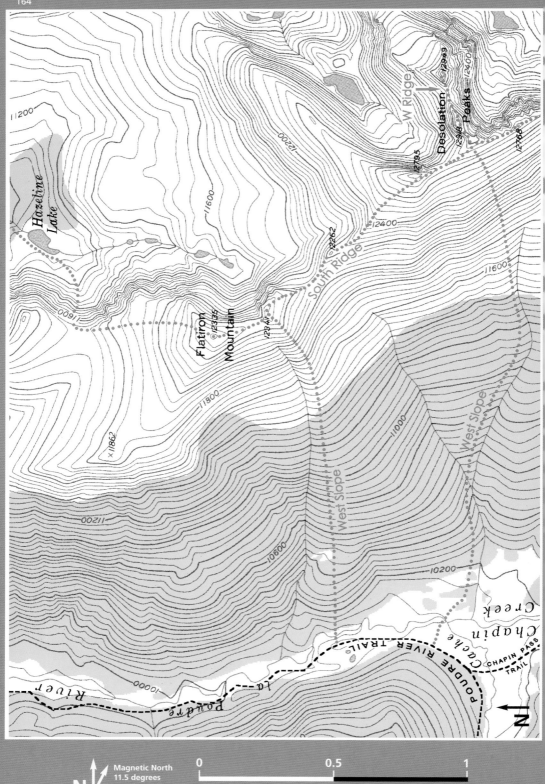

Magnetic North
11.5 degrees

N

0   0.5   1

Distance in miles

locate a gentle ridge that slopes southeast toward Point 11,545'. Leave the trail and hike cross-country up the ridge over tundra-and-grass slopes alive with wildflowers to an 11,800-foot rocky knob. This vantage offers a great view of Flint Pass, Comanche Peak, Fall Mountain, Skull Point, Icefield Pass, the grand expanse of Rowe Mountain, and the majestic Hague Creek drainage. Desolation Peaks, Flatiron Mountain, and Nokhu Crags also stand out. Descend southeast to the flat plateau of Flint Pass.

Pingree Park Access   From the Emmaline Lake/Mummy Pass Trailhead (p. 167) in Pingree Park, follow the Mummy Pass Trail (p. 172) for 6.8 miles to Mummy Pass. Leave the trail and turn south, hiking cross-country for 0.7 mile to gorgeous Flint Pass.

Flatiron Mountain   12,335 feet
T **OT**   *Regional map p. 120 (K, 13); hike map p. 164*

Flatiron Mountain lies 1.3 miles northwest of Desolation Peaks between the Hazeline Lake drainage and the Cache la Poudre River. It has a unique chevron-shaped band of light rock on its east face that makes it easily recognizable from afar.

South Ridge (Chapin Pass Access)   GRADE II CLASS 2   From Desolation Peaks (follow the route description below), hike northwest along the ridge either skirting three prominent 12,000-foot peaks on the west or hiking over the top of them. From Point 12,341', hike north for 0.3 mile to the summit.

West Slope (Poudre River Access)   GRADE II CLASS 2   From the Poudre River Trailhead (p. 169), follow the Poudre River Trail (p. 172) for 5.3 miles to the Cache back-country campsite, near the confluence of the Cache la Poudre River and Chapin Creek. Continue north along the trail for 0.4 mile as it skirts Point 10,855' on the east, past the point where the two creeks converge. Leave the trail and bushwhack through willows to the river. Cross the river and fight through thick willows and marshy bogs to more solid ground. Climb northeast up the west slope of Flatiron Mountain for 1.4 miles to the summit.

Desolation Peaks   12,949 feet
T **OT**   *Regional map p. 120 (M, 14); hike map p. 164*

Desolation Peaks (East Desolation Peak, 12,918 feet; and West Desolation Peak, 12,949 feet) are a pair of jagged buttresses that live up to their name. Remotely situated between Chapin Creek and Hague Creek, these peaks are hard to access and impart a feeling of wildness to any intrepid climber who stands upon their stately summits. The Class 3 scramble between the lower summit and the true summit is exposed and exciting.

West Ridge (Chapin Pass Access)   GRADE II CLASS 3+   From the Chapin Pass Trailhead (p. 166), follow the Chapin Creek Trail (p. 171) as it climbs steeply for 0.2 mile to Chapin Pass. From here, do not drop downhill (north) into the Chapin Creek drainage. Instead, take a right and follow a spur trail east through dense forest for 0.75 mile to treeline. A faint trail continues east, contouring along the northwest side of Mount Chapin and ending at the pass between Mounts Chapin and Chiquita. Skirt low on another faint trail and contour northeast below Mounts Chapin and Chiquita. Climb over boulders and tundra to the saddle between Mount Chiquita and Ypsilon Mountain. From here, skirt Ypsilon Mountain and contour northwest, climbing 0.9 mile to Point 12,718'.

Hike north along the ridge for 0.5 mile to Point 12,768', then continue north for 0.2 mile to the west ridge of Desolation Peaks. Turn east and scramble to the lower summit (12,918 feet), then continue heading east along the exposed, Class 3 west ridge for 0.3 mile to the base of the true summit block. A narrow, angling chimney leads 15 feet to the summit. Squeeze up the fissure (Class 3+) to top out on the high-point of Desolation Peaks for a remarkable view of Hague Creek and the west slopes of the Mummy Range's thirteeners.

West Ridge (Poudre River Access) GRADE II CLASS 3+ From the Poudre River Trailhead (p. 169), follow the Poudre River Trail (p. 172) for 5.3 miles to Cache backcountry campsite, near the confluence of the Cache la Poudre River and Chapin Creek. Continue north along the trail to the point where the two creeks join as one. This avoids a large, wet krummholz field and also makes it so only one stream crossing is necessary, though the river is slightly swifter and stronger north of the confluence.

Leave the trail and bushwhack through willows to the river. Cross the river and fight through thick willows and marshy bogs to more solid ground. Climb east up the west slope of Desolation Peaks for 2.1 miles to the lower summit (12,918 feet), then scramble east along the exposed, Class 3 west ridge for 0.3 mile to the base of the true summit block. A narrow, angling chimney leads 15 feet to the summit. Squeeze up the fissure (Class 3+) to top out on the highpoint of Desolation Peaks.

TRAILHEADS

Alluvial Fan Parking
From the Fall River Entrance Station on US 34, drive west 2.2 miles to the turnoff for Old Fall River Road. Turn right and drive west past the Lawn Lake Trailhead for 0.5 mile to the East Alluvial Fan Parking Area, on the north side of the road. Continue west on Old Fall River Road for 0.2 mile to the West Alluvial Fan Parking Area.

Alpine Visitor Center (AVC) at Fall River Pass
This visitor center is at Fall River Pass (11,796 feet) on scenic Trail Ridge Road. It can also be accessed via unpaved Old Fall River Road. It serves as a trailhead for hikes in the Fall River Pass area. From RMNP's Beaver Meadows Visitor Center near Estes Park, drive 4.2 miles west on US 36 until it turns into Trail Ridge Road (US 34) at Deer Ridge Junction. Continue west on Trail Ridge Road through the heart of RMNP for 17.4 miles to AVC, located on the east side of Trail Ridge Road. Or, from Grand Lake, drive north on US 34 for 22.3 miles to AVC. Or, from Endovalley Picnic Area, follow Old Fall River Road west for 9 miles to AVC.

Big South Trailhead
This trailhead lies at 8,440 feet in Roosevelt National Forest and provides access to the Big South Trail. It is located on CO 14 about 12 miles east of Cameron Pass and 47 miles west of the US 287/CO 14 junction northwest of Fort Collins.

Castle Mountain Parking
This roadside parking area lies at 7,700 feet and accesses Castle Mountain and Window Rock. From the junction of US 36 and US 34 in Estes Park, drive west on US 34 (Elkhorn Avenue) through the heart of town for 1.7 miles to the junction with the US 34 Bypass (Wonderview Avenue). Park along the shoulder of US 34, making sure vehicles are well off the roadway.

Chapin Pass Trailhead
This trailhead is at 11,020 feet on Old Fall River Road, the one-way dirt road (only open to vehicles during the summer months) that climbs 9 miles from Endovalley to Fall River Pass. The trailhead provides access to Chapin Pass, Chapin Creek Trail, and the west side of the Mummy Range. From the Lawn Lake Trailhead (p. 168), continue

west for 1.7 miles to the Endovalley Picnic Area. From here, follow unpaved Old Fall River Road west for 6.9 miles to the Chapin Pass Trailhead. The trailhead is on the north side of the road, and there is limited parking on the south (left-hand) side at a small pullout. Since Old Fall River Road is one way, from the Chapin Pass Trailhead, drive west up the road for 2.1 miles to Fall River Pass and the Alpine Visitor Center at 11,796 feet. Drive through the parking lot to reach Trail Ridge Road (US 34), the paved highway that connects Estes Park and Grand Lake. Follow Trail Ridge Road southeast to Estes Park.

Corral Creek Trailhead

This trailhead lies at 10,020 feet along Long Draw Road (Forest Route 156) in Roosevelt National Forest and provides access to the Corral Creek Trail (also called the Corral Park Trail), Mummy Pass Trail, Big South Trail, and Poudre River Trail. Long Draw Road leaves CO 14 between Chambers Lake and Joe Wright Reservoir, 5 miles east of Cameron Pass. Turn southeast onto unpaved Long Draw Road and drive 8.5 miles to the Corral Creek Trailhead.

Cow Creek Trailhead at McGraw Ranch

This trailhead lies at 7,820 feet and provides access to North Boundary, Cow Creek, and Black Canyon Trails. From the junction of US 34 and US 36 in Estes Park, drive west on US 34 Bypass (Wonderview Avenue) for 0.4 mile to MacGregor Avenue. Turn right on MacGregor Avenue (which turns into Devils Gulch Road), and drive northeast for 3.5 miles to McGraw Ranch Road. Turn north (left) onto the dirt road, pass the gate (if it is locked a sign will advise visitors how to open it), and follow the winding dirt road for 2.2 miles to McGraw Ranch and the Continental Divide Research Learning Center. The road dead-ends into a turn-around area. Signs on the west side of the dirt road indicate legal parking. Only parallel parking is permitted at this location, and there is room for about 15 cars.

Dunraven Trailhead

This trailhead lies in Roosevelt National Forest at 7,900 feet and provides access to the North Fork Trail (Trail 929, also known as the Dunraven Trail and the Lost Lake Trail) and the Stormy Peaks Pass Trail (Trail 980, also known as the Stormy Peaks Trail). From the junction of US 34 and US 36 in Estes Park, drive west on US 34 Bypass (Wonderview Avenue) for 0.4 mile to MacGregor Avenue. Turn right on MacGregor Avenue (which turns into Devils Gulch Road/CR 43), and drive northeast for 7 miles to Glen Haven. Drive east of Glen Haven for 1.9 miles to Dunraven Glade Road (CR 51B). Turn left and drive northwest for 2.2 miles to where the road dead-ends into a large gravel parking lot near the trailhead.

Emmaline Lake/Mummy Pass Trailhead

This trailhead lies in Roosevelt National Forest at 8,960 feet and provides access to the Emmaline Lake Trail and the Mummy Pass Trail. From the junction of CO 14 and Pingree Park Road (CR 63E), which is 34 miles east of Cameron Pass and 25 miles west of the US 287/CO 14 junction near Fort Collins, turn south (left) from CO 14 and cross a metal bridge. Follow the winding, dirt Pingree Park Road south for 15.7 miles to the turnoff for the Tom Bennett Campground. This turnoff is about a half mile before the Pingree Park Campus of Colorado State University (CSU). Turn right on Forest Road 145 and drive down a steep hill to the campground. Continue past the campground for 0.3 mile to the Emmaline Lake/Mummy Pass Trailhead. A 4WD road continues west 0.5 mile to a road closure at a green gate. Park at the trailhead (passenger cars) or along the road near the gate (high-clearance vehicles).

Endovalley Picnic Area

This large picnic area (8,640 feet) is in a wooded area along Fall River, 1.7 miles west of Lawn Lake Trailhead and immediately east of the start of unpaved Old Fall River Road. From RMNP's Fall River Entrance Station on US 34, drive west 2.2 miles to the junction with Old Fall River Road. Turn west (right) and drive 1.8 miles to the Endovalley Picnic Area. The charming picnic area is a nice spot to enjoy an afternoon.

Lawn Lake Trailhead

This trailhead lies at 8,540 feet and provides access to the Lawn Lake and Ypsilon Lake Trails. It can be reached from either US 34 or US 36. From RMNP's Beaver Meadows Visitor Center on US 36, drive west for 1.1 miles to the Beaver Meadows Entrance Station. Pass the kiosk and proceed west on US 36 past the turnoff to Bear Lake Road. Drive another 3.1 miles to Deer Ridge Junction. Turn right and drive north on US 34, descending for 1.8 miles to the turnoff for Old Fall River Road. Turn left and drive west 0.1 mile to the trailhead.

The Lawn Lake Trailhead can also be reached from US 34 (Fall River Road). From the junction of US 36 and US 34 in Estes Park, drive west on US 34 for 7.2 miles to Old Fall River Road. Take a right and head west for 0.1 mile to the trailhead.

Bronson MacDonald and Melissa Strong at Gem Lake

Lumpy Ridge Trailhead

This trailhead lies at 7,852 feet and provides access to Lumpy Ridge, the Twin Owls area, the Gem Lake Trail, the Black Canyon Trail, and the Cow Creek Trail.

From the junction of US 34 and US 36 in Estes Park, drive west on US 34 Bypass (Wonderview Avenue) for 0.4 mile to MacGregor Avenue. Turn right on MacGregor Avenue (which turns into Devils Gulch Road) and drive northeast for 1.3 miles to the turnoff for Lumpy Ridge Trailhead. Turn north and drive 0.3 mile to the parking area.

Steve Volker on the Signal Mountain Trail

Poudre River Trailhead

This trailhead lies at 10,720 feet and provides access to the Poudre River Trail. From RMNP's Beaver Meadows Visitor Center near Estes Park, drive 4.2 miles west on US 36 until it turns into Trail Ridge Road (US 34) at Deer Ridge Junction. Continue west on Trail Ridge Road through the heart of Rocky Mountain National Park for 21.2 miles to the unmarked Poudre River Trailhead, on the west side of the road. A paved pullout, large enough for several cars, represents the trailhead, which is located 0.6 mile northeast of Milner Pass. From Grand Lake, drive north on US 34 for 18.5 miles to the trailhead.

Signal Mountain Trailhead

This trailhead lies in Roosevelt National Forest at 8,194 feet and provides access to the Bulwark Ridge Trail (Trail 928, also known as the Signal Mountain Trail) and the Indian Trail (Trail 927). From the Dunraven Trailhead (p. 167), walk past the gate at the west end of the lot (the road beyond is closed to private vehicles) and hike northwest along the dirt road toward Cheley Camp for 0.2 mile to the Signal Mountain Trailhead.

Winter along the Poudre River Trail

Stormy Peaks Trailhead

This trailhead is in Pingree Park at 9,020 feet and provides access to the Stormy Peaks Pass Trail (Trail 980, also known as the Stormy Peaks Trail). From the junction of CO 14 and Pingree Park Road (CR 63E), which is 34 miles east of Cameron Pass and 25 miles west of the US 287/CO 14 junction near Fort Collins, turn south (left) onto Pingree Park Road and cross a metal bridge. Follow the winding dirt road south for 16 miles, past the turnoff to CSU's Pingree Park Campus, to where the road dead-ends at the trailhead parking area.

Alluvial Fan Trail
See Alluvial Fan, p. 129.

Alpine Ridge Trail
See 'Fall River Pass Mountain,' p. 123.

Big South Trail
This trail is within Roosevelt National Forest. From the Big South Trailhead on CO 14, the trail travels south along the Cache la Poudre River to the junction of Corral Creek Trail and Poudre River Trail, immediately north of RMNP's northwestern border. The Big South Trail can offer an interesting alternative for access to some of RMNP's trails, such as the Poudre River Trail, Mummy Pass Trail, and Mirror Lake Trail (also called the Comanche Peak Trail). The Big South Trail is long and rugged, and a crucial bridge washed away years ago, creating the challenge of crossing the swift Cache la Poudre River in order to continue following the trail. The bridge has not been replaced, and this trail is only for the most adventurous souls.

Black Canyon Trail
The Lumpy Ridge Trail leads 0.7 mile northwest from the Lumpy Ridge Trailhead to access the Black Canyon Trail near the open meadows above MacGregor Ranch. From here the trail leads northwest for 8.2 miles to join the Lawn Lake Trail 0.7 mile southeast of Lawn Lake. Cattle graze the sweeping landscape that provides open views of Longs Peak to the south. Lumpy Ridge's characteristic rock cliffs rise to the north of the trail in a striking geologic display.

From the Lumpy Ridge Trailhead (p. 168), follow the Lumpy Ridge Trail 0.7 mile northwest as it climbs and then descends to the open meadows above MacGregor Ranch. Continue along the Black Canyon Trail as it descends slightly and passes the open meadows. Travel west past trail junctions for the striking Lumpy Ridge rock formations 'The Book' and 'The Pear.' The trail skirts the open meadowland and enters the forest, climbing northwest and much more steeply to a pass between Dark Mountain and Lumpy Ridge. En route, it passes the junction with a climber's trail to Sundance Buttress, the largest rock formation on Lumpy Ridge. Continue to the junction with the trail that turns east toward Cow Creek. Turn west (left) and follow the Black Canyon Trail along Black Canyon Creek. The trail climbs northwest and passes over a saddle between McGregor and Dark Mountains, then it continues to Tileston Meadows before connecting with the Lawn Lake Trail.

Bulwark Ridge Trail
This trail, which is also known as Trail 928 and the Signal Mountain Trail, begins at the Signal Mountain Trailhead in Roosevelt National Forest. It climbs very steeply for 6 miles to a trail junction north of Signal Mountain where the Signal Mountain Trail (which travels north 5.2 miles to Pingree Park Road) and the Lookout Mountain Trail intersect.

From the Signal Mountain Trailhead, hike north for 0.7 mile to Bulwark Ridge and the junction with the Indian Trail (Trail 927), which leads into Miller Fork. Follow the Bulwark Ridge Trail as it climbs steeply and steadily through the forest (with intermittent rock outcroppings providing nice viewpoints) for 4.3 miles to a large saddle between Point 10,890' and South Signal Mountain. From here, follow the trail as it descends, then begins to climb again. The trail rises steadily, bypassing South Signal Mountain and continuing toward Signal Mountain. It skirts slightly east of Signal Mountain's summit and leads to the junction with Lookout Mountain Trail and Signal Mountain Trail, which originates in Pingree Park.

Chapin Creek Trail

Chapin Creek flows through a verdant, marshy valley speckled with flowering plants. The Chapin Creek Trail, no longer marked on updated maps, leads through the beautiful wetland and becomes obscured by bogs. The trail is not maintained, making it extremely difficult to follow in places. It leads from the Chapin Pass Trailhead for 3.3 miles to connect with the Poudre River Trail near the confluence of the Cache la Poudre River and Chapin Creek.

From the Chapin Pass Trailhead, follow the Chapin Creek Trail as it climbs steeply through the forest for 0.2 mile to Chapin Pass. Ignore the obvious spur trail that leads east through dense forest, and drop downhill (north) into the marshy Chapin Creek drainage in order to locate and follow the old, unmaintained the Chapin Creek Trail.

Corral Creek Trail

The Corral Creek Trail (also called the Corral Park Trail) leaves the Corral Creek Trailhead and travels east for 1 mile to the junction with Big South Trail.

Cow Creek Trail

Cow Creek flows through a peaceful valley in the secluded northeastern section of RMNP. The Cow Creek Trail parallels the creek for 2.5 miles and provides access to the Black Canyon Trail and Bridal Veil Falls. It begins as a doubletrack road and narrows to a beautiful singletrack path. It is very scenic and popular, though in spring ticks thrive in the meadows and forest near the trail.

Crystal Lakes Trail

This path leaves the trail to The Saddle (p. 136) 1 mile northwest of Lawn Lake and travels west past an unnamed pond for 0.4 mile to Little Crystal Lake, then skirts the northeastern shore and continues 0.2 mile to Crystal Lake.

Emmaline Lake Trail

This trail travels within both the Roosevelt National Forest and Comanche Peak Wilderness Area. From the Emmaline Lake/Mummy Pass Trailhead, it follows an old doubletrack road (closed to vehicles) southwest for 2.5 miles to the junction with the Mummy Pass Trail, then continues southwest 0.9 mile to beautiful Cirque Meadows. From here it turns into a narrow path and enters Comanche Peak Wilderness Area. It ascends through forest, enters a corridor of rock knobs, and climbs to a shelf above Cirque Lake, from which cairns lead up a granite shelf to Emmaline Lake.

Gem Lake Trail

This trail leaves the Lumpy Ridge Trailhead and climbs for 1.7 miles to Gem Lake. From the Lumpy Ridge Trailhead, it leads through a tiny rock canyon for 0.5 mile to the junction with the trail that leads toward Twin Owls. It turns northeast (right) and climbs through the forest to a rocky outcrop overlooking Estes Park. The trail sweeps into another rock canyon and climbs to Gem Lake, 1.2 miles from the junction.

Lawn Lake Trail

The Lawn Lake Trail leaves the broad valley of Horseshoe Park and climbs steadily north along the eastern bank of the Roaring River for 6.3 miles to Lawn Lake. From the Lawn Lake Trailhead, the trail traverses and ascends a steep ridge, topping out at an overlook of the Lawn Lake flood damage along the river. It continues to a junction with the Ypsilon Lake Trail, 1.5 miles from the trailhead. It then follows switchbacks through the forest to an open, sandy area near the junction with Black Canyon Trail, which is 5.6 miles from the trailhead. The trail then leads northwest for 0.7 mile to Lawn Lake.

Lumpy Ridge Trail
This is a 0.7-mile connector trail between Lumpy Ridge Trailhead and Black Canyon Trail.

Mirror Lake Trail
This trail is in both Roosevelt National Forest and RMNP. It leaves the Mummy Pass Trail 4.2 miles east of the Corral Creek Trailhead and heads north for 0.6 mile to a trail junction. Mirror Lake spur trail continues north for 1 mile to Mirror Lake, while the Mirror Lake Trail (also called Comanche Peak Trail from this point north) turns northeast to climb above treeline and traverse the tundra slopes southwest of Comanche Peak, then turns northwest and leaves RMNP to enter Comanche Peak Wilderness Area. Then it passes a junction with the Hourglass Trail and continues 4.6 miles northwest to the Flowers Trail, which is 4.1 miles northwest of Peterson Lake.

Mummy Pass Trail
This trail is in both Roosevelt National Forest and RMNP. From the Emmaline Lake/ Mummy Pass Trailhead, it follows an old doubletrack road (closed to vehicles) southwest for 2.5 miles to a trail junction. The road continues southwest to the Emmaline Lake Trail,

Mummy Pass Trail

while the Mummy Pass Trail leaves the road and then climbs southwest up a forested hillside. It then enters Comanche Peak Wilderness Area after 0.25 mile and RMNP after 2.8 miles.

From the RMNP boundary the trail climbs southwest along the eastern flank of Fall Mountain for 1.8 miles to Mummy Pass. From Mummy Pass, the trail turns west and becomes intermittent amid the marshland of Mummy Pass Creek, descending to enter the forest and meet the Mirror Lake Trail in 1.8 miles. The Mummy Pass Trail continues west for 2.4 miles to join with the Poudre River Trail. This junction is 1.8 miles east of the Corral Creek Trailhead.

North Boundary Trail
This trail originates at McGraw Ranch near the Cow Creek Trailhead and leads north for 6.5 miles to join with the North Fork Trail near a NPS patrol cabin. It climbs up and over three major ridges and is densely forested the entire way. It crosses West Creek, Fox Creek, and Grouse Creek, providing access to West Creek Falls and Fox Creek Falls. This trail also provides access to the North Fork Trail from the Estes Park area, eliminating the lengthy drive to the Dunraven Trailhead but adding 1.5 miles of hiking.

North Fork Trail
This trail (also known as Trail 929, the Dunraven Trail, and the Lost Lake Trail) leaves the Dunraven Trailhead and travels west for 9.7 miles to Lost Lake (see p. 150 for details).

Poudre River Trail
The Poudre River Trail runs northeast from Poudre Lake (at Milner Pass), the headwaters of the Cache la Poudre River, for 8.8 miles to the junction with Corral Creek

Trail near Long Draw Reservoir. It follows the Cache la Poudre River as it flows north-east between Specimen Mountain and Fall River Pass, staying west of and above the willow-choked corridor near the river, and meandering in and out of sections of forest and meadow. It then skirts Point 10,855' on the east and swings north through the Cache la Poudre valley, west of Flatiron Mountain and east of Willow Creek. It joins the Mummy Pass Trail at a junction 1.8 miles east of the Corral Creek Trailhead and 8.3 miles northeast of the Poudre River Trailhead.

Stormy Peaks Pass Trail

This trail (also known as Trail 980 and the Stormy Peaks Trail) leaves the North Fork Trail near Lost Falls and travels 6.9 miles to Pingree Park. It climbs northwest to Stormy Peaks Pass, skirting below and southwest of Stormy Peaks, then descends northeast to Pingree Park, near the Colorado State University (CSU) campus. Access to the south end of the trail is from the Dunraven Trailhead; follow the North Fork Trail 7.5 miles to the junction with the Stormy Peaks Pass Trail. Access to the north end of the trail is from the Stormy Peaks Trailhead in Pingree Park.

Trail to The Saddle

This trail leads northwest from Lawn Lake for 2.3 miles to The Saddle, a large pass between Fairchild Mountain and Hagues Peak. From Lawn Lake, the trail skirts the northeastern shore and climbs into a beautiful alpine valley above the trees. It passes the turnoff to Crystal Lakes 1 mile beyond Lawn Lake and continues to climb through rocky mounds and then up on talus to end at The Saddle.

Ypsilon Lake Trail

See Ypsilon Lake, p. 133.

See Ypsilon Lake, p. 133.

OTHER POINTS OF INTEREST

Black Canyon

Black Canyon Creek flows from the southern slopes of Mummy Mountain through a magnificent forested valley for 8.9 miles to join the Big Thompson River east of Lake Estes. Black Canyon is home to meadows, ponds, and waterfalls and is bordered on the north by Dark Mountain and the south by McGregor Mountain.

Cascade Lake

This lake no longer exists, but it was a 12-acre man-made lake on Fall River from 1908 to 1982. The lake (8,472 feet) was set amid a group of private inholdings within the boundaries of RMNP, just west of the Fall River Entrance Station on US 34. When the Lawn Lake flood raged down the Roaring River into Horseshoe Park, it inundated Cascade Lake with excessive force, destroying the dam that had been built to impound water for a hydroelectric plant. Cascade Lake was washed away, and the dam was not rebuilt. The river flows through the old lakebed, and the flood damage is still apparent.

Little Horseshoe Park

This tiny, secluded meadow lies at 8,660 feet between Horseshoe Park and Deer Ridge. A series of trails from Deer Ridge Junction and Horseshoe Park access the area. It was the site of a large Civilian Conservation Corps (CCC) camp from 1933 to 1942. The CCC was proposed in 1933 by President Roosevelt to recruit unemployed young men from cities and provide jobs for them in the nation's forests and parks. The men of the CCC worked to improve RMNP, which in turn provided opportunity and refuge for those affected by the depressed economy of the times.

Wild Basin

Mount Copeland from Meadow Mountain

Wild Basin represents the southeastern corner of RMNP and is a rugged wonderland of high peaks, secluded mountain lakes, and delightful waterfalls. Because this area is so isolated, most of the approaches to destinations in this region are long. Wild Basin is bordered on the south by the beautiful Indian Peaks Wilderness Area, on the west by the high peaks that line the Continental Divide, and on the north by the formidable mountains surrounding Longs Peak. A series of well-maintained trails services the area.

East face of Mount Alice

SUBREGIONS with Highlighted Hiking Destinations

MEEKER PARK 179
    Horsetooth Peak 179
    Lookout Mountain.............................. 179

HUNTERS CREEK 180
    Sandbeach Lake................................ 181
    Mount Orton 183

LOWER NORTH ST. VRAIN CREEK 184
    🚶 Copeland Falls................................ 184
    🚶 Calypso Cascades 185
    🚶 Ouzel Falls 185
    Twin Lakes 186

LION LAKES AREA 187
    Castle Lake 187
    Lion Lake No. 1 187
    Trio Falls...................................... 188
    Lion Lake No. 2 188
    Snowbank Lake................................ 188
    Mount Alice................................... 189

THUNDER LAKE AREA 191
    Thunder Lake 191
    Lake of Many Winds........................... 193
    Fan Falls 193
    Boulder–Grand Pass 194
    Tanima Peak 195

Eastward view from summit of Elk Tooth

EAGLE LAKE AREA................................. 197
    Mertensia Falls................................... 197
    Box Lake and Eagle Lake 197
    Frigid Lake.................................... 198
    Eagles Beak 199
    Moomaw Glacier 200

OUZEL CREEK................................... 200
    Ouzel Lake...................................... 200
    Bluebird Lake 201
    Pipit Lake...................................... 202
    Isolation Lake 202
    Mount Copeland 203
    Mahana Peak................................... 204
    Isolation Peak.................................. 205
    Ouzel Peak 206

CONY CREEK.................................... 208
    Finch Lake 208
    Pear Lake 208
    Elk Tooth 210
    Ogalalla Peak.................................. 212

ALLENSPARK AREA 214
    Meadow Mountain and St. Vrain Mountain 214

TRAILHEADS 215

TRAILS 216

OTHER POINTS OF INTEREST......... 219

Clint Lamb and Todd Brownell ascending Lookout Mountain

Ronny Campbell hikes down the North Ridge

Macey Bray descending Mount Copeland

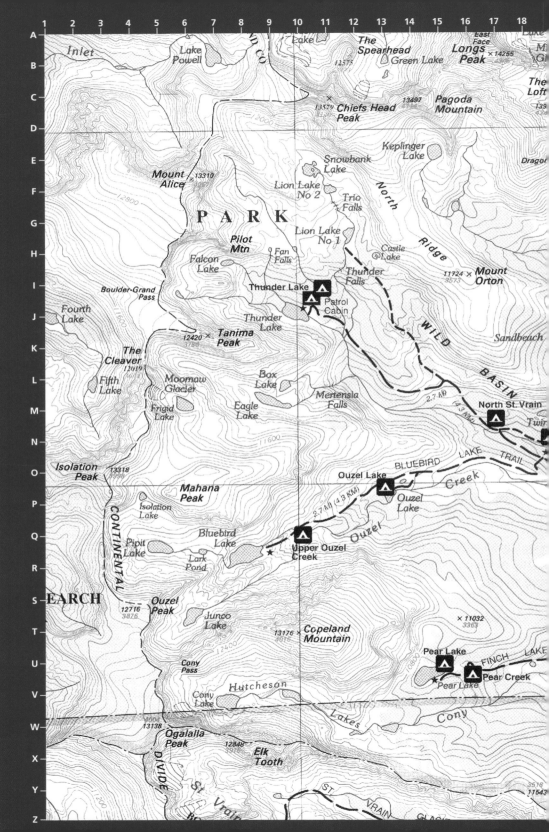

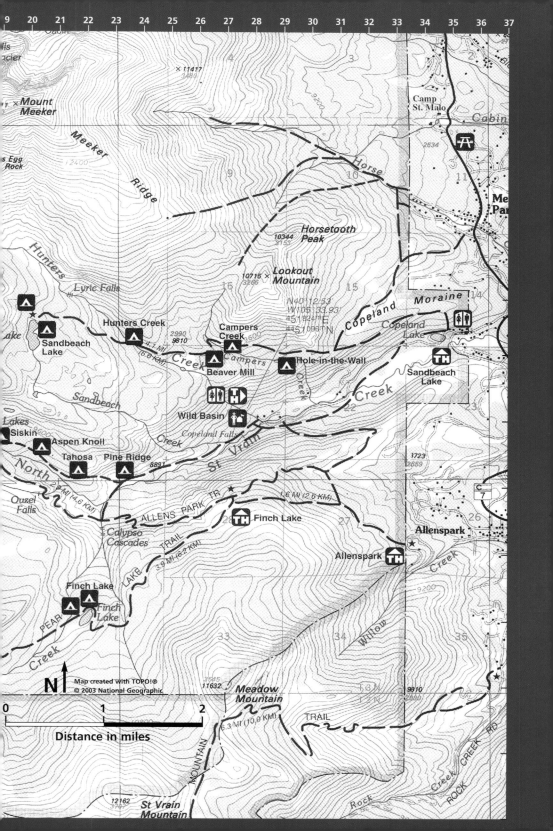

MEEKER PARK   *Regional map p. 177 (F, 37)*

PEAKS

Horsetooth Peak   10,344 feet
T **OT**   *Regional map p. 177 (G, 29)*

Horsetooth Peak is an appealing summit on the fringes of RMNP's southeastern boundary. Originally called "Chisel Top," the craggy summit block of this small mountain can easily be seen when driving south from Estes Park on CO 7. It is a jagged rock outcrop on the eastern edge of Meeker Ridge, which swoops from the summit of RMNP's second highest mountain like a natural flying buttress.

Mountains across the nation that are distinguished by characteristic rock notches are named after the teeth of animals or, in the case of "Teddy's Teeth" on Rams Horn Mountain near RMNP, after famous people such as Teddy Roosevelt. The Front Range is dotted with names like "Tiger's Tooth," "Wolf's Tooth," and more than one "Horsetooth Peak." Fort Collins' most notable landmark is aptly dubbed Horsetooth Mountain, and RMNP's smaller version is also suitably named.

Of the smaller orbital peaks that surround high-profile Longs Peak and Mount Meeker, Horsetooth is one of the most secluded. Tucked into the dense forest south of Horse and Cabin Creeks, the short but steep hike to the summit of Horsetooth offers solitude and adventure. Large boulders sculpted by weather form the unique rocky crest. Massive gaps create the blocky toothlike appearance of the ridge. The hike leads through a peaceful forest, ending with a fun and sporty scramble to the highpoint of the stony summit.

Southwest Ridge   GRADE I   CLASS 2   From the unmarked 'Horse Creek Trailhead' (p. 215) on CR 113N, follow the Lookout Mountain Trail as it leads west-northwest for 100 yards to RMNP's boundary. The trail crosses the creek and continues southwest, skirting Horsetooth Mountain, and then leads 2.3 miles to a small saddle between Lookout Mountain and Meeker Ridge. From the saddle, turn northeast and hike through the forest to gain the chiseled ridge that leads to Horsetooth Peak.

Scramble 0.5 mile along the ridge, gaining and losing elevation while steadily moving to the northeast. (Stay on the west side of the ridge where the scrambling is easier and less committing.) The outcroppings that define the summit area of Horsetooth Peak are so similar in height that it may be difficult to determine the absolute zenith. This charming mountaintop is strategically located to provide a sweeping view of the entire Tahosa Valley as it unfolds to the north of the peak. The distinctive granite block that defines the summit of Lookout Mountain lies to the southwest, and massive Meeker Ridge dominates the view to the northwest.

Ronny Campbell on the summit of Horsetooth Peak

Lookout Mountain   10,715 feet
T **OT**   *Regional map p. 177 (I, 28)*

Lookout Mountain is a captivating summit that lives up to its name. Throughout history, this peak has proved a perfect vantage from which to survey beautiful Wild Basin. The cap rock that guards the summit from easy access elevates those who stand upon it above the forest and provides impressive and far-reaching vistas. The short but steep

Opposite: Spirit Lake and Lake Verna from the west slope of Boulder–Grand Pass

The strategic location of this small but imposing summit drew botanist William S. Cooper to use it for triangulation when he surveyed Wild Basin in 1908. The information he gathered was recorded on the Cooper-Babcock map of 1911. Cooper studied wildflowers and alpine vegetation in the region, and just for fun, set out to be the first person to survey Wild Basin. He subsequently spent his career as the head of the botany department at the University of Minnesota and contributed to the research that helped establish Glacier Bay National Park in Alaska. Before Cooper incorporated the peak into his scientific research, Lookout Mountain was originally designated 'Triangulation Point' on the Burlington map of 1910.

hike to Lookout Mountain leads through a dense forest that receives few visitors. Solitude abounds in this secluded section of RMNP and imparts a refreshing experience far from the crowded trails of the Park's interior. The sporty scramble to gain the summit block involves a couple of semi-technical rock-climbing moves that may intimidate some hikers. Be cautious when attempting the final moves to the top.

Northwest Slope GRADE I CLASS 3   From the unmarked 'Horse Creek Trailhead' (p. 215) on CR 113N, follow the Lookout Mountain Trail west-northwest for 100 yards to the RMNP boundary. Continue along the trail as it parallels Horse Creek, then crosses it and leads southwest, skirting Horsetooth Mountain and climbing steadily through the thick forest. The path is well defined and pleasant, rising at a moderate grade. Continue to a small saddle between Lookout Mountain and Meeker Ridge, 2.3 miles from the trailhead. The plateau is a lowpoint on Meeker Ridge and is heavily treed with limited views.

From the saddle, hike southeast through the forest, following a coarse path of cairns. Clamber up steep sections of rock (Class 2) to the base of the large, stacked summit blocks. Execute a few extremely committing Class 3 moves to climb roughly 30 vertical feet to the top of Lookout Mountain. The moves are exposed and, if the rock is wet, can be slippery, so use caution when attempting this short but difficult scramble. The view from atop the blocks opens up into a spectacular panorama encompassing most of Wild Basin. A sweeping view of the entire Tahosa Valley unfolds to the north. Horsetooth Peak stands out above the forest to the northeast. Mount Meeker's distinctive eastern summit soars to the northwest. Massive Mount Copeland, along with Ouzel, Isolation, and Tanima Peaks, rises to the southwest.

Andrea Charlebeis and Carolyn Foster in Hunters Creek

HUNTERS CREEK
Regional map p. 177 (H, 20)

Hunters Creek is one of the most pristine and visually stunning drainages in the Rocky Mountains. Bordered on the northeast by Meeker Ridge and on the southwest by North Ridge, the river begins simply as snowmelt running down from the precipitous cliffs of Chiefs Head Peak and Pagoda Mountain, then it pools in isolated Keplinger Lake and spills into a lush marshland. After it enters the thick forest, the creek plummets over pretty Lyric Falls before rushing to join the mighty St. Vrain Creek on its journey to the thirsty plains. A beautiful, shallow, unnamed lake lies at 11,180 feet in the heart of the drainage. The entire valley is graced with a wealth of beauty. Much of the valley is reached by some difficult bushwhacking through marshy bogs that are choked with thick krummholz and willows.

LAKES AND FALLS

Lyric Falls   10,160 feet

T **OT** *Regional map p. 177 (I, 21)*

Lyric Falls is a modest cascade in a wooded setting along the meandering path of Hunters Creek. Finding the falls can be a bit challenging because the creek hosts numerous drops in elevation that could be mistaken for a named waterfall on the RMNP scale. The lyrical song of the water tumbling over rock slabs draws hikers to explore the river corridor and seek out the appealing cascade.

From the Sandbeach Lake Trailhead (p. 215), follow the Sandbeach Lake Trail (below) for 3.2 miles to a bridge that crosses Hunters Creek. From here, leave the main trail and locate a faint path that travels along the northeastern side of Hunters Creek, heading northwest into the heart of the drainage. The path dips and rises with the rolling topography, climbing steadily up the valley. Hunt along the creek for the falls, traveling about 0.75 mile to a noisy cascade that spills over a large rock slab. Lyric Falls is most impressive for the pleasing gibbering of the cascading water as it tumbles over the steps in the creek bed. To truly appreciate the majesty of Hunters Creek, travel upstream from Lyric Falls to an open meadow that affords views of the high peaks that border the blossoming and verdant valley.

Sandbeach Lake   10,283 feet

T *Regional map p. 177 (K, 20)*

Nestled in the shadow of Mount Meeker's expansive southern side, Sandbeach Lake provides a tranquil setting for a picnic, a day hike, or an overnight camping trip. It is the

Sandbeach Lake

headwaters of Sandbeach Creek, a tributary of the North St. Vrain Creek that flows east to the plains. The appealing, sandy beach and pleasing views make Sandbeach Lake a popular summertime destination.

From the Sandbeach Lake Trailhead (p. 215), follow the Sandbeach Lake Trail as it ascends steadily along the south side of Copeland Moraine. As the trail steeply rises from the valley floor, look back to the east for good views of the North St. Vrain Creek drainage, dotted with beaver ponds. An impressive view of Mount Copeland lies to the west. The trail crests Copeland Moraine after 1.1 miles to intersect the trail from Meeker Park.

Continue due west along the Sandbeach Lake Trail as it skirts the south side of Lookout Mountain. Several imposing rock outcroppings tower above the trail as it travels along a level, sandy bench that leads through a lovely spruce and pine forest. Continue hiking and cross Campers Creek on a footbridge. Follow the trail as it parallels the creek briefly, then heads west again toward Hunters Creek. This stretch of trail between the two creeks gains and loses elevation and passes through a pleasant aspen grove.

About 0.9 mile beyond Campers Creek, the trail crosses Hunters Creek, 3.2 miles from the trailhead. From its origin on the slopes of Pagoda Mountain, Hunters Creek flows through one of the most beautiful and pristine valleys in RMNP to cross the Sandbeach Lake Trail, then it continues southeast to join North St. Vrain Creek. West of Hunters Creek, the trail gets considerably steeper and climbs steadily for the last mile to Sandbeach Lake, which is hard to fully appreciate from just one vantage. Take a stroll around the shoreline, take in the views and marvel at the unique size and shape of this mountain gem. It is heavily treed on the west side, while the east and southeast sides offer the hallmark sandy beach. Views south to St. Vrain and Meadow Mountains are delightful. Longs Peak, Mount Meeker, the Keyboard of the Winds, and Pagoda Mountain stand out to the north. The lake's outlet flows from its southern end.

> Like many high-altitude lakes, Sandbeach Lake was dammed in the early 1900s to help provide water to Colorado's thirsty Eastern Plains, in this case, specifically for Longmont. Reservoir water obscured the sandy beach for many years. For preservation and restoration, the NPS bought the reservoir and dismantled the dam in the late 1980s. The sandy shore is revealed again below the "bathtub ring" that is characteristic of dammed lakes after they are returned to their natural state.

Keplinger Lake   11,686 feet
T **OT** *Regional map p. 176 (E, 15); hike map p. 192*

This high-alpine lake is tucked into a horseshoe-shaped cirque on the south side of Pagoda Mountain. The easiest approach is not the most direct way.

Hunters Creek Access   Bushwhacking up the length of Hunters Creek valley is a grueling exercise in backcountry slogging, but it travels through one of the most pristine and beautiful valleys in RMNP. From the Sandbeach Lake Trailhead (p. 215), follow the Sandbeach Lake Trail (p. 181) for 3.2 miles to a bridge that crosses Hunters Creek. Leave the main trail and locate a faint path that travels along the northeastern side of Hunters Creek, heading northwest into the heart of the drainage.

The path dips and rises with the rolling topography, climbing steadily up the valley. The trail disintegrates, but keep hiking along the creek for 2.4 miles to a beautiful, shallow, unnamed lake at 11,180 feet. Getting to this lake involves fighting through marsh and willow-choked terrain. From the unnamed lake, bushwhack west and around the butt of a small ridge for 0.25 mile to an unnamed pond south of Keplinger Lake. Turn north and scramble through a large boulder field for 0.6 mile to Keplinger Lake.

North Ridge and Pagoda Mountain

North Ridge Access   A longer but easier route from North Ridge provides more pleasant access to this secluded tarn. From the Sandbeach Lake Trailhead (p. 215), follow the Sandbeach Lake Trail (p. 181) for 4.2 miles to Sandbeach Lake. Hike around the north side of the lake and bushwhack northwest up the densely wooded slope of Mount Orton. Top out on the bulge of Mount Orton's east side at

11,600 feet, and skirt the rocky summit of Mount Orton on the north. From here, either contour along the northeast slope of North Ridge or walk along the crest of North Ridge for a mile, then descend to Hunters Creek as it flows between Keplinger Lake and a narrow, unnamed pool to the south. Scramble north through a field of large boulders to the shore of beautiful Keplinger Lake. The southwest face of Pagoda Mountain rises dramatically northeast of the lake.

PEAKS AND OTHER DESTINATIONS

North Ridge   11,800 feet
T **OT** *Regional map p. 176 (G, 14); hike map p. 192*

North Ridge is the massive, nearly 2-mile-long ridge that runs between Chiefs Head Peak and Mount Orton. It separates Hunters Creek from the Lion Lakes basin. The flat-topped ridge is more than a third of a mile wide and provides pleasant hiking over tundra and talus with outstanding views of the surrounding high peaks.

From the Sandbeach Lake Trailhead (p. 215), follow the Sandbeach Lake Trail (p. 181) for 4.2 miles to Sandbeach Lake. Hike around the north side of the lake and bushwhack northwest up the densely wooded slopes of Mount Orton. The trees give way to rocky tundra and big views of Wild Basin's rugged majesty. Top out on the bulge of Mount Orton's east side and follow the gentle rock and tundra slope northwest to the stony summit. Descend northwest to the expansive North Ridge.

Mount Orton   11,724 feet
T **OT** *Regional map p. 176 (I, 16); hike map p. 192*

Mount Orton is an obscure, rounded mountain tucked away in a rugged nook of Wild Basin, 2 miles south of Longs Peak. Mount Orton offers an up-close vantage of the south side of the three highest peaks in RMNP and an inspiring overview of the Hunters Creek and Sandbeach Creek drainages. It is a highpoint on the beautiful North Ridge that extends southeast from mighty Chiefs Head Peak. This broad ridge is bordered on the north by Hunters Creek and on the south by tributaries to North St. Vrain Creek. Wildflowers flourish on the tundra of the summit ridge and bighorn

Rocks near the summit of Mount Orton

sheep can often be seen in the vicinity. The route to the top of this strategically positioned summit climbs Copeland Moraine, passes scenic Sandbeach Lake, and requires an arduous off-trail hike up the southeast slope of the mountain.

Southeast Slope GRADE II CLASS 2   From the Sandbeach Lake Trailhead (p. 215), follow the Sandbeach Lake Trail (p. 181) for 4.2 miles to Sandbeach Lake. Hike around the north side of the lake and bushwhack northwest up the densely wooded slope of Mount Orton. The trees give way to rocky tundra and big views of Wild Basin's rugged majesty. Top out on the bulge of Mount Orton's east side, and follow the gentle rock and tundra slope northwest to the stony summit. From this impressive perch, seven of RMNP's 20 peaks above 13,000 are visible. Lakes and mountains spread out in every direction. Sandbeach Lake glistens below to the southeast. The Continental Divide rises to the west, and the cities at the base of the Front Range unfold to the east.

Dragons Egg Rock 12,200+ feet

T **OT** *Regional map p. 177 (E, 19)*

RMNP ranger Jack Moomaw must have been drunk when he named this rock formation on the south slope of Mount Meeker in 1921, but since he named it, people are
interested in climbing it. Dragons Egg Rock is identified on maps as one closed
contour line located west of the east fork of Hunters Creek, which originates on the
expansive southern slope of Mount Meeker. The rock is most practically identified by
studying the south face and locating the protruding cliff, then climbing up a steep talus
slope to the base of it. Dragons Egg Rock is not a round feature, but rather a short,
boxy cliff section amid the large boulder-strewn face of Mount Meeker.

South Slope GRADE II CLASS 2   From the Sandbeach Lake Trailhead (p. 215), follow
the Sandbeach Lake Trail (p. 181) for 3.2 miles to a bridge that crosses Hunters Creek.
Leave the trail and locate a faint path that leads northwest along the east side of the
creek. The trail climbs through the trees and is sometimes hard to follow. The trail
enters a large meadow at the base of Mount Meeker's south face. Dragons Egg Rock
is apparent to the northwest. Hike northwest to the point where a seasonal tributary
(often dry, but sometimes a small trickle) to Hunters Creek joins the main flow of
the stream. Follow this tributary north to the central gully that divides the massive
south face of Mount Meeker. Hike for 0.8 mile toward Dragons Egg Rock, located
on the boulder slope west of the drainage. Cross the shallow ravine and climb to the
small cliff. Skirt the broad south face of the cliff and hike northwest to the point
where the top of the formation meets the boulder slope. Scramble up a small gully to
the summit (Class 2).

LOWER NORTH ST. VRAIN CREEK *Regional map p. 177 (O, 25)*

LAKES AND FALLS

Copeland Falls 8,500 feet

T **[figure]** *Regional map p. 177 (N, 27)*

Copeland Falls is an alluring set of cascades and a great destination for families and
those seeking a moderate adventure. It involves a short walk along a relatively flat, wide
trail for 0.3 mile to the falls. The North St. Vrain Creek flows from the remote peaks
of the Continental Divide and plunges through some of the prettiest and most pristine
terrain in RMNP, eventually spilling over upper and lower Copeland Falls near the eastern border of RMNP. After plummeting over the short, pretty rock escarpments at the
falls, the river joins two other tributaries to merge into the famous St. Vrain Creek, which
is largely responsible for feeding Colorado's thirsty Eastern Plains.

From the Wild Basin Trailhead (p. 215), cross pretty Hunters Creek on a footbridge and follow the gentle grade of the Thunder Lake Trail (p. 191) as it weaves
through the forest. Hike for 0.3 mile to reach lower Copeland Falls. Here a spur trail
leads to the river and the lower portion of the cascades. Hike upstream along the path
for 100 yards to reach the upper falls. Upper Copeland Falls is slightly bigger and more
dramatic than the lower section. The water dances over a 10-foot drop then spills
through smaller riffles. A pool of open water swirls at the base of the falls, and granite
slabs line the riverbank, providing good viewing platforms.

'Hidden Falls'   8,920 feet
T **OT**   *Regional map p. 177 (O, 27)*

'Hidden Falls' is a damp seep that slowly trickles down overhanging rock in the summer. In winter, however, an impressive 100-foot ice column forms, enticing technical ice climbers to scale the tower. The "waterfall" lies on the south side of North St. Vrain Creek, and with no established trail leading there, a bridgeless river-crossing is required to reach it.

'Hidden Falls' can be seen from intermittent openings in the forest canopy along the trail. From the Wild Basin Trailhead (p. 215), follow the Thunder Lake Trail (p. 191) for 0.7 mile to a small rise along the trail. Before the trail descends, turn south and cross the river. Climb steeply for 0.3 mile through the forest to an obvious cliff band, and locate the recessed alcove of the falls.

Calypso Cascades   9,280 feet
T **🚶**   *Regional map p. 177 (Q, 23)*

This pretty cascade in Cony Creek dances and tumbles 200 feet over a low-angle series of boulders and downed trees, leaping over obstacles and spraying mist in all directions. It is a refreshing destination on a hot summer day. Cony Creek originates near the Continental Divide at the southwestern boundary of Wild Basin, meanders past Pear and Finch Lakes, then plunges through appealing Calypso Cascades to join the North St. Vrain Creek.

From the Wild Basin Trailhead (p. 215), follow the Thunder Lake Trail (p. 191) for 1.9 miles to Calypso Cascades. It was named for the delicate pink fairy slipper orchid, *Calypso bulbosa*. Look for this lovely flower blooming near the falls in June. A series of wooden bridges traverses the base of the falls.

Ouzel Falls   9,460 feet
T **🚶**   *Regional map p. 177 (P, 20)*

Ouzel Falls is the most popular destination in Wild Basin. It is a short cascade in Ouzel Creek that plunges dramatically over a small granite cliff. The main trail skirts below the waterfall, and a rough spur path leads to the base of the torrent, located in a shaded niche. The trail to Ouzel Falls passes two smaller cascades along different streams and travels through part of the prominent burned-out area from the 1978 Ouzel Fire. Enos Mills is given credit for naming Ouzel Creek in honor of the swift, gray water ouzel, or American Dipper. Commonly seen along Ouzel Creek, these birds bob up and down on rocks before diving completely under water in search of food. Later, Ouzel Falls, Ouzel Lake, and Ouzel Peak were named for their association with the creek.

From the Wild Basin Trailhead (p. 215), follow the Thunder Lake Trail (p. 191) for 2.7 miles to Ouzel Falls. The water drops 50 feet from a rocky shelf above Ouzel Creek. This beautiful plummet of water is particularly dazzling when spring snowmelt increases the volume and gushes over the drop. At any time of year, this magnificent setting is photogenic and aesthetic.

THE 1978 OUZEL BURN

Wild Basin showcases the most widespread burn in RMNP's history. In 1978, lightning started a fire near Ouzel Lake, and it slowly began to consume the thick forest. The fire was monitored and kept within a low-risk zone until high winds swept it out of control and pushed it eastward toward RMNP's boundary and private property. More than 500 firefighters battled the blaze and successfully contained it within RMNP. About 1,050 acres in RMNP were damaged and private property was threatened, causing Park officials to rethink existing fire-management policy.

Prescribed burning is now used as a tool to manage healthy forests and maintain the natural balance of fire in an ecosystem. Thunder Lake Trail and Finch Lake–Pear Lake Trail both travel through areas affected by the 1978 fire. New growth vies for footholds among charred trees, and the burned-out areas are good places to observe the regeneration of forest ecology. The lack of canopy also allows far-reaching views of the surrounding peaks.

Twin Lakes 9,860 feet
T **OT** *Regional map p. 177 (M, 19)*

'Upper' Twin Lake (9860 feet) and 'Lower' Twin Lake (9,820 feet) are a pair of obscure ponds off the beaten path in central Wild Basin. These small bodies of water are tucked into the hillside and offer a secluded experience with good views toward the

Steve Volker at Twin Lakes

Continental Divide. Finding these lakes is a bit of an orienteering challenge, as they are perched on a small bench midway up a forested ridge with no trails providing direct access. It seems obvious that these lakes were named for their proximity to each another, even though their shapes and sizes are different. The smaller one, referred to as 'Upper' Twin Lake, is a crescent-shaped shallow pond adorned with lily pads. Stands of colorful aspen surround this pool, enhancing the picturesque setting. The larger of the lakes lies a bit lower in elevation and is much deeper. Several interesting boulders highlight the deep blue waters that reflect the surrounding forest.

From the Wild Basin Trailhead (p. 215), follow the Thunder Lake Trail (p. 191) for 1.4 miles to the junction with the Campsite Shortcut Trail (p. 217). Follow the Campsite Shortcut Trail as it climbs through the forest and passes several NPS campsites before rejoining the main trail. From here, hike northwest along the main trail toward Thunder Lake for 0.3 miles to an obvious dip in the trail created by a seasonal creek. From here, hike northeast through the forest for 0.25 miles and about 300 vertical feet to a small but relatively flat bench that is home to the two lakes. Turn east on this bench and hike to the larger of the two Twin Lakes. Massive Mount Copeland dominates the view from the shore of this pretty pond, which also provides a unique vantage of the sheer 600-foot east face of Eagles Beak, the impressive rock spire at more than 12,000 feet that soars over of one of Wild Basin's isolated valleys. Hike slightly uphill along the bench to reach the upper lake.

LION LAKES AREA   *Regional map p. 176 (G, 11)*

LAKES AND FALLS

Castle Lakes   10,620 feet
T OT   *Regional map p. 176 (H, 13); hike maps pp. 192, 196*

Castle Lakes are a pair of tiny ponds located along the Lion Lake Trail, 0.75 mile south of the much larger Castle Lake. From the Wild Basin Trailhead (p. 215), follow the Thunder Lake Trail (p. 191) for 4.5 miles to the Lion Lake Trail. Follow the Lion Lake Trail northwest for 0.75 mile to 10,640 feet. The lakes lie just east and below the trail. Hike east and descend through sparse forest to the first tiny lake, then descend a short hill to the second, much larger, pond. Tall grasses and stands of trees surround the irregular-shaped lake.

   Note: The USGS topographical map shows the lakes on the west side of the trail, but the Lion Lake Trail is inaccurately represented on that map. A NPS volunteer hiked with a Global Positioning System (GPS) unit along the Lion Lake Trail and it actually takes a very different course than that depicted on the USGS topo. Castle Lakes actually lie immediately east of the trail.

Castle Lake   11,140 feet
T OT   *Regional map p. 176 (H, 13); hike map p. 192*

The fortresslike rock island in the middle of Castle Lake is ornamented by several stunted trees, and there is an outstanding view of Mount Alice's striking diamond-shaped east face. This scenic lake is rarely visited because of its proximity to the popular Lion Lakes, and the fact that there is no trail leading to it. It is situated on a bench below North Ridge, southeast of Lion Lake No. 1. From Lion Lake No. 1

Castle Lake and Mount Alice

(follow route description below), leave the trail and contour southeast along a prominent bench for 0.3 mile to Castle Lake, surrounded by trees. Mount Alice, Pilot Mountain and Tanima Peak stand out to the west.

Lion Lake No. 1   11,080 feet
T   *Regional map p. 176 (H, 12); hike map p. 192*

Lion Lake No. 1 is the lowest of a set of three alpine tarns south of Chiefs Head Peak and east of Mount Alice. This is one of the most scenic and beautiful places in all of RMNP. This exquisite basin is colorfully decorated with wildflower-laced tundra, short, stark cliffs that are garlanded with verdant growth, cascading waterfalls, and effervescent streams. From here, impressive views of Mount Alice and Chiefs Head Peak loom grandly at the head of the lake basin.

Jim Cleary and Michelle Chase hike toward Lion Lakes

From the Wild Basin Trailhead (p. 215), follow the Thunder Lake Trail (p. 191) for 4.5 miles to the Lion Lake Trail. Follow the Lion Lake Trail (p. 218) northwest as it rises steeply at an unforgiving gradient, climbing northwest into the heart of Wild Basin. The trail meanders through forest and marsh for 1.75 miles to Lion Lake No. 1.

Trio Falls   11,300 feet
T **OT**   *Regional map p. 176 (F, 11); hike map p. 192*

Wild Basin is blessed with an abundance of scenic waterfalls. Trio Falls is a symphonic display of nature's subtle pulchritude and powerful ability to shape and chisel the granite landscape. Situated in the tremendous basin below the southern flank of mighty Chiefs Head Peak, this triple stream cascades over a rocky shelf between Lion Lakes No. 1 and No. 2. Beautiful and secluded, this setting is a must-see for waterfall lovers. From Lion Lake No. 1 (follow route description, p. 187), a faint trail pushes beyond the lake toward Trio Falls and Lion Lake No. 2. The falls are visible from Lion Lake No. 1. Hike along the eastern shore of Lion Lake No. 1, then turn northwest and follow the drainage for 0.4 mile to a rocky shelf below the falls.

Lion Lake No. 2   11,420 feet
T **OT**   *Regional map p. 176 (F, 11); hike map p. 192*

This small alpine tarn lies on a shelf above Lion Lake No. 1. It is a lovely place for a high-altitude picnic, flanked on the north by the jagged, convoluted spires that riddle the southern face of Chiefs Head Peak. From Lion Lake No. 1 (follow route description, p. 187), a faint trail pushes beyond the lake toward Trio Falls and Lion Lake No. 2. Hike along the eastern shore of Lion Lake No. 1, then turn northwest and follow the drainage for 0.4 mile to Trio Falls. Climb north up the short rock wall and negotiate thick krummholz and dense vegetation for 0.2 mile to Lion Lake No. 2.

Snowbank Lake   11,521 feet
T **OT**   *Regional map p. 176 (E, 10); hike map p. 192*

This pristine alpine lake is surrounded by short granite walls and lies on a shelf slightly higher than the bench that holds Lion Lake No. 2. It has a pebble-strewn south shore and several small boulders resting in its chilly waters. From Lion Lake No. 2 (follow route description above), hike to the crest of the bench that holds Snowbank Lake. This lake lies directly east of the long, rising ramp that ascends to the saddle between Mount Alice and Chiefs Head Peak.

Thunder Falls

Thunder Falls   10,900 feet
T **OT**   *Regional map p. 176 (I, 12); hike map p. 192*

A beautiful, unnamed creek meanders south from Lion Lake No. 1, weaving its way through intermittent marsh and forest on its journey to join North St. Vrain Creek. Thunder Falls represents a vociferous break in the stream's passage, interrupting the peaceful flow as it dramatically plunges over a short cliff, forcefully spraying mist into the air. The scene is remote and engaging, with water rushing over the rock slab and shattering the silence of Wild Basin's dense forest. No small task to reach, Thunder Falls lies obscurely amid a remote finger of woodland tucked between the Thunder Lake and Lion Lakes Trail systems. The hike is lengthy, requiring a quarter-mile bushwhack along the beautiful brook that hosts this small, magnificent cascade.

From Lion Lake No. 1 (follow route description, p. 187), hike south along Lion Lake's eastern shore to the outlet, and follow the creek as it gradually descends through the forest. The stream winds through bogs and patches of downed trees, dropping more abruptly as it nears the falls. The noise of the water rushing over the granite cliff and the steepness of the topography are clues to finding the tumbling waterfall. The falls are framed by tall pine trees and highlighted by the dark granite cliff, located 0.3 mile south of Lion Lake No. 1.

PEAKS

Mount Alice 13,310 feet

T **OT** *Regional map p. 176 (F, 6); hike map p. 192*

Mount Alice

The sheer, 1,000-foot diamond-shaped east face of Mount Alice makes this peak easily recognizable. This bulky, massive mountain is on the Continental Divide, 1.8 miles southwest of Chiefs Head Peak. It has a lot of notable characteristics and imposes its enormous northern buttress into upper North Inlet basin. This is a fun peak to climb, and it affords panoramic views of a large section of RMNP.

Hourglass Ridge GRADE II CLASS 2+ This exciting route climbs along a narrow ridge between the dramatic east and north faces of this great mountain. From Snowbank Lake (follow route description, opposite), hike west toward the obvious, broad ramp that leads to the sizable saddle between Chiefs Head Peak and Mount Alice. The ramp is extremely scenic and ornamented with wildflowers in July. A faint path leads up the ramp to the saddle, 1.1 miles from Snowbank Lake.

Turn south and hike along tundra to Hourglass Ridge, the jagged rock neck that traverses to the expansive talus slope that leads to Mount Alice's summit. Descend along the ridge and negotiate some obstacles on the west side (Class 2+). This route is exciting and exposed, but easier than it looks. Reach the steep talus slope and climb steadily up the rocky incline to the summit, 0.6 mile from the Alice–Chiefs Head saddle.

South Ridge GRADE II CLASS 2 This is the easiest route to Mount Alice's grand summit. From Boulder–Grand Pass (follow route description, p. 194), head north and hike along the Continental Divide over grassy tundra for 1.2 miles to the summit. This gentle slope is long, but uncomplicated.

Southeast Slope GRADE II CLASS 2 From Lion Lake No. 1 (follow route description, p. 187), skirt the lake on the south and hike west cross-country for 0.6 mile to the base of a bowl below Pilot Mountain and Mount Alice. A large, wide gully between the two peaks leads to the Continental Divide. Climb up the grassy boulder slope for 1.2 miles to the Continental Divide. Turn north and hike up talus and tundra for 0.1 mile to Mount Alice's summit.

Pilot Mountain 12,200+ feet

T **OT** *Regional map p. 176 (H, 8); hike map p. 192*

This confusing little peak is not on the Continental Divide between Boulder–Grand Pass and Mount Alice, but it is the jagged apex of an arm that runs east from the Continental Divide, 0.6 mile southeast of Mount Alice. Pilot Mountain goes against the idea that a summit is the highest point on a particular feature, and it is not the highpoint on the ridge. Pilot is a difficult summit to reach, but has its rewards. The sharp, serrated ridge that runs east from the divide is a special feature, and the top of Pilot Mountain is a magical place. The Northeast Face and Northwest Ridge Route is a difficult route, but it is the easiest way to the summit of this little peak. From the Wild Basin Trailhead (p. 215), choose any of the three following approach routes to reach the base of Pilot Mountain's northeast face, then follow the detailed directions to the summit.

Lion Lake Access to base of route

From Lion Lake No. 1 (follow route description, p. 187), bushwhack west over mixed terrain of talus and boulders to the bowl below the northeast face of Pilot Mountain. From here, scramble southwest up a wide scree gully that gives way to a narrower scree gully and access a grassy ledge that traverses east along Pilot Mountain's northeast face (Class 3).

Thunder Lake Access to base of route

Follow the route description to Fan Falls via Thunder Lake (p. 193) and continue to the unnamed lake north of Fan Falls. Skirt this lake on the north and hike over mixed terrain to the bowl below the northeast face of Pilot Mountain. Scramble southwest up a wide scree gully that gives way to a narrower scree gully and accesses a grassy ledge that traverses east along Pilot Mountain's northeast face (Class 3).

Boulder–Grand Pass Access to base of route

From Boulder–Grand Pass (follow route description, p. 194), turn north and climb over talus and tundra along the Continental Divide to a saddle between Mount Alice and the beginning of the east ridge that forms Pilot Mountain. This saddle provides access to a small bowl on the south side of Mount Alice. Descend east through the steep gully over loose scree, rocks, and grass to where it really broadens out above Pilot Mountain, then traverse southeast on big boulders to a large, flat grassy slope that leads to a cliff section above Pilot. Descend a very steep gully (Class 3) through the cliff section, keeping close to the main ridge. Traverse east on loose boulders, aiming for the grassy ledge on Pilot's northeast face.

Northeast Face and Northwest Ridge Route GRADE II CLASS 4

From the west end of the grassy ledge on Pilot Mountain's northeast face (see previously described access routes), the knife-edge ridge just west of Pilot Mountain's summit rises magnificently above. It may be tempting to ascend directly to the ridgecrest of Pilot Mountain, but this is more difficult than traversing across the northeast face. To keep the climbing difficulty at a minimum, turn east on the grassy ledge and angle up to the base of a prominent notch between the knife-edge west ridge and the summit of Pilot Mountain.

About 10 yards below the cleft, a steep Class 4 chimney leads to narrow, slanting ramps on the northeast face of Pilot that lead diagonally to the summit. The chimney ascends vertically to the ramps, and presents difficult Class 4 climbing. Clamber to the top of the chimney and access the diagonal ledge system, riddled with upper Class 3 and lower Class 4 moves, which is very exposed to the north. Falling here is not an option, so use caution, as the rock is somewhat slick and laden with moss. Avoid climbing this section in wet or snowy conditions. Ascend to the tiny summit, which will only comfortably seat two or three people. Huge exposure to the south makes this unique perch very exciting.

THUNDER LAKE AREA   *Regional map p. 176 (I, 9)*

LAKES AND FALLS

Thunder Lake   10,574 feet

T *Regional map p. 176 (J, 10); hike maps pp. 192, 196*

From the Wild Basin Trailhead, the Thunder Lake Trail climbs west for 6.2 miles to Thunder Lake, providing access to numerous destinations in northern Wild Basin. From the Wild Basin Trailhead (p. 215), follow the Thunder Lake Trail and cross Hunters Creek on a foot-bridge. Follow the wide, flat trail to Copeland Falls, 0.3 mile from the trailhead. Named for an early homesteader, this small cascade in the North St. Vrain Creek is a nice resting stop.

Baby marmots, Thunder Lake Area

From Copeland Falls, the trail climbs more steadily through the forest for almost 1.2 miles to the junction with the Campsite Shortcut Trail (p. 217), which is an alternate trail that leads to several backcountry campsites and rejoins the Thunder Lake Trail 3.8 miles from the Wild Basin Trailhead. This alternate trail is 1.7 miles long, shortcutting the Thunder Lake Trail by 0.7 mile. Continue along the main trail to a bridge that crosses North St. Vrain Creek and continues south along Cony Creek to the intersection with the Allenspark–Wild Basin Trail. Turn west (right) at this junction to arrive at Calypso Cascades, 1.9 miles from the Wild Basin Trailhead.

Cross the base of the cascades on a series of bridges and continue hiking as the trail enters one of the areas affected by the Ouzel Fire. Charred dead trees and new growth denote the burn area, and the lack of canopy allows for outstanding views of Mount Meeker and Longs Peak above a ridge to the north. From here, the trail climbs switch-backs and ascends a ridge to Ouzel Falls. This beautiful 50-foot fall in Ouzel Creek is particularly dazzling when spring snowmelt pushes high volumes of water over the drop. Cross the bridge at Ouzel Falls and continue hiking to the junction with the Bluebird Lake Trail, 3.4 miles from the trailhead.

Continue along the Thunder Lake Trail and cross North St. Vrain Creek on a foot-bridge. Climb slightly to the junction with the northwest end of the Campsite Shortcut Trail. From here, hike northwest along the Thunder Lake Trail for 0.7 mile through thick forest to the junction with the Lion Lake Trail, 4.5 miles from the Wild Basin Trailhead. From here, continue northwest for 1.6 miles to Thunder Lake. Immediately before Thunder Lake, the trail crests a rise and then descends to a small meadow south-east of the lake. A NPS patrol cabin is located on the northeast-ern shore. Thunder Lake is mag-nificent, bordered on the south by Tanima Peak. Boulder–Grand Pass lies to the west and craggy Pilot Mountain and massive Mount Alice stand out to the northwest. This is a popular des-tination for hikers seeking a long trail hike to a pretty alpine lake.

Thunder Lake patrol cabin

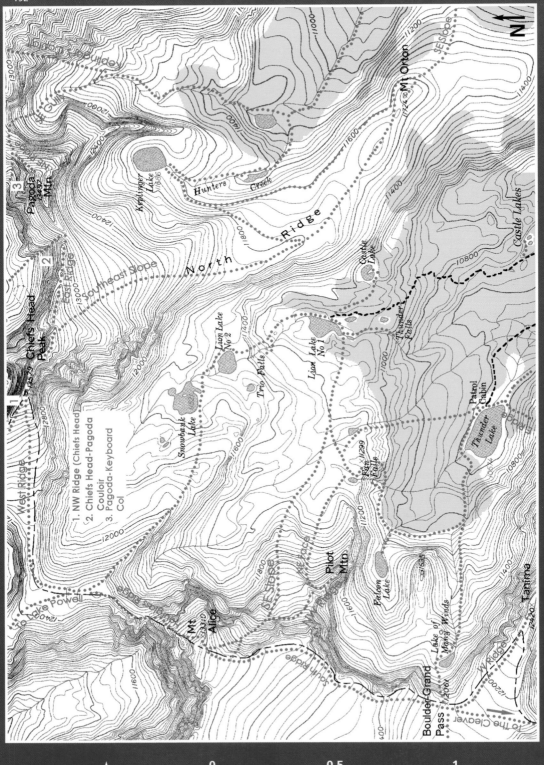

Magnetic North
11.5 degrees

Distance in miles

0   0.5   1

Falcon Lake 11,060 feet

T **OT** *Regional map p. 176 (H, 7); hike map p. 192*

Falcon Lake lies in a rocky cirque below the 900-foot south face of Pilot Mountain and is roughly a third the size of Thunder Lake. It is a splendid destination for the adventurous hiker. Stark granite surrounds the deep blue lake in a setting of alpine splendor. From the Wild Basin Trailhead (p. 215), follow the Thunder Lake Trail (p. 191) for 6.2 miles to Thunder Lake. At Thunder Lake, pass the NPS patrol cabin and continue along a well-worn trail that skirts the northern shore of the lake. This trail crosses the lake's inlet on a series of footbridges and continues west toward Lake of Many Winds at the foot of Boulder–Grand Pass. This is not the destination, so look sharply when hiking along the trail for a good place to break away from the path and travel cross-country in a northerly direction through beautiful alpine meadows and stunted trees to cross the stream that cascades out of Falcon Lake. Turn northwest and climb along rocky benches to Falcon Lake's outlet. Hike through krummholz to the eastern shore of the beautiful tarn. Boulder–Grand Pass stands out to the southwest.

Lake of Many Winds 11,620 feet

T **OT** *Regional map p. 176 (I, 6); hike map p. 192*

This gorgeous, round lake lies at the foot of majestic Boulder-Grand Pass and is one of three high-alpine tarns that drain into scenic Thunder Lake. Powerful winds often funnel over the Continental Divide at Boulder–Grand Pass, pushing eastward past the boulder-strewn shores of this isolated lake.

From the Wild Basin Trailhead (p. 215), follow the Thunder Lake Trail (p. 191) for 6.2 miles to Thunder Lake. At Thunder Lake, pass the NPS patrol cabin and continue on the well-worn trail that skirts the northern shore of the lake. This trail crosses the inlet on a series of footbridges and continues west through scenic topography. The trail leaves the trees and then enters a grassy alpine ravine between the creek that flows from Lake of Many Winds and Point 11,635' to the north. Wildflowers thrive in this gully in July. The trail becomes less distinct but is still manageable to follow as it ambles up the gorge. Climb steeply over boulders to the top of the rock bench that holds the lake, and behold a superb view of Boulder–Grand Pass.

Lake of Many Winds and Boulder–Grand Pass

Fan Falls 11,160 feet

T **OT** *Regional map p. 176 (H, 9); hike map p. 192*

Nestled at the foot of Pilot Mountain in a remote section of Wild Basin, Fan Falls thunders down broken granite cliffs in a raucous display of magnificence. This glorious cascade of rushing mountain water tumbles over at least three main tiers of jumbled rock shelves before fanning out through a hillside of cobblestones intermixed with tufts of lush, green plant communities. Scenic, overhanging crags tower over the landscape. The hike involves a long walk along the Thunder Lake Trail then a charming off-trail excursion over varied terrain to reach the refreshing spray of the waterfall.

Route to the base of Fan Falls From the Wild Basin Trailhead (p. 215), follow the Thunder Lake Trail (p. 191) for 6.2 miles to Thunder Lake. At Thunder Lake, pass the NPS patrol cabin and continue along a well-worn trail that skirts the northern

Alex Kostadinov and Katy Nye at Fan Falls

shore of the lake. This trail crosses the lake's inlet on a series of footbridges and continues west toward Lake of Many Winds at the foot of Boulder–Grand Pass. This is not the destination, so look carefully when hiking along the trail for a good place to break away from the path and travel cross-country through beautiful alpine meadows and stunted trees in a northerly direction to cross the stream that cascades out of Falcon Lake.

Continue hiking northeast toward Fan Falls over marshy ground. Outstanding views of Longs Peak, Mount Meeker, and Tanima Peak present themselves along the way. Climb the lush benches below Fan Falls to reach the base of the cascade. A stunning unnamed lake above the falls provides plenty of water, which plummets dramatically over the precipices in a vibrant display of natural beauty. Look to the south and southwest for views of Boulder–Grand Pass and Tanima Peak's north face. The far west end of Thunder Lake can be seen at the base of Tanima Peak. Pilot Mountain's steep granite walls rise to the west, highlighting the scenery around the falls. Alpine flowers abound in the wet regions below the main body of the falls, growing amid fields of green grasses and thick groups of plants.

To reach the unnamed lake and the origin of the waterfall, skirt to the east side of the cascade to avoid the cliffs that surround it. Climb at a moderate grade through the sparse forest to the lake basin below Pilot Mountain and Mount Alice. Walk to the south end of the unnamed lake to a cliff at the top of the falls for a wonderful view of the water gushing through a narrow channel and fanning out at the bottom.

Direct route to the top of Fan Falls   From Thunder Lake, turn north and bushwhack upslope for 0.75 mile through the forest to top out on a bench that holds the unnamed 11,220-foot lake. This lake is the headwaters of Fan Falls. Turn west and hike 0.1 mile to the top of the falls.

PEAKS AND OTHER DESTINATIONS

Boulder–Grand Pass   12,061 feet
T **OT**   *Regional map p. 176 (I, 5); hike maps pp. 192, 196*

This wonderful, tundra-laden pass is on the Continental Divide and provides access between East Inlet and Wild Basin. Breathtaking scenery and adventurous hiking draws countless trekkers to use it as a thoroughfare to access a myriad of destinations. One of the most enticing options is to cross the Continental Divide here on a through-hike from the Wild Basin Trailhead to the East Inlet Trailhead.

East Access GRADE II CLASS 2   From the Wild Basin Trailhead (p. 215), follow the Thunder Lake Trail (p. 191) for 6.2 miles to Thunder Lake. At Thunder Lake, pass the NPS patrol cabin and continue along a well-worn trail that skirts the northern shore of the lake. This trail crosses the inlet on a series of footbridges and continues west for 1.3 miles to Lake of Many Winds at the foot of Boulder–Grand Pass. Skirt this lake on the north shore and hike up dirt and talus to the base of the pass. A rough trail climbs the north side of the pass. The route is very steep with loose rocks and dirt that complicate the ascent. A snowfield at the southern headwall of the pass persists for much of the year. The route tops out on the lovely tundra of Boulder–Grand Pass.

West Access GRADE II CLASS 2   See Region 6, p. 283.

Alex Kostadinov and Katy Nye descend Boulder–Grand Pass

Tanima Peak 12,420 feet
T **OT** *Regional map p. 176 (K, 7); hike maps pp. 192, 196*

Tanima Peak is a long, modest hump that juts eastward from the Continental Divide south of Boulder–Grand Pass. It has a steep north face that rises above Thunder Lake and a precipitous south side that towers over Box and Eagle Lakes.

West Ridge GRADE II CLASS 2
This is the most straightforward route up Tanima Peak. From Boulder–Grand Pass (follow route description, opposite), hike south, then east, over pleasant tundra and talus for 0.6 mile to the humble summit of Tanima.

East Ridge GRADE II CLASS 3
From the Wild Basin Trailhead (p. 215), follow the Thunder Lake Trail (p. 191) for 6.2 miles to Thunder Lake. From Thunder Lake, cross the outlet, hike southwest, and bushwhack to the base of Tanima Peak's east ridge. Climb southwest up the steep, loose talus slope, bypassing short cliff bands (Class 3) for 1,000 vertical feet to the east ridge. Turn west and scramble along the east ridge (Class 2) for 0.8 mile to the summit.

Continental Divide Crossing (Wild Basin Trailhead to East Inlet Trailhead)
T **OT** *Regional map p. 176–177 (N, 28 to I, 1, and off of map to the west)*

This is a long, exciting, one-day hike (Grade II, Class 2) that leaves the Wild Basin Trailhead to penetrate the heart of Wild Basin, then climbs Boulder–Grand Pass and crosses the Continental Divide. It then descends to Fourth Lake and travels downhill along the East Inlet Trail to the East Inlet Trailhead. The route involves 3,600 vertical feet of elevation gain and 3,700 feet of elevation loss in 17.3 miles. It can be completed in reverse as well, from the East Inlet Trailhead to the Wild Basin Trailhead.

From the Wild Basin Trailhead (p. 215), follow the Thunder Lake Trail (p. 191) west for 6.2 miles to Thunder Lake. Climb west for 1.6 miles past Lake of Many Winds and up Boulder–Grand Pass (follow route description, opposite). Descend west and bushwhack to Fourth Lake (Region 6, p. 277), then follow a rough trail west along the north side of Spirit Lake to the east end of Lake Verna. Locate the East Inlet Trail at the west end of Lake Verna and follow it west for 6.9 miles to the East Inlet Trailhead.

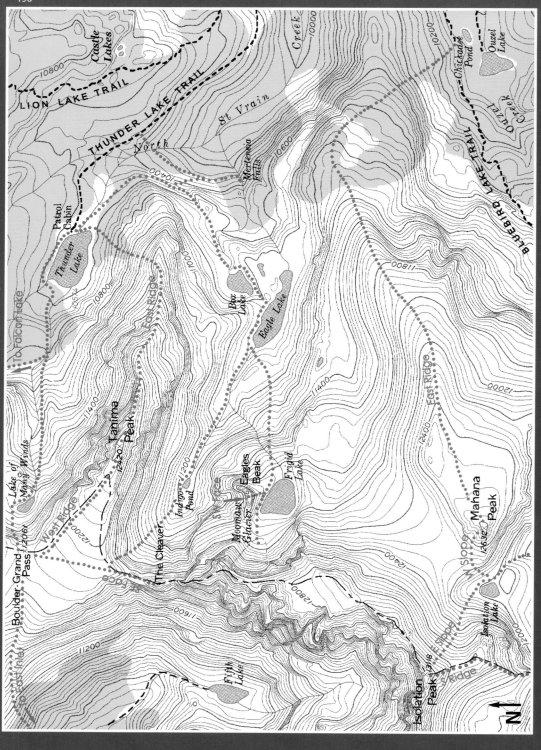

EAGLE LAKE AREA   Regional map p. 176 (M, 9)

LAKES AND FALLS

Mertensia Falls   10,360 feet

T **OT** *Regional map p. 176 (L, 11); hike map p. 196*

Of the 31 named waterfalls in RMNP, Mertensia Falls is an easy contender for the most spectacular. This magnificent feature is seen from above as a silvery ribbon through the trees from the popular Thunder Lake Trail, but the falls erupt into a massive, noisy display of rushing water in a superb alpine setting when viewed at close range. The creek spills through a narrow, rocky gorge, then fans out into a marshy area that promotes a profusion of the wildflowers that give the falls their name. Because it is difficult to access, few people ever see the grandeur of Mertensia Falls' secret splendor. "Mertensia" pertains to a genus of herbs belonging to the family *boraginaceae* that have blue or purple flowers shaped like funnels. Blue chiming bells prosper in the lush wetlands created by the waterfall. They are common throughout the Park and can be identified by their drooping, tube-shaped flower petals.

From the Wild Basin Trailhead (p. 215), follow the Thunder Lake Trail (p. 191) for 5.6 miles to a point 0.6 mile east of Thunder Lake. Look for Mertensia Falls, below and southwest of the trail. Leave the trail and bushwhack south, dropping steeply through thick forest toward North St. Vrain Creek. Find a way across the creek and

Mertensia Falls

bushwhack south below the steep cliffs of Tanima Peak's rocky east side. From here, hike southwest through lush, subalpine terrain and beautiful meadows to Mertensia Falls, just below the confluence of the two outlet streams flowing from Box and Eagle Lakes. In spring and early summer, the water rushes mightily through the rocky defile in an awesome exhibit of nature's power. Enjoy good views of Longs Peak and Mount Meeker framed by trees from the steep slope surrounding the falls.

Box Lake (10,740 feet) and Eagle Lake (10,820 feet)

T **OT** *Regional map p. 176 (M, 9); hike map p. 196*

Marvelously hidden deep within the splendor of Wild Basin, Box Lake and Eagle Lake are situated in a rugged cirque that showcases stark rock and prolific wildflowers. In addition to the lengthy trek along the Thunder Lake Trail, the hike to the two alpine tarns requires more than a mile of rugged off-trail hiking, and the absence of an improved pathway between the Thunder Lake Trail and these lakes helps keep them isolated and seldom visited. However, this picturesque setting is a must-see for the avid Rocky Mountain hiker and history buff.

Eagle Lake

From the Wild Basin Trailhead (p. 215), follow the Thunder Lake Trail (p. 191) for 6.2 miles to Thunder Lake. From Thunder Lake, cross the outlet and hike southeast, contouring low along Tanima Peak's east side. Be careful not to get too high on the steep, cliff-ridden slopes. Stay low and look for a faint trail leading south.

From the base of Tanima Peak's east side, hike southwest through lush, subalpine terrain, following the faint path as it weaves through a scenic basin. Beautiful meadows adorn the eastern regions near the lakes. The path leads to the northeastern edge of Box Lake, cradled in a rock basin at the foot of Tanima Peak's south face. From here, bushwhack south from Box Lake for 0.25 mile through nasty, low bushes and krummholz and over steep bedrock to Eagle Lake.

Much larger than Box Lake, Eagle Lake stretches 0.3 mile west to east and is a true alpine jewel. The Continental Divide lies to the west, and Eagles Beak, an imposing rock feature, stands out near the Divide. The slopes of Mahana Peak form the rocky ridge to the south. Tranquil views northeast toward Longs Peak and Mount Meeker, and east toward the valley of North St. Vrain Creek, contrast the striking, rocky terrain that surrounds the lakes. The quiet solitude found at these lakes is not easily forgotten.

Like many high-altitude lakes, Box and Eagle were involved in the struggle for water rights, and the remains of a water-diversion tunnel near the eastern end of Eagle Lake can still be investigated. Started in 1914, this tunnel project was part of C.S. Burford's plan to make a reservoir system out of Eagle, Box, Thunder, and Snowbank Lakes. After RMNP was established in 1915, authorities legally forced Burford and his partner to relinquish the claims on three of the four lakes in the proposed system, effectively ending the project and the tunnel was never completed.

Indigo Pond   11,180 feet

T **OT**   *Regional map p. 176 (L, 7); hike map p. 196*

This tiny pond lies in a rocky canyon near the headwall of the Continental Divide, below The Cleaver. From Eagle Lake (follow route description, p. 197), skirt the lake and fight through short, stunted trees, heading west into a wide ravine between Tanima Peak and Eagles Beak. Hike amid large boulder fields and grassy slopes to a long finger of water that leads west to round Indigo Pond.

Frigid Lake   11,820 feet

T **OT**   *Regional map p. 176 (M, 6); hike map p. 196*

Frigid Lake imparts a wild sense of Alaskan solitude to those who hike to it. Ice from Moomaw Glacier calves off into the deep, chilly lake, creating huge icebergs that float in the tarn even in midsummer. The lake lies in the shadow of craggy Eagles Beak, and the bitterly cold water lives up to its name. Steep snowfields on the south prevent hiking on that side of the tarn.

From Eagle Lake (follow route description, p. 197), skirt the lake on the south and hike west up rock benches, avoiding patches of low, stunted trees and krummholz. Gain a large field of boulders and hike west amid the rocks to the large bench that holds Frigid Lake, 0.8 mile from Eagle Lake. The steep, impressive Moomaw Glacier rises to the west of Frigid Lake.

The Cleaver   12,200+ feet

T **OT** *Regional map p. 176 (K, 5); hike map p. 196*

It's hard to get a good look at this mysterious rock pinnacle that is tucked away into a serrated ridgeline north of Isolation Peak's convoluted north ridge. The Cleaver is the southernmost gendarme in the jagged ridge along the Continental Divide south of Boulder–Grand Pass, and north of Isolation Peak. It is a rock tooth with a wide south-east face and an overhanging summit block that soars over East Inlet. Although the difficulty in reaching the summit of The Cleaver does not exceed Class 3 if the path of least resistance is followed, it is an exposed challenge that can be treacherous if the rock is snowy or wet.

Southeast Face GRADE II CLASS 3   This is the easiest route to the top of The Cleaver. The southeast face can be reached from Indigo Pond or Boulder–Grand Pass. From Indigo

Pond (follow route description, opposite), scramble up the steep, loose, dirt- and scree-filled gully for 850 vertical feet to the Continental Divide, north of The Cleaver. From Boulder–Grand Pass (follow route description, p. 194), hike slightly uphill and south over tundra, skirting Tanima Peak on the west.

The blocky ridgeline of The Cleaver stands out magnificently north of Isolation Peak's giant north ridge buttress. Descend a dirt slope to the southeast and work along the precipitous ridge. Indigo Pond glistens below to the east. Pass to the west side of the

Alex Kostadinov ascending The Cleaver's Southeast Face

ridge to skirt a small, pointy gendarme for a good view of the lakes of upper East Inlet. Scramble to the notch between the first and second gendarmes, and ascend a promi-nent slab ramp on the east side of the second spire to reach its top.

Descend a Class 3 gully to the base of the gendarme. Stay on the east side of the ridge and skirt another pinnacle and another cliff, traversing over boulders and on grassy ledges, working upward to the base of The Cleaver (Class 3). To ascend directly to the summit from here involves Class 4 climbing through a crack system. To keep the difficulty at Class 3, traverse south on the east side of The Cleaver to a small notch that provides access to an obvious system of ledges that breach the southeast face. Follow the path of least resistance and climb up the beautiful, fun, exposed, and exciting southeast face of The Cleaver. The face narrows toward the top and leads to a cap rock that dramatically overhangs to the west, overlooking the magnificent lakes of East Inlet. This is a special summit, with Isolation Peak's north ridge buttress looming overhead to the south and Wild Basin unfolding to the east.

Eagles Beak   12,200+ feet

T **OT** *Regional map p. 176 (L, 6); hike map p. 196*

This intriguing, craggy little peak lies north of Frigid Lake and overlooks the Box and Eagle Lake basin. It is a beautiful, pagodalike feature set amid an alpine world of rock and ice. Moomaw Glacier lies southwest, calving ice into chilly Frigid Lake and highlighting the scene below this superlative mountain of rock.

Southwest Face GRADE II CLASS 3+   This is the easiest route to the top of Eagles Beak. It ascends a Class 3+ gully up the southwest face. From Frigid Lake (follow route description, p. 198), scramble north to a grassy rock moraine on the southeast side of Eagles Beak. Climb north to the base of two prominent gullies. The eastern gully is blocked by a large chockstone midway up. The western gully is easier, ascending rock steps, loose dirt, and grass shelves (Class 3+) to the west ridge of Eagles Beak. Turn east and scramble up the west ridge (Class 2) to the summit, a mound of stacked granite blocks with a good view of Longs Peak and Mount Meeker. The panorama encompasses most of Wild Basin and more.

Legendary Jack C. Moomaw was a National Park Ranger whose colorful character is indelibly etched into RMNP's history. He was born in Nebraska in 1892, and his family relocated to a farm near Lyons the following year. The nine Moomaw children spent a good deal of time in the mountains near Estes Park. Jack joined J.W. Alexander on the second ascent of the East Face of Longs Peak in 1922. He made the first midwinter ascent of the peak in January of the same year, at which time he started out 30 miles away from the foothills on foot and on skis.

Moomaw's stint as a guide on Longs Peak and his subsequent career as a RMNP ranger produced an arsenal of interesting stories and experiences that he colorfully describes in his own whimsical memoir, *Recollections of a Rocky Mountain Ranger*, published in 1963. He is also responsible for naming several features in Wild Basin. U.S. Geological surveyors christened Moomaw Glacier in his honor in 1958, though Moomaw himself referred to this feature as Dresden Glacier.

Moomaw Glacier 12,320 feet
T **OT** *Regional map p. 176 (L, 5); hike map p. 196*
Sizable, impressive Moomaw Glacier lies southwest of Eagles Beak and is currently calving huge chunks of ice into appropriately named Frigid Lake. It wraps around the west and south sides of the lake and has a very steep headwall snuggled up against the Continental Divide below Isolation Peak's convoluted north ridge. It sports a flat base below the headwall that ends in a moraine and extends out into the lake. From Frigid Lake (follow route description, p. 198), skirt the north shore for 0.2 mile to the foot of Moomaw Glacier.

OUZEL CREEK   *Regional map p. 176 (P, 14)*

LAKES

Chickadee Pond   10,020 feet
T **OT** *Regional map p. 176 (O, 14); hike map p. 196*
Mountain chickadees are vocal birds with black, gray, and white feathers. These birds are prevalent in RMNP and are notorious for scolding intruders who infringe upon their domain. Their namesake pond is a stagnant, shallow pool ornamented with pond lilies, located northeast of Ouzel Lake and sandwiched between the Bluebird Lake Trail and the Ouzel Lake Trail. From the junction of Bluebird and Ouzel Lake Trails (see the Bluebird Lake Trail, p. 216), which is 4.6 miles from the Wild Basin Trailhead, turn south and hike 0.2 mile along the Ouzel Lake Trail to the point where the trail skirts Chickadee Pond. Leave the trail and hike north a short distance to the small body of water.

Ouzel Lake   10,020 feet
T *Regional map p. 176 (P, 13); hike maps pp. 196, 207*
Ouzel Lake lies in the shadow of Mount Copeland's precipitous north face and offers a diverse hike through one of the most beautiful areas in northern Colorado. The trail

to this picturesque lake passes three appealing waterfalls and travels through the prominent burned area left by the 1978 Ouzel Fire.

From the Wild Basin Trailhead (p. 215), follow the Thunder Lake Trail (p. 191) for 3.4 miles to the junction with the Bluebird Lake Trail. Turn southwest and follow the Bluebird Lake Trail for 1.2 miles to the junction with the Ouzel Lake Trail. Turn southwest and then descend along the Ouzel Lake Trail for 0.4 mile to Ouzel Lake. The pretty lake is snugly situated against Mount Copeland's northern flank. The peak's striking, craggy face provides an imposing backdrop to the serenity of the calm waters. The treed shore wraps around the somewhat heart-shaped lake and obscures portions of it from view. The shoreline is marshy, but several suitable picnic spots lie near the northern shore. Ouzel Peak lies in the distance to the west.

Bluebird Lake   10,978 feet
T *Regional map p. 176 (R, 8); hike map p. 207*

Steeped in controversial history, Bluebird Lake has undergone many phases of change in the last century. This high alpine tarn is cut deeply into granite bedrock amid a rock-strewn basin endowed with the mighty peaks of the Continental Divide as a backdrop. The contrast between the rocky shoreline and the striking blue water, interspersed with islands of green vegetation, is breathtaking. This is a setting of unparalleled alpine grandeur that was once drastically altered by ambitious water developers and eventually returned to its natural state for all RMNP visitors to enjoy.

From the Wild Basin Trailhead (p. 215), follow the Thunder Lake Trail (p. 191) for 3.4 miles to the junction with the Bluebird Lake Trail. Turn southwest and follow the Bluebird Lake Trail for 1.2 miles to the junction with the Ouzel Lake Trail. From here it is 1.75 miles and almost 1,000 vertical feet of elevation gain up to spectacular Bluebird Lake. Colorful wildflowers abound on this stretch of trail, which gets much steeper and leads over several rocky slabs. The trail becomes indistinct as it climbs the rock benches and slabs and can be somewhat tricky to follow.

The path winds among the steep, rocky topography, eventually climbing a series of switchbacks that rise through a narrow canyon to reach the lake. The trail pops out on a granite bench overlooking the lake. The deep lake is ornamented with a few small rock islands and peninsulas close to shore. Waterfalls above the west shore cascade down granite cliffs. Ouzel Peak's prominent rock buttresses stand out grandly to the southwest. The gray face of Mount Copeland rises to the south, while the orange-colored ramparts of Mahana Peak rise to the north. A noticeable "bathtub ring" encircles the lake—the high-water mark remaining from when this alpine tarn was dammed.

In 1902, local rancher Emma Arbuckle filed on five lakes in Wild Basin with the intent to construct dams on them. She and her son Frank started to build dams on Pear and Bluebird Lakes, but within two years they sold the water rights to a group of Longmont businessmen under the name "Arbuckle Reservoir Company." Beginning in 1914, the company began construction of a more substantial dam at Bluebird Lake. The undertaking was a considerable effort, and a rock crusher had to be disassembled and hauled in with mules to make cement sand from the abundance of granite found near the lake.

In 1933 the company sold the rights to the city of Longmont, and by the 1970s the neglected dam was deemed unsafe. RMNP fought to gain the water rights to this and other dammed lakes within its borders, and in 1987, the Park paid $1.9 million for Bluebird, Pear, and Sandbeach Reservoirs. In what proved to be a massive undertaking, RMNP crews deconstructed the dams and attempted to restore the lakes to their natural conditions. Aside from some leftover damage at the outlet, it is difficult to visualize a dam at Bluebird Lake—a testament to the success of the restoration effort.

Lark Pond   11,340 feet
T **OT** *Regional map p. 176 (R, 6); hike map p. 207*

Lark Pond is a tiny pool that lies midway between Pipit Lake and Bluebird Lake, high above treeline at the base of Ouzel Peak's northeastern rib. It is a pretty alpine tarn set amid the grandeur of the granite basin between Mahana and Ouzel Peaks. From Bluebird Lake (follow route description, p. 201), descend north into a small rock canyon at the outlet of the lake, and cross the stream on series of rocks, then climb up a gully on the other side of the gulch. Hike along the north side of Bluebird Lake and negotiate rock benches that are scattered with krummholz to reach the grassy boulder fields that lead to Lark Pond, 0.7 mile from Bluebird Lake.

Pipit Lake   11,420 feet
T **OT** *Regional map p. 176 (Q, 5); hike map p. 207*

Pipit Lake lies between Isolation and Ouzel Peaks in a basin of stark granite boulders east of the Continental Divide. Serving jointly with Junco Lake as the headwaters of Ouzel Creek, Pipit Lake is the most remote body of water in the drainage. This lovely, high-altitude lake was named for the American pipit, a bird that nests on the ground and breeds strictly on the alpine tundra. Because it lives in an area with no trees, the pipit sings while in flight.

From Bluebird Lake (follow the route description on p. 201), descend north into a small rock canyon at the outlet of the lake and cross the stream on series of rocks, then climb up a gully on the other side of the gulch. Hike along the north side of Bluebird Lake and negotiate rock benches scattered with krummholz to reach the scenic, grassy boulder fields that lead past tiny Lark Pond

Pipit Lake from the Continental Divide

and up to the rocky basin that cradles oval-shaped Pipit Lake. The stark topography reveals a desolate setting, with delicate alpine plants and flowers clinging to the barren landscape. The majestic backdrop of the Continental Divide headwall, with Isolation and Ouzel Peaks standing sentinel over the basin, is truly remarkable.

Isolation Lake   11,980 feet
T **OT** *Regional map p. 176 (P, 4); hike map p. 196*

Tiny Isolation Lake sits on a rocky perch between Isolation and Mahana Peaks. It is nestled on a grassy tundra bench below the barren, rocky saddle between the two summits, adding a splash of refreshing green color to the stark talus slopes that surround it. The grandeur and remote beauty of the area is breathtaking, and this is a nice site for a high-altitude picnic.

From Bluebird Lake (follow route description, p. 201), descend north into a small rock canyon at the outlet of the lake and cross the stream on series of rocks, then climb up a gully on the other side of the gulch. Hike along the north side of Bluebird Lake and negotiate rock benches scattered with krummholz to reach the grassy boulder fields that lead past tiny Lark Pond. Climb northwest over tundra and talus benches to Isolation Lake.

Junco Lake 11,620 feet
T **OT** *Regional map p. 176 (T, 6); hike map p. 207*

Named for a little songbird, this lake lies in a large alpine bowl northeast of Cony Pass, below the precipitous eastern buttresses of Ouzel Peak. A short rock rib lies between Bluebird Lake and the creek that flows from Junco Lake. From Bluebird Lake (follow route description, p. 201), hike south, skirting the rib by negotiating blobby cliffs. Scramble from the cliffs into the Junco Lake drainage, where the stream is so shallow and wide that it flows through a cobble field and is very scenic. Hike southwest up the drainage through a rock corridor and crest two small boulder hills that are often covered with snow, even in late summer.

Junco Lake drainage

At the top of the second hill lies a shallow, unnamed pond. Skirt the pond on the north side, following the grassy rock benches to a vantage overlooking the bowl that holds Junco Lake, which is surrounded by boulders and grassy meadows. The striking rock ramparts on Mount Copeland's northeastern face are impressive from this angle. Cony Pass and Ouzel Peak highlight the scenery surrounding this gorgeous mountain lake.

PEAKS

Mount Copeland 13,176 feet
T **OT** *Regional map p. 176 (T, 10); hike map p. 207*

Mount Copeland is a huge, bulky mountain that dominates the heart of magnificent Wild Basin. It stands between the drainages of Cony and Ouzel Creeks and is the major peak visible when entering Wild Basin on Wild Basin Road. The view from the summit is one of unparalleled grandeur and beauty, and on a clear day there is no finer vantage of southern Wild Basin. This massive peak is labeled "Mount Copeland" on the USGS Isolation Peak quadrangle, but all other maps and references refer to it as "Copeland Mountain." For the purposes of this book, USGS designations are used.

Northeast Slope from Ouzel Lake GRADE II CLASS 2   From Ouzel Lake (follow route description, p. 200), circumvent the lake and bushwhack south, ascending the steep and heavily treed northeastern slope of Mount Copeland. This slope is precipitous enough to avalanche, so assess the conditions before venturing onto the shoulder of this large mountain during winter. In summer, this is an arduous bushwhack. Climb to treeline, then continue southwest along the long, stark ridge over intermittent talus and tundra for a mile to the summit. Be prepared for the numerous false summits between treeline and the true highpoint.

Because this remarkable mountain is the highest point in southern Wild Basin, the view is panoramic, encompassing some of RMNP's wildest country. It's located 1.5 miles east of the Continental Divide, which provides a unique view of the other high area summits. Mount Copeland's immense loftiness combines with its steep, broken north face and jagged west ridge to make this one of the most aesthetic vantages in RMNP.

East Ridge from Pear Lake GRADE II CLASS 2   To climb Mount Copeland from Pear Lake is slightly more difficult than the route from Ouzel Lake. The steep cliffs of

Longs Peak and Mount Meeker from Mount Copeland

Mount Copeland's southeast face rise above Pear Lake, blocking easy access to the summit slopes. It is possible to route-find through the cliff band, but it is not the best hiking option. The easiest route from Pear Lake is to skirt the base of the east slope and gain the gentler northeastern aspect of the mountain.

From Pear Lake (follow route description, p. 208), bushwhack north along the base of the east slope for 0.7 mile. Turn west and ascend the large, nontechnical talus slope for 1.3 arduous miles to the summit.

Mahana Peak   12,632 feet

T **OT**   *Regional map p. 176 (P, 6); hike map p. 196*

Mahana Peak lies in the shadow of Isolation Peak, east of the Continental Divide, and is surrounded by alpine lakes. It has steep north and east faces and a sweeping talus field on the north. It is a difficult mountain to access and a challenging hike. Ellsworth Bethel, an early 20th-century historian, wanted to name this peak "Comanche," but the name was already taken for a summit in the northern section of what would become RNMP. The Taos Indians called the Comanche Tribe "Mahana," which became the acceptable substitute.

Mahana's massive slopes and ridges separate the Ouzel Creek drainage from the basin containing Box and Eagle Lakes. Even though higher peaks border it, Mahana dominates the region with sheer cliffs and long, sloping ridges. The climb up this bulky peak is perfectly suited for the ambitious hiker.

East Ridge   GRADE II   CLASS 2   From the Wild Basin Trailhead (p. 215), follow the Thunder Lake Trail (p. 191) for 3.4 miles to the junction with the Bluebird Lake Trail. Turn southwest and follow the Bluebird Lake Trail for 1.2 miles to the junction with the Ouzel Lake Trail. Mahana Peak's long east ridge extends eastward toward the trail. Continue west on the Bluebird Lake Trail for 0.2 mile to a likely spot to strike off-trail to the north. From this point, leave the trail and bushwhack north up the rolling ridge of Mahana Peak's eastern arm. Hike through dead timber and up the rocky slope for 0.8 mile to gain the top of the prominent ridge.

Turn west and hike along the dipping and rolling ridgeline through the forest and up a steep knoll to reach the rocky tundra slope that leads 1.6 miles west to the summit.

Several false summits must be overcome to reach the true peak, located on the west side of the rounded tableland that comprises the top of the mountain. Look into the Mahana–Isolation saddle for a great view of Isolation Peak, soaring to a height of 13,118 feet across the gap. Isolation Lake lies below the saddle, and outstanding views of Wild Basin's rich topography reveals glistening lakes and soaring peaks in every direction.

West Slope GRADE II CLASS 2   This route allows Isolation and Mahana Peaks to be climbed together. From Isolation Lake (follow route description, p. 202), hike north into the rocky saddle between Isolation Peak and Mahana Peak. Turn east and climb over talus to the summit of Mahana Peak.

Isolation Peak 13,118 feet

T **OT** *Regional map p. 176 (O, 3); hike map p. 196*

Isolation Peak is an intriguing thirteener with many different personalities. Remotely hidden on the Continental Divide and overlooking several drainages, the peak lives up to its name. It has a long, extremely convoluted north ridge that is riddled with steep cliffs and tall towers. In contrast to most of the other RMNP peaks along the Continental Divide, which have sharp, glacier-carved east faces and gentle western slopes, Isolation Peak has gentle eastern slopes and an intimidating northwest face that rises magnificently above Fifth Lake at the headwaters of East Inlet, west of the divide. Though Isolation offers a gentle eastern slope that is relatively easy to climb, the elevation gain required to stand atop this lofty mountain is nearly the same as the climb to Longs Peak, the most sought-after and highest summit in RMNP. The easiest approach is from Wild Basin and involves a long Class 2 hike to reach the summit of this splendid mountain.

View from the summit of Isolation Peak

Roger Toll, RMNP superintendent in the early 1900s, was a prominent name-giver to area features, and he originally called Isolation Peak "Clarence King." King was a man of great distinction in Colorado during the late 1800s, and several state geographic features bear his name. His credentials included being director of the U.S. Geological Survey and chief of the 40th Parallel Survey, which was partially conducted in the Estes Park region and produced an atlas responsible for naming mountains statewide. King visited the Estes Park area during the survey and climbed Longs Peak in 1871.

King and his survey crew blew the whistle on a scam by three con men who planted diamonds and other gemstones in Colorado soil to dupe political figures, gem appraisers, and the public into believing those riches existed where they didn't. King detected geological inconsistencies that thwarted the deceptive plan—regrettably, after it had already caused serious financial repercussions nationwide.

Because of King's popularity, many nominations were made for his moniker to grace natural features in Colorado, and King's name was in the running for Copeland Mountain and Lake Powell. Isolation Peak wasn't officially named until 1942 when an Arapaho National Forest supervisor proposed the current designation and it was accepted.

East Slope GRADE II CLASS 2   This long hike is the easiest way to reach the top of Isolation Peak. From Isolation Lake (follow route description, p. 202), climb north into the saddle between Isolation and Mahana Peaks. From the saddle, scramble west up the boulder field that comprises the 1,100-foot eastern face of Isolation Peak. Climb the final large blocks near the summit and crest onto the Continental Divide for an awe-inspiring view into the East Inlet drainage. Superior views from the summit are unobstructed by the lesser peaks that surround Isolation.

West Ridge to Southwest Slope GRADE II CLASS 2   This is an extremely long route that approaches Isolation Peak from the west. From the East Inlet Trailhead (Region 6, p. 303), follow the East Inlet Trail (Region 6, p. 304), then a faint path for 9.3 miles to Fifth Lake. Hike to the west side of the lake and scramble southwest over rocky terrain for 1.1 miles to an obvious 11,900-foot saddle on the ridge west of Isolation Peak. Stay west of any technical difficulties or cliff bands presented by the steep mass of Isolation Peak.

From the scenic saddle, it is 0.75 mile to the summit along Isolation's west ridge, which is easy at first but becomes more difficult when several problematic towers west of the summit interrupt easy passage. Scrambling into the clefts between the towers and traversing the towers is exposed Class 4 climbing. To avoid these problems along the west ridge, skirt these cliffs on the south. From the 11,900-foot saddle, scramble southeast for 0.3 mile, then turn east for 0.5 mile, staying below the obstacles on the west ridge. Scramble north for 0.2 mile to the summit.

South Ridge GRADE II CLASS 2   This route approaches the peak along the Continental Divide from the south and is usually combined with an ascent of Ouzel Peak. From Pipit Lake (follow route description, p. 202), climb west up the broad talus slope for 0.7 mile to the Continental Divide at 12,180 feet. Turn north and hike along the gentle south ridge for 0.5 mile to the summit to Isolation Peak.

Ouzel Peak   12,716 feet
T **OT**   *Regional map p. 176 (S, 5); hike map p. 207*
This modest summit stands between the two lakes that represent the headwaters of Ouzel Creek: Junco Lake and Pipit Lake. It is on the Continental Divide and separates Paradise Park from Wild Basin. From the Continental Divide, the summit of Ouzel is an easy hike from either the north or the south. There are several ways to reach the Continental Divide.

West Ridge GRADE II CLASS 2   This route ascends the west ridge from the Continental Divide. There are many access routes to the Continental Divide. Use the West Ridge when climbing Ouzel Peak from Isolation Peak, or use the following route description from Bluebird Lake. From Bluebird Lake (follow route description, p. 201), descend north into a small rock canyon at the outlet of the lake and cross the stream on series of rocks, then climb up a gully on the other side of the gulch. Hike along the north side of Bluebird Lake and negotiate rock benches scattered with krummholz to reach the grassy boulder fields that lead past tiny Lark Pond and onto the rocky basin that cradles oval-shaped Pipit Lake. Skirt the lake and climb southwest up boulders for 0.7 mile to the Continental Divide. From here, hike south, then west over gentle terrain for 1 mile to the summit.

North Slope GRADE II CLASS 2   This is the easiest route to the summit of Ouzel Peak. From Pipit Lake (follow route description, p. 202), skirt south along the east shore and climb the broad boulder slope of Ouzel Peak's north side for 0.6 mile to the top.

Southeast Slope to South Ridge GRADE II CLASS 2   From Junco Lake (follow the route description on p. 203), skirt the lake on the north, and scramble west to a grassy ramp that ascends a gully to the Continental Divide. The gully is scree-filled near the top. Turn north and hike over gentle terrain for 0.1 mile to the summit.

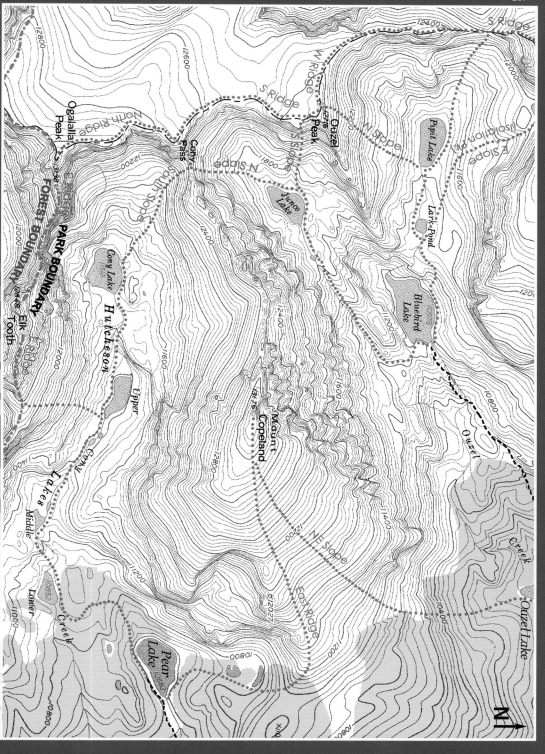

Magnetic North
11.5 degrees

N

0   0.5   1

Distance in miles

CONY CREEK   *Regional map p. 176 (V, 18)*

LAKES

Finch Lake   9,912 feet
T   *Regional map p. 177 (T, 22)*

Steve Volker at Finch Lake

Wild Basin is the home to 26 named alpine lakes, each with a different character and feel. All of them are surrounded by pristine wilderness and incredible beauty. Aside from Copeland Lake, which lies on the road, Finch Lake is Wild Basin's lowest-elevation lake and is bordered by a thick coniferous forest. Finch Lake is unique in that it has no permanent inlet or outlet. Lush marshland makes up much of the shoreline, which offers scenic views of Mount Copeland and Elk Tooth.

Finch Lake is frequented by the Cassin's finch, at home in the forested sections of RMNP. The lake is a rich environment for many kinds of flora and fauna, and the well-endowed forest along Cony Creek hosts a variety of indigenous and visiting birds. From the Finch Lake Trailhead (p. 215), follow the Finch Lake–Pear Lake Trail (p. 217) for 5 miles to Finch Lake. On calm days, Mount Copeland's grand image is reflected in the clear water.

Pear Lake

Pear Lake   10,582 feet
T   *Regional map p. 176 (V, 15); hike map p. 207*

Formerly called "Pear Reservoir," Pear Lake lies in a peaceful alpine setting near the southeastern flank of massive Mount Copeland. Along with several other high-elevation lakes in RMNP, it was dammed in the early 1900s to serve the agricultural needs of Colorado's thirsty Eastern Plains. Pear Lake offers a wonderful view of Elk Tooth, the steep, rocky peak that lies along the southern boundary of Wild Basin. Although this hike is long, it is neither

Joe Mills, along with his brother Enos, was instrumental in protecting the local wilderness. The brothers' writing, photography, and drawings led to the preservation of RMNP. Joe sketched Wild Basin from the top of Longs Peak, dubbing it the "Land of Many Waters." He christened Pear Lake by merit of its shape, noting that it bulged out at one end and reminded him of a plump pear. Wild Basin is indeed blessed with an abundance of lakes and streams, which caught the eye of developers in the early 1900s, resulting in the purchase and damming of several mountain lakes now within RMNP's boundaries. When the dams were dismantled, the water levels dropped, and the characteristic "bathtub rings" left from the previous high-water marks marred the landscape surrounding the lakes. At Pear Lake, the drop in water level formed an obvious shoreline ring devoid of dense vegetation.

technical nor difficult. It is accessed by a well-maintained trail that passes pretty Finch Lake and provides intermittent views of the surrounding high peaks.

From the Finch Lake Trailhead (p. 215), follow the Finch Lake–Pear Lake Trail (p. 217) for 5 miles to Finch Lake. The trail circles around the north side of Finch Lake and continues to climb steadily through thick forest for 2 miles to the shoreline of the former Pear Reservoir. Now that the water level has been restored to its natural state, a sandy depression surrounds the current waterline and effectively highlights the dramatic difference in water volume held in the basin since the removal of the dam. Numerous flat boulders offer good picnic spots with dramatic views to the west. Drop down into the "bathtub ring" and explore the rocky shore. The imposing slopes of colossal Mount Copeland dominate the backdrop to the lake, while Elk Tooth rises magnificently to the west.

Hutcheson Lakes and Cony Lake

T **OT** *Regional map p. 176 (W, 7-13); hike map p. 207*

At the extreme southern border of rugged Wild Basin lies a set of four pristine lakes ('Lower' Hutcheson Lake, 10,852 feet; 'Middle' Hutcheson Lake, 11,060 feet; 'Upper' Hutcheson Lake, 11,180 feet; and Cony Lake, 11,512 feet) strung out like pearls along the remote Cony Creek drainage. Not to be confused with "Coney Creek," another prominent waterway situated miles to the south in the neighboring Indian Peaks Wilderness Area, beautiful Cony Creek originates from a permanent snowfield nestled

Michelle and Bob Chase at Hutcheson Lakes

snugly against the Continental Divide north of magnificent Ogalalla Peak, the southernmost thirteener in RMNP. The hike to these beautiful alpine pools is long and moderately strenuous, passing through some of the most amazing countryside RMNP has to offer.

From the Finch Lake Trailhead (p. 215), follow the Finch Lake–Pear Lake Trail (see p. 217) for 5 miles to pretty Finch Lake. The trail circles around the north side of Finch Lake and then continues to climb steadily through thick forest for 2 miles up to Pear Lake. From here, locate and follow the unimproved and unmaintained but somewhat recognizable path southwest, then south, for 0.8 mile to lower Hutcheson Lake at 10,852 feet. Elk Tooth rises magnificently to the south. As the path fades out at the lower lake, hike along the northern shoreline and leave the trees behind as the terrain becomes quite marshy and plagued with thick krummholz. It is easy to bypass 'Middle' Hutcheson Lake, which is located

An Episcopal reverend from Kansas tried to attach the name "Lakes of the Archangels" to these tarns, but the U.S. Board on Geographic Names labeled them Hutcheson in the early 1950s. Henry Hutcheson moved from Michigan to Lyons in 1890 and procured mining claims in the upper Cony Creek area. He served as a contractor for several Wild Basin reservoirs, including Bluebird, Pear, and Sandbeach. Although he never attempted to name features in the Cony Creek drainage, he named Box Lake, located in another section of Wild Basin.

Hutcheson's desire to claim the water rights in the drainage north of Mahana Peak caused him to attempt to dig a tunnel between Eagle and Box Lakes, planning to drain Eagle Lake into Box. The tunnel still exists, though it only reached a length of about 50 feet and was never successful in transporting water.

0.2 mile up the creek at 11,060 feet. Hike over tundra and rocky marshland to an amazing vantage overlooking the largest of the Hutcheson Lakes. Mount Copeland stands out dramatically to the north, with Elk Tooth and Ogalalla Peak towering over the valley on the southwest. Descend over intermittent bedrock mixed with krummholz and marshland through striking alpine terrain to 'Upper' Hutcheson Lake, the largest of the ponds at more than 350 yards across. This is a wonderland of natural beauty on a grand scale. Huge peaks with jagged ridges soar in all directions, and the picturesque lake valley spreads out toward the plains in the east.

Cony Lake lies 0.5 mile above 'Upper' Hutcheson Lake, starkly situated at the head of the valley. Tundra graces the shores of this alpine tarn, elevated above treeline amid the barren rock. Cony Pass crowns this spectacular scene, rising ominously to a height of 12,380 feet. The pass is a lowpoint on the extraordinary ridge connecting the Continental Divide and Mount Copeland.

PEAKS AND OTHER DESTINATIONS

Elk Tooth   12,848 feet

T **OT** *Regional map p. 176 (X, 9); hike map p. 207*

Elk Tooth is a striking, precipitous-looking peak located 0.7 mile east of the Continental Divide along the southern boundary of RMNP in rugged Wild Basin. It has an extremely steep, convoluted south face, and its north and east sides consist of moderately steep scree slopes. Surprisingly, it is the only geographical feature in RMNP named for elk, which abound in the area. The sharpness of Elk Tooth's appearance from Pear Lake and the Cony Creek drainage reveals the reason for its name. It has a pointed summit ridge that resembles an incisor. It is connected to Ogalalla Peak and the Continental Divide by a dramatic ridge complete with tall spires and craggy rock walls. Elk Tooth is one of seven named peaks that lie in both RMNP and the Indian Peaks Wilderness Area. Elk Tooth is remote, and the approach from Wild Basin to the eastern slopes of the mountain is long and arduous. The peak itself, however, is easier to climb than it looks. It's a fun adventure, and the top offers a splendid vantage of neighboring high peaks in RMNP and an isolated section of Indian Peaks Wilderness Area.

East Ridge GRADE II CLASS 3   From the Finch Lake Trailhead (p. 215), follow the Finch Lake–Pear Lake Trail (p. 217) for 7 miles to Pear Lake. Elk Tooth rises magnificently to the west. From here, follow an unimproved but recognizable trail southwest, then west for a little more than half a mile to 'Lower' Hutcheson Lake at 10,852 feet. As the trail peters out at the lower lake, hike along the northern shoreline and leave the trees behind as the terrain becomes marshy and plagued with thick krummholz. It is easy to bypass 'Middle' Hutcheson Lake, located 0.2 mile up the creek at 11,060 feet. Hike on tundra and rocky marshland to an amazing vantage overlooking the largest of the Hutcheson Lakes. Descend over intermittent bedrock mixed with krummholz and marshland through striking alpine terrain to 'Upper' Hutcheson Lake.

When Abner Sprague, a prominent Estes Park lodge owner and historian, came to the area in 1875, he marveled at the number of elk he saw, stating that it was in the thousands. Unregulated hunting caused their numbers to decline, and by the late 1880s it was rare to see the animals in the Estes Park region. Beginning in 1913, elk were reintroduced to the area, transplanted from Montana. The first 29 elk were brought to Lyons by train, then loaded onto Stanley Steamers and driven to Estes Park. In 1915, 24 more elk arrived and were released directly into Little Horseshoe Park. From these populations grew the teeming numbers of elk that Estes Park residents and millions of visitors enjoy seeing every day.

Opposite: Josh Agan enjoys the view of Cony Lake and Elk Tooth as he hikes down Cony Pass

From here, hike south toward the prominent scree and talus fields of Elk Tooth's northeastern slopes. Work up the steep mountainside to a prominent shoulder on Elk Tooth's east ridge. Climb west along the ridge (Class 3) as it rises and dips, enjoying wonderful views of the Cony Creek drainage. Keep climbing along the ridge crest, passing any difficulties on the north side of the ridge. Avoid the south side of the ridge, as it is considerably steeper and more technical. Near the summit, a large talus slope extends to the top, offering easy passage to this magnificent mountain. Elk Tooth's striking south side is extraordinary, and the view into Indian Peaks Wilderness Area's St. Vrain Glaciers is breathtaking.

Cony Pass   12,420 feet
T OT *Regional map p. 176 (U, 6); hike map p. 207*

Cony Pass is a peculiar little lowpoint along the convoluted ridge between Mount Copeland and the Continental Divide. The best place to view it is either from Junco or Cony Lakes. The route is very steep but easier to climb than it looks. It's impossible not to kick off lots of rock when climbing or descending the scree slopes above Cony Lake, so this is not a good route for a large party.

From Cony Lake (follow route description, p. 209), circle to the lake's north side and hike northwest through a plane of large boulders to the base of Cony Pass. Spread out to avoid being hit by the small scree avalanches that will be set off by climbers above, and fight through ankle-deep dirt and scree to ascend the extremely loose slope to the top of the pass. Descending from the pass is easier because it is possible to boot-ski down the slope, but take care to maintain control while "screeing" on top of the moving debris. Rockfall from above is the real danger here, and it's hard to hear warnings because the sliding scree slope is noisy and drowns out communication with others.

At the top of Cony Pass, several options await: descending back to Cony Lake, descending to Junco Lake (Class 3), or climbing 350 vertical feet west to the Continental Divide (Class 4). To descend to Junco Lake, choose one of the moderate scree gullies that lead down the north side of Cony Pass. This may require some minor Class 3 scrambling, depending on the gully chosen. The north side of Cony Pass has steeper cliffs than the scree-filled south side. Descend a gully to the boulder fields southwest of Junco Lake. Hike northeast over boulders to the grassy shores of the lake. To reach the Continental Divide from the top of the pass, follow the path of least resistance and climb west up a broken cliff section (Class 2) to a Class 4 buttress that blocks easy access to the terrain above. This section requires several slightly exposed Class 4 moves, but there is no way around it. From the top of the buttress, climb southwest to the Continental Divide (Class 3).

Ogalalla Peak   13,138 feet
T OT *Regional map p. 176 (W, 6); hike map p. 207*

Located at the southwest corner of Wild Basin, this remote summit is the southernmost thirteener in RMNP and overlooks four separate drainages. It is the highest peak for many miles around, and because every approach is long, it sees few ascents. It is connected to Elk Tooth by a rugged ridge spiked with rock towers.

North Ridge GRADE II CLASS 2   From Ouzel Peak (follow route description, p. 206), amble south across tundra and talus for 1.4 miles to the summit of Ogalalla Peak.

Cony Pass to North Ridge GRADE II CLASS 4   From Cony Pass (follow route description above), follow the path of least resistance and climb west up a broken cliff section (Class 2) to a Class 4 buttress that blocks easy access to the terrain above. This section requires several slightly exposed Class 4 moves, but there is no way around it. From

Cony Creek drainage from Ogalalla Peak

the top of the buttress, climb southwest to the Continental Divide (Class 3). The steep eastern cirques below the Continental Divide are in sharp contrast to the broad tundra and talus slopes of the west side. From the Continental Divide at 12,550 feet, hike south along the gentle rocky tundra slope for 0.6 mile to the summit of Ogalalla Peak, which magnificently overlooks Paradise Park, Hell Canyon, the Middle St. Vrain drainage, and Wild Basin.

East Ridge GRADE II CLASS 4   This is an exciting way to reach the summit of Ogalalla and involves an ascent of Elk Tooth as well. From Elk Tooth, the tricky east ridge of Ogalalla rises impressively westward, riddled with stone towers and obstacles. Negotiating this 0.7-mile-long ridge requires careful route finding to keep the climbing at Class 4. It is a fun, exciting ridge that sparks interest in any mountaineer who is motivated to walk more than 9 miles (one way) for a challenge.

From the Finch Lake Trailhead (p. 215), follow the East Ridge Route for 9.2 miles to the summit of mighty Elk Tooth (follow route description, p. 210). From here, pick a route down the broken west ridge of Elk Tooth, negotiating Class 3 terrain and following the path of least resistance. This is not the most direct route—it loses a lot of elevation during the downclimb along the south side of the ridge, then it requires some additional climbing to reach the saddle; however, it avoids some large blocks, which can also be avoided on the north side of the ridge (also Class 3).

From the saddle, stay on the south side of the ridge and enjoy Class 2 terrain to the base of a big cliff. Skirt below the base of the cliff on the south, and choose a gully that leads north to the ridge crest (Class 4). Cross to the north side of the ridge and negotiate exposed Class 4 ledges west toward easier ground. The difficulty relents and a series of Class 3 ledges leads to the rounded boulder hump of Ogalalla's summit. The view of Elk Tooth is magnificent from here, with its strikingly steep south side dropping off dramatically into the Middle St. Vrain drainage. The St. Vrain Glaciers lie at the headwall of Middle St. Vrain Creek, and stupendous views of Indian Peaks, the Never Summer Mountains, Wild Basin, and, more remotely, Grays Peak, Torreys Peak, Mount Bierstadt, and Mount Evans unfold in the distance.

ALLENSPARK AREA   *Regional map p. 177 (R, 32)*

PEAKS

Meadow Mountain (11,632 feet) and St. Vrain Mountain (12,162 feet)
T **OT**   *Regional map p. 177 (Z, 24 and V, 28)*

Meadow Mountain and St. Vrain Mountain form the southeastern corner of Wild Basin and RMNP. These delightful summits are strategically positioned to offer an intriguing glimpse of the majestic Indian Peaks Wilderness Area, as well as an impressive view of eight of RMNP's named peaks that rise above 13,000 feet. The hike passes through plentiful aspen trees and travels over expansive tundra slopes. The St. Vrain Mountain Trail begins in Roosevelt National Forest south of Allenspark, passes into the Indian Peaks Wilderness Area, climbs past Meadow and St. Vrain Mountains, skirting inside the border of RMNP for a short distance between the peaks, then re-enters the wilderness area and descends south to connect with the Buchanan Pass Trail in the Middle St. Vrain drainage. The trail does not lead directly to the top of either mountain, necessitating some straightforward off-trail hiking to reach the summits.

Meadow Mountain South Slope   GRADE I   CLASS 2
and St. Vrain Mountain East Slope   GRADE II   CLASS 2

From the St. Vrain Mountain Trailhead (opposite), follow the St. Vrain Mountain Trail as it meanders pleasantly west through aspen trees and an aging, fire-damaged forest up numerous switchbacks along an east-facing hillside. Once above treeline, the trail bypasses the summit of Meadow Mountain and arcs to the south, 3.4 miles from the trailhead. Leave the trail and hike north 0.3 mile across boulders and tundra to the broad top. Meadow Mountain is the premier vantage point for Wild Basin. Intimate views of Pagoda Mountain, Longs Peak, and Mount Meeker to the northwest; and an overview of the Indian Peaks Wilderness Area to the south combine to make this a truly spectacular lookout.

To reach St. Vrain Mountain, hike south from the Meadow Mountain summit to regain the trail. Follow the trail south for 1 mile, then break off the beaten path and hike southwest through krummholz and over large boulders to reach the blocky top.

This is more strenuous than the ascent to Meadow Mountain, gaining 700 feet of elevation in 0.6 mile. St. Vrain Mountain's southerly position on RMNP's border presents wide-ranging views into the Indian Peaks Wilderness Area, another national treasure that is literally at RMNP's back door. The jagged peaks rise dramatically above deep valleys in a stunning display of natural beauty.

Steve Volker on Meadow Mountain

Allenspark Trailhead

This trailhead lies in Roosevelt National Forest at 8,935 feet and provides access to the Allenspark–Wild Basin Trail, which in turn accesses the Finch Lake–Pear Lake Trail, Thunder Lake Trail, and Bluebird Lake Trail. From the junction of US 36 and CO 7 in Estes Park, drive south on CO 7 for 14.6 miles to the town of Allenspark. Turn right and drive on Allenspark-Ferncliff Business Route (Washington Street) for 0.1 mile to the junction with CR 90. Turn right and continue 0.5 mile, bearing left (straight) at the first Y junction between CR 90 and S. Skinner Road. Stay on CR 90 and proceed 0.8 mile to the second Y junction (unmarked). Bear right and continue 0.1 mile to the Allenspark Trailhead, 1.4 miles from the town of Allenspark.

Finch Lake Trailhead

This trailhead lies at 8,480 feet and provides access to the Finch Lake–Pear Lake Trail. From the junction of US 36 and CO 7 in Estes Park, drive south on CO 7 for 12.5 miles to Wild Basin Road (CR 84W). Turn west and drive 0.3 mile to the turnoff for RMNP's Wild Basin. Take a right and drive less than 0.1 mile to the RMNP information and toll kiosk. Pass the kiosk and continue 1.8 miles to the Finch Lake Trailhead, on the south side of the road.

'Horse Creek Trailhead'

This unofficial trailhead lies in Roosevelt National Forest at 8,700 feet and is within a residential area near Meeker Park. From the junction of US 36 and CO 7 in Estes Park, drive south on CO 7 for 11.5 miles to Meeker Park. Turn west on CR 113N and continue for more than a half-mile, following handmade signs posted on trees directing the way. There is no official parking area, so park along CR 113N. Please don't block driveways or trespass on private property.

Sandbeach Lake Trailhead

This trailhead lies at 8,340 feet and is located 0.1 mile east of Copeland Lake. It provides access to the Sandbeach Lake Trail. From the junction of US 36 and CO 7 in Estes Park, drive south on CO 7 for 12.5 miles to Wild Basin Road (CR 84W). Turn west and drive 0.3 mile to the turnoff for RMNP's Wild Basin. Take a right and drive less than 0.1 mile to the RMNP information and toll kiosk. The Sandbeach Lake Trailhead is located immediately north of the kiosk. Pass the booth and turn north into the parking lot.

St. Vrain Mountain Trailhead

This trailhead lies in Roosevelt National Forest at 8,490 feet, and provides access to the St. Vrain Mountain Trail. From the junction of US 36 and CO 7 in Estes Park, drive south on CO 7 for 14.6 miles to the town of Allenspark. Turn right and drive on the Allenspark-Ferncliff Business Route for 0.1 mile to unpaved Ski Road (CR 107). Turn right and drive 1.5 miles to a prominent fork. Follow the right-hand fork 0.5 mile to the trailhead parking area. During winter months, the road is impassible beyond the fork.

Wild Basin Trailhead

The Wild Basin Trailhead (8,500 feet) provides access to the Thunder Lake Trail, Lion Lake Trail, Bluebird Lake Trail, and Allenspark–Wild Basin Trail, which connects with the Finch Lake–Pear Lake Trail. From the junction of US 36 and CO 7 in Estes Park, drive south on CO 7 for 12.5 miles to Wild Basin Road (CR 84W). Turn west and drive 0.3 mile to the turnoff for RMNP's Wild Basin. Take a right and drive less than 0.1 mile to the RMNP information and toll kiosk. Pass the kiosk and drive 2.1 miles to the Wild Basin Trailhead, located at the end of the road.

Wild Basin

Wild Basin Trailhead (Winter Access)

In winter, a seasonal gate closure 1 mile east of the Wild Basin Trailhead prevents vehicle access to the summer trailhead. A small lot on the south side of Wild Basin Road serves as the winter parking area. This site is 1.1 miles west of the RMNP information and toll kiosk. Using this access point adds 1 mile each way to all hiking destinations from the Wild Basin Trailhead.

TRAILS

Allenspark–Wild Basin Trail

From the Allenspark Trailhead, this trail travels west 1.7 miles to join the Finch Lake–Pear Lake Trail, then it continues west for 1.6 miles to join the Thunder Lake Trail slightly north of Calypso Cascades.

Bluebird Lake Trail

This trail leaves the Thunder Lake Trail 3.4 miles west of the Wild Basin Trailhead and climbs 2.9 miles southwest to Bluebird Lake. From the junction, turn southwest and follow the Bluebird Lake Trail up a steep ridge and onto its crest. Here the deforestation from the 1978 Ouzel Burn provides an opportunity to view the high peaks of Wild Basin. Mounts Copeland and Alice, along with Ouzel, Mahana, and Tanima Peaks come into view. Longs Peak and Mount Meeker rise to the north.

Continue hiking along the moraine to the junction between the Ouzel Lake and Bluebird Lake Trails. From here it is 1.75 miles and almost 1,000 vertical feet of elevation gain to spectacular Bluebird Lake. Wildflowers abound on this stretch of trail, which gets much steeper and leads over several rocky slabs. The trail is indistinct as it climbs the rock benches and slabs and can be somewhat tricky to follow. The path winds along the steep and rocky topography, eventually ascending a series of switchbacks that weave through a narrow canyon to reach Bluebird Lake.

Campsite Trail

This alternate trail leaves the Thunder Lake Trail 1.4 miles west of the Wild Basin Trailhead and leads to several backcountry campsites before rejoining the Thunder Lake Trail at a point 3.8 miles from the Wild Basin Trailhead. It is known as the Campsite Trail, and is 1.7 miles long, shortcutting the Thunder Lake Trail by 0.7 mile. It is a forested, rocky path that climbs steeply along a ridge. It is not an effective shortcut for those hiking to the Bluebird Lake Trail because it bypasses the turnoff for this trail.

Copeland Moraine to Meeker Park Trail

This trail climbs from Meeker Park through thick forest to connect with the Sandbeach Lake Trail at a junction 1.1 miles from the Sandbeach Lake Trailhead.

Finch Lake–Pear Lake Trail

From the Finch Lake Trailhead, the trail travels across about 50 yards of flat terrain, then rises steeply, climbing eastward along a lateral moraine through a heavy forest of pine and fir trees. The grade doesn't relent for 0.9 mile, where the trail finally tops out on the ridge as it takes a sharp turn and heads west through a gorgeous aspen grove. From here the trail meanders slightly downhill for 0.5 mile to a signed junction. A network of trails from the Allenspark area merges together here.

Continue west along the Finch Lake–Pear Lake Trail as it again begins to climb through the wooded countryside. Intermittent openings in the canopy reveal views of Chiefs Head Peak, Pagoda Mountain, and Mount Meeker. Longs Peak lies hidden behind the mass of Mount Meeker, and only a portion of the blocky summit

Michelle and Bob Chase on the Bluebird Lake Trail

Fire burnout area along the Finch Lake–Pear Lake Trail

can be seen peeking above it. About 2.6 miles from the trailhead, pass a junction with the Allenspark–Wild Basin Trail, which leads west to Calypso Cascades or east to the Allenspark Trailhead. Continue southwest along the Finch Lake–Pear Lake Trail as it enters an intriguing fire corridor that remains as a testament to the power of the 1978 fire that started at Ouzel Lake and burned 1,050 acres of Wild Basin before it was contained. Budding new growth, saplings, and a striking wildflower display augment the stark reality of the burned trees and charred landscape. This section of forest is truly remarkable and beautiful.

The trail reenters the unburned forest, skirting the base of Meadow Mountain and crossing several streams before cresting a small ridge. From here, the trail descends for a half-mile to the marshy shore of Finch Lake. The trail skirts along the northern shore of Finch Lake, passing the turnoff to several backcountry campsites, and continuing on for 2 miles to Pear Lake.

Lion Lake Trail

The Lion Lake Trail leaves the Thunder Lake Trail 4.5 miles west of the Wild Basin Trailhead and then leads 1.75 miles northwest to Lion Lake No. 1. From the junction, follow the Lion Lake Trail northwest up a very steep log stairway. It rises at an unforgiving gradient, then it levels slightly to climb and meander through forest and marsh to Lion Lake No. 1. A faint trail pushes beyond the lake toward Trio Falls and Lion Lake No. 2.

Lookout Mountain Trail

See Lookout Mountain, p. 179.

Ouzel Lake Trail

The Ouzel Lake Trail is a spur trail that leaves the Bluebird Lake Trail 4.6 miles from the Wild Basin Trailhead. The trail descends through the forest and goes past Chickadee Pond, then parallels Ouzel Creek and leads to the northeastern shore of the lake, 0.4 mile from the junction.

Sandbeach Lake Trail

See Sandbeach Lake, p. 181.

Thunder Lake Trail

See Thunder Lake, p. 191.

Copeland Lake

This small lake is located at 8,312 feet on Wild Basin Road. It was originally a small pond fed by springs but was enlarged in the late 1800s when John B. Copeland dug a diversion ditch from North St. Vrain Creek to the lake. Copeland homesteaded 320 acres near Copeland Lake in 1896 and got entangled in a legal tussle with state officials regarding stocking fish without a license. The lake, a moraine, a waterfall, and a mountain in Wild Basin were all named for him.

Though many people, including surveyor William Cooper and conservationist Enos Mills, tried to change these designations to honor men they considered more worthy, the U.S. Board on Geographic Names was partial to local history, and Copeland's name remains on the features. In 1913, Longmont bought 129 acres in the area and built a dam on the lake. Today, the road travels across the top of the dam before winding through the forest toward the Wild Basin Trailhead.

Copeland Moraine

This prominent mound, formed by the ancient Wild Basin Glacier, lies between Meeker Park and Copeland Lake. The Meeker Park–Copeland Moraine Trail climbs the north side of the ridge and the Sandbeach Lake Trail climbs the south side. The two trails meet at the western end of the moraine.

Meeker Ridge

Meeker Ridge is the large southeastern arm of Mount Meeker that separates Hunters Creek from Cabin Creek, with Lookout Mountain and Horsetooth Peak sitting at its southeastern end. An unmaintained path leads from Meeker Park to reach the northeastern side of the ridge.

A moraine east of Ouzel Lake

REGION FOUR

Longs Peak Group

Longs Peak is the monarch of RMNP and of northern Colorado.
It sits at the head of the Roaring Fork valley and draws thousands
of visitors each year to the area. It is the highest peak in RMNP
and is neighbored by Mount Meeker, the second highest. This
section of the book covers Longs Peak, Mount Meeker, and the
geographical features and peaks that surround them. Nearly every
aspect of Longs Peak is named—every bump, cleft, and ridge—
and the definitions of these features are included on pages 240-
245 for ease of reference.

*Knife-edge ridge,
Mount Meeker*

SUBREGIONS with Highlighted Hiking Destinations

CHASM LAKE AREA.................................. 223
    Peacock Pool and Columbine Falls................ 223
    🏔 Chasm Lake..................................... 223
    Chasm Meadows & Chasm Meadows Ranger Cabin.. 224
    🏔 Ships Prow 224
THE LOFT AREA.................................... 225
    The Loft 225
LONGS PEAK AREA 227
    Mount Lady Washington 227
    Storm Peak....................................... 227
    🏔 Longs Peak 229
MOUNT MEEKER 234
    Mount Meeker 234
MOORE PARK AREA 236
    🚶 Eugenia Mine 236
    Battle Mountain 236
    🚶 Moore Park..................................... 237

TRAILHEADS 238

TRAILS 238

OTHER POINTS OF INTEREST 240

ALPINE BROOK 240
ROARING FORK 240
BOULDER FIELD AREA............................ 240
    Boulder Field.................................... 240
    Agnes Vaille Memorial Shelter................... 240
    The Keyhole...................................... 241
LONGS PEAK EAST FACE 241
LONGS PEAK NORTH FACE 243
LONGS PEAK WEST FACE......................... 244
LONGS PEAK SOUTH FACE 245

Lambs Slide

*Bob Hostetler crossing
The Narrows in winter*

Opposite: Climbers ascending The Homestretch, Longs Peak

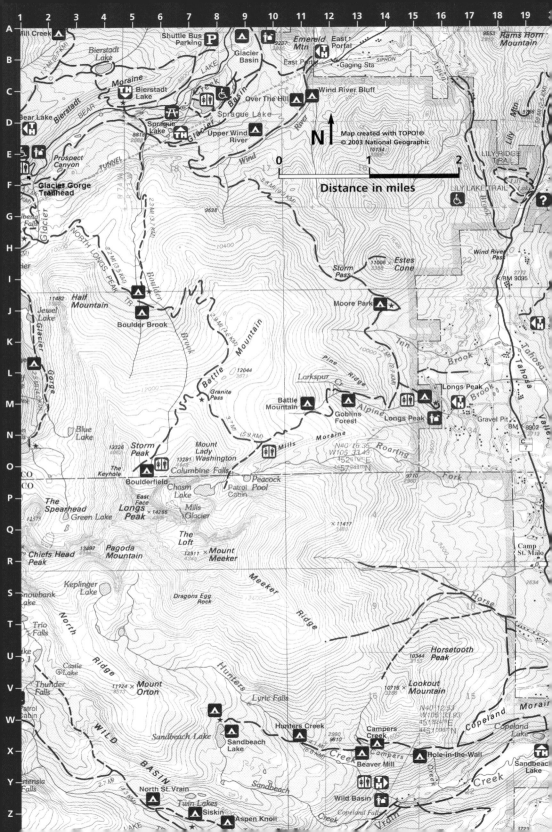

CHASM LAKE AREA   *Regional map p. 222 (P, 8)*

LAKES AND FALLS

Peacock Pool (11,300 feet) and Columbine Falls (11,440 feet)

T **OT** *Regional map p. 222 (O, 9); hike map p. 228*

Pretty Peacock Pool lies at the base of Columbine Falls in the Roaring Fork drainage, east of Longs Peak. Most hikers view it from above when hiking along the Chasm Lake Spur Trail between Chasm Junction and Chasm Meadows. The bird's-eye view from the trail reveals a multi-colored effect in the lake. The shallow shores and deep center cause different shades of soft colors to shimmer in the water. The sporty 260-vertical-foot descent from the trail to the lake involves a rough scramble down an unstable boulder field.

From the Longs Peak Trailhead (p. 238), follow the East Longs Peak Trail (p. 238) for 3.25 miles to Chasm Junction (p. 240). From here, hike southwest on the Chasm Lake Spur Trail for 0.5 mile to a point on the trail directly above Peacock Pool. Leave the trail and cautiously descend the unstable boulder field to the base of Columbine Falls. This is a popular technical ice-climbing area during winter. The falls roar magnificently over the dark, 100-foot cliffs to plunge into a rock basin and spill over a shelf into Peacock Pool. Scramble down a grassy, rock-laden shelf to the shores

Columbine Falls

of Peacock Pool, a lovely alpine tarn encircled with green vegetation and light-gray bedrock. Two distinctive Longs Peak hallmarks, the Diamond and the Beaver, rise beyond short, water-stained cliffs above the southwestern shore.

Chasm Lake   11,780 feet

T **[N]** *Regional map p. 222 (P, 8); hike map p. 228*

Tucked in a chasm formed by austere granite walls, Chasm Lake is appropriately named. This is one of the best places to view Colorado's most famous rock wall— The Diamond. From the Longs Peak Trailhead (p. 238), follow the East Longs Peak Trail (p. 238) for 3.25 miles to Chasm Junction (see p. 240). From here, hike southwest along the Chasm Lake Spur Trail as it descends gradually along the southeastern flank of Mount Lady Washington. A substantial drop-off on the south side of the trail overlooks Peacock Pool and Columbine Falls, two key features in the Roaring Fork drainage.

When dry, this section of trail descends gently and is generally horizontal. However, this area is often loaded with snow, which obscures the trail and creates a steep and unpredictable slope that can be prone to avalanches. Given these conditions, crossing this section can be treacherous, and the consequences of falling here are severe due to the considerable drop-off below the trail. In winter, spring, and early summer, an ice axe and crampons are recommended to aid crossing this section of trail.

Chasm Lake

The trail leads to a stepping-stone crossing of the Roaring Fork and enters Chasm Meadows, a pretty alpine bowl below the north face of Mount Meeker and the East Face of Longs Peak. Wildflowers thrive in this lush meadowland. A patrol cabin stands at the southeastern edge of the meadow. The sheer face of Ships Prow dominates the scene. Hike west and negotiate the broken cliffs that lead to Chasm Lake. Climb the short rock wall, following rock cairns along small ledges. Top out on rocky shelves above a stark, open bowl that is home to this dark, deep alpine lake. The arresting East Face of Longs Peak dominates the view, so look carefully to see climbers scaling the cliff above.

PEAKS AND OTHER DESTINATIONS

Chasm Meadows and Chasm Meadows Ranger Cabin 11,599 feet
T Regional map p. 222 (P, 8); hike map p. 228

Chasm Meadows is a pretty alpine bowl below the north face of Mount Meeker and the East Face of Longs Peak. Wildflowers thrive in this lush wetland, fed by snowmelt and the narrow, winding Roaring Fork. A patrol cabin stands at the southeastern edge of the meadow. This structure replaced the old Chasm Meadows Shelter Cabin, a charming stone hut built in 1931 (below). Rising beyond Chasm Meadows to the southwest is the blunt face of 'Ships Prow Buttress.' Chasm Meadows is the jumping-off point for numerous hikes and technical climbs on Longs Peak and Mount Meeker.

From the Longs Peak Trailhead (p. 238), follow the East Longs Peak Trail (p. 238) for 3.25 miles to Chasm Junction (p. 240). From here, follow the Chasm Lake Spur Trail for 0.7 mile southwest to Chasm Meadows.

Ships Prow 13,320+ feet
T **OT** **⚐** Regional map p. 222 (Q, 7); hike map p. 228

Ships Prow is the stately rock ridge separating the East Face of Longs Peak and the north face of Mount Meeker. Its blunt northeastern face (the Prow) rises above Chasm Meadows and its long, jagged ridge runs southwest toward The Loft.

⚐ 'Ships Prow Tower' (Technical)
GRADE II CLASS 5.4   The highpoint of Ships Prow (13,320+ feet) is near The Loft, where two distinct towers protrude skyward at the southwestern end of the Ships Prow ridge. These towers are technical, and a rope and helmet are recommended. The western tower is the higher of the two and requires 30 feet of Class 5.4 technical climbing on loose blocks to reach the summit.

From the top of The Loft (follow route description, opposite), hike northeast over boulders to the lowpoint between The Loft and the summit tower of Ships Prow. Skirt 'Ships Prow Tower' on the northwest side and

CHASM MEADOWS RANGER CABIN
The blizzard of March 2003 deposited more than 8 feet of snow in the Mount Meeker–Longs Peak cirque, loading the area between Ships Prow and Mount Meeker with literally tons of snow. Frequent high winds usually scour the walls of the cirque semi-clean of snow before any significant avalanche activity occurs, but the unusual amount of snow in a short period proved substantial enough to send a massive avalanche raging down the headwall of the cirque and into Chasm Meadows, overrunning and destroying the old stone patrol cabin built in 1931. Debris was scattered for more than a mile, and remnants of the old structure are still littered about the meadow, some of it now used to reinforce the trail.

A temporary cabin was built on the footprint of the old structure in late fall of 2003, but that building was removed entirely in 2009. The present-day edifice is located southeast of the historical cabin site, out of view of the trail. The new construction is much more practical than the original stone hut, and more functional. Wind constantly pushed snow into the historic cabin through gaps in the mortar, and the cold stone walls of the building lacked insulation. The new cabin is warmer and has a more efficient use of space. The NPS used natural stone to imitate the historic cabin and blend in with the natural environment.

As before, the NPS structure houses rescue equipment and serves as a patrol cabin as well as a staging ground for rescue operations. One of the most notable rescues came in January 1968 when Dr. Sam Luce performed a successful brain surgery operation at the old cabin, miraculously saving the life of a victim who had slipped down Lambs Slide.

Alex Kostadinov approaches 'Ships Prow Tower'

access a gully that rises between the two summit pinnacles. Ascend slabs and ledges (Class 3) to the obvious notch between the blocky spires. From here, climb up a chimney filled with large, loose blocks to the summit (Class 5.4), which overhangs the abyss to the southeast.

'Ships Prow Buttress' GRADE II CLASS 3+   This route accesses the top of the blunt northeastern face of Ships Prow (12,000 feet) and is one of the descent routes for technical climbs on the east face of Ships Prow. From Chasm Meadows (follow route description, opposite), hike southwest over tundra and boulders toward the bottom of Ships Prow. Skirt 'Ships Prow Buttress' and hike southwest into the wide gorge below The Loft.

Locate the only obvious nontechnical gully that ascends the southeastern side of 'Ships Prow Buttress.' Hike over grass and gravel ledges to access the gully. Climb up Class 3 terrain to a big chockstone blocking easy access to a large ramp. This is the crux of the route. A horizontal crack system on the lower half of the boulder allows decent footing, while the top of the boulder provides large handholds. These few steps are exposed, exciting Class 3+. The rest is an easy walk up a wide ramp to the high point on the buttress. The imposing walls of Ships Prow ridge soar above this imperial location.

THE LOFT AREA   *Regional map p. 222 (Q, 7)*

OTHER DESTINATIONS

The Loft   13,460 feet
T **OT**   *Regional map p. 222 (Q, 7); hike map p. 228*

This is the broad saddle between Longs Peak and Mount Meeker and provides access to hiking routes up both. The top of the saddle is a nearly flat boulder field 0.3 mile wide and 0.4 mile long. It is a glorious place to spend time gazing into Wild Basin, reveling in the majesty of the convoluted southeast ridge of Longs Peak, or observing the rounded rock stack that represents the summit of Mount Meeker. The Loft is located southwest of Chasm Meadows and is guarded from direct passage (for hikers) by a sheer cliff band topped with a sloping snowfield. However, a wonderful Class 3 hiking route skirts this cliff band on the south to access The Loft with moderate effort.

The Loft Route GRADE II CLASS 3   This route ascends the broad saddle between Longs and Meeker and allows the two peaks to be climbed together. Following the path of least resistance, the route does not exceed Class 3. However, when snow or ice forms on the ledges below The Loft, this route becomes extremely hazardous.

From the Longs Peak Trailhead (p. 238), follow the East Longs Peak Trail (p. 238) for 3.25 miles to Chasm Junction (p. 240). From here, follow the Chasm Lake Spur Trail 0.7 mile southwest to Chasm Meadows. From Chasm Meadows, leave the trail and hike southwest over tundra, grass, and talus to the funneled boulder field between the north face of Mount Meeker and Ships Prow. Turn southwest and climb boulders toward The Loft, following an obvious dirt "trail" that snakes its way up toward the cliffs of The Loft.

The major cliffs below The Loft snowfield are extremely steep and technical. A long waterfall spills down the cliffs to fan out and cascade over the broken steps at the base of the cliffs. Climb these wet, broken steps (Class 3) with rivulets cascading down them to the bottom of the sheer wall. A 12-foot-wide ramp turns to the south and climbs across the southern edge of the cliff band; this ramp is the key to finding relatively easy access up The Loft. From the base of the serious cliffs, access the south-angling ramp and climb along the southern edge of the cliff band. It sports a huge drop-off on the east and a broken wall on the west that provides convenient handholds. The ramp leads to a large boulder that blocks direct passage to easier ground. Skirt this boulder on the east side for serious exposure, or climb up a V-slot between the boulder and the wall (Class 3).

Continue angling south up the ramp to a series of broken rock bulges, and look for a 3-foot-wide grassy ledge that cuts back to the north (right) and gives nontechnical (Class 2) access to

The Loft Route

the upper Loft boulder field. Follow cairns up the boulder-strewn slope to the flat area of The Loft, nestled between Mount Meeker and the Beaver. A great view of a tower called Zumie's Thumb can be seen from here.

LONGS PEAK AREA   *Regional map p. 222 (P, 6)*

Mount Lady Washington   13,281 feet

T **OT** *Regional map p. 222 (O, 7); hike map p. 228*

This stalwart summit is comprised of massive granite blocks, strategically seated on the eastern flank of Longs Peak. The best thing about hiking to the top of this rounded pile of boulders is the exciting and close-up views of Longs Peak's impressive East Face, Mount Meeker's dramatic north face, and the stark contrast between the high peaks and the flat plains that stretch out to the east.

East Ridge GRADE II CLASS 2   From the Longs Peak Trailhead (p. 238), follow the East Longs Peak Trail (p. 238) for 3.25 miles to Chasm Junction (p. 240), where Mount Lady Washington rises to the west and the Roaring Fork drainage sweeps below to the southeast. From Chasm Junction leave the trail and hike west over boulders and through patches of krummholz to access the east ridge. Boulder-hop up the steep ridge to a point where it merges with the broad east face. This steep slope is unrelenting and riddled with large, loose boulders. Mount several humps that lead to more boulders until a final, steep section stands just east of the summit. Gain 1,200 vertical feet in 0.9 mile to crest the top of the slope, then scramble southwest along weathered granite slabs to the summit. In winter this is a great place to view the long ice smear that drops vertically down the center of the lower East Face of Longs Peak and is appropriately named the "Smear of Fear."

History was made in 1873 when the Hayden Party effectively put the first woman on top of Longs Peak. Anna Dickinson was invited on the expedition and successfully climbed to the top, out-hiking the other ladies who started the climb but weren't able to finish it.

After the climb, the party bantered together about naming some of the surrounding peaks. In the book *High Country Names,* Louisa Arps and Elinor Kingery speculate that Anna Dickinson named the peak "Mount Washington" after New Hampshire's highest summit, which she reportedly had climbed 26 times. They further speculate that Nathan Meeker, who was also on the expedition, named Mount Meeker for his father, and inserted the designation "Lady" into the name Mount Washington in honor of Anna Dickinson.

Mount Lady Washington and Chasm Lake

West Slope GRADE II CLASS 2   This route ascends Mount Lady Washington from the Boulder Field. From the Longs Peak Trailhead (p. 238), follow the East Longs Peak Trail (p. 238) for 5.9 miles to the Boulder Field. Leave the trail and boulder-hop up the western slope of Mount Lady Washington for 0.5 mile to the summit.

Storm Peak   13,326 feet

T **OT** *Regional map p. 222 (O, 5); hike map p. 228*

This pyramid-shaped summit lies at the western edge of the Boulder Field and is a highpoint along the long ridge that runs north from Longs Peak to Half Mountain. This ridge forms the steep, formidable eastern wall of Glacier Gorge. Storm Peak is comprised of large boulders and overlooks the Boulder Field, offering a great view of

Larkspur Creek

Jims Grove TRAIL

LONGS PEAK Mills Moraine

Granite Pass

11600

11000

11400

11408 C

12200

North Slope

Storm Peak
13326

North Ridge

West Slope

E Slope

Boulder Field

Mount Lady Washington
13281

Chasm View

The Keyhole

The Keyhole Route

The Trough

The Loft

Longs Peak
14255 × △14259

East Face

Chasm View

Mills Glacier

Lambs Slide

Glacier Ridge

Ships Prow

Iron Gates

Chasm Lake

Columbine Falls

Peacock Pool

12000

12000

12200

13000

12400

12000

12400

12800

13000

Keyboard of the Winds

6

Ice Gully

The Loft

Clarks Arrow

Rock Ridge

Mt Meeker
13911

East Slope

10800

11600

12800

13

13400

5 Pagoda Mtn
13497

14473

10600

1. Ships Prow Buttress
2. Ships Prow Tower
3. South Ridge (Meeker)
4. Meeker Ridge
5. Pagoda-Keyboard Col (Pagoda)
6. Keyboard of the Winds

N

Magnetic North
11.5 degrees

N

0   0.5   1

Distance in miles

Longs Peak's mighty North Face. Though thousands of people pass below Storm Peak's eastern slopes each year, few take the time to climb it. Most are focused on an ascent of Longs and don't take much notice of the other notable peaks in the area.

East Slope GRADE II CLASS 2   From the Boulder Field, this is a straightforward ascent up the steep talus slope to the top. From the Longs Peak Trailhead (p. 238), follow the East Longs Peak Trail (p. 238) for 5.9 miles to the Boulder Field (p. 240). Leave the trail and boulder-hop west up the steep slope for 0.4 mile to the summit.

North Slope to North Ridge GRADE II CLASS 2   From the Glacier Gorge Trailhead (Region 1, p. 109), hike southwest for 0.25 mile to Glacier Gorge Junction (p. 114). Turn south and follow the Loch Vale/Glacier Gorge Trail past Alberta Falls for 1.3 miles to reach the junction with the North Longs Peak Trail. Turn east and cross Glacier Creek on a bridge. Follow the North Longs Peak Trail as it climbs across and up the vast, open slopes of Half Mountain, Storm Peak, and Battle Mountain to the junction with the Boulder Brook Trail. Leave the trail and hike south, then southwest, across a large boulder field for 1.6 miles to the north ridge of Storm Peak. Climb along the ridge for 0.2 mile to the summit.

Longs Peak   14,259 feet

T **OT** ⛰   *Regional map p. 222 (P, 5); hike map p. 228*

The name Longs Peak is recognized all over the world. It's the highest summit in RMNP and Boulder County, the 15th highest mountain in Colorado, and, more notably, the northernmost 14,000-foot peak in the Rocky Mountains (thus the highest peak from Estes Park north in the Rockies). The sheer, intimidating East Face of Longs Peak combines with the giant north face of Mount Meeker to form the most inspiring mountain cirque in the state. It is the only fourteener in RMNP and is one of the most sought-after summits in Colorado.

Longs Peak sees a large number of successful ascents each year, but it has also been the site of many tragedies. It is a numinous mountain with many person-alities and also seems to have a deeply spiritual effect on those who climb it. It has a distinct look, crowned by a huge block of granite with a striking East Face that towers nearly 2,000 feet above Chasm Lake, and is in the running for the most characteristic landmark in Colorado. Longs Peak's broad profile and flat summit are highly visible from most angles, and the routes that penetrate the summit are riddled with complexities. Seen from the southeast, including the Denver metro area, the massive slopes of Mount Meeker hide the bulk of Longs Peak, with only Longs' blocky top seen rising higher than Meeker's summit.

Longs Peak was named in honor of Major Stephen Harriman Long, a young army officer who led a survey expedition in the Colorado Rockies in 1820. The team traveled southward along the foothills of the Front Range, and though they only saw Longs Peak from the distant plains, Long's men made the first recorded sighting of it. Later, though Major Long didn't come within 30 miles of Longs Peak, it was named in his honor. The Arapaho Indians called Longs Peak and Mount Meeker "The Two Guides," using the landmarks as bearing points during their travels on the plains. French-speaking fur trappers called them "Les Deux Oreilles," meaning "The Two Ears."

Major John Wesley Powell is usually credited with the first ascent of the peak, though it is likely that Indians and even other European settlers reached the summit before he did. Powell is the notorious one-armed army veteran who pioneered the visionary boat exploration of the Green River and Colorado River through the Grand Canyon in 1869. Powell's 1868 expedition to Colorado resulted in a successful ascent of Longs Peak after four days of tedious route finding from a remote start at Grand Lake. The party climbed over the Continental Divide and dropped into Hunters Creek to scale the peak from the south. Even today, with maintained trails and modern gear, the route they took is an arduous adventure into rugged terrain. However, substantial evidence supports theories that others reached the peak before Powell. Whatever the truth, these early pioneers forged the way for thousands of people in modern times to test their grit against the will of the mountain.

Climbers and hikers travel great distances to attempt a summit bid on this great mountain, which offers climbs of varying difficulties. In ideal conditions the easiest routes up Longs Peak are simply exposed scrambles, but in adverse weather or the presence of snow and ice, all routes become technical. Severe weather plagues Longs Peak year-round, and the NPS advises hikers and climbers to leave early enough to reach the summit and return below treeline before predictable early afternoon thundershowers set in. A clear, cloudless morning can quickly turn into a violent, storm-battered afternoon on any summer day, transforming a pleasant climb into an epic adventure on wet, snowy, or icy rock. As a result, typical start times range from 1 a.m. to 5 a.m., with 3 a.m. being the standard time for starting The Keyhole Route.

Climbers have the option of camping out or starting early, depending on party fitness. Camping requires a NPS permit. Most ascents are done in a day, though distance, altitude, and exposure combine to make it an extremely strenuous one-day trip. The NPS-designated "nontechnical climbing season" for Longs is short, usually between mid-July and September. In some years, such as the wet summer of 2004, the peak never received nontechnical designation from the NPS. An ascent of Longs Peak is a genuine challenge, close to technical even on the best days.

The hike passes through three zones: montane, subalpine, and alpine. The large, flat summit, which is the highest point around, resembles a huge football field full of boulders, many of them level. Grand views abound in every direction.

Longs Peak from the south

◸ The Keyhole Route GRADE II CLASS 3+

This is the standard "hiking route" up Longs Peak. It spirals three-quarters of the way around the mountain to access the least difficult passages to the summit. It is a lengthy, demanding climb and should not be underestimated, and a helmet is

Any ascent of Longs Peak is a serious affair. The Keyhole Route is a mountaineer's route, not a hike. Class 3+ scrambling combines with extreme exposure and temperamental weather to make this a difficult and arduous climb. Climbers should be prepared for the heightened risks of the numerous objective dangers inherent in ascending a 14,000 foot peak.

recommended to protect the hiker against rockfall set off by fellow climbers. Once the summit is attained, hikers are faced with the long, difficult descent, and many people experience fatigue, which can cause carelessness and accidents. The average estimated time it takes to complete The Keyhole Route is between 8–14 hours round trip.

From the Longs Peak Trailhead (p. 238), follow the East Longs Peak Trail (p. 238) for 5.9 miles to the Boulder Field (p. 240). From the trail's end, about midway through the Boulder Field, continue southwest over boulders of varying size toward The Keyhole (p. 241). The route gets gradually steeper until the final hill below the opening of The Keyhole.

From The Keyhole, Glacier Gorge spreads out magnificently nearly 3,000 feet below. Scramble over the large blocks of The Keyhole to the west side of the ridge and locate the Ledges (p. 244), which provide access into The Trough (p. 244). From here to the summit the route is marked with red and yellow paint blazes called "bulls-eyes" or "fried eggs." Scramble across the Ledges (the obvious broken ledge system), following the paint blazes, to a steep corner of rock. The trail climbs this corner and then traverses above steep slabs. A section of steel reinforcement bar aids leverage in the trickiest section. The route traverses, climbing and descending, to a point where the Ledges join the Trough.

From The Keyhole to The Trough is 0.4 mile of exposed traversing on ledges above steep rock slabs. The Trough typically contains snow until mid-July, and when it is completely filled in, an ice axe is recommended. When exposed rocks melt out on the north and south sides of The Trough, scramble up the rocks to avoid the snow, providing that no technical climbing is encountered. The most difficult sections of this route should not exceed Class 3+, so if it's harder than that, you are off-route. The Trough constricts near the top, and just below the point where it meets the Narrows (p. 244) a short but steep rock step presents the crux of the route. This 15-foot vertical scramble involves difficult Class 3+ moves, so take time to figure out the easiest way up the blockade. Climb up blocks to the crook between The Trough and the Narrows of the south face. A dramatic drop-off is unnerving, but the ledge is wide enough (3 feet at its narrowest) for safe passage. Turn the corner and walk along the skinny ledge until it widens out, then gives way to a larger ledge system that climbs east to the base of the Homestretch (p. 245).

From here, the route is obvious as it climbs the parallel cracks that ascend steep slabs directly to the summit. These boxy, double-sided, 3-foot-wide cracks require the use of both hands and feet to safely ascend them. Choose the path of least resistance to avoid much harder climbing on the smooth slabs that surround the cracks. Top out on the summit and hike north over flat rocks to the boulder that represents the highest point. A tube tethered to the boulder by a cable holds the summit register. Acres of rock stretch out along the flat summit. Hike to each end of the summit plane to take in dramatic drop-off views down different aspects of this mighty mountain. This is the top of the world from Northern Colorado through the northern Rocky Mountains, and affords a 360-degree panorama of the plains and scores of mountains in the distance. Revel in the grand views and your accomplishment.

◸ The Trough GRADE II CLASS 3+ MODERATE SNOW

This route climbs more than 2,000 vertical feet up The Trough (p. 244), a moderately steep couloir that rises from upper Glacier Gorge to a notch on the west ridge of Longs Peak, where it meets the Narrows (p. 244). It is wide at the bottom and climbs up to an impressive curve before it heads north, getting narrower as it progresses. The Trough is often filled with snow, which sometimes melts out entirely to reveal a rubble-filled gully. This route is best in early summer. Crampons, an ice axe, and a helmet are recommended for the ascent.

From Black Lake in Glacier Gorge (see Region 1, p. 49), skirt the lake on the northeast shore and follow a trail that climbs east up the scenic creek drainage. At the top of the gully, the trail crosses the creek and turns south, breaching a short granite cliff and topping out on the broad glacial shelf of upper Glacier Gorge. The trail ends at the crest of the plateau. Bushwhack south through dense bushes and over large rock slabs, then angle southeast over boulders and talus toward the base of the west slope of Longs Peak. Climb up into The Trough, skirting short cliffs that may present more technical challenges. Climb moderate snow for 0.6 mile to the point where The Trough meets the Narrows at 13,865 feet. From here, follow The Keyhole Route (p. 231) to the summit.

⚐ **Clarks Arrow** GRADE II CLASS 4   This magnificent route, like The Keyhole Route, spirals three-quarters of the way around the peak to reach the Homestretch; but Clarks Arrow does it by circling around the opposite side. In late summer, when dry conditions prevail, Clarks Arrow is only slightly harder than The Keyhole Route, and it is 1.5 miles shorter. Even so, it receives little attention and is rarely crowded. When this route is snowy or icy, it becomes a severe technical challenge. Even in prime conditions, the main difficulty is the route finding. Whereas The Keyhole Route has multiple paint blazes leading the way through confusing sections, this route has only one extremely faded white arrow painted inside a circle. A RMNP ranger named John Clark placed the arrow at the most crucial passageway on the route—hence the name. Because of potential rockfall, a helmet is advised when attempting this route.

The route ascends The Loft, the broad saddle between Longs and Meeker. From The Loft, the route gets tricky to find, but when the path of least resistance is located, the route does not exceed Class 4. However, when snow or ice forms on the ledges below The Loft and on the slabs between the Homestretch and upper Keplinger's Couloir (opposite), this route becomes extremely hazardous.

From the top of The Loft (follow route description, p. 225) hike northwest toward Longs Peak across the expansive boulder field, but do not gain elevation. Lose roughly 150 vertical feet of elevation and locate the top section of a narrow gully that leads down to the scree-filled couloirs on the south side of Longs Peak. Cairns mark the route to this gully. The gully is Class 3 overall but has two sections of Class 4 moves, and descends almost 200 feet to a basin at the bottom of the Palisades (p. 245). Descend the gully to an obvious ledge that cuts across the base of the Palisades. Clarks Arrow cannot be seen from this direction, as it is on a west-facing boulder directing traffic to the cleft that provides access from the ledge below the Palisades to the Class 4 gully that ascends to The Loft. The arrow is quite faded and difficult to see. The ledge descends into easy terrain and open, dirt-filled gullies at the base of the Palisades.

From here, traverse open gullies upward toward Keplinger's Couloir. Some scrambling is necessary to access the couloir (Class 3). Get into the couloir and climb up loose boulders and scree toward The Notch (p. 243), the deep cleft between Longs Peak's summit and the southeast ridge. About 400 vertical feet below The Notch, look northwest for a wide ramp that traverses across the top of some steep cliffs and skirts below the large south face of Longs Peak. Make an easy transition from the couloir to the wide ramp, and scramble (Class 3) over a horizontal section of broken rock to the bottom of the Homestretch. Here Clarks Arrow Route joins The Keyhole Route (p. 231) and climbs the parallel cracks of the Homestretch (p. 245) for 450 vertical feet to the summit.

Keplinger's Couloir GRADE II CLASS 3 MODERATE SNOW This approach to Longs Peak from Wild Basin is a long route up the south side of the mountain. It is usually climbed from a high camp in Hunters Creek. L.W. Keplinger was a college student and member of the 1868 Powell expedition that ascended Longs Peak. Keplinger scouted a viable route up the peak for the other expedition members, and consequentially, the route and a nearby lake were named in his honor.

From the Sandbeach Lake Trailhead (see Region 3, p. 215), follow the Sandbeach Lake Trail (see Region 3, p. 181) for 3.2 miles to a bridge that crosses Hunters Creek. Leave the trail and locate a faint path that leads northwest along the east side of the creek. The trail climbs through the trees and is sometimes hard to follow. When the path disappears, keep bushwhacking northwest to break out of the trees and negotiate marshy terrain to a shallow, unnamed lake at 11,200 feet. Hiking to this lake requires arduous bushwhacking through thick willows and over deep, soggy terrain. The Hunters Creek drainage is worth it, however, because it is one of the most pristine, picturesque places in RMNP.

From the shallow lake, hike north through willows, krummholz, large boulder fields, and marshy areas into the mighty, high-alpine basin at the base of Pagoda Mountain, Longs Peak, and Mount Meeker. This is a magical place. The sheer, striated walls of Pagoda Mountain's southern rib are astoundingly beautiful. Keplinger's Couloir is the largest, most obvious gully on the south face of Longs Peak. It is located farthest to the west of all the smaller gullies. It snakes up the peak in a grand, curving sweep and ends at The Notch (p. 243) on the northwest side of the Palisades (p. 245). The gully is snow-filled through June, and scree-filled when it is dry. When snow is present,

the ascent ranges from a moderate snow climb to a steep, intimidating ascent on hard snow or ice. A rope, crampons, a helmet, and an ice axe are recommended when the gully contains snow. When the snow melts out, it's a tedious climb through loose scree, dirt and boulders for 1,600 vertical feet to a point about 400 vertical feet below The Notch.

Here Keplinger's Couloir joins Clarks Arrow Route. Look northwest for a wide ramp that traverses the top of some steep cliffs and skirts below the large south face of Longs Peak. Make an easy transition from the couloir to the wide ramp, and scramble (Class 3) over a horizontal section of broken rock to the bottom of the Homestretch. When these ledges and slabs are covered with snow or ice, this is a difficult and dangerous section. When dry, it is an exposed but easy scramble. At the base of the Homestretch, join The Keyhole Route (p. 231) and climb the parallel cracks of the Homestretch (p. 245) to reach the summit.

Keplinger's Couloir

Mount Meeker and Longs Peak

MOUNT MEEKER   *Regional map p. 222 (R, 8)*

PEAKS

Mount Meeker   13,911 feet
T **OT**   *Regional map p. 222 (R, 8); hike map p. 228*

Mount Meeker is Longs Peak's closest neighbor and is the second-highest mountain in RMNP. The immense north face of Mount Meeker combines with the sheer, intimidating East Face of Longs Peak to form the most inspiring mountain cirque in the state. Mount Meeker has an east and west summit, with the western hump 40 feet higher than the eastern. The two summits are separated by an intimidating knife-edge ridge made up of huge granite blocks with vertical plunges that sweep downward on either side of the pointed crest. The enormous south, east, and west slopes of the mountain are more gentle and comprised of large boulders stacked haphazardly on top of one another. The north face is vertical and has numerous technical routes that scale the precipice.

Loft Route to Northwest Ridge   GRADE II   CLASS 3   This route climbs The Loft Route and ascends directly to the higher, western summit of Mount Meeker. From the Longs Peak Trailhead (p. 238), follow the East Longs Peak Trail (p. 238) for 3.25 miles to Chasm Junction (p. 240). From here, follow the Chasm Lake Spur Trail 0.7 mile southwest to Chasm Meadows. From Chasm Meadows, follow the route up The Loft (follow route description, p. 225) to the top of the saddle. From the flat, broad area of The Loft, hike southeast over large boulders to the northwestern shoulder of Mount Meeker's western summit. Climb Class 2 terrain to the top.

Iron Gates   GRADE II   CLASS 3   This route provides access to the lower, eastern summit of Mount Meeker. From there, a Class 3 traverse of the knife-edge ridge between the two high points must be made to access the true (western) summit.

From the Longs Peak Trailhead (p. 238), follow the East Longs Peak Trail (p. 238) for 3.25 miles to Chasm Junction (p. 240). From here, follow the Chasm Lake Spur Trail 0.7 mile southwest to Chasm Meadows. From Chasm Meadows, leave the trail and boulder-hop south toward the massive north face of Mount Meeker. A large gully ascends to a cleft between two towerlike buttresses on the eastern margin of Mount Meeker's steep north face. The two towers form the outer posts of the "iron gates." Climb the loose talus to the top of the gully, where it tapers and some Class 3 scrambling is required to overcome large blocks. Top out on Mount Meeker's east ridge and hike up talus to the eastern summit.

From here, negotiate west along the extremely exposed knife-edge ridge for 300 yards to the western summit. This section is extremely tricky and the exposure is unnerving. This ridge is not recommended in high winds. When dry, the ridge is Class 3, but when snow or ice is present the traverse becomes technical. Traverse along large blocks and scramble over the pointy crest, skirting the summit on the north and coming back at it from the west side to avoid an airy Class 3 move required to reach the summit from the east side.

East Slope to East Ridge GRADE II CLASS 3   This route ascends the expansive eastern slope of Mount Meeker to reach the east ridge that leads to the eastern summit. From Camp St. Malo, located 10.5 miles south of Estes Park on CO 7, follow a faint trail east along Cabin Creek into Meeker drainage. The trail peters out in the trees, but keep following the creek toward the obvious S-shaped gully that snakes down the east slope of Mount Meeker. (This is a low-angle gully, but it makes a nice ski descent for the hearty mountaineer.) Climb up the vast boulder field (Class 2) to the east ridge, then follow the ridge to Meeker's east summit. It is 3.8 miles from Camp St. Malo to the lower, eastern summit of Mount Meeker via this route. From here, negotiate west along the extremely exposed knife-edge ridge (Class 3) for 300 yards to the higher western summit, at 13,911 feet.

South Ridge GRADE II CLASS 2   This approach from Wild Basin is extremely long, but it is the easiest route (in terms of climbing difficulty) to the top of Mount Meeker. It is longer, entails more arduous bushwhacking, and requires more elevation gain than any of the routes from the Longs Peak Trailhead, but it is only Class 2. This route climbs directly to the higher, western summit of the peak.

From the Sandbeach Lake Trailhead (see Region 3, p. 215), follow the Sandbeach Lake Trail (see Region 3, p. 181) for 4.2 miles to Sandbeach Lake. Leave the trail and bushwhack northwest through difficult terrain to Hunters Creek. Large boulder fields and densely forested sections plague this route. Cross Hunters Creek and fight through the tough terrain, heading north toward the large south ridge of Mount Meeker. Hike up talus and scramble over boulders to reach the ridge. Stay below the crest of the ridge to avoid complicated cliffs along the top of it. Continue upward to the western summit.

Meeker Ridge GRADE II CLASS 3   This route climbs from Meeker Park to the east (lower) summit of Mount Meeker (Class 2). From the unmarked 'Horse Creek Trailhead' on CR 113N near Meeker Park (see Region 3, p. 215), follow the Lookout Mountain Trail (see Region 3, p. 179) as it leads west-northwest for 100 yards to RMNP's boundary. The trail crosses the creek and continues southwest, skirting Horsetooth Mountain, and leads 2.3 miles to a small saddle between Lookout Mountain and Meeker Ridge. From the saddle, turn northwest and climb for 2.5 miles along broad Meeker Ridge to the east summit of Mount Meeker. From here, negotiate west along the extremely exposed knife-edge ridge (Class 3) for 300 yards to the higher, western summit.

MOORE PARK AREA   *Regional map p. 222 (J, 12)*

PEAKS AND OTHER DESTINATIONS

Eugenia Mine   9,908 feet
T 🏃 *Regional map p. 222 (K, 13)*

Unlike much of Colorado's high country, the RMNP region is only mildly scarred by mines, tailings, and man-made debris. Though some mining took place within the existing borders of RMNP, little ore was reaped and most of the hearty, diehard miners were forced to move on to more promising prospects in other areas of the state. Eugenia Mine was the largest prospect on the east side of RMNP, located on the banks of Inn Brook on the northeastern flank of Longs Peak's smaller neighbor, Battle Mountain. Evidence of the mining efforts still exists at a pretty site along the creek, accessed by a pleasant hike along a well-maintained trail from the Longs Peak Trailhead. The remains of a log cabin, rusted metal pieces, and mine tailings remind visitors of the brief mining history in this section of the Rocky Mountains.

Apparently searching for gold, Carl P. Norwall, a prosperous miner from California, partnered with Edward A. Cudahy in 1905 and tunneled more than 1,000 feet into a hillside in the Longs Peak region. Though the prospect bore nothing of reportable value, they recorded their claim on the mine with the Larimer County Clerk in 1908. Together with his wife and two daughters, Norwall lived in a log cabin near the mine site, surrounded by comfortable furnishings that included a piano. Tales of musical evenings spent at the Norwall house, told by young mountain guides who worked at neighboring lodges such as the Longs Peak and Hews-Kirkwood Inns, are legendary. Norwall filed his last claim in 1919, and after years of fruitless toiling and discouragement, the lack of production caused him to pack up and leave the area. The designation "Eugenia" remains a mystery, as there is no evidence showing a relevant reason for the name.

From the Longs Peak Trailhead (p. 238), follow the well-worn East Longs Peak Trail (p. 238) for 0.5 mile to the junction with the trail that leads toward Eugenia Mine, Storm Pass, and Estes Cone. Turn north (right) and hike through a beautiful aspen grove. The trail continues through coniferous forest, undulating and rolling along the hilly topography that parallels the heavily wooded Pine Ridge (p. 240). Pass a spur trail that leads to private property and continue north toward Inn Brook, which originates amid the avalanche scar high on the eastern slope of Battle Mountain.

The trail crosses Inn Brook on a footbridge and leads to the remains of an old log cabin, 1.4 miles beyond the trailhead. Head upstream from the cabin to take a look at the mine site itself. Situated less than a hundred yards upstream, the mine tailings and rusted metal of disintegrating equipment reveal the location of the mine. Though it is unimpressive compared to the large mining sites near Leadville and in southern Colorado, the Eugenia Mine is one of RMNP's historical landmarks, telling the story of those who attempted to make a living and strike it rich in this rocky, barren landscape. They learned that RMNP's bounty is in its scenery and not in the ore buried in its rocky slopes.

Battle Mountain   12,044 feet
T **OT** *Regional map p. 222 (L, 9)*

Intriguing Battle Mountain lies in the shadow of Longs Peak and is seldom visited. Enos Mills lived at the foot of Longs Peak and keenly observed the elements of nature shaping and changing the appearance of the peaks. He named both Battle Mountain and Storm Peak for the intense storms, fire, wind, and avalanches that altered the peaks throughout history. Popular with locals for the quality of its skiing, Battle Mountain has several small avalanches each winter, making it a dangerous place for the inexperienced hiker or skier. In April 1993, a large-scale avalanche ripped down the east side of Battle Mountain. The deluge of snow followed the existing avalanche path on the mountain's east side, but the magnitude of the slide enlarged the scar by a third, digging up hundreds of trees and making the damage visible from CO 7.

West Slope GRADE II CLASS 2   This is the easiest route up Battle Mountain. From the Longs Peak Trailhead (p. 238), follow the East Longs Peak Trail (p. 238) for 4.3 miles to Granite Pass (p. 240). From the junction, hike along the North Longs Peak Trail for 0.3 mile, then strike off the trail and hike east over gentle talus and tundra for 0.4 mile to the summit.

Northeast Slope GRADE II CLASS 2   This route explores the remarkable avalanche scar on the east side. From the Longs Peak Trailhead (p. 238), follow the East Longs Peak Trail (p. 238) for 0.5 mile to the junction with the trail to Eugenia Mine and Storm Pass. Turn north (right) and hike through an aspen grove. Continue through coniferous forest as the trail gains and loses elevation, and then crosses Inn Brook on a footbridge 1.4 miles from the trailhead. Just ahead lie the remains of an old log cabin where Carl Norwall lived with his wife and two daughters in the early 1900s while he worked the Eugenia Mine.

At the point where the trail crosses Inn Brook, head west and bushwhack upstream for about 0.5 mile to reach the base of the avalanche area. The opening in the forest represents an active avalanche path. (This route is not recommended in winter.) Forest openings caused by fires, high winds, and avalanches can regenerate themselves in as little as a decade or two if climate and soil conditions are favorable. However, active avalanche paths like this one sustain damage yearly and take much longer to repair. Bushwhack up the steep, difficult terrain of the damaged area, hiking over downed trees and across upturned earth, noting the new growth taking root in the scarred area. Above the avalanche debris, continue hiking southwest along the tundra to the summit plateau. The true summit is not obvious and is just a small outcrop of rocks. The view of Longs Peak and the surrounding high peaks is rewarding from the summit.

Moore Park 9,760 feet
T **[figure]** *Regional map p. 222 (J, 14)*

This pretty meadow lies between Inn Brook and Estes Cone, and provides a lovely view of Estes Cone. It is a nice spot for a family picnic. From the Longs Peak Trailhead (p. 238), follow the well-worn East Longs Peak Trail (p. 238) for 0.5 mile to the junction with the trail to Eugenia Mine and Storm Pass. Turn north (right) and hike through a lovely aspen grove. The trail continues through coniferous forest, undulating and rolling along the hilly topography that parallels the heavily wooded Pine Ridge. Continue north toward Inn Brook, which originates amid the avalanche scar high on the eastern slope of Battle Mountain. The trail crosses Inn Brook on a footbridge and leads to the remains of an old log cabin, 1.4 miles beyond the trailhead. Continue north along the Storm Pass Trail for 0.4 mile to Moore Park.

The inquisitive marmot is commonly seen in RMNP

TRAILHEADS/TRAILS

TRAILHEADS

Glacier Gorge Trailhead
See Region 1, p. 109.

Longs Peak Trailhead
This trailhead lies at 9,400 feet and provides access to the East Longs Peak Trail and the Storm Pass Trail. It is one of the busiest trailheads in RMNP, and the ranger station here is staffed regularly during the summer. The East Longs Peak Trail is very popular and provides access to routes on every side of Longs Peak. From the junction of US 36 and CO 7 in Estes Park, drive south on CO 7 for 8.8 miles to the turnoff for Longs Peak. Turn right and drive west 1 mile to the trailhead.

TRAILS

Chasm Lake Spur Trail
This is the spur trail that begins at Chasm Junction and leads southwest for 0.9 mile to Chasm Lake. See Chasm Lake, p. 223.

East Longs Peak Trail
From the Longs Peak Trailhead, the East Longs Peak Trail climbs northwest for 0.5 mile to the junction with the trail to Eugenia Mine and Storm Pass, which also provides access to Estes Cone. The East Longs Peak Trail swings southwest and climbs switchbacks through the forest. The trail meets Alpine Brook and turns northwest to climb a switchback before gaining a flat area and turning west to climb through Goblins Forest, a dense section of woodland with multitudes of fantastic, twisted limber pines. The trail crosses tiny Larkspur Creek and ascends more switchbacks to pop out near treeline and cross a footbridge that spans beautiful Alpine Brook.

From here the East Longs Peak Trail travels south among stunted trees and provides a high perspective overlooking the cities on the plains to the southeast. With a predawn start, hikers usually reach this section before sunrise, and the bright city lights are

Bighorn sheep alongside the Chasm Lake Spur Trail

East Longs Peak Trail

quite spectacular. The dual humps of Twin Sisters Peaks stand out to the east. The trail enters open, treeless terrain and offers dramatic views of Longs Peak, with the Diamond's sheer 1,000-foot face rising behind the shoulder of Mount Lady Washington. The trail climbs steadily to Battle Mountain Junction, then cuts southwest along the basin, paralleling Mills Moraine (p. 240). It surmounts Mills Moraine near its western end where the trail splits. Chasm Lake Spur Trail leads southwest to Chasm Lake. The East Longs Peak Trail swings northwest to skirt the eastern flank of Mount Lady Washington and climbs to Granite Pass, the point where the North Longs Peak Trail joins the East Longs Peak Trail.

From Granite Pass, the East Longs Peak Trail turns southwest and climbs long, shallow switchbacks through tundra to the Boulder Field (p. 240). This famous landmark is a giant field of granite boulders at the base of Longs' North Face, northeast of The Keyhole (p. 241). The trail crosses the Boulder Field to reach an arena of crude, manmade rock walls that shelter tent sites for campers. Here the trail ends; the continuation of The Keyhole Route (p. 231) up Longs Peak becomes a route, not a trail.

North Longs Peak Trail

This gorgeous trail climbs along the slopes of Half and Battle Mountains to approach Longs Peak from the north. It is 2.9 miles longer, but less crowded, than the East Longs Peak Trail. This distance can be shortened to 1.8 miles longer by hiking from Storm Pass Trail Parking on Bear Lake Road and using the Boulder Brook Trail to shortcut a portion of the North Longs Peak Trail.

From the Glacier Gorge Trailhead (see Region 1, p. 109), hike southwest for 0.25 mile to Glacier Gorge Junction (p. 114). Turn south and follow the Loch Vale/Glacier Gorge Trail past Alberta Falls for 1.3 miles to the junction with the North Longs Peak Trail. Turn east and cross Glacier Creek on a bridge. Follow the North Longs Peak Trail as it climbs across and up the vast, open slopes of Half Mountain, Storm Peak, and Battle Mountain toward Granite Pass (p. 240). This section of the trail is breathtaking. It is 7.2 miles from the Glacier Gorge Trailhead to Granite Pass, where the North Longs Peak Trail meets the East Longs Peak Trail.

ALPINE BROOK

Jims Grove   11,120 feet

T *Regional map p. 222 (M, 11); hike map p. 228*

Jims Grove is a pretty section of forest south of Mills Moraine and north of Point 11,408'. The area used to shelter NPS campsites, but they have now been closed for revegetation. A nebulous spur trail angles west and uphill through the grove to join the East Longs Peak Trail immediately south of Granite Pass. The NPS no longer classifies this route as an established or designated trail, and discourages its use.

Pine Ridge   *Regional map p. 222 (L, 12)*

This wooded ridge is the eastern arm of Battle Mountain and separates Alpine Brook from Inn Brook.

Granite Pass   12,060 feet

T *Regional map p. 222 (M, 7); hike map p. 228*

Granite Pass, where the North Longs Peak Trail meets the East Longs Peak Trail, is a small saddle between the north ridge of Mount Lady Washington and the southwestern rib of Battle Mountain. It is located 4.3 miles from the Longs Peak Trailhead and 6.9 miles from the Glacier Gorge Trailhead, and provides wonderful views of Hallett Peak and the Mummy Range. The pass was gouged from veins of volcanic rock sandwiched between the much harder granite that comprises the bulk of Longs Peak's great mass. The softer volcanic layers were eaten away faster than the granite, forming a depression between the two ridges and creating a passageway between them.

ROARING FORK

Mills Moraine and Chasm Junction   11,540 feet

T *Regional map p. 222 (N, 10); hike map p. 228*

Mills Moraine is a lateral moraine that lies east of Longs Peak and separates Roaring Fork from Alpine Brook. Chasm Junction lies at the west edge of Mills Moraine and is the point where the East Longs Peak Trail turns northwest toward Granite Pass, and the Chasm Lake Spur Trail leads southwest to Chasm Lake.

BOULDER FIELD AREA

Boulder Field   12,800 feet

T *Regional map p. 222 (O, 5); hike map p. 228*

This relatively flat plateau of jumbled granite boulders lies above treeline at almost 13,000 feet. It stretches 1.2 miles in length and reaches 0.8 mile at its widest point. It is bordered on the west by Storm Peak, on the east by Mount Lady Washington, and on the south by the mighty North Face of Longs Peak. It is where the hiking trail ends and the rough scramble up the latter part of The Keyhole Route begins. Recent scientific hypotheses have proposed the existence of a glacier below the rock and tundra of the Boulder Field, but nothing has been proven and many geologists disagree with this theory.

Agnes Vaille Memorial Shelter   13,160 feet

T **OT** *Regional map p. 222 (O, 4); hike map p. 228*

Below the southeastern margin of The Keyhole is a conical-topped stone hut fashioned out of the same granite that litters the Boulder Field. In January 1925, after three previous attempts, Agnes Vaille and the experienced Swiss mountaineer Walter Kiener made the first winter ascent of the East Face. Vaille, age 35, was so exhausted by the summit bid that she stumbled while descending the North Face and fell about 150 feet. Kiener rushed to her aid, but she was battered and too fatigued to continue, and he went to seek help.

Kiener and three other rescuers attempted to climb back to Vaille, but two of the men were insufficiently dressed and eventually turned back. One of those reached a shelter cabin near Jims Grove, while the other, Herbert Sortland, became hopelessly lost. It is believed that Sortland fell and broke his hip, and, at the mercy of the fierce weather, he perished within a short distance of Longs Peak Inn, where he had been caretaker. Vaille also succumbed to the elements and died before help could reach her. Kiener survived with severe frostbite that claimed several fingers, part of one foot, and all of his toes. A sobering plaque bolted to the Agnes Vaille Memorial Shelter commemorates Vaille and Sortland and warns others of the dangers presented by climbing this prodigious peak.

The Keyhole 13,160 feet

T **OT** *Regional map p. 222 (O, 4); hike map p. 228*

This remarkable feature is the "key" to The Keyhole Route. It is a gaping, oval-shaped hole in the ridge between Longs and Storm Peaks, providing nontechnical access to the west side of Longs Peak. It is open at the top—framed by dramatic, overhanging rock fins that don't quite meet to complete the oval shape. Without this striking feature providing a break in the steep ridge, climbers would be forced onto technical terrain to use this route to summit the mountain. The exhilarating, unsurpassed view of Glacier Gorge from The Keyhole is a principal highlight on the ascent of Longs Peak. The glistening lakes lie nearly 3,000 feet below and are ringed with the 13,000-foot peaks of Glacier Gorge, creating a dazzling panorama of alpine glory.

LONGS PEAK EAST FACE

Mills Glacier 12,300 feet

T **OT** **◩** *Regional map p. 222 (P, 7); hike map p. 228*

Together with Lambs Slide, Mills Glacier forms an L-shaped body of snow and ice. Disputes between geologists have shed doubt on the status of modern-day Mills Glacier and whether or not it moves—a characteristic of a true glacier. During the intense drought of 2002, the ice and snow that usually can be seen above ground disappeared completely.

Mills Glacier lies directly below the Diamond at the base of the mighty East Face of Longs Peak. A hike to the base of the glacier from Chasm Lake is a rough trek into a wild area of RMNP. From Chasm Lake, skirt the lake on the north and locate a coarse, cairned trail that weaves through the boulder field above the lake. The trail ends on the west side of the lake, below the East Face. The glacier is steep, and technical skills are needed to ascend it.

Lambs Slide 12,300–13,280 feet

◩ *Regional map p. 222 (Q, 7); hike map p. 228*

This is the 1,000-foot snow couloir that ascends from Mills Glacier to the top of Glacier Ridge. It is bordered on the east by Glacier Ridge and is used to access Broadway, the horizontal ledge at the base of the Diamond. An ascent of Lambs Slide is a technical venture, and crampons, a helmet, a rope, and an ice axe are recommended. The condition of this steep slope is widely variable—from soft snow to bulletproof ice—and Lambs Slide has been the scene of numerous injuries and multiple fatalities.

The feature was named for Reverend Elkanah Lamb, who homesteaded 160 acres east of Longs Peak in 1875. He and his son Carlyle were early Longs Peak mountain

Lambs Slide

guides. After a solo ascent of the mountain in 1871, Lamb decided to descend the then-unclimbed East Face. In downclimbing he concluded that he had made a mistake, and though he wished to return to the summit and go down the standard route, he had bypassed several technical difficulties he didn't think he could reclimb. He decided to "face the music," as he wrote in a report 34 years later, and ended up at the top of today's Lambs Slide. He slipped as he tried to cross it, and with death imminent, he somehow grabbed a conical-shaped boulder and arrested his fall. His self-rescue from this precarious position is an entertaining tale of a mountaineer who took chances and got lucky enough to escape a near-fatal fall relatively unscathed. Lamb's legacy lives on in the name of this notable snow and ice gully.

Glacier Ridge 13,190 feet
Regional map p. 222 (Q, 7); hike map p. 228

This is the prominent rock rib that borders Lambs Slide on the east and rises from Mills Glacier to a saddle at the top of Lambs Slide. All aspects of this ridge are technical.

East Face and the Diamond
Regional map p. 222 (P, 5); hike map p. 228

The East Face of Longs Peak stretches from Lambs Slide to Chasm View and encompasses such features as The Notch, Diagonal Wall, Chasm View Wall, Devils Staircase, and the Diamond. The Diamond is the awesome diamond-shaped vertical wall in the middle of the East Face. It rises for nearly 1,000 vertical feet from Broadway (a long, horizontal ledge that traverses the East Face) to the apex near the summit of Longs Peak. Chasm Lake (see the route description on p. 223) is one of the best places to view this magnificent wall. The East Face sports a multitude of technical climbing routes that entice climbers to test their mettle against nature and ascend a very unforgiving side of the peak. There are no hikes on this aspect of the mountain. Note that everything west of Ships Prow requires technical climbing skills.

The Diamond

The Beaver 14,004 feet

The Beaver is a distinct rock formation on the south ridge of Longs Peak. The Beaver was named in 1974 when James Michener identified the feature in his acclaimed classic novel, Centennial. Michener referred to Longs Peak as the mountain upon which a giant stone beaver seemed to be climbing upward. The deep cleft between the summit plateau and the southeast ridge borders the nose of the Beaver as it is looking up at the peak. The Beaver has an obvious brow and a large head, which drops down to a depression between the animal's shoulder and back. The Beaver's tail ends near The Loft.

◹ The Notch 13,830 feet

The Notch is a large, 200-foot cleft in the southeast ridge of Longs Peak. It is a distinct gap located between the summit plateau and the "nose" of the Beaver that can be seen for miles away. It also separates the Palisades from the summit of Longs Peak. It can be accessed from the top of Keplinger's Couloir on the south side and from Notch Couloir on the East Face. Both of these access routes are technical. There are no hiking routes to, or up, The Notch.

LONGS PEAK NORTH FACE

Chasm View 13,500 feet

T OT *Regional map p. 222 (P, 5); hike map p. 228*

Chasm View is a small gap in the ridge at the base of Longs Peak's great North Face. It provides a wonderful vantage from which to view the mighty East Face of Longs Peak, where it is common to see technical climbers ascending the sheer wall of the Diamond. Chasm View has a dramatic 800-foot vertical drop-off on the east, and it is thrilling to gaze into the abyss of Chasm Lake. A rough, off-trail hike across the Boulder Field leads to Chasm View. A tiny hole in the floor of the ledge looks straight down into the void. Chasm View overlooks the Diamond about midway up the 1,000-foot face and showcases the North Face and the Boulder Field as well. From the campsites at the Boulder Field, leave the trail and hike southeast across large boulders for 0.4 mile to Chasm View.

The Dove 13,240 feet

Regional map p. 222 (P, 5); hike map p. 228

The Dove is a distinct pattern of snow and ice located between The Keyhole and the North Face that looks roughly like a bird in flight when viewed from above. The formation is the only aboveground, permanent ice feature near the Boulder Field.

◹ North Face 13,540 feet

Longs Peak's sweeping North Face rises above the Boulder Field and is a popular climbing destination. It is considered technical, with a rating of Class 5.4. It used to be the most popular hiking route up the mountain, when the technical sections of rock were fitted with strong metal cables to assist hikers in climbing the face. These stiff handrails were in place from 1925 to 1973, but the NPS finally removed the cables and returned the route to its original difficulty in an effort to reduce accidents (serious rockfall was common, resulting in injuries and fatalities) and to reinstate the pristine, natural condition of the mighty North Face. The North Face is still commonly referred to as 'The Cable Route,' but has been replaced by The Keyhole Route (Class 3+) as the most popular "hiking" route up the mountain.

LONGS PEAK WEST FACE

The Ledges 13,170 feet

The Ledges are a series of horizontal rock shelves above slick granite slabs that connect The Keyhole to The Trough. The Ledges are located about midway up The Trough between Glacier Gorge and the Narrows. Painted circles of yellow and red dye referred to as "bulls-eyes" or "fried eggs" serve as landmarks to guide climbers along the route. A steep V-shaped niche between boulders marks the crux of the Ledges, reinforced with an iron rod serving as a handhold. From the V slot, the route descends slightly, then climbs into The Trough.

◪ The Trough 11,800–13,865 feet

This moderately steep couloir rises from upper Glacier Gorge to a notch on the west ridge of Longs Peak, where it meets the Narrows. It is wide at the bottom and then climbs up to an impressive curve. Then it leads north and gets narrower as it progresses. The Keyhole Route (p. 231) intersects The Trough midway up the couloir and ascends the upper section to the Narrows. The Trough is often filled with snow, but sometimes it melts out entirely to reveal a rubble-filled gully. A chockstone just below the point where The Trough meets the Narrows is the crux of The Keyhole Route and presents a move or two of semi-technical climbing (Class 3+). The exposure makes these moves seem harder than they really are. The principal danger in The Trough is rockfall that is kicked off by hikers and climbers, so a helmet is recommended for protection. Take extreme care when ascending or descending this couloir, as the welfare of others may depend upon your actions.

The Narrows 13,865 feet

At the top of The Trough, the steep walls of Longs Peak's west and south faces extend upward to the summit. The gap between The Trough and the Narrows gives a wonderful view into Wild Basin. The Narrows, a 3-foot-wide ledge, provides an exposed but straightforward route across the initial section of the south face. A sheer drop-off to the south strikes fear into the hearts of many hikers at this point, but a broken rock wall on the opposite side provides good handholds and presents the option of leaning into the wall, away from the abyss. The Narrows give way to a wider ledge system that leads east to the base of the Homestretch.

Sandy White and Dale Hatcher traverse The Narrows

LONGS PEAK SOUTH FACE

The Homestretch 13,980 feet

The Homestretch is a series of perpendicular cracks that provide passage up the steep south face of Longs Peak. The fissures run parallel to one another and are the only weaknesses in the upper cliffs of Longs Peak that provide relative nontechnical access to the summit. All the easiest routes up Longs Peak converge at the base of the Homestretch to utilize this relatively "easy" passage to the summit. The smooth slabs that surround the cracks present harder climbing, so to keep the difficulty at a minimum, the cracks must be used. The route is highly exposed and Class 3 when dry. Wet or icy conditions alter the scope of this "hike" to the top of Longs Peak, turning it into a technical challenge.

Steve Lawlor on The Homestretch

The Palisades 13,990 feet

The Palisades are a series of beautiful west-facing cliffs high on the southeast side of Longs Peak. They are most easily viewed from the Narrows and Homestretch of The Keyhole Route (p. 231). The two largest towers are about 400 feet high. The Palisades are the obstacles that must be skirted when using the Clarks Arrow Route (p. 232) to ascend Longs Peak. All climbs up these buttresses are technical.

The Palisades

Eastern Perimeter

The eastern border of RMNP butts up against civilization in nearby Allenspark, Meeker Park, and Estes Park. Numerous worthwhile destinations lie outside RMNP boundaries in National Forest Service land near these towns. This region includes these destinations and those immediately inside the RMNP boundary at the eastern edge.

Homer Rouse Trail

SUBREGIONS with Highlighted Hiking Destinations

GLEN HAVEN AREA 249
    Crosier Mountain 249

BIG THOMPSON CANYON 250
    Sheep Mountain 250

LION GULCH 251
    Homestead Meadows 251

ESTES PARK AREA 252
    Lake Estes..................................... 252
    Oldman Mountain 252

EAST PORTAL AREA 255
    Emerald Mountain 255
    Storm Pass 255

FISH CREEK ROAD AREA 258
    Homer Rouse Trail............................. 258

LILY LAKE AREA 259
    Lily Lake...................................... 259
    Lily Mountain 259
    Twin Sisters Peaks on Twin Sisters Mountain....... 261
    Estes Cone 262

PIERSON PARK 263

View from 'Lightning Peak'

TRAILHEADS 266

TRAILS 268

OTHER POINTS OF INTEREST 269

Old Man Mountain

Opposite: Lily Lake (see p. 259)

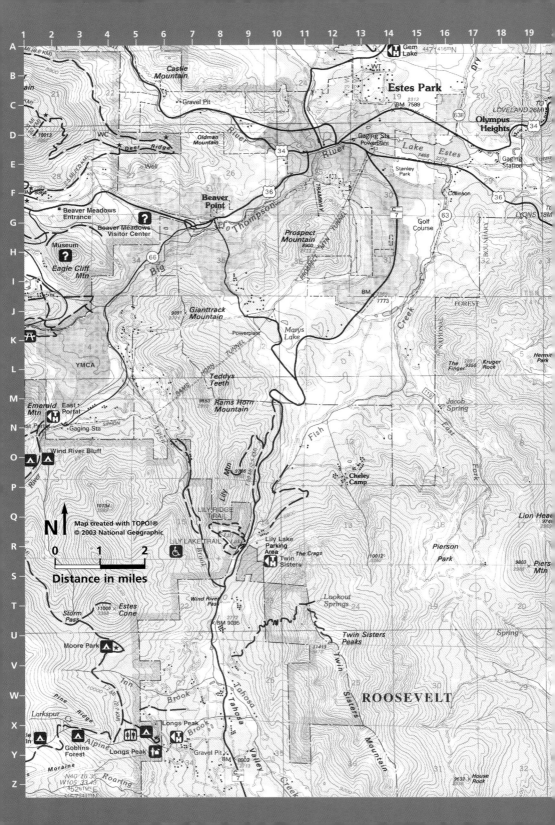

GLEN HAVEN AREA   *Regional map p. 248 (not shown on map)*

PEAKS

Crosier Mountain   9,250 feet

T   *Regional map p. 248 (not shown on map)*

This rounded foothill lies east of RMNP in Roosevelt National Forest, south of CR 43 and north of US 34. Four trailheads provide access to the peak: Garden Gate, Glen Haven, Crosier Mountain Gravel Pit, and Sullivan Gulch. Crosier Mountain is a popular location enjoyed by hunters, hikers, bicyclists, and dog and horse enthusiasts. It's a good year-round destination, especially when higher-

Steve Volker and Ken Godowski on Crosier Mountain

elevation destinations are difficult to access because of ice and snow. It is strategically located with good views of the high peaks and a nice sampling of the diversity of the low-elevation woodlands that make up Roosevelt National Forest. The well-traveled trails lead to a rocky outcrop at the top. The trails are quite steep in some sections and fairly wide and deeply rutted in others.

Glen Haven Access GRADE I CLASS 2   This is the closest approach to Crosier Mountain from Estes Park. From the Glen Haven Trailhead (p. 267), a dirt road winds past the stables and private residences to a narrow path that marks the start of the trail. From here, the Crosier Mountain Trail (Trail 931) climbs up the hillside along a deeply rutted trail, then descends and crosses a creek that flows from Piper Meadows. It then climbs to a lovely open meadow where it is common to see deer and elk. The trail traverses along the edge of the meadow, providing wonderful views of RMNP's magnificent Mummy Range to the northwest. Follow the Crosier Mountain Trail and pass several trail junctions. The trail becomes considerably steeper and rises through an amazingly dense lodgepole pine forest. The trees are straight and beautiful, seemingly the same size and age, creating an enchanting, dark, impenetrable woodland. The trail breaks out of the uniformity of the pines and levels on a bench were a large rock cairn marks the last trail junction. Follow the sign and turn west for the final 0.5-mile climb that ascends 480 vertical feet to Crosier Mountain. The trail negotiates several steep switchbacks and climbs to a level open area topped by a small rock outcrop that represents the zenith of this forested mountain. Views of Longs Peak and the eastern skyline of RMNP are stunning.

Crosier Mountain Gravel Pit Trailhead Access GRADE I CLASS 2   From the Crosier Mountain Gravel Pit Trailhead (p. 266), hike south on Trail 1013 for 1.9 miles to the junction with the Crosier Mountain Trail (above). Turn east and follow the Crosier Mountain Trail 1.3 miles to the junction with the summit spur trail. Turn west and negotiate the steep trail for 0.5 mile to the summit.

Garden Gate Access GRADE I CLASS 2   From the Garden Gate Trailhead (p. 267) hike south, then west along the Crosier Mountain Trail (above) for 3.7 miles to the junction with the summit spur trail. Turn west and negotiate the steep trail for 0.5 mile to the summit.

Sullivan Gulch Access GRADE I CLASS 2   At the Sullivan Gulch Trailhead (p. 268), a small sign indicates the start of the Sullivan Gulch Trail in a scenic, narrow draw. Follow the trail north as it climbs relentlessly and very steeply to the area near Sullivan Park. The trail is indistinct in many areas and generally difficult to follow. It virtually disappears in Sullivan Park. Hike to the junction with the Crosier Mountain Trail (see p. 249; 1.5 miles from the trailhead) and follow it west for 2.9 miles to the junction with the summit spur trail. Turn west and negotiate the steep trail for 0.5 mile to the summit.

BIG THOMPSON CANYON   *Regional map p. 248 (not shown on map)*

PEAKS

Sheep Mountain 8,450 feet
T *Regional map p. 248 (not shown on map)*

Jim Cleary on Sheep Mountain's summit

This lovely peak is a high point along the forested ridges that border the Big Thompson canyon. A small clearing near the top offers good views of RMNP. The trailhead is 16 miles east of Estes Park on US 34.

Round Mountain Trailhead Access GRADE I CLASS 1
From the Round Mountain Trailhead (p. 268), the Foothills Nature Trail and the Summit Adventure Trail strike out west along a double-track road. Pass a gate and follow the road for 0.3 mile to a marked junction where the summit trail cuts back to the east. The nature trail leads to a scenic overlook. Follow the summit trail as it climbs the hillside overlooking the Big Thompson River.

The canyon stretches impressively below the trail, with the river and road noise echoing off the canyon walls. Interpretive signs along the trail explain facts about plant life and the mountain ecosystem. The thick ponderosa pine forest on the south side of the canyon contrasts the more sparsely treed hillside across the river. Bitterbrush, the main staple of mule deer, covers the slope. Common and Rocky Mountain juniper, yucca, and prickly pear cactus abound in this environment. The trail climbs through the forest at a steady grade, gradually turning southwest and away from the river corridor. Look for pasqueflowers in spring, and Colorado blue grouse year-round. Continue to a beautiful, wet glade created by a small spring.

Several unique rock formations line the path, including one in the shape of a holy water basin that stands in the middle of the trail. The pathway weaves through some interesting rock walls before angling up the long, final stretch that skirts broken rock faces near the top. A large summit cairn made of mid-sized rocks stands nearly 8 feet high and marks the forested summit area. There are no views from the highest point because the trees are too thick. Hike west of the summit cairn to a small opening in the trees to enjoy views of RMNP's Hallett Peak, Mummy Mountain, and Mount Dickinson. The small clearing is a pleasant spot to have lunch and read the interpretive sign that directs the eye to distant Mount Meeker and Longs Peak, the two highest peaks in the region.

LION GULCH   *Regional map p. 248 (not shown on map)*

OTHER DESTINATIONS

Homestead Meadows   8,660 feet

T **[figure]** *Regional map p. 248 (not shown on map)*

A homesteader cabin in Homestead Meadows

Homestead Meadows is home to eight ranch sites established by early settlers in the late 1800s. Interpretive signs provide photographs and information about the pioneers who built cabins, barns, outbuildings, and sawmills in a series of meadows now located within Roosevelt National Forest, just 8 miles southeast of Estes Park. The area's low elevation keeps the trail free of snow for much of the year. Horse enthusiasts frequent the area, and many locals opt for this hike because dogs are permitted, a limited luxury on the public land near Estes Park. First established in 1889, almost 30 years after the Homestead Act of 1862 began to entice settlers to the Western states with the promise of free land, Homestead Meadows saw individuals and families struggle to make a living cattle ranching, timber harvesting, and farming. Multiple ownerships ended in the 1960s, when the Holnholz family purchased all the area homesteads, consolidating them into one. In 1978 the Forest Service bought the southern section of their large estate, which showcases ruins of early ranches established near the turn of the 20th century.

From the Lion Gulch Trailhead (p. 267), follow the broad Lion Gulch Trail (p. 269) as it descends a hill and crosses the Little Thompson River. Continue as the trail climbs at a steady, moderate grade to a broad meadow. The first homestead is 2.8 miles from the trailhead. A sign directs hikers to the respective homesteads, located on a series of loop trails that are relatively flat and easy, accessing the eight historic home sites. Some of the trails follow original wagon roads created by the early settlers. Several sites feature cabins and barns that are still standing; others have old farm machinery and crumbling foundations. Most of the structures were built with lumber cut and milled by the settlers.

The first ruin site along the Lion Gulch Trail system is the Walker Homestead. Sarah Walker was the only woman to homestead in the area, and she worked the land for more than 15 years, making a living by selling her fresh eggs and cream in Lyons. Well-marked loop trails direct the hiker to the other homesteads. The Griffith Homestead is east of the Walker property. North of the Walker Homestead is the Irvin Homestead, which was home to several early residents. R. J. Nettleton and his daughter Peg raised rabbits there. The pelts from Peg's rabbits were used as lining for military parkas during World War II. The Brown Homestead is also located in the northern section of the meadows. The Brown family made a living out of cattle ranching, owning this property for nearly 40 years. The Engert, Laycook, Boren, and Hill homesteads are situated in the southern end of the valley.

All of these sites are historically significant and interesting to see in person. The rotting structures, old sawmills, and abandoned farm machinery all tell a tale of hardy settlers paving the way for future generations to prosper in the area. The 1990 nomination of this parcel of land to the National Register of Historic Places is an appropriate testimony to the historical significance of these ranch sites and to the stories of the energetic folk who sought to make a living from this rocky, inhospitable landscape. Experiencing the sites firsthand is an educational experience that makes it easier to imagine what it was like for families ranching and homesteading in the early 1900s.

ESTES PARK AREA *Regional map p. 248 (B, 15)*

LAKES

Lake Estes 7,468 feet
T 🚶 ♿ *Regional map p. 248 (D, 16)*

Olympus Dam blocks the flow of Big Thompson River to create Lake Estes, located between US 36 and US 34 at the east end of Estes Park. A scenic, paved path circles the lake, providing recreation to hikers, runners, and bicyclists. The loop is 3.8 miles long and gains a total of 120 feet. There are multiple well-marked parking lots that service the trail, which can be accessed conveniently from either highway. The trail runs east along the north shore and crosses the inlet stream on a footbridge. It continues east and passes the marina, then loops around and below Olympus Dam, and crosses the outlet stream on a footbridge. Anglers frequent this area. The path climbs to Mall Road, then swings west along the south shore and parallels US 36. It passes the fire station and power plant and continues to loop around to the north shore of the lake.

PEAKS AND OTHER DESTINATIONS

Oldman Mountain 8,310 feet
OT *Regional map p. 248 (D, 8)*

Oldman Mountain is a notable peak located on the western edge of Estes Park, sandwiched between the Fall and Big Thompson River corridors. This prominent local landmark sports sloping rock walls and ledges on all sides, and the upper section, a conical granite knob, resembles a rock beehive from most vantages. Though relatively low-angle, the smooth granite slabs that comprise the bulk of the mountain prevent easy access to the top, and even the least difficult routes require some rock scrambling. The easiest route is sometimes marked by squares of orange paint that guide the hiker through the precipitous rock bulges that guard the summit. The paint fades over time, but often gets repainted. Grand views of Estes Park and RMNP abound from the top of this small but high-profile peak.

European settlers took note of the rock outline that resembles a human face, and unofficially called this peak "Oldman Mountain" decades before the U.S. Board on Geographic Names formally recognized it in 1965. The Arapaho Indians called it "Sitting Man," as they also identified the manlike figure that is obvious when viewed from the north. When interviewed by Oliver Toll in 1914, members of the tribe remembered that fellow clansmen fasted on the summit. The site was sacred to prehistoric Native Americans, where they conducted ritual "vision quests" that would bring healing power and good fortune. Projectile points and ceremonial artifacts that were found on and near Oldman Mountain tell a history of intermittent Native American occupation of the Estes Park area, with hunters traveling back and forth across the Continental Divide. Seasonal hunting opportunities and the prospect of escaping the heat on the plains during the summer may have been the reason they traveled regularly to the region.

Southwest Slope GRADE I CLASS 2+

From the roadside parking at the end of Old Ranger Drive (p. 267), pass the gate at Oldman Mountain Estates and follow a faint path uphill past the UNC buildings to a wide, prominent gully on the south side of the mountain. This gully is adorned with ponderosa pines, Douglas fir, and rock slabs. A few cairns mark the route up the moderately steep ravine. At the highpoint of the main gully, a small saddle offers a sneak peak of the Fall River corridor. Turn northwest (left) and hike over low angle slabs to a prominent overlook that provides impressive views of Fall River and Estes Park. From here the route gets more technical and can be daunting if the rock is wet or snowy. From the overlook, look sharply for a route through the rock blobs that ascends the upper slopes of the mountain, sometimes marked by rectangles of orange paint. Scramble up the rocks and top out on the summit, composed of large, horizontal slabs of granite. Mountaintop weathering pits, or large rock basins, fill with rainwater during the summer. Lumpy Ridge and Lake Estes stand out over Estes Park to the north and east. To the west, Stones Peak is nicely framed by the gap between Deer Ridge and Beaver Mountain. The Longs Peak group looms to the south. Directly west and below the summit is a gentle meadow laced with horse trails that lead to Deer Ridge.

Mount Olympus 8,808 feet

`OT` *Regional map p. 248 (not shown on map)*

One of the most famous photos taken by Enos Mills in the early 1900s depicts a winding river snaking its way through a spacious, pristine valley rimmed with high mountain peaks. The photo exudes serenity and illustrates the reason he fought so hard to preserve so much land near Estes Park by establishing RMNP. The sublime beauty of this unique mountain landscape has stirred the hearts of millions since Mills stood atop Mount Olympus and composed that photo.

A hiker on rocks west of Mount Olympus' summit

In Greek mythology, Mount Olympus is the home of the gods. It is easy to see why this modest peak was named for such a lofty place. Though the beauty and magnitude of the Continental Divide and the grandeur of the Big Thompson River has changed little since RMNP was established in 1915, the Estes Park valley has expanded into a maze of roads and housing developments, business corridors and power lines. The most notable difference between today's view from Mount Olympus and Enos' photograph is Lake Estes, which swallowed the bulk of the Big Thompson River as if flowed through the valley and buried it under a large body of water.

Mount Olympus is a worthwhile destination that offers spectacular views of the Continental Divide, Estes Park, and its foothills. Surrounded on three sides by private land, the only legal access near this sculptured granite mountaintop is from Roosevelt National Forest on US 34. The summit of Mount Olympus is private property and is off-limits. Crocker Ranch, located in a beautiful valley between Mount Olympus and Mount Pisgah, owns much of the mountain, including the summit and the region about 100 yards north of it. Even without reaching the summit, this is a fun bushwhack up a beautiful mountain, and several rock outcrops on public land (see photo above) offer good views of Estes Park.

Northwest Slope GRADE I CLASS 2 From the junction of US 36 and US 34 in Estes Park, drive east on US 34 for 3 miles to a small dirt pullout on the south side of the road. This parking area is located at the brown Roosevelt National Forest sign and is big enough for about four cars. There is no trail to the top of this peak, and the route is steep, leading up the northwest slope.

Leave the parking area and bushwhack up the hillside, dodging dense brush and climbing over rock slabs. A shallow ravine provides easier passage for the first few hundred yards. Climb out of the ravine and gain the broad forested slope. Continue bushwhacking through the trees, as the forest thins out slightly. Pick a route over rock slabs, through thick trees, and upward over nasty bushes. Continue to climb steadily in a southeasterly direction to the granite domes that make up the summit. Use caution not to trespass on private land, which includes the entire summit. The rocks on the west offer the best views of Estes Park, but are not the true summit blocks. If permission is somehow procured, climb up the steep granite knobs to the summit ridge and hop east along the rocky spine to the top. Mount Olympus' south side is a craggy wonderland of deep cracks and sheer slabs interspersed with blocky outcrops. Crocker Ranch lies in the lush valley to the south. The Big Thompson River winds through the canyon to the north. Hike over to the rocks on the western-most side of the summit ridge to view the vantage from which Enos Mills took his famous photograph.

Mount Pisgah 8,630 feet
OT *Regional map p. 248 (not shown on map)*

Mount Pisgah is one of the few entirely privately owned mountains near Estes Park. It is a small, forested peak immediately north of US 36, near the top of Park Hill and south of Mount Olympus. It is owned by Crocker Ranch and, historically, public access has been denied. The original Mount Pisgah, located east of the Dead Sea, was a biblical site from which Moses looked down on the Promised Land (a place he couldn't enter) before his death. It's ironic that Moses could only look at the Promised Land but not enter it, whereas visitors can look up to Mount Pisgah but not climb it. This is unfortunate because it's a fun hike to a rocky little summit.

Prospect Mountain 8,900 feet
R *Regional map p. 248 (H, 11)*

This large, forested dome lies immediately south of downtown Estes Park and is privately owned. An aerial tramway ascends the north side of the peak to a sub-summit with good views of the Continental Divide. A service road snakes up the east side of the mountain but is blocked midway by a gate. Two rock features, The Thumb and The Needle, are located on the southeast aspect and are popular with technical rock climbers. Access to these rock outcrops is via a trail that leaves the service road imme-diately before the gate and climbs extremely steeply for 0.2 mile to the base of the rocks. Permission from either the company that operates the aerial tramway or the administrators of the Colorado–Big Thompson Project, which has a tunnel that goes underneath Prospect Mountain from Marys Lake to Lake Estes, is necessary to hike the 1.6-mile-long road to the summit of this mountain. From the junction of US 36 and CO 7 near Estes Park, drive south on CO 7 for 1.6 miles to Peak View Drive. Turn right and drive west for 0.9 mile to Curry Drive. Turn right and drive up the steep road for 0.5 mile to the gate.

Gianttrack Mountain 9,091 feet
OT *Regional map p. 248 (J, 7)*

This forested dome lies in Roosevelt National Forest, west of Marys Lake and north of Rams Horn Mountain near Estes Park. The summit is on Forest Service land, but it is completely landlocked by private parcels that circle the base of this pretty peak. There is no legal access to Forest Service property from either CO 66 or Marys Lake Road. A highly visible dirt road leads west from Marys Lake Road to the broad saddle between Gianttrack Mountain and Rams Horn Mountain, but the road is private and off-limits to the public. The only ways to get there are via helicopter or to get permission from one of the local landowners at the base. If permission is granted, there are a few horse trails that traverse low on the peak, but reaching the summit involves a steep bushwhack to the forested summit. Several scenic meadows grace the north side of the mountain.

EAST PORTAL AREA   Regional map p. 248 (N, 3)

PEAKS AND OTHER DESTINATIONS

Emerald Mountain   9,237 feet
T **OT**   *Regional map p. 248 (M, 1)*

Tucked neatly within an irregular
panhandle of land just inside RMNP's
eastern border, Emerald Mountain
is located between the YMCA of the
Rockies and Glacier Basin. Its strategic
placement offers great views of the
Continental Divide as well as a lovely
panorama of the low-lying mountains
of the Estes Park valley. The mostly
off-trail hike is short and quite steep,
climbing through sage and a sparse
ponderosa pine forest. Much of the land
that surrounds this tiny peak is private,

Amber Greathouse on the summit of Emerald Mountain

but the south side is publicly accessible via
the East Portal Trailhead. East Portal lies at
the southwest end of CO 66, and there is a
circular drive with parking allowed on the
shoulder.

The Alva B. Adams Tunnel traverses beneath
the Continental Divide for 13.1 miles from
Grand Lake to East Portal, located at the base
of Emerald Mountain. Extremely controversial
at the time, the Colorado–Big Thompson
Project diverts water from Lake Granby,
Shadow Mountain Lake, and Grand Lake by
sending it underground to the thirsty east
side of the Continental Divide. Most of the
water from Adams Tunnel is diverted through
the Aspen Creek Siphon and the Rams Horn
Tunnel to the Marys Lake power plant. A small
portion passes through the gauging station
and joins Wind River at East Portal Reservoir,
which then flows into Big Thompson River.
The project was approved by President Franklin
Roosevelt in 1937 and completed 10 years later.

South Slope   GRADE I   CLASS 2   From the
circular drive near the East Portal Trailhead
(p. 266), a trail leaves the roadbed and
heads north across a meadow. The trail
enters the trees and begins to climb west up
the dusty hillside. After 0.25 mile, the trail
passes a sign and enters RMNP. About 100
yards farther is a junction with several other
trail systems: the Wind River Trail, routes
to the YMCA and the Glacier Basin Campground, and an alternate course to East
Portal. Here the trail loops upon itself, with the right-hand fork sweeping higher on
the hillside to reconnect with the original trail 50 yards later. Continue hiking west
toward Glacier Basin for 0.1 mile to an obvious rock outcrop on the north (right-hand)
side of the trail. Immediately past the boulders, take a right and follow a faint path
that climbs steeply up the southern flank of Emerald Mountain. The path becomes
indistinct and splits in different directions. Keep hiking uphill between sage and ponderosa pines to a wide gap in the rock outcrops near the top of the mountain. Pass
through the gap and continue as the trail levels slightly, traveling through a forested
area. The trail leaves the trees and again climbs steeply, quickly gaining the rocky summit.

Storm Pass   10,260 feet
T   *Regional map p. 248 (T, 3)*

Storm Pass is a wooded lowpoint between Estes Cone and Battle Mountain, separating
Wind River drainage on the north from Tahosa Creek tributaries on the south. A system
of trails converge at the top of Storm Pass: A spur trail leads 2.8 miles northeast to Lily

Lake (p. 259), while the Storm Pass Trail (p. 261) leads 3 miles northwest to Wind River and 4.5 miles to Bear Lake Road (see Storm Pass Trail Parking, Region 1, p. 110), or 2.6 miles southeast to the Longs Peak Trailhead (Region 4, p. 238). The trail to Estes Cone climbs very steeply for 0.7 mile to the summit.

'Lightning Peak' 10,567 feet

T **OT** *Regional map p. 248 (S, 4)*

This unofficially named mountain is one of RMNP's unheralded gems. It has a summit area made up of two rocky teeth, and scrambling between them is adventurous and fun. It is advantageously located to provide incomparable vistas in a stunning 360-degree panorama that is utterly breathtaking and is worth the arduous trek through forest and over rock, without the benefit of any trails, to the top of this seemingly modest and anonymous peak. Because the peak is officially unnamed, it offers seclusion that is rarely found on the lower foothill peaks of the region.

In 1907, when officials from the Young Men's Christian Association (YMCA) were searching for a location for their western conference grounds, they spied Ypsilon Mountain's 'Y-Couloir,' a set of gullies that cut down the striking east face and form a snowy Y. They believed that God had led them to the site, and established what is now the largest YMCA in the world. The staff and guests of the YMCA have been climbing the peaks near their campus ever since and are responsible for naming numerous area features, such as Teddy's Teeth on Rams Horn Mountain. They christened two small but regal summits directly north of their property 'Thunder Peak' and 'Lightning Peak,' and YMCA hike masters have for many years taken groups to the summits. Locals know the distinctive hills by these names, though they have never been officially recognized.

Northwest Ridge GRADE I CLASS 2   From the East Portal Trailhead (p. 266), follow the trail for a few hundred yards to a tiny canyon that harbors a weir and a small reservoir. Hike up the Wind River Trail for 50 yards to a trail junction. Continue along the Wind River Trail as it parallels the creek and passes along some bluffs adorned with interesting rock formations. The trail passes near a fork in the river. The eastern stream is a tributary of Wind River that flows from Storm Pass. Leave the trail and cross Wind River here, following the tributary until it is possible to gain an obvious ridge to the east. Climb to the crest of the ridge and follow it to a rock outcrop and a small saddle that allows a visual of the entire ridge leading up toward 'Lightning Peak.' To the east the rock fins and walls of 'Thunder Peak' can be seen. Drop down into the saddle and cross a seasonal drainage. Follow the forested ridge for 1.2 laborious miles as it crests numerous false summits. The west side of the ridge is denser and more difficult to hike through than the east. Follow the ridge as it dips and rises to a level rock outcropping north of a large saddle. This is the most convincing false summit, but it is not the true peak. Descend 160 feet into the saddle and hike up the forested slope to a jumbled boulder field that leads to the rocky teeth that make up the summit. The southern tooth is higher. A stony saddle separates the two summit knobs. Scrambling between the two highpoints is steep and somewhat exposed. An incredible panorama stretches from Mount Meeker and Longs Peak to the Continental Divide, the entire Mummy Range, Estes Park, and an impressive view of Lily Lake.

'Thunder Peak' 10,134 feet

T **OT** *Regional map p. 248 (Q, 4)*

This unofficially named summit is located southwest of Estes Park near the YMCA of the Rockies and has been a local landmark for years. Large rock fins and impressive granite outcrops rise out over the thick forest, making it a unique-looking foothill. This summit offers a stunning 360-degree panorama that is hard to beat. No trails lead up this mountain, making the hike a difficult exercise in bushwhacking.

Northwest Ridge GRADE I CLASS 2   From the East Portal Trailhead (p. 266), follow the trail for a few hundred yards to a tiny canyon that harbors a weir and a small reservoir. Hike up the Wind River Trail for 50 yards to a trail junction. Continue along the Wind River Trail as it parallels the creek and passes by some bluffs adorned with interesting rock formations. The trail passes near a fork in the river. Below the fork, leave the trail and cross Wind River, then bushwhack southeast through the thick forest for 0.6 mile to the northwest ridge of 'Thunder Peak.' Scramble along the crest of the distinctive rock rib, or avoid the craggy difficulties along the spine by descending slightly on the east side and traversing south through the forest. Top out at a saddle between the rock rib, ornamented by bulging granite outcrops, and the summit slope. The final trudge to the peak ascends through sparse forest inundated with downed timber to a boulder field that leads to a prominent rock outcrop. This is an obvious false summit. Dip down to a small depression immediately before the summit rocks, then scramble to the top of the rock shelf to reach the highpoint of 'Thunder Peak.' The summit is composed of a semiflat area of rock slabs and offers a commanding view of the area. The panorama encompasses Estes Cone, intimately situated to the south; the Longs Peak area; Stones Peak and Forest Canyon; the entire Mummy Range; the Windcliff housing development; Teddy's Teeth; Estes Park; Mount Olympus; and Lily Lake.

Tour de Estes Cone

T *Regional map p. 248 (T, 4)*

This circuit route orbits 11,006-foot Estes Cone, the unique, conical-shaped dome west of CO 7. Estes Cone is surrounded by a series of trails that sweep around the west, south, and east sides and offer pleasant hiking opportunities. Unfortunately, private land on the northern end of the Aspen Brook Trail prevents one from legally finishing a complete circuit of the peak, but a car shuttle at Lily Lake suffices to allow hikers to experience the beauty of this trail

Lindsey Landers on the Aspen Brook Trail

system without breaking the law. A pleasant detour to the summit of Estes Cone or a diversion along Aspen Brook to a beautiful series of meadows and some disintegrating cabins are added bonuses to this modest trail hike.

East Portal Trailhead Access GRADE I CLASS 2   From the East Portal Trailhead (p. 266), follow the trail for a few hundred yards to a trail junction. Follow the Wind River Trail (p. 269) to the Storm Pass Trail. The north (right hand) fork leads to Sprague Lake and Bear Lake Road. Turn south (left) and climb southeast along the Storm Pass Trail as it rises at a steeper grade and leads up a sparsely treed slope that offers good views of the surrounding peaks. Follow the Storm Pass Trail for 3 miles to Storm Pass, the site of a major trail junction. Storm Pass is not a dramatic place, as it is completely surrounded by forest with no views. Continue east, then northeast on the trail to Lily Lake. This trail ambles along the southeastern slope of Estes Cone and is mostly downhill. After 2.4 miles, the trail comes to a prominent junction at a substantial footbridge that spans Aspen Brook. A wonderful trail descends north along Aspen Brook but this reaches private property after 1.7 miles. Otherwise, this would be a logical loop back to the East Portal Trailhead and would eliminate the need for a car shuttle. From the bridge, follow the main trail as it climbs steeply for 0.6 mile to Lily Lake. A car shuttle at Lily Lake completes the day.

FISH CREEK ROAD AREA *Regional map p. 248 (O, 12)*

PEAKS AND OTHER DESTINATIONS

Homer Rouse Trail
T **Ⓗ** *Regional map p. 248 (O, 11)*

The Homer Rouse Trail was named for a popular RMNP superintendent, who served from 1992 to 1995. Part of the Estes Valley Trail System, this public trail through private property climbs south 1.8 miles from the Fish Creek valley near Estes Park to CO 7 near Lily Lake. The road incline is moderate, and this is a wonderful hike for families. It showcases superb wildflower displays in spring, and during autumn the numerous aspen stands turn vivid orange and yellow.

From the Fish Creek Trailhead (p. 266), hike south for 0.6 mile along the dirt road to a gate at the start of the Homer Rouse Trail. Pass the gate and walk south along the dirt road for 0.2 mile to a detour that skirts private property and leads to a narrow, pretty trail lined with aspen trees. Shortly thereafter, the trail rejoins the road and winds upward through the forest. Round a corner to marvel at an ideal view of Estes Cone perfectly framed between the road and the treetops. Continue uphill and revel in several more open viewpoints, especially a magnificent vista of Longs Peak and the Diamond. The road passes a famous local landmark, The Baldpate Inn, which is a pleasant spot to have lunch, then leads to a parking lot on the east side of CO 7, across the highway from scenic Lily Lake.

'Christmas Tree Mountain' 8,586 feet
OT *Regional map p. 248 (N, 13)*

This rock mound stands out in a flat, open field southeast of Fish Creek near Estes Park. Though its diminutive height seems trivial, it stands solo in the middle of the valley and therefore has a dominating presence. Possession of the dual rock humps that comprise the summit is split between two private owners. Additionally, any access to the mountain crosses private property. The most logical way to approach the mountain is from Cheley Camp, but permission must be gained before using this access. Even then, the problem of identifying the owners of the summits (one of the owners is listed as "Christmas Tree Mountain") and procuring permission to legally stand on either summit of this tiny peak is unlikely. So, at present, it's off-limits.

However, things change, and with the possibility of land exchanges or ownership transfers, in the future event that pretty little 'Christmas Tree Mountain' becomes public property, here's how to access it. Sometimes called Christmas Rock or Christmas Tree Rock, it is situated just north of the famous Cheley Camp and is very scenic when viewed from above, especially from CO 7. The hike to the base of the rocks is pleasant, and an exciting rock scramble is required to reach the top of the steep rock knobs. The higher summit if more difficult to climb, with unavoidable sections of hard Class 4+ climbing. The lower summit is easier, with moderate Class 4 climbing leading to the top.

Southwest Slope GRADE I CLASS 4+ From the Fish Creek Trailhead (p. 266), hike south for 0.6 mile to the gate at the start of the Homer Rouse Trail, then turn east along the Cheley Camp road. Stay left at all junctions and hike toward a small pond, which provides a good view of 'Christmas Tree Mountain.' Hike northeast through a meadow, cross a horse trail, and ascend the hillside, following a fenceline to where it dead-ends into a rock wall. Take a left at the gap between the fence and the rock and hike north, following a faint trail marked by cairns to a gully located south of the main summit. This gully is the easiest access to the main summit, but the climbing is too difficult to be classified as a 'hike.' Ascend the rock slabs, climbing over Class 4 terrain, with a couple short sections of harder scrambling. Good views of the Fish Creek valley and The Crags on Twin Sisters Mountain can be seen from the top. From the gully, descend and skirt the main summit on the west side to access the prominent cleft between the two highest knobs. This gully is wide and filled with trees. From the cleft, ascend the lesser summit with moderate Class 4 scrambling.

LILY LAKE AREA   *Regional map p. 248 (R, 9)*

LAKES

Lily Lake   8,927 feet
T 🚻 ♿   *Regional map p. 248 (R, 9)*

The Lily Lake Trail hugs the shore of Lily Lake, circling it completely. The hike is short and simple, but the dramatic scenery and the tranquility of the lake make it enjoyable for everyone, even experienced hikers. This walk is especially gratifying at sunrise or at sunset. Located immediately north of Wind River Pass, this pleasant destination is the origin of Fish Creek, which flows north into Lake Estes. Views of the two highest peaks in RMNP are outstanding from the lake, which is a popular spot for anglers, picnickers, and

Fishermen try their luck at Lily Lake

hikers. The wheelchair accessible trail around Lily Lake is wide and level, lined by logs, and made of hard-packed dirt and gravel. In spring and summer, wildflowers flourish in the area. Ducks frequent this lake and can be seen diving for food. Often, anglers line the shore in the evenings. Several wooden resting benches along the path allow visitors to relax and enjoy the serenity of the lake and awe-inspiring vistas.

From the Lily Lake Parking Area (p. 267), access the Lily Lake Trail and follow the path as it circles for 0.8 mile around the lake. From the southwest side of the lake, dense trees offer welcome shade on hot afternoons, and a spur trail heads south to a picnic area with several picnic tables. This trail leads through a lovely aspen grove and loops back to the Lily Lake Parking Area. On the main trail, a fishing pier and observation deck on the lake's southeast shore provide good views of Lily Mountain, Estes Cone, Longs Peak, and Mount Meeker.

PEAKS AND OTHER DESTINATIONS

Lily Mountain   9,786 feet
T   *Regional map p. 248 (P, 9)*

Lily Mountain lies north of Lily Lake and south of Rams Horn Mountain in Roosevelt National Forest. A well-maintained trail leads to the base of the summit rocks, then a short but somewhat challenging Class 2 scramble is required to reach the top. Though this small summit is considered "easy" compared to most summit climbs in and around

RMNP, 1,000 feet of elevation gain combine with mild route-finding near the summit to make this a moderately difficult hike. Outstanding views of the surrounding high peaks reward those who make it to the top of this captivating peak.

Lily Mountain Trailhead Access GRADE I CLASS 2   From the Lily Mountain Trailhead (p. 267), follow the Lily Mountain Trail as it ambles along the eastern flank of Lily Mountain. Because the trail is located on Forest Service land, dogs are allowed on a leash. Though the summit is actually only 0.5 mile northwest of the trailhead, the Lily Mountain Trail traverses north and then south in long switchbacks to minimize the steepness of the ascent. The trail descends slightly before cutting back to the south to ascend a lengthy, angling line to the base of the summit outcrops. This roundabout route saves hikers from a steep and arduous ascent up the abrupt eastern slope. Because of this, the trail is relatively gentle and spreads out the elevation gain over 1.5 miles. Hike along the gentle grade of the trail and enter the forest, paralleling the highway. Intriguing rock outcrops highlight the initial section of the hike. Climb a short hill and follow the trail as it descends along the eastern slope of Lily Mountain. The trail passes over intermittent bedrock, and there are several viewpoints from rocky overlooks suspended high above CO 7. The trail switches back to the south rather abruptly near some boulders and begins to climb steadily through the forest. A viewpoint provides good vistas of neighboring Rams Horn and Gianttrack Mountains to the north.

The path peters out near the summit cliffs, marked by intermittent rock cairns. Scramble up the short, broken cliffs that guard the summit (Class 2). Climb to a prominent cleft that divides the summit blocks and scramble up the northern hump to reach the highpoint. Outstanding views abound in every direction from this small peak. Breathtaking, intimate views of Longs Peak and Mount Meeker rise to the southwest. The distinct summits of Twin Sisters Peaks stand out to the east, while Meadow and St. Vrain Mountains can be seen to the south. The Mummy Range is impressive to the north, and the Continental Divide stretches from McHenrys Peak to a view of Flattop Mountain. Stones Peak stands alone, towering over Forest Canyon. Loveland and Fort Collins are visible to the northeast.

Rams Horn Mountain/Teddy's Teeth 9,553 feet

T **OT**   *Regional map p. 248 (M, 8)*

This pretty peak lies between Gianttrack Mountain and Lily Mountain in Roosevelt National Forest. Teddy's Teeth are the prominent granite outcrops on the mountain's west side, named by boys at the YMCA in the early 1900s for President Theodore Roosevelt's teeth, which were at the time depicted by cartoonists as very large, protruding pearly-whites. The summit of Rams Horn Mountain and the ridge south of it are on Forest Service property, but the west, east, and north slopes are surrounded by private land. The only legal access to this peak is from the south, most conveniently accessed from the Lily Mountain Trail. A trail built by Molly Kemper and her mother leaves from Marys Lake Road and climbs along the east side of the peak to the summit, but this trail leaves from private property and permission is difficult to gain.

South Ridge GRADE I CLASS 2   From the Lily Mountain Trailhead (p. 267), follow the Lily Mountain Trail (see route description above) for 1.2 miles to 9,000 feet, below the north ridge of Lily Mountain. Leave the trail and bushwhack west to the saddle between Lily and Rams Horn Mountains. Turn north at the saddle and bushwhack for 0.7 mile to the summit of Rams Horn Mountain.

The Crags 10,831 feet

OT *Regional map p. 248 (R, 11)*

The Crags are a pretty maze of rock buttresses, towers, and fins located north of Point 10,831', a protruding bump on the northwestern shoulder of Twin Sisters Mountain. Situated within Roosevelt National Forest, the freestanding rock protrusions are mostly made up of schist and gneiss and are scattered throughout a large talus field below two large main walls—the Upper Great Face and Lower Great Face. The region is unique and resembles a "forest" of rock pinnacles. There is no trail to the area, and aside from a few die-hard technical rock climbers, it is seldom visited. The Crags are highly visible from Fish Creek Road (CR 63) and Cheley Camp near Estes Park. The area is dotted with private property, so use caution to stay on public land when accessing The Crags.

East Lily Lake Parking Area Access GRADE I CLASS 2   From the East Lily Lake Parking Area (p. 267), bushwhack east through the thick forest for 0.25 mile, then turn northeast and hike 0.5 mile to the bottom of a prominent talus field that leads to the spires. Ascend the talus to explore the intriguing rock labyrinth.

Lily Ridge Trail

T **▶** *Regional map p. 248 (Q, 8)*

The Lily Ridge Trail is 0.8 mile long and loops above and north of Lily Lake (p. 259). From the east end of Lily Lake, follow the Lily Lake Trail north, then west for 0.4 mile to a junction. The Lily Lake Trail continues to circle the lake, while the trail toward Aspen Brook leads north. Turn north (right) and hike 0.1 mile to the junction with the Lily Ridge Trail. Turn east (right) and follow Lily Ridge Trail as it traverses a hillside above Lily Lake and provides nice overviews of the area. Continue to follow the loop trail back to the starting point.

Twin Sisters Peaks on Twin Sisters Mountain:
East Summit (11,428 feet) and West Summit (11,413 feet)

T *Regional map p. 248 (U, 13)*

Located on an island of NPS property bordering Tahosa Valley, this extremely popular and delightful mountain affords a marvelous panorama of its lofty neighbors, including a close-up, unobstructed view of Longs Peak. Twin Sisters Mountain has several distinct summits, but the trail leads to the second highest. A long ridge runs southeast for 1.6 miles from Point 11,428' (the true summit) to Point 10,432'. Twin Sisters Peaks are the two highest points on the mountain.

Twin Sisters Trailhead Access GRADE I CLASS 2   From the Twin Sisters Trailhead (p. 268), follow the Twin Sisters Trail as it climbs through the dense forest that opens occasionally to afford good views of Longs Peak to the southwest. The trail climbs steadily along switchbacks for 2.5 miles to a small saddle between The Crags and the bulk of Twin Sisters' northern hump. Here an unmarked path leads east to Lookout Springs. Turn south along the main trail and climb more switchbacks that lead to treeline where the views of the Continental Divide to the west are stupendous. The rest of the trail is above treeline and leads up several long switchbacks on the north side of the peak.

The rocky, cobbled northern slopes of Twin Sisters Mountain are both stark and beautiful. Follow the trail through the outcrops to a rocky saddle between Twin Sisters Peaks: the 11,428-foot eastern summit and the 11,413-foot western summit. The true summit is the more easterly of the two. Point 11,376', another prominent highpoint, lies to the south. The trail leads to the most commonly visited western summit. Pass a small historic rock cabin and follow the trail as it climbs the rock outcroppings that crown Twin Sisters' western summit. An old fire lookout tower used to be located here but was removed in 1977. On top, the views are extraordinary. An unparalleled view of Longs Peak rises dramatically to the southwest. Mount Meeker, the East Face of Longs Peak, and Mount Lady Washington combine to create a truly spectacular vista. Estes Park is visible to the north, with Indian Peaks to the south. To reach the true summit, leave the trail at the saddle between Twin Sisters Peaks and hike

Historic Rock cabin on Twin Sisters Mountain
Note: This cabin is used for administrative purposes
only and is not a shelter cabin for hikers

east over rock cobbles to the small cliff at the base of Point 11,438'. Clamber up the rock outcrop (Class 2) to the summit.

Lookout Springs   10,550 feet
T **OT**   *Regional map p. 248 (T, 12)*

These natural springs are located on the north side of Twin Sisters Mountain between The Crags and Twin Sisters Peaks. It is likely that the natural water source was used to provide water for the old fire lookout tower that stood on top of Twin Sisters Mountain until 1977. Water seeps from this little spring for much of the year. From the Twin Sisters Trailhead (p. 268), follow the Twin Sisters Trail (see route description, p. 261) as it climbs steadily along switchbacks for about 2.5 miles to a small saddle between The Crags and the bulk of Twin Sisters' northern hump. Here an unmarked, faded path leaves the main trail near a horse hitch rack and descends east to Lookout Springs.

Estes Cone   11,006 feet
T   *Regional map p. 248 (T, 4)*

Located about 4 miles northeast of Longs Peak, this modest mountain is strategically positioned to showcase panoramic views of the Estes Park valley and the east side of RMNP. This is a rewarding and pleasant day hike that passes through dense forest to a pretty mountain meadow, then climbs steeply up the "cone," which is the rounded summit crag.

Longs Peak Trailhead Access GRADE I CLASS 2   From the Longs Peak Trailhead (see Region 4, p. 238), follow the East Longs Peak Trail (see Region 4, p. 238) for 0.5 mile to the junction with the trail to Eugenia Mine and Estes Cone. Turn north (right) and hike through an aspen grove, then enter coniferous forest as the trail gains and loses elevation on its route toward Estes Cone. The trail crosses Inn Brook on a footbridge and leads to the remains of an old log cabin, 1.4 miles beyond the trailhead (see Eugenia Mine, Region 4, p. 236). Follow the trail north past the cabin site as it travels downhill to a lovely meadow. This is Moore Park, where wildflowers flourish in summer, and the open field provides a wonderful view of Estes Cone.

Proceed from the meadow and pass a faint spur trail that leads east to private property. Bear northwest along the Storm Pass Trail, which offers intermittent views of Longs Peak and Mount Lady Washington to the southwest. The trail climbs steadily to Storm Pass, 2.6 miles from the Longs Peak Trailhead and the site of a major trail junction. The trail to Estes Cone heads northeast for 0.7 mile to the summit. Follow the trail toward Estes Cone as climbs abruptly through the forest. The last 0.5 mile of the trail is difficult and sustained, climbing quite steeply up a series of switchbacks for 600 vertical feet to the top. This is a tough section of trail for many unwary hikers. Rock cairns mark the trail as it negotiates the steep hillside to a large rock outcropping that caps the summit of Estes Cone. Clamber up the rocks to gain a small plateau, then scramble east to the summit. The panoramic views from the top are rewarding.

Lily Lake Parking Area Access   GRADE I   CLASS 2   From the east end of Lily Lake (see p. 259), hike southwest to the trail toward Storm Pass. This trail descends along a ridge for 0.6 mile a junction at the Aspen Brook footbridge. Cross the bridge and follow the trail toward Storm Pass as it climbs through the forest. The trail climbs a series of scenic rock steps that lead through a rock garden with wonderful views of Lily Mountain and the Aspen Brook drainage. Continue to climb along the trail to Storm Pass, the site of a major trail junction. The trail to Estes Cone heads northeast for 0.7 mile to the summit. The final push to the top is extremely steep and sustained.

Storm Pass Trail Parking Access   GRADE I   CLASS 2   From the Storm Pass Trail parking on Bear Lake Road (see Region 1, p. 110), follow the Storm Pass Trail (p. 269) southeast for 4.5 miles to Storm Pass. Turn northeast and follow the steep trail for 0.7 mile to Estes Cone.

East Portal Access   GRADE I   CLASS 2   From the East Portal Trailhead (p. 266), follow the Wind River Trail (p. 269) southwest for 2.5 miles to the junction with Storm Pass Trail. Turn southeast (left) and follow the Storm Pass Trail 3 miles to Storm Pass. Turn northeast and follow the steep trail for 0.7 mile to Estes Cone.

PIERSON PARK   *Regional map p. 248 (R, 19)*

PEAKS AND OTHER DESTINATIONS

House Rock   9,632 feet
R OT *Regional map p. 248 (Z, 17)*

House Rock is an appealing little foothill located in Roosevelt National Forest near Meeker Park, across the highway from Wild Basin. Few people visit this intriguing nugget of rock because it remains out of sight of all major roads, tucked away on the east side of Twin Sisters Mountain. It has a wonderful little rocky top that showcases big views of Twin Sisters, Pierson Mountain, Big Elk Meadows, Kenny Mountain, Coffin Top, Wild Basin, Indian Peaks, and more. It is one of the few summits in the area without a view of Longs Peak and Mount Meeker, because they are blocked by the bulk of Twin Sisters Mountain.

From the junction of US 36 and CO 7 in Estes Park, drive south on CO 7 for 11.2 miles to Cabin Creek Road, near the village of Meeker Park. Turn east (left) on Cabin Creek Road and drive for 0.9 mile to a T in the road (the junction of CR 82E and Cabin Creek Road). Take a right at the T and continue along the dirt road for another mile to a sign that announces FR 119. One fork of FR 119 continues east (straight) toward Johnny Park, and the other turns north (left) toward Pierson Park. Turn north (left) and drive for 0.1 mile to a small dirt parking area on the east (right-hand) side of the road. Park and walk up the steep dirt road for 150 yards to the first gate. When the first gate is open, those with 4WD vehicles may continue north along the rough road for 3.2 miles to the second gate at the base of House Rock.

Donald Smitherman, who bought Elk Park Ranch in 1962, published a historical book in 1999 entitled *Elk Park Ranch: Human Interest Stories.* The work chronicles his experience in the area, including fanciful tales of ranch events and depictions of the lively characters he encountered through the years. He tells the history of the House family, who homesteaded 160 acres west of the current Elk Park Ranch entrance around 1907. Bob House built a log house in the little box canyon at the base of Twin Sisters. He farmed oats on the House property and operated a sawmill on the Engert property. He married Nettie Engert, daughter of Charles Engert, who "proved up" (fulfilled obligations for homesteaded land that, over time, allowed legal acquisition) the Engert homestead. Bob and Nettie had seven children, including William Turner House, who eventually bought the Engert Homestead. Turner House's wife, Lucille House, was the schoolteacher at a little schoolhouse near Wilson Spring, in the northeast corner of the Smitherman Ranch. She also taught for a time in Sarah Walker's cabin. Turner House bought Engert Homestead from his grandparents and lived at the Laycook Homestead from 1933 to 1952, making it the longest continuous stay of any area resident in the Homestead Meadows area. He also bought the Engert, Boren, and Walker Homesteads in conjunction with nearby Pullen property. He operated a ranch and timber business in the area.

West Slope GRADE I CLASS 2

The route to House Rock follows FR 119 (also called Pierson Park Road) north from the first gate for 3.2 miles to the second gate, then leaves the road and climbs 0.25 mile up the peak. When the road is open to vehicles, it's a quick drive to the second gate and a short 320-vertical-foot climb up the rocky, forested western slope of House Rock. From the first gate, hike or drive up the road to the junction with FR 325. Stay on FR 119 and keep following it to a dramatic curve in the road. Look back (west) at this point for an incredible view of Mount Meeker. FR 119 curves to the north (left), passing several closed side roads, and continues to undulate through the forest. Beautiful scenery and interesting rock formations can be seen from the roadside. Keep following FR 119 to the second gate and the start of the ascent. From here the road continues north past the gate to Pierson Park. Park all 4WD vehicles at the road edge to avoid blocking the gate.

From the gate, hike east and bushwhack up the western aspect of House Rock. Though the route is short, there is no trail, and it is relatively steep. When the summit blocks come into view, stay on the north side of the peak and scramble up to the tiny summit ridge. Move south along the mountain's spine to the top. A summit register is tucked into a glass jar among the summit boulders. Grand views stretch out in every direction. Big Elk Park lies to the east. The fire damage from the 2002 Kenny Mountain Fire is obvious. Copeland Mountain stands out prominently in Wild Basin, with Elk Tooth looming behind it. Mount Audubon highlights the view of Indian Peaks. Lookout Mountain and Horsetooth Peak are noticeable to the southwest.

Pierson Mountain 9,803 feet
T **OT** *Regional map p. 248 (S, 19)*

The forested twin summits of Pierson Mountain are located southeast of Estes Park in Roosevelt National Forest. The dual humps are most distinctive when viewed from the Lake Estes area. Pretty rock outcroppings on the mountain's northwest side offer unobstructed views of Marys Lake, Twin Sisters Mountain, and the open meadowland of Pierson Park. The hike wanders through the arid forest that characterizes the foothills surrounding Estes Park.

Southwest Slope GRADE I CLASS 2   From the Pierson Park Trailhead (p. 268), follow the Pierson Park Trail (Trail 1000) as it ambles downhill, leading toward Homestead Meadows and Lion Gulch. Follow the trail for 0.65 mile to a small open area. From this point the Pierson Park Trail bends to the southeast and climbs along the southern slope of Pierson Mountain. Leave the trail 200 yards beyond an interpretive sign and bushwhack northeast through the forest. Scarred tree stumps and other signs of logging tell the tale of the homesteaders who thinned the forest with handsaws for fuel and building materials. Climb upslope through the peaceful forest for 600 vertical feet to reach the southern, higher summit of Pierson Mountain. The northern summit is less than 40 feet lower and provides easy access to Lion Head.

Lion Head 9,740 feet
T **OT** *Regional map p. 248 (Q, 20)*

Lion Head is a modest, rocky prominence located between Pierson Park and Lion Gulch in Roosevelt National Forest. From its stony top, Hill Homestead, one of eight ranch sites established in Homestead Meadows (p. 251) by early settlers in the late 1800s, is visible below in a scenic draw. This pleasant peak is enjoyable to climb and offers a great view of the twin summits of Pierson Mountain, as well as Fish Creek, Hermit Park, and Twin Sisters Mountain.

Southwest Slope GRADE I CLASS 2   From the Pierson Park Trailhead (p. 268), follow the Pierson Park Trail (Trail 1000) as it ambles downhill, leading toward Homestead Meadows and Lion Gulch. Follow the trail for 0.65 mile to a small open area. From this point the Pierson Park Trail bends to the southeast and climbs along the southern slope of Pierson Mountain. Leave the trail and follow a dirt road that leads north. After a short distance, leave the road and bushwhack northeast through the thinned forest toward the saddle between Pierson Mountain and Lion Head. From the saddle, a well-cairned trail zigzags up the southwestern slope of Lion Head. Avoid the steeper southeastern side, as it is adorned with the precipitous rock cliffs that give Lion Head its name as the western headwall of Lion Gulch. Follow the path for 0.2 mile and 500 vertical feet to the top of the small mountain. Meander out to a rocky overlook on the eastern edge of the summit to view the homesteads in the valley below.

Kruger Rock 9,355 feet
T *Regional map p. 248 (L, 18)*

Kruger Rock is a beautiful rocky-topped mountain located north of Pierson Park and east of Fish Creek in Roosevelt National Forest. The views from the summit are outstanding, as Kruger Rock presents a 360-degree panorama that is utterly breathtaking.

Hermit Park Open Space offers a pleasant two-mile trail to the top of the peak. The trail is very scenic with several overlooks of the Estes Park Valley and the high peaks of Rocky Mountain National Park.

Kruger Rock used to be a difficult peak to access because it was almost landlocked by private property. However, in 2008, Hermit Park Open Space was opened to the public, allowing legal access the summit of Kruger Rock on a wonderful, well-maintained trail. Aside from the trail from Hermit Park, the only other legal access to Kruger Rock is from Pierson Park, which requires a lengthy cross-country bushwhack.

nita Prinzmetal and Munchkin, summit area, Kruger Rock

Hermit Park Open Space consists of 1,362 acres of prime property set amid a beautiful forest with numerous rocky outcrops. Visitors can hike, bike and camp in the Open Space. There is a year round entrance fee for each vehicle, bicycle or walk-in.

Hermit Park Open Space was once a part of Crocker Ranch, but was purchased by Hewlett Packard (HP) in 1967. It was used as a private retreat for HP employees until it was taken over by Agilent Technologies, and thereafter used by employees of that company until 2007. The land was purchased in cooperation with numerous public entities and private individuals in a community supported partnership by the Larimer County Department of Natural Resources, and it opened to the public in 2008.

Hermit Park is located 3.5 miles east of Estes Park on US 36. The entrance is located on the south side of the highway. Turn into the Hermit Park Open Space and pass the self-registration kiosk. Here visitors may purchase entrance permits, which are required year round. A visitor information center is located in a small house near the kiosk. Continue on the dirt road as it climbs a steep hill and winds around, passing several turnoffs for camping. Follow signs that direct traffic to the Kruger Rock Trail Parking Area, located near the Pavilion, 2.4 miles from the turnoff from US 36.

From the parking area, hike past the bathrooms and the Pavilion on a spur trail that leads to the road where the Kruger Rock Trail is identified by a sign. The Kruger Rock Trail climbs steadily through open parkland before it enters the forest and leads to a beautiful overlook of the Estes Park Valley. From this overlook, the trail continues to climb through the forest, offering intermittent views of the high peaks and the surrounding valley.

The trail continues to a conspicuous rock landing on the south side of Kruger Rock. A narrow gully leads between the two major summit blocks to a small plateau at the top of the mountain. Climbing through the cleft to reach the top involves short, easy scrambling up large boulders.

An astounding view stretches toward Longs Peak, the Continental Divide to Stones Peak, Sundance Mountain, Forest Canyon, the magnificent Mummy Range, and a brilliant overview of Estes Park and its foothills. Dollar Lake shimmers below to the southwest.

TRAILHEADS Crosier Mountain Gravel Pit Trailhead

This trailhead lies at 6,950 feet and provides access to Trail 1013, which connects to the Crosier Mountain Trail (Trail 931) after 1.9 miles. The trailhead is located on the south side of CR 43, 2.1 miles east of Glen Haven, in a large gravel pit.

East Portal Trailhead

This trailhead is at 8,260 feet and provides access to Glacier Basin, the Glacier Creek Trail, the Storm Pass Trail, the Wind River Trail, Emerald Mountain, and two unofficially named summits, 'Thunder Peak' and 'Lightning Peak.' From the junction of US 36 and CO 66 by Beaver Point near Estes Park, drive southwest for 3.3 miles to East Portal. The road (CO 66) ends at a circular drive with parking allowed on the shoulder. A small Larimer County Park on the north side of the road also offers parking. From the circular drive, a trail leaves the roadbed and heads north across a meadow. Follow this trail past the reservoir and enter RMNP, marked by a trailhead sign.

Fish Creek Trailhead

This trailhead lies at 8,106 feet and provides access to the Homer Rouse Trail. From the junction of US 36 and CO 7 in Estes Park, drive east on US 36 for 0.9 mile to Fish Creek Road. Turn south (right) and drive for 4.2 miles to Cheley Road. This is an unmarked dirt road that leads to famous Cheley Camp. It's easy to miss the turn, which is 0.2 mile south of Marys Lake Road (CO 7). Turn south (left) on the dirt road and locate the parking lot on the east side of the road, which is the Fish Creek Trailhead. The trailhead is 0.6 mile north of the gate at the start of the Homer Rouse Trail.

Garden Gate Trailhead

This trailhead is at 6,420 feet and provides access to the Crosier Mountain Trail (Trail 931), which leads 7 miles from the Garden Gate Trailhead to the Glen Haven Trailhead, but also connects with the trail to Crosier Mountain's summit. The trailhead is located on the south side of CR 43, 2.2 miles west of Drake and 5.9 miles east of Glen Haven, and is marked by a small parking area and a gate.

Glen Haven Trailhead

This trailhead lies at 7,240 feet and provides access to the Crosier Mountain Trail (Trail 931), which leads 7 miles between the Glen Haven Trailhead and the Garden Gate Trailhead, but also connects with the trail to Crosier Mountain's summit. It is located in Glen Haven just east of the post office near the livery stable, marked by a brown Forest Service sign. A dirt road winds past the stables and private residences to a narrow path that marks the start of the trail.

Lily Lake Parking Area

This parking area lies at 8,940 feet and provides access to the Lily Lake Trail, Lily Ridge Trail, Aspen Brook, and Storm Pass. From the junction of CO 7 and US 36 in Estes Park, drive south on CO 7 for 6.2 miles to the Lily Lake Parking Area, located on the west side of the road at Lily Lake.

East Lily Lake Parking Area

From the junction of US 36 and CO 7 in Estes Park, drive south 6.2 miles on CO 7 to a parking lot on the east side of CO 7, across the highway from Lily Lake.

Lily Mountain Trailhead

This trailhead lies at 8,780 feet and provides access to the Lily Mountain Trail. It is simply a small dirt pullout on the west side of CO 7, complete with an emergency call box. From the junction of US 36 and CO 7 in Estes Park, drive south on CO 7 for 5.7 miles to the trailhead.

Lion Gulch Trailhead

This trailhead lies at 7,360 feet in Roosevelt National Forest, providing access to the Lion Gulch Trail. From the junction of US 34 and US 36 in Estes Park, drive east on US 36 for 8 miles to the Lion Gulch Trailhead, located on the south side of the road.

Old Ranger Drive Hiking Access

This access point lies at 7,800 feet and provides access to Oldman Mountain and 'Oldman Mountain Caves.' From the junction of US 36 and US 34 in Estes Park, continue west along US 34 through the heart of Estes Park for 1.1 miles to Old Ranger Drive. Turn left, cross Fall River, and continue up the road for 0.4 mile to a dead end. There is limited parking on the south side of the road.

Do not park in private driveways or on University of Northern Colorado (UNC) property. This was the site of a former U.S. Forest Service ranger station and was given to the university in the 1950s. Presently UNC administers 80 acres on the mountain's south side, including a retreat with rental of the buildings open to the public. UNC currently allows individuals and small groups to hike across their property to access Oldman Mountain.

East of UNC property, the notorious 'Oldman Mountain Caves' and the rough path leading up the gully in which they lie are located on private property. The current owners also allow hikers to use their land as long as visitors are respectful and don't litter. Not true caves, this maze of narrow slots offers some sunlight through the openings in the top of the "caves." Popular with high school students, the area sees a lot of traffic. The entrance to the "caves" is difficult to locate, and a short scramble provides access to the start. The "caves" require a bit of climbing experience to navigate.

Pierson Park Trailhead

This trailhead lies at 9,060 feet and provides access to the Pierson Park Trail (Trail 1000). From the junction of US 36 and Fish Creek Road in Estes Park, drive south on Fish Creek Road for 2.8 miles to Little Valley Road. Take a left onto unpaved Little Valley Road and follow it 2 miles to a Forest Service gate at the intersection of FR 119 and Moss Rock Drive. This is the winter parking area, with room for several vehicles to park on a slanted pull-off near the gate. In summer, those with high-clearance vehicles may continue to the Pierson Park Trailhead, 1.8 miles farther along FR 119, and park at the main trailhead near a scenic meadow.

Round Mountain Trailhead

This trailhead lies at 5,743 feet on US 34 (Big Thompson Canyon), 10 miles west of Loveland in Roosevelt National Forest. Two trails leave from the well-marked parking lot on the south side of the river, immediately west of Viestenz-Smith Mountain Park. The Foothills Nature Trail leads northeast to a stone hut, while the Round Mountain National Recreation Trail (the Summit Adventure Trail or Trail 831) leads southwest for 3 miles to the summit of Sheep Mountain.

Sullivan Gulch Trailhead

This trailhead is found at 6,560 feet and provides access to the Sullivan Gulch Trail, which is a faint path that can be hard to follow. It connects with the Crosier Mountain Trail (Trail 931) after 1.5 miles. The unmarked trailhead is located up a short, steep dirt road on the north side of US 34, 2.1 miles west of Drake and immediately west of Waltonia Road.

Twin Sisters Trailhead

This trailhead lies at 9,110 feet and provides access to the Twin Sisters Trail. From the junction of US 36 and CO 7 in Estes Park, drive south on CO 7 for 6.2 miles to the trailhead turnoff. Turn east (left) and drive up a dirt road for 0.4 mile to the Twin Sisters Trailhead. Parking is also available at the East Lily Lake Parking Area (p. 267).

Aspen Brook Trail

From the east end of Lily Lake, hike southwest for 0.6 mile to connect with the Aspen Brook Trail. Turn north and follow the Aspen Brook Trail as it descends through the forest to pretty open meadows. Aspen Brook is nestled in a lush green canyon bordered by Lily Mountain to the east and scenic unnamed outcroppings to the west. It is a beautiful valley that hosts several scenic meadows and ends in private property on the north. At the private property signs, there are several old cabins, one of them falling down and the other two in decent repair. The cabins are what remains of Anna Wolfrom's homestead, where she entertained guests at the Wigwam Tea Room and sold Indian trinkets in the 1920's. From this point, the trail continues north, past the signs that warn of no exit to public land, and eventually turns into a doubletrack road that leads past houses and exits onto paved CO 66, east of the East Portal Trailhead. It is also possible to access the Aspen Brook Trail from the south. To do so, locate the start of the unmarked trail at a point 0.2 mile north of Wind River Pass on CO 7.

Crosier Mountain Trail
See Crosier Mountain, p. 249.

Homer Rouse Trail
See Homer Rouse Trail, p. 258.

Lily Lake Trail
See Lily Lake Area, p. 259.

Lily Mountain Trail
See Lily Mountain, p. 259.

Lily Ridge Trail
See Lily Lake Area, p. 261.

Lion Gulch Trail
This low-elevation trail lies in Roosevelt National Forest and begins at the Lion Gulch Trailhead. It leads 2.8 miles to picturesque Homestead Meadows. It is a scenic trail reserved for nonmotorized recreation, including hikers, bicyclists, and equestrians.

Andy Neff on the Twin Sisters Trail

Storm Pass Trail
The Storm Pass Trail leaves Bear Lake Road 7.8 miles from the Beaver Meadows Visitor Center and climbs 4.5 miles to Storm Pass, then descends 0.8 mile to Moore Park.

Twin Sisters Trail
See Twin Sisters Peaks on Twin Sisters Mountain, p. 261.

Wind River Trail
This trail begins at the East Portal Trailhead and parallels the Wind River southwest for 2.5 miles to connect with the Storm Pass Trail.

OTHER POINTS OF INTEREST

Butterfly Burn
Butterfly Burn is a fire-damaged area on the western slope of Twin Sisters Mountain. A forest fire in the late 1920s scarred a region shaped roughly like a butterfly, until aspen trees reclaimed the area, highlighting the interesting shape with green leaves in summer and gold leaves in autumn. The burn is difficult to see now, but a strategic vantage from CO 7 provides the opportunity to attempt to pick out the butterfly shape amid the densely forested hillside.

Wind River Pass
R This 9,130-foot pass is located on CO 7 between Aspen Brook and Tahosa Creek.

West Side Central

Ten Lake Park

This chapter covers the RMNP region on the west side of the Continental Divide that is south of Milner Pass, east of Trail Ridge Road, and north of the Indian Peaks Wilderness Area. It excludes the small section of land south of East Inlet and west of Paradise Creek, which is covered in the Southwest Corner chapter (Region 7). Accessed by well-maintained trails from numerous trailheads, the west side of RMNP is centered around five major drainages: East Inlet, North Inlet, Tonahutu Creek, Onahu Creek, and Timber Creek. The nearest town to local destinations in this chapter is Grand Lake, and the region is typically less crowded than the busy east side that is accessed from Estes Park. The west side of the Continental Divide generally gets more moisture than the east, resulting in more lush greenery to enhance the hiking experience.

Above Haynach Lakes

SUBREGIONS with Highlighted Hiking Destinations

EAST INLET 275
   📷 Adams Falls 275
      Lone Pine Lake 276
      Lake Verna 276
      Spirit Lake 276
      Fourth Lake 277
      Fifth Lake 277
   📷 East Meadow 277
      Mount Enentah................................ 277
      Mount Cairns 278
      Mount Wescott 278
      Ptarmigan Mountain 280
      Andrews Peak 281
      Mount Craig 281
      Boulder–Grand Pass........................... 283

PARADISE CREEK 284
      Paradise Park 284
      Ten Lake Park 285

NORTH INLET 286
   📷 Cascade Falls 286
      Big Pool 286
      Lake Nokoni 287
      Lake Nanita 287
      Lake Powell 289
   📷 Summerland Park 289

Lake Verna

PTARMIGAN CREEK 291
    War Dance Falls 291
    Bench Lake 291

TONAHUTU CREEK............................... 292
    Granite Falls.................................. 292
    Haynach Lakes 293
    Green Mountain 294
    Mount Patterson............................... 294
    Big Meadows 295
    Nakai Peak 296
    Bighorn Flats 296
    Snowdrift Peak 296

ONAHU CREEK 297
    Julian Lake 298
    Long Meadows 298

TIMBER CREEK.................................. 299
    Timber Lake 299
    Jackstraw Mountain 300

MILNER PASS 300
    Lake Irene.................................... 301
    Sheep Rock 302
    'Poudre Lake Spires' 302

TRAILHEADS 303

TRAILS 304

Mount Craig

Crossing Paradise Creek

East Inlet Trail

Map created with TOPO!®
© 2003 National Geographic
Distance in miles
0
1
2
N
Shadow Mountain Lake
Grand Lake
Colorado
River
Green Ridge Campground
Pine Beach
Shadow Mountain Dam
Shadow Mountain
Lookout
Grand Lake Entrance
Kawuneeche Visitor Center
Columbine Lake
Golf Course
Winding River Ranch
Green Mountain
Lodgepole
Paint Brush
South Meadows
Big Meadows
Tonahutu
Tonahutu / North Inlet
Filtration Plant
East Inlet
West Portal
Adams Falls
East Meadow
Summerland Park
Mount Bryant
Echo Creek
Ranger Creek
Pole Creek
Mount Enentah
Nisa Mountain
Mount Patterson
Cascade Falls
Twinberry
Big Pool
Lower East Inlet
Mount Wescott
Cats Lair
Mount Cairns
Gray Jay
Lone Pine Lake
Slickrock
Solitaire
Upper East Inlet
Lake Verna
Spirit Lake
Fourth Lake
Fifth Lake
Mount Craig
Ten Lake Park
Paradise
Ptarmigan Mountain
Pettingell Lake
Lake Solitude
North Inlet
Grouseberry
North Inlet
Foot Bridge
Porcupine
Ptarmigan
War Dance
North Inlet Falls
North Inlet Junction
Pine Marten
July
Hallett Creek
Bench Lake
Ptarmigan Creek
Snowdrift Peak
Snowdrift Lake
Andrews Peak
Andrews Pass
Andrews Glacier
Taylor Peak
Taylor Glacier
Otis Peak
Hallett Peak
Tyndall Glacier
Powell Peak
Mc Henrys Peak
Sky Pond
The Sharkstooth
Glass Lake
Loch Vale
Icy Brook
Lake Powell
Mount Alice
Boulder-Grand Pass
The Cleaver
Isolation Peak
Moomaw Glacier
Frigid Lake
Falcon Lake
Pilot Mtn
Tanima Peak
NATIONAL
MOUNTAIN
VALLEY TRAIL
EAST INLET TRAIL
NORTH INLET TRAIL
TUNNEL
1.3 MI (2.1 KM)
3.2 MI (5.3 KM)
4.8 MI (7.6 KM)
1 2 3 4 5 6 7 8 9 10 11 12 13 14 15 16 17 18 19
A B C D E F G H I J K L M N O P Q R S T U V W X Y Z

EAST INLET   *Regional map p. 272 (R, 6)*

East Inlet is the name for the beautiful creek that originates on the north slope of Isolation Peak and meanders for 9.4 miles to empty its waters on the eastern shore of Grand Lake. Concurrently, North Inlet supplies water to the north side of Grand Lake.

LAKES AND FALLS

Adams Falls   8,460 feet
T **[符]** *Regional map p. 272 (J, 7)*

This is the west side's equivalent to Alberta Falls —a short walk to a beautiful waterfall. It is very popular and often crowded. A scenic loop trail and viewing platform for the falls enhance the site. From the East Inlet Trailhead (p. 303), follow the wide trail for 0.3 mile to the lower entrance to the loop. Take a right and head south along the path to the viewing over-look, augmented by impressive rockwork and a railing. The top section of Adams Falls is a set of cascades that sweeps through two channels in times of high water. The creek then takes a sharp turn and flows over a cliff for about 15 feet in a narrow rock-walled ravine. Scramble below the overlook on rock slabs to look down on the steep drop. From the viewing platform, the loop trail continues up a well-crafted rock stairway and climbs along East Inlet creek, pass-ing two smaller cascades. The path then levels out and intersects the East Inlet Trail, 0.5 mile from the trailhead.

East Inlet

'East Inlet Falls'   8,960 feet
T **OT** *Regional map p. 272 (N, 6); hike map p. 279*

Set amid a deep, dark, pine forest, 'East Inlet Falls' is the unofficial name for a tumbling cascade in East Inlet creek. From the East Inlet Trailhead (p. 303), follow the East Inlet Trail (p. 304) for 3 miles to 9,000 feet, just west of the first major switchback in the trail that skirts an exposed rock outcrop. Leave the trail and bushwhack southeast for 0.1 mile to the babbling falls.

Texan Jay Adams built several houses in Grand Lake in the late 1800s. One of them was only accessible by boat and became abandoned in later years. People used to row across the lake to picnic on the property, dubbing it the "House on the Rock." In 1917, Adams treated the Grand Lake community to a lavish picnic on the shore of the lake, then solicited his guests to name this nearby waterfall. A unanimous vote christened it Adams Falls in honor of their host.

Opposite: Timber Lake (see p. 299)

Lone Pine Lake   9,900 feet

T *Regional map p. 272 (Q, 6);*
hike maps pp. 279, 288

This popular destination is the first of a long chain of lakes in the upper East Inlet drainage. It has a significant rock island in the southwest section of the lake, ornamented with not one, but several trees. Ranger Fred McLaren named it 'Lone Pine' in the 1930s because at the time a lone tree had taken root in the rocky crevices. From the East Inlet Trailhead (p. 303), follow the extremely scenic and leg-pumping East Inlet Trail (p. 304) for 5.3 miles to Lone Pine Lake. Inviting rock slabs on the southwest shore provide a nice overview of the lake. Mount Craig rises to the south.

Lake Verna   10,180 feet

T *Regional map p. 272 (T, 5);*
hike maps pp. 279, 288

This distinctly long, pretty lake is the largest in the East Inlet drainage. It is unique among RMNP's high-alpine lakes in that it has a superb sandy beach on the east shore. Grandiose views of the striking tower 'Aiguille de Fleur' rise to the south. A short and powerful waterfall cascades

Lone Pine Lake

down some large granite blocks on the south side of the lake. From the East Inlet Trailhead (p. 303), follow the East Inlet Trail (p. 304) for 6.6 miles to a long, shallow, unnamed lake west of Verna that showcases big boulders in shallow waters. The trail climbs above this unique body of water and continues for 0.3 mile to Lake Verna.

Spirit Lake

Spirit Lake   10,300 feet

T *Regional map p. 272 (U, 5)*

Half the size of Lake Verna but twice the size of Fourth Lake, Spirit Lake offers hikers amazing views of the sharpness of the rock tower, 'Aiguille de Fleur.' A huge boulder field spills down toward the lake on the south side, and scenic grassy meadows adorn the east side. A noticeable boulder sits in the shallow water's edge of this oval-shaped lake. From the East Inlet Trailhead (p. 303), follow the East Inlet Trail (p. 304) for 6.9 miles to Lake Verna. Here the maintained trail ends. Continue hiking along an unmaintained path that follows the north shore of Verna and hike 0.9 mile to Spirit Lake.

Fourth Lake   10,380 feet
T *Regional map p. 272 (V, 4)*

Shallow Fourth Lake is round with a grassy shoreline. Verdant marshy wildflower meadows decorate the east and west sides. Steep rock slabs with small waterfalls filtering down them on the south side and a nice, lush forest on the north make a tremendously scenic setting. From the East Inlet Trailhead (p. 303), follow the East Inlet Trail (p. 304) for 6.9 miles to Lake Verna. Here the maintained trail ends. Hike along the unmaintained path that follows the north shore of Verna and continue for 0.9 mile to Spirit Lake. The trail becomes progressively harder to follow as it leads eastward. Hike along the north shore of Spirit Lake and continue for 0.6 mile to Fourth Lake.

Fourth Lake

Fifth Lake   10,860 feet
T *Regional map p. 272 (W, 3); hike map, Region 3, p. 196*

This high-altitude, sandy-bottomed lake lies in a remarkable alpine basin at the base of Isolation Peak's jagged and complicated north ridge. A flat, grassy shoreline and wind-battered stands of trees highlight the scene against the drama of the sheer rock walls rising above. From Fourth Lake (follow route description above), the trail deteriorates rapidly through high grass but leads into a beautiful alpine basin below Boulder–Grand Pass and The Cleaver. This creek-inspired wildflower basin is one of the most special places in RMNP. A dramatic curve in East Inlet prompts the hiker to turn south and climb through boulder fields overgrown with grasses and wildflowers. The route leads to a vantage slightly higher than Fifth Lake. Drop down to the grassy shoreline to enjoy the majesty of this far-off place.

PEAKS AND OTHER DESTINATIONS

East Meadow   8,535 feet
T 🚶 *Regional map p. 272 (L, 7)*

From the East Inlet Trailhead (p. 303), follow the East Inlet Trail (p. 304) for 1.6 miles to East Meadow, a pretty meadow with good views of Mount Craig. The East Inlet creek meanders lazily through the grassy meadow in big, sweeping, horseshoe-shaped curves. Look for signs of muskrat and beaver.

Mount Enentah   10,781 feet
T **OT** *Regional map p. 272 (M, 10)*

Mount Enentah is the lower, forested point on a ridge extending northwest from beautiful unnamed Point 11,588', which is located between Mount Cairns and Ptarmigan Mountain. Mount Enentah has a steep, convoluted north face and a forested, gentler east face. It separates the lower sections of North and East Inlet drainages. Interestingly, the Alva B. Adams Tunnel (see Region 5, p. 255) runs right under Mount Enentah's summit. The tunnel is a massive water-diversion project that transfers water eastward through the mountains from Grand Lake to Estes Park. It was named for the Colorado senator who submitted legislation on the project to the U.S. Congress in 1937. Building such tunnel in a national park met a lot of controversy, but pressure from farmers and businesses started a political momentum that could not be stopped. Completed in 1947, the 13.1-mile-long tunnel is a marvel of engineering. It travels northeast from the West Portal at Grand Lake through RMNP. It crosses beneath the Continental Divide at Andrews Pass and ends at the East Portal near Emerald Mountain.

Southwest Slope GRADE II CLASS 2   From the East Inlet Trailhead (p. 303), hike east on the East Inlet Trail (p. 304) for 0.8 mile to a marshy area near Point 8,508'. Leave the trail and bushwhack northeast up the steep, forested slope, aiming for Point 9,976'. Skirt the numerous short cliff sections along the way. From Point 9,976', continue northeast through the trees to the top of Mount Enentah. The summit is unremarkable, decorated with pine duff, flat rocks, and trees. Slightly northeast of the summit is a rock overlook that provides good views of the North Inlet valley. Snowdrift and Nakai Peaks, Mount Patterson, and Nisa Mountain can be seen. Ptarmigan Mountain looks inviting to the east.

Mount Cairns 10,880 feet

T **OT** *Regional map p. 272 (O, 7); hike map p. 279*

Mount Cairns' most notable characteristics are the striking south-facing cliffs that flank the mountain's western aspect. The sheer walls rise above the East Inlet valley and can be seen for miles around. These cliffs are the salient feature of the lower East Inlet valley.

Southeast Slope GRADE II CLASS 2   From the East Inlet Trailhead (p. 303), hike along the East Inlet Trail (p. 304) for 4.1 miles to a bridge that crosses the unnamed creek that flows south from Ptarmigan Mountain. Leave the trail and bushwhack north through the dense forest, skirting the numerous cliffs and large boulders that block the way. The forest is more reasonable to penetrate on the east side of the creek. Hike 0.5 mile to 10,200 feet, then angle northwest and cross the creek. Climb up the short, but steep, hillside to the summit of Mount Cairns. Mount Cairns is *not* the more prominent rock outcrop to the northeast, but is nestled in the trees with limited views.

Mount Wescott

Mount Wescott 10,421 feet

T **OT** *Regional map p. 272 (O, 4); hike map p. 279*

This small fortress of rock is guarded on all sides by granite cliffs and is difficult to climb. Broken cracks and weaknesses in the granite grace the southwest side and provide the most reasonable hiking options. Mount Wescott is a low rock dome littered with pine trees. From many vantages it is dwarfed by the higher summits near it, and it seems to blend into the densely forested ridgeline that is sandwiched between East Inlet and Echo Creek. However, this is a respectable mountain and a worthy goal.

Southwest Face GRADE II CLASS 3   From the East Inlet Trailhead (p. 303), follow the East Inlet Trail (p. 304) for 4.4 miles to the bridge that spans East Inlet. Search the forest on the south for the start of the Paradise Park Trail (p. 306). Locate the trail and hike south for 0.6 mile to a point slightly southeast of Mount Wescott's summit. Cross Paradise Creek where it is flat and wide, using fallen logs to aid crossing. From here, bushwhack west, aiming for a prominent notch between Mount Wescott's summit and the unnamed 10,200-foot rock mounds to the south. Scramble through forest and up rock slabs over nontechnical terrain of steep dirt and downed trees. Climb on benches to gain the notch where the rock mound ridge meets the main cliff band of Mount Wescott. In the saddle of

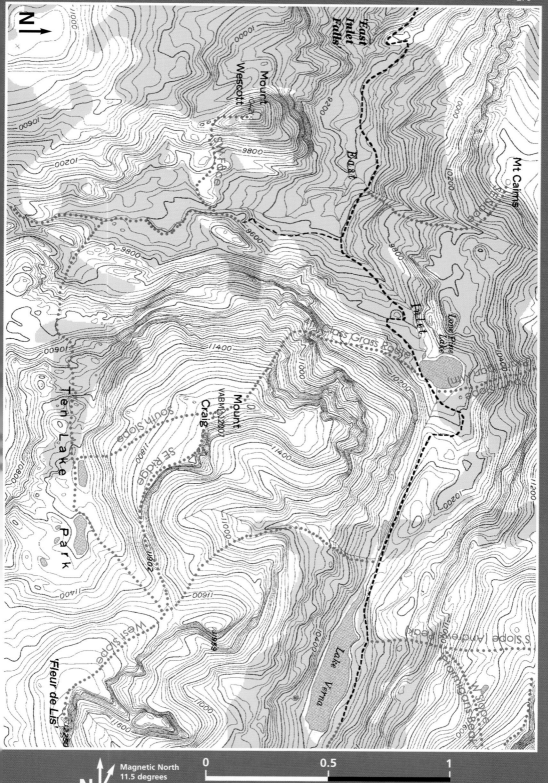

N

East Inlet Falls

Mount Wescott

SW Face

Mt Cairns

East Inlet

Lone Pine Lake

Grass Route

Teno Lake

11400

11000

Mount Craig

VABM 13007

South Slope

SE Ridge

11600

11800

Park

West Slope

11902

11959

Fleur de Lis

11600

Lake Verna

S Slope Andrews Peak

W Slope Thompson's Peak

Magnetic North
11.5 degrees

0   0.5   1

Distance in miles

the notch, steep, overhanging walls guard upward passage. Continue west through the cleft and pass a sizable black pool. Hike 150 yards to the southwestern aspect of the mountain where some prominent weaknesses present themselves. Turn northeast toward the summit and climb along steep dirt and grass ledges and up occasional rock slabs to the summit ridge. Several sections of Class 3 climbing must be overcome in this section. A very pleasurable Class 2 scramble along the summit spine leads to a large balanced boulder on top. An opportune break in the trees offers an awesome view of Grand Lake and Shadow Mountain. Mount Craig rises grandly to the east. The Paradise Creek valley unfolds to the southeast. This is a wonderful, secluded, seldom-visited summit. Enjoy.

View from Ptarmigan Mountain

Ptarmigan Mountain 12,324 feet

T **OT** *Regional map p. 272 (Q, 10); hike map p. 288*

This large peak has steep north and east sides but gentle south and west aspects. It stands between the North and East Inlets, and can be approached from either drainage. From North Inlet, Ptarmigan is most impressive when viewed from Lake Nanita because of the five craggy towers that rise magnificently west of the lake. These unofficially named 'Ptarmigan Towers' have many interesting technical challenges on them. The easiest routes up Ptarmigan Mountain don't exceed Class 2, but are long and arduous.

South Slope GRADE II CLASS 2   This is the shortest route up Ptarmigan Mountain, but because of laborious bush-whacking, it's more difficult than the Northwest Ridge Route. From the East Inlet Trailhead (p. 303), follow the East Inlet Trail (p. 304) for 5.3 miles to Lone Pine Lake. Leave the trail and bushwhack northwest through the thick forest, skirting short cliff bands when necessary. Above treeline, hike up a ridge to gain the long, arcing talus slope that leads to the summit, inset from the dramatic north and east aspects of the mountain. The mountain looks like a rounded talus field from this side, but once on the summit, hike north to gaze over the sharp, precipitous face and down on Lake Nokoni. Panoramic views showcase the Never Summer Mountains, Mummy Range, Longs Peak, the Continental Divide, and Wild Basin.

Northwest Ridge GRADE II CLASS 2
Although very long, this is the easiest route up Ptarmigan Mountain. From the North Inlet Trailhead (p. 303), follow the North Inlet Trail (p. 306) for 7.7 miles to the junction with the Lake Nanita Trail. Follow the Lake Nanita Trail south for 2.5 miles, then scramble west for 0.1 mile to Lake Nokoni. From the northeast shore, bushwhack northwest to a scree field that leads 0.25 mile to the saddle between Point 11,322' and Point 11,733'. This route becomes slightly convoluted in order to skirt the cliffs on the north side of Ptarmigan Mountain. Turn southwest and hike for 0.3 mile to gain Point 11,733', then descend from this point to the open talus slopes that provide easy access to the summit of Ptarmigan Mountain. Contour south, then southeast up the broad talus slope for 0.8 mile to the top. From here, Andrews Peak is a two-mile walk southeast over open tundra slopes.

Andrews Peak 12,565 feet

T **OT** *Regional map p. 272 (T, 8); hike map p. 288*

This is the highest peak along the impressive ridge that separates the East and North Inlet drainages. It is located on the west side of the Continental Divide and is a huge mountain. A long, uncomplicated hike with some arduous bushwhacking from East Inlet is the easiest way to the summit. A mammoth summit cairn, more than 7 feet tall, adorns the top of this regal peak.

Summit cairn on Andrews Peak

South Slope GRADE II CLASS 2   From the East Inlet Trailhead (p. 303), follow the East Inlet Trail (p. 304) for 6.9 miles to Lake Verna. Continue east on the trail as it travels along the lake's north shore. At roughly the midpoint of the lake, leave the trail and bushwhack through thick timber up a steep slope for 0.4 mile to treeline. Skirt any cliffs that bar the way. Once above treeline, the broad south slope of Andrews Peak rises for another mile over talus and tundra to the top.

'Ptarmigans Beak' 12,241 feet

T **OT** *Regional map p. 272 (U, 7); hike map p. 288*

This noteworthy, unofficially named peak rises above the east end of Lake Verna, located 0.9 mile southeast of Andrews Peak. It has a dramatic northeast face that rises above a beautiful, unofficially named lake ('Lake Catherine') that feeds a tributary of North Inlet.

West Slope GRADE II CLASS 2   The best way to reach 'Ptarmigans Beak' is from Andrews Peak. From the summit of Andrews (follow route description above), hike southeast along the gentle tundra slope for 0.9 mile to the top. Or, follow the South Slope Route on Andrews Peak to treeline, then hike northeast over talus for 0.9 mile to the top of 'Ptarmigans Beak.'

Mount Craig 12,007 feet

T **OT** *Regional map p. 272 (Q, 4); hike map p. 279*

This massive mountain dominates the view from the town of Grand Lake (where locals call it Mount Baldy, because of its treeless rock-and-tundra summit) and lies between East Inlet and Paradise Creek. It's a fun peak to climb and provides incredible views of the southwestern region of RMNP.

South Slope GRADE II CLASS 2   This route involves a considerable time commitment to complete it in a day. It requires bushwhacking to Ten Lake Park, then ascending a long talus slope to the top. It is an exquisite adventure into a wild, remote, pristine area. No camping is permitted in Paradise or Ten Lakes Parks. From the East Inlet Trailhead (p. 303), follow the East Inlet Trail (p. 304) for 4.4 miles to the Paradise Park Trail (p. 306). Follow this trail south until it disappears, then bushwhack east through difficult terrain to reach a grouping of rock knobs that stand between Paradise Creek and Ten Lake Park, about 1.4 miles south of the East Inlet Trail. This route is rough going, but is shorter than hiking into Paradise Park, then ascending to Ten Lake Park from there. Negotiate the rugged terrain and climb east through the rock knobs, gaining elevation to the bench north of Paradise Creek that is home to Ten Lake Park. Here, heavy forest is interspersed with rock slabs and domes. Immediately west of Ten Lake Park, pick a route and hike north up the abrupt base of Mount Craig to gain access to the more gentle talus slope that leads to the summit.

Fourth Class Grass Route GRADE II CLASS 3+   This route is a fun adventure up a steep, beautiful gully to the summit ridge. It ascends the steep northwest face of Mount Craig. From the East Inlet Trailhead (p. 303), follow the East Inlet Trail (p. 304) for 5.3 miles to Lone Pine Lake. From the west end of the lake, leave the trail and bushwhack south through thick forest, avoiding any small cliffs along the way. Hike into a broad, central basin with a picturesque waterfall rushing over sheer walls. A beautiful avalanche-scarred meadow lies at the base of an obvious gully that rises southeast. The impressive cliffs of Mount Craig tower above. Climb up the gully, which is extremely steep and funnels into a narrow channel filled with dirt and loose rocks. Gain the northwest face, characterized by extremely steep grass slopes (the "fourth-class" grass!) with intermittent rock slabs that provide stability when climbing. This is not a desirable descent route because it is so steep. The grade relents and becomes more reasonable, leading through stunted trees and over tundra to the lower, north summit of Mount Craig. Hike south along the blocky ridge crest to the true summit.

Southeast Ridge GRADE II CLASS 3   From the East Inlet Trailhead (p. 303), follow the East Inlet Trail (p. 304) for 6.4 miles to the point where an unnamed creek flows north into East Inlet at the east end of a long, rocky, unnamed pond that lies west of Lake Verna. Leave the trail and cross to the south side of East Inlet creek. Bushwhack up the steep, forested slope over large boulders into an unnamed creek drainage and follow it south toward a bowl formed by Mount Craig and Points 11,902' and 11,959'. Hike southeast up steep scree (Class 3) to the saddle between the two unnamed points. Turn west and hike over Point 11,902', then hike along the gentle south side of the ridge for 0.9 mile to Mount Craig.

Joanne Skidmore and Marisa Howe hiking on Mount Craig

'Fleur de Lis' (12,250 feet) and 'Aiguille de Fleur' (11,940 feet)

T OT *Regional map p. 272 (U, 3–4); hike map p. 279*

These beautiful, unofficially named features lie along the imposing ridge between Mount Craig and Isolation Peak. 'Fleur de Lis' is the highpoint on the ridge west of Isolation Peak. The hike to this peak is a rugged one. 'Aiguille de Fleur' is the sheer tower at the terminus of the sharp ridge running north from 'Fleur de Lis,' and is technical. It is prominent and beautiful when viewed from Lake Verna.

'Fleur de Lis' West Slope GRADE II CLASS 3   From the East Inlet Trailhead (p. 303), follow the East Inlet Trail (p. 304) for 6.4 miles to the point where an unnamed creek flows north into East Inlet at the west end of a long, rocky unnamed pond that lies east of Lake Verna. Leave the trail and cross to the south side of the East Inlet creek. Bushwhack up the steep, forested slope over large boulders into an unnamed creek drainage and follow it south toward a bowl formed by Mount Craig and Points 11,902' and 11,959'. Hike southeast up steep scree to the saddle between the two unnamed points. Turn east and hike over along the gentle tundra-and-talus slope for 0.8 mile to the top.

Mountaineers Route, Aiguille de Fleur

'Fleur de Lis' East Slope GRADE II CLASS 2   This is the preferred route up 'Fleur de Lis.' It's longer, more scenic, and easier than the West Slope route. From the East Inlet Trailhead (p. 303), follow the East Inlet Trail (p. 304) for 9.3 miles to Fifth Lake. Hike to the west side of the lake and scramble southwest over rocky terrain for 1.1 miles to an obvious 11,900-foot saddle on the ridge west of Isolation Peak. Stay west of any technical difficulties or cliff bands presented by the steep mass of Isolation. From the scenic saddle, hike west across the gentle talus-and-tundra slope for 0.6 mile to the top.

Boulder–Grand Pass   12,061 feet

T OT *Regional map p. 272 (X, 5); hike maps, Region 3, pp. 192, 196*

This wonderful, tundra-laden pass provides access between East Inlet and Wild Basin. Breathtaking scenery and adventurous hiking draw countless trekkers to use it as a thoroughfare to access a myriad of destinations.

West Access From the East Inlet Trailhead (p. 303), follow the East Inlet Trail (p. 304) for 6.9 miles to Lake Verna. Continue east on a rough path for 0.9 mile to Spirit Lake, then hike along the north shore and continue for 0.6 mile to Fourth Lake on a deteriorating

Upper East Inlet valley, below Boulder–Grand Pass

trail. From Fourth Lake, bushwhack northeast through the dense forest to top out above treeline. From treeline, climb east over open tundra slopes to the magnificent flat saddle of Boulder–Grand Pass, 1.1 miles from Fourth Lake.

East Access See Region 3, p. 194.

PARADISE CREEK   *Regional map p. 272 (P, 1)*

OTHER DESTINATIONS

Paradise Park   10,500 feet
T OT   *Regional map p. 272 (R, 1)*

Recognized early on as a treasure trove of pristine riparian beauty, officials have protected this area from overuse by man. It is truly a wonderland of remote, untouched natural wilderness. Moose frolic in the shelter of the forest, and Paradise Creek provides a wonderful habitat for flora and fauna. This area is not easy to reach. An unmaintained trail follows Paradise Creek for only about 1 mile of its 3.7-mile course. Scientists believe that the forest has developed without interruption since the last glacial period. The homogeneous tree stands and the uniformity of the forest floor give evidence of undisturbed growth. Hiking into the area is an adventure.

Paradise Park is classified as a Research Natural Area—one of three such zones in RMNP. These research sites were established by the International Biological Program and included in a worldwide system of natural areas for scientific and educational purposes. In these areas, natural processes are allowed to predominate and act as a baseline for man-caused changes measured elsewhere. Foot traffic is allowed but not encouraged, with only day-use activities authorized (no camping allowed).

East Inlet Access   From the East Inlet Trailhead (p. 303), hike east along the East Inlet Trail (p. 304) for 4.4 miles to a bridge that crosses East Inlet. Locate and follow the Paradise Park Trail (p. 306) south along the creek initially, then as it climbs along a steep hillside and drops down near some unnamed cascades to enter a bog. Here the trail peters out. Hike south through the bog and fight through along the trailless route to a sweeping curve in Paradise Creek. Head east through marshland festooned with wildflowers. Explore Paradise Park by bushwhacking through thick forest choked with fallen timber and rotting logs. Trudge over soggy subalpine meadows and through deep bogs to your heart's desire.

Roaring Fork Access   From Watanga Lake (follow route description, Region 7, p. 312), skirt along the western shore and follow Watanga Creek north, then east, to the headwall between Mount Adams and Watanga Mountain. Climb northeast up the steep hill and over tundra to the long, broad saddle and ridgeline between the two peaks. Adams Lake is visible to the northeast on a large bench above Paradise Park. Drop down from the ridgeline, descending the steep, loose terrain to the bench. Continue to descend through difficult terrain for 1.2 miles to Paradise Creek.

Paradise Park

Ten Lake Park 11,200 feet
T **OT** *Regional map p. 272 (R, 3); hike map p. 279*

Imagine a verdant shelf set high on a stately mountainside above an unspoiled, heavenly creek valley. Add a series of lovely lakes to ornament the shelf and place it in a location so remote that few humans would ever have the ambition to go there. Put it all together and you've got Ten Lake Park. The 1958 USGS quadrangle "Isolation Peak" identifies two major lakes and three small ponds on the map. The other five lakes must be the numerous shallow ponds and small puddles that dot the bench, rife with tall grasses, abundant wildflowers, and marshy bogland. These lofty lakes are all between 11,200 and 11,400 feet. Graced with unparalleled mountain views, nestled below the southeastern flank of mighty Mount Craig and soaring above the rapture of Paradise Park, Ten Lake Park is a true paradise.

Paradise Creek Access From the East Inlet Trailhead (p. 303), follow the East Inlet Trail (p. 304) for 4.4 miles to the Paradise Park Trail. Follow this trail until it disappears, then bushwhack east through difficult terrain to reach a grouping of rock knobs that stand between Paradise Creek and Ten Lake Park, about 1.4 miles south of the East Inlet Trail. This route is rough going but is shorter than hiking into Paradise Park, then ascending to Ten Lake Park from there. Negotiate the rugged terrain and climb east through the rock knobs, gaining elevation to the bench north of Paradise Creek that is home to Ten Lake Park. Here, heavy forest is interspersed with rock slabs and domes. Continue west to the lakes of Ten Lake Park, set on an open shelf with outstanding views.

Lake Verna Access From the East Inlet Trailhead (p. 303), follow the East Inlet Trail (p. 304) for 6.4 miles to the point where an unnamed creek flows north into East Inlet at the west end of a long, rocky, unnamed pond that lies east of Lake Verna. Leave the trail and cross to the south side of East Inlet creek. Bushwhack up the steep, forested slope over large boulders into an unnamed creek drainage, and follow it south toward a bowl formed by Mount Craig and Points 11,902' and 11,959'. Hike southeast up steep scree to the saddle between the two unnamed points. From here, descend southwest for 0.5 mile to Ten Lake Park.

Ten Lake Park

NORTH INLET   *Regional map p. 272 (M, 12)*

North Inlet is the name for the magnificent creek that originates west of Chiefs Head Peak at the Continental Divide. The drainage is an extremely rugged testimony to wilderness. Upper North Inlet, between Lake Powell and Solitude Lake, is wild and special, made more so because it is exceedingly difficult to access. Lower North Inlet is accessed by a well-maintained trail and offers a cornucopia of wonderful destinations to explore. North Inlet flows for 12.8 miles from Lake Powell to empty its waters into Grand Lake from the north. Concurrently, East Inlet supplies water to the east side of Grand Lake.

LAKES AND FALLS

Cascade Falls   8,800 feet
T 🏞 *Regional map p. 272 (N, 13)*

North Inlet creek rushes noisily over broken granite steps for nearly 100 feet in a raucous display of splendor at Cascade Falls. From the North Inlet Trailhead (p. 303), follow the North Inlet Trail (p. 306) for 3.6 miles to Cascade Falls. A small loop in the trail near the falls presents uphill travel on the southeast fork and downhill travel on the northwest fork. This helps prevent conflicts between horse traffic and hikers on the narrow, rocky path near the falls. The view of the falls from the trail is minimal. Scramble off-trail a short distance to get a better vantage of the gushing waterfall.

Lisa Foster jumping into Big Pool

Big Pool   8,920 feet
T *Regional map p. 272 (N, 15)*

Big Pool is a water-scoured natural basin in North Inlet. A tiny waterfall drops off a short cliff into the swirling pool. Bordered on one side by a 15-foot-high granite cliff and on the other by sloping boulders, the creek rushes out of the pool and continues descending through the thick forest. From the North Inlet Trailhead (p. 303), follow the North Inlet Trail (p. 306) for 4.8 miles to Big Pool. A nearby NPS campsite was named for this feature. The trail overlooks the churning landmark, with slabs offering restful picnic spots.

> Note: Jumping into rushing mountain streams is not recommended and is a dangerous practice that can lead to hypothermia, injury, or drowning.

Pettingell Lake   10,500 feet
T **OT** *Regional map p. 279 (P, 13)*

This secluded lake lies on a bench 1,200 vertical feet above the North Inlet valley. The first time I went there, I bushwhacked southeast through extremely dense timber from North Inlet along the outlet stream from Pettingell Lake. There's no need to do this, though, because there is an easier way. From Lake Nokoni, located just northwest of the Lake Nanita Trail, it is a short off-trail hike up and over a rocky ridge to Pettingell.

From the North Inlet Trailhead (p. 303), follow the North Inlet Trail (p. 306) for 7.7 miles to the junction with the Lake Nanita Trail. Turn south and follow the Lake Nanita Trail for 2.6 miles to Lake Nokoni. From the north side of Lake Nokoni, leave the trail and then hike north for 0.25 mile to a saddle located between Point 11,322' and Point 11,733'. From the saddle, contour northwest and then descend 0.5 mile to

Pettingell Lake

Pettingell Lake. Tucked snugly between the forest to the north and a rocky cirque to the south, this attractive lake rests in isolated glory.

'North Inlet Falls'   9,480 feet
T *Regional map p. 272 (R, 14)*

This is the unofficial name for a short, pretty waterfall in North Inlet along the Lake Nanita Trail. A nearby campsite was named for this charming little drop in the creek. From the North Inlet Trailhead (p. 303), follow the North Inlet Trail (p. 306) for 7.7 miles to the junction with the Lake Nanita Trail. Follow the Lake Nanita Trail south for 0.2 mile to a bridge over a dark, picturesque gorge that is home to the tiny waterfall.

Lake Nokoni   10,780 feet
T *Regional map p. 272 (Q, 12); hike map p. 288*

Lake Nokoni is a fine alpine tarn, carved into a glacially scoured bowl at the base of Ptarmigan Mountain's steep north face. From the North Inlet Trailhead (p. 303), follow the North Inlet Trail (p. 306) for 7.7 miles to the junction with the Lake Nanita Trail. Follow the Lake Nanita Trail south for 2.5 miles to a point on the trail immediately east of Lake Nokoni. Leave the trail and scramble 0.1 mile to the east shore.

Lake Nanita   10,780 feet
T *Regional map p. 272 (S, 10); hike map p. 288*

Lake Nanita is undoubtedly one of the most beautiful tarns in RMNP. Nestled at the flank of the spectacular northeast-facing ridge between Ptarmigan Mountain and Andrews Peak, this elongated lake is a pearl of natural beauty. The stately spires of 'Ptarmigan Towers' add majesty to this exciting place. From Lake Nokoni (follow the route description above), the trail continues southeast toward Lake Nanita, climbing steeply for 0.3 mile to a small saddle between Point 11,218' and Ptarmigan Mountain. From here it descends for 0.6 mile to Lake Nanita's western shore.

'Lake Catherine'   10,600 feet
T **OT** *Regional map p. 272 (V, 8)*

'Lake Catherine' is an extremely remote, gorgeous lake in upper North Inlet, set in a deep bowl below the north face of 'Ptarmigans Beak' and the convoluted west face of Mount Alice. Due to its isolated, rugged location, it is one of the most rarely visited lakes in RMNP. From Lake Nanita (above) hike southeast and climb to a prominent 11,380-foot saddle between Andrews Peak and Point 11,603'. The route is steep and it is easier to access a ridge to the north than to follow the drainage proper from Lake Nanita. Traverse south along the ridge to reach the saddle. From here, descend southeast over tundra to treeline, then turn northeast and hike through the forest to the shore of beautiful 'Lake Catherine.'

Lake Solitude   9,740 feet
T **OT** *Regional map p. 272 (T, 12)*

RMNP is home to two lakes christened "solitude." Lake Solitude is a shallow pond in a quiet meadow amid the wilderness of upper North Inlet. Solitude Lake is the stark alpine tarn on a rocky shelf high above Glacier Gorge. Both lakes require off-trail

hiking to reach. Lake Solitude lies southwest of North Inlet creek in a remote field of grass and wildflowers. The 1961 RMNP map shows a trail leading southeast from the Lake Nanita Trail to Lake Solitude, but it has degenerated to an intermittent angler's path that is difficult to follow. From the North Inlet Trailhead (p. 303), follow the North Inlet Trail (p. 306) for 7.7 miles to the junction with the Lake Nanita Trail. Turn south and follow the Lake Nanita Trail for 0.9 mile to the first major switchback along the trail. Leave the trail and bushwhack southeast, crossing the stream from Lake Nokoni and continuing through increasingly thick forest for 0.4 mile to reach the meadow and Lake Solitude. Tall grasses ornament the pretty little pond, encircled by abundant wildflowers.

Lake Powell 11,540 feet
T **OT** *Regional map p. 272 (Y, 10)*

Austere and frigid, Lake Powell is a classic example of a high-altitude tarn cut into a stone basin by the power of ice. Surrounded by huge peaks in a barren gorge, this deep, teardrop-shaped lake lies in a commanding position at the headwaters of mighty North Inlet. Reached by either an arduous bushwhack up the hard-to-penetrate North Inlet valley or a strenuous hike over the saddle between Mount Alice and Chiefs Head Peak from Wild Basin, this remote tarn is reserved for determined lake-seekers.

North Inlet Access Follow the route description, p. 287, to lovely Lake Solitude. From here, the intense bushwhacking adventure begins. Crossing and recrossing North Inlet may seem easier in a continual effort to reach easier ground, but the grueling bush-whacking is the same on both sides of the stream. Marsh, tall plants, thick forest, and fallen timber choked with bramble all present obstacles to easy passage. Fight through it and cross the stream that flows from Lake Nanita, continuing through the dense forest. Cross a stream from the outlet of 'Lake Catherine', then cross North Inlet where it angles east and keep moving upward. Climb steeply out of the forest into a beautiful basin surrounded by steep rock walls to the north and a remote canyon to the south. Ascend grassy ledges through avalanche debris to granite slabs slick with rushing water. Climb to the top of a bench with unnamed ponds amid grassy fields. McHenrys Notch soars magnificently upward to the north. Negotiate a route up slabs and large boulders to Lake Powell, cupped into a basin below the Chiefs Head–Mount Alice saddle.

Wild Basin Access This is the easiest route to Lake Powell. From Snowbank Lake (see Region 3, p. 188), hike northwest toward the obvious, broad ramp that leads to the sizable saddle between Chiefs Head Peak and Mount Alice. The ramp is extremely scenic and ornamented with wildflowers in July. A faint path leads up the ramp to the saddle, 1.1 miles from Snowbank Lake. At the saddle, hike north over broad tundra slopes to a rib of rock that juts out to the northwest from the Continental Divide, 900 vertical feet above Lake Powell. This is the least steep option for descending to the lake. Downclimb over boulders and loose talus to the rocky lake basin, 0.9 mile from the saddle.

OTHER DESTINATIONS

Summerland Park 8,520 feet
T **[hikers]** *Regional map p. 272 (J, 11)*

The rushing waters of North Inlet slow down to meander lazily through Summerland Park, a pretty, wide-open meadow along the trail. From the North Inlet Trailhead (p. 303), follow the North Inlet Trail (p. 306) east along a doubletrack road closed to

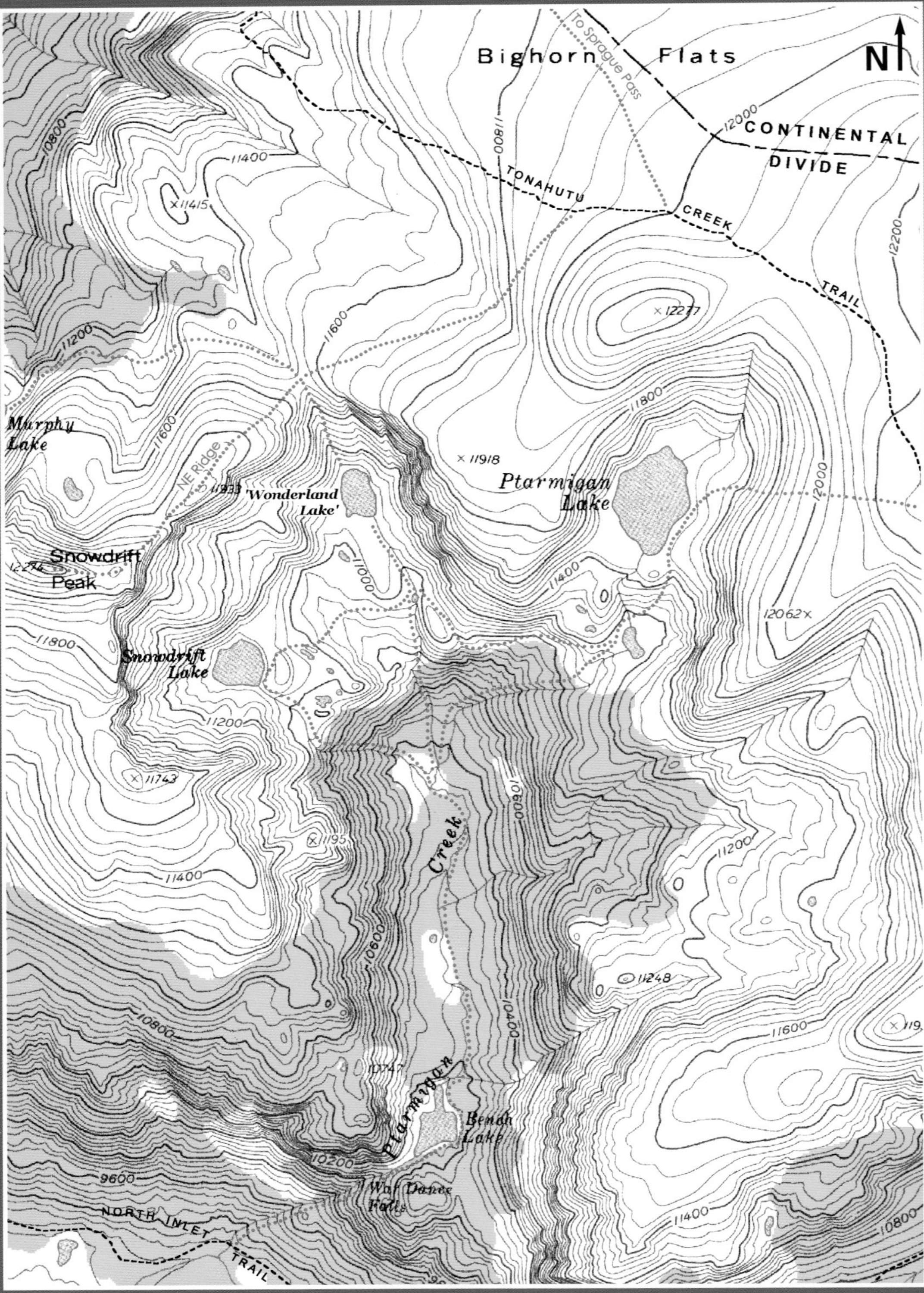

Bighorn Flats

To Sprague Pass

CONTINENTAL DIVIDE

N

TONAHUTU

CREEK

TRAIL

10800

11400

11600

11200

× 11415

× 12277

Murphy Lake

NE Ridge

11933

'Wonderland Lake'

× 11918

Ptarmigan Lake

11800

12000

Snowdrift Peak

12274

1000

1400

12062 ×

11800

Snowdrift Lake

11200

× 11743

× 11951

10600

11200

11400

10600

11248

10800

11600

× 119

Creek

PTARMIGAN

11400

10400

11747

Benah Lake

10200

War Dance Falls

9600

NORTH INLET TRAIL

11400

10800

Magnetic North
11.5 degrees

N

0   0.5   1

Distance in miles

unauthorized vehicles. Initially the road follows RMNP's southern boundary, and the land south of the road is private. The road descends about 50 feet near the trailhead, then levels off for an easy 1.3-mile stroll to Summerland Park.

PTARMIGAN CREEK *Regional map p. 272 (R, 18)*

Ptarmigan Creek originates from three large lakes tucked into fingerlike gorges between Snowdrift Peak and Ptarmigan Point. The brook flows through a verdant canyon of incomparable splendor and pools into pretty Bench Lake before tumbling over a steep, forested slope and then cascading through War Dance Falls to join North Inlet. Unanimously christened 'The Wonderland' by all who visit, this mystifying and remote basin beckons hardy hikers to explore its exquisite, virtually unmatched natural beauty.

LAKES AND FALLS

War Dance Falls 9,900 feet
T **OT** *Regional map p. 272 (R, 16); hike map p. 290*
This mighty waterfall prances over granite blocks amid a dense forest 500 vertical feet above the valley floor. It's fun and exciting to climb the steep slope beside the dancing cascade. From the North Inlet Trailhead (p. 303), follow the North Inlet Trail (p. 306) for 6.7 miles to the bridge that crosses Ptarmigan Creek. Cross the bridge and strike off-trail to the northeast, bushwhacking up the east side of Ptarmigan Creek. A faint trail ascends this slope but it is somewhat hard to follow. Cairns mark the route in some sections. Climb 0.4 mile to War Dance Falls. Enjoy the intimate setting of tight forest encompassing a wonderfully steep waterfall.

Bench Lake 10,140 feet
T **OT** *Regional map p. 272 (R, 16); hike map p. 290*
Bench Lake lies at the southern end of an unbelievably beautiful hanging valley that's known as 'The Wonderland,' 850 vertical feet above the North Inlet Trail. The crystal blue waters of Bench Lake are surrounded by lush greenery, augmented by the gushing outlet stream that plummets through War Dance Falls to join North Inlet on the valley floor. From War Dance Falls (follow route description above), climb north past the cascade for 0.6 mile to top out on the verdant shelf that is home to Bench Lake.

Bench Lake

Snowdrift Lake (11,060 feet), **Ptarmigan Lake** (11,460 feet), and **'Wonderland Lake'** (11,060 feet)
T **OT** *Regional map p. 272–273 (Q, 19; S, 20; and R, 20); hike map p. 290*
The headwaters of Ptarmigan Creek originate from the three large alpine lakes at the north end of the pristine valley called 'The Wonderland.' Ptarmigan Lake is the largest, located east of Ptarmigan Point in a beautiful cirque headwall fed by snowmelt from Point 12,227' on the south side of Bighorn Flats. Snowdrift Lake is located in a bowl

southeast of Snowdrift Peak. Large, unofficially named 'Wonderland Lake' sits in the middle gorge between the other two. Numerous other unnamed pools adorn the stark basins below these magnificent lakes.

Ptarmigan Creek Access From the North Inlet Trailhead (p. 303), follow the North Inlet Trail (p. 306) for 6.7 miles to a bridge that crosses Ptarmigan Creek. Leave the trail and bushwhack northeast up the steep slope on the east side of Ptarmigan Creek. A faint trail ascends the slope but it is somewhat hard to follow. Cairns mark the route in some sections. The route climbs steeply to War Dance Falls, then continues upward to Bench Lake. Bushwhack north for 0.8 mile up Ptarmigan Creek to the point where the tributaries from the three lakes converge. From here hike northwest for 0.7 mile to reach Snowdrift Lake, or north for 0.6 mile to reach 'Wonderland Lake,' or northeast for 0.7 mile to access Ptarmigan Lake. Reaching the lakes involves slogging through marshland and bushwhacking into stunted forest, then scrambling over rough talus fields to boulder-strewn granite benches.

Bighorn Flats Access From Flattop Mountain (see Region 1, p. 75), hike west for 0.3 mile to the junction with the Tonahutu Creek Trail. Follow the Tonahutu Creek Trail (p. 307) west for about a mile to a point directly east of the Ptarmigan Lake cirque. Leave the trail and hike across talus and tundra to the rim of the cirque at 12,000 feet. Descend over steep talus and boulders for 0.3 mile to Ptarmigan Lake. Skirt Ptarmigan Lake and descend south along the outlet stream to a small, unnamed lake at 11,180 feet. From here, descend slightly and traverse at 11,000 feet to the outlet stream for 'Wonderland Lake.' Turn north and scramble 0.2 mile to 'Wonderland Lake,' or traverse west and descend 100 vertical feet to reach Snowdrift Lake.

TONAHUTU CREEK   *Regional map p. 272 (H, 16)*

LAKES AND FALLS

Granite Falls   9,800 feet
T *Regional map p. 273 (L, 21)*

Granite Falls cascades over tiers of polished boulders in Tonahutu Creek as it flows through thick timber north of Mount Patterson. It is a noisy, scenic spot for a picnic with the added benefit of refreshing spray coming from the rushing water on hot afternoons. Viewpoints above and below the falls offer different perspectives from which to enjoy the scenery.

Green Mountain Trailhead Access From the Green Mountain Trailhead (p. 303), follow the Green Mountain Trail (p. 304) east for 1.8 miles to the Tonahutu Creek Trail (p. 307). Follow the Tonahutu Creek Trail north, then east, for 3.3 miles to Granite Falls. A spur path leads south down a rocky, hard-packed trail to sloping rock slabs at the base of the main tier of cascades, level with a rushing pool. Below this, the water tumbles down four shallower steps.

Bear Lake Access The falls can also be reached from the east via the Tonahutu Creek Trail. From Flattop Mountain (see Region 1, p. 75), hike west for 0.3 mile to the Tonahutu Creek Trail (p. 307). Follow the Tonahutu Creek Trail for 6.1 miles to Granite Falls.

Haynach Lakes 11,060 feet

T *Regional map p. 273 (N, 25)*

In 1914, two elderly Arapaho Indians who had spent their youth in the Estes Park area were invited on an extended pack trip in what is now RMNP to identify Arapaho names for local features. The Arapaho word for "snow water" is *haanach,* which was adapted to "Haynach" to complement these cold high-altitude lakes.

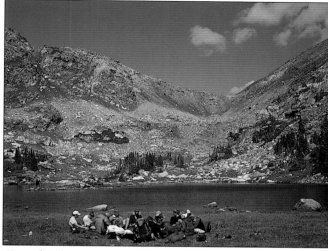

Haynach Lakes

Green Mountain Trailhead Access

From the Green Mountain Trailhead (p. 303), follow the Green Mountain Trail (p. 304) east for 1.8 miles to the Tonahutu Creek Trail (p. 307). Turn north on Tonahutu Creek Trail and travel along the perimeter of Big Meadows. The trail angles east for 3.3 miles to Granite Falls. Past the falls, follow the Tonahutu Creek Trail for 2 miles to the junction with the spur trail that leads northwest to Haynach Lakes. Turn north and follow the Haynach Lakes Trail for 1.5 miles to Haynach Lakes. The trail leads to the largest, horseshoe-shaped lake. Lush grass and medium-sized boulders adorn the shoreline. Multiple clumps of small pines enrich the scenery surrounding the lake. Point 12,052' dominates the view to the west. Three smaller ponds are situated south of the largest lake. Additionally, three more pools lie above treeline at the base of the sensational east face of Nakai Peak.

Bear Lake Access   Haynach Lakes can also be reached from the east via the Tonahutu Creek Trail. From Flattop Mountain (see Region 1, p. 75), hike west for 0.3 mile to the Tonahutu Creek Trail (p. 307). Follow the Tonahutu Creek Trail for 4.1 miles to the Haynach Lakes Trail. Turn north and follow the Haynach Lakes Trail for 1.5 miles to Haynach Lakes.

Murphy Lake 11,220 feet

T **OT** *Regional map p. 273 (O, 20)*

Murphy Lake is nestled up against a permanent snowfield set deeply within a rock cirque formed by the sharp northwest ridge of Snowdrift Peak. Boulder fields line the shore of this frigid lake, and the snowfield rises to a deep notch in the ridge. This high-alpine setting is magnificent and can be reached from either the Flattop Mountain Trail (see Region 1, p. 75) or the Tonahutu Creek Trail (p. 307). Follow either one of these trails to

Unnamed pond enroute to Murphy Lake

Bighorn Flats. From 11,600 feet on the Tonahutu Creek Trail as it crosses Bighorn Flats, contour south across open country for 0.8 mile to the obvious 11,540-foot saddle between the northeast ridge of Snowdrift Peak and Bighorn Flats. Angle southwest for 0.8 mile to Murphy Lake.

PEAKS AND OTHER DESTINATIONS

Green Mountain 10,313 feet
T **OT** *Regional map p. 272 (G, 17)*

This small, forested peak is merely a stone's throw from Trail Ridge Road, over which millions of people travel annually, yet only a handful of people have climbed Green Mountain this century. Limited views are undoubtedly the reason, but a stroll through the sparse, magical forest makes it worthwhile.

Northwest Slope GRADE I CLASS 2   From the Green Mountain Trailhead (p. 303), follow the Green Mountain Trail (p. 304) for 0.6 mile to a meadow on the south side of the trail. Leave the trail and hike south through the marshy meadow. Hike cross-country and upward through the sparse forest of small lodgepole pines. Any fallen logs are easy to hike over, because they are small and on the ground instead of suspended between live trees. Branch bramble is at a minimum here. Gain a forested ridge that rises southeast to the northern summit of Green Mountain. Descend from this knob and hike south to the true summit. Views of Kawuneeche Valley and Trail Ridge Road can be seen through the trees.

Northeast Slope GRADE I CLASS 2   This route approaches the peak from Big Meadows. From the Green Mountain Trailhead (p. 303), follow the Green Mountain Trail (p. 304) for 1.8 miles to the Tonahutu Creek Trail. Turn south (right) and follow the trail for 0.3 mile to a logical point on the northeast side of Green Mountain. Leave the trail and bushwhack southwest through the sparse forest for 0.6 mile to the top.

Nisa Mountain 10,788 feet
T **OT** *Regional map p. 272 (J, 16)*

Nisah is the Arapaho word for "twins." Nisa Mountain's twin summits (Points 10,741' and 10,788') are two bumps on a ridge extending southwest from Mount Patterson. Nisa lies between the lower North Inlet and lower Tonahutu Creeks. Both streams have tributaries that originate on Nisa Mountain's forested slopes.

Northwest Slope GRADE I CLASS 2   From the Green Mountain Trailhead (p. 303), follow the Green Mountain Trail (p. 304) east for 1.8 miles to the Tonahutu Creek Trail near Big Meadows. Turn south and follow the Tonahutu Creek Trail for 1.4 miles to 9,200 feet. Leave the trail, hike east to cross Tonahutu Creek, and begin climbing the west slope of Nisa Mountain. This cross-country travel is moderate in difficulty, passing through a sparse forest with no tricky bushwhacking. Rock outcrops along the slope provide good views of Big Meadows below, with Shadow Mountain Lake and Lake Granby visible through the trees. The slope gets very steep near the top, then mellows out and leads to a rock outcrop that represents the summit, from which a nice vantage of neighboring Mount Patterson can be seen.

Mount Patterson 11,424 feet
T **OT** *Regional map p. 272 (K, 18)*

The bald summit of this strategically located peak overlooks North Inlet and Tonahutu Creeks and dominates the forest between Big Meadows and Snowdrift Peak. It is a quiet point off the beaten path.

West Slope to Northwest Ridge GRADE 1 CLASS 2 From the Green Mountain Trailhead (p. 303), follow the Green Mountain Trail (p. 304) for 1.8 miles to the Tonahutu Creek Trail at Big Meadows. Leave the trail, hike east into Big Meadows, and cross Tonahutu Creek. Continue east and climb through the sparse forest to Point 11,008'. From here, descend slightly southeast to an open saddle, then climb a forested ridge southeast for 0.7 mile to the summit of Mount Patterson.

Big Meadows 9,400 feet

T ⫟ *Regional map p. 272 (H, 19)*

Tonahutu means "big meadows" in Arapaho. Tonahutu Creek flows south through Big Meadows, lazily meandering through the elongated glacial valley ornamented with tall, swaying grasses. This is the largest montane meadow in RMNP. Nakai Peak rises beyond the meadow to the northeast. Two dilapidated cabins lie along the Tonahutu Creek Trail on the west edge of the meadow, evidence of the settlers who tried to make a living from this rugged landscape. This is a nice spot for a picnic, with pleasant views of Mount Patterson and with wildflowers growing copiously throughout the scenic meadow.

From the Green Mountain Trailhead (p. 303), follow the Green Mountain Trail (p. 304) east for 1.8 miles to the Tonahutu Creek Trail. Turn north on the Tonahutu Creek Trail and hike for 0.1 mile to two deteriorating log structures. Trees have taken root in the floors, and nature is at work to reclaim this meadowside area. Leave the trail and then hike east into Big Meadows to explore Tonahutu Creek and revel in the views.

Alex Kostadinov and Michelle Chase cross a stream in Big Meadows

Nakai Peak 12,216 feet
T OT *Regional map p. 273 (L, 25)*

Located 1.7 miles south of the tight grouping of Continental Divide high peaks, Nakai Peak stands alone. Its large, bulky mass reigns over the forested region in an uncontested monarchy. Nakai's rocky slopes overlook Onahu Creek to the north and Tonahutu Creek to the south.

Northeast Ridge GRADE II CLASS 2+ This is the easiest route to the top, but is a long day hike. It can be made less demanding by a high camp at Haynach Lakes. From Haynach Lakes (follow the route description on p. 293), locate the end of the trail at the largest, horseshoe-shaped lake, then hike 0.5 mile northwest over large boulders to the obvious saddle at the headwall of the tiny stream that flows into the lake. This saddle lies between the Continental Divide and Point 12,052', offering a grand view into the Julian Lake valley. From the saddle it is 0.8 mile to the top of Nakai. Turn southwest and scramble up large boulders along the Class 2+ ridge, past a false summit, to Point 12,052'. Drop down to a grassy saddle, then ascend the tundra slope to the summit.

Bighorn Flats 11,900 feet
T *Regional map p. 273 (S, 23)*

This large summit upland stretches from Sprague Pass to Ptarmigan Point and slopes slightly—about 300 feet per mile. An impressive expanse of high country, it spans the Continental Divide and provides access between the Tonahutu Creek Trail (p. 307) and the Flattop Mountain Trail (see Region 1, p. 75). This is the site of a water-diversion ditch that was dug in 1902 to collect water and redirect it into Spruce Canyon. The ditch has since been filled in by the NPS after a creative agreement regained the water rights for RMNP. Good grazing on the flats attracts hordes of elk and bighorn sheep.

Bighorn Flats

Snowdrift Peak 12,274 feet
T OT *Regional map p. 272 (P, 19); hike map p. 290*

Named for its hallmark snowdrift that persists nearly year-round on the northeast ridge, this mountain harbors numerous alpine lakes in the nooks of its convoluted ridges. The abrupt south face soars 3,000 vertical feet above North Inlet, while the precipitous north face rises 2,000 feet above Tonahutu Creek. A gentle ridge provides easy access from Bighorn Flats, and the summit area consists of open tundra that is bordered by glacial cliffs on the northwest.

Northeast Ridge GRADE II CLASS 2 This is the easiest route to the top of Snowdrift Peak. Take either the Flattop Mountain Trail (see Region 1, p. 75) or the Tonahutu Creek Trail (p. 307) to Bighorn Flats. From 11,600 feet on the Tonahutu Creek Trail as it crosses Bighorn Flats, contour south across open country for 0.8 mile to the obvious 11,540-foot saddle between the northeast ridge of Snowdrift Peak and Bighorn Flats. This beautifully rounded ridge with a snowfield at a lowpoint leads gently toward the summit, 0.8 mile away. From the saddle, hike southwest up the ridge to Point 11,933'. Descend slightly and climb southwest to the summit plane of Snowdrift. Turn west to climb blocky talus to the summit.

Ptarmigan Creek Access GRADE II CLASS 2   From the North Inlet Trailhead (p. 303), follow the North Inlet Trail (p. 306) for 6.7 miles to a bridge that crosses Ptarmigan Creek. Cross the bridge and locate a faint path that leads northeast up the east side of the creek. The route climbs steeply to War Dance Falls, a lovely cascade tucked away in an abrupt, dense forest. Continue upward to Bench Lake, located at the start of a pristine hanging basin almost 800 vertical feet above the valley floor. Skirt Bench Lake on the east and hike north through the incredible, lush wonderland of Ptarmigan Creek. The headwaters of Ptarmigan Creek originate from three large alpine lakes tucked into finger valleys at the headwall of the gorge. Hike north to the unnamed lake in the middle, unofficially called 'Wonderland Lake.' Climb north up loose talus and scree to the obvious saddle northeast of Snowdrift's summit. Follow the Northeast Ridge Route (above) to the top.

ONAHU CREEK   *Regional map p. 273 (F, 23)*

| LAKES |

Chickaree Lake   9,260 feet
T OT *Regional map p. 273 (E, 23)*

This sizable lake is tucked away on a forested bench slightly north of Onahu Creek. It is surrounded by dog hair stands of lodgepole pines and is a charming, secluded destination with no trails leading to it. With no inlet or outlet, finding the lake through the unvarying forest is challenging.

> The red squirrel, or chickaree, is an extremely vocal creature that lives in virtually all dense montane and subalpine forests. It characteristically builds up middens, which are piles of pinecone fragments often several feet deep, and chatters and scolds intruders to its territory.

Onahu Creek Trailhead Access From the Onahu Creek Trailhead (p. 303), follow the Onahu Creek Trail (p. 306) for 1.9 miles to 9,480 feet. Leave the trail and bushwhack northwest through the forest of even-sized lodgepole pines that resemble Pick-Up Sticks. Cross Onahu Creek and traverse across multiple scenic draws and hollows, littered with these "Pick-Up Sticks." Cross a tributary to Onahu Creek and continue northwest through the sparsely treed and vegetated forest. Gain a very large, relatively flat bench and hike around the perimeter to Chickaree Lake. The pretty, green lake is huge considering it has no inlet or outlet and is on an elevated shelf amid a forest, far from any other water source. It is nearly the size of Black Lake in Glacier Gorge. Pond lilies grace the water's edge, and the forested summits to the northeast of the lake stack upon each other in Smoky Mountain –type relief. Dirt hillsides on the north shore and a forest of crisscrossed standing and fallen lodgepole pines create a mystical setting.

Trail Ridge Road Access This is the most direct route to Chickaree Lake, but there is no convenient parking available along Trail Ridge Road. From a point 1.6 miles south of the Bowen/Baker Trailhead (see Region 8, p. 356) on Trail Ridge Road, leave the road and bushwhack northeast up a steep, forested hillside for 0.9 mile to Chickaree Lake.

Julian Lake 11,100 feet
T **OT** *Regional map p. 273 (K, 28)*

Julian Lake lies southwest of Chief Cheley Peak at the head of Onahu Creek. It is quiet, secluded, and difficult to reach. Access is either from the Timber Lake Trail and up over a high saddle southwest of Mount Ida, or from a long, demanding bushwhack up Onahu Creek.

Onahu Creek Access From the Onahu Creek Trailhead (p. 303), follow the Onahu Creek Trail (p. 306) for 3.3 miles to the junction with the Timber Creek Trail. Turn north and follow the Timber Creek Trail for 0.5 mile to 9,840 feet. Leave the trail and bushwhack along Onahu Creek, up into the lush valley formed by the steep cliff walls of Nakai Peak, Chief Cheley Peak, and Point 11,880'. Julian Lake lies at the northern head of this gorge. Travel off-trail and fight through bogland choked with willows along the stream. Wildflowers abound in the valley. Climb above treeline to stand on the boxy shoreline of Julian Lake. The rugged cliffs on the south side of Chief Cheley Peak tower above the scenic, boulder-strewn basin.

Timber Lake Access From Timber Lake (follow route description, opposite), hike southeast for 0.75 mile to the prominent 11,740-foot saddle between Timber Creek and Onahu Creek drainages. Descend southeast over steep scree to a large boulder bench, then descend grassy slopes to Julian Lake, 0.6 mile from the saddle.

OTHER DESTINATIONS

Long Meadows 10,300 feet
T *Regional map p. 273 (H, 27)*

Of the named meadows in RMNP, Long Meadows ranks as one of the most impressive. Set amid the healthy pine forest that lies between Timber Creek and Onahu Creek,

Inspecting plant life in Long Meadows

Long Meadows is an extraordinary plat of wide-open grassland. True to its name, it stretches for over 1.5 miles, festooned with verdant grasses and home to several small ponds. Too wet to support a large community of trees, it offers a wonderful, open visual relief set against fields of evergreen trees and the azure Colorado sky. The meadow is flat and luxuriant, bordered by thick stands of green trees. The best way to explore it is to hike along the perimeter of the trees, since the grassland is boggy for most of the summer. Several scenic ponds provide good photo opportunities. Access to the meadow is from the Timber Creek Trail, which can be reached via the Timber Lake Trail, Onahu Creek Trail, or Tonahutu Creek Trail.

Onahu Creek Access From the Onahu Creek Trailhead (p. 303), follow the Onahu Creek Trail (p. 306) for 3.3 miles to the junction with the Tonahutu Creek Trail, which comes in from the south, and the Timber Creek Trail, which comes in from the north. Then turn onto the Timber Creek Trail and hike north for 1.2 miles to Long Meadows. The trail becomes very indistinct and disappears before reaching the meadows. Fight through the bog and dense vegetation to reach the southern end of Long Meadows. Skirt the meadow in the trees on the east, then hike to the north end of the meadow to locate the Timber Creek Trail (also called the Long Meadows Trail).

Timber Creek Access From the Timber Lake Trailhead (p. 304), follow the the Timber Lake Trail (below) for 3.8 miles to the junction with the Timber Creek Trail, also called the Long Meadows Trail. Turn south on the Timber Creek Trail and cross Timber Creek. Continue as the trail climbs through thick forest for 1.6 miles to the northern end of Long Meadows, then peters out in the marsh. Though very difficult to locate amid the bogs and low-lying vegetation, it picks up again south of the meadow and continues southward to meet the Onahu and Tonahutu Creek Trails.

Green Mountain Trailhead Access From the Green Mountain Trailhead (p. 303), follow the Green Mountain Trail (p. 304) for 1.8 miles to the Tonahutu Creek Trail. Turn north and follow the Tonahutu Creek Trail for 0.75 mile to the Timber Creek Trail. Travel north on the Timber Creek Trail for 1.6 miles to the junction with the Onahu Creek Trail. Continue north on the Timber Creek Trail for 1.2 miles until it becomes very indistinct and obscured by bogs at the southern end of Long Meadows.

TIMBER CREEK   *Regional map p. 273 (F, 30)*

LAKES

Timber Lake   11,060 feet
T *Regional map p. 273 (J, 30)*

Timber Lake is a marvelous place to spend an afternoon picnicking and enjoying the gentle alpine scenery of the western slope. Moose and elk frequent the lush forest along the trail. From the Timber Lake Trailhead (p. 304), the Timber Lake Trail leads southeast through a large stand of mature aspen trees and across a level meadow to a bridge over cascading Beaver Creek. It then climbs steeply along the southwestern flank of Jackstraw Mountain through a thick forest of lodgepole pine, spruce, and fir. Vehicle

Mike Arneson overlooks Timber Lake

noise from Trail Ridge Road filters through the trees until the trail turns eastward and parallels Timber Creek, obscured from view by the dense forest. The trail connects with the Timber Creek Trail 3.8 miles from the trailhead. The Timber Lake Trail climbs northeast up some steep switchbacks to a scenic meadow, unofficially called 'Jackstraw Meadow.' The trail leads into the forest and contours southeast along the creek to another set of switchbacks that leads to Timber Lake. The area near the lake's outlet is marshy and thriving with globeflowers, bog laurel, and marsh marigolds. The north shore is lined with trees, with the south side rocky and barren. Some rocky cliffs on Mount Ida's west side rise behind the lake to the east.

PEAKS

Jackstraw Mountain   11,704 feet

T **OT**   *Regional map p. 273 (H, 33)*

This beautiful mountain has three summits, all above 11,000 feet. The rounded humps, technically below treeline but now devoid of vegetation, can be seen from Trail Ridge Road. The slopes of Jackstraw Mountain are thought to have been affected by active landslides in loose glacial debris. Dead trees standing barren and toppled logs cluttered

on top of each other look like a large-scale game of jackstraws, the pastime in which narrow strips of plastic or wood are tossed into a jumbled heap and players try to remove them one at a time without disturbing any of the others. The two main summits of this peak are flat, expansive fields of tundra.

Southeast Slope GRADE II CLASS 2

From the Timber Lake Trailhead (p. 304), follow the Timber Lake Trail (p. 299) for 4.2 miles to 'Jackstraw Meadow' at 10,800 feet. Leave the trail and bushwhack northwest along a small tributary into a stunning, wide-

Jackstraw Mountain

open basin between the two main summits of Jackstraw Mountain. Green grass, thriving wildflower gardens, and deep, narrow channels of water zigzagging through the lush landscape highlight the scene. The cliffs of Jackstraw's lower, southern summit rise to the northwest. Follow the creek up mellow terrain to the saddle between the two summits. The northern summit (11,704 feet) is higher and grassier, while the southern summit (11,679 feet) is lower and adorned with flat rocks and tundra. From the northern summit the barren hillsides of the northwestern aspect of the mountain stand out prominently.

MILNER PASS   *Regional map p. 273 (H, 38)*

At 10,758 feet, Milner Pass is a lowpoint on the Continental Divide immediately southwest of Poudre Lake. The parking lot at Milner Pass is right on the Continental Divide. The divide separates river drainage to the Atlantic Ocean from drainage to the Pacific. On the west side of the pass, Beaver Creek flows into the Colorado River, which travels 1,400 miles to the Gulf of California and the Pacific Ocean. On the east side of the pass, Poudre Lake feeds the Cache la Poudre River, which flows into the Missouri River, which joins the Mississippi and merges into to the Gulf of Mexico and the Atlantic Ocean.

LAKES

Lake Irene 10,600 feet

T 👫 *Regional map p. 273 (G, 36)*

This small, oval-shaped lake lies below Lake Irene Picnic Area (p. 303) to the southwest and is the source of Phantom Creek. A short, steep path leads down to the lake and then levels out to circle around it. The trail then returns to the trailhead in a 0.5-mile loop. From the parking area, notice the view of Sheep Rock across Trail Ridge Road to northeast. Several picnic sites are located near the lot. A log cabin still stands from the 1930s. From the southwest corner of the parking lot, locate the trail and descend steeply to the lake. Surrounded by grass and pines, this is a pretty destination. Follow the trail as it circles the lake and leads back to the short, steep hill that climbs to the parking lot. A bridge on the lake's southwest side spans Phantom Creek as it flows from the outlet. From here the old Ute Trail continues for 1.3 miles to the southwest to Farview Curve on Trail Ridge Road, where it ends.

"Squeaky Bob" Wheeler named Lake Irene for a guest at his resort. Squeaky Bob established one of the first dude ranches on the North Fork of the Grand River, now the Colorado River. His fishing camp and tent house resort was officially called Camp Wheeler, but Squeaky Bob liked to refer to it as "Hotel de Hardscrabble." Most locals simply called it "Squeaky Bob's Place." Established in 1907, it offered crude accommodations laced with a sense of humor. Squeaky Bob was notorious for not changing the sheets on the beds, but merely scenting them with talcum powder. His high, squeaky voice cracked when he got excited, resonating with a falsetto note, thus establishing his nickname. The name for Squeak Creek is all that is left of the legacy of this famous local resort.

Lake Irene

Bighorn Lake (No Public Access)   11,060 feet

T **OT** *Regional map p. 273 (H, 38)*

This inconspicuous, oval-shaped lake is located merely 0.8 mile from Milner Pass within the Specimen Mountain Bighorn Sheep Protection Area, which is closed to public use year-round. An old, forgotten trail leaves from Trail Ridge Road midway between the Lake Irene Picnic Area (opposite) and Milner Pass (see Region 1, p. 109). It follows the creek that spills down the hillside from the slopes of the unnamed 11,000-foot peak to the northeast of Bighorn Lake. The trail is well worn in some spots and sparse in others, leading to the little basin northeast of Bighorn Lake. Bighorn Lake is the headwaters to Squeak Creek, a tributary of the Colorado River. It lies in a quaint marshy valley out of sight and earshot of Trail Ridge Road.

OTHER DESTINATIONS

Sheep Rock   10,920+ feet

T **OT** **[图]** *Regional map p. 273 (I, 37)*

This rock knob is a good example of a *roche moutonnée* (French for "sheep-shaped rock" or "fleecy rock"). A roche moutonnée is a bare hummock of rock that was abraded, shaped, and smoothed by glacial action. Groups of these hummocks resemble the backs of scattered sheep, which is where the name originated. As the glacier flowed over Sheep Rock, it ground and polished the southwest side of the rock but plucked rocks away from the northeast side, leaving it rough and jagged. Sheep Rock lies southwest of Poudre Lake and rises 170 vertical feet above Trail Ridge Road at Milner Pass.

East Slope GRADE I CLASS 2   From the Poudre Lake Trailhead at Milner Pass (see Region 1, p. 109), hike on the Ute Trail for 0.4 mile to 10,880 feet, marked by a major switchback. An old trail leads to the top of Sheep Rock but is now closed. Break away from the trail and bushwhack southwest 0.1 mile to the top of Sheep Rock. The rounded summit mound is a wonderful lookout with good views of the Never Summer Mountains, Poudre Lake, Specimen Mountain, and Trail Ridge Road.

'Poudre Lake Spires'   10,820 feet

T **[图]** *Regional map p. 273 (I, 37)*

This is an unofficial name for the interesting rock cliffs on the Continental Divide southeast of Milner Pass. These 60-foot-high, jagged towers lie on the initial stretch of the Ute Trail south of Poudre Lake and can be seen from Trail Ridge Road. The spires consist of ancient Precambrian metamorphic rocks. From the Poudre Lake Trailhead at Milner Pass (see Region 1, p. 109), follow the Ute Trail south for 0.2 mile to the site.

Steve Lawlor at 'Poudre Lake Spires'

East Inlet Trailhead

This trailhead lies at 8,400 feet and provides access to the East Inlet Trail. It is 2.4 miles from Grand Lake. From the junction of US 34 and CO 278 in Grand Lake, drive east for 0.3 mile to the Y junction of Grand Avenue and West Portal Road. Continue east on West Portal Road for 2.1 miles to the East Inlet Trailhead.

Green Mountain Trailhead

This trailhead is at 8,800 feet and provides access to the Green Mountain and Tonahutu Creek Trails. From the RMNP Beaver Meadows Visitor Center near Estes Park, drive 4.2 miles west on US 36 until it turns into Trail Ridge Road (US 34) at Deer Ridge Junction. Continue west on Trail Ridge Road through the heart of RMNP for 35.2 miles to the Green Mountain Trailhead, located on the east side of the road. From Grand Lake, drive north on US 34 for 4.5 miles to the trailhead.

Kawuneeche Visitor Center (KVC)

This visitor center lies at 8,715 feet, 0.3 mile south of the Grand Lake Entrance Station to RMNP. From the RMNP Beaver Meadows Visitor Center near Estes Park, drive 4.2 miles west on US 36 until it turns into Trail Ridge Road (US 34) at Deer Ridge Junction. Continue west on Trail Ridge Road through the heart of RMNP for 38.3 miles to KVC, located on the east side of the road. From Grand Lake, drive north on US 34 for 1.4 miles to the visitor center. From the south end of the parking lot, the Tonahutu Spur Trail travels east for 0.6 mile to connect to the Tonahutu Creek Trail. The trail basically provides a shortcut, saving a quarter mile on destinations normally accessed by the Tonahutu Trailhead.

Lake Irene Picnic Area

This trailhead lies at 10,660 feet and provides access to Lake Irene, the lower Ute Trail, and Phantom and Squeak Creeks. From the RMNP Beaver Meadows Visitor Center near Estes Park, drive 4.2 miles west on US 36 until it turns into Trail Ridge Road (US 34) at Deer Ridge Junction. Continue west on Trail Ridge Road through the heart of RMNP for 22.3 miles to the Lake Irene Picnic Area, located on the west side of the road. From Grand Lake, drive north on US 34 for 17.4 miles to the picnic area.

North Inlet Trailhead

This trailhead lies at 8,500 feet and provides access to the North Inlet Trail, Lake Nanita Trail, and the rough, unmaintained path that climbs into the Ptarmigan Creek drainage. From the junction of US 34 and CO 278 in Grand Lake, drive east for 0.3 mile to the Y junction of Grand Avenue and West Portal Road. Continue east on West Portal Road for 0.8 mile to the turnoff for the Tonahutu and North Inlet Trailheads. Turn left on CR 663 and drive for 0.3 mile to the North Inlet Trailhead.

Onahu Creek Trailhead

This trailhead is at 8,780 feet and provides access to the Onahu Creek Trail. From the RMNP Beaver Meadows Visitor Center near Estes Park, drive 4.2 miles west on US 36 until it turns into Trail Ridge Road (US 34) at Deer Ridge Junction. Continue west on Trail Ridge Road through the heart of RMNP for 34.7 miles to the Onahu Creek Trailhead, located on the east side of the road. From Grand Lake, drive north on US 34 for 5.1 miles to the trailhead.

Poudre Lake Trailhead at Milner Pass

See Region 1, p. 109.

TRAILHEADS/TRAILS

Timber Lake Trailhead
This trailhead is at 9,060 feet and provides access to the Timber Lake Trail and the Timber Creek Trail (also called the Long Meadows Trail). From the RMNP Beaver Meadows Visitor Center near Estes Park, drive 4.2 miles west on US 36 until it turns into Trail Ridge Road (US 34) at Deer Ridge Junction. Continue west on Trail Ridge Road through the heart of RMNP for 28.4 miles to Timber Creek Trailhead, located on the east side of the road. From Grand Lake, drive north on US 34 for 11.3 miles to the trailhead.

Tonahutu Trailhead
This trailhead lies at 8,500 feet and provides access to the Tonahutu Creek Trail. From the junction of US 34 and CO 278 in Grand Lake, drive east for 0.3 mile to the Y junction of Grand Avenue and West Portal Road. Continue east on West Portal Road for 0.8 mile to the turnoff for the Tonahutu and North Inlet Trailheads. Turn left on CR 663 and drive 0.2 mile to the Tonahutu Trailhead.

TRAILS

Connecting trail between the Onahu Creek and Green Mountain Trailheads
A well-defined forested trail connects the Onahu Creek Trailhead to the Green Mountain Trailhead. From the Onahu Creek Trailhead, locate the trail at the south end of the parking lot and follow it south for 0.6 mile to the Green Mountain Trailhead.

East Inlet Trail
The East Inlet Trail climbs east up the East Inlet valley, paralleling East Inlet creek. It provides access to five named lakes, two waterfalls, and numerous high peaks. The trail is well maintained for 6.9 miles to Lake Verna, then becomes an unmaintained path to Spirit Lake and deteriorates to a rough course that is somewhat difficult to follow farther east. This lower section of the trail is popular and very scenic. Lovely stands of brilliant aspen trees, water flowing over smooth rock, thriving communities of wildflowers, steep cliff sections, grand overviews of lakes, and soaring high peaks combine to make the trail memorable. The trail is a real leg-pumper, with some considerable climbs in short steps making it strenuous in some sections.

Michelle Chase on the East Inlet Trail

Green Mountain Trail
This trail leads east from Trail Ridge Road through dense forest, skirting the northern flank of Green Mountain and connecting to the Tonahutu Creek Trail near the midpoint of Big Meadows. The trail basically provides a shortcut to the Tonahutu Creek Trail (which originates at the Tonahutu Trailhead, above); saving 2.4 miles on destinations located in the northern section of Tonahutu Creek drainage. It begins steeply, then travels along a moderate, steady grade to Big Meadows.

Haynach Lakes Trail

This spur trail penetrates the striking lake basin below the east face of Nakai Peak. It is not marked on the 1958 USGS topographic maps. From the Green Mountain Trailhead, follow the Green Mountain Trail east for 1.8 miles to the junction with the Tonahutu Creek Trail. From the Tonahutu Trailhead, follow the Tonahutu Creek Trail north for 4.3 miles to the junction with the Green Mountain Trail. Continue north, then east along the Tonahutu Creek Trail for 5.3 miles to the junction with the Haynach Lake Trail. A sign announcing the trail to several NPS campsites indicates this junction. Turn northwest to access the Haynach Lakes Trail. The trail climbs quite steeply at first, then levels somewhat and travels northwest through an ancient forest to a gorgeous alpine valley. The jagged southeast ridge of Nakai Peak comes into view. Travel through long meadows and crest a rise to enter the lake basin. The trail bypasses the smaller lakes and leads to the largest, horseshoe-shaped lake, where it ends. The rocky promontory that rises to the west of the largest lake is Point 12,052', not the summit of Nakai Peak. Nakai Peak lies southwest of this point, and the top is hidden from view at the lake.

Lake Nanita Trail

The Lake Nanita Trail leaves the North Inlet Trail 7.7 miles from the trailhead and climbs into a classic lake basin that is home to two remote, picturesque alpine tarns. From the junction with the North Inlet Trail, turn south and follow the Lake Nanita Trail to a bridge that spans a dark gorge with unofficially named 'North Inlet Falls' cascading through it. The trail continues south through the forest as it climbs above North Inlet to offer a view of Lake Solitude, a small pond in a low-lying meadow along the creek. The trail goes upward to a point where it turns southwest and ascends multiple switchbacks along a forested ridge to a stark rock basin that holds Lake Nokoni. The trail continues southeast toward Lake Nanita, climbing steeply to a small saddle between Point 11,218' and Ptarmigan Mountain. From here it descends to a marshy meadow below the sharp, imposing 'Ptarmigan Towers,' which are five east-facing spires on the northeast ridge of Ptarmigan Mountain. The trail reenters the trees and leads to Lake Nanita's western shore.

Approaching Ptarmigan Mountain from the south

North Inlet Trail

Pond by the North Inlet Trail

From the North Inlet Trailhead, the North Inlet Trail heads east 1.25 miles to Summerland Park, then climbs along the narrow, swift creek for 2.3 miles to Cascade Falls. It continues for 3.1 miles to the confluence of Ptarmigan Creek and North Inlet. From here a rough path strikes off to the north to access the Ptarmigan Creek drainage. The North Inlet Trail continues southeast for a mile to the junction with the Lake Nanita Trail, which bears south to two alpine lakes. Here the North Inlet Trail leaves North Inlet and climbs steeply northeast along Hallett Creek to the expansive tundra slopes on the west side of the Continental Divide between Flattop Mountain and Andrews Pass. It climbs the open, treeless slope to meet the Tonahutu Creek Trail on the Continental Divide, 0.3 mile west of Flattop Mountain. Heavy horse traffic is common on the lower North Inlet Trail. This is one of the major trails used for trans–Continental Divide through-hikes from Estes Park to Grand Lake.

Onahu Creek Trail

This trail leads northeast from Trail Ridge Road through a substantial forest and parallels Onahu Creek. It connects to the Tonahutu Creek and Timber Creek Trails. In 1914, Onahu Creek was called 'Fish Creek,' but as a result of an interview with two elderly Arapahos, the name was changed to Onahu. *Onah hu* was the Arapaho word meaning "warms himself." One of the Arapaho's biggest and fastest horses was notorious for sneaking up to the campfire to warm himself on cold evenings. The horse died near the creek.

Paradise Park Trail

This trail provides access to Paradise Park and Ten Lake Park on the south side of Mount Craig. These two parks are extremely isolated and generally untrammeled by man. Designated as the Paradise Park Research Natural Area, which is restricted for world research projects, this region is sensitive and pristine. Please keep it that way. Day hiking is allowed in the area but camping is not.

From the East Inlet Trailhead, hike east along the East Inlet Trail for 4.4 miles to a bridge that crosses East Inlet. Here, an old abandoned trail heads south along the east side of Paradise Creek. It is unmarked and unmaintained. The trail can be faint in places, but is generally manageable to follow as it leads up the valley between Mount Wescott and Mount Craig. It peters out in the vicinity of the sweeping curve in Paradise Creek, about 1 mile from the East Inlet Trail. From here, bushwhack up the drainage through varied terrain, which ranges from thick forest to boggy, marshy wetlands.

Timber Creek Trail

This trail, also called the Long Meadows Trail, connects the Timber Lake Trail to the Tonahutu Creek Trail and provides access to Long Meadows. It becomes indistinct and difficult to follow through Long Meadows.

Timber Lake Trail

See Timber Lake, p. 299.

Tonahutu Creek Trail

This scenic trail leads 12 miles from Grand Lake to Bighorn Flats. From the Tonahutu Trailhead it travels north for 0.8 mile to the junction with the Tonahutu Spur Trail from the Kawuneeche Visitor Center (p. 303). It continues north through the valley between Green and Nisa Mountains and into Big Meadows, where it connects with the trail from Green Mountain Trailhead, 4.3 miles from the Tonahutu Trailhead. It parallels Big Meadows on the west and leads 0.75 mile to the junction with the Timber Creek Trail. From here, the Tonahutu Creek Trail swings eastward, leading 2.6 miles to pretty Granite Falls. Beyond the falls the trail continues northeast and climbs steeply through the forest 2 miles to the junction with the Haynach Lakes Trail. It continues to climb steeply out of the trees to top out on Bighorn Flats and lead southeast across the open tundra, connecting with the North Inlet Trail and the Flattop Mountain Trail east of Ptarmigan Pass. This is one of the major trails used for trans–Continental Divide through-hikes from Estes Park to Grand Lake.

Unmaintained Trail to Ptarmigan Creek

From the North Inlet Trailhead, follow the North Inlet Trail for 6.7 miles to the point where the trail crosses Ptarmigan Creek on a footbridge. Leave the trail and locate the unofficial, unmaintained path or bushwhack northeast up the steep slope on the east side of Ptarmigan Creek. Cairns mark the route in some sections. The route climbs steeply for 0.4 mile to War Dance Falls, a lovely cascading waterfall tucked away in a dense forest. Continue upward for 0.3 mile to Bench Lake, located at the start of the pristine hanging basin almost 800 vertical feet above the valley floor. Here the unmaintained trail ends. Skirt Bench Lake on the east and bushwhack north through the incredible, lush wonderland.

Alex Kostadinov and Michelle Chase in Big Meadows

REGION SEVEN

Southwest Corner

This region covers a secluded section of RMNP located south of the East Inlet Trail, west of the Continental Divide, north of Indian Peaks Wilderness Area (IPWA), and east of Shadow Mountain Lake. This region's interior is thickly forested, isolated, and virtually trailless. Well-maintained trails that start outside RMNP access the perimeter of this area. Be prepared for off-trail travel for most destinations in this region.

East Shore Trail

Watanga Lake (IPWA) 312
Adams Lake 312
Shadow Mountain Lookout 314
Shadow Mountain.................................. 314
Mount Bryant 315
Mount Acoma 315
Mount Adams 316
'Roaring Peak'................................... 316
Twin Peaks 316
Watanga Mountain................................ 317
Hiamovi Mountain (IPWA) 317
Mount Irving Hale (IPWA) 318

TRAILHEADS 318

TRAILS 319

OTHER POINTS OF INTEREST 321

Columbine Creek

Indian Peaks Wilderness Area

Opposite: Shadow Mountain Lookout Tower (see p. 314)

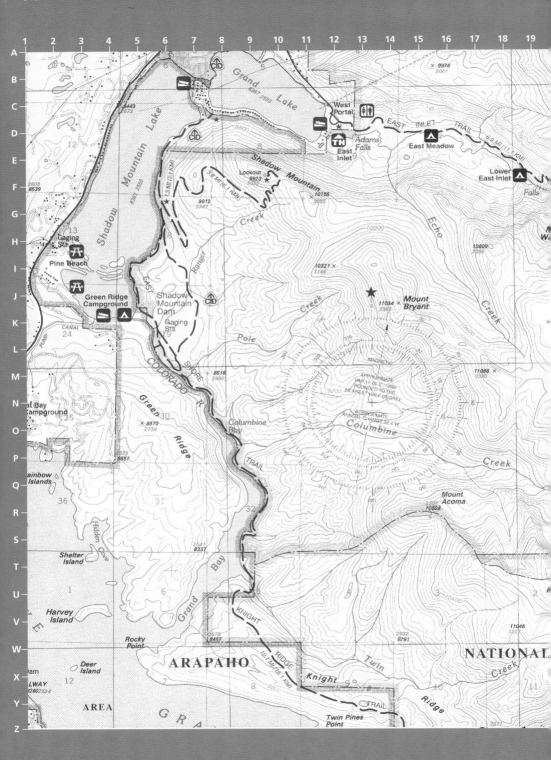

Grand Lake

West Portal

East Inlet

Adams Falls

East Meadow

Shadow Mountain

Lookout
9923
3022

East Inlet Trail 6.9 Mi (11.1 KM)

Lower East Inlet

Falls

10155
3095

10321 ×
3146

Echo Creek

10000

10809
3296

Gaging Sta

Pine Beach

Green Ridge Campground

Shadow Mountain Dam

Gaging Sta

East Creek

Ranger Creek

Pole Creek

Mount Bryant
11034 ×
3363

MAGNETIC

APPROXIMATE
VAR 11 06 E 1980
ROUNDED TO THE
NEAREST HALF DEGREE

9200

APPROXIMATE
ANNUAL CHANGE 02.4 W

11088 ×
3380

8518
2596

Bay Campground

COLORADO R.

SHORE TRAIL

Green Ridge

8970
2734

8657

Columbine Bay

Columbine Creek

Mount Acoma
10508

10400

Rainbow Islands

Hidden Cove

Shelter Island

2541
8337

Grand Bay

TRAIL

KNIGHT

11046

Harvey Island

Rocky Point

8578
8457

KNIGHT RIDGE TRAIL 10.1 Mi (16.1 KM)

2832
9291

Twin Ridge

NATIONAL

ARAPAHO

Knight

Deer Island

Dam
2780 2524

SPILLWAY

TRAIL

Twin Pines Point

2971

AREA

GRA

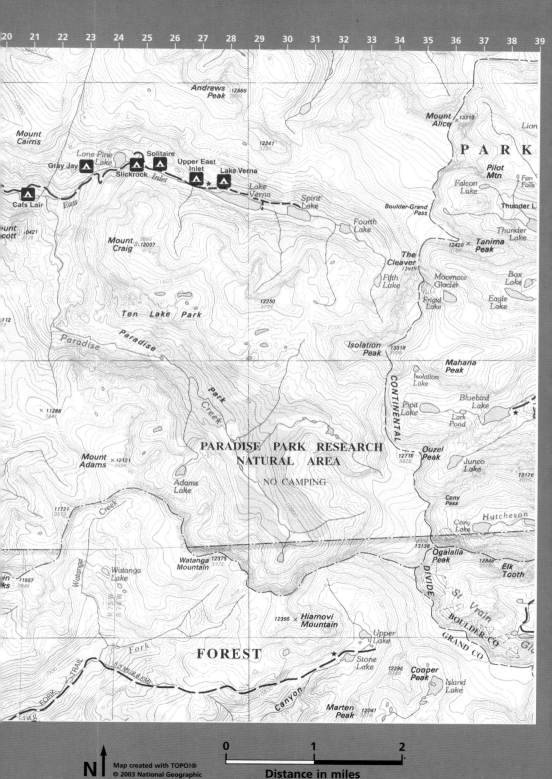

N

Map created with TOPO!®
© 2003 National Geographic

Distance in miles

0   1   2

LAKES

Watanga Lake   10,780 feet

T   *Regional map p. 311 (U, 24); hike map p. 313*

This pretty lake lies in Indian Peaks Wilderness Area, one mile south of RMNP's boundary. It is the jumping-off point for numerous scenic destinations along the IPWA-RMNP border. From the Roaring Fork Trailhead (p. 319), hike on the Roaring Fork Trail (p. 320) for 3.5 miles to the signed junction with the Watanga Lake Trail. Not marked on outdated maps, this well-defined trail climbs north very steeply from the junction for 1.25 miles to pretty Watanga Lake. Two smaller lakes and several marshy ponds lie southeast of Watanga Lake. Hike cross-country over a hill to reach them. Watanga Creek originates at the head of a wonderful mountain basin formed by the slopes of Mount Adams, Twin Peaks, and Watanga Mountain. The precipitous face of Twin Peaks' eastern buttress rises to the west of the lake.

Adams Lake   11,180 feet

T **OT**   *Regional map p. 311 (P, 27); hike map p. 313*

This is one of the most remote and inaccessible lakes in the Park. Together with three unnamed lakes, it lies to the north of the impressive ridgeline of peaks that form the southwestern border of RMNP. Not only is there no trail to this lake, but also there are no maintained trails for miles in any direction. Located in pristine Paradise Park Research Natural Area, this large, alpine lake is located on a bench above the unspoiled, heavenly valley of Paradise Park. It is reached either via Paradise Park (see Region 6, p. 284) or from the Watanga Lake area of Indian Peaks Wilderness Area.

Steve Lawlor at Watanga Lake

N

ROCKY MOUNTAIN NATIONAL PARK

INDIAN PEAKS WILDERNESS

Twin Peaks 11957

Northeast Ridge

Watanga

Watanga Lake

Creek

Columbine Creek

'Roaring Peak' 11721

East Ridge

Mt Adams 12121

South Slope

PARK BOUNDARY

WILDERNESS BOUNDARY

West Slope

Northwest Ridge

Watanga Mtn 12375

Adams Lake

Roaring Fork

Paradise Creek

N
Magnetic North
11.5 degrees

0   0.5   1

Distance in miles

Watanga Lake Access   From Watanga Lake (follow route description, p. 312), skirt along the western shore and follow Watanga Creek north, then east, to the headwall between Mount Adams and Watanga Mountain. Climb northeast up the steep hill and over tundra to the long, broad saddle and ridgeline between the two peaks. Adams Lake is visible to the northeast on a large bench above Paradise Park. Drop down from the ridgeline, descending the steep, loose terrain to the bench. Though steep, this route is manageable and doesn't present any technical difficulties.

Paradise Park Access   From the East Inlet Trailhead (see Region 6, p. 303), hike east along the trail for 4.4 miles to a bridge that crosses East Inlet. Here, an old abandoned trail heads south along the east side of Paradise Creek. The trail is faint in places but generally manageable to follow as it leads up the valley between Mount Wescott and Mount Craig. It peters out in the vicinity of the sweeping curve in Paradise Creek, about 1.5 miles from the East Inlet Trail. From here, bushwhack up the drainage through varied terrain—from thick forest to boggy, marshy wetlands. Continue for 1.8 miles to the confluence with the stream that flows from Adams Lake. Head south and fight through difficult terrain for 1.2 miles to the bench that holds the lake. This route is long and strenuous, but worth the arduous effort because the isolated splendor of the lake is something to behold.

PEAKS AND OTHER DESTINATIONS

Shadow Mountain Lookout   9,923 feet
T *Regional map p. 310 (F, 10)*

This is the most popular destination from the East Shore Trailhead. The charming old fire lookout tower was built in 1932 on the lower summit of Shadow Mountain and is listed on the National Register of Historic Places. The building has wooden steps that wrap around the attractive stone tower and lead to an observation deck that provides panoramic views of Shadow Mountain Lake, Lake Granby, and Grand Lake. The true summit of Shadow Mountain lies 0.5 mile southeast, but does not offer the same grand views because it is heavily wooded.

East Shore Trailhead Access GRADE I CLASS 1   From the East Shore Trailhead (p. 318), the hike begins on Forest Service land and crosses into RMNP after 0.6 mile. The trail follows along the shore of Shadow Mountain Lake and is flat and scenic. This enjoyable section of the hike provides wonderful views out over the water. Hike for 1.4 miles to the junction with the trail to the Shadow Mountain Lookout (also called the Shadow Mountain Trail). Follow the Shadow Mountain Trail as it climbs steadily up long switchbacks toward Shadow Mountain. The trail ascends a ridge and switches back near tiny Ranger Creek. Continue to climb steep switchbacks and follow the trail as it circles around to the east side of the tower, 4 miles from the trail junction. Walk up the tower steps to the wooden platform. The tower rises above the dense forest and is strategically located to offer extensive views in all directions. Grand Lake village and Grand Lake, the largest natural lake in Colorado, lie to the north. Shadow Mountain Lake spreads out to the west, with massive Lake Granby to the south. The striking Never Summer Mountains unfold to the northwest.

Shadow Mountain   10,155 feet
T **OT** *Regional map p. 310 (F, 11)*

This double-topped peak rises above Grand Lake in a wave of evergreen trees. The lower summit is home to Shadow Mountain Lookout, an old fire lookout tower with a good trail leading to it. The higher summit is a forested rock pile without many views.

Northwest Ridge GRADE I CLASS 2   From the Shadow Mountain Lookout (follow the route description on the opposite page), backtrack along the trail, hiking southeast to the second switchback from the top. Leave the trail and bushwhack southeast through thick trees for 0.4 mile to the true summit of Shadow Mountain (10,155 feet).

Mount Bryant 11,034 feet
T **OT** *Regional map p. 310 (J, 14)*

Tucked deeply into a primitive forest between Echo and Columbine Creeks, this lonely mountain receives few visitors. The Bryant family from Redmond, Oregon, hiked the peak in 1981 and commented, "Everyone should climb their own mountain." A good thought indeed.

Northwest Slope GRADE II CLASS 2   From the Shadow Mountain Lookout (follow the route description on the opposite page), backtrack along the trail, hiking southeast to the second switchback from the top. From here, leave the trail and bushwhack southeast through heavy trees for 0.4 mile to the true summit of Shadow Mountain (10,155 feet). It is possible to contour below the summit of Shadow Mountain, but the forest is quite thick, and the somewhat open view at the highpoint is a nice position from which to sight a route to Mount Bryant. From Shadow Mountain, descend to a densely forested saddle and fight through the trees to climb a long hill leading to Mount Bryant. It's easy to get disoriented in the woods, so keep the compass handy. Continue southeast to Point 10,827', a wonderful sub-summit of Mount Bryant with a lovely rock outcrop that is devoid of trees, showcasing views of Isolation Peak, Mount Craig, Columbine Bay on Lake Granby, and Shadow Mountain Lake. Continue hiking southeast along a delightful, flat-topped ridge, sparsely laced with lodgepole pines. Strike uphill to gain a distinct spine with several high rocky points and keep meandering upward to the summit. The top is a boulder pile in the trees. Through the foliage views of Mount Adams, Watanga Mountain, and Mount Craig can be seen.

Mount Acoma 10,508 feet
T **OT** *Regional map p. 310 (R, 16)*

This low-elevation, forested peak lies on the southwest border of RMNP and overlooks the beautiful and remote Columbine Creek drainage. The summit provides good views of Shadow Mountain Lake and the southern section of the Never Summer Mountains. Access is either from the Shadow Mountain Dam along the East Shore Trail or the Knight Ridge Trail from Arapaho Bay.

Shadow Mountain Dam Access From the Shadow Mountain Dam (p. 319), follow the East Shore Trail (p. 319) south for 3.3 miles to the extreme southwestern corner of RMNP. Most boundaries in RMNP are well marked by U.S. Department of the Interior Boundary Line signs. From here, follow the Southwest Ridge route (p. 316) to the summit.

Ellsworth Bethel (1863–1925) was a Denver high-school teacher who championed the cause of naming area peaks for Native American tribes. In 1914 he sketched a map of northern Colorado, complete with his recommendations for names of mountains at the time unnamed. He sent it to the U.S. Board on Geographic Names in Washington, D.C. His main goal was to represent 10 tribes connected with Colorado history by peaks visible from Denver. The board accepted some of his recommendations (such as the one for Mount Acoma) but rejected others. Bethel was angry and disappointed by the board's decision to throw out some of his ideas, but they accepted enough of his suggestions that his influence still lives today in the mountains of the Indian Peaks Wilderness Area. Though little evidence of the Acoma Indian tribe remains in the United States, the ancient ruins of one Acoma pueblo still exist in New Mexico.

Roaring Fork to Southwest Ridge Route GRADE II CLASS 2   From the Roaring Fork Trailhead (p. 319), hike for 3.9 miles along the Knight Ridge Trail (p. 320) to the Twin Creek Ranger Station, located just south of RMNP's border. Cross Twin Creek and follow the trail for 0.5 mile to the RMNP boundary line.

From RMNP's southwest border, leave the trail and hike east to gain the prominent, forested ridge that leads to the summit of Mount Acoma. This is a pleasant walk through the forest, which is sparsely timbered with a few downed trees to climb over or around. Hike over pine duff through this beautiful forest, lamentably plagued with mountain pine beetle infestation. The view from the hillside overlooking the Twin Creek Ranger Station shows the widespread damage to the trees from this native bug. The ridge turns northeast and leads to the summit of Mount Acoma, gradually getting steeper as it climbs higher. For navigation, follow the well-spaced NPS boundary signs since the forest provides few views of the surrounding terrain for reference.

Mount Acoma's summit is slightly anticlimactic, simply a small rock outcrop that is significantly lower than the more prominent unnamed Point 11,293' to the east. However, it provides splendid views of rugged Columbine Creek and a nice vantage of Mount Bryant, Mount Adams, and Shadow Mountain. With binoculars the Shadow Mountain Lookout tower can also be seen.

Mount Adams   12,121 feet
T OT *Regional map p. 311 (P, 23); hike map p. 313*

Set near the southwestern border of RMNP, this tundra-covered peak overlooks the unspoiled Columbine and Paradise Creek drainages. It provides a commanding view of the southwestern section RMNP.

South Slope GRADE II CLASS 2   From Watanga Lake (follow route description, p. 312), skirt along the western shore and hike north up Watanga Creek to the pronounced saddle between Mount Adams and Point 11,721' (unofficially named 'Roaring Peak'). From the saddle, climb east over grass to the broad tundra and talus slope of Mount Adams. Continue north over easy terrain to the boulder hump that represents the rounded top.

'Roaring Peak'   11,721 feet
T OT *Regional map p. 311 (S, 22); hike map p. 313*

This unofficially named peak lies at the north end of the Watanga Lake basin between Mount Adams and Twin Peaks. It is worthy of a side trip when in the area.

East Ridge GRADE II CLASS 2   From Watanga Lake (follow route description, p. 312), skirt along the western shore, then hike north for 1 mile up Watanga Creek to the pronounced saddle between Mount Adams and 'Roaring Peak' (Point 11,721'). Turn west and climb up the steep eastern ridge for 0.1 mile to reach the summit.

Twin Peaks   11,957 feet
T OT *Regional map p. 311 (U, 20); hike map p. 313*

Located on the southern border of RMNP between Mount Acoma and Watanga Mountain, Twin Peaks' double summit is adorned with rock outcrops and krummholz. A stellar overlook of Lake Granby combines with views of the Never Summer Mountains, the peaks of East Inlet, Indian Peaks, and a wonderful vantage of Longs Peak to make this summit outstanding. Pleasurable tundra walking characterizes the hike to the top of this mountain.

Northeast Ridge GRADE II CLASS 2   From Watanga Lake (follow the route description on p. 312), skirt along the shore and hike northwest, then west for 0.7 mile to the obvious saddle between Twin Peaks and 'Roaring Peak' (Point 11,721'). Stay north to skirt the steep cliffs on the east side of Twin Peaks. From the saddle, hike southwest over gentle tundra and boulders to a small depression, then climb more steeply to the flat summits of Twin Peaks.

Watanga Mountain   12,375 feet

T **OT** *Regional map p. 311 (T, 27); hike map p. 313*

Watanga means "black coyote" in Arapaho. Watanga Mountain separates the Paradise Creek and Roaring Fork drainages. A commanding view of Paradise Park, Indian Peaks, East Inlet peaks, the Longs Peak group, and much more can be seen from the top.

Parry primrose

Northwest Ridge GRADE II CLASS 2   From Watanga Lake (follow route description, p. 312), skirt along the shore and hike northeast toward the ridge between Mount Adams and Watanga Mountain. Climb the steep ridge and gain the tundra slope above. Hike southeast along tundra toward Watanga Mountain. Skirt the 12,254-foot rocky bump along the ridge and continue across long tundra slopes to Watanga Mountain. To reach the summit, cross a slender neck of rock that spans a rock-cut chasm, then gain a blocky ridge that leads to the highpoint. Large blocks of granite make up the summit, marked by a USGS survey marker. Upper Paradise Park unfolds to the northeast.

West Slope GRADE II CLASS 2   Skirt the south shore of Watanga Lake (follow route description, p. 312) and climb southeast up a small hill to a grouping of unnamed ponds. Continue southeast past the ponds for almost 0.5 mile, then turn northeast and climb up Watanga Mountain's western slope for a mile to the summit.

Hiamovi Mountain   12,395 feet

T **OT** *Regional map p. 311 (V, 30)*

This rocky summit is located in the Indian Peaks Wilderness Area, 0.3 mile south of RMNP's border. It is an important summit and also fun to climb. Sandwiched between Roaring Fork and Hell Canyon, this peak offers spectacular mountain vistas. Hiamovi's western slope is moderate, but all of its other sides are steep and broken. A jagged ridge runs east from the top to an unnamed 12,220-foot pinnacle called 'Hiamovi Tower.'

Southwest Slope GRADE II CLASS 2   From the Roaring Fork Trailhead (p. 319), follow the Roaring Fork Trail (p. 320) for 3.5 miles to the junction with the Watanga Lake Trail. Bypass this turnoff and continue east on the Roaring Fork Trail as it climbs very steeply for 1.25 miles through the forest to break out of the trees at the obvious, broad tundra saddle between Mount Irving Hale and Hiamovi Mountain. Leave the trail and hike northeast over glorious tundra, which gives way to charming mounds of earth ornamented with trees and rocks. Climb upward to the expansive boulder field that leads to the summit. 'Hiamovi Tower' is the awesome, stark rock pinnacle to the east. The sharp, jagged ridge between the two peaks is rated Class 4, and is greatly exposed.

Steve Lawlor approaching Mount Irving Hale, IPWA

Mount Irving Hale 11,754 feet

T **OT** *Regional map p. 311 (south of Z, 27; off of map)*

This pointy peak is a petite prize among the higher peaks of the area. Its gentle west slope provides admission to gaze down the mountain's sheer east face into Hell Canyon.

North Ridge GRADE II CLASS 2 From the Roaring Fork Trailhead (opposite), follow the Roaring Fork Trail (p. 320) for 3.5 miles to the junction with the Watanga Lake Trail. Bypass this turnoff and continue east on the Roaring Fork Trail as it climbs extremely steeply for 1.25 miles through the forest to break out of the trees at the gorgeous, broad saddle between Mount Irving Hale and Hiamovi Mountain. Leave the trail and hike south through clumps of trees and over the amazing tundra slope to a rocky spine that leads to a boulder field. Climb up the boulder field to the summit and an overlook of Long and Crawford Lakes. Open views of Indian Peaks and the southern section of RMNP abound.

TRAILHEADS

East Inlet Trailhead
See Region 6, p. 303.

East Shore Trailhead
This trailhead is at 8,420 feet and provides access to East Shore Trail. It is 1.2 miles from Grand Lake. From the junction of US 34 and CO 278 (the main road leading to the town of Grand Lake), head east for 0.2 mile to Center Drive. Turn right and drive for 0.2 mile to Marina Drive. Turn left and drive 0.1 mile to Shadow Mountain Drive (which turns into Lake Side Drive). Turn right and drive 0.2 mile to Jericho Drive. Turn right and cross the bridge between Grand Lake and Shadow Mountain Lake. Continue for 0.4 mile to Shoreline Way. Turn left and drive 0.1 mile, then park in a gravel lot on the right.

Roaring Fork Trailhead

This trailhead is at 8,300 feet and provides access to the Roaring Fork and Watanga Lake Trails. It is 19 miles from Grand Lake. From the junction of US 34 and US 36 in Estes Park, drive 47 miles to Grand Lake. From Grand Lake, continue south on US 34 for 9.2 miles to the Arapaho Bay turnoff. Turn left and drive on CR 6 for 8.9 miles to the junction with CR 637. Turn left and drive 0.9 mile to the Roaring Fork Trailhead. The area is located outside RMNP in Arapaho Bay National Recreation Area, and fees apply for use.

Shadow Mountain Dam

This location provides access to the East Shore Trail midway between Shadow Mountain Lake and the southwest corner of RMNP. From Grand Lake, drive south on US 34 for 2.7 miles to the turnoff for the Green Ridge Campground complex. Turn left on CR 66 and drive 1.2 miles to the Green Ridge Campground, then turn left again to reach a T junction. Turn right at the T junction and drive 0.1 mile to the Shadow Mountain Reservoir and Dam parking area. Hike west across the dam to reach the the East Shore Trail.

TRAILS

Columbine Creek Trail

This unmaintained trail is difficult to follow and remains mostly neglected. It leaves the East Shore Trail where Columbine Creek empties into Columbine Bay and leads east, following Columbine Creek for about 2 miles until it peters out in a forested marsh.

East Shore Trail

The East Shore Trail (also called the Outlet Trail for the first 3.5 miles) begins at the isthmus between Shadow Mountain Lake and Grand Lake. It runs south along the eastern shore of Shadow Mountain Lake for 3.5 miles to Shadow Mountain Dam. From

East Shore Trail

there, it continues south along the Colorado River, then leads along Columbine Bay to the extreme southwestern corner of RMNP. From here the trail name changes to the Knight Ridge Trail and continues south through Arapaho National Forest to Arapaho Bay on Lake Granby, 11.3 miles from the start.

Knight Ridge Trail

From the Roaring Fork Trailhead, follow a confusing maze of signs and trails westward, or, more simply, hike along the road to the Arapaho Bay Ranger Station at the Roaring Fork Loop of Arapaho Bay Campground. Pass the ranger station and follow the sign to the Knight Ridge/East Shore Trail system. At the northern end of the campground, the trail crosses a bridge and travels along the shore of Lake Granby, then climbs a ridge for a nice overview of the lake. The Knight Ridge Trail becomes faint and hard to follow, but stay on track by identifying sawn-off logs that indicate trail improvement. From the Roaring Fork Trailhead, the Knight Ridge Trail travels northwest for 4.5 miles to RMNP's southwest boundary.

Roaring Fork Trail

The Roaring Fork Trail isn't marked on the 1958 USGS quadrangle, but it is well defined as it penetrates Hell Canyon, a gorgeous lake basin in the northern section of the Indian Peaks Wilderness Area. The trail is extremely steep and rocky initially, ascending short, abrupt switchbacks to the top of a ridge, where it parallels Roaring Fork and the grade lessens. From here, it crosses the creek several times and ambles through a quiet forest. After 3.5 miles it reaches a signed trail junction (also unmarked on USGS maps) with the Watanga Lake Trail. The Roaring Fork Trail continues east for 3.2 miles to Stone Lake.

Shadow Mountain Trail

See Shadow Mountain Lookout, p. 314.

Watanga Lake Trail

See Watanga Lake, p. 312.

The Knight Ridge Trail overlooking Arapaho Bay

Grand Lake

OTHER POINTS OF INTEREST

Arapaho Bay
This pretty cove lies at the southeastern limit of Lake Granby, outside RMNP. It is the starting point for the Knight Ridge Trail.

Columbine Bay
This slender finger of water represents the northernmost backup of water resulting from the Granby Dam. It is just outside the southwest boundary of RMNP. Completed in 1954, Granby Dam blocked the flow of the Colorado River and created the huge lake. Accessible from the East Shore Trail, the bay lies just west of RMNP and is a great place to view eagles.

Grand Lake
The town of Grand Lake was named after this beautiful, 1.5-mile-long lake that lies at 8,367 feet and is more than 0.7 mile wide. Grand Lake is the largest natural lake in Colorado. The level of Grand Lake and neighboring man-made Shadow Mountain Lake are kept equal by pumping water from Lake Granby.

Lake Granby
This huge, man-made body of water at 8,280 feet is outside RMNP and administered by the U.S. Forest Service within Arapaho National Recreation Area.

Shadow Mountain Lake
Also man-made, this lake lies outside RMNP between Grand Lake and Lake Granby. Ornamented by large islands on the southern end, this lake is within Arapaho National Recreation Area and is administered by the U.S. Forest Service. It lies at 8,367 feet.

Never Summer Mountains

Given the colorful name *ni-chébē-chíi* ("never-no-summer") by the Arapaho Indians, the Never Summer Mountains are a small range that stretch from Cameron Pass in the north to Ruby Mountain in the south. The range is within RMNP, Arapaho and Routt National Forests, and Neota and Never Summer Wilderness Areas. The Never Summer peaks, nestled along the Continental Divide, form part of RMNP's western boundary.

A huge, sweeping turn in the Continental Divide starts at La Poudre Pass and travels south along the RMNP border, turning the conventional idea of what is east and west upside down. This rotation causes the west side of the Continental Divide to be on the east, and the east side to be on the west. For example, Lake Agnes and Mount Cindy (both west of RMNP) physically lie to the west of the Continental Divide, but are actually on the east side of the Continental Divide, with their waters draining to the Gulf of Mexico and the Atlantic Ocean. Additionally, Lake of the Clouds physically lies immediately east of the Continental Divide, but its waters drain westward into the Colorado River, and then to the Gulf of California and the Pacific Ocean.

In contrast to the solid granite peaks that make up most of RMNP, the Never Summer Mountains are of volcanic origin and are characterized by crumbling, rotten rock. This makes hiking in the area more taxing, less stable, and more dangerous. However, stunning scenery, challenging objectives, and isolation combine to make the Never Summer Mountains an attractive area for hikers.

Skeleton Gulch

Pinnacle Pool

SUBREGIONS with Highlighted Hiking Destinations

LAKE AGNES 326
    Lake Agnes 326

MICHIGAN LAKES 326
    American Lakes (Michigan Lakes) 326
    Snow Lake 328
    Thunder Pass 328
  ⬩ Nokhu Crags 329
    Static Peak 330

LA POUDRE PASS 331
    Little Yellowstone 331
    Lulu Mountain, Thunder Mountain,
      and Mount Neota 332

SKELETON GULCH 333
    Mount Richthofen 333
  ⬩ Tepee Mountain 333
    Lead Mountain 334

Kawuneeche Valley

Opposite: Alex Kostadinov on the North ridge of Lead Mountain (see p. 334)

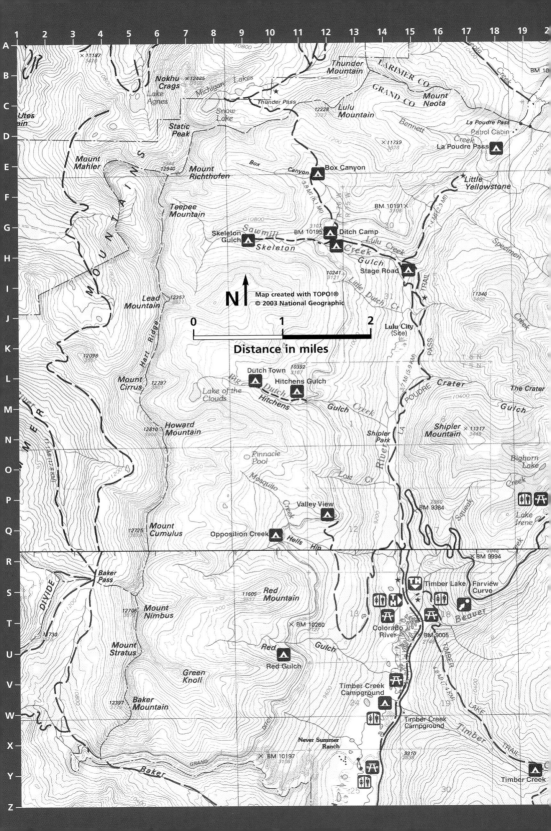

HITCHENS GULCH.................................. 336
    Lake of the Clouds............................. 336
    Mount Cirrus 338
    Howard Mountain 338

MOSQUITO CREEK................................ 339
    Pinnacle Pool.................................. 339

OPPOSITION CREEK............................... 339
    Mount Cumulus................................ 339

RED GULCH 340
    Red Mountain................................. 340
    Mount Nimbus................................. 342
    Green Knoll 343
    Mount Stratus 343

BAKER GULCH 344
    Parika Lake.................................... 344
    Baker Pass..................................... 344
    Baker Mountain 345
    Parika Peak.................................... 346
    Farview Mountain 346

BOWEN GULCH 347
    Blue Lake 347
    Bowen Lake 347
    Bowen Pass.................................... 347
    Mineral Point.................................. 348
    Bowen Mountain 349

SPECIMEN MOUNTAIN GROUP.................... 350
    🚶 The Crater 350
    Specimen Mountain (no public access) 351
    Shipler Mountain 351

COLORADO RIVER 352
    🚶 Lulu City and Shipler Park Cabins.............. 352

KAWUNEECHE VALLEY............................ 353
    🚶 ♿ Holzwarth Historic Site (Never Summer Ranch) ... 353
    🚶 Valley Trail and River Trail 354
    🚶 ♿ Coyote Valley Trail 354

TRAILHEADS 356

TRAILS 358

OTHER POINTS OF INTEREST 361

*Outlet stream,
Parika Lake*

Shipler Park cabins

*Karla Mosier hiking
to Mineral Point*

LAKE AGNES
Regional map p. 324 (C, 5)

LAKES

Lake Agnes (10,663 feet)
T *Regional map p. 324 (C, 5);*
hike map p. 327

Lake Agnes

This gorgeous lake lies on the western flank of jagged Nokhu Crags, just outside of the northwestern border of RMNP in Colorado State Forest. A pretty forested island in the lake, along with dramatic vistas of RMNP's Mount Richthofen, and the very prominent, unofficially named 12,493-foot 'Mahler Peak' make this setting very special. From the old log cabin at Lake Agnes Day Use Area parking lot (see the Lake Agnes Trailhead, p. 357), follow the Lake Agnes Trail as it climbs up through the forest to a junction. Nokhu Crags' steep slopes rise dramatically skyward. The trail is quite steep in some places but very well maintained. From the junction, follow the Lake Agnes Trail for 0.5 mile to pop out above the lake. Hike down to the shoreline and enjoy the views of the surrounding peaks.

MICHIGAN LAKES   *Regional map p. 324 (C, 8)*

LAKES

American Lakes (Michigan Lakes): 'Lower Michigan Lake' (11,208 feet) and 'Middle Michigan Lake' (11,210 feet)
T *Regional map p. 324 (C, 9); hike map p. 327*

The Michigan Lakes are a chain of three large lakes strung out along the Michigan River just outside the northern border of RMNP. They have been renamed American Lakes but remain "Michigan Lakes" on most maps. From the American Lakes Trailhead (p. 357), follow the doubletrack American Lakes Road (closed to motorized vehicles) southeast for 1.1 miles to Michigan Ditch, a water diversion channel from the slopes near Lake Agnes to the Cache la Poudre River drainage. Cross the ditch and continue along the American Lakes Trail, through the trees, to a footbridge spanning the creek. The trail climbs more steeply into Michigan Lakes' drainage, ascending above treeline through a scenic landscape of rolling tundra hills festooned with wildflowers and intermittent clumps of trees. Arrive at Michigan Lakes, 3.3 miles from the trailhead. The main trail crosses the outlet near 'Lower Michigan Lake' and turns southeast toward Thunder Pass. A spur trail travels along the northwest shore of 'Lower Michigan Lake.'

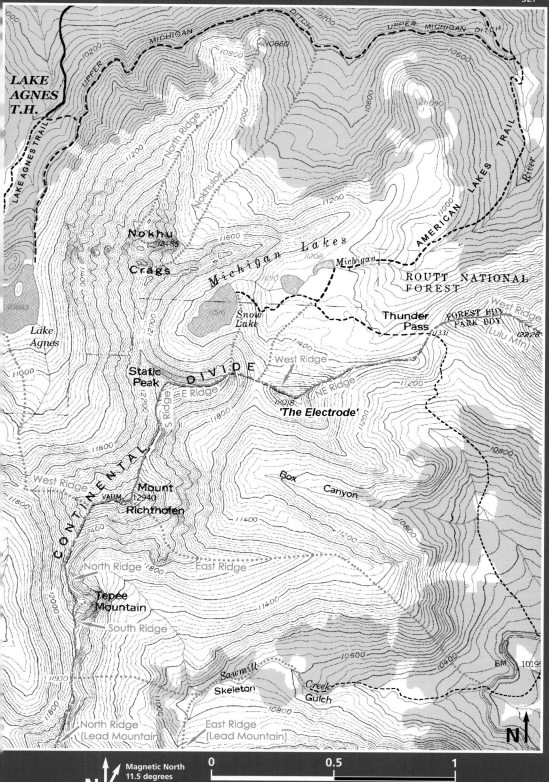

LAKE AGNES T.H.

Nokhu Crags 12485

Michigan Lakes

Michigan

ROUTT NATIONAL FOREST

Lake Agnes

Snow Lake

Thunder Pass

FOREST BDY
PARK BDY (Lulu Min)

West Ridge
12228

Static Peak

DIVIDE

West Ridge

'The Electrode'
12018

NE Ridge

E Ridge

S Ridge

Box Canyon

C O N T I N E N T A L

West Ridge

Mount Richthofen
VABM 12940

North Ridge

East Ridge

Tepee Mountain

South Ridge

Sawmill

Skeleton

Creek Gulch

BM 10195

North Ridge (Lead Mountain)

East Ridge (Lead Mountain)

Magnetic North 11.5 degrees

N

0   0.5   1

Distance in miles

Snow Lake 11,516 feet

T **OT** *Regional map p. 324 (C, 8); hike map p. 327.*

'Lower' and 'Middle' Michigan Lakes are shallow meres surrounded by grassy shore-lines, located below the 300-foot rock headwall of the glacial bench that holds Snow Lake, the highest tarn in the Michigan Lake chain. A cascading waterfall flows from Snow Lake over this headwall to feed the other two lakes. From the American Lakes Trailhead (p. 357), follow the American Lakes Trail for 3.5 miles to the point where the main trail turns southeast toward Thunder Pass. Leave the main trail and hike cross-country (following a faded, intermittent path) toward Snow Lake. Ascend the moraine along a rough trail on the south (left) side of the waterfall for 0.4 mile to top out in a stark alpine gorge, devoid of vegetation. Snow Lake is magnificently cupped in a dramatic stone basin formed by Static Peak and Nokhu Crags.

PEAKS AND OTHER DESTINATIONS

Thunder Pass 11,331 feet

T *Regional map p. 324 (C, 10); hike map p. 327*

Thunder Pass is a magnificent lowpoint along the Continental Divide between Lulu Mountain and Point 12,018'. The pass is right on the border between Colorado State Forest and RMNP. It overlooks the Colorado River drainage and the Never Summer Mountains to the south and the Michigan Lakes basin to the northwest. The pass is flat and covered with velvet tundra and scattered wildflowers.

American Lakes Trailhead Access   From the American Lakes Trailhead (p. 357), follow the American Lakes Trail for 3.5 miles to the point where the main trail turns southeast toward Thunder Pass. Continue for 0.6 mile along the smooth trail as it climbs over tundra hills and ascends a steep embankment to the top of the pass.

La Poudre Pass Access   From the Never Summer Trailhead near La Poudre Pass (p. 357), hike to the gate at La Poudre Pass, along the RMNP boundary. Pass the gate and hike southwest along level Grand Ditch Road (p. 358) for 3.4 miles to the point where the Thunder Pass Trail crosses the ditch (along the way, pass Ditch Camp). Cross the ditch on a log bridge and hike north into beautiful Box Canyon. Follow the Thunder Pass Trail (p. 360) for 0.6 mile to an open meadow near a NPS camp-site. Continue north as the trail gets steeper and rises above the trees. Follow the scenic, winding trail to Thunder Pass, 1.7 miles from the Grand Ditch.

Colorado River Access   From the Colorado River Trailhead (p. 356), hike north along the Colorado River Trail–La Poudre Pass Trail (p. 358) for 3.5 miles to Lulu City.

Continue north for 0.25 mile to the Thunder Pass Trail. Follow the Thunder Pass Trail (p. 360) northwest for 1.6 miles to Grand Ditch Road. Cross the ditch on a log bridge and hike north for 1.7 miles to Thunder Pass.

'The Electrode' 12,018 feet

T **OT** *Regional map p. 324 (D, 8); hike map p. 327*

This noteworthy, unofficially named summit was labeled 'The Electrode' because of its proximity to Static Peak. It is an interesting-looking peak made of loosely stacked red rocks. It provides nice views of Static Peak and Mount Richthofen.

Cliffs on 'The Electrode'

Northeast Ridge GRADE I CLASS 2 From Thunder Pass (follow route description, opposite), leave the trail and climb west over tundra to a small rocky highpoint, then continue climbing up steep grass dotted with rocks to the summit.

West Ridge GRADE I CLASS 2 The west ridge of 'The Electrode' is riddled with tiny rock spires and pinnacles made of loose shale, separated by shallow gullies. Traversing these slopes is only Class 2, but tricky because it is so loose. From the American Lakes Trailhead (p. 357), follow the American Lakes Trail for 3.5 miles to the point where the main trail turns southeast toward Thunder Pass. Leave the trail and travel cross-country to the saddle between Static Peak and 'The Electrode.' From the saddle, climb loose red talus to the west ridge and negotiate past the spires to the summit.

Nokhu Crags: North Summit (12,485 feet) and South Summit (12,480+ feet)

T **OT**  *Regional map p. 324 (B, 7); hike map p. 327*

Nokhu Crags are a collection of serrated spires grouped together to form an inspiring-looking mountain. They are in the northern section of the Never Summer Mountains, located slightly north of the RMNP boundary. Alluring and mysterious, Nokhu Crags have two main summits and are nothing more than a set of tottering rubble piles stacked majestically to heights well over 12,000 feet. Because of the unconsolidated, loose rock that comprises the mountain, the south summit is best climbed in late May or early June, when snow conditions stabilize and avalanche danger is low, but before the snow completely melts out of the gullies that provide access to the top. This is not true for the north summit, which is best climbed when there is no snow on the west face. Any route on Nokhu Crags qualifies as an extremely strenuous ascent of a rotten, unstable mountain. Rockfall is common, and warrants the use of a helmet. An ice axe is recommended for snow ascents.

North Ridge and West Face

GRADE I CLASS 4 This is a convoluted route up the higher, northern summit of Nokhu Crags. It is the easiest route to the highest summit, and requires tricky route finding combined with good climbing skills on loose rock. From the Lake Agnes Trailhead (p. 357), bushwhack east for 0.1 mile to a service road that parallels man-made Michigan Ditch. Follow the ditch northeast (away from the mountain) for

Descending 'Nokhuloir,' Nokhu Crags

0.9 mile to a point where the north ridge meets the ditch road at 10,380 feet. Leave the road and climb south for 1 mile up the north ridge to reach a group of rotten gendarmes at 12,200 feet that interrupt passage along the final section of the north ridge. Leave the north ridge and descend diagonally southwest for 100 vertical feet to gain the west face. From here, traverse south and upward along the west face for about 100 yards over loose scree to the base of several steep gullies that lead eastward to the summit. Do not take the most obvious gully that rises south to the summit. Instead, turn east (left) and enter a broad gully riddled with unstable scree. Climb for about 100 yards and look sharply for a narrow Class 4 passageway that cuts back southeast (right) toward the summit. Scramble carefully up the channel to easier ground and ascend loose scree to the top.

East Face 'Nokhuloir' GRADE I CLASS 3 MODERATE SNOW

The eastern side of Nokhu Crags provides access to the southern summit. There are two gullies, or couloirs, that split the striking east face. The 'Grand Central Couloir' is the more difficult and steep of the two, while the route described here takes the wider, lower angle 'Nokhuloir', which sports a grade of Class 3 with moderate snow climbing. This route is best attempted in May or early June. When the snow in the gully melts, hideous scree and loose blocks make the route dangerous. From Lake Agnes Trailhead (p. 357), bushwhack east for 0.1 mile to a service road that parallels man-made Michigan Ditch. Follow the ditch northeast (away from the mountain) for 1.3 miles as it loops around the northern aspect of Nokhu Crags. Leave the trail and bushwhack southwest for a mile into the basin below the mighty east face. Identify 'Nokhuloir,' located south of the other, steeper couloir. Climb moderate snow for 550 vertical feet to a saddle south of the southern summit. Turn north and scramble along loose blocks to the southern summit of Nokhu Crags. The loose shale that is haphazardly stacked atop the mountain provides an unsteady stance from which to take in the stupendous panorama. Lake Agnes and Michigan Lakes shine below. Static Peak is impressive to the south. The northern summit of Nokhu Crags stands sentinel to the north. Traversing between the two summits is not recommended because the crumbling rock towers are dangerous and exposed.

Static Peak 12,560 feet
T OT *Regional map p. 324 (D, 7); hike map p. 327*

This stately peak lies along the Continental Divide on the northwest border of RMNP and offers one of the best ridge climbs in RMNP. It is unusual in contrast with other Never Summer peaks because its gray granite is generally stable and relatively reliable. Climbing up the aesthetic, exciting East Ridge is a classic mountaineering adventure. Had John Muir been in the area, he would have climbed this mountain to get its good tidings.

East Ridge GRADE I CLASS 3   This ridge rises north above Snow Lake before taking a sweeping turn to the west to reach the summit. It is extremely fun to climb. Much of it is a knife-edge ridge with exciting exposure, but easy climbing on relatively stable rock. From the American Lakes Trailhead (p. 357), follow the American Lakes Trail for 3.5 miles to the point where the main trail turns southeast toward Thunder Pass. Leave the main trail and hike cross-country toward Snow Lake. Ascend the moraine on a rough trail on the south (left) side of the waterfall for 0.4 mile to Snow Lake. Boulder-hop south along Snow Lake's east shore to the ridge, initially grassy and nontechnical. The ridge takes a turn and leads west to become much steeper, providing full-on Class 3 scrambling and sections of sheer knife-edge rock. This is sporty scrambling with huge exposure but the climbing is very easy. Though the rock is

better than that of other Never Summer peaks, be wary of possible unstable rock along the steep ridge. On the final leg to the summit the ridge mellows to a Class 2 walk to the top. A huge cairn 4 feet tall and 3 feet wide graces the summit, which overlooks Lake Agnes.

South Ridge GRADE II CLASS 2 This is the easiest (least technical) route up Static Peak, but it first requires an ascent of Mount Richthofen and is a long route. Static lies 0.5 mile north of Richthofen. From the summit of Mount Richthofen (follow route description, p. 333), descend scree and hefty boulders northward to a large saddle between the two peaks. Climb north to the summit of Static Peak. The easiest descent route from Static is to reclimb Richthofen and return to the starting point from there.

LA POUDRE PASS Regional map p. 324 (D, 18)

La Poudre Pass (10,175 feet) is a strategic lowpoint along the Continental Divide on the northern border of RMNP. It lies at the northern end of the Grand Ditch Road and is the point where the Grand Ditch empties its stolen, precious liquid load into La Poudre Pass Creek, which transports it to the Cache la Poudre River and on to the thirsty Eastern Plains.

LAKES

La Poudre Pass Lake (Historical)
Regional map p. 324 (D, 19)
Once located directly south of La Poudre Pass, beaver dams probably formed this large lake. After the beavers moved on, the lake drained, and now only a scenic meadow remains. A small pond located northwest of the original site of this lake is visible from the La Poudre Pass Ranger Cabin.

PEAKS AND OTHER DESTINATIONS

Little Yellowstone 10,100 feet
T Regional map p. 324 (E, 17)
This scenic canyon is southwest of La Poudre Pass, cut by the diminutive Colorado River near its source, below the confluence of Bennett Creek and a northern tributary to Specimen Creek. It is a severely eroded area of yellow and white volcanic rock, dating back to an ashflow eruption that occurred around 28 million years ago in the vicinity of Lulu Mountain. The area was named by a RMNP ranger for its resemblance to the Grand Canyon of the Yellowstone River in Wyoming. The La Poudre Pass Trail leads to an overlook on the canyon rim, showcasing colorful substrata and eroding rock pillars.

La Poudre Pass Access From the Never Summer Trailhead near La Poudre Pass (p. 357), hike to the gate at La Poudre Pass along the RMNP boundary to access Grand Ditch Road (p. 358). Follow the road southwest for 1.3 miles to the La Poudre Pass Trail, marked by a sign. Descend from the road to follow the trail downhill through a serene forest for 0.4 mile to Little Yellowstone.

Colorado River Trail Access This route is longer than the route from La Poudre Pass but is more logical for people in the Estes Park–Grand Lake region, because the drive from there to La Poudre Pass is long. From Colorado River Trailhead (p. 356), follow Colorado River Trail–La Poudre Pass Trail (p. 358) north for 3.7 miles to the junction with Thunder Pass Trail and La Poudre Pass Trail. Follow La Poudre Pass Trail north for 1.5 miles to Little Yellowstone.

Lulu Mountain (12,228 feet), Thunder Mountain (12,040+ feet), and Mount Neota (11,734 feet)

T **OT** *Regional map p. 324 (C, 12; B, 13; and C, 15)*

These three mountains are located along the Continental Divide on the northwestern border of RMNP. They lie in close proximity to one another and are separated by gentle passes. They are typically climbed together. Access is either from La Poudre Pass or Thunder Pass. Depending on the trailhead used, the ratings for each mountain may be Grade I or Grade II (see ratings in the Destinations Chart, Appendix B). Lulu Mountain is the remnant of a volcano that erupted about 28 million years ago. Lulu and Thunder Mountains are scenic, rounded tundra-and-talus humps with outstanding views of Nokhu Crags and Static Peak. Mount Neota is an unremarkable talus hump that does not stand out obviously as a summit.

Thunder Pass Access GRADE I CLASS 2   From Thunder Pass (follow route description, p. 328), leave the trail and hike northeast for 0.5 mile up dirt, tundra, and talus to the rounded summit of Lulu Mountain. From here it is 0.6 mile to Thunder Mountain and 1.2 miles to Mount Neota. Lulu Mountain is the highest of the three peaks, making it a downhill tundra walk to the other two mountains. From Lulu Mountain, descend northeast over talus to a pretty saddle, and then climb steeply to Thunder Mountain. This view into American Lakes (Michigan Lakes) basin is unsurpassed. From Thunder Mountain, descend southeast along an aesthetic ridge to Mount Neota. Lush, scenic creek drainages highlight the view on both sides of the ridgeline.

La Poudre Pass Access GRADE I CLASS 2   From the Never Summer Trailhead near La Poudre Pass (p. 357), hike to the gate at La Poudre Pass along the RMNP boundary. Leave the road and strike off through the relatively thick forest, heading west along the well-marked NPS boundary line. Climb through the forest to the open dirt slopes of Mount Neota and ascend the ridge to the indistinct top, 1.4 miles from La Poudre Pass. Nokhu Crags peeks out from the gap between Thunder and Lulu Mountains. Hike northwest along a broad ridge and climb for 0.6 mile to Thunder Mountain, where outstanding views of the surrounding peaks unfold. Descend to a pretty saddle and climb in an ascending traverse for 0.6 mile to Lulu Mountain, which has a rock windbreak big enough for six people. Thunder Pass lies distinctly below.

Kari Lennartson and Belle Morris on Thunder Mountain

SKELETON GULCH
Regional map p. 324 (H, 12)

Skeleton Gulch

PEAKS

Mount Richthofen 12,940 feet
T **OT** *Regional map p. 324 (E, 7);*
hike map p. 327

This majestic summit is the highest peak
in the Never Summer Mountains and
also the highest peak from Milner Pass
north along the Continental Divide in
Colorado. A popular summit and a fun
peak to climb, it's located on the border of
RMNP in the northern Never Summer
Mountains. Access is from Lake Agnes
or the Colorado River Trailhead.

Lake Agnes Access: West Ridge GRADE I CLASS 2   This is the shortest route up Mount
Richthofen and also the most popular. From Lake Agnes (follow route description,
p. 326), follow a short trail around the west shore of the lake and scramble uphill
over boulders to the creek that flows north from unofficially named 'Mahler Peak'
(12,493 feet) into Lake Agnes. Fight upward through loose scree to gain the prominent
11,980-foot saddle between Mount Richthofen and 'Mahler Peak' to the west. Turn
east and climb steeply up the abrupt ridge to the Continental Divide and continue
east to the top of Richthofen.

Colorado River Trailhead Access: East Ridge GRADE II CLASS 2   This is a long route, but
the outstanding scenery and a magical walk along the mountain's broad east ridge
make it worthwhile. From the Colorado River Trailhead (p. 356), follow the Colorado
River Trail (p. 358) north for 0.5 mile to an open meadow and the trail junction
between the Red Mountain Trail, Colorado River Trail, and La Poudre Pass Trail.
Continue north on the Colorado River Trail–La Poudre Pass Trail for 3.7 miles to the
junction with the Thunder Pass Trail. Follow the Thunder Pass Trail (p. 360) for
1.6 miles to the Grand Ditch. Turn south on Grand Ditch Road (p. 358) and hike
for 0.5 mile to a bridge that crosses Grand Ditch and enters Skeleton Gulch.

   Follow the Skeleton Gulch Trail (p. 360) for 0.7 mile to a point where it is
advantageous to leave the trail and hike northwest to the broad, velvety east ridge of
Mount Richthofen. Climb the ridge and walk west along the luscious tundra to the
rocky east face of Richthofen. Climb west over steep but nontechnical terrain and
through gullies to the summit.

Tepee Mountain 12,360+ feet
T **OT** 🏔 *Regional map p. 324 (F, 6); hike map p. 327*

A showy set of towers comprises this fortress of crumbling rock located 0.5 mile
south of Mount Richthofen on the Continental Divide. Tepee has eastern and western
summits. The western peak is located along the main ridge, and the summit cairn and
register are located on the more dramatic, conical-shaped eastern spire, which is separated from the main ridge by a large gap. The saddle between the summits is a scenic
nook that is ornamented with a slender tower of vertical rock covered in yellow lichen.
A helmet is recommended for this route due to the poor quality of the rock.

South Ridge: West Summit GRADE II CLASS 3 and **East Summit** GRADE II CLASS 4
From the Colorado River Trailhead (p. 356), follow the Colorado River–La Poudre
Pass Trail (p. 358) for 3.7 miles to the junction with the Thunder Pass Trail. Follow

the Thunder Pass Trail (p. 360) for 1.6 miles to the Grand
Ditch. Turn south on Grand Ditch Road (p. 358) and hike for
0.5 mile to a bridge that crosses the ditch and enters Skeleton
Gulch. Follow the Skeleton Gulch Trail for 1.2 miles until it
dissipates in a meadow. Hike west up rock benches with trees
and grass on them to the base of an obvious, wide, grass-and-
rock gully that ascends to the 11,930-foot saddle between
Tepee and Lead Mountain.

    This is a nontechnical route but it's very steep and loose.
Turn north on the ridge and climb toward Tepee, skirting a
large bump on its west side. This ridge is more easily traversed
slightly below ridgetop on the west side. Climb through a
maze of bumps and unstable spires to a point between the
western and eastern summits. Turn northwest and scramble
up to the west summit (Class 3). Turn east to descend to the
saddle with the yellow tower. Tepee's eastern summit wall looks
formidable from here. Follow cairns to an unlikely-looking
weakness in the cliff. Climb Class 4 steps up a narrow gully
that angles southward. The initial climbing is difficult, but

Tepee Mountain

the gully spills out on easier ground of blocky ledges that lead
to the summit. Wonderful views of Skeleton Gulch and the high peaks of the northern
Never Summer Mountains abound.

North Ridge GRADE II CLASS 3   This route requires a climb of Mount Richthofen first.
From the summit of Richthofen (follow route description, p. 333), scramble downhill along the Continental Divide (west), then turn south and descend the jagged,
exposed south ridge of Richthofen to the lowpoint, then climb south over rough,
blocky terrain to the western summit of Tepee.

Lead Mountain 12,537 feet
T OT *Regional map p. 324 (J, 6); hike map p. 337*
This beautiful mountain is on the Continental Divide and offers relatively (for the
Never Summers) solid rock. It can be reached from either Skeleton Gulch or Hitchens
Gulch. A significant, unofficially named summit, 'Jiffy Pop Peak' (Point 12,438') [a.k.a
'Cloudview Peak'], fans out east of Lead Mountain and separates the two drainages.
An exciting Class 4 ridge connects Lead to Tepee Mountain, offering one of the supe-
rior challenges in the Never Summer Mountains.

East Ridge from Hitchens Gulch GRADE II CLASS 3   From the Colorado River Trailhead
(p. 356), hike north for 0.5 mile to the Red Mountain Trail. Follow the Red Mountain
Trail (p. 360) west for 3.5 miles to Grand Ditch. Turn north and follow Grand
Ditch Road (p. 358) for 1.7 miles to Hitchens Gulch. Cross the ditch on a bridge
and follow the Lake of the Clouds Trail (p. 359) west to treeline. Leave the trail and
hike northwest over grassy slopes that give way to a large rock moraine below the
Continental Divide. From here choose an ascent of the south face or the east ridge.
For the south face, hike to the headwall of the gorge and ascend a ledge system that
leads to low-angle slabs topped with loose scree. Follow the path of least resistance
and scramble to the talus field that leads directly to the summit. For the east ridge

route, climb over pretty tundra benches to access the steep scree slope below the obvious 11,980-foot saddle between Lead Mountain and 'Jiffy Pop Peak' (Point 12,438') [a.k.a 'Cloudview Peak']. Animal trails zigzag up this slope. Climb north to the saddle, then turn west and negotiate the fun, narrow ridge for 0.3 mile to the top.

East Ridge from Skeleton Gulch GRADE II CLASS 3   From the Colorado River Trailhead (p. 356), follow the Colorado River–La Poudre Pass Trail (p. 358) for 3.7 miles to the junction with the Thunder Pass Trail. Follow the Thunder Pass Trail (p. 360) for 1.6 miles to the Grand Ditch. Turn south on Grand Ditch Road (p. 358) and hike for 0.5 mile to a bridge that crosses the ditch and enters Skeleton Gulch. Follow the Skeleton Gulch Trail for 1.2 miles until it dissipates in a meadow. Turn south and climb up loose scree (or snow in early summer) for 0.8 mile to the 11,980-foot saddle between Lead Mountain and 'Jiffy Pop Peak' (a.k.a 'Cloudview Peak'). Turn west and negotiate the fun, narrow ridge for 0.3 mile to the top.

North Ridge GRADE II   CLASS 4   Most of this ridge between Tepee and Lead Mountains is enjoyable Class 2 climbing, but an exciting, exposed Class 4 section makes it interesting. This section is south of the obvious 11,930-foot saddle between Tepee and Lead Mountains. It is nearly vertical on the east side and consists of extremely steep slabs on the west side. Follow the South Ridge Route on Tepee Mountain (opposite) to access the 11,930-foot saddle between Tepee and Lead Mountains. Hike south along the initially easy ridge, staying below the ridge crest on the west. Enter the tricky Class 4 section and climb exposed slabs and loose blocks along the west side of the ridge. Climb south to the 12,400-foot hump north of Lead. From here, hike south (enjoyable Class 2) across the aesthetic ridge as it dips and rises for 0.4 mile to Lead Mountain.

Alex Kostadinov on the summit of Lead Mountain

'Jiffy Pop Peak' (a.k.a. 'Cloudview Peak')   12,438 feet
T OT   *Regional map p. 324 (J, 8); hike map p. 337*

This enormous, unofficially named summit stands between Hitchens and
Skeleton Gulches and has massive north, east, and south sides. It is connected to
Lead Mountain by a half-mile-long ridge.

West Ridge   GRADE II   CLASS 2   Follow the route description for East Ridge on Lead
Mountain (p. 334) from either Hitchens Gulch or Skeleton Gulch. From the 11,980-
foot saddle, turn east and climb 0.25 mile to the summit of 'Jiffy Pop Peak' (a.k.a.
'Cloudview Peak').

HITCHENS GULCH   *Regional map p. 324 (M, 11)*

LAKES

Lake of the Clouds   11,430 feet
T OT   *Regional map p. 324 (M, 7); hike map p. 337*

Lake of the Clouds is the largest lake west of the Continental Divide in the Never
Summer Mountains. It lies grandly in a rock basin at the base of Howard Mountain
and Mount Cirrus, within the domain of 'Cloud Mountains' that runs south along the
Continental Divide from Mount Cirrus to Mount Stratus.

It is the most highly visited destination in the Never Summer Mountains. From
the Colorado River Trailhead, hike north for 0.5 mile to the junction with the Red
Mountain Trail. Follow the Red Mountain Trail as it climbs through Hells Hip Pocket,
crossing Opposition Creek twice and Mosquito Creek once. Follow the meandering
trail through subalpine forest for 3.5 miles to the Grand Ditch. Head north along the
road that parallels the Grand Ditch for 1.7 miles to Hitchens Gulch. The level road
offers an easy walk, with good views of Red Mountain and Mount Cumulus to the
southwest, and Kawuneeche Valley to the south. Cross the Grand Ditch at Hitchens
Gulch on a bridge and follow the Lake of the Clouds Trail (p. 359) along Big Dutch
Creek for about a mile. Big Dutch Creek flows east out of Lake of the Clouds and cascades down into Hitchens Gulch in the form of a lovely waterfall. The trail ends in a
boulder field at the base of the waterfall. Scramble southwest over the boulders, staying
on the northwestern side (right-hand side) of the waterfall. Top out on a somewhat
level bench made of tundra and scattered bedrock. Hike west to the shoreline of the
scenic lake.

Lake of the Clouds

Jiffy Pop Peak'
(a.k.a 'Cloudview Peak')

Lead
Mountain

Mount
Cirrus

Howard
Mtn

Lake of the
Clouds

Hitchens
Big
Dutch
Gulch
Creek

Pinnacle
Pool

Mosquito
Creek

Mount
Cumulus

E Slope (Mt Cumulus)

N

Magnetic North
11.5 degrees

N

0   0.5   1

Distance in miles

PEAKS

Mount Cirrus 12,797 feet

T OT *Regional map p. 324 (L, 5); hike map p. 337*

This large mountain lies along the Continental Divide at the head of Hitchens Gulch, above Lake of the Clouds. Cirrus is a type of cloud that resembles a wispy filament, and is found at high altitudes, consisting of ice crystals. James Grafton Rogers named Mount Cirrus in 1914, along with Mounts Cumulus and Nimbus, after cloud formations. Mount Cirrus doesn't present any technical challenges and is really just a large talus heap.

Southwest Ridge GRADE II CLASS 2 From Lake of the Clouds (follow route description, p. 336), circle the lake and climb west over talus and up very steep, loose scree for 0.8 mile to the very prominent 12,380-foot saddle south of Cirrus. Turn north at the saddle and walk for 0.3 mile over pleasant tundra-and-talus slopes to the top.

Hart Ridge GRADE II CLASS 2 This is the ridge between Lead Mountain and Mount Cirrus. From Lead Mountain (follow route description, p. 334), hike south along scenic Hart Ridge for 1.1 miles to the top of Mount Cirrus.

The summit of Mount Cirrus

Howard Mountain 12,810 feet

T OT *Regional map p. 324 (N, 6); hike map p. 337*

This is the second highest peak in the Never Summer Mountains and is located along the Continental Divide. It towers over the only two named lakes in the range west of the divide. It has an uneven eastern arm that juts out on the south side of Hitchens Gulch and is made up of crumbling, unstable rock. Another ridge parallels this one to the south and is often mistaken for Howard's east ridge when viewed from Mosquito Creek.

East Ridge GRADE II CLASS 3 From Lake of the Clouds (follow the route description on p. 336), skirt the eastern shore and climb for 0.5 mile south up steep blocks to the east ridge of Mount Howard. This ridge is riddled with wobbly blocks and unstable talus, complete with ample exposure to the valleys below. Negotiate west along the ridgetop over Class 3 terrain for 0.6 mile to the summit.

Northwest Ridge GRADE II CLASS 2 From Lake of the Clouds (follow route description, p. 336), circle the lake and climb west over talus and up very steep scree for 0.8 mile to the prominent saddle between Mount Cirrus and Howard Mountain. Turn south at the saddle and hike for 0.4 mile along talus slopes to the top.

MOSQUITO CREEK   *Regional map p. 324 (P, 10)*

`LAKES`

Pinnacle Pool   11,300 feet
T **OT** *Regional map p. 324 (O, 9); hike map p. 337*

Michelle Chase above Pinnacle Pool

Of the numerous lakes and ponds that grace the east side of the Continental Divide in the Never Summer Mountains, only two are named. Pinnacle Pool is one of these, set like a gemstone among the mazelike topography between Mosquito Creek and the dramatic east ridge of Howard Mountain. From the Colorado River Trailhead (p. 356), hike north for 0.5 mile to the Red Mountain Trail. Follow the Red Mountain Trail (p. 360) west for 3.5 miles to the Grand Ditch. Turn south and hike to the bridge near Valley View campsite. From here, choose to either cross the bridge at Valley View or continue along the Grand Ditch Road to the point where Mosquito Creek drains into the ditch. There is no bridge at Mosquito Creek, so this option forces the hiker to wade across the ditch, which is very cold and difficult in times of high water. From Valley View, cross the bridge and bushwhack west through the thick forest to Mosquito Creek. Follow the impressive but appropriately named stream (bug repellent recommended) northwest through beautiful marshlands, meadows, and forest to a bench at the terminus of a prominent unnamed ridge that juts eastward from the Continental Divide. Contour north around the ridge to gain the rolling basin south of Howard Mountain's striking east ridge. Pinnacle Pool lies well protected on a verdant shelf between the east ridge of Howard Mountain and the unnamed ridge to the south. The round, scenic pool is surrounded by a flat field of green grass and flourishing plants, ornamented with rock shards that lie in and near the shallow waters of the lake edge.

OPPOSITION CREEK   *Regional map p. 324 (Q, 9)*

`PEAKS`

Mount Cumulus   12,725 feet
T **OT** *Regional map p. 324 (Q, 6); hike maps pp. 337, 341*

This massive mountain is a monster of scree located on the Continental Divide between Howard Mountain and Mount Nimbus. A beautiful, flat summit area is composed of medium-sized, lichen-covered blocks on two distinct highpoints, about 300 yards apart. The southern summit is higher. From the northern summit, it is a scrappy Class 3 scramble with occasional exposure for 1.4 miles north to Mount Howard. From the southern summit, it's a Class 2 walk down a wide talus ridge to saddle between Mounts Cumulus and Nimbus.

East Slope GRADE II CLASS 2   This is the shortest route up the mountain. From the Colorado River Trailhead (p. 356), hike north for 0.5 mile to the Red Mountain Trail. Follow the Red Mountain Trail (p. 360) west for 3.5 miles to the Grand Ditch. Follow the road south for 1 mile to the bridge near the Opposition Creek campsite. Cross the footbridge and bushwhack west to treeline. Climb the broad talus slope to the broad east ridge of Mount Cumulus, which leads west over an unstable scree slope for 1.2 miles to the summit.

South Ridge GRADE II CLASS 2   This is the logical route when climbing Cumulus and Nimbus together. From the Colorado River Trailhead (p. 356), hike north for 0.5 mile to the Red Mountain Trail. Follow the Red Mountain Trail (p. 360) west for 3.5 miles to the Grand Ditch. Follow Grand Ditch Road southwest for 1 mile to Opposition Creek. Cross the ditch on a log bridge and follow a trail west to its end, then bushwhack west to treeline. Climb through the scenic, rocky gully and past unnamed ponds, following Opposition Creek to its headwaters. Climb up steep, loose talus slopes to the Continental Divide at a 12,060-foot saddle between Mounts Cumulus and Nimbus. From the saddle, turn north and climb the wide talus-and-scree ridge for 0.6 mile to the expansive summit.

RED GULCH   *Regional map p. 324 (U, 11)*

PEAKS

Red Mountain   11,605 feet
T OT   *Regional map p. 324 (S, 10); hike map p. 341*

This small but worthy peak lies at the eastern end of the rocky red ridge that runs east from Mount Nimbus. Red Mountain has steep north, east, and south sides. It is one

Ridge between Red Mountain and Mount Nimbus

of the top 100 peaks in order of elevation in RMNP, which is why it gets climbed a fair bit. It's characterized by sharp-edged red rock. Legend has it that Indians used dirt from this red mountain for war paint.

East Slope GRADE II CLASS 2   This is the shortest route up Red Mountain, but a very steep climb on dirt and rocks, and also through thick trees, makes it less logical than the longer West Ridge Route. From the Colorado River Trailhead (p. 356), hike north for 0.5 mile to the Red Mountain Trail. Follow the Red Mountain Trail (p. 360) west for 3.5 miles to Grand Ditch. Turn south and follow Grand Ditch Road (p. 358) for 1.6 miles to the base of Red Mountain's steep east face. There is no bridge across the ditch in the immediate vicinity, so wade through the chilly, swift waters. This is a dangerous practice, so take extreme care. Bushwhack west up the steep slope for a tough 0.7 mile to the top.

West Ridge GRADE II CLASS 2   This is the easiest route to the top of Red Mountain. From the Holzwarth Historic Site (formerly Never Summer Ranch) Trailhead (p. 357), follow 'Ditch Road' (p. 358) for 3.1 miles to Grand Ditch Road. Turn north on Grand Ditch Road (p. 358) and hike for 1.8 miles to Red Gulch. Cross the ditch on a footbridge and follow the steep trail to a NPS campsite. Here the trail ends. Leave the trail and bushwhack north for 100 yards to cross the creek. Continue northwest to the base of a boulder field directly south of the prominent saddle between

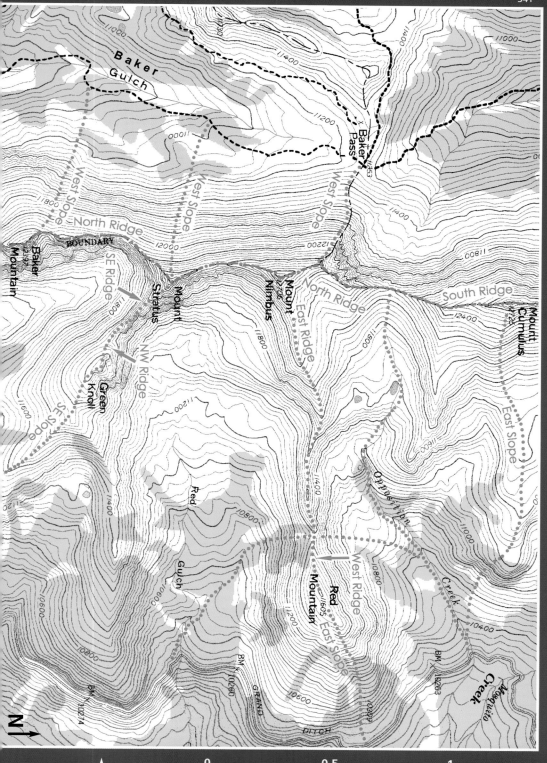

Baker Gulch

11000

11400

11200

11000

Baker Pass

11253

West Slope

West Slope

West Slope

11400

11800

North Ridge

12000

12200

11800

BOUNDARY

Baker Mountain
12397

SE Ridge

Mount Stratus
11800

Mount Nimbus
12726

Mount Cumulus
12725

North Ridge

South Ridge

12400

East Ridge

East Slope

11800

NW Ridge

Green Knoll

11600

11800

11200

SE Slope

11400

11200

Red

Opposition

11600

11000

10800

Gulch

10600

11400

10800

11200

Red Mountain
11605

West Ridge

East Slope

Creek

10800

10600

10400

10800

Mosquito

Creek

BM 10274

BM 10260

GRAND

DITCH

BM 10263

N

Magnetic North
11.5 degrees

0   0.5   1

Distance in miles

Red Mountain and Point 11,600'. Climb northward on the east side of the major red scree slope along the perimeter of the trees to avoid thick forest farther east or fighting upward through the loose scree. Steep grass with intermittent trees leads to the 11,380-foot saddle, green and lush on the south side and red and rocky on the north. Turn east from the saddle and climb a gentle, open ridge to the summit. The summit cairn and register are on a lower hump to the east that offers a better view than the true summit, which is a nondescript flat area.

The West Ridge Route can also be reached from Opposition Creek. From the Colorado River Trailhead (p. 356), hike north for 0.5 mile to the Red Mountain Trail. Follow the Red Mountain Trail (p. 360) west for 3.5 miles to the Grand Ditch. Turn south and follow Grand Ditch Road 1 mile to Opposition Creek. Cross the ditch on a footbridge and bushwhack up the valley for 0.6 mile. Turn south and scramble up loose, rocky slopes for 0.5 mile to the west ridge. Turn east and climb a gentle, open ridge to the summit.

Mount Nimbus 12,706 feet
T **OT** *Regional map p. 324 (T, 6); hike map p. 341*

Mount Nimbus is the western head of a gorgeous 1.4-mile-long east-west ridgeline between Red Gulch and Opposition Creek. This peak is exciting to climb because it is scenic and remote. The top is a huge blob of rocks, with marvelous views of the Never Summer Wilderness and the southern Never Summer Mountains in RMNP.

North Ridge GRADE II CLASS 2   From the saddle between Mounts Cumulus and Nimbus (follow the South Ridge Route on Mount Cumulus, p. 340), hike south along a very enjoyable nontechnical ridge past two beautiful knobs that jut upward from the crest. The ridge narrows and leads to the summit, 0.6 mile from the Cumulus-Nimbus saddle.

West Slope GRADE II CLASS 2   From the Bowen/Baker Trailhead (p. 356), follow the Baker Gulch Trail (follow Baker Pass route description, p. 344) west for 3.9 miles to the junction with the Parika Lake Trail. Continue north on the Baker Gulch Trail for 2.2 miles to lovely Baker Pass. Leave the trail and climb east over steep, unstable scree for 0.7 mile to the top.

East Ridge GRADE II CLASS 2   This is a fun and stimulating route. From the Holzwarth Historic Site (formerly Never Summer Ranch) Trailhead (p. 357), follow 'Ditch Road' (p. 358) for 3.1 miles to Grand Ditch Road. Turn north on Grand Ditch Road (p. 358) and hike north for 1.8 miles to Red Gulch. Cross the ditch on a footbridge and follow the steep trail to a NPS campsite. Here the trail ends. Leave the trail and bushwhack north 100 yards to cross the creek. Continue northwest to the base of a boulder field directly south of the prominent saddle between Red Mountain and Point 11,600'. Climb on the east side of the major red scree slope along the perimeter of the trees to avoid thick forest farther east or fighting upward through the loose scree. Steep grass with intermittent trees lead to the saddle, green and lush on the south side and red and rocky on the north. Turn west and hike along the narrow ridge crest toward Mount Nimbus. Surmount two scree bumps with beautiful rotten flutes snaking down each side. Loose volcanic rock is stacked along the V-shaped ridge, providing enjoyable scrambling. The sharp, loose ridge gives way to a broad, grassy talus ridge that climbs a false summit jutting over the Red Gulch drainage, then continues to climb west to the true summit.

This route can also be reached from Opposition Creek. From the Colorado River Trailhead (p. 356), hike north for 0.5 mile to the Red Mountain Trail. Follow the Red Mountain Trail (p. 360) west for 3.5 miles to the Grand Ditch. Turn south and follow Grand Ditch Road for 1 mile to Opposition Creek. Cross the ditch on a foot-bridge and bushwhack up the valley for 0.6 mile. Turn south and scramble up loose, rocky slopes for 0.5 mile to the east ridge. Turn west and hike along the narrow ridge crest for 1.2 miles to Mount Nimbus.

Green Knoll 12,280+ feet
T **OT** *Regional map p. 324 (V, 7); hike map p. 341*
Green Knoll is a lovely, rounded summit on the south side of Red Gulch, separated from Mount Stratus by a sharp, turreted Class 3 ridge. Just as Red Mountain looks red from a distance, the velvety-green tundra carpet that blankets this peak stands out prominently when viewed from southern Kawuneeche Valley.

Southeast Slope GRADE I CLASS 2
From the Holzwarth Historic Site (formerly Never Summer Ranch) Trailhead (p. 357), follow 'Ditch Road' (p. 358) for 3.1 miles to Grand Ditch Road. Either wade across the ditch here or hike north a short distance to a dirt-covered culvert and cross to a level bench on the northwest side. There is a cairned, faint trail across the ditch from the point where 'Ditch Road' meets Grand Ditch Road. This trail is difficult to follow and leads to an avalanche path full of debris,

Green Knoll from the west

then disappears. Bushwhack northwest through sparse forest and up an extremely steep slope to an open area on the southeastern side of Green Knoll. Hike up steep, wildflower-laced tundra to a false summit that overlooks a beautiful unnamed lake in Red Gulch. Continue northwest over two more tundra humps to the summit of Green Knoll, 1.4 miles from Grand Ditch Road.

Northwest Ridge GRADE II CLASS 3 This is the beautiful, steep ridge that separates Mount Stratus and Green Knoll. Reverse the route description for Mount Stratus, Southeast Ridge, (p. 344), to access Green Knoll from Mount Stratus.

Mount Stratus 12,520 feet
T **OT** *Regional map p. 324 (U, 5); hike map p. 341*
Three ridges join together on the broken summit area of Mount Stratus, forming a kind of triangle: the ridge north to Mount Nimbus, the ridge south to Baker Mountain, and the tower-ridden ridge southeast to Green Knoll.

West Slope GRADE II CLASS 2 From the Bowen/Baker Trailhead (p. 356), follow the Baker Gulch Trail (follow Baker Pass route description, p. 344) west for 3.9 miles to the junction with the Parika Lake Trail. Continue north on the Baker Gulch Trail for 1.4 miles to 11,000 feet. Leave the trail and bushwhack east a short distance through thick, wet forest to an open talus slope on the west side of Stratus. Climb east over unstable scree for 0.7 mile to the top.

North Ridge GRADE II CLASS 2 This is a fun route up Stratus. From the summit of Mount Nimbus (follow route description, opposite), descend south over a rocky slope with picturesque rock fins that frame the scenery to the east. Descend to a small saddle on the ridge, then scramble south, first over rock points and then along narrow grass ledges. Enjoy the high-alpine feeling, complete with major exposure on the east and gentle exposure toward Baker Pass on the west. The aesthetic ridge undulates for 0.5 mile to Mount Stratus, which is almost anticlimactic after the beauty of the ridge. However, the view is outstanding.

Southeast Ridge GRADE II CLASS 3   From Green Knoll, Mount Stratus lies 0.5 mile northwest on the opposite end of an exciting, narrow ridge that is riddled with rock gendarmes. This is a fun Class 3 scramble with plenty of exposure. From Green Knoll (follow route description, p. 343), descend to a small saddle between the knoll and the ridge. The crest of the ridge presents technical challenges. To keep the difficulty at Class 3, stay below the ridge crest for most of the traverse. Climb northwest on the south side of the ridge and come to a spot where it's necessary to traverse steep rock across a cleft of sheer ramparts with a rotten dirt saddle between the walls. This is the crux of the route. Continue to traverse along the south side, staying below the Class 5 gendarmes along the ridge top. Angle along dirt and grass ledges to a point where it is logical to climb to the ridge crest. From here it gets easier. Climb toward Mount Stratus over blocky terrain, choosing the path of least resistance. Several areas are easier to negotiate on the north side of the ridge. Ascend a dirty rock-filled channel to the summit.

BAKER GULCH   *Regional map p. 324 (Z, 7)*

LAKES

Parika Lake   11,380 feet
T *Regional map p. 324 (west of V, 1; off of map)*

This scenic lake lies on the west side of the Continental Divide in Never Summer Wilderness, east of Parika Peak and Farview Mountain. From the Bowen/Baker Trailhead (p. 356), follow a dirt road (closed to private vehicles) northwest across the Colorado River and the meadowland of Kawuneeche Valley to the junction between the Baker and Bowen Gulch Trails. Take the right-hand fork and follow the Baker Gulch Trail for 3.5 miles to Grand Ditch Road. Cross the ditch on a footbridge and continue along the Baker Gulch Trail for 0.5 mile to the junction with the Parika Lake Trail. Immediately before the junction is a crude log crossing of the creek that flows south from Baker Pass. From the junction, follow the very steep Parika Lake Trail northwest for 1.4 miles to Parika Lake. This shallow lake is quite scenic, surrounded by smooth tundra and throngs of wildflowers. The beautiful saddle between Farview Mountain and Parika Peak rises to the west, while the significant, unofficially named 12,253-foot 'Paprika Peak' lies splendidly to the north.

PEAKS AND OTHER DESTINATIONS

Baker Pass   (11,253 feet)
T *Regional map p. 324 (S, 4); hike map p. 341*

The Baker Gulch Trail leads northwest from Kawuneeche Valley to Baker Pass. Baker Gulch is forested in the lower region, giving way to a lush open basin decorated with luxurious meadowland below the pass. Baker Pass is along the Continental Divide west of RMNP in Never Summer Wilderness. It's a vast, treeless area, showcasing an abandoned mine site and sweeping views of the surrounding topography. It's atypical of most of the scenery found in RMNP, as it is more wide open and surrounded by green valleys contrasted with red, volcanic mountainsides. It is a magical place that receives few visitors, even though it has a trail leading right to it.

From the Bowen/Baker Trailhead (p. 356), follow a dirt road (closed to private vehicles) northwest across the Colorado River and the meadowland of the Kawuneeche Valley to the junction between the Baker and Bowen Gulch Trails. Take the right-hand fork and follow the Baker Gulch Trail into Arapaho National Forest and Never Summer

Wilderness. The trail rises steeply through the dense forest to Grand Ditch Road, 3.5 miles from the trailhead. Cross the ditch on a footbridge and continue along the Baker Gulch Trail through forest and lush meadows for 0.5 mile to the junction with the Parika Lake Trail. Immediately before the junction is a crude log crossing of the creek that flows south from Baker Pass. From the junction, continue north on the Baker Gulch Trail through the trees until it leads into open, grassy meadows that stretch from Baker Pass through a wide valley formed by the western slope of Mount

Hiking in Baker Gulch

Nimbus to the east and Point 11,730' to the west. From the junction it is 2.1 miles to Baker Pass.

From Baker Pass a trail leads southwest toward Parika Lake, skirting below the Continental Divide. Pass mining deposits and old cabin ruins and follow the faint trail through rolling topography, laced with streams cascading down from snow-laden cliffs on the Continental Divide. As the trail becomes hard to follow, stay northwest of the trees. Keep traversing southwest to the junction with Parika Lake Trail. Follow the Parika Lake Trail southwest to Parika Lake, or turn left and follow the Parika Lake Trail southeast back to the junction with the Baker Gulch Trail.

Baker Mountain   12,397 feet

T **OT**   *Regional map p. 324 (W, 5); hike map p. 341*

This pointy, pyramid-shaped peak is the southernmost summit in RMNP's section of the Never Summer Mountains.

West Slope   GRADE II CLASS 2   From the Bowen/Baker Trailhead (p. 356), follow the Baker Gulch Trail for 3.5 miles to Grand Ditch Road. Cross the ditch on a footbridge and continue along the Baker Gulch Trail for 0.5 mile to the junction with the Parika Lake Trail. Continue north on the Baker Gulch Trail toward Baker Pass for 0.8 mile to 10,680 feet. Leave the trail and bushwhack southeast through a short section of dense forest mixed with marshy wetlands to reach the gentlest aspect of Baker Mountain's western slopes. Climb a steep, long, scree-and-grass slope for 0.9 mile to the summit.

North Ridge   GRADE II CLASS 2   From the summit of Mount Stratus (follow route description, p. 343), Baker Mountain is 0.8 mile south along a jagged ridge. The ridge has a lot of up-and-down maneuvers along it, with several technical rock outcrops that are best skirted on the west side. It is the most difficult ridge walk south of Lead Mountain in the Never Summers along the north-south crest. The summit offers spectacular views of the Never Summer Wilderness, Parika Lake, Kawuneeche Valley, Lake Granby, Winter Park Ski Area, Longs Peak, Trail Ridge Road, and the Mummy Range.

'Paprika Peak'   12,253 feet
T **OT** *Regional map p. 324 (not shown on map)*

This unofficially named summit is in the Never Summer Wilderness and is a significant mountain rising to a respectable height from the north shore of beautiful Parika Lake.

West Ridge GRADE II CLASS 2   This route is used when climbing Parika Peak and 'Paprika Peak' together. From Parika Lake (follow route description, p. 344), leave the trail and hike around the north shore to a point below the obvious 11,740-foot saddle between Parika Peak and 'Paprika Peak.' Turn north and scramble for 0.3 mile up scree to the saddle. From the saddle, climb east along a mellow ridge for 0.4 mile to the summit.

South Slope GRADE II CLASS 2   From Parika Lake (follow route description, p. 344), leave the trail and climb north up the steep tundra-and-talus slope for 0.4 mile to the summit of 'Paprika Peak.'

Parika Peak   12,394 feet
T **OT** *Regional map p. 324 (not shown on map)*

Parika Peak is a joyful tundra summit along the Continental Divide on the border between the Never Summer Wilderness and Routt National Forest. It has a grassy, flowery top with stunning views of Wyoming and the entire southern section of the Never Summer Mountains.

South Slope GRADE II CLASS 1   From Parika Lake (follow route description, p. 344), circle the south shore along a trail that climbs grassy moraines and traverses long switchbacks to ascend a beautiful earthen headwall to the Continental Divide. The trail parallels sections of mining cart rails, tangible history of our mining heritage. Climb for 0.8 mile to the 12,000-foot saddle between Parika Peak and Farview Mountain. Leave the trail and hike north up incredibly verdant tundra slopes to a false summit, which leads to a sweeping green ridge with a short rock face on the east side. Ascend the smooth ridge to the summit of Parika Peak, 0.4 mile from the saddle.

East Ridge GRADE II CLASS 2   This route is used when climbing Parika Peak and 'Paprika Peak' together. From Parika Lake (follow route description, p. 344), leave the trail and hike around the north shore to a point below the obvious 11,740-foot saddle between Parika Peak and 'Paprika Peak.' Turn north and scramble for 0.3 mile up scree to the saddle. From the saddle, turn west and hike for 0.3 mile to the summit of Parika Peak.

Farview Mountain   12,246 feet
T *Regional map p. 324 (not shown on map)*

Farview Mountain lies along the Continental Divide between the Never Summer Wilderness and Routt National Forest. This gentle, rounded talus hump provides far-reaching views of the southern Never Summer Mountains, along with good views of Jack Park and the Illinois River drainage in Routt National Forest.

North Slope and Northwest Slope GRADE II CLASS 1   From Parika Lake (follow route description, p. 344), circle the south shore along a trail that climbs grassy moraines and traverse long switchbacks to ascend a beautiful earthen headwall to the Continental Divide. Climb for 0.8 mile to the 12,000-foot saddle between Parika Peak and Farview Mountain. From here, leave the trail and hike south for 0.2 mile to Farview Mountain, or follow the trail as it swings west, then south around Farview Mountain, descending into the Illinois River drainage. A spur trail breaks away from the main trail, and leads southeast to hit the indistinct summit of Farview Mountain. The main trail loses a considerable amount of elevation and descends into Illinois River drainage to a trail junction between the Illinois River Trail and the Bowen Gulch (Bowen Pass) Trail. Turn east (left) and follow the Bowen Gulch Trail as it climbs through a rugged alpine bowl and crosses two seasonal streams. The scenery in this basin is stupendous. Climb along the trail up a steep slope to Bowen Pass.

BOWEN GULCH *Regional map p. 324 (not shown on map)*

LAKES

Blue Lake 10,690 feet
T *Regional map p. 324 (not shown on map)*

Blue Lake sits in the Never Summer Wilderness amid a small, forested basin ringed by the steep cliffs of several high peaks. Bowen Mountain and Point 12,084' rise steeply beyond gentle, rolling terrain northwest of the pretty lake. A trail leads directly to the forested shoreline. Another section of the trail skirts the east side of the lake to climb a ridge between Bowen Mountain and Mineral Point. This trail is intermittent and difficult to follow. From the Bowen/Baker Trailhead (p. 356), follow a dirt road (closed to private vehicles) northwest across the Colorado River and the meadowland of the Kawuneeche Valley to the junction between the Baker and Bowen Gulch Trails. Take the left-hand fork and follow the Bowen Gulch Trail (see Bowen Pass below) for 5.9 miles to the junction with the Blue Lake Trail. Follow the Blue Lake Trail north through open, treeless, slanted meadows along a moderately steep incline for 0.7 mile to round Blue Lake, forested on one side and lined with rocky areas on the other.

Bowen Lake 11,019 feet
T *Regional map p. 324 (not shown on map)*

This large lake lies in Never Summer Wilderness, southeast of Cascade Mountain. From the Bowen/Baker Trailhead (p. 356), follow a dirt road (closed to private vehicles) northwest across the Colorado River and the meadowland of the Kawuneeche Valley to the junction between the Baker and Bowen Gulch Trails. Take the left-hand fork and follow the Bowen Gulch Trail (see Bowen Pass below) for 5.9 miles to the junction with the Blue Lake Trail. Continue west on the Bowen Gulch Trail for 1 mile to a T junction with the Bowen Lake Trail and the Bowen Gulch (Bowen Pass) Trail, which leads north. Turn south and climb along the trail through dense forest for 1.2 miles to boxy Bowen Lake, flanked on the west side by nearly vertical fields of grass that lead up to the southeast ridge of Cascade Mountain.

PEAKS AND OTHER DESTINATIONS

Bowen Pass 11,476 feet
T *Regional map p. 324 (not shown on map)*

Bowen Gulch lies within the Never Summer Wilderness and extends northwest from the Kawuneeche Valley to Bowen Pass. It is heavily forested in the lower gulch and is wide open and lush in the upper creek valley formed by Bowen and Ruby Mountains. It's a wonderful, secluded destination, accessed by an adequate trail. From the Bowen/Baker Trailhead (p. 356), follow a dirt road (closed to private vehicles) north-west across the Colorado River and the meadowland of the Kawuneeche Valley to the junction between the Baker and Bowen Gulch Trails. Take the left-hand fork and then follow the Bowen Gulch (Bowen Pass) Trail into Arapaho National Forest and Never

Bowen Pass Trail

Summer Wilderness. The trail travels south through the forest, paralleling the Kawuneeche Valley to a trail junction, 2.4 miles from the trailhead.

Here the Bowen Gulch Trail leads northwest into Bowen Gulch, and a spur trail leads southeast to Gaskil Site, a tiny mining settlement that lasted a few years longer than Lulu City, but was finally abandoned in 1886. The headquarters for the Wolverine Mine in Bowen Gulch, Gaskil Site had a population that never exceeded 50. There are no buildings or relics left at the site, though a hotel and a saloon both existed there. From here, the Bowen Gulch Trail follows the path of an old mining road that traveled from Gaskil Site to the Wolverine Mine on the southern flank of Point 12,084', south of Bowen Mountain. The trail is wide, and the remains of an old vehicle bridge span the creek.

The trail heads west through the forest to the junction with the Blue Lake Trail, then continues west for 1 mile to a T junction. Here, the Bowen Lake Trail leads south for 1.2 miles to Bowen Lake, and the Bowen Gulch (Bowen Pass) Trail turns north and climbs through a marshy garden bejeweled with hundreds of Indian paintbrush and other flowers. Beautiful Ruby Lake lies northeast of Ruby Mountain above the basin and is the stream source for the gulch. Medium-sized rock cairns mark the route through a bog, leading to a set of switchbacks that ascend to the top of the pass. From the T junction it is 1.5 miles to Bowen Pass.

Mineral Point 11,488 feet

T **OT** *Regional map p. 324 (not shown on map)*

Mineral Point is a nondescript summit plateau at the end of a long ridge running east from Bowen Mountain and separating Baker and Bowen Gulches in Never Summer Wilderness. Adorned with gnarled, mini tree clumps and graced with wonderful, dramatic views of Baker Mountain, Mount Stratus, Green Knoll, and the obvious scar of the Grand Ditch, this small peak reigns over the eastern section of the gulches. To avoid a long, arduous bushwhacking adventure to the top of this small peak, the easiest route is to hike to the ridge between Bowen Mountain and Mineral Point, then descend a beautiful tundra ridge to the summit.

West Ridge GRADE II CLASS 2   From Blue Lake (follow route description, p. 347), skirt the lake on the east side and either bushwhack north through the forest to a grassy avalanche chute, or locate the faint trail that leads north and switchbacks up a steep slope to the ridge between Bowen Mountain and Mineral Point. Climb the avalanche chute or along the trail to the flat area of the ridge. Hike northeast over tundra and talus to Point 11,960'. From here descend northeast over tundra slopes to a scenic mining shaft ruin, still largely intact. Continue to descend along the ridge as it swings to the southeast and settles in a small saddle. Climb southeast through weathered tree clusters and locate an animal trail that leads to Mineral Point.

Bowen Mountain 12,524 feet

T **OT** *Regional map p. 324 (not shown on map)*

This beautiful peak lies southeast of the Continental Divide in Never Summer Wilderness. It is the highest summit south of Baker Pass in the Never Summer Mountains and offers an excellent view of the entire region. Bowen Mountain has steep, rotten faces that are difficult to climb. The easiest route is up the nontechnical south ridge.

South Ridge GRADE II CLASS 2 From Blue Lake (follow route description, p. 347), skirt the lake on the west side and bushwhack northwest through forest and marshland, staying on the west side of a creek, to an open basin below Bowen Mountain's southeast face. Climb west over talus fields to a prominent saddle between Bowen Mountain and Point 12,084'. A fun side-hike is to turn south and climb for 0.2 mile along the ridge to reach Point 12,074', which is very pretty. From the saddle, turn north and scramble over steep Class 2 terrain for 0.5 mile to Bowen Mountain's grand summit. The far-reaching views from this peak are magnificent.

Northwest Ridge GRADE II CLASS 3   This route puts the hiker in a strategic position to climb unofficially named 'Never Summer Peak' (12,442 feet) and Farview Mountain (12,246 feet). From the Bowen/Baker Trailhead (p. 356), follow a dirt road (closed to private vehicles) northwest across the Colorado River and the meadowland of the Kawuneeche Valley to the junction between the Baker and Bowen Gulch Trails. Take the left-hand fork and follow the Bowen Gulch (Bowen Pass) Trail for 8.4 miles to Bowen Pass on the Continental Divide. From Bowen Pass, leave the trail and climb northeast for 0.4 mile to Point 12,285'. From this unnamed summit, it is 0.5 mile to Bowen Mountain, across a beautiful ridge spiked with rock towers. Bypass these towers and scramble along Class 3 terrain to the summit. To reach the neighboring summits, scramble back to Point 12,285' on the Continental Divide, then climb north along a mellow ridge for 0.4 mile to noteworthy 'Never Summer Peak,' which overlooks the Parika Lake basin to the north. From 'Never Summer Peak,' it is an easy descent along a rocky tundra ridge for 0.7 mile to Farview Mountain, which is located on a trail. Either descend along the trail south to Bowen Pass or northeast to Baker Gulch.

Karla Mosier on Bowen Mountain

SPECIMEN MOUNTAIN GROUP   *Regional map p. 324 (east of M, 20; off of map)*

Sandwiched between the Colorado River and the Cache la Poudre River, this group of destinations lies east of the Never Summer Mountains and is included in this chapter because of its proximity to the range. All the destinations lie within the Specimen Mountain Bighorn Sheep Protection Area, which provides seasonal and year-round closures to protect sensitive herds of bighorn sheep from human disturbance. This district is also part of the Specimen Mountain Research Natural Area, one of three such zones in RMNP established by the International Biological Program and included in a world-wide system of natural areas for scientific and educational purposes. In these areas, natural processes are allowed to predominate and act as a baseline for man-caused changes measured elsewhere. Foot traffic is allowed but is not encouraged, with only day-use activities authorized. Horse use and camping are prohibited. The Research Natural Area is only slightly larger than the Bighorn Sheep Protection Area, resulting in very limited public access to this entire region.

PEAKS AND OTHER DESTINATIONS

The Crater   (11,460 feet)

T   🚶   *Regional map p. 324 (L, 19)*

The Crater is a sculptured natural bowl showcasing exposed layers of volcanic debris at the head of Crater Gulch, east of the Colorado River. It was named from the previous belief that it was the mouth of a volcano. More recent discoveries have determined that the volcanic ashflow rock and underlying obsidian, which cover Specimen Mountain and neighboring summits, came from another volcano's eruption, which flowed over Specimen Mountain and solidified into rock while still hot. The Crater Trail is one of the premier short hikes in RMNP, leading steeply northwest for 0.8 mile through forest to open tundra and ending at a fine viewpoint of the gaping, craterlike bowl at the head of Crater Gulch. The Crater Trail is closed from May 1 to July 15 (or longer) to protect bighorn sheep during lambing season.

Photographing The Crater from the south

From the Crater Trailhead (p. 356), follow the Crater Trail into the trees and climb very steeply through a forest of subalpine fir and Engelmann spruce. The trail levels out on the broad, open tundra slopes south of Specimen Mountain. Follow the trail to the chasm rim for incredible views of the majestic Never Summer Mountains.

Specimen Mountain (No Public Access) 12,489 feet
Regional map p. 324 (not shown on map)

Specimen Mountain is flanked by two unnamed summits that form the noticeable alpine ridge of Specimen Mountain massif. 'South Specimen Mountain' (12,269 feet) is the unnamed summit that rises prominently north of The Crater. 'North Specimen Mountain' (12,307 feet) is the notable summit located 0.75 mile north of Specimen. In fact, seven distinct summits lie in the Specimen Mountain Group along the Continental Divide ridge crest between La Poudre Pass and Milner Pass, all of them significant at elevations above 11,000 feet, with only Specimen being officially named. A rough trail leads north from The Crater to summit 'South Specimen Mountain,' then descends to a saddle and climbs along the ridgeline to Specimen Mountain, 1.1 miles from The Crater. This trail is closed year-round to public use.

Shipler Mountain 11,320+ feet
T **OT** *Regional map p. 324 (N, 17)*

This out-of-the-way, tundra-topped mountain is a subtle peak strategically located to offer unparalleled views of the entire length of the mighty Never Summer Mountains. Located between Crater Gulch and the Squeak Creek drainage, Shipler Mountain forms the incredibly steep headwall above Shipler Park and overlooks the Colorado River, including the lush Kawuneeche Valley. In contrast to its west side, it has a gentle eastern slope that offers a moderate hike along a tundra-laden ridge to the top. This route is the only legal way to reach Shipler Mountain. The NPS allows periodic access along the ridge west of Crater Overlook to Shipler Mountain's summit. This route is closed from May 1 to August 15 (or longer). Hikers must stay along the ridge crest when using this route. Any variance from the ridgeline violates the year-round closure of the Bighorn Sheep Protection Area.

Southeast Ridge GRADE I CLASS 2   From the Crater Trailhead (p. 356), follow the Crater Trail (opposite) for 0.8 mile to Crater Overlook. From here, follow the ridge south to Point 11,618'. Continue south and follow the ridgeline as it swings west and descends along the beautiful, narrow tundra hump that soon climbs to the summit of Shipler Mountain. An incredible density of alpine plants and flowers abound on this stretch of the route. The terrain is fragile and vulnerable, so step lightly when crossing this amazing landscape. The western aspect of Shipler Mountain is extremely steep and drops down to Shipler Park quite unexpectedly, especially compared with the gentle tundra slope of the east side. The summit offers a great overview of the Never Summer Mountains and is a wonderful spot to sit and contemplate routes up neighboring peaks.

COLORADO RIVER   *Regional map p. 324 (T, 14)*

OTHER DESTINATIONS

Lulu City (9,360 feet) and Shipler Park Cabins (9,140 feet)

T **[⁂]** *Regional map p. 324 (J, 15; N, 15)*

Little evidence remains of this old mining boomtown, but close inspection of the meadow near the site reveals the remains of dilapidated cabins, rotted foundations, and scattered mine tailings. The real prize of this hike is a visit to the lovely, open valley created by the braided, shallow Colorado River flowing lazily through it. Several footpaths lead from the main trail to the water's edge. Small gravel beaches offer pleasant picnic sites and safe, easy access for children to explore this mellow section of the mighty Colorado River.

Lulu City was a real town for four short years. The city planners intended more longevity for the settlement, hopeful that the mining boom would pay off. It was soon evident, however, that the gold, silver, and lead ore was of poor quality, resulting in the lowest output from any of Colorado's mining counties. Today it is hard to believe that the town boomed from 1879 to 1883, consisting of 19 streets and 100 square blocks. At its height, the Kawuneeche Valley had 500 residents, 200 of whom lived in Lulu City. Stagecoaches arrived five times weekly from Grand Lake and Fort Collins. The elegant Godsmark and Parker Hotel supplied linen, silver, crystal, and fine china to their wealthy guests. Liquor, hardware, clothing, and grocery stores served the town. A post office, barbershop, and even a two-cabin brothel thrived. Two sawmills operated to keep up with the demand for lumber. The demise of the boomtown was hastened, however, by harsh winters that caused many prospectors to desert their claims,

Melissa Martin at the Lulu City site

while the absence of a nearby smelter compounded the problems with ore quality. The most hazardous legacy of this mining heritage lies along the banks of the Colorado River in the form of orange deposits of iron manganese precipitate. The state is currently seeking solutions to rid endangered waterways of this major pollutant.

From the Colorado River Trailhead (p. 356), hike north and immediately climb a short, steep hill. The trail levels off in trees and continues to a pretty, open meadow after 0.5 mile. From the trail junction, continue north on the Colorado River Trail–La Poudre Pass Trail as it parallels the Colorado River and passes below the western slope of Shipler Mountain, on which numerous mineshafts were dug between 1870 and 1900. Several spur paths lead east up steep slopes to the mines. Almost a mile from trailhead, cross tailings from the unsuccessful Shipler Mine. Access this mine by climbing the loose, steep slope on north side of the tailings. (It's never a good idea to enter an old mine. Unstable rocks and deteriorating structure beams can be hazardous.) The trail cuts across the mine tailings and passes rusted-out relics, such as an old mining car. Hike another 0.4 mile to Shipler Park and Joe Shipler's cabin.

Here the ruins of two tiny cabins lie on the edge of pretty meadow. This is a nice family destination. Joseph L. Shipler was a silver mining pioneer along the North Fork of the Grand River (now the Colorado River). He built a cabin in Shipler Park in 1876, which had the distinction of being the first structure erected in the valley. He helped discover the Wolverine Mine on Bowen Mountain, and he owned the Tiger Mine and Collins Lode Mine on the west-facing slope of Shipler Mountain. The Wolverine Mine was shut down in 1883, but Shipler was still living in his cabin as late as 1914, when members of the Colorado Mountain Club made the trek from Grand Lake to Shipler Park, where Mr. Shipler extended warm hospitality to the campers. Beyond the cabins, 100-year-old wagon-wheel ruts provide evidence of the stagecoach road that transported mail and provisions to Lulu City. Continue north for 1.5 miles to the trail junction between the Lulu City spur trail and the west fork to Little Yellowstone. Take the east fork and hike downhill for 0.2 mile to the Lulu City site.

KAWUNEECHE VALLEY *Regional map p. 324 (Z, 13)*

OTHER DESTINATIONS

Holzwarth Historic Site (Never Summer Ranch) 8,884 feet
T **[*]** **[&]** *Regional map p. 324 (X, 12)*

Located in the flat, glacially carved Kawuneeche Valley at the foot of the Never Summer Mountains, the rustic buildings of the Holzwarth Historic Site offer a history lesson about pioneers at the turn of the 20th century. The wheelchair- and stroller-friendly hike features a 0.5-mile walk (one-way) on a level, dirt road. A visit to this site is a step back into time to a rural western dude ranch. One of the cabins is located right at the trailhead. From here, go west along the level dirt road to a bridge across the Colorado River, very scenic amid the swaying grasses of the Kawuneeche Valley. Continue west to the homestead.

On display are a group of cabins, including the Holzwarth home. The site show-cases bunkhouses, kitchens, an ice-storage room, a taxidermy shop, old sleds, wagons, and farm machinery. During summer months, the buildings are open to public, staffed by NPS employees and volunteers. Inquire at the visitor center for a tour schedule. John Holzwarth Senior, a German immigrant, started a cattle ranch here in 1918. After a visit from a group of drunken fishermen, Mrs. Sophia Holzwarth insisted that future guests must pay to stay. From this episode, the couple opened as a guest ranch called

Brian Biggs at the Holzwarth Historic Site Trailhead

Holzwarth Trout Lodge, which featured Sophia's tasty home cooking. The dude ranch was later expanded and renamed Never Summer Ranch in 1929. John Holzwarth Junior, who operated the ranch from the 1920s, insisted on preservation of the site for public use and denied many lucrative offers for development, eventually selling the property to the Nature Conservancy in 1974. The following year the land was annexed by RMNP.

Valley Trail and River Trail 8,700 feet

T 👫 *Regional map p. 324 (south of Z, 13; off of map)*

These two trails combine to make a nice 4.7-mile loop that explores the southern section of the Kawuneeche Valley. A connecting trail cuts across the lower end of the loop, creating a north loop (2.4 miles) and a south loop (2.3 miles) that may be hiked individually. From the Harbison Picnic Area (p. 357), hike west along a path into the woods to access the Valley Trail. Turn north (right) and hike along the level, well-defined horse trail as it parallels Trail Ridge Road. The Valley Trail is within earshot of the road for its entire 2.2 miles; sometimes leading through the trees, sometimes out in the open alongside the highway. Hike for 0.4 mile to a junction with a connecting trail that leads west for 0.3 mile to the River Trail.

Continue north on the Valley Trail as it gains elevation and leads to a junction with a trail that comes in from Trail Ridge Road to the north. Hike northwest as the trail swings around and leads to the NPS Green Mountain Housing Area, where it is called the "Stock Trail." As the trail turns south, it becomes the River Trail and parallels the Colorado River as it meanders through the gorgeous Kawuneeche Valley. Views of Baker Mountain, Mount Stratus, Green Knoll, Bowen Mountain, and Mineral Point stand out grandly. Tall, lush grasses of red, yellow, and green blow in the breeze along the river. Pass the remains of an old log cabin, still standing with a doorway and walls up to chest level. The trail starts to climb away from the river to the junction with the Powerline Trail, which parallels the River Trail for a short distance. Pass a fresh oxbow lake and arrive at the connecting path to the Valley Trail. Continue south on the River Trail as it travels close to the river, then rises into the woods to a trail junction on the south end of the loop. Circle east and then north to the Valley Trail and hike back to the Harbison Picnic Area.

These trails can also be reached from the Green Mountain Trailhead. From the Green Mountain Trailhead (see Region 6, p. 303), cross Trail Ridge Road to the east and access the Valley Trail at its northern end.

Coyote Valley Trail 8,840 feet

T 👫 ♿ *Regional map p. 324 (south of Z, 13; off of map)*

This level, 0.5-mile-long trail parallels the Colorado River as it flows through the scenic Kawuneeche Valley. It travels between the river and the meadow with wonderful views of Baker Mountain and Green Knoll. Numerous log benches offer resting places, and written wayside exhibits provide information about the history, geology, flora, and fauna of the region. The incline of the trail is less than 5 percent, and the surface is firmly compact gravel, conducive to trouble-free use of wheelchairs and strollers.

From the Coyote Valley Trailhead (p. 356), hike west, then cross the Colorado River on a stone bridge. Past the bridge is a picnic area to the southwest. The start of the nature trail is directly north. The trail leads into the expansive riparian habitat of the Kawuneeche Valley. The vast floodplain is home to grasses and sedges; it's too wet to support communities of trees. An ideal habitat for wildlife, the meadow showcases deer, elk, moose, coyotes, and smaller mammals like chipmunks and ground squirrels. Golden eagles and red-tailed hawks can frequently be seen hunting in the meadow. The U-shaped valley was created by glaciation and continued erosion. Glaciers in the Never Summer Mountains flowed east to merge with the glaciers inching west from the Continental Divide to form the largest river of ice in the RMNP region. The Colorado River Glacier stretched for 20 miles from La Poudre Pass to its terminus at the chain of islands on the south end of Shadow Mountain Lake. Explore the river ecosystem and enjoy views of the southern section of the Never Summer

"Kah ah wu-na chee" is an Arapaho word that means "coyote creek." This was the Arapaho word for the north fork of the Grand River (now the Colorado River), since there were many coyotes there. In 1914, members of the Colorado Mountain Club invited two elderly Arapaho men, who were then living on a reservation in Wyoming, to return to the Estes Park–Grand Lake region, where they had spent some time in their youth. Together with an interpreter, they conducted a two-week pack trip through the mountains. Oliver Toll diligently recorded the stories they told and in particular, the regional place names they remembered from their childhood. Although his important book, *Arapaho Names and Trails,* was not published until 1962, dozens of Indian names were placed on area features as a direct result of this trip. Today, RMNP showcases one of the greatest concentrations of Indian place names in the United States. Other Indian names were suggested for the valley, but the Colorado Geographic Board decided on Kawuneeche because they deemed it the most pronounceable.

Mountains, which represent the headwaters to the mighty Colorado River. This is just the beginning of the Colorado River's 1,400-mile course to the Gulf of California. The trail leads north to a small turnaround loop, then doubles back on the same path to end at the stone bridge near the trailhead.

Coyote Valley Trail

Bowen/Baker Trailhead

This trailhead lies at 8,850 feet and provides access to the Baker and Bowen Gulch Trails. The trailhead is located within RMNP, but the trails lead to destinations both in RMNP and in the Never Summer Wilderness of Arapaho, Roosevelt and Routt National Forests. From the RMNP Beaver Meadows Visitor Center near Estes Park, drive 4.2 miles west on US 36 until it turns into Trail Ridge Road (US 34) at Deer Ridge Junction. Continue west on Trail Ridge Road through the heart of RMNP for 31.6 miles to the Bowen/Baker Trailhead, located on the west side of the road. From Grand Lake, drive north on US 34 for 8.1 miles to the trailhead.

Colorado River Trailhead

This trailhead is at 9,040 feet and provides access to the Colorado River Trail, Red Mountain Trail, La Poudre Pass Trail, Thunder Pass Trail, Grand Ditch Road, Skeleton Gulch Trail, and Lake of the Clouds Trail. From the RMNP Beaver Meadows Visitor Center near Estes Park, drive 4.2 miles west on US 36 until it turns into Trail Ridge Road (US 34) at Deer Ridge Junction. Continue west on Trail Ridge Road through the heart of RMNP for 28.3 miles to the Colorado River Trailhead, located on the west side of the road. From Grand Lake, drive north on US 34 for 11.4 miles to the trailhead.

Coyote Valley Trailhead

This trailhead lies at 8,820 feet and provides access to the Kawuneeche Valley and the Coyote Valley Trail. From the RMNP Beaver Meadows Visitor Center near Estes Park, drive 4.2 miles west on US 36 until it turns into Trail Ridge Road (US 34) at Deer Ridge Junction. Continue west on Trail Ridge Road through the heart of RMNP for 32.2 miles to the Coyote Valley Trailhead, located on the west side of the road. From Grand Lake, drive north on US 34 for 7.5 miles to the trailhead. From US 34, turn west and drive downhill on a dirt road for 0.1 mile to the trailhead.

Crater Trailhead

This trailhead lies at 10,740 feet and provides access to the Crater Trail. It is located 0.3 mile northeast of Milner Pass. From the RMNP Beaver Meadows Visitor Center near Estes Park, drive 4.2 miles west on US 36 until it turns into Trail Ridge Road (US 34) at Deer Ridge Junction. Continue west on Trail Ridge Road through the heart of RMNP for 21.4 miles to the Crater Trailhead, located on the west side of the road. From Grand Lake, drive north on US 34 for 18.2 miles to the trailhead.

The Crater Trail

Harbison Picnic Area

This picnic area is at 8,708 feet and provides access to two scenic Kawuneeche Valley trails: the Valley Trail and the River Trail. These two trails make a nice 4.7-mile loop. From the RMNP Beaver Meadows Visitor Center near Estes Park, drive 4.2 miles west on US 36 until it turns into Trail Ridge Road (US 34) at Deer Ridge Junction. Continue west on Trail Ridge Road through the heart of RMNP for 37.1 miles to the Harbison Picnic Area, located on the west side of the road. From Grand Lake, drive north on US 34 for 2.6 miles to the picnic area.

Holzwarth Historic Site (Never Summer Ranch) Trailhead

This trailhead lies at 8,884 feet and provides access to Holzwarth Ranch and the Grand Ditch via 'Ditch Road.' From the RMNP Beaver Meadows Visitor Center near Estes Park, drive 4.2 miles west on US 36 until it turns into Trail Ridge Road (US 34) at Deer Ridge Junction. Continue west on Trail Ridge Road through the heart of RMNP for 30.3 miles to the Holzwarth Historic Site turnoff, located on the west side of the road. Turn west and drive less than 0.1 mile to the trailhead. From Grand Lake, drive north on US 34 for 9.4 miles to the trailhead.

Lake Agnes and American Lakes (Michigan Lakes) Trailheads

These two trailheads are located just outside the northern border of RMNP in Colorado State Forest. Fees apply to use this area. The Lake Agnes Trailhead lies at 10,250 feet and provides access to the Lake Agnes Trail. The American Lakes (Michigan Lakes) Trailhead is at 9,780 feet and provides access to the Michigan Ditch Trail and the American Lakes Trail. From Cameron Pass on CO 14, drive west on CO 14 for 2.5 miles to CR 62 and the turnoff for Colorado State Forest State Park. Turn south and follow the dirt road for 0.6 mile to the junction with the roads to American Lakes and Lake Agnes. To reach Lake Agnes, turn right and drive south up a steep hill for 1.1 miles to the Lake Agnes Trailhead. This dirt road is extremely steep but passable by passenger cars, unless the road is deeply rutted after a storm. To reach the American Lakes (Michigan Lakes) Trailhead, continue straight from the American Lakes–Lake Agnes junction and drive east for 0.8 mile to the trailhead.

Never Summer Trailhead near La Poudre Pass

This trailhead is located on Long Draw Road (a gravel road only open in the summer) east of the Continental Divide at 10,175 feet. It provides access to the northern Never Summer Mountains, Skeleton Gulch Trail, and the eastern ends of Grand Ditch Road, La Poudre Pass Trail, and Thunder Pass Trail. Vehicle access to this trailhead is only from the east side of the Continental Divide since the Grand Ditch Road is permanently closed to unauthorized vehicles. From the junction of CO 14 and CR 27 (Stove Prairie Road) in Poudre Canyon, drive west for 37 miles to Long Draw Road turnoff (FR 156). Follow Long Draw Road for 13 miles (past Long Draw Reservoir) to the Never Summer Trailhead, where the road dead-ends into the parking lot. A spur road that is closed to unauthorized vehicles approaches the gate at La Poudre Pass directly, but there is no parking allowed there. From the trailhead a path leads across a pretty meadow (no camping) to the service road northeast of La Poudre Pass. Follow the road to the gate at La Poudre Pass. Pass the gate to enter RMNP and cross to the west side of the Continental Divide.

American Lakes (Michigan Lakes) Trail
See American Lakes (Michigan Lakes), p. 326.

Baker Gulch Trail
See Baker Pass, p. 344.

Blue Lake Trail
See Blue Lake, p. 347.

Bowen Gulch (Bowen Pass) Trail
See Bowen Pass, p. 347.

Bowen Lake Trail
See Bowen Lake, p. 347.

Colorado River Trail
This trail used to run the length of Colorado River from the Green Mountain Trailhead to a point 0.5 mile north of the present-day Colorado River Trailhead, but is now closed south of the Colorado River Trailhead. The NPS recognizes the Colorado River Trail as the section running north from the Colorado River Trailhead to the junction with the Thunder Pass Trail, located 0.25 mile north of Lulu City, even though most of this trail is marked as the La Poudre Pass Trail on the USGS topographical maps. Suffice it to say that the Colorado River Trail and the La Poudre Pass Trail overlap.

From the Colorado River Trailhead, the trail immediately climbs a steep hill, which represents the most dramatic incline along the trail. It levels off in the trees and travels north for 0.5 mile to an open meadow at the junction with the Red Mountain Trail, Colorado River Trail, and La Poudre Pass Trail. Follow the Colorado River Trail–La Poudre Pass Trail north past Shipler Park and through the Colorado River valley for 3 miles to Lulu City. Continue north for 0.25 mile to the junction with the La Poudre Pass Trail and the Thunder Pass Trail.

Crater Trail
See The Crater, p. 350.

Coyote Valley Trail
See Coyote Valley Trail, p. 354.

'Ditch Road'
This access road climbs steeply from the Holzwarth Homestead to connect with Grand Ditch Road. From the Holzwarth Historic Site (formerly Never Summer Ranch), hike along the wide, dirt road (closed to public vehicles) for 0.3 mile to a junction immediately prior to reaching the Holzwarth Homestead. Take the right-hand fork for "official vehicles only" and hike past the backside of the ranch buildings. This is the 'Ditch Road,' which the Water Supply and Storage Company and RMNP use for authorized access to Grand Ditch Road. It is a rough 4WD road and quite steep. It climbs at a substantial, steady grade through numerous switchbacks for 2.7 miles to Grand Ditch Road.

Grand Ditch Road and Ditch Camp
This "trail" is actually a dirt road that parallels the Grand Ditch and traverses 14.3 miles along the lower section of the east side of the Never Summer Mountains. The level service road provides easy walking, but the trails that access it are typically long and

steep. Log bridges span the ditch at strategic points. Crossing the ditch by any other means proves difficult and cold in times of high water. The Water Supply and Storage Company, which owns and operates the Grand Ditch, maintains the road. In the summer, company employees inhabit Ditch Camp, a small group of buildings along the northern section of the ditch, reminiscent of the numerous construction camps that existed along the canal from 1894 to 1936 to house the crews who built it.

Hiking the length of the ditch is pleasurable but presents transportation problems, since the starting points are in drastically different locales, and the northern end is almost three hours by road from Estes Park. All in all, traversing the length of the ditch is an adventure, highlighted by oddities such as a rocky grave and a cross that lie across the ditch from Ditch Camp. At one point, wooden planks line the ditch, and a bowling pin and six colorful bowling balls are partially submerged in the cement reinforcements. This area is curiously termed 'McFall Balls.' Along the way, handcrafted signs crudely state the names of creeks that flow into the ditch.

La Poudre Pass Trail

This trail leaves Grand Ditch Road 1.3 miles south of La Poudre Pass and descends into the Colorado River valley, passing Little Yellowstone on the way. It then follows the Colorado River south through Lulu City and Shipler Park to end at the major junction of the Colorado River, Red Mountain, and La Poudre Pass Trails, located 0.5 mile north of the Colorado River Trailhead. What's considered the present-day Colorado River Trail overlaps much of this route. It is a very scenic trail to many enticing destinations.

Lake Agnes Trail

See Lake Agnes, p. 326.

Lake of the Clouds Trail

This trail starts on Grand Ditch Road and travels a mile west into Hitchens Gulch, below the rock bowl holding beautiful Lake of the Clouds. The trail then dissipates in upper Hitchens Gulch, and a rough path leads west another 0.3 mile to the lake. Hitchens Gulch was the site of Dutchtown, a mining camp abandoned in 1884. It was manned by a group of former Lulu City miners exiled after an evening's drunken brawl at a Lulu City saloon, where a woman suffered a broken arm and a man lost an eye.

Lake of the Clouds

Parika Lake Trail
See Parika Lake, p. 344.

Red Mountain Trail
This trail leaves the Colorado River Trail 0.5 mile north of the Colorado River Trailhead and climbs up to Grand Ditch Road. From the Colorado River Trailhead, hike north for 0.5 mile to an open meadow and the junction with the start of the Red Mountain Trail. Follow the Red Mountain Trail west and cross the Colorado River on a footbridge. The trail climbs steadily through the forest to a prominent viewpoint of Hells Hip Pocket, which is the steep forested drainage of Opposition and Mosquito Creeks. The trail crosses Opposition Creek twice and Mosquito Creek once and climbs across a couple of rocky moraines. Instead of multiple switchbacks, the trail makes an unusual lengthy ascending traverse southwest to some small ponds, then bends back sharply to arc upon itself and climb upslope in the opposite direction (north). It tops out on Grand Ditch Road north of Red Mountain, 3.9 miles from the Colorado River Trailhead.

Skeleton Gulch

Skeleton Gulch Trail
This trail starts on Grand Ditch Road and travels for 1.2 miles west into Skeleton Gulch, the gorgeous alpine valley at the base of the remarkable ridge between Tepee and Lead Mountains. Skeleton Gulch is the headwaters to Sawmill Creek. The bridge that crosses the ditch is high and narrow, exciting for those with a fear of heights.

Thunder Pass Trail
This trail is located in both the Colorado State Forest and RMNP. The northern end begins near Michigan Lakes, and the southern end starts at a junction north of Lulu City. From the Colorado River Trailhead, follow the Colorado River Trail north for 0.5 mile to the junction of the Red Mountain Trail and the La Poudre Pass Trail. Continue north on the Colorado River Trail–La Poudre Pass Trail for 3 miles to Lulu City.

Hike north for 0.25 mile to the junction between the La Poudre Pass Trail and the Thunder Pass Trail. Follow the Thunder Pass Trail for 1.6 miles as it climbs very steeply through the dense forest between Lulu and Sawmill Creeks to top out on Grand Ditch Road. Cross Grand Ditch on a log bridge and follow the scenic Thunder Pass Trail as it climbs steeply through Box Canyon to rise above treeline and reach Thunder Pass after 1.7 miles. Box Canyon is very pretty, with open meadows and plenty of elk and deer. From Thunder Pass on the Continental Divide, the trail descends west into the Colorado State Forest and connects with the American Lakes Trail after 0.6 mile.

Valley Trail and River Trail
See Valley Trail and River Trail, p. 354.

Colorado River

This river begins modestly in the Kawuneeche Valley, fed by runoff from the high peaks of the Never Summer Mountains. Here it begins its 1,400-mile journey south to the Gulf of California. Fed by multiple vital tributaries along the way, it becomes one of the most significant rivers in the USA. It passes through seven Western states and carves deep rifts in the landscape, of which the Grand Canyon is the deepest and most notable. This mighty river is the lifeblood of the arid Southwest, and the demand for this water sparked a water war that rages on today. The important book *Cadillac Desert: The American West and Its Disappearing Water* by Marc Reisner is an interesting resource on the water war. The Colorado River supplies municipal water, hydroelectric power, farmland irrigation, and recreation to millions of people.

Grand Ditch

The Grand Ditch is a man-made earthen canal approximately 20 feet wide and 6 feet deep that was dug by hand at the turn of the 20th century as part of a substantial water-diversion project that steals stream runoff from creeks in the Never Summer Mountains and diverts it to the eastern slope before it has a chance to contribute to the Colorado River. Highly visible because of the 14.3-mile scar that traverses the mountains and causes unavoidable, evident erosion on the lower forested hillsides, the project has always been surrounded by controversy. Used as a supplemental water source for Front Range cities and farms, the ditch starts in Baker Gulch at the southern end of the Never Summer Mountains and carries water across the Continental Divide at La Poudre Pass to Long Draw Reservoir, located on the north side of the Never Summer Mountains.

In 2003, water eroded the service road north of Lulu Creek and breached the ditch, sending a large-scale flood raging through the forest and into Lulu Creek and the Colorado River, eventually burying the wetlands below Lulu City in 3 feet of gravel and debris. Thousands of trees were uprooted, acres of parkland damaged, and trails and bridges washed out.

The Grand Ditch

APPENDIX A: GLOSSARY

Alluvial fan: A sloping, fan-shaped mass of loose rock debris deposited by a stream or flood where it leaves a narrow mountain valley and enters a plain or broad valley.

Alpine: Characteristic of or resembling the European Alps or any high-altitude mountainous region, especially those above treeline.

Arête: A sharp, narrow ridge or crest of a mountain.

Basin: A wide, depressed area in which the topography inclines toward a center.

Bedrock: The solid, undisturbed rock uncovered by erosion, or rock that is beneath soil or gravel.

Bench: A fairly level terrace cut in the earth that interrupts the upward momentum of a slope.

Bergschrund: A type of glacial crevasse that separates the moving ice and snow from the snowfield at the top of a mountain valley.

Boulder: Any large rock worn smooth and rounded by weather and water, typically larger than a volleyball and reaching sizes greater than a house.

Bushwhacking: Hiking off-trail through a densely vegetated area where it might be necessary to fight one's way through thick bramble or interlaced tree branches.

Buttress: A projecting fin of rock or earth that is situated against a mountain wall, seeming to support or reinforce it.

Cairn: A conical heap of stones built as a monument or landmark, used to mark a trail or route.

Chockstone: A stone block or wedge that fills in a space between rock walls.

Cirque: A natural semicircle amphitheater caused by glacial erosion, located high on the side of a mountain and formed by steep walls.

Col: A gap between peaks in a mountain range, used as a pass.

Continental Divide: A long ridge of the Rocky Mountains that divides North America into two massive watersheds and separates rivers flowing in an easterly direction from those flowing in a westerly direction. Precipitation falling on the western side flows into the Gulf of California and the Pacific Ocean. Precipitation falling on the eastern side flows into the Gulf of Mexico and the Atlantic Ocean.

Contour line: A line on a map connecting all points of the same elevation in a particular area.

Contour interval: The difference in value between adjacent contour lines on a map.

Couloir: A narrow mountain gorge or gully, usually closely delimited by rock walls, and often filled with snow or ice.

Crampons: A pair of spiked metal plates fastened on climbers' boots to prevent slipping when walking on ice or snow.

Crevasse: A deep crack or fissure in a snowfield or glacier.

Crux: The hardest part of a climb or route.

Erratic: A boulder or rock formation that was transported from its original source by a glacier.

Fourteener: A 14,000-foot mountain.

Gendarme: A rock tower that guards passage along a ridge.

Glacier: A large, moving mass of ice and snow formed on land by the compaction and recrystallization of snow. A glacier forms in areas where the rate of snowfall constantly exceeds the rate at which the snow melts. The mass moves slowly outward from the center of accumulation or down a mountain because of the force resulting from its own weight.

Ice axe: A mountaineering tool used for safely moving on snow and ice. The axe has a shaft with a spike on the bottom and a sharp pick on top.

Krummholz: This German word for "crooked wood." It refers to the stunted, gnarled, and windswept trees found near treeline.

Massif: A mountainous mass broken up into separate but connected peaks that form the backbone of a mountain range.

Moraine: A mound or ridge of debris such as soil, sand, clay, or boulders that was carried and deposited directly by glaciers during an ice age. A lateral moraine was deposited at the side of a glacier and a terminal moraine was deposited at the end of a glacier. When two glaciers merged, two lateral moraines joined to form a medial moraine.

Park: A level, open area surrounded by mountains or forest.

Pass: A natural passage or opening between mountains.

Range: A series of connected peaks, ridges, and their valleys, considered as a single system.

Roche moutonnée: This is French for "fleecy rock" or "sheep-shaped rock." It is used to describe glaciated rock outcrops that look like sheep when seen from a distance. The bare hummocks of rock are usually smoothed on the upstream side and grooved on the other by glacial action.

Rock glacier: A mass of boulders and fine rock debris cemented by ice, occurring in high mountains and extracted from steep cliffs by frost action. It has the same general appearance and slow movement as a small alpine glacier.

Saddle: A depression in the crest of a ridge between two summits, often forming a pass.

Scree: Loose gravel and stones on a hillside, typically smaller than talus.

Self-arrest: To stop or check the motion of one's slide down a snow slope by digging the pick of an ice axe into the snow.

Summit register: A canister placed on a mountain summit that holds note paper upon which climbers or hikers write their names to keep a record of who climbed the peak and when. Registers are sometimes placed by individuals, and sometimes by organizations such as the Colorado Mountain Club.

Talus: An accumulated heap of rock fragments derived from and lying at the base of a cliff or very steep slope.

Tarn: A small, deep lake filling a bedrock basin carved by a glacier in high mountains.

Thirteener: A 13,000-foot peak.

Treeline: Also called timberline. The elevation above which trees do not grow. In RMNP, treeline is about 11,400 feet.

Tundra: A Lapp word referring to any of the vast, nearly level, treeless plains of the Arctic regions. In the mountains it refers to a treeless ecosystem above upper treeline.

Wetland: An area of land characterized by bogs and marshes where water is at or near the land surface.

APPENDIX B: DESTINATIONS CHART

ORGANIZATION AND METHODOLOGY

The following Destinations Chart (pages 366–385) covers Rocky Mountain National Park and selected neighboring destinations surrounding the national park boundary. The entries have generally been arranged alphabetically by proper name, so that related features (e.g., Rock Lake and Little Rock Lake, listed as "Rock Lake, Little") will be presented in proximity to one another.

OFFICIAL AND UNOFFICIAL NAMES

Official names of hiking destinations are derived from the USGS 7.5-minute series maps when available. Numerous unofficial names are included for notable features that have no official USGS name. These are shown in single quotes. For example, the unofficially named 12,018-foot summit between Thunder Pass and Static Peak is commonly known as 'The Electrode.'

    Certain groups of lakes that have official names only in a collective sense but have unofficial, relational names itemized in the chart (i.e., 'Upper,' 'Middle,' and 'Lower') are also shown in single quotes. These instances include: Fay Lakes, Hutcheson Lakes, Michigan Lakes, Spectacle Lakes, and Twin Lakes.

CALCULATION OF ELEVATIONS

Summit elevations have been obtained from the USGS 7.5-minute quadrangle maps when available. If no elevation is given, the elevation is calculated as the highest contour line shown on the map, with a "+" character indicating that the summit is less than 40 feet higher than the last shown contour interval. For example, Hayden Spire does

Michelle Chase enjoys an evening at Bear Lake

View from the summit of Elk Tooth

not have a stated elevation on the McHenrys Peak quadrangle, but the highest contour interval shown for Hayden Spire is 12,480 feet. The summit is therefore between 12,480 feet and 12,520 feet (40-foot contour interval). The elevation provided in the chart is thus 12,480+ feet.

All other features on the maps, including trailheads, lakes, ponds, tarns, meadows, passes, and other features, have been interpolated at half-contour-interval increments from the 7.5-minute maps when an exact elevation is not stated. For example, Lonesome Lake at the foot of Hayden Spire lies between the 11,680-foot and 11,720-foot contour intervals, so the elevation is given as 11,700 feet.

The elevation of glaciers, falls, cascades, meadows, parks, and other topographic features that extend over a range of contour intervals is calculated at their intermediate elevation. The elevation for glaciers is particularly difficult to calculate as their extent changes over the course of a year and because of year-to-year climatic variations. The convention used here is to calculate the average elevation of the glacier from the extent shown on the USGS 7.5-minute map. For example, Sprague Glacier, located southeast of Hayden Spire, extends from 'Sprague Tarn' at 11,860 feet to 12,340 feet, with a total height of 480 feet. The elevation is calculated as 11,860 feet plus half of 480 feet, or 12,100 feet.

The elevation stated for trails is the maximum elevation reached along the route.

The Gain/Loss column in the Destinations Chart is calculated as the absolute change between the trailhead and the destination. This number *does not* reflect any elevation gain or loss encountered while en route to the destination, which could be considerable.

HIKE DISTANCES

Distances presented in the table are one-way except for loop trails (Lily Lake, Lily Ridge, Adams Falls, Lake Estes, Bear Lake, and Sprague Lake).

DESTINATION	PAGE	ONE-WAY DISTANCE (MILES)	TRAILHEAD	TRAIL/ROUTE	TRAILHEAD ELEVATION (FEET)	DESTINATION ELEVATION (FEET)	GAIN/LOSS ELEVATION (FEET)	GRADE	CLASS	SNOW/ICE
Acoma, Mt.	315	6.7	Roaring Fork TH	SW Ridge	8,300	10,508	2,208	II	2	
Acoma, Mt.	315	6.0	Shadow Mtn. Dam	SW Ridge	8,380	10,508	2,128	II	2	
Adams Falls	275	0.3	East Inlet TH	Trail	8,400	8,460	60	–	–	
Adams Falls	275	1.0	East Inlet TH	Viewing Loop Trail (round-trip from Trailhead)	8,400	8,480	80	–	–	
Adams Lake	312	6.5	Roaring Fork TH	Watanga Lake Access	8,300	11,180	2,880*	–	–	
Adams Lake	312	8.9	East Inlet TH	Paradise Park Access	8,400	11,180	2,780	–	–	
Adams, Mt.	316	6.6	Roaring Fork TH	S Slope from Watanga Lake	8,300	12,121	3,821	II	2	
Agnes Vaille Memorial Shelter	240	6.3	Longs Peak TH	From Boulder Field	9,400	13,160	3,760	–	–	
Agnes, Lake	326	0.8	Lake Agnes TH	Trail	10,250	10,663	413	–	–	
Alberta Falls	46	0.8	Glacier Gorge TH	Trail	9,180	9,400	220	–	–	
Alice, Mt.	189	8.8	Wild Basin TH	Hourglass Ridge	8,500	13,310	4,810	II	2+	
Alice, Mt.	189	9.0	Wild Basin TH	S Ridge from Boulder–Grand Pass	8,500	13,310	4,810	II	2	
Alice, Mt.	189	10.7	East Inlet TH	S Ridge from Boulder–Grand Pass	8,400	13,310	4,910	II	2	
Alice, Mt.	189	8.2	Wild Basin TH	SE Slope from Lion Lake No. 1	8,580	13,310	4,810	II	2	
Alluvial Fan	129	0.2	East Alluvial Fan Parking Area	Trail	8,580	8,640	60	–	–	
'Amore, Lake'	104	6.4	Poudre Lake TH at Milner Pass	From N Slope of 'Jagor Point'	10,758	11,380	622*	–	–	
'Amore, Lake'	104	7.8	Poudre Lake TH at Milner Pass	From Mt. Ida–Chief Cheley Peak saddle	10,758	11,380	622*	–	–	
'Amore, Lake'	104	2.9	Rock Cut Parking Area	Forest Canyon Access	12,110	11,380	–730*	–	–	
'Amore, Lake'	104	7.2	Alpine Visitor Center	Forest Canyon Pass	11,796	11,380	–416*	–	–	
Andrews Glacier	66	4.8	Glacier Gorge TH	Glacier Gorge Access	9,180	11,680	2,500	II	2	MS
Andrews Glacier	66	6.0	Bear Lake TH	Flattop Mtn. Access	9,450	11,680	2,230	II	2	MS
Andrews Pass	67	5.1	Glacier Gorge TH	Via Andrews Glacier	9,180	11,980	2,800	–	–	
Andrews Pass	67	6.0	Bear Lake TH	Via Flattop Mtn.	9,450	11,980	2,530	–	–	
Andrews Pass	67	11.4	North Inlet TH	W Slope from North Inlet Trail	8,500	11,980	3,480	–	–	
Andrews Peak	281	8.2	East Inlet TH	S Slope from Lake Verna	8,400	12,565	4,165	II	2	
Andrews Tarn	65	4.6	Glacier Gorge TH	Trail	9,180	11,380	2,200	–	–	
Arch Rocks	39	1.2	Fern Lake TH	Trail	8,150	8,220	70	–	–	
Arrowhead	54	5.9	Glacier Gorge TH	NW Face	9,180	12,640+	3,460	II	3+	
Arrowhead Lake	105	6.7	Poudre Lake TH at Milner Pass	From Mt. Ida–Chief Cheley Peak saddle	10,758	11,120	362*	–	–	
Arrowhead Lake	105	6.6	Poudre Lake TH at Milner Pass	From N Slope of 'Jagor Point' (from Love Lake)	10,758	11,120	362*	–	–	
Arrowhead Lake	105	6.4	Poudre Lake TH at Milner Pass	From saddle SW of 'Jagor Point'	10,758	11,120	362*	–	–	
Arrowhead Lake	105	2.8	Rock Cut Parking Area	Forest Canyon Access	12,110	11,120	–990*	–	–	
Arrowhead Lake	105	7.6	Alpine Visitor Center	Forest Canyon Pass	11,796	11,120	–676*	–	–	
Azure Lake	105	5.4	Poudre Lake TH at Milner Pass	From Mt. Ida–Chief Cheley Peak saddle	10,758	11,900	1,142*	–	–	
Azure Lake	105	5.1	Poudre Lake TH at Milner Pass	From saddle SW of 'Jagor Point'	10,758	11,900	1,142*	–	–	
Azure Lake	105	4.6	Rock Cut Parking Area	Forest Canyon Access	12,110	11,900	–210*	–	–	

RATING

* = absolute change only. This destination requires a considerable amount of elevation gain and elevation loss and is more strenuous than is indicated by the absolute change

DESTINATION	PAGE	ONE-WAY DISTANCE (MILES)	TRAILHEAD	TRAIL/ROUTE	TRAILHEAD ELEVATION (FEET)	DESTINATION ELEVATION (FEET)	GAIN/LOSS ELEVATION (FEET)	RATING GRADE CLASS	RATING SNOW/ICE
Azure Lake	105	9.3	Alpine Visitor Center	Forest Canyon Pass	11,796	11,900	104*	–	–
Baker Mtn.	345	5.6	Bowen/Baker TH	W Slope from Baker Gulch	8,850	12,397	3,547	II	2
Baker Mtn.	345	6.7	Bowen/Baker TH	N Ridge from Mt. Stratus	8,850	12,397	3,547	II	2
Baker Pass	344	6.1	Bowen/Baker TH	Trail	8,850	11,253	2,403	II	1
'Balanced Rock'	144	4.0	Cow Creek TH	Trail	7,820	8,863	1,043	–	–
'Balanced Rock'	144	4.2	Lumpy Ridge TH	Trail	7,852	8,863	1,011	–	–
Battle Mtn.	236	4.8	Longs Peak TH	W Slope from Granite Pass	9,400	12,044	2,644	II	2
Battle Mtn.	236	2.8	Longs Peak TH	NE Slope from Eugenia Mine	9,400	12,044	2,644	II	2
Bear Lake	72	100 yards	Bear Lake TH	Trail	9,450	9,475	25	–	–
Bear Lake	72	0.65	Bear Lake TH	Loop trail	9,450	9,475	25	–	–
Bear Lake	72	17.7	North Inlet TH	North Inlet/Flattop Mtn. Trails	8,500	9,475	975*	–	–
Bear Lake	72	18.5	Tonahutu TH	Tonahutu/Flattop Mtn. Trails	8,500	9,475	975*	–	–
Bear Lake	72	0.7	Glacier Gorge TH	Connecting Trail	9,180	9,475	295	–	–
Bear Lake	72	8.7	Fern Lake TH	Trail including side trip to Odessa Lake	8,150	9,475	1,325	–	–
Beaver Meadows	44	6.3	Ute Crossing	Ute Trail via Tombstone Ridge and Timberline Pass	11,440	8,440	-3,000	–	–
Beaver Mtn.	40	2.6	Upper Beaver Meadows TH	E Slope	8,440	10,491	2,051	I	2
Bench Lake	291	7.3	North Inlet TH	Ptarmigan Creek Access	8,500	10,140	1,640	–	–
Bierstadt Lake	34	1.3	Bierstadt Lake TH	Trail	8,860	9,416	556	–	–
Bierstadt Lake	34	1.5	Bierstadt Moraine TH at Park and Ride	Trail	8,820	9,416	596	–	–
Bierstadt Lake	34	3.0	Hollowell Park TH	Trail	8,180	9,416	1,236	–	–
Bierstadt Lake	34	2.0	Bear Lake TH	Trail	9,450	9,416	-34*	–	–
Big Meadows	295	2.0	Green Mtn. TH	Trail	8,800	9,400	600	–	–
Big Pool	286	4.8	North Inlet TH	Trail	8,500	8,920	420	–	–
Bighorn Flats	296	6.8	Bear Lake TH	From Tonahutu Creek Trail	9,450	11,900	2,450	–	–
Bighorn Flats	296	9.6	Green Mtn. TH	From Tonahutu Creek Trail	8,800	11,900	3,100	–	–
Bighorn Lake	302	0.9	Lake Irene Picnic Area	No Legal Public Access	10,660	11,060	400	–	–
Bighorn Mtn.	135	3.9	Lawn Lake TH	NW Slope	8,540	11,463	2,923	II	2
Black Lake	49	4.9	Glacier Gorge TH	Trail	9,180	10,620	1,440	–	–
Black Pool	95	2.9	Fern Lake TH	Bushwhack from Fern Lake Trail	8,150	9,060	910*	–	–
Blue Lake	50	5.5	Glacier Gorge TH	From Black Lake	9,180	11,140	1,960	–	–
Blue Lake	347	6.9	Bowen/Baker TH	Trail	8,850	10,690	1,840	–	–
Bluebird Lake	201	6.3	Wild Basin TH	Trail	8,500	10,978	2,478	–	–
Boulder Field	240	5.9	Longs Peak TH	Trail	9,400	12,800	3,400	II	2
Boulder–Grand Pass	194	7.8	Wild Basin TH	E Access from Lake of Many Winds	8,500	12,061	3,561	II	2
Boulder–Grand Pass	283	9.5	East Inlet TH	W Access from Fourth Lake	8,400	12,061	3,661	II	2

* = absolute change only. This destination requires a considerable amount of elevation gain and elevation loss and is more strenuous than is indicated by the absolute change

DESTINATION	PAGE	ONE-WAY DISTANCE (MILES)	TRAILHEAD	TRAIL/ROUTE	TRAILHEAD ELEVATION (FEET)	DESTINATION ELEVATION (FEET)	GAIN/LOSS ELEVATION (FEET)	GRADE	CLASS	SNOW/ICE
Bowen Lake	347	8.2	Bowen/Baker TH	Trail	8,850	11,019	2,169	—	—	
Bowen Mtn.	349	9.1	Bowen/Baker TH	S Ridge from Blue Lake	8,850	12,524	3,674	II	2	
Bowen Mtn.	349	9.3	Bowen/Baker TH	NW Ridge from Bowen Pass	8,850	12,524	3,674	II	3	
Bowen Pass	347	8.4	Bowen/Baker TH	Trail	8,850	11,476	2,626	II	1	
Box Lake	197	7.0	Wild Basin TH	From Thunder Lake	8,500	10,740	2,240	—	—	
Bridal Veil Falls	145	3.1	Cow Creek TH	Trail	7,820	8,880	1,060	—	—	
Bryant, Mt.	315	7.3	East Shore TH	NW Slope from Shadow Mtn.	8,420	11,034	2,614	II	2	
Cairns, Mt.	278	4.9	East Inlet TH	SE Slope from East Inlet	8,400	10,880	2,480	II	2	
Calypso Cascades	185	1.9	Wild Basin TH	Trail	8,500	9,280	780	—	—	
Cascade Falls	286	3.6	North Inlet TH	Trail	8,500	8,800	300	—	—	
Castle Lake	187	6.6	Wild Basin TH	From Lion Lake No. 1	8,500	11,140	2,640	—	—	
Castle Lakes	187	5.4	Wild Basin TH	From Lion Lake Trail	8,500	10,620	2,120	—	2	
Castle Mtn.	138	0.8	Castle Mtn. parking	SE Slope	7,700	8,834	1,134	I	2	
Castle Rock	92	5.7	Fern Lake TH	S Gully to W Ridge	8,150	10,640+	2,490	I	2	
Castle Rock on Castle Mtn.	139	0.5	Castle Mtn. parking	To base of formation	7,700	8,669	969	—	—	
'Catherine, Lake'	287	12.8	North Inlet TH	From Lake Nanita	8,800	10,600	1,800	—	—	
Chaos Canyon Cascades	69	1.8	Bear Lake TH	From Lake Haiyaha Trail	9,450	9,840	390	—	—	
'Chaotic Glacier'	72	3.7	Bear Lake TH	From Lake Haiyaha	9,450	11,810	2,360	II	2	AI 2 SS
Chapin Pass	124	0.2	Chapin Pass TH	Trail	11,020	11,140	120	—	—	
Chapin, Mt.	124	2.4	Chapin Pass TH	N Slope from Chapin–Chiquita saddle	11,020	12,454	1,434	I	2	
Chapin, Mt.	124	2.7	Endovalley Picnic Area	E Ridge	8,640	12,454	3,814	II	2	
Chasm Falls	124	0.1	Old Fall River Road	Trail	9,080	9,060	−20	—	—	
Chasm Falls	124	1.5	Endovalley Picnic Area	Road/Trail	8,640	9,060	420	—	—	
Chasm Lake	223	4.2	Longs Peak TH	Trail	9,400	11,780	2,380	—	—	
Chasm Meadows	224	4.0	Longs Peak TH	Trail	9,400	11,599	2,199	—	—	
Chasm View	243	6.3	Longs Peak TH	From Boulder Field	9,400	13,500	4,100	—	—	
Chickadee Pond	200	4.8	Wild Basin TH	From Ouzel Lake Trail	8,500	10,020	1,520	—	—	
Chickaree Lake	297	0.9	Trail Ridge Road (1.6 mi S of Bowen/Baker TH)	Bushwhack from Trail Ridge Road	8,800	9,260	460	—	—	
Chickaree Lake	297	2.6	Onahu Creek TH	Onahu Creek Trail Access	8,780	9,260	480	—	—	
Chief Cheley Peak	107	5.3	Poudre Lake TH at Milner Pass	NW Ridge from Mt. Ida	10,758	12,804	2,046	II	2	
Chiefs Head Peak	59	9.4	Wild Basin TH	W Ridge from Lion Lakes	8,500	13,579	5,079	II	2	
Chiefs Head Peak	59	7.9	Sandbeach Lake TH	SE Slope from Mt. Orton	8,340	13,579	5,239	II	2	
Chiefs Head Peak	59	7.8	Glacier Gorge TH	NW Ridge from Stone Man Pass	9,180	13,579	4,399	II	3	
Chiefs Head Peak	59	7.3	Glacier Gorge TH	E Ridge from Chiefs Head–Pagoda Couloir	9,180	13,579	4,399	II	2	SS
Chiefs Head–Pagoda Couloir	60	6.6	Glacier Gorge TH	From Green Lake	9,180	12,860	3,680	II	2	SS
Chipmunk Lake	133	4.2	Lawn Lake TH	Trail	8,540	10,660	2,120	—	—	
Chiquita Lake	134	5.5	Lawn Lake TH	Bushwhack from Ypsilon Lake	8,540	11,340	2,800	—	—	

DESTINATION	PAGE	ONE-WAY DISTANCE (MILES)	TRAILHEAD	TRAIL/ROUTE	TRAILHEAD ELEVATION (FEET)	DESTINATION ELEVATION (FEET)	GAIN/LOSS ELEVATION (FEET)	RATING GRADE	CLASS	SNOW/ICE
Chiquita, Mt.	125	3.0	Chapin Pass TH	SW slope from Chapin–Chiquita saddle	11,020	13,069	2,049	I	2	
Chiquita, Mt.	125	6.0	Lawn Lake TH	E Ridge	8,540	13,069	4,529	II	2	
'Christmas Tree Mtn.'	258	1.4	Fish Creek TH	SW Slope	8,225	8,586	361	I	4+	
Cirque Lake	159	5.8	Emmaline Lake–Mummy Pass TH	Trail	8,960	10,940	1,980	–	–	
Cirque Meadows	160	3.5	Emmaline Lake–Mummy Pass TH	Trail	8,960	9,780	820	–	–	
Cirrus, Mt.	338	8.1	Colorado River TH (Red Mtn. Trail)	SW Ridge from 12,380' saddle	9,040	12,797	3,757	II	2	
Cirrus, Mt.	338	9.3	Colorado River TH (Red Mtn. Trail)	Hart Ridge from Lead Mtn. via Hitchens Gulch	9,040	12,797	3,757	II	2	
Cleaver, The	199	8.2	Wild Basin TH	SE Face from Boulder–Grand Pass	8,500	12,200+	3,700	II	3	
Cleaver, The	199	9.9	East Inlet TH	SE Face from Boulder–Grand Pass	8,400	12,200+	3,800	II	3	
Cleaver, The	199	8.6	Wild Basin TH	SE Face from Indigo Pond	8,500	12,200+	3,700	II	3	
Clouds, Lake of the	336	7.0	Colorado River TH (Red Mtn. Trail)	Trail	9,040	11,430	2,390	–	–	
Columbine Falls	223	3.9	Longs Peak TH	Trail	9,400	11,440	2,040	–	–	
Comanche Peak	162	7.2	Emmaline Lake– Mummy Pass TH	SE Face to NE Ridge from Emmaline Lake	8,960	12,702	3,742	II	2	
Comanche Peak	162	7.2	Corral Creek TH	W Slope from Mirror Lake Trail	10,020	12,702	2,682	II	2	
Cony Lake	209	9.2	Finch Lake TH	From Hutcheson Lakes	8,480	11,512	3,032	–	–	
Cony Pass	212	7.9	Wild Basin TH	N Slope from Junco Lake	8,500	12,420	3,920	II	3	
Cony Pass	212	10.0	Finch Lake TH	S Slope from Cony Lake	8,480	12,420	3,940	II	2	
Copeland Falls	184	0.3	Wild Basin TH	Trail	8,500	8,500	0	–	–	
Copeland, Mt.	203	7.0	Wild Basin TH	NE Slope via Ouzel Lake	8,500	13,176	4,676	II	2	
Copeland, Mt.	203	10.0	Wild Basin TH	E Ridge via Pear Lake	8,500	13,176	4,676	II	2	
Coyote Valley Trail	354	0.5	Coyote Valley TH	Loop Trail	8,820	8,840	20	–	–	
Cracktop	100	6.0	Poudre Lake TH at Milner Pass	SW Ridge from Mt. Ida	10,758	12,766	2,008	II	2+	
Cracktop	100	5.9	Poudre Lake TH at Milner Pass	Cracktop Couloir	10,758	12,766	2,008	III	5.0–5.6	SS
Crags, The	261	0.7	East Lily Lake Parking	W Slope to Base of Crags	8,920	10,831	1,911	I	2	
Craig, Mt.	281	8.5	East Inlet TH	SE Ridge from Lake Verna	8,400	12,007	3,607	II	3	
Craig, Mt.	281	6.4	East Inlet TH	Fourth Class Grass Route from Lone Pine Lake	8,400	12,007	3,607	II	3+	
Craig, Mt.	281	7.8	East Inlet TH	S Slope from Ten Lake Park	8,400	12,007	3,607	II	2	
Crater, The	350	0.8	Crater TH	Trail	10,740	11,460	720	–	–	
Crosier Mtn.	249	4.2	Garden Gate TH	Trail	6,420	9,250	2,830	I	2	
Crosier Mtn.	249	3.8	Crosier Mtn. Gravel Pit TH	Trail	6,950	9,250	2,300	I	2	
Crosier Mtn.	249	3.9	Glen Haven TH	Trail	7,240	9,250	2,010	I	2	
Crosier Mtn.	249	4.4	Sullivan Gulch	Trail	6,720	9,250	2,530	I	2	
Crystal Lake	133	7.9	Lawn Lake TH	Trail	8,540	11,500	2,960	–	–	
Crystal Lake, Little	133	7.7	Lawn Lake TH	Trail	8,540	11,500	2,960	–	–	

DESTINATION	PAGE	ONE-WAY DISTANCE (MILES)	TRAILHEAD	TRAIL/ROUTE	TRAILHEAD ELEVATION (FEET)	DESTINATION ELEVATION (FEET)	GAIN/LOSS ELEVATION (FEET)	RATING GRADE	RATING CLASS	RATING SNOW/ICE
Cub Creek Beaver Ponds	38	0.9	Cub Lake TH	Trail	8,080	8,120	40	—	—	—
Cub Lake	38	2.4	Cub Lake TH	Trail	8,080	8,620	540	—	—	—
Cumulus, Mt.	339	6.5	Colorado River TH (Red Mtn. Trail)	E Slope from Opposition Creek	9,040	12,725	3,685	II	2	2
Cumulus, Mt.	339	7.3	Colorado River TH (Red Mtn. Trail)	S Ridge from 12,060' saddle	9,040	12,725	3,685	II	2	2
Dark Mtn.	147	4.5	Cow Creek TH	SE Slope	7,820	10,859	3,039	I	2	2
Deer Mtn.	40	3.1	Deer Mtn./Deer Ridge TH	Trail	8,920	10,013	1,093	I	1	1
Deserted Village	152	3.0	Dunraven (North Fork) TH	Trail	7,900	8,180	280	—	—	—
Desolation Peaks	165	5.1	Chapin Pass TH	W Ridge from Chapin Pass	11,020	12,949	1,929	II	3	3+
Desolation Peaks	165	8.0	Poudre River TH	W Ridge from Cache la Poudre River	10,720	12,949	2,229	II	3	3+
Dickinson, Mt.	153	7.8	Dunraven (North Fork) TH	NE Slope from Happily Lost campsite	7,900	11,831	3,931	II	2	2
Dickinson, Mt.	153	14.8	Dunraven (North Fork) TH	W Ridge from Mt. Dunraven	7,900	11,831	3,931	II	2	2
Doughnut Lake	105	6.8	Poudre Lake TH at Milner Pass	From Mt. Ida–Chief Cheley Peak saddle	10,758	11,260	502*	—	—	—
Doughnut Lake	105	6.5	Poudre Lake TH at Milner Pass	From saddle SW of 'Jagor Point'	10,758	11,260	502*	—	—	—
Doughnut Lake	105	3.6	Rock Cut Parking Area	Forest Canyon Access	12,110	11,260	–850*	—	—	—
Doughnut Lake	105	8.4	Alpine Visitor Center	Forest Canyon Pass	11,796	11,260	–536*	—	—	—
Dragons Egg Rock	184	5.5	Sandbeach Lake TH	S Slope to N side of rock	8,340	12,200+	3,860	II	2	2
Dream Lake	73	1.1	Bear Lake TH	Trail	9,450	9,900	450	—	—	—
Dunraven, Lake	152	11.1	Dunraven (North Fork) TH	From Lost Lake	7,900	11,260	3,360	II	2	—
Dunraven, Mt.	153	12.5	Dunraven (North Fork) TH	NW Slope from Lake Dunraven	7,900	12,571	4,671	II	2	2
Dunraven, Mt.	153	10.1	Dunraven (North Fork) TH	E Ridge from Mt. Dickinson	7,900	12,571	4,671	II	2	2
Eagle Cliff Mtn.	39	0.5	Moraine Park Museum	NW Slope	8,120	8,906	786	I	1	—
Eagle Lake	197	7.2	Wild Basin TH	From Thunder Lake	8,500	10,820	2,320	—	—	—
Eagles Beak	199	8.3	Wild Basin TH	SW Face	8,500	12,200+	3,700	II	3	3+
'East Inlet Falls'	275	3.1	East Inlet TH	Trail	8,400	8,960	560	—	—	—
East Meadow	277	1.3	East Inlet TH	Trail	8,400	8,540	140	—	—	—
'Eleanor, Mt.'	100	9.5	Bear Lake TH	SE Ridge from Sprague Pass via Flattop Mtn.	9,450	12,360+	2,910	II	2	2
'Eleanor, Mt.'	100	7.5	Poudre Lake TH at Milner Pass	NW Ridge from Chief Cheley Peak	10,758	12,360+	1,602	II	2	2
'Electrode, The'	328	4.2	American Lakes (Michigan Lakes) TH	W Ridge from Static–'Electrode' saddle	9,780	12,018	2,238	I	1	—
'Electrode, The'	328	4.5	American Lakes (Michigan Lakes) TH	NE Ridge from Thunder Pass	9,780	12,018	2,238	I	1	2
Elk Tooth	210	9.2	Finch Lake TH	E Ridge from Hutcheson Lakes	8,480	12,848	4,368	II	3	3
Embryo Lake	63	3.7	Glacier Gorge TH	Bushwhack from jct. of Icy Brook and Andrews Creek	9,180	10,380	1,200	—	—	—
Emerald Lake	74	1.8	Bear Lake TH	Trail	9,450	10,100	650	—	—	—
Emerald Mtn.	255	0.8	East Portal TH	S Slope	8,260	9,237	977	I	1	—
Emmaline Lake	159	5.9	Emmaline Lake–Mummy Pass TH	From Cirque Lake	8,960	11,020	2,060	—	—	—
Enentah, Mt.	277	2.8	East Inlet TH	SW slope from meadow near Point 8,508'	8,500	10,781	2,281	II	2	2

* = absolute change only. This destination requires a considerable amount of elevation gain and elevation loss and is more strenuous than is indicated by the absolute change

DESTINATION	PAGE	ONE-WAY DISTANCE (MILES)	TRAILHEAD	TRAIL/ROUTE	TRAILHEAD ELEVATION (FEET)	DESTINATION ELEVATION (FEET)	GAIN/LOSS ELEVATION (FEET)	RATING GRADE	CLASS	SNOW/ICE
Estes Cone	262	5.2	Storm Pass Trail parking	Trail	8,820	11,006	2,186	I	2	
Estes Cone	262	6.1	East Portal TH	Trail	8,260	11,006	2,746	I	2	
Estes Cone	262	3.3	Longs Peak TH	Trail	9,400	11,006	1,606	I	2	
Estes Cone	262	3.4	Lily Lake Parking Area	Trail	8,940	11,006	2,066	I	2	
Estes Cone, Tour de	257	11.5	East Portal TH	Trail	8,260	10,260	2,000			MS
Estes, Lake	252	3.8	Multiple parking lots to access trail	Loop Trail	–	7,468	120			
Eugenia Mine	236	1.4	Longs Peak TH	Trail	9,400	9,908	508	–	–	
Eureka Ditch	94	6.8	Bear Lake TH	Via Flattop Mtn.	9,450	11,870	2,420	–	–	
Fairchild Mtn.	136	8.9	Lawn Lake TH	NE Slope	8,540	13,502	4,962	II	2	
Fairchild Mtn.	136	7.0	Lawn Lake TH	Hourglass Couloir, S Face from Fay Lakes	8,540	13,502	4,962	II	2	
Fairchild Mtn.	136	8.8	Lawn Lake TH	SE Ridge	8,540	13,502	4,962	II	2	
Falcon Lake	193	7.2	Wild Basin TH	From Thunder Lake	8,500	11,060	2,560	–	–	
Fall Mtn.	161	6.2	Emmaline Lake/Mummy Pass TH	E Ridge from Mummy Pass Trail	8,960	12,258	3,298	II	2	
Fall Mtn.	161	6.9	Corral Creek TH	S Slope from Mummy Pass	10,020	12,258	2,238	II	2	
Fall Mtn.	161	8.2	Corral Creek TH	NW Slope from Comanche Peak	10,020	12,258	2,238	II	2	
Fall River Pass	123	–	On Old Fall River Road At Alpine Visitor Center		11,796	11,796	0	–	–	
Fall River Pass	45	4.7	Poudre Lake TH at Milner Pass	Ute Trail to Alpine Visitor Center	10,758	11,796	1,038	I	1	
'Fall River Pass Mtn.'	123	0.3	Alpine Visitor Center	Alpine Ridge Trail	11,796	12,005	209	I	1	
Fan Falls	193	7.4	Wild Basin TH	From Thunder Lake, Route to base of falls	8,500	11,160	2,660	–	–	
Fan Falls	193	7.1	Wild Basin TH	From Thunder Lake, Route to top of falls	8,500	11,160	2,660	–	–	
Fan Lake (Historic)	129	0.1	West Alluvial Fan Parking Area	This lake no longer exists	8,580	8,560	-20	–	–	
Farview Mtn.	346	6.3	Bowen/Baker TH	N Slope from Farview–Parika saddle	8,850	12,246	3,396	II	1	
Farview Mtn.	346	6.5	Bowen/Baker TH	NW Slope via Summit Spur Trail	8,850	12,246	3,396	II	1	
Fay Lake (Lower)	134	5.3	Lawn Lake TH	From Ypsilon Lake	8,540	10,740	2,200	–	–	
Fay Lake (Middle)	134	5.8	Lawn Lake TH	From Ypsilon Lake	8,540	11,020	2,480	–	–	
Fay Lake (Upper)	134	6.1	Lawn Lake TH	From Ypsilon Lake	8,540	11,220	2,680	–	–	
Fern Falls	78	2.6	Fern Lake TH	Trail	8,150	8,800	650	–	–	
Fern Falls	79	3.8	Fern Lake TH	From Fourth Lake	8,150	9,540	1,390	–	–	
Fifth Lake	277	9.3	East Inlet TH	Trail	8,400	10,860	2,460	–	–	
Finch Lake	208	5.0	Finch Lake TH	Trail	8,480	9,912	1,432	–	–	
Flatiron Mtn.	165	6.1	Corral Creek TH	From Hazeline Lake	10,020	12,335	2,315	II	2	
Flatiron Mtn.	165	6.4	Chapin Pass TH	S Ridge from Desolation Peaks	11,020	12,335	1,315	II	2	
Flatiron Mtn.	165	7.4	Poudre River TH	W Slope from Cache la Poudre River	10,720	12,335	1,615	II	2	
Flattop Mtn.	75	4.4	Bear Lake TH	Flattop Mtn. Trail	9,450	12,324	2,874	II	1	
Flattop Mtn.	75	13.3	North Inlet TH	North Inlet Trail	8,500	12,324	3,824	II	1	
Flattop Mtn.	75	11.7	Green Mtn. TH	Green Mtn./Tonahutu Creek Trails	8,800	12,324	3,524	II	1	
'Fleur de Lis'	283	8.4	East Inlet TH	W Slope from East Inlet (W of Lake Verna)	8,400	12,250	3,850	II	3	

DESTINATION	PAGE	ONE-WAY DISTANCE (MILES)	TRAILHEAD	TRAIL/ROUTE	TRAILHEAD ELEVATION (FEET)	DESTINATION ELEVATION (FEET)	GAIN/LOSS ELEVATION (FEET)	RATING GRADE	CLASS	SNOW/ICE
'Fleur de Lis'	283	11.0	East Inlet TH	E Slope from Fifth Lake	8,400	12,250	3,850	II	–	2
Flint Pass	163	7.5	Emmaline Lake–Mummy Pass TH	Pingree Park Access from Mummy Pass	8,960	11,630	2,670	–	–	–
Flint Pass	163	6.2	Corral Creek TH	Corral Creek Access	10,020	11,630	1,610	–	–	–
Forest Canyon Pass	42	2.4	Poudre Lake TH at Milner Pass	Trail	10,758	11,320	562	–	–	–
Forest Canyon Pass	42	2.3	Alpine Visitor Center	Trail	11,796	11,320	–476	–	–	–
Forest Lake	97	1.7	Forest Canyon Overlook	Bushwhack	11,716	10,298	–1,418*	–	–	–
Fourth Lake	277	8.4	East Inlet TH	From North Boundary Trail	8,400	10,380	1,980	–	–	–
Fox Creek Falls	148	3.0	Cow Creek TH	From Thunder Lake	7,820	8,420	600	–	–	–
Frigid Lake	198	8.0	Wild Basin TH	From Thunder Lake	8,500	11,820	3,320	–	–	–
Frozen Lake	50	6.1	Glacier Gorge TH	From Black Lake	9,180	11,580	2,400	–	–	–
Gable, The	88	5.8	Fern Lake TH	N Slope from Spruce Lake	8,150	11,040+	2,890	I	–	2
Gabletop Mtn.	88	7.2	Bear Lake TH	SW Slope via Flattop Mtn.	9,450	11,939	2,489	I	–	2
Gabletop Mtn.	88	6.3	Fern Lake TH	SE Slope from Tourmaline Lake	8,150	11,939	3,789	I	–	2
Gash, The	66	4.8	Glacier Gorge TH	From Andrews Creek	9,180	11,540	2,360	–	–	–
Gem Lake	140	1.7	Lumpy Ridge TH	Trail	7,852	8,820	968	–	–	–
Gianttrack Mtn.	254	1.0	Marys Lake	S Slope (Private Access)	8,060	9,091	1,031	I	–	2
'Gibraltar Mtn.'	155	12.9	Dunraven (North Fork) TH	Icefield Pass Access	7,900	13,300	5,400	II	–	2
'Gibraltar Mtn.'	155	9.1	Stormy Peaks TH (Pingree Park)	Icefield Pass Access	9,020	13,300	4,280	II	–	2
Glacier Falls	47	2.3	Glacier Gorge TH	Trail/Off Trail	9,180	9,880	700	–	–	–
Glacier Knob, East	65	2.3	Glacier Gorge TH	W Slope from Loch Vale Trail	9,180	10,225	1,045	I	–	2
Glacier Knob, West	65	2.6	Glacier Gorge TH	S Slope from Loch Vale Trail	9,180	10,280+	1,100	I	–	2
Glass Lake ('Lake of Glass')	64	4.2	Glacier Gorge TH	Trail	9,180	10,820	1,640	–	–	–
Grace Falls	79	3.4	Bear Lake TH	From Fern-Odessa Trail	9,450	10,260	810*	–	–	–
Granite Falls	292	5.3	Green Mtn. TH	Trail	8,800	9,800	1,000	–	–	–
Granite Falls	292	10.8	Bear Lake TH	Trail	9,450	9,800	350*	–	–	–
Granite Pass	240	4.3	Longs Peak TH	East Longs Peak Trail	9,400	12,060	2,660	I	–	1
Granite Pass	240	6.9	Glacier Gorge TH	North Longs Peak Trail	9,180	12,060	2,880	I	–	1
Granite Pass	240	6.1	Storm Pass Trail parking	Boulder Brook/North Longs Peak Trails	8,820	12,060	3,240	I	–	1
Green Knoll	343	4.5	Holzwarth Historic Site (Never Summer Ranch)	SE Slope	8,900	12,280+	3,380	–	–	2
Green Knoll	343	6.4	Bowen/Baker TH	NW Ridge	8,850	12,280+	3,430	II	–	3
Green Lake	51	6.0	Glacier Gorge TH	From Black Lake	9,180	11,540	2,360	–	–	–
Green Mtn.	294	3.4	Green Mtn. TH	NE Slope from Big Meadows	8,800	10,313	1,513	I	–	2
Green Mtn.	294	1.7	Green Mtn. TH	NW Slope	8,800	10,313	1,513	I	–	2
Hagues Peak	137	9.4	Lawn Lake TH	SW Ridge from The Saddle	8,540	13,560	5,020	II	–	2
Hagues Peak	137	8.7	Lawn Lake TH	E Ridge	8,540	13,560	5,020	II	–	2
Haiyaha, Lake	71	2.1	Bear Lake TH	Trail	9,450	10,220	770	–	–	–

* = absolute change only. This destination requires a considerable amount of elevation gain and elevation loss and is more strenuous than is indicated by the absolute change.

DESTINATION	PAGE	ONE-WAY DISTANCE (MILES)	TRAILHEAD	TRAIL/ROUTE	TRAILHEAD ELEVATION (FEET)	DESTINATION ELEVATION (FEET)	GAIN/LOSS ELEVATION (FEET)	RATING GRADE	CLASS	SNOW/ICE
Haiyaha, Lake	71	3.3	Glacier Gorge TH	Trail	9,180	10,220	1,040	–	–	–
Half Mtn.	52	2.9	Glacier Gorge TH	N Slope from North Longs Peak Trail	9,180	11,482	2,302	I	2	–
Hallett Peak	76	5.1	Bear Lake TH	W Slope from Flattop Mtn.	9,450	12,713	3,263	II	2	–
Hallett Peak	76	3.3	Bear Lake TH	E Ridge, SE Gully, and E Slope	9,450	12,713	3,263	II	2	–
Hayden Lake	98	8.2	Poudre Lake TH at Milner Pass	Continental Divide Access via Mt. Ida	10,758	11,140	382*	–	–	–
Hayden Lake	98	9.6	Bear Lake TH	Continental Divide Access via Flattop Mtn. and Sprague Pass	9,450	11,140	1,690*	–	–	–
Hayden Lake	98	4.2	Ute Crossing	Hayden Gorge Access from Ute Crossing	11,440	11,140	–300*	–	–	–
Hayden Spire	99	9.4	Bear Lake TH	NE Ridge from Continental Divide	9,450	12,480+	3,030	II	5.6	
Hayden Spire	99	9.0	Green Mtn. TH	NE Ridge from Continental Divide	8,800	12,480+	3,680	II	5.6	
Hayden Spire	99	9.5	Bear Lake TH	SE Face and NE Ridge from Lonesome Lake	9,450	12,480+	3,030	II	5.4	
Hayden Spire	99	5.1	Ute Crossing	SE Face and NE Ridge from Lonesome Lake	11,440	12,480+	1,040*	II	5.4	
Haynach Lakes	293	8.7	Green Mtn. TH	Trail	8,800	11,060	2,260	–	–	
Haynach Lakes	293	10.3	Bear Lake TH	Trail	9,450	11,060	1,610*	–	–	
Hazeline Lake	163	5.0	Corral Creek TH	From Mummy Pass Trail	10,020	11,100	1,080	–	–	
Helene, Lake	81	3.2	Bear Lake TH	Trail	9,450	10,580	1,130	–	–	
Helene, Lake	81	5.7	Fern Lake TH	Trail	8,150	10,580	2,430	–	–	
Hiamovi Mtn.	317	6.4	Roaring Fork TH	SW Slope (from Hiamovi-Irving Hale saddle)	8,300	12,395	4,095	II	2	
'Hidden Falls'	185	0.4	Wild Basin TH	Bushwhack from Thunder Lake Trail (winter only)	8,500	8,920	420	–	–	
Hidden Valley Beaver Wetlands	42	0.1	Beaver Wetlands parking	Boardwalk	9,140	9,160	20	–	–	
Highest Lake	106	5.5	Poudre Lake TH at Milner Pass	From Mt. Ida–Chief Cheley Peak saddle	10,758	12,420	1,662*	–	–	
Highest Lake	106	5.6	Poudre Lake TH at Milner Pass	From saddle SW of 'Jagor Point'	10,758	12,420	1,662*	–	–	
Highest Lake	106	4.4	Rock Cut Parking Area	Forest Canyon Access	12,110	12,420	310*	–	–	
Highest Lake	106	9.6	Alpine Visitor Center	Forest Canyon Pass	11,796	12,420	624*	–	–	
Holzwarth Historic Site	353	0.5	Holzwarth Historic Site (Never Summer Ranch)	Trail	8,884	8,900	16	–	–	
Homer Rouse Trail	258	2.4	Fish Creek Trailhead	Trail to Lily Lake Visitor Center	8,233	8,960	727	–	–	
Homestead Meadows	251	2.8	Lion Gulch TH	Trail	7,360	8,660	1,300	–	–	
Horseshoe Falls	129	0.3	East Alluvial Fan Parking Area	Trail	8,580	8,900	320	–	–	
Horseshoe Park, Little	111	1.3	Deer Ridge Junction	Deer Ridge Trail System	8,920	8,660	–260	–	–	
Horsetooth Peak	179	2.8	'Horse Creek TH'	SW Ridge	8,700	10,344	1,644	I	2	
Hourglass Lake	91	9.1	Bear Lake TH	From ridge E of 'Sprague Tarn'	9,450	11,220	1,770	–	–	
Hourglass Lake	91	7.2	Fern Lake TH	From Spruce Canyon	8,150	11,220	3,070	–	–	
House Rock	263	0.2	USFS Parking Area on FR 119	W Slope	9,300	9,632	332	I	2	
Howard Mtn.	338	8.2	Colorado River TH (Red Mtn. Trail)	NW Ridge	9,040	12,810	3,770	II	2	

* = absolute change only. This destination requires a considerable amount of elevation gain and elevation loss and is more strenuous than is indicated by the absolute change

DESTINATION	PAGE	ONE-WAY DISTANCE (MILES)	TRAILHEAD	TRAIL/ROUTE	TRAILHEAD ELEVATION (FEET)	DESTINATION ELEVATION (FEET)	GAIN/LOSS ELEVATION (FEET)	RATING GRADE	RATING CLASS	RATING SNOW/ICE
Howard Mtn.	338	8.1	Colorado River TH (Red Mtn. Trail)	E Ridge	9,040	12,810	3,770	II	1	3
Husted, Lake	152	10.4	Dunraven (North Fork) TH	From Lost Lake	7,900	11,088	3,188	–	–	–
Hutcheson Lake (Lower)	209	7.8	Finch Lake TH	From Pear Lake	8,480	10,852	2,372	–	–	–
Hutcheson Lake (Middle)	209	8.0	Finch Lake TH	From Pear Lake	8,480	11,060	2,580	–	–	–
Hutcheson Lake (Upper)	209	8.6	Finch Lake TH	From Pear Lake	8,480	11,180	2,700	–	–	–
Iceberg Lake	42	0.2	Lava Cliffs Pullout	Descend from parking area	12,080	11,860	–220	–	–	–
Icefield Pass	154	11.6	Dunraven (North Fork) TH	Lake Louise Access	7,900	11,840	3,940	II	2	2
Icefield Pass	154	11.9	Dunraven (North Fork) TH	Stormy Peaks Access	7,900	11,840	3,940	II	2	2
Icefield Pass	154	7.9	Stormy Peaks TH (Pingree Park)	Stormy Peaks Access	9,020	11,840	2,820	II	2	2
Ida, Mt.	106	4.9	Poudre Lake TH at Milner Pass	N Ridge from Milner Pass	10,758	12,880+	2,122	I	2	2
Ida, Mt.	106	6.6	Timber Lake TH	W Slope from Timber Lake	9,060	12,880+	3,820	II	2	2
'Ikoko, Mt.'	162	6.7	Corral Creek TH	S Slope from Mirror Lake	10,020	12,232	2,212	II	2	2
Indigo Pond	198	7.5	Wild Basin TH	From Eagle Lake	8,500	11,180	2,680	–	–	–
Inkwell Lake	105	5.8	Poudre Lake TH at Milner Pass	From Mt. Ida–Chief Cheley Peak saddle	10,758	11,460	702*	–	–	–
Inkwell Lake	105	5.5	Poudre Lake TH at Milner Pass	From saddle SW of 'Jagor Point'	10,758	11,460	702*	–	–	–
Inkwell Lake	105	4.1	Rock Cut Parking Area	Forest Canyon Access	12,110	11,460	–650*	–	–	–
Inkwell Lake	105	8.8	Alpine Visitor Center	Forest Canyon Pass	11,796	11,460	–336*	–	–	–
Irene Lake	90	8.4	Bear Lake TH	From ridge E of 'Sprague Tarn'	9,450	11,860	2,410*	–	–	–
Irene Lake	90	7.5	Fern Lake TH	Rainbow Lake Access from Spruce Canyon	8,150	11,860	3,710	–	–	–
Irene, Lake	301	0.5	Lake Irene Picnic Area	Loop Trail	10,660	10,660	–60	–	–	–
Irving Hale, Mt.	318	5.5	Roaring Fork TH	N Ridge	8,300	11,754	3,454	II	2	2
Isolation Lake	202	7.8	Wild Basin TH	From Bluebird Lake	8,500	11,980	3,480	–	–	–
Isolation Peak	205	8.3	Wild Basin TH	E Slope from Isolation Lake	8,500	13,118	4,618	II	2	2
Isolation Peak	205	8.5	Wild Basin TH	S Ridge	8,500	13,118	4,618	II	2	2
Isolation Peak	205	11.4	East Inlet TH	W Ridge to SW Slope	8,400	13,118	4,718	II	2	2
'Italy Lake'	51	6.2	Glacier Gorge TH	From Black Lake	9,180	11,620	2,440	–	–	–
Jackstraw Mtn.	300	5.1	Timber Lake TH	SE Slope from 'Jackstraw Meadow'	9,060	11,704	2,644	II	2	2
'Jade, Pool of'	74	2.9	Bear Lake TH	From Emerald Lake	9,450	11,580	2,130	–	–	–
'Jagor Point'	106	5.1	Poudre Lake TH at Milner Pass	W Slope	10,758	12,632	1,874	I	1	2
'Jaws Falls'	37	1.1	Fern Lake TH	View from Fern Lake Trail (winter only)	8,150	9,000	850	–	–	–
Jewel Lake	49	3.1	Glacier Gorge TH	Trail	9,180	9,940	760	–	–	–
'Jiffy Pop Peak' a.k.a 'Cloudview Peak'	336	7.9	Colorado River TH (Red Mtn. Trail)	W Ridge from Hitchens Gulch (11,980' saddle)	9,040	12,438	3,398	II	2	2
'Jiffy Pop Peak' a.k.a 'Cloudview Peak'	336	8.2	Colorado River TH (Thunder Pass Trail)	W Ridge from Skeleton Gulch (11,980' saddle)	9,040	12,438	3,398	II	2	2
Jims Grove	240	2.8	Longs Peak TH	Trail	9,400	11,120	1,720	–	–	–

* = absolute change only. This destination requires a considerable amount of elevation gain and elevation loss and is more strenuous than is indicated by the absolute change

DESTINATION	PAGE	ONE-WAY DISTANCE (MILES)	TRAILHEAD	TRAILHEAD ELEVATION (FEET)	TRAIL/ROUTE	DESTINATION ELEVATION (FEET)	GAIN/LOSS ELEVATION (FEET)	RATING GRADE	CLASS	SNOW/ICE
Joe Mills Mtn.	82	2.9	Bear Lake TH	9,450	S Slope	11,078	1,628	I	2	–
Julian Lake	298	6.4	Timber Lake TH	9,060	Timber Lake Access	11,100	2,040	–	–	–
Julian Lake	298	5.9	Onahu Creek TH	8,780	Onahu Creek Access	11,100	2,320	–	–	–
Julian, Mt.	102	6.7	Poudre Lake TH at Milner Pass	10,758	SW Ridge	12,928	2,170	II	3	3
Julian, Mt.	102	4.0	Forest Canyon Overlook	11,716	NE Ridge via Terra Tomah Mtn.	12,928	1,212	II	3	3
Julian, Mt.	102	5.1	Ute Crossing	11,440	S Gully to NE Ridge	12,928	1,488	II	3	3
Junco Lake	203	7.2	Wild Basin TH	8,500	From Bluebird Lake	11,620	3,120	–	–	–
Keplinger Lake	182	7.2	Sandbeach Lake TH	8,340	North Ridge Access (Descend into Hunters Creek)	11,686	3,346	–	–	–
Keplinger Lake	182	6.5	Sandbeach Lake TH	8,340	Bushwhack up Hunters Creek	11,686	3,346	–	–	–
'Kettle Tarn'	149	5.3	Dunraven (North Fork) TH	7,900	From North Fork Trail	9,220	1,320	–	–	–
Keyboard of the Winds	61	6.8	Glacier Gorge TH	9,180	Via Pagoda–Keyboard Col	13,200+	4,020	II	3	3
Keyhole, The	241	6.3	Longs Peak TH	9,400	Via Boulder Field	13,160	3,760	II	2	2
Knobtop Mtn.	86	6.4	Bear Lake TH	9,450	SW Slope via Flattop Mtn	12,331	2,881	I	2	2
Kruger Rock	265	2.0	Hermit Park	8,420	Trail	9,355	935	I	2	2
La Poudre Pass	331	–	Never Summer TH near La Poudre Pass	10,175	Via Long Draw Road	10,175	0	–	–	–
La Poudre Pass	359	7.0	Colorado River TH (La Poudre Pass Trail)	9,040	Via Colorado River–La Poudre Pass Trail	10,175	1,135	–	–	–
Lady Washington, Mt.	227	4.2	Longs Peak TH	9,400	E Ridge	13,281	3,881	II	2	2
Lady Washington, Mt.	227	6.3	Longs Peak TH	9,400	W Slope	13,281	3,881	II	2	2
Lark Pond	202	7.0	Wild Basin TH	8,500	From Bluebird Lake	11,340	2,840	–	–	–
Lava Cliffs	43	0.3	Lava Cliffs Pullout	12,080	Descend to the base of the cliffs	12,000	–80	–	–	–
Lawn Lake	131	6.3	Lawn Lake TH	8,540	Lawn Lake Trail	10,987	2,447	–	–	–
Lawn Lake	131	9.6	Lumpy Ridge TH	7,852	Black Canyon Trail	10,987	3,135*	–	–	–
Lead Mtn.	334	8.0	Colorado River TH (Red Mtn. Trail)	9,040	E Ridge from Hitchens Gulch (11,980' saddle)	12,537	3,497	II	2	2
Lead Mtn.	334	8.2	Colorado River TH (Thunder Pass Trail)	9,040	E Ridge from Skeleton Gulch (11,980' saddle)	12,537	3,497	II	2	2
Lead Mtn.	334	8.5	Colorado River TH (Thunder Pass Trail)	9,040	N Ridge from Tepee–Lead saddle	12,537	3,497	II	4	4
'Lightning Peak'	256	2.3	East Portal TH	8,260	NW Ridge	10,567	2,307	II	2	2
Lily Lake	259	0.8	Lily Lake Parking Area	8,940	Loop Trail	8,927	–13	–	–	–
Lily Mtn.	259	1.8	Lily Mtn. TH	8,780	Trail	9,786	1,006	I	2	2
Lily Ridge Trail	261	0.8	Lily Lake Parking Area	8,940	Loop Trail	9,120	180	–	–	–
Lion Head	265	2.0	Pierson Park TH	9,060	SW Slope	9,740	680	I	2	2
Lion Lake No. 1	187	6.3	Wild Basin TH	8,500	Trail	11,080	2,580	–	–	–

* = absolute change only. This destination requires a considerable amount of elevation gain and elevation loss and is more strenuous than is indicated by the absolute change

DESTINATION	PAGE	ONE-WAY DISTANCE (MILES)	TRAILHEAD	TRAIL/ROUTE	TRAILHEAD ELEVATION (FEET)	DESTINATION ELEVATION (FEET)	GAIN/LOSS ELEVATION (FEET)	RATING GRADE	CLASS	SNOW/ICE
Lion Lake No. 2	188	6.9	Wild Basin TH	From Lion Lake No. 1	8,500	11,420	2,920	–	–	–
Little Matterhorn	87	4.2	Bear Lake TH	SW Ridge from Grace Falls	9,450	11,586	2,136	I	3	–
Little Matterhorn	87	7.0	Bear Lake TH	SW Ridge from Continental Divide	9,450	11,586	2,136	I	3	–
Little Matterhorn	87	6.2	Fern Lake TH	SW Ridge from Tourmaline Lake	8,150	11,586	3,436	I	3	–
Little Yellowstone	331	1.6	Never Summer TH near La Poudre Pass	La Poudre Pass Access	10,175	10,100	–75	I	1	–
Little Yellowstone	331	5.9	Colorado River Trailhead	Colorado River–La Poudre Pass Trail Access	9,040	10,100	1,060	I	1	–
Loch, The	62	2.9	Glacier Gorge TH	Trail	9,180	10,180	1,000	–	–	–
Loft, The	225	5.2	Longs Peak TH	The Loft Route from Chasm Lake	9,400	13,460	4,060	II	3	–
Lone Pine Lake	276	5.3	East Inlet TH	Trail	8,400	9,900	1,500	–	–	–
Lonesome Lake	99	9.2	Bear Lake TH	Sprague Mtn. Access	9,450	11,700	2,250*	–	–	–
Lonesome Lake	99	4.5	Ute Crossing	Hayden Gorge Access from Ute Crossing	11,440	11,700	260*	–	–	–
Long Meadows	298	5.5	Timber Lake TH	Trail	9,060	10,300	1,240	–	–	–
Long Meadows	298	4.5	Onahu Creek TH	Trail	8,780	10,300	1,520	–	–	–
Long Meadows	298	5.4	Green Mtn. TH	Trail	8,800	10,300	1,500	–	–	–
Longs Peak	229	7.4	Longs Peak TH	The Keyhole Route	9,400	14,259	4,859	III	3+	–
Longs Peak	229	5.9	Longs Peak TH	Clarks Arrow	9,400	14,259	4,859	III	4	–
Longs Peak	229	9.2	Storm Pass Trail parking	North Longs Peak Trail to The Keyhole Route	8,820	14,259	5,439	III	3+	–
Longs Peak	229	7.3	Glacier Gorge TH	The Trough	9,180	14,259	5,079	III	3+	MS
Longs Peak	229	7.7	Sandbeach Lake TH	Keplinger's Couloir	8,340	14,259	5,919	III	3	MS
Lookout Mtn.	179	3.2	'Horse Creek TH'	NW Slope	8,700	10,715	2,015	I	3	–
Lookout Springs	262	2.5	Twin Sisters TH	Faint trail from horse hitch rack at 10,620'	9,160	10,550	1,390	–	–	–
Loomis Lake	90	5.6	Fern Lake TH	From Spruce Lake	8,150	10,220	2,070	–	–	–
Lost Falls	150	7.5	Dunraven (North Fork) TH	Bushwhack from Lost Lake Trail	7,900	9,840	1,940	–	–	–
Lost Lake	150	9.7	Dunraven (North Fork) TH	Trail	7,900	10,714	2,814	–	–	–
Louise, Lake	152	10.9	Dunraven (North Fork) TH	From Lost Lake	7,900	11,020	3,120	–	–	–
Love Lake	105	6.6	Poudre Lake TH at Milner Pass	From N Slope of 'Jagor Point'	10,758	11,260	502*	–	–	–
Love Lake	105	7.4	Poudre Lake TH at Milner Pass	From Mt. Ida–Chief Cheley Peak saddle	10,758	11,260	502*	–	–	–
Love Lake	105	2.4	Rock Cut Parking Area	Forest Canyon Access	12,110	11,260	–850*	–	–	–
Love Lake	105	7.4	Alpine Visitor Center	Forest Canyon Pass	11,796	11,260	–536*	–	–	–
Lulu City	352	3.5	Colorado River TH	Trail	9,040	9,360	320	–	–	–
Lulu Mtn.	332	4.6	American Lakes (Michigan Lakes) TH	W Ridge (From Thunder Pass)	9,780	12,228	2,448	I	2	–
Lulu Mtn.	332	2.6	Never Summer TH near La Poudre Pass	NE Ridge (From Thunder Mtn.)	10,175	12,228	2,053	I	2	–
Lulu Mtn.	332	7.7	Colorado River TH (Thunder Pass Trail)	W Ridge (From Thunder Pass)	9,040	12,228	3,188	II	2	–
Lumpy Ridge Loop	141	10.7	Lumpy Ridge TH	Loop Trail	7,852	9,127	1,275*	–	–	–
Lyric Falls	181	4.0	Sandbeach Lake TH	Bushwhack up Hunters Creek	8,340	10,160	1,820	–	–	–

* = absolute change only. This destination requires a considerable amount of elevation gain and elevation loss and is more strenuous than is indicated by the absolute change

DESTINATION	PAGE	ONE-WAY DISTANCE (MILES)	TRAILHEAD	TRAIL/ROUTE	TRAILHEAD ELEVATION (FEET)	DESTINATION ELEVATION (FEET)	GAIN/LOSS ELEVATION (FEET)	RATING GRADE	CLASS	SNOW/ICE
'MacGregor Falls'	140	3.2	Lumpy Ridge TH	Trail/Off-trail meadow crossing	7,852	8,380	528*	–	–	
Mahana Peak	204	8.1	Wild Basin TH	W Slope from Isolation lake	8,500	12,632	4,132	II	2	
Mahana Peak	204	7.2	Wild Basin TH	E Ridge	8,500	12,632	4,132	II	2	ES
Many Winds, Lake of	193	7.5	Wild Basin TH	From Thunder Lake	8,500	11,620	3,120	–	–	
Marguerite Falls	78	3.9	Fern Lake TH	Bushwhack from Fern Lake	8,150	9,420	1,270	–	–	
Marigold Lake	81	3.9	Bear Lake TH	From Fern-Odessa Trail	9,450	10,220	770*	–	–	SS
Marigold Pond	82	3.1	Bear Lake TH	From Two Rivers Lake	9,450	10,580	1,130	–	–	
Marmot Point	123	0.4	Old Fall River Road (0.7 mi below Fall River Pass)	W Slope	11,560	11,909	349	I	2	
Marmot Point	123	1.1	Alpine Visitor Center	Walk down Fall River Road to access W Slope	11,796	11,909	113	I	2	
McGregor Mtn.	144	1.2	Fall River Visitor Center	SW Slope	8,180	10,486	2,306	I	2	
McHenrys Notch	57	7.8	Glacier Gorge TH	Via Andrews Glacier	9,180	12,820	3,640	II	2	
McHenrys Notch	57	8.5	Bear Lake TH	Via Flattop Mountain	9,450	12,820	3,370	II	2	
McHenrys Notch	57	15.3	Glacier Gorge TH	Loop via McHenrys Peak	9,180	12,820	3,640	II	5.3	
McHenrys Notch	57	6.0	Glacier Gorge TH	McHenrys Notch Couloir	9,180	12,820	3,640	II	2	
McHenrys Peak	56	7.1	Glacier Gorge TH	S Slope from Stone Man Pass	9,180	13,327	4,147	II	3	
McHenrys Peak	56	6.0	Glacier Gorge TH	Arrowhead Arête	9,180	13,327	4,147	II	4+	
Meadow Mtn.	214	3.7	St. Vrain Mtn. TH	S Slope	8,490	11,632	3,142	I	2	
Meeker, Mt.	234	4.3	Camp St. Malo	E Slope to E Ridge	8,660	13,911	5,251	II	3	
Meeker, Mt.	234	5.4	Longs Peak TH	Iron Gates	9,400	13,911	4,511	II	3	
Meeker, Mt.	234	5.1	Longs Peak TH	The Loft Route to NW Ridge	9,400	13,911	4,511	II	3	
Meeker, Mt.	234	5.0	'Horse Creek TH'	Meeker Ridge	8,700	13,911	5,211	II	3	
Meeker, Mt.	234	6.5	Sandbeach Lake TH	S Ridge	8,340	13,911	5,571	II	2	
Mertensia Falls	197	6.2	Wild Basin TH	From Thunder Lake Trail	8,500	10,360	1,860	–	–	
Michigan Lake (Lower)	326	3.3	American Lakes (Michigan Lakes) TH	Trail	10,250	11,208	958	–	–	
Michigan Lake (Middle)	326	3.5	American Lakes (Michigan Lakes) TH	Trail	10,250	11,210	960	–	–	
Mill Creek Basin	35	1.9	Hollowell Park TH	Trail from Hollowell Park	8,180	9,000	820	–	–	
Mill Creek Basin	35	4.4	Fern Lake TH	Trail From The Pool	8,150	9,000	850	–	–	
Mill Creek Basin	35	2.2	Bear Lake TH	Trail from Bear Lake	9,450	9,000	–450*	–	–	
Mills Glacier	241	4.8	Longs Peak TH	From Chasm Lake	9,400	12,300	2,900	–	–	
Mills Lake	49	2.7	Glacier Gorge TH	Trail	9,180	9,940	760	–	–	
Mineral Point	348	8.4	Bowen/Baker TH	W Ridge from Blue Lake	8,850	11,488	2,638	II	2	
Mirror Lake	160	5.8	Corral Creek TH	Trail	10,020	11,020	1,000	–	–	
Mirror Lake	160	10.2	Emmaline Lake/Mummy Pass TH	Trail	8,960	11,020	2,060	–	–	

* = absolute change only. This destination requires a considerable amount of elevation gain and elevation loss and is more strenuous than is indicated by the absolute change

DESTINATION	PAGE	ONE-WAY DISTANCE (MILES)	TRAILHEAD	TRAIL/ROUTE	TRAILHEAD ELEVATION (FEET)	DESTINATION ELEVATION (FEET)	GAIN/LOSS ELEVATION (FEET)	RATING GRADE	CLASS	SNOW/ICE
Moomaw Glacier	200	8.2	Wild Basin TH	From Thunder Lake	8,500	12,320	3,820	–	–	–
Moore Park	237	1.8	Longs Peak TH	Trail	9,400	9,760	360*	–	–	–
Mummy Mtn.	137	7.2	Lawn Lake TH	SE Slope	8,540	13,425	4,885	II	2	–
Mummy Mtn.	137	8.9	Lawn Lake TH	NW Slope	8,540	13,425	4,885	II	2	–
Mummy Pass	161	6.0	Corral Creek TH	Trail (Corral Creek Access)	10,020	11,260	1,240	I	1	–
Mummy Pass	161	6.8	Emmaline Lake/Mummy Pass TH	Trail (Pingree Park Access)	8,960	11,260	2,300	I	2	–
Murphy Lake	293	8.3	Bear Lake TH	From Tonahutu Creek Trail	9,450	11,220	1,770*	I	2	–
Murphy Lake	293	11.2	Green Mtn. TH	From Tonahutu Creek Trail	8,800	11,220	2,420	–	–	–
Nakai Peak	296	10.0	Green Mtn. TH	NE Ridge	8,800	12,216	3,416	II	2	2+
Nanita, Lake	287	11.1	North Inlet TH	Trail	8,500	10,780	2,280	–	–	–
Needles, The	143	3.2	Lumpy Ridge TH	S Gully to N Ridge	7,852	10,068	2,216*	I	1	2+
Needles, The	143	4.8	Lumpy Ridge TH	NW Slope	7,852	10,068	2,216*	I	1	2+
Neota, Mt.	332	1.4	Never Summer TH near La Poudre Pass	E Ridge (from La Poudre Pass)	10,175	11,734	1,559	I	2	–
Neota, Mt.	332	8.9	Colorado River Trailhead	NW Ridge (from Thunder Mtn.)	9,040	11,734	2,694	II	2	–
Neota, Mt.	332	5.8	American Lakes (Michigan Lakes) TH	NW Ridge (from Thunder Mtn.)	9,780	11,734	1,954	I	2	–
Nimbus, Mt.	342	6.8	Bowen/Baker TH	W Slope from Baker Pass	8,850	12,706	3,856	II	2	–
Nimbus, Mt.	342	7.1	Colorado River TH (Red Mtn. Trail)	E Ridge from Opposition Creek	9,040	12,706	3,666	II	2	–
Nimbus, Mt.	342	7.3	Colorado River TH (Red Mtn. Trail)	N Ridge from Cumulus–Nimbus saddle	9,040	12,706	3,666	II	2	–
Nimbus, Mt.	342	7.1	Holzwarth Historic Site (Never Summer Ranch)	E Ridge from Red Gulch	8,884	12,706	3,822	II	2	–
Nisa Mtn.	294	4.2	Green Mtn. TH	NW Slope	8,800	10,788	1,988	I	2	–
'No Name, Little'	155	8.3	Stormy Peaks TH (Pingree Park)	Via Icefield Pass	9,020	12,530	3,510	II	2	–
'No Name, Little'	155	12.1	Dunraven (North Fork) TH	Via Icefield Pass	7,900	12,530	4,630	II	2	–
'No Name, Middle'	155	8.6	Stormy Peaks TH (Pingree Park)	Via Icefield Pass	9,020	12,760+	3,740	II	2	–
'No Name, Middle'	155	12.5	Dunraven (North Fork) TH	Via Icefield Pass	7,900	12,760+	4,860	II	2	–
Nokhu Crags (N Summit)	329	2.4	Lake Agnes TH	N Ridge and W Face	10,250	12,485	2,235	I	4	–
Nokhu Crags (S Summit)	329	3.1	Lake Agnes TH	E Face 'Nokhuloir'	10,250	12,480+	2,230	I	3	MS
Nokoni, Lake	287	10.3	North Inlet TH	Trail	8,500	10,780	2,280	–	–	–
'North Inlet Falls'	287	7.8	North Inlet TH	Trail	8,500	9,480	980	–	–	–
Notchtop Mtn.	84	6.1	Bear Lake TH	Continental Divide to NW Ridge	9,450	12,160+	2,710	I	4	–
Notchtop Mtn.	84	4.3	Bear Lake TH	SE Gully to NW Ridge	9,450	12,160+	2,710	I	4	–
Nymph Lake	73	0.6	Bear Lake TH	Trail	9,450	9,700	250	–	–	–
Odessa Lake	80	4.8	Fern Lake TH	Trail	8,150	10,020	1,870	–	–	–
Odessa Lake	80	3.9	Bear Lake TH	Trail	9,450	10,020	570*	–	–	–
Ogalalla Peak	212	9.3	Wild Basin TH	N Ridge from Ouzel Peak	8,500	13,138	4,638	II	2	–
Ogalalla Peak	212	9.9	Wild Basin TH	E Ridge from Elk Tooth	8,500	13,138	4,638	II	4	–

* = absolute change only. This destination requires a considerable amount of elevation gain and elevation loss and is more strenuous than is indicated by the absolute change

DESTINATION	PAGE	ONE-WAY DISTANCE (MILES)	TRAILHEAD	TRAILHEAD ELEVATION (FEET)	TRAIL/ROUTE	DESTINATION ELEVATION (FEET)	GAIN/LOSS ELEVATION (FEET)	GRADE	CLASS	SNOW/ICE
Ogalalla Peak	212	8.7	Wild Basin TH	8,500	N Ridge from Cony Pass via Junco Lake	13,138	4,638	II	4	
Oldman Mtn.	252	0.3	Old Ranger Drive	7,800	SW Slope	8,310	510	I	2+	
Olympus, Mt.	253	0.7	US 34	7,370	NW Slope	8,808	1,438	I	2	
Orton, Mt.	183	5.7	Sandbeach Lake TH	8,340	SE Slope	11,724	3,384	II	2	
Otis Peak	71	5.6	Glacier Gorge TH	9,180	W Slope from Andrews Pass	12,486	3,306	II	2	
Otis Peak	71	6.0	Bear Lake TH	9,450	W Slope from Flattop Mtn.	12,486	3,036	II	2	
Otis Peak	71	3.8	Bear Lake TH	9,450	NE Slope from Lake Haiyaha	12,486	3,036	II	2	
Ouzel Falls	185	2.7	Wild Basin TH	8,500	Trail	9,460	960	–	–	
Ouzel Lake	200	5.0	Wild Basin TH	8,500	Trail	10,020	1,520	–	–	
Ouzel Peak	206	7.8	Wild Basin TH	8,500	SE Slope to S. Ridge from Junco Lake	12,716	4,216	II	2	
Ouzel Peak	206	7.9	Wild Basin TH	8,500	N Slope from Pipit Lake	12,716	4,216	II	2	
Ouzel Peak	206	9.0	Wild Basin TH	8,500	W Ridge from Continental Divide	12,716	4,216	II	2	
Pagoda Mtn.	60	6.8	Glacier Gorge TH	9,180	Pagoda–Keyboard Col to NE Ridge	13,497	4,317	II	3	
Pagoda Mtn.	60	7.6	Sandbeach Lake TH	8,340	SE Gully to NE ridge	13,497	5,157	II	2	
'Paprika Peak'	346	5.8	Bowen/Baker TH	8,850	S Slope from Parika Lake	12,253	3,403	II	2	
'Paprika Peak'	346	6.3	Bowen/Baker TH	8,850	W Ridge from Parika Lake	12,253	3,403	II	2	
Paradise Park	284	7.7	Roaring Fork TH	8,300	From Adams Lake	10,500	2,200*	–	–	
Paradise Park	284	7.7	East Inlet TH	8,400	From East Inlet	10,500	2,100	–	–	
Parika Lake	344	5.4	Bowen/Baker TH	8,850	Trail	11,380	2,530	–	–	
Parika Peak	346	6.5	Bowen/Baker TH	8,850	S Slope from Farview–Parika saddle	12,394	3,544	II	1	
Parika Peak	346	6.3	Bowen/Baker TH	8,850	E Ridge from Parika Lake	12,394	3,544	II	2	
Patterson, Mt.	294	3.7	Green Mtn. TH	8,800	W Slope to NW Ridge	11,424	2,624	I	2	
'Paul Bunyan's Boot'	144	1.4	Lumpy Ridge TH	7,852	Trail	8,560+	708	–	–	
Peacock Pool	223	3.9	Longs Peak TH	9,400	From Chasm Lake Trail	11,300	1,900	–	–	
Pear Lake	208	7.0	Finch Lake TH	8,480	Trail	10,582	2,102	–	–	
Pettingell Lake	286	11.1	North Inlet TH	8,500	From Lake Nokoni	10,500	2,000	–	–	
Pierson Mtn.	264	1.5	Pierson Park TH	9,060	SW Slope	9,803	743	I	2	
Pilot Mtn.	189	7.6	Wild Basin TH	8,500	NE Face and NW Ridge, Lion Lakes Access	12,200+	3,700	II	4	
Pilot Mtn.	189	7.6	Wild Basin TH	8,500	NE Face and NW Ridge, Thunder Lake Access	12,200+	3,700	II	4	
Pilot Mtn.	189	9.4	Wild Basin TH	8,500	NE Face and NW Ridge, Boulder–Grand Pass Access	12,200+	3,700	II	4	
Pinnacle Pool	339	5.7	Colorado River TH (Red Mtn. Trail)	9,040	Via Mosquito Creek	11,300	2,260	–	–	
Pipit Lake	202	7.2	Wild Basin TH	8,500	From Bluebird Lake	11,420	2,920	–	–	
Pisgah, Mt.	254	0.4	Pole Hill Road off US 36	8,380	SE Slope (No Legal Public Access)	8,630	250	I	2	
Pool, The	37	1.7	Fern Lake TH	8,150	Trail	8,300	150	–	–	
Potts Puddle	130	6.5	Lawn Lake TH	8,540	From Tileston Meadows	10,900	2,360	–	–	
Poudre Lake	42	–	Poudre Lake TH at Milner Pass	10,758	On Road	10,758	0	–	–	

* = absolute change only. This destination requires a considerable amount of elevation gain and elevation loss and is more strenuous than is indicated by the absolute change.

DESTINATION	PAGE	ONE-WAY DISTANCE (MILES)	TRAILHEAD	TRAIL/ROUTE	TRAILHEAD ELEVATION (FEET)	DESTINATION ELEVATION (FEET)	GAIN/LOSS ELEVATION (FEET)	RATING GRADE	CLASS	SNOW/ICE
'Poudre Lake Spires'	302	0.1	Poudre Lake TH at Milner Pass	Trail	10,758	10,800	42	—	—	—
Powell Peak	68	7.5	Glacier Gorge TH	W Slope via Andrews Glacier	9,180	13,208	4,028	II	2	—
Powell Peak	68	8.2	Bear Lake TH	W Slope via Flattop Mtn.	9,450	13,208	3,758	II	2	—
Powell Peak	68	5.6	Glacier Gorge TH	Powell Couloir	9,180	13,208	4,028	II	2	SS
Powell Peak	68	4.8	Glacier Gorge TH	Thatchtop-Powell Ridge	9,180	13,208	4,028	II	5.2	—
Powell, Lake	289	9.1	Wild Basin TH	Via Mt. Alice–Chiefs Head Peak saddle	8,500	11,540	3,040	—	—	—
Powell, Lake	289	12.2	North Inlet TH	Long Bushwhack up North Inlet (from Lake Solitude)	8,500	11,540	3,040	—	—	—
'Primrose Pond'	90	5.4	Fern Lake TH	From Spruce Lake	8,150	10,140	1,990	—	—	—
Prospect Mtn.	254	1.8	Thumb and Needle parking	Hike up service road	8,160	8,900	740	I	2	—
'Ptarmigan Glacier'	83	4.2	Bear Lake TH	Via Lake Helene to base of snowfield	9,450	11,900	2,450	I	2	MS
Ptarmigan Lake	291	5.9	Bear Lake TH	Bighorn Flats Access	9,450	11,460	2,010*	—	—	—
Ptarmigan Lake	291	9.4	North Inlet TH	Ptarmigan Creek Access	8,500	11,460	2,960	—	—	—
Ptarmigan Mtn.	280	11.6	North Inlet TH	NW Ridge	8,500	12,324	3,824	II	2	—
Ptarmigan Mtn.	280	7.6	East Inlet TH	S Slope from Lone Pine Lake	8,500	12,324	3,824	II	2	—
Ptarmigan Pass	83	5.1	East Inlet TH	Trail	9,450	12,180	2,730	I	1	—
Ptarmigan Pass	83	4.5	Bear Lake TH	Up 'Ptarmigan Glacier' via Lake Helene	9,450	12,180	2,730	I	1	—
Ptarmigan Point	83	5.3	Bear Lake TH	Tonahutu Creek Trail Access from Flattop Mtn.	9,450	12,363	2,913	I	1	—
'Ptarmigans Beak'	281	8.0	East Inlet TH	W Slope from Lake Verna	8,400	12,241	3,841	II	2	—
'Ptarmigans Beak'	281	9.2	East Inlet TH	W Slope from Andrews Peak	8,400	12,241	3,841	II	2	—
'Rabbit Ears'	147	1.5	Cow Creek TH	Trail	7,820	8,290	470	—	3	—
Rainbow Lake	90	8.5	Bear Lake TH	From ridge E of 'Sprague Tarn'	9,450	11,740	2,290	II	3	—
Rainbow Lake	90	7.5	Fern Lake TH	Spruce Canyon Access	8,150	11,740	3,590	—	—	—
Rams Horn Mtn.	260	2.9	Lily Mtn. TH	S Ridge from Lily Mtn.	8,780	9,553	773	I	2	—
Ramsey Peak	157	6.0	Stormy Peaks TH (Pingree Park)	S Slope from Sugarloaf Mtn.	9,020	11,582	2,562	II	2	—
Ramsey Peak	157	11.4	Dunraven (North Fork) TH	S Slope from Sugarloaf Mtn.	7,900	11,582	3,682	II	2	—
Ramsey Peak	157	4.3	Stormy Peaks TH (Pingree Park)	NE Slope	9,020	11,582	2,562	II	2	—
Raspberry Park	97	4.1	Fern Lake TH	From Black Pool	8,150	9,000	850*	—	—	—
Red Mtn.	340	6.1	Holzwarth Historic Site (Never Summer Ranch)	W Ridge from Red Gulch (11,380' saddle)	8,884	11,605	2,721	II	2	—
Red Mtn.	340	6.2	Colorado River TH (Red Mtn. Trail)	E Slope	9,040	11,605	2,565	II	2	—
Red Mtn.	340	6.2	Colorado River TH (Red Mtn. Trail)	W Ridge from Opposition Creek (11,380' saddle)	9,040	11,605	2,565	II	2	—
Ribbon Falls	47	4.8	Glacier Gorge TH	Trail	9,180	10,580	1,400	—	—	—
Richthofen, Mt.	333	2.1	Lake Agnes TH	W Ridge from 11,980' saddle	10,250	12,940	2,690	I	1	—
Richthofen, Mt.	333	7.8	Colorado River TH (Thunder Pass Trail)	E Ridge from Skeleton Gulch	9,040	12,940	3,900	II	2	—
River Trail	354	2.1	Harbison Picnic Area	Trail	8,708	8,800	92	—	—	—
'Roaring Peak'	316	5.9	Roaring Fork TH	E Ridge	8,300	11,721	3,421	II	2	—

* = absolute change only. This destination requires a considerable amount of elevation gain and elevation loss and is more strenuous than is indicated by the absolute change

DESTINATION	PAGE	ONE-WAY DISTANCE (MILES)	TRAILHEAD	TRAIL/ROUTE	TRAILHEAD ELEVATION (FEET)	DESTINATION ELEVATION (FEET)	GAIN/LOSS ELEVATION (FEET)	RATING GRADE	CLASS	SNOW/ICE
Rock Lake	104	7.0	Poudre Lake TH at Milner Pass	From saddle SW of 'Jagor Point'	10,758	10,300	-458*	–	–	–
Rock Lake	104	7.8	Poudre Lake TH at Milner Pass	From Mt. Ida-Chief Cheley Peak saddle	10,758	10,300	-458*	–	–	–
Rock Lake	104	2.3	Rock Cut Parking Area	Forest Canyon Access	12,110	10,300	-1,810*	–	–	–
Rock Lake	104	7.7	Alpine Visitor Center	Forest Canyon Pass	11,796	10,300	-1,496*	–	–	–
Rock Lake, Little	104	6.9	Poudre Lake TH at Milner Pass	From saddle SW of 'Jagor Point'	10,758	10,300	-458*	–	–	–
Rock Lake, Little	104	7.9	Poudre Lake TH at Milner Pass	From Mt. Ida-Chief Cheley Peak saddle	10,758	10,300	-458*	–	–	–
Rock Lake, Little	104	2.2	Rock Cut Parking Area	Forest Canyon Access	12,110	10,300	-1,810*	–	–	–
Rock Lake, Little	104	7.8	Alpine Visitor Center	Forest Canyon Pass	11,796	10,300	-1,496*	–	–	–
Round Pond	81	2.4	Bear Lake TH	From Fern-Odessa Trail	9,450	10,340	890	–	–	–
Rowe Glacier/ 'Rowe Glacier Lake'	156	8.8	Lawn Lake TH	Hagues Peak Access	8,540	13,200	4,660	II	2	
Rowe Glacier/ 'Rowe Glacier Lake'	156	13.1	Dunraven (North Fork) TH	From Lake Dunraven	7,900	13,200	5,300	II	2	
Rowe Glacier/ 'Rowe Glacier Lake'	156	10.0	Stormy Peaks TH (Pingree Park)	Icefield Pass Access	9,020	13,200	4,180	II	2	
Rowe Mtn.	154	9.6	Lawn Lake TH	Hagues Peak Access	8,540	13,184	4,644	II	2	
Rowe Mtn.	154	12.9	Dunraven (North Fork) TH	Icefield Pass Access	7,900	13,184	5,284	II	2	
Rowe Mtn.	154	9.3	Stormy Peaks TH (Pingree Park)	Icefield Pass Access	9,020	13,184	4,164	II	2	
Rowe Peak	155	9.1	Lawn Lake TH	Hagues Peak Access	8,540	13,400+	4,860	II	2	
Rowe Peak	155	13.4	Dunraven (North Fork) TH	Icefield Pass Access	7,900	13,400+	5,500	II	2	
Rowe Peak	155	9.7	Stormy Peaks TH (Pingree Park)	Icefield Pass Access	9,020	13,400+	4,380	II	2	
Saddle, The	136	8.6	Lawn Lake TH	Trail	8,540	12,398	3,858	–	–	
Sandbeach Lake	181	4.2	Sandbeach Lake TH	Trail	8,340	10,283	1,943	–	–	
'Scotch Lake'	152	11.7	Dunraven (North Fork) TH	From Lake Dunraven	7,900	11,620	3,720	–	–	
Shadow Mtn.	314	5.6	East Shore TH	NW Ridge from Shadow Mtn. Lookout	8,420	10,155	1,735	I	2	
Shadow Mtn. Lookout	314	5.4	East Shore TH	Trail	8,420	9,923	1,503	I	1	
Sharkstooth, The	66	5.2	Glacier Gorge TH	Technical (no hiking access)	9,180	12,630	3,450	II		5.4
Sheep Lakes	129	0	Sheep Lakes parking on US 34	View from road	8,560	8,508	-52	–	–	
Sheep Mtn.	146	2.2	Cow Creek TH	E Slope	7,820	9,794	1,974	I	2	
Sheep Mtn.	146	2.1	Cow Creek TH	SE Slope	7,820	9,794	1,974	I	2	
Sheep Mtn./ Round Mtn.	250	4.7	Round Mtn. TH	Trail	5,743	8,450	2,707	I	1	
Sheep Rock	302	0.5	Poudre Lake TH at Milner Pass	E Slope	10,758	10,920+	162	I	2	
Shelf Lake	51	4.7	Glacier Gorge TH	Follow Shelf Creek	9,180	11,220	2,040	–	–	
Shipler Mtn.	351	2.8	Crater TH	SE Ridge from The Crater	10,740	11,320+	580	1	2	
Shipler Park Cabins	352	1.8	Colorado River TH	Trail	9,040	9,140	100	–	–	
Ships Prow	224	5.2	Longs Peak TH	'Ships Prow Tower' via The Loft Route	9,400	13,320+	3,920	II		5.4
Ships Prow	224	4.9	Longs Peak TH	'Ships Prow Buttress' via SE Gully	9,400	12,000	2,600	II		3+

* = absolute change only. This destination requires a considerable amount of elevation gain and elevation loss and is more strenuous than is indicated by the absolute change

DESTINATION	PAGE	ONE-WAY DISTANCE (MILES)	TRAILHEAD	TRAIL/ROUTE	TRAILHEAD ELEVATION (FEET)	DESTINATION ELEVATION (FEET)	GAIN/LOSS ELEVATION (FEET)	RATING GRADE	CLASS	SNOW/ICE
Signal Mtn.	159	6.0	Dunraven (North Fork) TH	SW Slope	7,900	11,262	3,362		II	2
Signal Mtn., South	159	5.6	Dunraven (North Fork) TH	SE Slope	7,900	11,248	3,348		II	2
Skull Point	157	11.5	Dunraven (North Fork) TH	From Stormy Peaks Pass	7,900	12,040+	4,140		II	2
Skull Point	157	7.5	Stormy Peaks TH (Pingree Park)	From Stormy Peaks Pass	9,020	12,040+	3,020		II	2
Sky Pond	64	4.4	Glacier Gorge TH	Trail	9,180	10,900	1,720		–	–
Snow Lake	328	3.9	American Lakes (Michigan Lakes) TH	Trail	9,780	11,516	1,736		–	–
Snowbank Lake	188	7.1	Wild Basin TH	From Lion Lakes	8,500	11,521	3,021		–	–
Snowdrift Lake	291	7.6	Bear Lake TH	Bighorn Flats Access	9,450	11,060	1,610*		–	–
Snowdrift Lake	291	8.9	North Inlet TH	Ptarmigan Creek Access	8,500	11,060	2,560		–	–
Snowdrift Peak	296	8.3	Bear Lake TH	NE Ridge via Flattop Mtn.	9,450	12,274	2,824		II	2
Snowdrift Peak	296	11.2	Green Mtn. TH	NE Ridge via Tonahutu Creek Trail	8,800	12,274	3,474		II	2
Snowdrift Peak	296	10.4	North Inlet TH	Ptarmigan Creek Access	8,500	12,274	3,774		II	2
Solitude Lake	51	5.0	Glacier Gorge TH	Follow Shelf Creek	9,180	11,420	2,240		–	–
Solitude, Lake	287	9.0	North Inlet TH	North Inlet via Lake Nanita Trail	8,500	9,740	1,240		I	2
South Lateral Moraine	36	0.3	Hollowell Park TH	S Slope	8,180	8,720	540		I	–
Spearhead, The	58	6.6	Glacier Gorge TH	NW Slope via Frozen Lake	9,180	12,575	3,395		II	4
Spearhead, The	58	6.6	Glacier Gorge TH	E Gully via Green Lake	9,180	12,575	3,395		II	4
Specimen Mtn.	351	1.9	Crater TH	Trail (no legal public access)	10,740	12,489	1,749		I	2
Specimen Mtn.	351	3.2	Poudre River TH	N Slope (no legal public access)	10,720	12,489	1,769		I	2
'Specimen Mtn., North'	351	2.8	Poudre River TH	S Slope (no legal public access)	10,720	12,307	1,587		I	2
'Specimen Mtn., South'	351	1.9	Crater TH	Trail (no legal public access)	10,740	12,269	1,529		I	2
Spectacle Lake (Lower)	134	5.3	Lawn Lake TH	From Ypsilon Lake	8,540	11,340	2,800		–	–
Spectacle Lake (Upper)	134	5.7	Lawn Lake TH	From Ypsilon Lake	8,540	11,340	2,800		–	–
Spirit Lake	276	7.8	East Inlet TH	Trail	8,400	10,300	1,900		–	–
Sprague Glacier	92	8.4	Bear Lake TH	From ridge E of 'Sprague Tarn'	9,450	12,100	2,650		–	–
Sprague Glacier	92	7.8	Fern Lake TH	Rainbow Lake Access from Spruce Canyon	8,150	12,100	3,950		–	–
Sprague Lake	33	0.5	Sprague Lake	Loop Trail	8,700	8,700	0		–	–
Sprague Mtn.	93	8.7	Bear Lake TH	SE Ridge from Sprague Pass via Flattop Mtn.	9,450	12,713	3,263		II	2
Sprague Mtn.	93	8.7	Fern Lake TH	SE Ridge from Sprague Pass via Spruce Canyon	8,150	12,713	4,563		II	2
Sprague Mtn.	93	9.0	Green Mtn. TH	S Slope via Tonahutu Creek Trail	8,800	12,713	3,913		II	2
Sprague Pass	93	7.6	Fern Lake TH	Spruce Canyon Access from Spuce Lake	8,150	11,708	3,558		II	2
Sprague Pass	93	7.5	Bear Lake TH	From Flattop Mtn.	9,450	11,708	2,258		II	2

DESTINATION	PAGE	ONE-WAY DISTANCE (MILES)	TRAILHEAD	TRAIL/ROUTE	TRAILHEAD ELEVATION (FEET)	DESTINATION ELEVATION (FEET)	GAIN/LOSS ELEVATION (FEET)	RATING GRADE	CLASS	SNOW/ICE
'Sprague Tarn'	92	8.3	Bear Lake TH	From ridge E of 'Sprague Tarn'	9,450	11,860	2,410	—	—	
'Sprague Tarn'	92	7.7	Fern Lake TH	Rainbow Lake Access from Spruce Canyon	8,150	11,860	3,710	—	—	
Spruce Lake	89	4.8	Fern Lake TH	Trail	8,150	9,660	1,510	—	—	
St. Vrain Mtn.	214	4.8	St. Vrain Mtn. TH	E Slope	8,490	12,162	3,672	II	2	
Static Peak	330	4.6	American Lakes (Michigan Lakes) TH	E Ridge from Snow Lake	9,780	12,560	2,780	I	3	
Static Peak	330	8.4	Colorado River TH	S Ridge from Mt. Richthofen	9,040	12,560	3,520	II	2	
Steep Mtn.	36	1.2	Hollowell Park TH	E Slope	8,180	9,538	1,358	I	2	
Stone Man Pass	56	6.7	Glacier Gorge TH	NE Slope via Black Lake	9,180	12,500	3,320	II	2	
Stones Peak	94	9.8	Bear Lake TH	SW Ridge from Sprague Mtn.	9,450	12,922	3,472	II	2	
Stones Peak	94	8.2	Fern Lake TH	Hourglass Lake Access	8,150	12,922	4,772	II	2	
Stones Peak	94	7.8	Fern Lake TH	Spruce Canyon Access from SE Ridge of Point 12,736'	8,150	12,922	4,772	II	2	
Storm Pass	255	4.5	Storm Pass Trail parking	Trail	8,820	10,260	1,440	I	1	
Storm Pass	255	5.5	East Portal TH	Trail	8,260	10,260	2,000	I	1	
Storm Pass	255	2.6	Longs Peak TH	Trail	9,400	10,260	860*	I	1	
Storm Pass	255	2.8	Lily Lake Parking Area	Trail	8,940	10,260	1,320	I	1	
Storm Peak	227	6.3	Longs Peak TH	E Slope from the Boulder Field	9,400	13,326	3,926	II	2	
Storm Peak	227	5.5	Glacier Gorge TH	N Slope to N Ridge	9,180	13,326	4,146	II	2	
Stormy Peaks	156	9.5	Dunraven (North Fork) TH	S Slope from Stormy Peaks Pass	7,900	12,148	4,248	II	2	
Stormy Peaks	156	5.5	Stormy Peaks TH (Pingree Park)	S Slope from Stormy Peaks Pass	9,020	12,148	3,128	II	2	
Stormy Peaks Pass	156	9.1	Dunraven (North Fork) TH	Trail	7,900	11,660	3,760	I	2	
Stormy Peaks Pass	156	5.2	Stormy Peaks TH (Pingree Park)	Trail	9,020	11,660	2,640	I	2	
Stratus, Mt.	343	7.6	Colorado River TH	N Ridge from Mt. Nimbus	9,040	12,520	3,480	II	2	
Stratus, Mt.	343	5.0	Holzwarth Historic Site (Never Summer Ranch)	SE Ridge from Green Knoll	8,884	12,520	3,636	II	3	
Stratus, Mt.	343	5.9	Bowen/Baker TH	W Slope	8,850	12,520	3,670	II	2	
Sugarloaf Mtn.	157	10.7	Dunraven (North Fork) TH	E Slope from Stormy Peaks Pass	7,900	12,120	4,220	II	2	
Sugarloaf Mtn.	157	5.3	Stormy Peaks TH (Pingree Park)	N Slope to E Slope from Stormy Peaks Trail	9,020	12,120	3,100	II	2	
Sugarloaf Mtn.	157	6.8	Stormy Peaks TH (Pingree Park)	E Slope from Stormy Peaks Pass	9,020	12,120	3,100	II	2	
Summerland Park	289	1.3	North Inlet TH	Trail	8,500	8,520	20	—		
Sundance Mtn.	44	0.3	Trail Ridge Road (pullout S of summit)	S Slope	11,900	12,466	566	I	2	
Sundance Mtn.	44	1.8	Ute Crossing	SE Slope	11,440	12,466	1,026	I	2	
Tanima Peak	195	8.4	Wild Basin TH	W Ridge from Boulder–Grand Pass	8,500	12,420	3,920	II	2	
Tanima Peak	195	7.4	Wild Basin TH	E Ridge from Thunder Lake	8,500	12,420	3,920	II	3	
Taylor Glacier	67	5.2	Glacier Gorge TH	From Sky Pond	9,180	11,800	2,620	II	3	AI 3 SS
Taylor Peak	67	6.1	Glacier Gorge TH	NW Slope via Andrews Glacier	9,180	13,153	3,973	II	2	

* = absolute change only. This destination requires a considerable amount of elevation gain and elevation loss and is more strenuous than is indicated by the absolute change.

DESTINATION	PAGE	ONE-WAY DISTANCE (MILES)	TRAILHEAD	TRAIL/ROUTE	TRAILHEAD ELEVATION (FEET)	DESTINATION ELEVATION (FEET)	GAIN/LOSS ELEVATION (FEET)	RATING GRADE	RATING CLASS	RATING SNOW/ICE
Taylor Peak	67	7.1	Bear Lake TH	NW Slope via Flattop Mtn.	9,450	13,153	3,703	II	2	
Ten Lake Park	285	8.1	East Inlet TH	From Lake Verna	8,400	11,200	2,800	–	–	
Ten Lake Park	285	7.4	East Inlet TH	From Paradise Creek	8,400	11,200	2,800	–	–	
Tepee Mtn., E Summit	333	8.0	Colorado River TH (Thunder Pass Trail)	S Ridge from Tepee–Lead saddle	9,040	12,360+	3,320	II	4	
Tepee Mtn., W Summit	333	2.6	Lake Agnes TH	N Ridge from Mt. Richthofen	10,250	12,360+	2,110	II	3	
Tepee Mtn., W Summit	333	8.0	Colorado River TH (Thunder Pass Trail)	S Ridge from Tepee–Lead saddle	9,040	12,360+	3,320	II	3	
Terra Tomah Mtn.	102	3.3	Forest Canyon Overlook	NE Ridge from Forest Lake	11,716	12,718	1,002	II	3	
Terra Tomah Mtn.	102	7.4	Poudre Lake TH at Milner Pass	SW Ridge from Mt. Julian	10,758	12,718	1,960	II	3	
Thatchtop	53	3.7	Glacier Gorge TH	S–shaped Gully via Loch Vale Trail	9,180	12,668	3,488	II	2	
Thatchtop	53	5.6	Glacier Gorge TH	S Slope from Solitude Lake	9,180	12,668	3,488	II	2	
Thousand Falls	123	0.3	Endovalley Picnic Area	Follow Sundance Creek	8,640	9,160	520	–	–	
Thunder Falls	188	6.6	Wild Basin TH	From Lion Lake No. 1	8,500	10,900	2,400	–	–	
Thunder Lake	191	6.2	Wild Basin TH	Trail	8,500	10,574	2,074	–	–	
Thunder Mtn.	332	8.3	Colorado River TH	SW Ridge (from Lulu Mtn.)	9,040	12,040+	3,000	II	2	
Thunder Mtn.	332	2.0	Never Summer TH near La Poudre Pass	SE Ridge (from Mt. Neota)	10,175	12,040+	1,865	I	2	
Thunder Mtn.	332	5.3	American Lakes (Michigan Lakes) TH	SW Ridge (from Lulu Mtn.)	9,780	12,040+	2,260	I	2	
Thunder Pass	328	4.1	American Lakes (Michigan Lakes) TH	Trail	9,780	11,331	1,551	I	1	
Thunder Pass	328	7.1	Colorado River TH (Thunder Pass Trail)	Trail	9,040	11,331	2,291	I	1	
Thunder Pass	328	5.1	Never Summer TH near La Poudre Pass	Grand Ditch Road and Trail	10,175	11,331	1,156	I	1	
'Thunder Peak'	256	2.0	East Portal TH	NW Ridge	8,260	10,134	1,874	I	2	
Tileston, Mt.	135	5.8	Lawn Lake TH	NW Slope from Lawn Lake Trail	8,540	11,254	2,714	II	2	
Timber Lake	299	5.0	Timber Lake TH	Trail	9,060	11,060	2,000	–	–	
Timberline Falls	63	3.9	Glacier Gorge TH	Trail	9,180	10,480	1,300	–	–	
Timberline Pass	46	1.9	Ute Crossing	Trail	11,440	11,484	44	–	–	
Timberline Pass	46	4.2	Upper Beaver Meadows TH	Trail	8,440	11,484	3,044	–	–	
Toll Memorial	43	0.5	Rock Cut Parking Area	Tundra World Nature Trail	12,110	12,304	194	–	–	
Tombstone Ridge	46	0.5	Ute Crossing	Point 11,691'	11,440	11,691	251	–	–	
Tombstone Ridge	46	0.9	Ute Crossing	Point 11,630'	11,440	11,630	190	–	–	
Tombstone Ridge	46	1.9	Ute Crossing	Point 11,722'	11,440	11,722	282	–	–	
Tourmaline Lake	87	5.4	Fern Lake TH	From Odessa Lake	8,150	10,580	2,430	–	–	
Trio Falls	188	6.7	Wild Basin TH	From Lion Lake No. 1	8,500	11,300	2,800	–	–	
Tuxedo Park	114	–	On Bear Lake Road	–	–	7,920	–	–	–	

DESTINATION	PAGE	ONE-WAY DISTANCE (MILES)	TRAILHEAD	TRAIL/ROUTE	TRAILHEAD ELEVATION (FEET)	DESTINATION ELEVATION (FEET)	GAIN/LOSS ELEVATION (FEET)	RATING GRADE	RATING CLASS	RATING SNOW/ICE
Twin Lake (Lower)	186	3.6	Wild Basin TH	From Thunder Lake Trail	8,500	9,820	1,320	–	–	
Twin Lake (Upper)	186	3.8	Wild Basin TH	From Thunder Lake Trail	8,500	9,860	1,360	–	–	
Twin Owls, The	142	1.2	Lumpy Ridge TH	Bowels of the Owls	7,852	8,789	937	I	5.0	
Twin Peaks	316	6.5	Roaring Fork TH	NE Ridge from Watanga Lake	8,300	11,957	3,657	II	2	
Twin Sisters Peaks, E Summit	261	3.4	Twin Sisters TH	Trail to NW Slope	9,160	11,428	2,268	I	2	
Twin Sisters Peaks, W Summit	261	3.4	Twin Sisters TH	Trail	9,160	11,413	2,253	I	2	
Two Rivers Lake	81	3.1	Bear Lake TH	Bushwhack from Fern-Odessa Trail	9,450	10,620	1,170	–	–	
Tyndall Glacier	77	4.7	Bear Lake TH	Overlook at top of Glacier from Flattop Mtn.	9,450	12,200	2,750	I	2	
Tyndall Glacier	77	3.2	Bear Lake TH	Tyndall Glacier via Emerald Lake	9,450	12,200	2,750	II	2	SS
Ute Trail	44	6.3	Upper Beaver Meadows TH	Trail to Ute Crossing	8,440	11,440	3,000	–	–	
Ute Trail	44	5.5	Ute Crossing	Trail to Gore Range Overlook	11,440	12,010	570	–	–	
Ute Trail	44	5.9	Gore Range Overlook	Trail to Farview Curve	12,010	10,120	-1,890	–	–	
Ute Trail	44	4.5	Alpine Visitor Center	Trail to Milner Pass	11,796	10,758	-1,038	–	–	
Valley Trail	354	2.2	Harbison Picnic Area	Trail	8,708	8,800	92	–	–	
Verna, Lake	276	6.9	East Inlet TH	Trail	8,400	10,180	1,780	–	–	
War Dance Falls	291	7.0	North Inlet TH	Ptarmigan Creek Access	8,500	9,900	1,400	–	–	
Watanga Lake	312	4.8	Roaring Fork TH	Trail	8,300	10,780	2,480	–	–	
Watanga Mtn.	317	7.1	Roaring Fork TH	NW Ridge from Watanga Lake	8,300	12,375	4,075	II	2	
Watanga Mtn.	317	6.3	Roaring Fork TH	W Slope from Watanga Lake	8,300	12,375	4,075	II	2	
Wescott, Mt.	278	5.7	East Inlet TH	SW Face	8,400	10,421	2,021	II	3	
West Creek Falls	147	2.4	Cow Creek TH	Trail	7,820	8,140	320*	–	–	
'Whiskey Lake'	152	11.5	Dunraven (North Fork) TH	From Lake Dunraven	7,900	11,540	3,640	–	–	
Window Rock on Castle Mtn.	139	0.6	Castle Mtn. parking	To base of formation	7,700	8,530	830	–	–	
Windy Gulch Cascades	37	0.5	Fern Lake TH	Fern Lake Trail to Windy Gulch	8,150	8,600	450	–	–	
'Wonderland Lake'	291	7.8	Bear Lake TH	Bighorn Flats Access	9,450	11,060	1,610*	–	–	
'Wonderland Lake'	291	9.1	North Inlet TH	Ptarmigan Creek Access	8,500	11,060	2,560	–	–	
Wuh, Mt.	82	2.7	Bear Lake TH	S Slope from Fern-Odessa Trail	9,450	10,761	1,311	I	2	
Ypsilon Lake	133	4.7	Lawn Lake TH	Trail	8,540	10,540	2,000	–	–	
Ypsilon Mtn.	125	4.0	Chapin Pass TH	SW Slope	11,020	13,514	2,494	I	2	
Ypsilon Mtn.	125	6.6	Lawn Lake TH	Donner Ridge	8,540	13,514	4,974	II	3	

* = absolute change only. This destination requires a considerable amount of elevation gain and elevation loss and is more strenuous than is indicated by the absolute change

Mike Poland winter camping

INDEX

Note: Citations followed by the letter "p" denote photos; citations followed by the letter "m" denote maps.

A

Acoma, Mount, 310m, 315–316

Adams, Mount, 311m, 313m, 316

Adams Falls, 272m, 275

Adams Lake, 311m, 312, 313m, 314

Agnes, Lake, 324m, 326, 326p, 327m

Agnes Vaille Memorial Shelter, 240–241

'Aiguille de Fleur,' 272m, 279m, 283, 283p

Alberta Falls, 30m, 32p, 46–47, 48m

Alice, Mount, 26p, 174p, 176m, 187p, 189, 189p, 192m

Allenspark Area hiking destinations, 177m, 214

Allenspark Trailhead, 215

Allenspark-Wild Basin Trail, 216

Alluvial Fan, 121m, 129

Alluvial Fan Parking, 166

Alluvial Fan Trail, 170

Alpine Brook, 240

Alpine Ridge Trail, 170

Alpine Visitor Center (AVC) at Fall River Pass, 166

altitude sickness, 18

American Lakes, 324m, 326, 327m

American Lakes and Lake Agnes Trailheads, 357

American Lakes (Michigan Lakes) Trail, 358

Andrews Creek Trail, 110

Andrews Glacier, 30m, 66–67, 70m

Andrews Pass, 30m, 67, 70m

Andrews Peak, 272m, 281, 281p, 288m

Andrews Tarn, 28p, 30m, 65, 70m

animals, 19, 21

Arapaho Bay, 321

Arch Rocks, 30m, 39

Arrowhead, 30m, 54, 54p, 55m

Arrowhead Lake, 31m, 101m, 105, 105p

Aspen Brook Trail, 257p, 268

Azure Lake, 31m, 101m, 105

B

Baker/Bowen Trailhead, 356

Baker Gulch hiking destinations, 324m, 344–347, 345p

Baker Gulch Trail, 358

Baker Mountain, 324m, 341m, 345

Baker Pass, 324m, 341m, 344–345

'Balanced Rock,' 121m, 144

Battle Mountain, 222m, 236–237

Bear Lake, 30m, 48m, 72–73, 72p

Bear Lake Nature Trail, 110

Bear Lake Trailhead, 108

Beaver, The, 243

Beaver Meadows hiking destinations, 31m, 40

Beaver Meadows Trail System, 110–111

Beaver Mountain, 31m, 40

Beaver Wetlands Parking, 108

Bench Lake, 12p, 272m, 290m, 291, 291p

Bierstadt Lake, 30m, 34–35

Bierstadt Lake Trail, 111

Bierstadt Lake Trailhead, 108

Bierstadt Moraine hiking destinations, 30m, 34–35

Bierstadt Moraine Trailhead, 108

Bighorn Flats, 273m, 296, 296p

Bighorn Lake, 273m, 302

Bighorn Mountain, 121m, 135

Big Meadows, 272m, 295, 295p, 307p

Big Pool, 272m, 286, 286p

Big South Trail, 170

Big South Trailhead, 166

Big Thompson Canyon hiking destinations, 248m, 250

Big Thompson River, 6p

Black Canyon, 173

Black Canyon Trail, 170

Black Lake, 30m, 49–50, 50p, 55m

Black Pool, 31m, 95
Bluebird Lake, 176m, 201, 207m
Bluebird Lake Trail, 216, 217p
Blue Lake, 30m, 50, 50p, 55m, 324m, 347
Blue Lake Trail, 358
Boulder Brook Trail, 111
Boulder Field, 240
Boulder Field Area, 240–241
Boulder-Grand Pass, 176m, 192m, 193p, 194, 195p, 196m, 272m, 283, 283p
Bowen/Baker Trailhead, 356
Bowen Gulch (Bowen Pass) Trail, 358
Bowen Gulch hiking destinations, 324m, 347–349
Bowen Lake, 324m, 347
Bowen Lake Trail, 358
Bowen Mountain, 324m, 349, 349p
Bowen Pass, 324m, 347–348
Bowen Pass Trail, 348p
Box Lake, 176m, 196m, 197–198
Bridal Veil Falls, 119p, 121m, 145–146, 145p
Bryant, Mount, 310m, 315
Bulwark Ridge hiking destinations, 121m, 159
Bulwark Ridge Trail, 170
Butterfly Burn, 269

C
Cairns, Mount, 272m, 278, 279m
Calypso Cascades, 177m, 185
Campsite Shortcut Trail, 217
Cascade Falls, 272m, 286
Cascade Lake, 173
Castle Lake, 176m, 187, 187p, 192m
Castle Lakes, 176m, 187, 192m, 196m
Castle Mountain, 121m, 138–139
Castle Mountain hiking destinations, 121m, 138–139
Castle Mountain Parking, 166
Castle Rock, 30m, 85m, 89p, 92–93, 92p, 121m, 139

Cathedral Spires, 34p
'Catherine, Lake,' 272m, 287
CCY Route, 120m, 126m, 127–128
Chaos Canyon Cascades, 30m, 69, 69p
Chaos Canyon hiking destinations, 30m, 69, 71–72
'Chaotic Glacier,' 30m, 70m, 72
Chapin, Mount, 119p, 120m, 124–125, 124p
Chapin Creek Trail, 171
Chapin Pass, 120m, 124
Chapin Pass Trailhead, 166–167
Chasm Falls, 120m, 124
Chasm Junction, 240
Chasm Lake, 222m, 223–224, 223p, 227p, 228m
Chasm Lake Area hiking destinations, 222m, 223–225
Chasm Lake Spur Trail, 23p, 238
Chasm Meadows, 222m, 224, 228m
Chasm Meadows Ranger Cabin, 222m, 224, 228m
Chasm View, 243
Chickadee Pond, 176m, 196m, 200
Chickaree Lake, 273m, 297
Chief Cheley Peak, 31m, 101m, 107
Chiefs Head-Pagoda Couloir, 30m, 55m, 60, 192m, 228m
Chiefs Head Peak, 30m, 55m, 59–60, 192m
child-friendly hiking destinations. See family-friendly hiking destinations
Chipmunk Lake, 120m, 126m, 133
Chiquita, Mount, 120m, 125, 126m
Chiquita Lake, 120m, 126m, 134
'Christmas Tree Mountain,' 248m, 258–259
Cirque Lake, 120m, 158m, 159–160
Cirrus, Mount, 324m, 337m, 338, 338p
class scale, 25–26
Cleaver, The, 176m, 196m, 199, 199p
Clouds, Lake of the, 8p, 324m, 336, 336p, 337m, 359p

Colorado River, 361

Colorado River hiking destinations, 324m, 352–353

Colorado River Trail, 358

Colorado River Trailhead, 356

Columbine Bay, 321

Columbine Creek, 309p

Columbine Creek Trail, 319

Columbine Falls, 222m, 223, 228m

Comanche Peak, 120m, 158m, 162

Comanche Peak Area hiking destinations, 120m, 159–163

Continental Divide Crossing, 30m, 76, 176m–177m, 195

Continental Divide Traverse, 30m–31m, 107–108, 107p

Cony Creek drainage, 213p

Cony Creek hiking destinations, 176m, 208–213

Cony Lake, 176m, 207m, 209–210, 211p

Cony Pass, 176m, 207m, 211p, 212

Copeland, Mount, 174p, 175p, 176m, 203–204, 207m

Copeland Falls, 177m, 184

Copeland Lake, 219

Copeland Moraine, 219

Copeland Moraine to Meeker Park Trail, 217

Corral Creek Trail, 171

Corral Creek Trailhead, 167

Cow Creek hiking destinations, 121m, 145–147

Cow Creek Trail, 171

Cow Creek Trailhead at McGraw Ranch, 167

Coyote Valley Trail, 324m, 354–355, 355p, 358

Coyote Valley Trailhead, 356

Cracktop, 31m, 100, 101m

Crags, The, 248m, 261

Craig, Mount, 271p, 272m, 279m, 281–282, 282p

Crater, The, 324m, 350–351, 350p

Crater Trail, 356p, 358

Crater Trailhead, 356

Crosier Mountain, 248m, 249–250, 249p

Crosier Mountain Gravel Pit Trailhead, 266

Crosier Mountain Trail, 269

Crystal Lake, 118p, 121m, 132m, 133

Crystal Lakes Trail, 171

Cub Creek Beaver Ponds, 30m, 38

Cub Lake, 30m, 38, 38p, 113p

Cub Lake Trail, 111

Cub Lake Trailhead, 108–109

Cumulus, Mount, 324m, 337m, 340–341, 341m

D

Dark Mountain, 121m, 147

Deer Mountain, 31m, 40–41, 41p

Deer Mountain/Deer Ridge Trailhead, 109

Deer Ridge hiking destinations, 31m, 40–41

Deer Ridge Junction, 115

Deer Ridge Trail System, 111

dehydration, 18

Deserted Village, 121m, 152–153, 152p

Desolation Peaks, 120m, 164m, 165–166

Desolation Peaks Area hiking destinations, 120m, 163, 165–166

Diamond, 242, 242p

Dickinson, Mount, 121m, 153

disability-friendly hiking destinations
    Alluvial Fan, 121m, 129
    Bear Lake, 30m, 48m, 72–73, 72p
    Coyote Valley Trail, 324m, 354–355, 355p, 358
    Estes, Lake, 248m, 252
    Hidden Valley Beaver Wetlands, 31m, 42, 108p
    Holzwarth Historic Site/Never Summer Ranch, 117, 324m, 353–354, 354p
    Lily Lake, 246p, 248m, 259, 259p
    Sprague Lake, 30m, 33, 33p
    Toll Memorial, 31m, 43, 43p

Ditch Camp and Grand Ditch Road, 358–359

'Ditch Road,' 358

dogs, 19

Doughnut Lake, 31m, 101m, 105

Dove, The, 243

Dragons Egg Rock, 177m, 184

Dream Lake, 30m, 48m, 73–74, 73p

Dunraven, Lake, 121m, 151m, 152

Dunraven, Mount, 121m, 151m, 153

Dunraven Trailhead, 167

E

Eagle Cliff Mountain, 31m, 39

Eagle Lake, 176m, 196m, 197–198, 198p

Eagle Lake Area hiking destinations, 176m, 197–200

Eagles Beak, 176m, 196m, 199–200

East Glacier Knob, 30m, 48m, 65–66

'East Inlet Falls,' 272m, 275, 279m

East Inlet hiking destinations, 272m, 275–278, 275p, 280–283

East Inlet Trail, 271p, 304, 304p

East Inlet Trailhead, 303, 318

East Lily Lake Parking Area, 267

East Longs Peak Trail, 238–239, 239p

East Meadow, 272m, 277

East Portal Area hiking destinations, 248m, 255–257

East Portal Trailhead, 266

East Shore Trail, 309p, 319–320, 319p

East Shore Trailhead, 318

'Eleanor, Mount,' 31m, 96m, 100, 101m

'Electrode, The,' 324m, 327m, 328–329, 328p

Elk Tooth, 3p, 176m, 207m, 210, 211p, 212

Embryo Lake, 30m, 48m, 63, 70m

Emerald Lake, 30m, 48m, 70m, 74, 74p

Emerald Lake Trail, 111

Emerald Mountain, 248m, 255, 255p

Emmaline Lake, 120m, 158m, 159–160

Emmaline Lake/Mummy Pass Trailhead, 167

Emmaline Lake Trail, 171

Endovalley Picnic Area, 168

Enentah, Mount, 272m, 277–278

equipment, 21

Estes, Lake, 248m, 252

Estes Cone, 248m, 262–263

Estes Park Area hiking destinations, 248m, 252–254

Eugenia Mine, 222m, 236

Eureka Ditch, 30m, 94

F

Fairchild Mountain, 1p, 118p, 120m, 132m, 136–137, 136p

Falcon Lake, 176m, 192m, 193

Fall Mountain, 120m, 158m, 161, 161p

Fall River Pass/Alpine Visitor Center, 116

Fall River Pass hiking destinations, 120m, 123

'Fall River Pass Mountain,' 120m, 123

family-friendly hiking destinations

  Adams Falls, 272m, 275

  Alberta Falls, 30m, 32p, 46–47, 48m

  Alluvial Fan, 121m, 129

  Arch Rocks, 30m, 39

  Bear Lake, 30m, 48m, 72–73, 72p

  Big Meadows, 272m, 295, 295p, 307p

  Bridal Veil Falls, 119p, 121m, 145–146, 145p

  Calypso Cascades, 177m, 185

  Cascade Falls, 272m, 286

  Chasm Falls, 120m, 124

  Copeland Falls, 177m, 184

  Coyote Valley Trail, 324m, 354–355, 355p, 358

  The Crater, 324m, 350–351, 350p

  Cub Creek Beaver Ponds, 30m, 38

  Cub Lake, 30m, 38, 38p, 113p

  Deserted Village, 121m, 152–153, 152p

  Dream Lake, 30m, 48m, 73–74, 73p

  East Meadow, 272m, 277

family-friendly hiking destinations *continued*
   Emerald Lake, 30m, 48m, 70m, 74, 74p
   Estes, Lake, 248m, 252
   Eugenia Mine, 222m, 236
   'Fall River Pass Mountain,' 120m, 123
   Fan Lake, 121m, 129
   Fern Falls, 30m, 78
   Gem Lake, 121m, 140–141
   Glacier Falls, 30m, 47, 48m
   Haiyaha, Lake, 30m, 48m, 70m, 71
   Hidden Valley Beaver Wetlands, 31m, 42, 108p
   Holzwarth Historic Site/Never Summer Ranch, 117, 324m, 353–354, 354p
   Homer Rouse Trail, 247p, 248m, 258, 269
   Homestead Meadows, 248m, 251, 251p
   Horseshoe Falls, 121m, 129
   Irene, Lake, 273m, 301, 301p
   Jewel Lake, 30m, 48m, 49
   Lily Lake, 246p, 248m, 259, 259p
   Lily Ridge Trail, 248m, 261, 269
   The Loch, 30m, 48m, 62–63, 62p
   Lulu City, 324m, 352–353, 352p
   'MacGregor Falls,' 121m, 140
   Marmot Point, 120m, 123
   Mills Lake, 30m, 48m, 49, 49p
   Moore Park, 222m, 237
   Nymph Lake, 30m, 48m, 73
   Ouzel Falls, 177m, 185
   'Paul Bunyan's Boot,' 121m, 144, 144p
   The Pool, 30m, 37
   'Poudre Lake Spires,' 273m, 302, 302p
   'Rabbit Ears,' 121m, 147
   River Trail, 324m, 354
   Sheep Rock, 273m, 302
   Shipler Park Cabins, 324m, 325p, 352–353
   Sprague Lake, 30m, 33, 33p
   Summerland Park, 272m, 289, 291
   Toll Memorial, 31m, 43, 43p
   Valley Trail, 324m, 354

Fan Falls, 176m, 192m, 193–194, 194p
Fan Lake, 121m, 129
Farview Curve, 117
Farview Mountain, 324m, 346–347
Fay Lakes, 120m, 126m, 134–135
fees, 21
Fern Creek, 80p
Fern Falls, 30m, 78
Fern Lake, 30m, 79–80, 85m
Fern Lake Trailhead, 108–109
Fern-Odessa Trail, 111
Fifth Lake, 196m, 272m, 277
Finch Lake, 177m, 208, 208p
Finch Lake-Pear Lake Trail, 217
Finch Lake Trailhead, 215
'Fire Trail,' 112
Fish Creek Road Area hiking destinations, 248m, 258–259
Fish Creek Trailhead, 266
Flatiron Mountain, 120m, 164m, 165
Flattop Mountain, 30m, 70m, 75–76
Flattop Mountain Trail, 75p, 112
'Fleur de Lis,' 272m, 279m, 283
Flint Pass, 120m, 163, 165
Forest Canyon hiking destinations, 31m, 94–95, 95p, 97
Forest Canyon Overlook, 116
Forest Canyon Pass, 31m, 42–43, 45p
Forest Lake, 31m, 97
Fourth Lake, 272m, 277, 277p
Fox Creek Falls, 121m, 148–149
Frigid Lake, 176m, 196m, 198
Frozen Lake, 30m, 50–51, 55m

G

Gable, The, 13p, 30m, 85m, 88–89
Gabletop Mountain, 29p, 30m, 85m, 88, 88p
Garden Gate Trailhead, 267
Gash, The, 30m, 66, 70m
gear, 21

Gem Lake, 121m, 140–141
Gem Lake Trail, 171
Gem Lake Trailhead, 168
Gianttrack Mountain, 248m, 254
Giardia lamblia, 18
'Gibraltar Mountain,' 121m, 151m, 155
Glacier Basin, 114
Glacier Basin hiking destinations, 30m, 33
Glacier Creek, 112p
Glacier Creek Trail, 112
Glacier Falls, 30m, 47, 48m
Glacier Gorge hiking destinations, 30m, 46–47, 49–54, 56–62, 60p
Glacier Gorge Junction, 114
Glacier Gorge Trail, 112
Glacier Gorge Trailhead, 109, 238
Glacier Ridge, 242
Glass Lake, 30m, 48m, 64, 70m
Glen Haven Area hiking destinations, 248m, 249–250
Glen Haven Trailhead, 267
Gore Range Overlook, 116
Gorge Lakes hiking destinations, 31m, 103–108
Grace Falls, 30m, 79, 85m
grade scale, 26
Granby, Lake, 321
Grand Ditch, 361, 361p
Grand Ditch Road and Ditch Camp, 358–359
Grand Lake, 321, 321p
Granite Falls, 273m, 292
Granite Pass, 240
Green Knoll, 324m, 341m, 343, 343p
Green Lake, 30m, 51, 55m, 58p
Green Mountain, 272m, 294
Green Mountain Trail, 304
Green Mountain Trailhead, 303, 304

H
Hagues Peak, 121m, 132m, 137
Haiyaha, Lake, 30m, 48m, 70m, 71
Half Mountain, 30m, 34p, 48m, 52–53
Hallett Peak, 30m, 70m, 76–77, 76p
handicaps, hiking destinations for persons with. See disability-friendly hiking destinations
Harbison Picnic Area, 357
Hayden Gorge hiking destinations, 31m, 97–100, 97p, 102–103
Hayden Lake, 31m, 96m, 98, 101m
Hayden Spire, 28p, 30m, 96m, 99–100
Haynach Lakes, 270p, 273m, 293, 293p
Haynach Lakes Trail, 305
Hazeline Lake, 120m, 163, 164m
Helene, Lake, 30m, 81, 85m
Hiamovi Mountain, 311m, 317
'Hidden Falls,' 177m, 185
Hidden Valley, 115
Hidden Valley Beaver Wetlands, 31m, 42, 108p
Hidden Valley hiking destinations, 31m, 41–42
Highest Lake, 31m, 101m, 106
Hitchens Gulch hiking destinations, 324m, 336, 338
Hollowell Park hiking destinations, 30m, 35–36
Hollowell Park Trailhead, 109
Holzwarth Historic Site/Never Summer Ranch, 117, 324m, 353–354, 354p
Holzwarth Historic Site/Never Summer Ranch Trailhead, 357
Homer Rouse Trail, 247p, 248m, 258, 269
Homestead Meadows, 248m, 251, 251p
Homestretch, The, 220p, 245, 245p
Hondius Park, 114
'Horse Creek Trailhead,' 215
Horseshoe Falls, 121m, 129
Horseshoe Park hiking destinations, 121m, 128–130

Horsetooth Peak, 177m, 179, 179p
'Hourglass Fire,' 159p
Hourglass Lake, 30m, 91–92, 91p, 96m
House Rock, 248m, 263–264
Howard Mountain, 324m, 337m, 338
Hunters Creek hiking destinations, 177m, 180–184, 180p
Husted, Lake, 121m, 151m, 152
Hutcheson Lakes, 176m, 207m, 209–210, 209p
hypothermia, 18

I

Iceberg Lake, 31m, 42, 42p
Iceberg Pass to Tundra Curves, 116
Icefield Pass, 121m, 151m, 154, 154p
icons, 22, 27
Ida, Mount, 31m, 101m, 106
Indigo Pond, 176m, 196m, 198
Inkwell Lake, 31m, 101m, 105
insects, 21
Irene, Lake, 273m, 301, 301p
Irene Lake, 30m, 90, 96m
Irving Hale, Mount, 311m, 318, 318p
Isolation Lake, 176m, 196m, 202
Isolation Peak, 176m, 196m, 205–206
'Italy Lake,' 30m, 51, 55m

J

Jackstraw Mountain, 273m, 300, 300p
'Jagor Point,' 31m, 101m, 106–107
'Jaws Falls,' 30m, 37–38, 37p
Jewel Lake, 30m, 48m, 49
'Jiffy Pop Peak' (a.k.a. 'Cloudview Peak'), 324m, 336, 337m
Jims Grove, 240
Joe Mills Mountain, 30m, 82–83, 85m
Julian, Mount, 31m, 96m, 101m, 102
Julian Lake, 273m, 298
Junco Lake, 176m, 203, 203p, 207m

K

Kawuneeche Valley hiking destinations, 323p, 324m, 353–355
Kawuneeche Visitor Center (KVC), 303
Keplinger Lake, 176m, 182–183
Keplinger's Couloir, 233p
'Kettle Tarn,' 121m, 149
Keyboard of the Winds, 30m, 60p, 61–62, 61p, 228m
Keyhole, The, 241
Knight Ridge Trail, 320, 320p
Knobtop Mountain, 30m, 85m, 86
Kruger Rock, 248m, 265, 265p

L

Lady Washington, Mount, 222m, 227, 227p, 228m
Lake Agnes and American Lakes Trailheads, 357
Lake Agnes hiking destinations, 324m, 326
Lake Agnes Trail, 359
'Lake Amore,' 31m, 101m, 104, 104p
Lake Haiyaha Trail, 112
Lake Irene Picnic Area, 303
Lake Nanita Trail, 305
Lake of the Clouds Trail, 359
Lambs Slide, 221p, 241–242, 242p
La Poudre Pass hiking destinations, 324m, 331–332
La Poudre Pass Lake, 324m, 331
La Poudre Pass Trail, 359
Lark Pond, 176m, 202, 207m
Lava Cliffs, 4p, 31m, 43
Lava Cliffs Pullout, 116
Lava Cliffs Pullout on Trail Ridge Road, 109
Lawn Lake, 119p, 121m, 131, 131p, 132m
Lawn Lake Trail, 171–172
Lawn Lake Trailhead, 168
Lead Mountain, 322p, 324m, 334–335, 335p, 337m

Leave No Trace, 21
Ledges, The, 244
lightning, 19
'Lightning Peak,' 248m, 256
Lily Lake, 246p, 248m, 259, 259p
Lily Lake Area hiking destinations, 248m, 259–263
Lily Lake Parking Area, 267
Lily Lake Trail, 269
Lily Mountain, 248m, 259–260
Lily Mountain Trail, 269
Lily Mountain Trailhead, 267
Lily Ridge Trail, 248m, 261, 269
Lion Gulch hiking destinations, 248m, 251
Lion Gulch Trail, 269
Lion Gulch Trailhead, 267
Lion Head, 248m, 265
Lion Lake No. 1, 176m, 187–188, 192m
Lion Lake No. 2, 176m, 188, 192m
Lion Lakes Area hiking destinations, 176m, 187–190
Lion Lake Trail, 218
Little Crystal Lake, 121m, 132m, 133
Little Horseshoe Park, 173
Little Matterhorn, 30m, 85m, 87–88
'Little No Name,' 121m, 151m, 155
Little Rock Lake, 31m, 101m, 104
Little Yellowstone, 324m, 331
Loch, The, 30m, 48m, 62–63, 62p
Loch Vale, 29p
Loch Vale hiking destinations, 30m, 62–69
Loch Vale Trail, 112, 112p
Loft, The, 222m, 225–226, 226p, 228m
Loft Area hiking destinations, 222m, 225–226
Lone Pine Lake, 272m, 276, 276p, 279m, 288m
Lonesome Lake, 30m, 96m, 99, 99p
Long Meadows, 273m, 298–299, 298p
Longs Peak, 13p, 16p, 204p, 220p, 222m, 228m, 229–233, 230p, 234p

Longs Peak Area hiking destinations, 222m, 227, 229–233
Longs Peak East Face, 241–243
Longs Peak North Face, 243
Longs Peak South Face, 245
Longs Peak Trailhead, 238
Longs Peak West Face, 244
Lookout Mountain, 175p, 177–178, 177m
Lookout Mountain Trail, 218
Lookout Springs, 248m, 262
Loomis Lake, 30m, 85m, 90
Lost Falls, 121m, 150, 150p
Lost Lake, 121m, 150, 151m
Louise, Lake, 121m, 151m, 152
Love Lake, 31m, 101m, 105, 105p
'Lower Michigan Lake,' 324m, 326, 327m
Lower North St. Vrain Creek hiking destinations, 177m, 184–186
Lulu City, 324m, 352–353, 352p
Lulu Mountain, 324m, 332
Lumpy Ridge hiking destinations, 121m, 139–145, 139p
Lumpy Ridge Loop, 121m, 141–142
Lumpy Ridge Trail, 172
Lumpy Ridge Trailhead, 168
Lyric Falls, 177m, 181

M
'MacGregor Falls,' 121m, 140
Mahana Peak, 176m, 196m, 204–205
Many Parks Curve, 115
Many Winds, Lake of, 176m, 192m, 193, 193p
map symbols, 27
Marguerite Falls, 30m, 78–79, 85m
Marigold Lake, 30m, 81, 85m
Marigold Pond, 30m, 82, 85m
Marmot Point, 120m, 123
McGregor Mountain, 121m, 144–145
McHenrys Notch, 30m, 55m, 57–58
McHenrys Peak, 25p, 30m, 50p, 55m, 56–57, 58p

Meadow Mountain, 177m, 214, 214p

Medicine Bow Curve, 117

Meeker, Mount, 27p, 204p, 221p, 222m, 228m, 234–235, 235p

Meeker Park hiking destinations, 177m, 179–180

Meeker Ridge, 219

Mertensia Falls, 176m, 196m, 197, 197p

Michigan Lakes (American Lakes) Trail, 358

Michigan Lakes hiking destinations, 324m, 326, 328–331

'Middle Michigan Lake,' 324m, 326, 327m

'Middle No Name,' 121m, 151m, 155

mileages, 26–27

Mill Creek Basin, 30m, 35–36

Mill Creek Basin Trail, 113

Mills Glacier, 241

Mills Lake, 30m, 48m, 49, 49p

Mills Moraine, 240

Milner Pass, 117p

Milner Pass hiking destinations, 273m, 300–302

Milner Pass/Poudre Lake, 117

Mineral Point, 324m, 325p, 348

Mirror Lake, 120m, 158m, 160

Mirror Lake Trail, 172

Moomaw Glacier, 176m, 196m, 200

Moore Park, 222m, 237

Moore Park Area hiking destinations, 222m, 236–237

Moraine Park hiking destinations, 31m, 36–39

Mosquito Creek hiking destinations, 324m, 339

Mount Ida Trail, 113

'Mount Ikoko,' 120m, 158m, 162–163, 162p

Mount Meeker hiking destinations, 222m, 234–235

Mummy Kill, 120m–121m, 128

Mummy Mountain, 121m, 132m, 137–138

Mummy Pass, 120m, 161

Mummy Pass/Emmaline Lake Trailhead, 167

Mummy Pass Trail, 118p, 172, 172p

Mummy Range, 115p

Murphy Lake, 273m, 293–294

N

Nakai Peak, 273m, 296

Nanita, Lake, 272m, 287, 288m

Narrows, The, 221p, 244, 244p

Needles, The, 121m, 143

Neota, Mount, 324m, 332

Never Summer Ranch/Holzwarth Historic Site, 117, 324m, 353–354, 354p

Never Summer Trailhead near La Poudre Pass, 357

Nimbus, Mount, 324m, 341m, 342–343

Nisa Mountain, 272m, 294

Nokhu Crags, 324m, 327m, 329–330, 329p

Nokoni, Lake, 272m, 287, 288m

North Boundary hiking destinations, 121m, 147–149

North Boundary Trail, 172

North Fork of the Big Thompson River hiking destinations, 121m, 149–150, 152–157

North Fork Trail, 172

'North Inlet Falls,' 272m, 287

North Inlet hiking destinations, 272m, 286–287, 289, 291

North Inlet Trail, 306

North Inlet Trailhead, 303

North Longs Peak Trail, 112p, 239

North Ridge, 175p, 176m, 182p, 183, 192m

Notch, The, 243

Notchtop Mountain, 20p, 30m, 84, 84p, 85m, 86

Nymph Lake, 30m, 48m, 73

O

Odessa-Fern Trail, 111

Odessa Gorge hiking destinations, 30m, 78–84, 86

Odessa Lake, 20p, 30m, 80, 85m

Ogalalla Peak, 176m, 207m, 212–213

Old Fall River Road hiking destinations, 120m, 123–125, 127–128

Oldman Mountain, 247p, 248m, 252–253

Old Ranger Drive Hiking Access, 267–268

Olympus, Mount, 248m, 253–254

Onahu Creek hiking destinations, 273m, 297–299

Onahu Creek Trail, 306

Onahu Creek Trailhead, 303, 304

Opposition Creek hiking destinations, 324m, 339–340

Orton, Mount, 176m, 183, 192m

Otis Peak, 30m, 34p, 48m, 70m, 71

Ouzel Creek hiking destinations, 176m, 200–206

Ouzel Falls, 177m, 185

Ouzel Lake, 176m, 196m, 200–201, 207m

Ouzel Lake Trail, 218

Ouzel Peak, 176m, 206, 207m

P

Pagoda Couloir-Chiefs Head, 30m, 55m, 60, 192m, 228m

Pagoda Mountain, 30m, 55m, 60–61, 182p, 192m, 228m

Palisades, The, 245, 245p

'Paprika Peak,' 324m, 346

Paradise Creek, 271p

Paradise Creek hiking destinations, 272m, 284–285

Paradise Park, 272m, 284, 284p

Paradise Park Trail, 306

Parika Lake, 324m, 325p, 344

Parika Lake Trail, 360

Parika Peak, 324m, 346

Patterson, Mount, 272m, 294–295

'Paul Bunyan's Boot,' 121m, 144, 144p

Peacock Pool, 222m, 223, 223p, 228

Pear Lake, 176m, 207m, 208–209, 208p

Pear Lake-Finch Lake Trail, 217

permits, 21

Petit Grepon, 66p

pets, 19

Pettingell Lake, 279m, 286–287, 287p

Pierson Mountain, 248m, 264–265

Pierson Park hiking destinations, 248m, 263–266

Pierson Park Trailhead, 268

Pilot Mountain, 176m, 189–190, 192m

Pine Ridge, 240

Pinnacle Pool, 323p, 324m, 337, 337p

Pipit Lake, 176m, 202, 202p, 207m

Pisgah, Mount, 248m, 254

Pool, The, 30m, 37

'Pool of Jade,' 30m, 70m, 74–75, 74p

Potts Puddle, 121m, 130

Poudre Lake, 31m, 42

Poudre Lake/Milner Pass, 117

'Poudre Lake Spires,' 273m, 302, 302p

Poudre Lake Trailhead at Milner Pass, 109, 303

Poudre River Trail, 169p, 172–173

Poudre River Trailhead, 169

Powell, Lake, 272m, 289

Powell Peak, 30m, 55m, 68–69

Powell-Thatchtop Ridge, 68p

'Primrose Pond,' 30m, 85m, 90

Prospect Canyon, 114

Prospect Mountain, 248m, 254

Ptarmigan Creek hiking destinations, 272m, 291–292

'Ptarmigan Glacier,' 30m, 70m, 83–84

Ptarmigan Lake, 272m–273m, 290m, 291–292

Ptarmigan Mountain, 272m, 280, 288m, 305p
Ptarmigan Pass, 30m, 83
Ptarmigan Point, 30m, 70m, 83
'Ptarmigans Beak,' 272m, 281, 288m

R

'Rabbit Ears,' 121m, 147
Rainbow Curve, 116
Rainbow Lake, 7p, 30m, 90–91, 91p, 96m
Ramsey Peak, 121m, 157
Rams Horn Mountain/Teddy's Teeth, 248m, 260
Raspberry Park, 31m, 97
ratings, 23–26
Red Gulch hiking destinations, 324m, 340, 342–344
Red Mountain, 324m, 340, 341m, 342
Red Mountain Trail, 360
regulations, 21
Ribbon Falls, 30m, 47, 47p, 55m
Richthofen, Mount, 324m, 327m, 333
River Trail, 324m, 354, 360
Roaring Fork, 240
Roaring Fork Trail, 320
Roaring Fork Trailhead, 319
'Roaring Peak,' 311m, 313m, 316
Roaring River hiking destinations, 121m, 130–131, 133–138
Rock Cut, 116
Rock Cut Parking Area, 109
Rock Lake, 31m, 101m, 104
Rocky Mountain National Park
  overview of, 17
  permits, fees, and regulations, 21
  regional map, 14m–15m
Round Mountain Trailhead, 268
Round Pond, 30m, 81, 85m
Rowe Glacier, 121m, 151m, 156, 156p
'Rowe Glacier Lake,' 121m, 151m, 156, 156p
Rowe Mountain, 121m, 151m, 154–155
Rowe Peak, 121m, 151m, 155

S

Saddle, The, 120m, 132m, 136
Saddle, Trail to The, 173
Sandbeach Lake, 177m, 181–182, 181p
Sandbeach Lake Trail, 218
Sandbeach Lake Trailhead, 215
'Scotch Lake,' 121m, 151m, 152
Shadow Mountain, 310m, 314–315
Shadow Mountain Dam, 319
Shadow Mountain Lake, 321
Shadow Mountain Lookout Tower, 307p, 310m, 314
Shadow Mountain Trail, 320
Sharkstooth, 30m, 66, 66p, 70m
Sheep Lakes, 121m, 129–130
Sheep Mountain, 121m, 146–147, 248m, 250, 250p
Sheep Rock, 273m, 302
Shelf Lake, 30m, 48m, 51–52, 51p
Shipler Mountain, 324m, 351
Shipler Park Cabins, 324m, 325p, 352–353
Ships Prow, 222m, 224–225, 225p, 228m
Signal Mountain, 121m, 159
Signal Mountain Trail, 169p
Signal Mountain Trailhead, 169
Skeleton Gulch hiking destinations, 323p, 324m, 333–336, 333p, 360p
Skeleton Gulch Trail, 360
Skull Point, 121m, 151m, 157
Sky Pond, 28p, 30m, 48m, 64, 66p, 70m
Snowbank Lake, 176m, 188, 192m
Snowdrift Lake, 272m–273m, 290m, 291–292
Snowdrift Peak, 273m, 296–297
Snow Lake, 324m, 327m, 328
Solitude, Lake, 272m, 287, 289
Solitude Lake, 30m, 48m, 51–52, 51p
South Lateral Moraine, 30m, 36
South Signal Mountain, 121m, 159
Spearhead, The, 30m, 55m, 58–59, 58p

Specimen Mountain, 324m, 351

Specimen Mountain Group hiking destinations, 324m, 350–351

Spectacle Lakes, 120m, 126m, 134

Spirit Lake, 178p, 272m, 276, 276p

Sprague Glacier, 30m, 92, 96m

Sprague Lake, 30m, 33, 33p

Sprague Lake Nature Trail, 113

Sprague Lake Trailhead, 110

Sprague Mountain, 30m, 93, 96m

Sprague Pass, 30m, 93, 96m

'Sprague Tarn,' 7p, 30m, 91p, 92, 96m

Spruce Canyon hiking destinations, 30m, 89–94

Spruce Lake, 5p, 29p, 30m, 85m, 89–90, 89p

St. Vrain Mountain, 177m, 214

St. Vrain Mountain Trailhead, 215

Static Peak, 324m, 327m, 330–331

Steep Mountain, 30m, 36

Stone Man Pass, 30m, 55m, 56

Stones Peak, 31m, 94, 96m

Storm Pass, 248m, 255–256

Storm Pass Trail, 269

Storm Pass Trail Parking, 110

Storm Peak, 222m, 227, 228m, 229

Stormy Peaks, 121m, 156–157

Stormy Peaks Pass, 121m, 156

Stormy Peaks Pass Trail, 173

Stormy Peaks Trailhead, 169

Stratus, Mount, 324m, 341m, 343–344

Sugarloaf Mountain, 121m, 151m, 157

Sullivan Gulch Trailhead, 268

Summerland Park, 272m, 289, 291

Sundance Mountain, 31m, 44

sun protection, 18

symbols, 22, 27

T

Tanima Peak, 176m, 192m, 195, 196m

Taylor Glacier, 30m, 55m, 67–68, 70m

Taylor Peak, 30m, 55m, 67, 70m

Teddy's Teeth/Rams Horn Mountain, 248m, 260

Ten Lake Park, 270p, 272m, 279m, 285, 285p

Tepee Mountain, 324m, 327m, 333–334, 334p

Terra Tomah Mountain, 31m, 96m, 101m, 102–103, 102p

Thatchtop, 30m, 34p, 48m, 53–54, 53p, 55m

Thatchtop-Powell Ridge, 68p

Thousand Falls, 120m, 123

Thunder Falls, 176m, 188–189, 188p, 192m

Thunder Lake, 176m, 191, 192m, 196m

Thunder Lake Area hiking destinations, 176m, 191, 193–195

Thunder Lake Trail, 218

Thunder Mountain, 324m, 332, 332p

Thunder Pass, 324m, 327m, 328

Thunder Pass Trail, 360

'Thunder Peak,' 248m, 256–257

thunderstorms, 19

Tileston, Mount, 121m, 135–136, 135p

Timber Creek hiking destinations, 273m, 299–300

Timber Creek Trail, 306

Timber Lake, 273m, 274p, 299–300, 299p

Timber Lake Trail, 306

Timber Lake Trailhead, 304

Timberline Falls, 30m, 48m, 63–64, 63p, 70m

Timberline Pass, 31m, 46

Toll Memorial, 31m, 43, 43p

Tombstone Ridge, 31m, 46

Tonahutu Creek hiking destinations, 272m, 292–297

Tonahutu Creek Trail, 307

Tonahutu Trailhead, 304

Tour de Estes Cone, 248m, 257

Tourmaline Gorge hiking destinations, 30m, 86–89

Tourmaline Lake, 30m, 85m, 86p, 87
Trail Ridge hiking destinations, 31m, 42–46
Trail Ridge Road, 115–117
Trio Falls, 176m, 188, 192m
Trough, The, 244
Tundra World Nature Trail, 113
Tuxedo Park, 114
Twin Lakes, 177m, 186, 186p
Twin Owls, The, 121m, 142–143, 142p
Twin Owls Trailhead, 168
Twin Peaks, 311m, 313m, 316–317
Twin Sisters Peaks, 248m, 261–262, 262p
Twin Sisters Trail, 269, 269p
Twin Sisters Trailhead, 268
Two Rivers Lake, 30m, 81–82, 85m
Tyndall Glacier, 30m, 70m, 77–78
Tyndall Gorge hiking destinations, 30m, 72–78

U
Upper Beaver Meadows Trailhead, 110
Ute Crossing, 110
Ute Trail, 31m, 44–45, 113

V
Valley Trail, 324m, 354, 360
Verna, Lake, 178p, 270p, 272m, 276, 279m, 288m

W
War Dance Falls, 272m, 290m, 291
Watanga Lake, 311m, 312, 312p, 313m
Watanga Lake Trail, 320
Watanga Mountain, 311m, 313m, 317
water, drinking, 18
weather, 18–19
Wescott, Mount, 272m, 278, 278p, 279m, 280
West Creek Falls, 121m, 147–148, 148p
West Glacier Knob, 30m, 48m, 65–66
'Whiskey Lake,' 121m, 151m, 152

Wild Basin, 216p
Wild Basin-Allenspark Trail, 216
Wild Basin Trailhead, 215, 216
wildlife, 19, 21
Willow Park, 120m, 124
Window Rock, 121m, 139, 139p
Wind River Pass, 269
Wind River Trail, 269
Windy Gulch Cascades, 31m, 37
'Winter Loch Vale Trail,' 113–114
'Wonderland Lake,' 272m–273m, 290m, 291–292
Wuh, Mount, 30m, 82

Y
Yosemite Decimal System (YDS), 23–26
Ypsilon Lake, 120m, 126m, 133–134
Ypsilon Lake Trail, 173
Ypsilon Mountain, 1p, 120m, 125, 126m, 127, 127p, 134p

ABOUT THE AUTHOR/PHOTOGRAPHER

photo by Les Moore

Lisa Foster is a widely renowned expert on the subject of hiking in Rocky Mountain National Park (RMNP). She has explored every facet of RMNP, personally hiking or climbing to every named destination, including peaks, parks, passes, lakes, meadows, and other features. A former RMNP employee, Foster has been instrumental in a series of Park-based scientific studies. She has spent months searching for endangered species in remote areas, and for years she hiked regularly into the back-country to collect water and precipitation samples for the National Atmospheric Deposition Program. Foster is the author of hundreds of newspaper and magazine articles on hiking in RMNP. Additionally, she has hosted numerous hiking videos about RMNP, including the multiple award-winning *Climb Longs Peak!* and *Across the Divide.* Foster is an avid hiker and a skilled technical rock and ice climber. She lives in Estes Park, Colorado with her husband and daughter. This is her first book.